Technical Analysis Explained

Technical Analysis Analysis Explained

THE SUCCESSFUL INVESTOR'S GUIDE TO SPOTTING INVESTMENT TRENDS AND TURNING POINTS

FIFTH EDITION

MARTIN J. PRING

New York   Chicago   San Francisco   Athens   London
Madrid   Mexico City   Milan   New Delhi   Singapore
Sydney   Toronto

1 2 3 4 5 6 7 8 9 0 DOC/DOC 1 9 8 7 6 5 4 3

ISBN   978-0-07-182517-7
MHID   0-07-182517-7

e-ISBN 978-0-07-182655-6
e-MHID 0-07-182655-6

This publication is designed to provide accurate and authoritative information in regard to the subject matter covered. It is sold with the understanding that neither the author nor the publisher is engaged in rendering legal, accounting, securities trading, or other professional services. If legal advice or other expert assistance is required, the services of a competent professional person should be sought.

—From a Declaration of Principles Jointly Adopted by a Committee of the American Bar Association and a Committee of Publishers and Associations

Library of Congress Cataloging-in-Publication Data

Pring, Martin J.
  Technical analysis explained / by Martin J. Pring.—Fifth edition.
      pages cm
  ISBN 978-0-07-182517-7 (alk. paper)—ISBN 0-07-182517-7 (alk. paper)
  1. Investment analysis. I. Title.
  HG4529.P75 2014
  332.63'22—dc23   2013024562

McGraw-Hill Education books are available at special quantity discounts to use as premiums and sales promotions or for use in corporate training programs. To contact a representative, please visit the Contact Us pages at www.mhprofessional.com.

To my son, Thomas William Pring

CONTENTS

Part II: Market Structure

Part III: Other Aspects of Market Analysis

PREFACE

There is no reason why anyone cannot make a substantial amount of money in the financial markets, but there are many reasons why many people will not. As with most endeavors in life, the key to success is knowledge and action. This book has been written in an attempt to shed some light on the internal workings of the markets and to help expand the *knowledge* component, leaving the *action* to the patience, discipline, and objectivity of the individual investor.

The mid- to late-1980s saw the expansion of investment and trading opportunities to a global scale in terms of both the cash and the futures markets. In the 1990s, innovations in the communications industry enabled anyone to plot data on an intraday basis for relatively little cost. Today, numerous charting sites have sprung up on the Internet, so now virtually anyone has the ability to practice technical analysis. Indeed, the technology of teaching technical analysis has progressed since the first edition of this book in 1979. We pioneered the teaching of the subject in video format in the mid-1980s, but I'll venture to guess that technological progress and the acceptance of new media formats will mean that e-book sales of this edition will outstrip traditional sales of the physical book before it runs its course. Already, the written word is in competition with audiovisual presentations, such as my recently introduced online interactive technical analysis video course at pring.com; others are sure to follow!

As a consequence of the technological revolution, time horizons have been greatly shortened. I am not sure that this is a good thing because short-term trends experience more random noise than longer-term ones. This means that the technical indicators, while still the most effective tool, are not generally as successful when applied to longer-term trends. The fifth edition of *Technical Analysis Explained* has been expanded and totally revised to keep abreast of many of these changes, and to include some technical innovations and evolvement in my own thinking since the publication of the fourth edition. Nearly every chapter has been thoroughly reworked and expanded. In the interest of efficiency, some have been dropped and others substituted.

Considerable attention continues to be focused on the U.S. equity market, but many of the marketplace examples feature international stock indexes, currencies, commodities, and precious metals. Special chapters also feature technical analysis of the credit markets and global equities. Our focus has also been expanded to include analysis of the secular, or very long-term, trends of stocks, bonds, and commodities. In most cases, the marketplace examples have been updated, but some older ones from previous editions have been left in deliberately to give the book some historical perspective. These historical examples also underscore the point that nothing has really changed in the last 100 years. The same tried-and-true principles are as relevant today as they always were. I have no doubt whatsoever that this will continue to be so in the future.

Thus, technical analysis could be applied in New York in 1850, in Tokyo in 1950, and in Moscow in 2150. This is true because price action in financial markets is a reflection of human nature, and human nature remains more or less constant. Technical principles can also be applied to any freely traded entity in any time frame. A trend-reversal signal on a 5-minute bar chart is based on the same indicators as one on a monthly chart; only the significance is different. Shorter time frames reflect shorter trends and are, therefore, less significant.

The chronological sequence of some of the opening chapters differs from previous editions. In *Martin Pring on Price Patterns* (McGraw-Hill, 2005), I approached the subject by first describing the building blocks of price formations, peak-and-trough analysis, support and resistance, trendlines, and volume characteristics. This same logical sequence has been applied here, so when anyone proceeds to the explanation of price patterns they will be in a far stronger position to understand how these formations are constructed and interpreted.

Two new chapters have been added in this edition. One on secular trends has already been referred to. The secular, or very long-term, trend is the granddaddy of them all and exists for each of the three primary asset classes: bonds, stocks, and commodities. The more I study markets, the more I become impressed with the fact that the direction of the secular trend influences the characteristics of the trends that fall directly below it. In secular uptrends, primary bull (business cycle–associated) trends generally have greater magnitude and duration than do bear markets and vice versa. Understanding the characteristics of secular trends and how their reversal might be identified is therefore a key objective of Chapter 23.

Our second new chapter discusses indicators and relationships that measure confidence in the U.S. equity market. The discussion points out that market reversals are often signaled ahead of time in a subtle way by changes in relationships that monitor investor confidence. Other important items that have been inserted in existing chapters include my Special K indicator. This momentum series is calculated from the summed cyclicality of the short-term, intermediate-term, and long-term Know Sure Thing (KST) and offers a series that on most occasions peaks and troughs simultaneously with the price series it is monitoring. Another feature of the fifth edition is the inclusion of many exchange-traded funds (ETFs) as illustrative examples. These innovative products now allow investors and traders to purchase a basket of stocks or bonds reflecting popular indexes, sectors, or countries—and this is just the beginning. Indeed, active ETFs, such as the Pring Turner Business Cycle ETF (symbol DBIZ), allow investors to participate in various strategies, such as the approach discussed in Chapter 2. The introduction and widespread acceptance of ETFs make it so much easier for investors to gain exposure to individual country equity markets, credit market instruments, practice sector rotation, purchase inverse funds if they believe prices are headed lower, etc.

In addition, recent years have seen the launch of exchange-traded notes, which allow the purchase of selected commodities. However, investors need to be careful to check tax implications and to make sure that swings in carrying costs in the futures markets truly reflect the ups and downs of the commodities in question.

Since the 1970s, the time horizon of virtually all market participants has shrunk considerably. As a result, technical analysis has become very popular for implementing short-term timing strategies. This use may lead to great disappointment: In my experience, there is a rough correlation between the reliability of the technical indicators and the time span being monitored. This is why most of the discussion here has been oriented toward intermediate-term and long-term trends. Even short-term traders with a 1- to 3-week time horizon need to have some understanding of the direction and maturity of the main or primary trend. This is because mistakes are usually made by taking on positions that go against the direction of the main trend. If a whipsaw (false signal) is going to develop, it will usually arise from a contratrend signal. Think of it as paddling upstream against the current. It can be done, but with great difficulty. Far better to have the current behind you.

To be successful, technical analysis should be regarded as the art of assessing the technical position of a particular security with the aid of several scientifically researched indicators. Although many of the mechanistic techniques described in this book offer reliable indications of changing market conditions, all suffer from the common characteristic that they can, and occasionally do, fail to operate satisfactorily. This attribute presents no problem to the consciously disciplined investor or trader, since a good working knowledge of the principles underlying major price movements in financial markets and a balanced view of the overall technical position offer a superior framework within which to operate.

There is, after all, no substitute for independent thought. The action of the technical indicators illustrates the underlying characteristics of any market, and it is up to the analyst to put the pieces of the jigsaw puzzle together and develop a working hypothesis.

The task is by no means easy, as initial success can lead to overconfidence and arrogance. Charles H. Dow, the father of technical analysis, once wrote words to the effect that "pride of opinion caused the downfall of more men on Wall Street than all the other opinions put together." This is true because markets are essentially a reflection of people in action. Normally, such activity develops on a reasonably predictable path. Since people can—and do—change their minds, price trends in the market can deviate unexpectedly from their anticipated course. To avoid serious trouble, investors, and especially traders, must adjust their attitudes as changes in the technical position emerge. That does not mean that one should turn negative because prices are falling. Rather, one should take a bearish tack because the evidence has also done so.

In addition to pecuniary rewards, a study of the market can reveal much about human nature, both from observing other people in action and from the aspect of self-development. As investors react to the constant struggle through which the market will undoubtedly put them, they will also learn a little about their own makeup. Washington Irving might well have been referring to this challenge of the markets when he wrote, "Little minds are taxed and subdued by misfortune but great minds rise above it."

Martin J. Pring
October 2013

INTRODUCTION

To investors willing to buy and hold common stocks for the long term, the stock market has offered excellent rewards over the years in terms of both dividend growth and capital appreciation. The market is even more challenging, fulfilling, and rewarding to resourceful investors willing to learn the art of market timing through a study of technical analysis.

The advantages of this over the "buy-and-hold" approach were particularly noticeable between 1966 and 1982. The market made no headway at all, as measured by the Dow Jones Industrial Average (DJIA), in the 16 years between 1966 and 1982. Yet, there were some substantial price fluctuations. Although the DJIA failed to record a net advance between 1966 and 1982, the period included five major advances totaling over 1,500 Dow points. The potential rewards of market timing were, therefore, significant.

A long-term investor fortunate enough to sell at the five tops in 1966, 1968, 1973, 1979, and 1981 and to reinvest the money at the troughs of 1966, 1970, 1974, 1980, and 1982 would have seen the total investment (excluding transaction costs and capital gains tax) grow from a theoretical $1,000 (i.e., $1 for every Dow point) in 1966 to over $10,000 by October 1983. In contrast, an investor following a buy-and-hold approach would have realized a mere $250 gain over the same period. In inflation-adjusted terms, the loss for the more broadly based S&P Composite was 62 percent. A similar experience developed after the 2000 top, for while the monthly average of the S&P Composite gained 13 percent between its March 2000 peak and the July 2013 level, when adjusted for inflation, it lost 18 percent. During that period, it experienced two gains between its September 2002 closing low and the October 2007 high and between the January 2009 low and July 2013 (latest data) high of 94 percent and 120 percent, respectively.

Even during major advances, such as that which developed between 1982 and 2000, technical analysis would have proved useful, since that period witnessed a considerable variation in performance between different industry groups. Buy and hold would have worked for this very long-term trend, known as a secular bull market, but a conservative policy of sector rotation would have done even better.

In the previous edition of this book, I said, "A bull market, like the one that occurred in the 1980s and 1990s, is a once-in-a-generation affair; in fact, it was a record in 200 years of U.S. stock market history. This implies that the opening decade of the twenty-first century will be a more difficult and challenging period and that market timing will prove to be of crucial importance." These secular or very long-term trends typically last between 15 and 20 years, so the second decade of the twenty-first century could well turn out to be an extension of the first. We will have a lot more to say on that subject later on.

In practice, of course, it is impossible to buy and sell consistently at exact turning points, but the enormous potential of this approach still leaves plenty of room for error even when slippage, commission costs, and taxes are included in the calculation. The rewards for identifying major market junctures and taking the appropriate action can be substantial.

Originally, technical analysis was applied only in the equity market, but its popularity has gradually expanded to embrace commodities, debt instruments, currencies, and non-U.S. equity markets. While the contents of the fifth edition of this book continue to be largely focused on U.S. equities, we have expanded coverage to embrace other asset classes. Never forget that the basic technical principles can be applied to any freely traded entity and time frame for which data are available.

In days of old, market participants had a fairly long time horizon, stretching over months or years. There have always been short-term traders and scalpers, but the technological revolution in communications has shortened the time horizon of just about everyone involved in markets. When holding periods are lengthy, it is possible to indulge in the luxury of fundamental analysis, but when time is short, timing is everything. In such an environment, technical analysis really comes into its own.

To be successful, the technical approach involves taking a position contrary to the expectations of "the crowd." This requires the patience, objectivity, and discipline to acquire a financial asset at a time of depression and gloom and liquidate it in an environment of euphoria and excessive optimism. This is easier said than done, of course. The level of pessimism or optimism will depend on the turning point. Short-term peaks and troughs are associated with more moderate extremes in sentiment than longer-term ones. The aim of this book is to explain the technical characteristics expected at all types of market turning points, particularly major ones, and to help you assess them as objectively as possible.

Technical Analysis Defined

The technical approach to investment is essentially a reflection of the idea that prices move in trends that are determined by the changing attitudes of investors toward a variety of economic, monetary, political, and psychological forces. The art of technical analysis, for it is an art, is to *identify trend changes at an early stage and to maintain an investment or trading posture until the weight of the evidence indicates that the trend has reversed.*

I use the word "art" deliberately because there has been a big debate among technicians as to whether technical analysis is an art or a science. My belief is that it is an art form that utilizes many scientifically derived indicators. Viewed in this way, both sides are correct.

At this time, a housekeeping note is in order—when it is time to emphasize a specific but important point, it will be highlighted in the following way:

> **Major Technical Principle** Technical analysis deals in probabilities, never certainties.

Human nature remains more or less constant and tends to react to similar situations in consistent ways. By studying the nature of previous market turning points, it is possible to develop some characteristics that can help identify market tops and bottoms. Technical analysis, therefore, is based on the assumption that people will continue to make the same mistakes as they have in the past. Human relationships are extremely complex and never repeat in identical combinations. The markets, which are a reflection of people in action, never duplicate their performance exactly. Nevertheless, the recurrence of similar characteristics provides technicians with sufficient evidence to identify juncture points. Since no single indicator has signaled, or indeed could signal, every top or bottom, technical analysts have developed an arsenal of tools to help isolate these points—hence the words "weight of the evidence" used in our definition earlier. It is also a fact that turning points are not created equal since some are blessed with a greater amount of evidence than others.

At any one point in time, equity prices are influenced by four drivers. They are monetary, economic, technical, and psychological. The vast majority of the time-equity market tops and bottoms correspond to peaks and troughs in the growth rate of leading economic indicators. But there are a few notable exceptions, such as the 1926–1927 recession, throughout which prices continued to rally. Another developed between November 2001 and October 2002, when the economy pulled out of a recession yet prices extended their decline.

Those are important examples, and the more I study market action, the greater the realization that prices are determined by the changing attitudes of traders and investors to the emerging fundamentals rather than the fundamentals themselves. It's all about psychology and confidence, or the lack thereof. When we look at charts, the best approach is not to blindly follow the rules but to use some common sense, always asking the question "What is the price action telling me about the basic underlying psychology?"

Three Branches of Technical Analysis

Technical analysis can be broken down into three essential areas: sentiment, flow-of-funds, and market structure indicators. Data and indicators for all three areas are available for the U.S. stock market and growing for those non-U.S. ones. For most financial markets, the statistics are more or less confined to the market structure indicators. The major exceptions are futures markets for which short-term sentiment and commitment of traders* data are available.

Sentiment Indicators

Sentiment or *expectational indicators* monitor the actions of different market participants, e.g., insiders, mutual funds, traders, newsletter writers,

---

*Biweekly reports published by the CFTC containing the reporting positions of various categories of market participants.

and so forth. Just as the pendulum of a clock continually moves from one extreme to another, so do the sentiment indexes (which monitor the emotions of investors) move from one extreme at a bear market bottom to another at a bull market top. The assumption is that different groups of investors are consistent in their actions at major market turning points. For example, insiders (i.e., key employees or major stockholders of a company) and commercial users in the futures markets, as a group, have a tendency to be correct at market turning points; in aggregate, their transactions are on the buy side toward market bottoms and on the sell side toward tops.

Conversely, advisory services as a group are often wrong at market turning points, since they consistently become bullish at market tops and bearish at market troughs. Indicators derived from such data show that certain readings have historically corresponded to market tops, while others have been associated with market bottoms. Since the consensus or majority opinion is normally wrong at market turning points, these indicators of market psychology are a useful basis from which to form a contrary opinion. Because it is not possible to know how far these indicators will stretch before a market peak or trough develops, it's often a good idea to wait for them to show some signs of reversing. Unfortunately, this is not an exact science, as major turning points can be associated with less intensive readings, setting up what technicians refer to as "divergences."

When actual sentiment data are not available, momentum indicators or oscillators can be substituted. I will have a lot to say on that aspect later on.

Major Technical Principle When everyone thinks alike on a specific market, it's already been factored into the price.

Flow-of-Funds Indicators

The area of technical analysis that involves what are loosely termed flow-of-funds indicators analyzes the financial position of various investor groups in an attempt to measure their potential capacity for buying or selling stocks. Since there has to be a purchase to offset each sale, the "ex post," or actual dollar balance between supply and demand, for any security must always be equal. The price at which a transaction takes place has to be the same for the buyer and the seller, so naturally, the amount of money flowing out of any freely traded entity must equal that put in. The flow-of-funds approach is, therefore, concerned with the before-the-fact balance between supply and demand, known as the *ex ante relationship*. If at a given price there is a preponderance of buyers over sellers on an ex ante basis, it follows that the actual (ex post) price will have to rise to bring buyers and sellers into balance.

Flow-of-funds analysis for U.S. equities is concerned, for example, with trends in mutual fund cash positions and other major institutions, such as pension funds, insurance companies, foreign investors, bank trust accounts, and customers' free balances, which are normally a source of cash on the buy side; and new equity offerings, secondary offerings, and margin debt, when it is liquidated, on the supply side.

This money flow analysis also suffers from disadvantages. For example, the data measure the availability of money for the stock market, e.g., mutual fund cash position or pension fund cash flow, but they give no indication of the inclination of market participants to use this money for the purchase of stocks, or of their elasticity or willingness to sell at a given price on the sell side. On the other hand, if the trend of these money flows is analyzed in conjunction with their levels, it is often possible to come up with some meaningful conclusions. Historically, the data for the major institutions and foreign investors have not been sufficiently detailed to be of much use, and in addition, they are typically reported well after the fact. In spite of these drawbacks, flow-of-funds statistics may be used as background material.

Fortunately, data for cash flows into specific mutual funds and ETFs have recently become more available and may also be used for analytical purposes, serving as both flow-of-funds and sentiment indicators. The main drawback to using ETF inflows and outflows is that this information does not have a long-term track record covering many cycles. It's interpretation-based on a few data points and should, therefore, be used more cautiously than indicators with a long and consistent record.

Market Structure Indicators

The area of technical analysis, which is the main concern of this book, embraces *market structure* or the *character of the market indicators*. They monitor the trend of various price indexes, market breadth, cycles, volume, etc., in order to evaluate the health of bull and bear markets. This type of analysis can be applied to any equity market, or indeed to any entity consisting of divergent components, such as credit markets, commodities, and so forth. However, given the depth of data available for the U.S. equity market, this is the area we will principally be focusing on, while at the same time recognizing that these same principles can be applied to any market.

Most of the time, price and internal measures, such as market breadth, momentum, and volume, rise and fall together, but toward the end of market movements, the paths of many of them diverge from the price. Such discrepancies offer omens of technical deterioration during advances and technical strength following declines. Through judicious observation of these signs of latent strengths and weaknesses, technically oriented investors are alerted to the possibility of a reversal in the trend of the market itself.

Since the technical approach is based on the theory that the price is a reflection of mass psychology—"the crowd"—in action, it attempts to forecast future price movements on the assumption that crowd psychology moves between panic, fear, and pessimism on the one hand and confidence, excessive optimism, and greed on the other. As discussed here, the art of technical analysis is concerned with identifying these changes at an early phase, since these swings in emotion take time to accomplish. Studying these market trends enables technically oriented investors and traders to buy or sell with a degree of confidence on the principle that once a trend is set in motion, it will perpetuate itself.

Price movements may be classed as primary, intermediate, and short-term. Major movements, sometimes called *primary* or *cyclical,* typically work themselves out in a period of 9 months to 2 years and are a reflection of investors' attitudes toward the business cycle. *Intermediate movements* usually develop over a period of 6 weeks to 9 months, sometimes longer. While not of prime importance, they are, nevertheless, useful to identify. It is clearly important to distinguish between an intermediate reaction in a bull market and the first down leg of a bear market, for example. *Short-term movements,* which last less than 3 or 6 weeks, tend to be random in nature. Secular, or very long-term, trends embracing several primary trend movements and intraday trends lasting a few minutes to a few hours round out the possibilities for price movements.

Swing and intraday traders would be quick to point out that much smaller trends develop during the course of a trading session. Those with an eye to history and greater perspective would also observe that very long-term trends lasting 15 to 20 years or more also exist. Indeed, I consider these secular trends to be of such significance that they are the subject of an individual chapter.

Discounting the Mechanism of the Market

All price movements have one thing in common: They are a reflection of the trend in the hopes, fears, knowledge, optimism, and greed of market participants. The sum total of these emotions is expressed in the price level, which is, as Garfield Drew noted, "Never what they [stocks] are worth, but what people think they are worth."

This process of market evaluation was well expressed by an editorial in *The Wall Street Journal:*

> The stock market consists of everyone who is "in the market" buying or selling shares at a given moment, plus everyone who is not "in the market," but might be if conditions were right. In this sense, the stock market is potentially everyone with any personal savings.
>
> It is this broad base of participation and potential participation that gives the market its strength as an economic indicator and as an allocator of scarce capital. Movements in and out of a stock, or in and out of the market, are made on the margin as each investor digests new information. This allows the market to incorporate all available information in a way that no one person could hope to. Since its judgments are the consensus of nearly everyone, it tends to outperform any single person or group. …[The market] measures the after-tax profits of all the companies whose shares are listed in the market, and it measures these cumulative profits so far into the future one might as well say the horizon is infinite. This cumulative mass of after-tax profits is then, as the economists will say, "discounted back to present value" by the market. A man does the same thing when he pays more for one razor blade than another, figuring he'll get more or easier shaves in the future with the higher-priced one, and figuring its present value on that basis.
>
> This future flow of earnings will ultimately be affected by business conditions everywhere on earth. Little bits of information are constantly flowing into the market from around the world as well as throughout the United States, and the market is much more efficient in reflecting these bits of news than are government statisticians. The market relates this information to how much American business can earn in the future. Roughly speaking, the general level of the market is the present value of the capital stock of the U.S.

This implies that investors are looking ahead and taking action so that they can liquidate at a higher price when the anticipated news or development actually takes place. If expectations are better or worse than originally thought, then through the market mechanism, investors sell, either sooner or later, depending on the particular circumstances. Thus, the familiar maxim "sell on good news" applies when the "good" news is right on or below the market's (i.e., the investors') expectations. If the news is good but not as favorable as expected, a quick reassessment will take place, and the market (other things being equal) will fall. If the news is better than anticipated, the possibilities are obviously more favorable. The reverse will, of course, be true in a declining market. This process explains the paradox of equity markets peaking out when economic conditions are strong, and forming a bottom when the outlook is most gloomy.

> **Major Technical Principle**   The market never discounts the same thing twice.

The reaction of any market to news events can be most instructive, for if it ignores supposedly bullish news and sells off, the event was well discounted, i.e., already built into the price mechanism, and the reaction should, therefore, be viewed bearishly. If a market reacts more favorably to bad news than might be expected, this in turn should be interpreted as a positive sign. There is a good deal of wisdom in the saying "A bear argument known is a bear argument understood."

The Financial Markets and the Business Cycle

The major movements in bond, stock, and commodity prices are caused by long-term trends in the emotions of the investing public. These emotions reflect the anticipated level and growth rate of future economic activity and the attitude of investors toward that activity.

For example, there is a definite link between primary movements in the stock market and cyclical movements in the economy because trends in corporate profitability are an integral part of the business cycle. If basic economic forces alone influenced the stock market, or any other asset class, the task of determining the changes in primary trend movements would be relatively simple. In practice, it is not and this is due to several factors.

First, changes in the direction of the economy can take some time to materialize. As the cycle unfolds, other psychological considerations—for example, political changes or purely internal factors such as a speculative buying wave or selling pressure from margin calls—can affect markets. Such developments often result in misleading rallies and reactions of 5 to 10 percent or more.

Second, changes in the equity market usually precede changes in the economy by 6 to 9 months, but the lead time can sometimes be far shorter or longer. In 1921, 1929, and 2002, the economy turned before the market did. The "economy" consists of many different sectors that are often moving in different directions. Housing, a leading indicator, might be rising, while capital spending, a latecomer, may still be declining. Consequently, when we talk about "the" economy, we are referring to a sector that moves in the middle, known as "coincident indicators." Examples might include nonfarm payrolls, industrial production, gross domestic product (GDP), etc. Thus, the equity market *anticipates* changes between a positive and negative *coincident* number, but *coincides* with reversals in the growth rate of *leading* economic indicators.

Third, even when an economic recovery is in the middle of its cycle, doubts about its durability often arise. When these misgivings coincide with political or other adverse developments, sharp and confusing countercyclical price movements usually result.

Fourth, profits may increase, but investors' attitudes toward those profits may change. For example, in the spring of 1946 the DJIA stood at 22 times the price/earnings ratio. By 1948, the comparable ratio was 9.5 when measured against 1947 earnings. In this period, profits had almost doubled and price/earnings ratios had fallen, but stock prices were lower.

Changes in bond and commodity prices are linked much more directly to economic activity than are stock market prices, but even here, psychological influences on price are very important. Currencies do not fit well into business cycle analysis. Data reported several months after the fact are very good at explaining currency movements, but technical analysis has been most useful for timely forecasts and the identification of emerging trends.

Technical Analysis Trend Determination

Since technical analysis involves a study of the action of markets, it is not concerned with the difficult and subjective tasks of forecasting trends in the economy or assessing the attitudes of investors toward those changes.

Technical analysis tries to identify turning points in the *market's* assessment of these factors.

Since this art form can be applied successfully to any freely traded entity such as stocks, market averages, commodities, bonds, currencies, etc., I will frequently use the term "security" as a generic one embracing all of these entities and avoiding unnecessary repetition.

The approach taken here differs from that found in standard presentations of technical analysis. The various techniques used to determine trends and identify their reversals will be examined in Part I, "Trend-Determining Techniques," which deals with price patterns, trendlines, moving averages (MAs), momentum, etc.

Major Technical Principle The basic principles of technical analysis apply to all securities and time frames, from 20-minute to 20-year trends.

Part II, "Market Structure," is principally concerned with analysis of the U.S. equity market, although examples using other securities are included to demonstrate that the principles are universally applicable. All that is required is the appropriate data. This section offers a more detailed explanation of the various indicators and indexes. It also shows how they can be combined to build a framework for determining the quality of the internal structure of the market. A study of market character is a cornerstone of technical analysis, since reversals of price trends in the major averages are almost always preceded by latent strengths or weaknesses in the market structure. Just as a careful driver does not judge the performance of a car from the speedometer alone, so a technical analyst looks further than the price trends of the popular averages. Trends of investor confidences are responsible for price movements, and this emotional aspect is examined from four viewpoints, or dimensions, namely, price, time, volume, and breadth.

Changes in prices reflect changes in investor attitude, and *price*, the first dimension, indicates the level of that change.

Time, the second dimension, measures the recurrence and length of cycles in investor psychology. Changes in confidence go through distinct cycles, some long and some short, as investors swing from excesses of optimism toward deep pessimism. The degree of price movement in the market is usually a function of the time element. *The longer it takes for investors to move from a bullish to a bearish extreme, the greater the ensuing price change is likely to be.* The examples in two of the chapters on time relate mainly to the U.S. stock market, but are equally valid for commodities, bonds, currencies, or stocks.

Volume, the third dimension, reflects the intensity of changes in investor attitudes. For example, the level of enthusiasm implied by a price rise on low volume is not nearly as strong as that implied by a similar price advance accompanied by very high volume.

The fourth dimension, *breadth,* measures the extent of the emotion. This is important, for as long as stocks are advancing on a broad front, the trend in favorable emotion is dispersed among most stocks and industries, which indicates a healthy and broad economic recovery and a widely favorable attitude toward stocks in particular. On the other hand, when interest narrows to a few blue-chip stocks, the quality of the trend deteriorates, and a continuation of the bull market is highly suspect.

Technical analysis measures these psychological dimensions in a number of ways. Most indicators monitor two or more aspects simultaneously; for instance, a simple price chart measures both price (on the vertical axis) and time (on the horizontal axis). Similarly, an advance/decline line measures breadth and time.

Part III, "Other Aspects of Market Analysis," deals with more specialized subjects. These include interest rates and the stock market, sentiment, automated trading systems, individual stock selection, and technical analysis as applied to global markets.

Conclusion

Financial markets move in trends caused by the changing attitudes and expectations of investors with regard to the business cycle. Since investors continue to repeat the same type of behavior from cycle to cycle, an understanding of the historical relationships between certain price averages and market indicators can be used to identify turning points. No single indicator can ever be expected to signal all trend reversals, so it is essential to use a number of them together to build up a consensus.

This approach is by no means infallible, but a careful, patient, and objective use of the principles of technical analysis can put the odds of success very much in favor of the investor or trader who incorporates these principles into an overall strategy.

Part I

TREND-DETERMINING TECHNIQUES

1

THE DEFINITION
AND INTERACTION
OF TRENDS

In the introduction, *technical analysis* was defined as the art of identifying trend changes at an early stage and to maintain an investment or trading posture until the weight of the evidence indicates that the trend has reversed. In order to identify a trend reversal, we must first know what that trend is. This chapter explains and categorizes the principal trends, and concludes with a discussion of one of the basic building blocks of technical analysis: *peak-and-trough progression*. This technique is arguably the simplest of trend-determining techniques, but in my book, certainly one of the most effective.

Time Frames

We have already established the link between psychology and prices. It is also a fact that human nature (psychology) is more or less constant. This means that the principles of technical analysis can be applied to any time frame, from one-minute bars to weekly and monthly charts. The interpretation is identical. The only difference is that the battle between buyers and sellers is much larger on the monthly charts than on the intraday ones. This means that such trend-reversal signals are far more significant. As we proceed, it will be evident that this book contains a huge variety of examples featuring many different time frames. *For the purpose of interpretation, the time frame really doesn't matter; it's the character of the pattern that does.*

For example, if you are a long-term trader and see a particular example featured on a 10-minute bar chart, the principles of interpretation are the same when applied to a weekly chart. A long-term investor would never initiate an investment based on a 10-minute chart, but can and should take action when that same type of technical evidence appears on a weekly or monthly one, and vice versa.

Three Important Trends

A trend is a period in which a price moves in an irregular but persistent direction. It may also be described as a time measurement of the direction in price levels covering different time spans. There are many different classifications of trends in technical analysis. It is useful to examine the more common ones, since such an understanding will give us perspective on the significance of specific technical events. The three most widely followed trends are primary, intermediate, and short-term. Whenever we talk of any specific category of trend lasting for such and such a time period, please remember that the description offered is a rough guide encompassing most, but not all, of the possible durations for that particular type. Some specific trends will last longer, and others for less time.

Primary

The primary trend generally lasts between 9 months and 2 years, and is a reflection of investors' attitudes toward unfolding fundamentals in the business cycle. The business cycle extends statistically from trough to trough for approximately 3.6 years, so it follows that rising and falling primary trends (bull and bear markets) last for 1 to 2 years. Since building up takes longer than tearing down, bull markets generally last longer than bear markets. The direction of the secular or very long-term trend will also affect the magnitude and duration of a primary trend. Those that move in the direction of the secular trend will generally experience greater magnitude and duration than those that move in the opposite direction. The characteristics of secular trends are discussed later in this chapter and more fully in Chapter 23.

The primary trend cycle is operative for bonds, equities, and commodities. Primary trends also apply to currencies, but since they reflect investors' attitudes toward the interrelationship of two different economies,

FIGURE 1.1 The Market Cycle Model

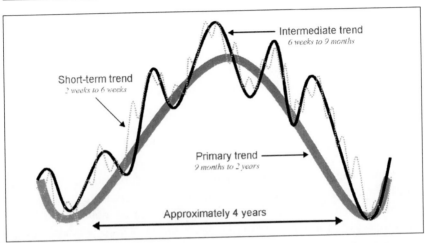

Note: Adapted from an idea first brought to my attention by the late Ian S. Notley of Yelton Fiscal Ridgefield, Connecticut.

analysis of currency relationships does not fit neatly into the business cycle approach discussed in Chapter 2.

The primary trend is illustrated in Figure 1.1 by the thickest line. In an idealized situation, the primary uptrend (bull market) is the same size as the primary downtrend (bear market), but in reality, of course, their magnitudes are different. Because it is very important to position both (short-term) trades and (long-term) investments in the direction of the main trend, a significant part of this book is concerned with identifying reversals in the primary trend.

Intermediate

Anyone who has looked at prices on a chart will notice that they do not move in a straight line. A primary upswing is interrupted by several reactions along the way. These countercyclical trends within the confines of a primary bull market are known as *intermediate price movements*. They last anywhere from 6 weeks to as long as 9 months, sometimes even longer, but rarely shorter. Countercyclical intermediate trends are typically very deceptive, often being founded on very believable but false assumptions. For example, an intermediate rally during a bear market in equities may very well be founded on a couple of unexpectedly positive economic numbers, which make it appear that the economy will avoid that much-feared recession.

When subsequent numbers are reported and found to be wanting, the bear market resumes. Intermediate-term trends of the stock market are examined in greater detail in Chapter 4 and are shown as a thin solid line in Figure 1.1.

It is important to have an idea of the direction and maturity of the primary trend, but an analysis of intermediate trends is also helpful for improving success rates in trading, as well as for determining when the primary movement may have run its course.

Short-Term Trends

Short-term trends typically last 3 to 6 weeks, sometimes shorter and sometimes longer. They interrupt the course of the intermediate cycle, just as the intermediate-term trend interrupts primary price movements. Short-term trends are shown in the market cycle model (Figure 1.1) as a dashed line. They are usually influenced by random news events and are far more difficult to identify than their intermediate or primary counterparts.

> **Major Technical Principle** As a general rule, the longer the time span of a trend, the easier it is to identify. The shorter the time span, the more random it is likely to be.

The Market Cycle Model

By now, it is apparent that the price level of any market is influenced simultaneously by several different trends, and it is important to understand which type is being monitored. For example, if a reversal in a short-term trend has just taken place, a much smaller price movement may be expected than if the primary trend had reversed.

Long-term investors are principally concerned with the direction of the primary trend, and, thus, it is important for them to have some perspective on the maturity of the prevailing bull or bear market. However, *long-term investors must also be aware of intermediate and, to a lesser extent, short-term trends.* This is because an important step in the analysis is an examination and understanding of the relationship between short- and intermediate-term trends and how they affect the primary trend. Also, if it is concluded that the long-term trend has just reversed to the upside, it may pay to wait before committing capital because the short-term trend could be overextended on the upside. Ignoring the position of the short-term trend could therefore prove costly at the margin.

Short-term traders are principally concerned with smaller movements in price, but they *also need to know the direction of the intermediate and primary trends*. This is because of the following principle.

> **Major Technical Principle** Surprises occur in the direction of the main trend, i.e., on the upside in a bull market and on the downside in a bear market.

In other words, rising short-term trends within the confines of a bull market are likely to be much greater in magnitude than short-term downtrends, and vice versa. Losses usually develop because the trader is in a countercyclical position against the main trend. In effect, *all market participants need to have some kind of working knowledge of all three trends*, although the emphasis will depend on whether their orientation comes from an investment or a short-term trading perspective.

> **Major Technical Principle** The direction of the primary trend will affect the character of intermediate and short-term trends.

Two Supplementary Trends

Intraday

The post-1990 development of real-time trading enabled market participants to identify hourly and even tick-by-tick price movements. *The principles of technical analysis apply equally to these very short-term movements, and are just as valid.* There are two main differences. First, reversals in the intraday charts only have a very short-term implication and are not significant for longer-term price reversals. Second, extremely short-term price movements are much more influenced by psychology and instant reaction to news events than are longer-term ones. Decisions, therefore, have a tendency to be emotional, knee-jerk reactions. Intraday price action is also more susceptible to manipulation. As a consequence, price data used in very short-term charts are much more erratic and generally less reliable than those that appear in the longer-term charts.

The Secular Trend

The primary trend consists of several intermediate cycles, but the secular, or very long-term, trend is constructed from a number of primary trends. This "super cycle," or long wave, extends over a substantially greater period, usually lasting well over 10 years, and often as long as 25 years, though most average between 15 and 20 years. It is discussed at great length in Chapter 23. A diagram of the interrelationship between a secular and a primary trend is shown in Figure 1.2.

It is certainly very helpful to understand the direction of the secular trend. Just as the primary trend influences the magnitude of the

FIGURE 1.2 The Relationship Between Secular and Primary Trends

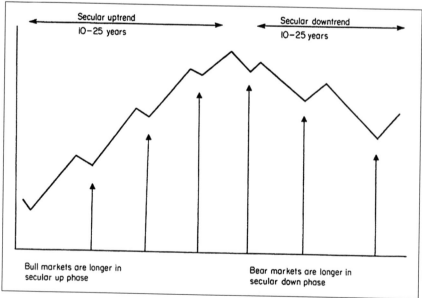

intermediate-term rally relative to the countercyclical reaction, so, too, does the secular trend influence the magnitude and duration of a primary-trend rally or reaction. For example, in a rising secular trend, primary bull markets will be of greater magnitude than primary bear markets. In a secular downtrend, bear markets will be more powerful, and will take longer to unfold, than bull markets. It is certainly true to say that long-term surprises will develop in the direction of the secular trend.

Bonds and commodities are also subject to secular trends, and these feed back into each other as well as into equities. I will have much more to say on this subject later.

Peak-and-Trough Progression

Earlier, we established that technical analysis is the art of identifying a (price) trend reversal based on the weight of the evidence. As in a court of law, a trend is presumed innocent until proven guilty! The "evidence" is the objective element in technical analysis. It consists of a series of scientifically derived indicators or techniques that work well most of the time in the trend-identification process. The "art" consists of combining these indicators into an overall picture and recognizing when that picture resembles a market peak or trough.

Widespread use of computers has led to the development of some very sophisticated trend-identification techniques. Some of them work reasonably well, but most do not. The continual search for the "Holy Grail," or perfect indicator, will undoubtedly continue, but it is unlikely that such a technique will ever be developed. Even if it were, news of its discovery would soon be disseminated and the indicator would gradually be discounted. It is as well to remember that prices are determined by swings in crowd psychology. People can and do change their minds, and so do markets!

Major Technical Principle Never go for perfection; always shoot for consistency.

In the quest for sophisticated mathematical techniques, some of the simplest and most basic techniques of technical analysis are often overlooked. Arguably the simplest technique of all, and one that has been underused, is peak-and-trough progression (see Chart 1.1).

CHART 1.1 Moody's AAA bond yields and peak-and-trough analysis. In Chart 1.1, the solid line above the yield corresponds to primary bull and bear markets. The series of rising peaks and troughs extended from the end of World War II until September 1981. This was a long period even by secular standards. Confirmation of the post-1981 downtrend was given in 1985, as the series of rising peaks and troughs was reversed. The signal simply indicated a change in trend, but gave no indication as to its magnitude.

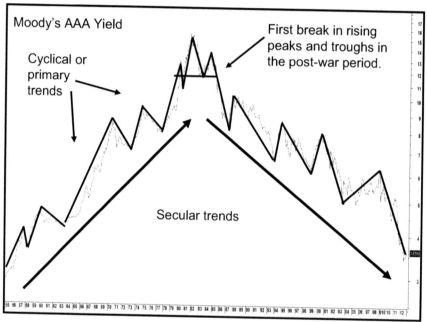

Source: From *Martin Pring's Intermarket Review.*

This principle reflects Charles Dow's original observation that a rising market moves in a series of waves, with each rally and reaction being higher than its predecessor. When the series of rising peaks and troughs is interrupted, a trend reversal is signaled. To explain this approach, Dow used an analogy with the ripple effect of waves on a seashore. He pointed out that just as it was possible for someone on the beach to identify the turning of the tide by a reversal of receding wave action at low tide, so, too, could the same objective be achieved in the market by observing the price action.

In Figure 1.3, the price has been advancing in a series of waves, with each peak and trough reaching higher than its predecessor. Then, for the first time, a rally fails to move to a new high, and the subsequent reaction pushes it *below the previous trough.* This occurs at point X, and gives a signal that the trend has reversed.

FIGURE 1.3 Reversal of Rising Peaks and Troughs

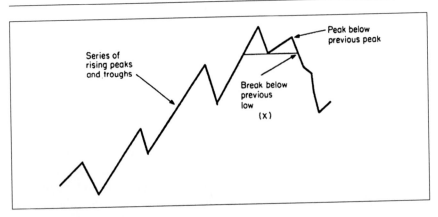

FIGURE 1.4 Reversal of Falling Peaks and Troughs

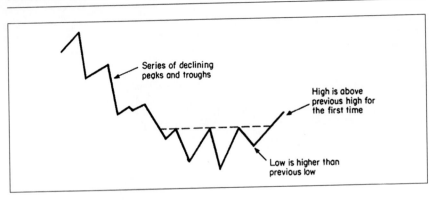

Figure 1.4 shows a similar situation, but this time, the trend reversal is from a downtrend to an uptrend.

The idea of the interruption of a series of peaks and troughs is the basic building block for both Dow theory (Chapter 3) and price pattern analysis (Chapter 8).

Major Technical Principle The significance of a peak-and-trough reversal is determined by the duration and magnitude of the rallies and reactions in question.

For example, if it takes 2 to 3 weeks to complete each wave in a series of rallies and reactions, the trend reversal will be an intermediate one, since intermediate price movements consist of a series of short-term (2- to 6-week) fluctuations. Similarly, the interruption of a series of falling intermediate peaks and troughs by a rising one signals a reversal from a primary bear to a primary bull market.

A Peak-and-Trough Dilemma

Occasionally, peak-and-trough progression becomes more complicated than the examples shown in Figures 1.3 and 1.4. In Figure 1.5, example *a*, the market has been advancing in a series of rising peaks and troughs, but following the highest peak, the price declines at point X to a level that is below the previous low. At this juncture, the series of rising troughs has been broken, but *not* the series of rising peaks. In other words, *at point X,*

FIGURE 1.5 Half-Signal Reversals

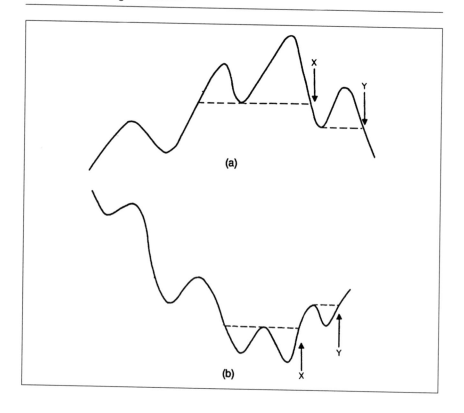

(a)

(b)

only half a signal has been generated. The complete signal of a reversal of both rising peaks and troughs arises at point Y, when the price slips below the level previously reached at point X.

At point X, there is quite a dilemma because the trend should still be classified as positive, and, yet, the very fact that the series of rising troughs has been interrupted indicates underlying technical weakness. On the one hand, we are presented with half a bearish signal, while on the other hand, waiting for point Y would mean giving up a substantial amount of the profits earned during the bull market.

The dilemma is probably best dealt with by referring back to the second half of the definition of technical analysis given at the beginning of this chapter "and riding that trend until the *weight of the evidence* proves that it has been reversed."

In this case, if the "weight of the evidence" from other technical indicators, such as, moving averages (MAs), volume, momentum, and breadth (discussed in later chapters), overwhelmingly indicates a trend reversal, it is probably safe to anticipate a change in trend, even though peak-and-trough progression has not completely *confirmed* the situation. It is still a wise policy, though, to view this signal with some degree of skepticism until the reversal is confirmed by an interruption in *both* series of rising peaks as well as troughs.

Figure 1.5, example *b*, shows this type of situation for a reversal from a bear to bull trend. The same principles of interpretation apply at point X as in Figure 1.5, example *a*. Occasionally, determining what constitutes a rally or reaction becomes a subjective process. One way around this problem is to choose an objective measure, such as categorizing rallies greater than, say, 5 percent. This can be a tedious process, but some software programs (such as MetaStock with its zig-zag tool) enable the user to establish such benchmarks almost instantly in graphic format.

What Constitutes a Legitimate Peak and Trough?

Most of the time, the various rallies and reactions are self-evident, so it is easy to determine that these turning points are legitimate peaks and troughs. Technical lore has it that a reaction to the prevailing trend should retrace between one-third and two-thirds of the previous move. Thus, in Figure 1.6, the first rally from the trough low to the subsequent peak is 100 percent. The ensuing reaction appears to be just over half, or a 50 percent retracement of the previous move. Occasionally, the retracement can reach 100 percent. Technical analysis is far from precise, but if a retracement

FIGURE 1.6 Identifying Peaks and Troughs (Magnitude)

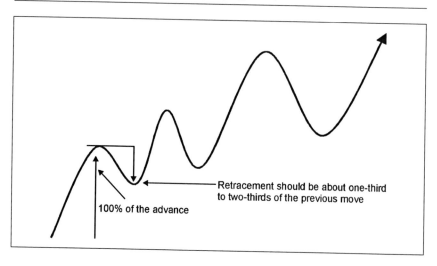

move is a good deal less than the minimum one-third, then the peak or trough in question is held to be suspect.

Sometimes though, it takes the form of a line or trading range. The depth of the trading range can fall short of the minimum "approximate one-third retracement" requirement and, in such instances, the correction qualifies more on the basis of time than on magnitude. A rule of thumb might be for the correction to last between one-third and two-thirds of the time taken to achieve the previous advance or decline. In Figure 1.7, the time distance between the low and the high for the move represents 100 percent. The consolidation prior to the breakout should constitute roughly two-thirds, or 66 percent, of the time taken to achieve the advance, ample time to consolidate gains and move on to a new high.

These are only rough guidelines, and in the final analysis, it is a judgment call based on experience; *common sense*; a bit of intuition; and perhaps most important of all, a review of other factors such as volume, support and resistance principles, etc. The words *common sense* have been italicized because the charts should always be interpreted with a bit of poetic license. For example, the rule states that a one-third retracement is required for a legitimate turning point, but it turns out to be 32 percent. If other factors suggest the move qualifies as a valid retracement, always take the common sense interpretation over the strict rules-based one. That is why we should regard technical analysis as both a science and an art.

FIGURE 1.7 Identifying Peaks and Troughs (Time)

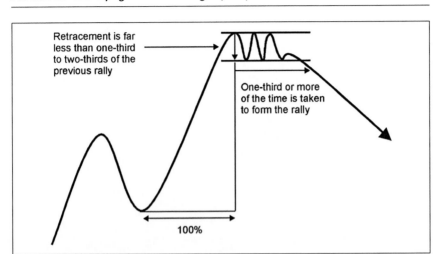

We have mainly been studying these concepts in a rising trend. However, the principles work exactly the same in a declining trend, in that rallies should retrace one-third to two-thirds of the previous decline.

It is also important to categorize what kind of trend is being monitored. Obviously, a reversal derived from a series of rallies and reactions, each lasting, say, 2 to 3 weeks, would be an intermediate reversal. This is because the swings would be short-term in nature. On the other hand, peak-and-trough reversals that develop in intraday charts are likely to have significance over a much shorter period. How short would depend on whether the swings were a reflection of hourly or, say, 5-minute bars.

Summary

1. A number of different trends simultaneously influence the price level of any market.
2. The three most important trends are primary, intermediate, and short-term.
3. The principles of technical analysis apply to intraday trends, but since they are more random in nature, the analysis is generally less reliable than that for longer-term trends.

4. Very long-term, or secular, trends influence the magnitude of primary bull and bear markets.

5. Peak-and-trough progression is the most basic trend-identification technique, and is a basic building block of technical analysis.

6. As a general rule, in order to qualify as a new legitimate peak or trough, the price should retrace between one-third and two-thirds of the previous move.

7. Lines or consolidations also qualify as peaks and troughs where they form between one-third and two-thirds of the time taken to produce the previous advance or decline.

2

FINANCIAL MARKETS AND THE BUSINESS CYCLE

Introduction

Our principal objective here is to explain the benefits of the technical approach, but it is also important to understand that primary trends of stocks, bonds, and commodities are determined by the *attitude* of investors toward unfolding events in the business cycle. Each market has a tendency to peak and trough at different points during the cycle in a consistent, chronological manner. An understanding of the interrelationship of credit, equity, and commodity markets provides a useful framework for identifying major reversals in each.

The Discounting Mechanism of Financial Markets

The primary trend of all financial markets is essentially determined by investors' expectations of movements in the economy, the effect those changes are likely to have on the price of the asset in which a specific financial market deals, and the psychological attitude of investors to these fundamental factors. Market participants typically anticipate future economic and financial developments and take action by buying or selling the appropriate assets, with the result that a market normally reaches a major turning point well ahead of the actual development.

Expectations of an expanding level of economic activity are usually favorable for stock prices. Anticipation of a weak economy is bullish

FIGURE 2.1 The Idealized Business Cycle

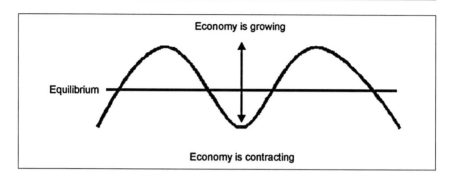

for bond prices, and prospects for capacity constraints offer a favorable tailwind for industrial commodity prices. These three markets often move in different directions simultaneously because they are discounting different things.

An economy is rarely stable; generally, it is either expanding or contracting. As a result, financial markets are in a continual state of flux. A hypothetical economy, as shown in Figure 2.1, revolves around a point of balance known as *equilibrium*. Roughly speaking, equilibrium can be thought of as a period of zero growth in which business activity is neither expanding nor contracting. In practice, this state of affairs is rarely, if ever, attained, since an economy as a whole possesses tremendous momentum in either the expansionary or the contractionary phase, so that the turnaround rarely occurs at an equilibrium level. In any event, the "economy" consists of a host of individual sectors, many of which are operating in different directions at the same time. Thus, at the beginning of the business cycle, leading economic indicators, such as housing starts, might be rising, while lagging indicators, such as capital spending, could be falling.

Major Technical Principle The business cycle is nothing less than a set series of chronological events that are continually repeating.

Market participants in financial markets are not concerned with periods of extended stability or equilibrium, for such environments do not produce volatile price swings and opportunities to make quick profits. The ever-changing character of the economic cycle creates tremendous opportunities for investors and traders because it means that different industries are experiencing different economic conditions simultaneously. Since housing leads the economy, housing stocks do well at the start of the recovery, when capital-intensive stocks such as steels tend to underperform. Later in the cycle, the tables are turned and housing peaks first, usually in an absolute sense, but occasionally as measured by its relative performance to a market average such as the S&P Composite. Different equity sectors discounting their specific area of the economy give rise to the sector rotation process, which is discussed at length in Chapter 22.

Since the financial markets lead the economy, it follows that the greatest profits can be made just before the point of maximum economic distortion, or disequilibrium. Once investors realize that an economy is changing direction and returning toward the equilibrium level, they discount this development by buying or selling the appropriate asset. Obviously, the more dislocated and volatile an economy becomes, the greater is the potential, not only for a return toward the equilibrium level, but also for a strong swing well beyond it to the other extreme. Under such conditions, the possibilities for making money in financial markets are greater because they, too, will normally become subject to wider price fluctuations. Two of the wildest post–World War II economic swings (1973–1974 and 2007–2008) certainly provided traders and investors with a roller coaster ride, with great profit possibilities were they able to identify the two respective bear market lows.

Market Movements and the Business Cycle

The major movements of interest rates, equities, and commodity prices are related to changes in the level of business activity. Please note that the term "commodity prices" refers to industrial prices that are sensitive to business conditions, as opposed to weather-driven commodities such as grains. Figure 2.2 represents a business cycle, which typically has a life of between 3 and 5 years between troughs. The horizontal line reflects a level of zero growth, above which are periods of expansion and below which are periods of contraction. After the peak is experienced, the economy continues to grow, but at a declining rate, until the line crosses below the equilibrium level and contraction in economic activity takes place. The arrows in Figure 2.2 show the idealized peaks and troughs of the financial markets as they relate to the business cycle.

FIGURE 2.2 The Idealized Business Cycle and Financial Market Turning Points
(B = Bonds; S = Stocks; C = Commodities)

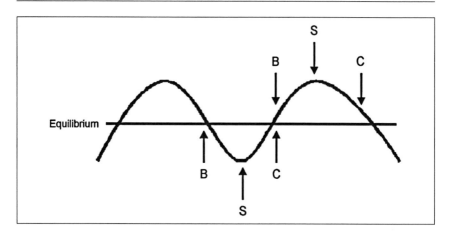

Periods of expansion generally last longer than periods of contraction because it takes longer to build something up than to tear it down. For this reason, bull markets for equities generally last longer than bear markets do. The same could be said for interest rates and commodities, but in all cases, the magnitude and duration of primary trends depend on the direction of the secular trend, as discussed in Chapters 1 and 23.

Figure 2.3 shows the hypothetical trajectories of bond prices, commodities, and equities during the course of a typical business cycle.

FIGURE 2.3 Idealized Sine Curves for the Three Financial Markets

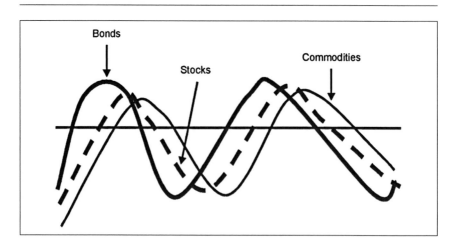

Referring back to Figure 2.2, we can see that the bond market is the first financial market to begin a bull phase. This usually occurs after the growth rate in the economy has slowed down considerably from its peak rate, and quite often is delayed until the initial stages of the recession. Generally speaking, the sharper the economic contraction, the greater the potential for a rise in bond prices will be (i.e., a fall in interest rates). Alternatively, the stronger the period of expansion, the smaller the amount of economic and financial slack, and the greater the potential for a decline in bond prices (and a rise in interest rates).

Following the bear market low in bond prices, economic activity begins to contract more sharply. At this point, participants in the equity market are able to "look through" the trend of deterioration in corporate profits, which are now declining sharply because of the recession, and to begin accumulating stocks. Generally speaking, the longer the lead between the low in bonds and that of stocks, the greater the potential for the stock market to rally. This is because the lag implies a particularly deep recession in which extreme corporate belt tightening is able to drop breakeven levels to a very low level. During the recovery, increases in revenue are therefore able to quickly move to the bottom line.

After the recovery has been under way for some time, capacity starts to tighten, resource-based companies feel some pricing power return, and commodity prices bottom. Occasionally, after a commodity boom of unusual magnitude, industrial commodity prices bottom out during the recession as a result of severe margin liquidation due to excessive speculation during the previous boom. However, this low is often subsequently tested, with a sustainable rally only beginning after the recovery has been under way for a few months. At this point, all three financial markets are in a rising trend.

Gradually, the economic and financial slack that developed as a result of the recession is substantially absorbed, putting upward pressure on the price of credit, i.e., interest rates. Since rising interest rates mean falling bond prices, the bond market peaks out and begins its bear phase. Because some excess plant and labor capacity still exists, rising business activity results in improved productivity and a continued positive outlook. The stock market discounts trends in corporate profits, so it remains in an uptrend until investors sense that the economy is becoming overheated and the potential for an improvement in profits is very low. At this point, there is less reason to hold equities, and they, in turn, enter into a bear phase. Later on, the rise in interest rates takes its toll on the economy, and commodity prices begin to slip.

Once this juncture has been reached, all three financial markets begin to fall. They will continue to decline until the credit markets bottom. This final stage, which develops around the same time as the beginning of the recession, is usually associated with a free-fall in prices in at least one of the financial markets. If a panic is to develop, this is one of the most likely points for it to take place.

The Six Stages

Since there are three financial markets and each has two turning points, it follows that there are conceptually six turning points in a typical cycle. I call these the six stages, and they can be used as reference points for determining the current phase of the cycle. The six stages are indicated in Figure 2.4.

When identifying a stage, it is important to look at the long-term technical position of all three markets so they can act as a cross-check on each other. The stages are also useful, in that specific industry groups outperform the market at particular times and vice versa. For example, defensive and liquidity-driven early-cycle leaders tend to do well in Stages I and II. On the other hand, earnings-driven or late-cycle leaders perform

FIGURE 2.4 The Six Stages of the Typical Business Cycle

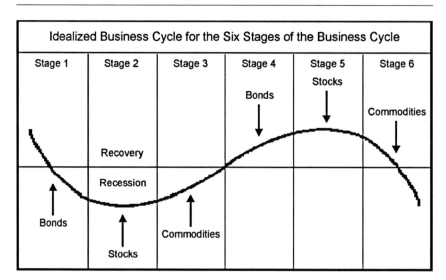

well in Stages IV and V when commodity prices are rallying. These aspects are covered more fully in Chapter 22 on sector rotation.

Longer Cycles

Some expansions encompass much longer periods, and they usually include at least one slowdown in the growth rate followed by a second round of economic expansion. This has the effect of splitting the overall expansion into two or three parts, each of which results in a complete cycle in the financial markets. I call this a double cycle. An example of this phenomenon is illustrated in Figure 2.5. A double cycle developed in the 1980s and another in the 1990s. In the mid-1980s, for example, commodity and industrial parts of the country were very badly affected as a result of the unwinding of the commodity boom that ended in 1980, but the east and west coasts continued their expansions unabated. The strong areas more than offset the weaker ones, and so the country as a whole avoided a recession.

FIGURE 2.5 Financial Market Peaks and Troughs in a Double Cycle

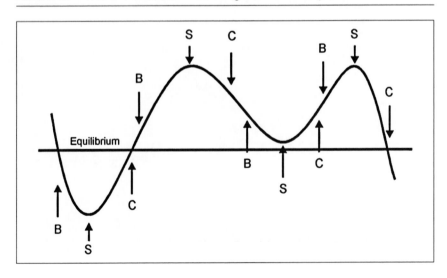

The Role of Technical Analysis

Technical analysis comes into play by helping to determine when the various markets have turned in a primary way. This is achieved by applying the various techniques outlined in subsequent chapters, moving average crossovers, changes in the direction of long-term momentum, and so forth. Each market can then be used as a cross-check against the other two. For example, if the weight of the technical evidence suggests that bonds have bottomed but that commodity prices remain in a bear market, then the next thing to do would be to look for technical signs pointing to a stock market bottom and so forth.

This analysis has also formed the basis of the Dow Jones Pring U.S. Business Cycle Index (symbol DJPRING) as shown in Chart 2.1. The index uses models to identify the six stages and then allocates assets and equity sectors based on their historical performance in each stage since the mid-1950s. It is far from perfect, but does show consistent long-term results. This methodology is also used in the Pring Turner Business Cycle

CHART 2.1 The Dow Jones Pring Business Cycle Index Performance versus Three Asset Classes

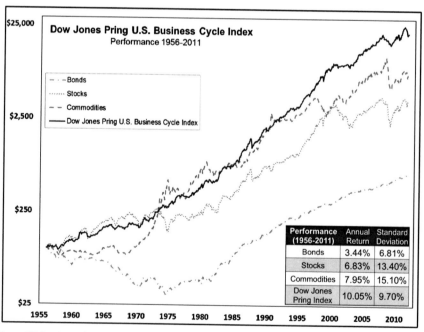

Source: S&P Dow Jones Indexes

ETF (Symbol DBIZ). The exchange-traded fund (ETF) does not seek to replicate the index, but rather to beat it on a risk-adjusted basis.

Market Experience, 1966–2001

Chart 2.1 shows how peaks and troughs developed for the various markets between 1966 and 1977.

Please note that inversely plotted short-term interest rates have been substituted for bond prices. There is a much closer link between equity prices and short-term rates than with longer-term ones. That is because corporations do more of their borrowing in the money markets than in the bond markets. Short-term rates are also more volatile than those at the end of the yield spectrum. The peaks and troughs turned out very much as expected. While the chronological sequence was more or less perfect, the leads and lags in each cycle varied considerably because of the different characteristics in each cycle.

In 1966, for instance, bonds and stocks bottomed more or less simultaneously, whereas the lag for the commodity market bottom was well over a year.

Chart 2.2 shows the same markets, but this time we are looking at the 1980s. The two small upward-pointing arrows in 1982 and 1990 reflect

CHART 2.2 Three Financial Markets, 1966–1977

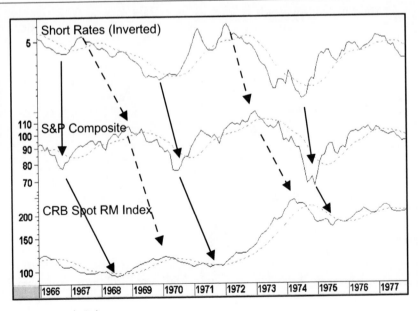

Source: From *Intermarket Review*

recessions. Such environments represent good buying opportunities for bonds, but terrible ones for owning commodities. The series of three bottoms that developed between 1984 and 1986 reflect the mid-1980s growth recession.

Generally speaking, the chronological sequence works satisfactorily until we get to the late 1980s, where the 1989 bottom in rates is juxtaposed with the stock market peak. Unfortunately, these out-of-sequence events are a fact of life. In my experience studying the 200 years of out-of-sequence relationships, I find they represent the exception rather than the rule.

Chart 2.3 shows the closing years of the twentieth century. This is the most difficult period I have encountered because of the record performance by the stock market and the strong deflationary forces associated with the technological revolution. This had the effect of reducing the normal cyclical fluctuation in the equity market. In the fourth edition of this book, I said, "Since the stock market boom was unprecedented, it is unlikely that the normal chronological sequences have been more than temporarily interrupted."

Chart 2.4 proves that conclusion to be mostly correct, except for the late 2001 low in commodities that preceded equities.

CHART 2.3 Three Financial Markets, 1980–1992

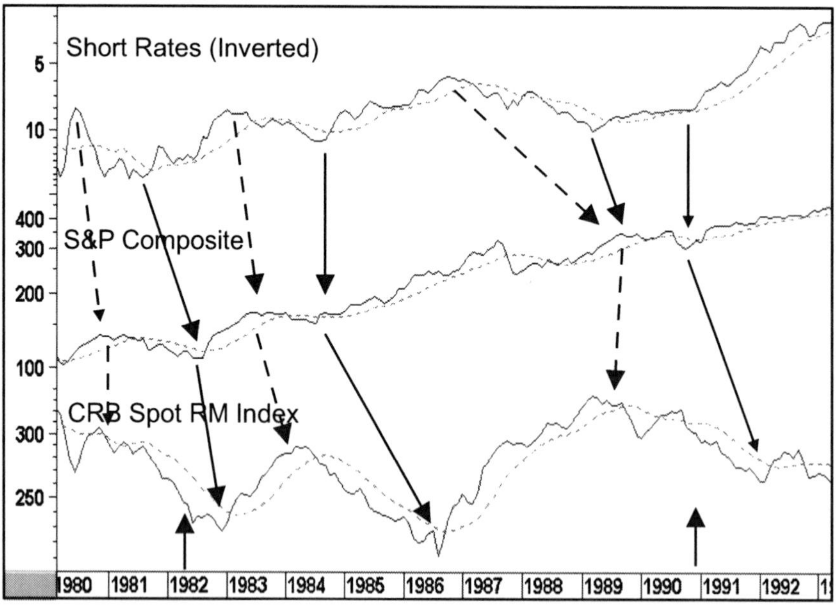

Source: From *Intermarket Review*

CHART 2.4 Three Financial Markets, 1989–2001

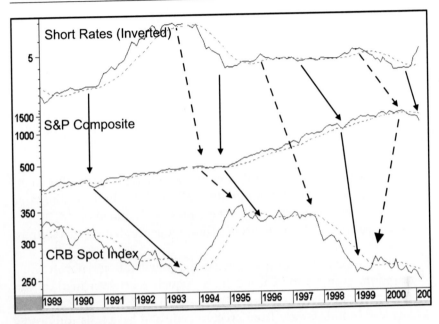

Source: From *Intermarket Review*

CHART 2.5 Three Financial Markets, 1999–2013

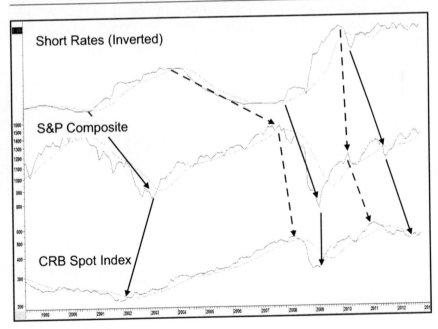

Source: From *Intermarket Review*

One could still argue, though, that the equity market lagged because it was still in the process of unwinding the tech bubble. Remember it continued to decline even *after* the 2001 recession ended. Note the double cycle that developed between 2010 and 2012 in Chart 2.5.

Summary

1. A typical business cycle embraces three individual cycles for interest rates, equities, and commodities. All are influenced by the same economic and financial forces, but each responds differently.
2. These markets undergo a chronological sequence that repeats in most cycles.
3. Some cycles experience a slowdown in the growth rate and not an actual recession. Even so, the chronological sequence between markets still appears to operate.
4. The leads and lags vary from cycle to cycle and have little forecasting value.
5. The chronological sequence of peaks and troughs in the various financial markets can be used as a framework for identifying the position of a specific market within its bull or bear cycle.

3

DOW THEORY

Introduction

The Dow theory is the oldest, and by far the most publicized, method of identifying major trends in the stock market. An extensive account will not be necessary here, as there are many excellent books on the subject. A brief explanation, however, is in order because the basic principles of the Dow theory are used in other branches of technical analysis.

The goal of the theory is to determine changes in the primary, or major, movement of the market. Once a trend has been established, it is assumed to exist until a reversal is proved. Dow theory is concerned with the *direction* of a trend and has no forecasting value as to the trend's ultimate duration or size.

It should be recognized that the theory does not always keep pace with events; it occasionally leaves the investor in doubt, and it is by no means infallible, since losses, as with any other technical approach, are occasionally incurred. These points emphasize that while mechanical devices can be useful for forecasting the stock market, there is no substitute for obtaining additional supportive analysis on which to base sound, balanced judgment. Remember there are no certainties in technical analysis because we are always dealing in probabilities.

The Dow theory evolved from the work of Charles H. Dow, which was published in a series of *Wall Street Journal* editorials between 1900 and 1902. Dow used the behavior of the stock market as a barometer of business conditions rather than as a basis for forecasting stock prices themselves. His successor, William Peter Hamilton, further developed Dow's principles and organized them into something approaching the theory as we know it today. These principles were outlined rather loosely in Hamilton's book *The Stock Market Barometer,* published in 1922. It was not until Robert Rhea published *Dow Theory,* in 1932, that a more complete and formalized account of the principles finally became available.

The theory assumes that the majority of stocks follow the underlying trend of the market most of the time. In order to measure "the market," Dow constructed two indexes, which are now called the *Dow Jones Industrial Average,* which was originally a combination of 12 (but now includes 30) blue-chip stocks, and the *Dow Jones Rail Average,* comprising 12 railroad stocks. Since the Rail Average was intended as a proxy for transportation stocks, the evolution of aviation and other forms of transportation has necessitated modifying the old Rail Average in order to incorporate additions to this industry. Consequently, the name of this index has been changed to *Transportation Average.*

Interpreting the Theory

In order to interpret the theory correctly, it is necessary to have a record of the daily closing[2] prices of the two averages and the total of daily transactions on the New York Stock Exchange (NYSE). The six basic tenets of the theory are discussed in the following sections.

1. The Averages Discount Everything

Changes in the daily closing prices reflect the aggregate judgment and emotions of all stock market participants, both current and potential. It is, therefore, assumed that this process discounts everything known and predictable that can affect the demand/supply relationship of stocks. Although acts of God are obviously unpredictable, their occurrence is quickly appraised and their implications are discounted.

2. The Market Has Three Movements

There are simultaneously three movements in the stock market.

---

[1]This assumes that the averages were available in 1897. Actually, Dow theory was first published in 1900.

[2]It is important to use closing prices, since intraday fluctuations are more subject to manipulation.

Primary Movement   The most important is the *primary* or *major trend,* more generally known as a bull (rising) or bear (falling) market. Such movements last from less than one year to several years.

A *primary bear market* is a long decline interrupted by important rallies. It begins as the hopes on which the stocks were first purchased are abandoned. The second phase evolves as the levels of business activity and profits decline. In the third stage, the bear market reaches a climax when stocks are liquidated, regardless of their underlying value (because of the depressed state of the news or because of forced liquidation caused, for example, by margin calls).

A *primary bull market* is a broad upward movement, normally averaging at least 18 months, which is interrupted by secondary reactions. The bull market begins when the averages have discounted the worst possible news and confidence about the future begins to revive. The second stage of the bull market is the response of equities to known improvements in business conditions, while the third and final phase evolves from over-confidence and speculation when stocks are advanced on projections that usually prove to be unfounded.

Secondary Reactions   A *secondary* or *intermediate reaction* is defined as "an important decline in a bull market or advance in a bear market, usually lasting from three weeks to as many months, during which interval, the movement generally retraces from 33 to 66 percent of the primary price change since the termination of the last preceding secondary reaction."[3] This relationship is shown in Figure 3.1.

Occasionally, a secondary reaction can retrace the whole of the previous primary movement, but normally, the move falls in the one-half to two-thirds area, often at the 50 percent mark. As discussed in greater detail later, the correct differentiation between the first leg of a new primary trend and a secondary movement within the existing trend provides Dow theorists with their most difficult problem.

Minor Movements   The *minor movement* lasts from a week or two up to as long as six weeks. It is important only in that it forms part of the primary or secondary moves; it has no forecasting value for longer-term investors. This is especially important since short-term movements can be manipulated to some extent, unlike the secondary or primary trends.

---

[3]Robert Rhea, *Dow Theory*, Barron's: New York, 1932.

FIGURE 3.1 Secondary Retracements

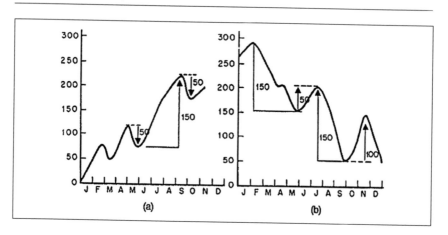

3. Lines Indicate Movement

Rhea defined a line as "a price movement two to three weeks or longer, during which period, the price variation of both averages moves within a range of approximately 5 percent (of their mean average). I see no reason why the 5 percent rule cannot be exceeded. After all, it really represents a digestion of gains or losses or a pause in the trend. Such a movement indicates either accumulation [*stock moving into strong and knowledgeable hands and therefore bullish*] or distribution [*stock moving into weak hands and therefore bearish*]."[4]

An advance above the limits of the "line" indicates accumulation and predicts higher prices, and vice versa. When a line occurs in the middle of a primary advance, it is really forming a horizontal secondary movement and should be treated as such.

My own view is that the formation of a legitimate line should probably take longer than 2 to 3 weeks. After all, a line is really a substitute for an intermediate price trend and 2 to 3 weeks is the time for a short-term or minor price movement.

4. Price/Volume Relationships Provide Background

The normal relationship is for volume to expand on rallies and contract on declines. If it becomes dull on a price advance and expands on a decline, this

---

[4]Ibid.

is a warning that the prevailing trend may soon be reversed. This principle should be used as background information only, since the conclusive evidence of trend reversals can be given only by the price of the respective averages.

5. Price Action Determines the Trend

Bullish indications are given when successive rallies penetrate peaks while the trough of an intervening decline is above the preceding trough. Conversely, bearish indications come from a series of declining peaks and troughs.

Figure 3.2 shows a theoretical bull trend interrupted by a secondary reaction. In example *a*, the index makes a series of three peaks and troughs, each higher than its respective predecessor. The index rallies following the third decline, but is unable to surpass its third peak. The next decline takes the average below its low point, confirming a bear market as it does so, at point X. In example *b*, following the third peak in the bull market, a bear market is indicated as the average falls below the previous secondary trough. In this instance,

FIGURE 3.2 Primary Trend Reversals

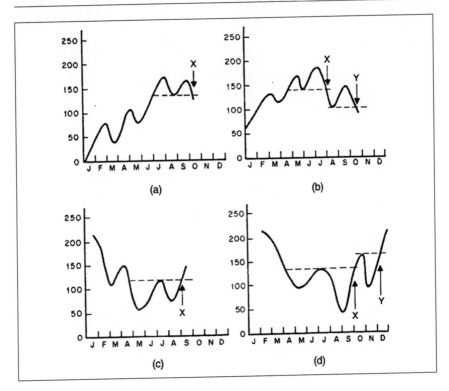

the preceding secondary was part of a bull market, not the first trough in a bear market, as shown in example *a*. Many Dow theorists do not consider penetration at point X in example *b* to be a sufficient indication of a bear market. They prefer to take a more conservative position by waiting for a rally and subsequent penetration of that previous trough marked as point Y in example *b*.

In such cases, it is wise to approach the interpretation with additional caution. If a bearish indication is given from the volume patterns and a clearly identifiable speculative stage for the bull market has already materialized, it is probably safe to assume that the bearish indication is valid. In the absence of such characteristics, it is wiser to give the bull market the benefit of the doubt and adopt a more conservative position. Remember, technical analysis is the art of identifying trend reversals based on *the weight of the evidence*. Dow theory is one piece of evidence, so if four or five other indicators are pointing to a trend reversal, it is usually a good idea to treat the "half" signal at point X as an indication that the trend has reversed. Examples *c* and *d* represent similar instances at the bottom of a bear market.

The examples in Figure 3.3 show how the primary reversal would appear if the average had formed a line at its peak or trough. The importance of being able to distinguish between a valid secondary correction and the first leg of a new primary trend is now evident. This is perhaps the most difficult part of the theory to interpret, and unquestionably the most critical.

It is essential to establish that the secondary reaction has retraced at least one-third of the ground of the preceding primary movement, as measured from the termination of the preceding secondary. The secondary should also extend for at least three to four weeks.

FIGURE 3.3 Lines Being Formed at a Peak and Trough

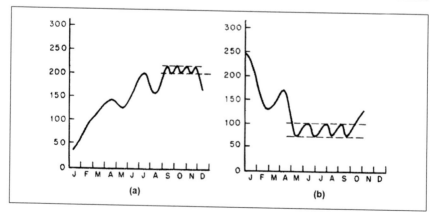

(a)　　　　　　　　　(b)

Vital clues can also be obtained from volume characteristics and from an assessment of the maturity of the prevailing primary trend. The odds of a major reversal are much greater if the market has undergone its third phase, characterized by speculation and false hopes during a primary upswing, or a bout of persistent liquidation and widespread pessimism during a major decline. A change in the primary trend can occur without a clearly identifiable third phase, but generally, such reversals prove to be relatively short-lived. On the other hand, the largest primary swings usually develop when the characteristics of a third phase are especially marked during the preceding primary movement. Hence, the excessive bouts of speculation in 1919, 1929, 1968, and 2000 in the NASDAQ were followed by particularly sharp setbacks. Intermediate-term movements are discussed more extensively in Chapter 4. Quite often, a reversal in an 18-month rate of change (ROC) from a reading in excess of 200 percent is reflective of such an exhaustion of buying power.

6. The Averages Must Confirm

One of the most important principles of Dow theory is that *the movement of the Industrial Average and the Transportation Average should always be considered together*; i.e., the two averages must confirm each other.

The need for confirming action by both averages would seem fundamentally logical, for if the market is truly a barometer of future business conditions, investors should be bidding up the prices, both of companies that produce goods and of companies that transport them, in an expanding economy. It is not possible to have a healthy economy in which goods are being manufactured but not sold (i.e., shipped to market). This principle of confirmation is shown in Figure 3.4.

FIGURE 3.4 Dow Theory Requires Both Averages to Confirm

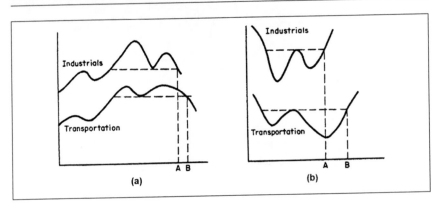

In example *a*, the Industrial Average is the first to signal a bear trend (point *A*), but the actual bear market is not indicated until the Transportation Average confirms at point *B*. Example *b* shows the beginning of a new bull market. Following a sharp decline, the industrials make a new low. A rally then develops, but the next reaction holds above the previous low. When prices push above the preceding rally, a bull signal is given by the industrials at point *A*. In the meantime, the Transportation Average makes a series of two succeeding lows. The question that arises is which average is correctly representing the prevailing trend? Since it is always assumed that a trend is in existence until a reversal is proved, the conclusion should be drawn at this point that the Transportation Average is indicating the correct outcome.

It is only when this average exceeds the peak of the preceding secondary at point *B* that a new bull market is confirmed by both averages, resulting in a Dow theory buy signal.

The movement of one average unsupported by the other can often lead to a false and misleading conclusion, which is well illustrated in Figure 3.5, which shows the 1930 price action in wave form.

The 1929–1932 bear market began in September 1929 and was confirmed by both averages in late October. In June 1930, each made a new low and then rallied and reacted in August. Following this correction, the industrials surpassed their previous peak. Many observers believed that this signaled the end of a particularly sharp bear market and that it was only a matter of time before the rails would follow suit. As it turned out, the action of the industrials was totally misleading; the bear market still had another two years to run.

FIGURE 3.5 1930 Example

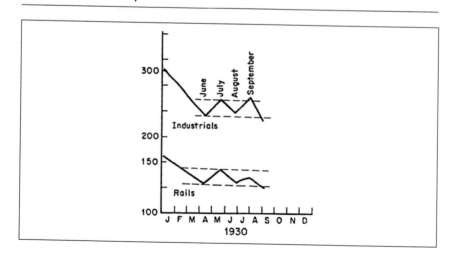

The Theory in Action: 1998–2013

Chart 3.1 compares the Industrials to the Transports between 1997 and 2013. The chart opens during the tail end of the 1982–2000 secular bull market.

The Transports gave a nonconfirmed sell signal in 1998 following a zig-zag down. The Industrials also broke to a new low, but since the previous July's high was above the April one, our strict interpretation said a nonconfirmed bear market. Since the Transports remained in a bearish mode until 2004, all that was required for a sell signal was Industrial confirmation, and that came in October 2000 as this average broke down from a line formation. Fortunes were reversed in early 2003 as the Industrials went bullish, but the Transports were unable to follow suit since they made a new low in early 2003 (C), unlike their industrial counterparts, who were able to give an unconfirmed bull signal at (D). Consequently, it was not until the Transports broke out of a line formation at (E) that a new bull market was signaled. The next event developed at (F) when the Industrials broke below their previous intermediate low. The Transportations eventually confirmed in November 2008 at (G). The subsequent bull market was signaled

CHART 3.1 Dow Theory Signals: 1997–2012

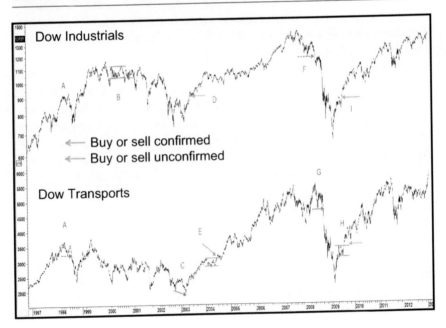

Source: Martin Pring's Intermarket Review.

by the Transports with a line breakout in early 2009 (H) and subsequently confirmed by the Industrials in June at (I). This buy signal is arguably controversial since the intermediate correction only lasted for 4 weeks—acceptable but somewhat on the low side. Also, the correction retraced just 30 percent of the previous advance, 33⅓ to 66⅔ being the normal accepted limits.

Additional Considerations

Dow theory does not specify a time period beyond which a confirmation of one average by the other becomes invalid. Generally, *the closer the confirmation, the stronger the following move is likely to be.* I have noticed that this principle can be extended to other techniques used in technical analysis, especially in conjunction with momentum/price considerations (see Chapter 13). For example, confirmation of the 1929–1932 bear market was given by the Rail Average just one day after the Industrial Average. The sharp 1962 break was confirmed on the same day.

One of the major criticisms of Dow theory is that many of its signals have proved to be late, often 20 to 25 percent after a peak or trough in the averages has occurred. One rule of thumb that has enabled Dow theorists to anticipate probable reversals at an earlier date is to observe the dividend yield on the Industrials. When the yield on the Industrial Average has fallen to 3 percent or below, it has historically been a reliable indicator at marker tops. This was certainly true prior to the mid-1990s and has been more questionable since then. Similarly, a yield of 6 percent has been a reliable indicator at market bottoms. Dow theorists would not necessarily use these levels as actual buying or selling points, but would probably consider altering the percentage of their equity exposure if a significant nonconfirmation developed between the Industrial Average and the Transportation Average when the yield on the Dow reached these extremes. This strategy would help to improve the investment return of the Dow theory, but would not always result in a superior performance. At the 1976 peak, for example, the yield on the Dow never reached the magic 3 percent level, and prices fell 20 percent before a mechanical signal was confirmed by both averages. In addition the 3 percent top would have missed the mark by about 5 years in the late 1990s.

Over the years, many criticisms have been leveled at the theory on the basis that from time to time (as in periods of war) the rails have been overregulated, or that the new Transportation Average no longer reflects investors' expectations about the future movement of goods. The theory has stood the test of time, however, as Table 3.1 indicates.

TABLE 3.1 Dow Theory Analysis

Buy Signals*			Sell Signals*		
Date of Signal	Price of Dow	Percentage gain from sell signal when short	Date of Signal	Price of Dow	Percentage gain from buy signal
Jul. 1897	44		Dec. 1899	63	43
Oct. 1900	59	6	Jun. 1903	59	0
Jul. 1904	51	14	Apr. 1906	92	80
Apr. 1908	70	24	May 1910	85	21
Oct. 1910	82	4	Jan. 1913	85	3
Apr. 1915	65	24	Aug. 1917	86	32
May 1918	82	5	Feb. 1920	99	22
Feb. 1922	84	16	Jun. 1923	91	8
Dec. 1923	94	(loss) 3	Oct. 1929	306	226
May 1933	84	73	Sep. 1937	164	95
Jun. 1938	127	23	Mar. 1939	136	7
Jul. 1939	143	5	May 1940	138	(loss) 7
Feb. 1943	126	8	Aug. 1946	191	52
Apr. 1948	184	4	Nov. 1948	173	(loss) 6
Oct. 1950	229	(loss)32	Apr. 1953	280	22
Jan. 1954	288	(loss) 3	Oct. 1956	468	63
Apr. 1958	450	4	Mar. 1960	612	36
Nov. 1960	602	2	Apr. 1962	683	13
Nov. 1962	625	8	May 1966	900	43
Jan. 1967	823	9	Jun. 1969	900	9
Dec. 1970	823	9	Apr. 1973	921	12
Jan. 1975	680	26	Oct. 1977	801	18
Apr. 1978	780	3	Jul. 1981	960	23
Aug. 1982	840	13	Feb. 1984	1,186	41
Jan. 1985	1,261	(loss) 6	Oct. 1989	2,510	104
Dec. 1990	2,610	(loss) 1	Oct. 2000	10,034	60
Jul. 2003	9,223	8	Nov. 2007	12,829	39
Jul. 2009	8,848	58			
Average of all cycles 39%			Average all cycles 11%		

*When considering the results, note that these signals are the result of my interpretation, in some cases with the benefit of hindsight. Some Dow theorists would disagree with my interpretation, but none would dispute the fact that, in general, the theory works.

Indeed, criticism is perfectly healthy, for if the theory gained widespread acceptance and its signals were purely mechanistic instead of requiring experienced judgment, they would be instantly discounted, which would render Dow theory useless for profitable investment.

In any event, it is important to note that it is far from perfect, and in any case, Dow theory should be regarded as one indicator that should be used with others in the technical arsenal.

Summary

1. Dow theory is concerned with determining the direction of the primary trend of the market, not its duration or size. Once confirmed by both averages, the new trend is assumed to be in existence until an offsetting confirmation by both averages takes place.
2. Major bull and bear markets each have three distinct phases. Both the identification of these phases and the appearance of any divergence in the normal volume/price relationship offer useful indications that a reversal in the major trend is about to take place. Such supplementary evidence is particularly useful when the action of the price averages themselves is inconclusive.

4

TYPICAL PARAMETERS FOR INTERMEDIATE TRENDS

Some Basic Observations

The two previous chapters discussed the main or primary trend, i.e., the price movement that corresponds to changes in economic activity over the course of a typical 3- to 4-year business cycle. Though it is clearly important to have an idea of the direction and maturity of the primary trend, it is also helpful to have some understanding of the typical character and duration of the intermediate trend for the purpose of improving success rates in trading, and also to help assess when the primary movement may have run its course. This chapter focuses on intermediate trends in the U.S. stock market, but the principles outlined here apply to any freely traded entity.

Successful analysis of intermediate trends for any market or stock offers the following advantages:

1. Changes in intermediate trends aid in identification of turning points in the primary trend.
2. Intermediate-term trading involves fewer transactions than trading of minor price movements and, therefore, results in lower commission and execution costs.
3. Intermediate-trend reversal points occur several times a year and can, if properly interpreted, allow a relatively high and quick return on capital.

Intermediate Cycles Defined

A primary trend typically consists of five intermediate trends, three of which form part of the prevailing trend, while the remaining two run counter to that trend. In a bull market, the intermediate countertrends are represented by price declines; in a bear market, they form rallies that separate the three intermediate down waves, as shown in Figure 4.1.

It is apparent from this discussion that there are essentially two types of intermediate price movements. The first, which goes in the direction of the primary trend, may be called a *primary intermediate price movement.* The second is an important price movement that lasts from 3 weeks to 3 months, occasionally longer. It normally retraces between one-third and two-thirds of the preceding primary intermediate trend. This price movement, which runs counter to the main trend, is called a *secondary movement* or *reaction.* Since a primary intermediate price movement operates in the same direction as the primary or main market trend, it almost always lasts longer than its secondary counterpart. Its price magnitude is normally much greater as well.

These countertrends, or reactions against the main trend, are notoriously difficult to forecast in terms of character, magnitude, and duration. Therefore, they should generally be avoided from a trading point of view, as they will almost invariably be subject to confusing whipsaws. By their very nature, they tend to fool the majority and are usually extremely treacherous. It is possible to design successful mechanized systems based

FIGURE 4.1 Intermediate Cycles in a Primary Trend

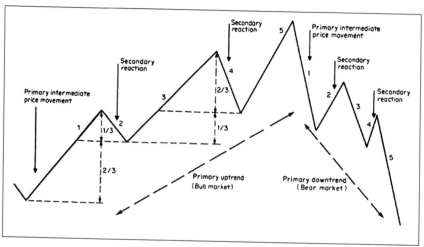

on intermediate price movements, but poor or losing signals usually come from secondary market movements that occur against the main trend. Intermediate-term trends that move in the same direction as the primary trend are generally easier to profit from. Those who do not have the patience to invest for the longer term will find that successful analysis of intermediate movements offers superior results, especially as the day-to-day or minor swings are, to a large degree, random in nature and, therefore, even more difficult to capitalize on. This tendency has been most pronounced in recent years when increasingly sharp price movements have resulted from emotional knee-jerk reactions to the release of unexpected economic data.

A secondary reaction does not have to be a decline in a bull market or a bear market rally. It can also take the form of a sideways movement or consolidation, under the same idea as Charles Dow's line formation (see the discussion in Chapter 3).

Intermediate movements can go either with or against the main trend, which means that there is an intermediate cycle similar to a primary one. An intermediate cycle consists of a primary intermediate price movement and a secondary reaction. It extends from the low of one intermediate trend to the low of the other, as shown in Figure 4.2.

In a bull market, the up phase of the cycle should be longer in time and greater in magnitude. The low on the secondary reaction should be higher than its predecessor. In a bear market, the reverse conditions hold

FIGURE 4.2 Intermediate-Term Cycles

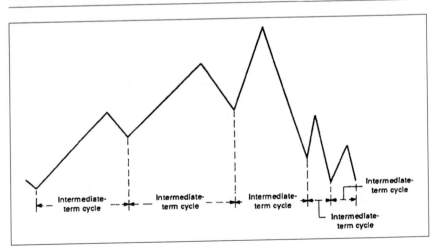

true; i.e., declines are longer and greater, while rallies are shorter and sharper, but of less magnitude. Accordingly, technicians are alerted first to the possibility of a reversal in the primary trend when a third intermediate cycle is nearing completion. It is also important to note whether the overall technical structure looks weak (strong in a bear market) as the previous intermediate low (high) is approached and, finally, to note whether that level is decisively broken on the downside (upside).

This does not mean that primary movements can never encompass more or fewer than three primary intermediate price movements, for often they do. Expect three as a normal event, but do not be caught off guard if there are fewer or more.

Causes of Secondary Reactions

Since the primary trend of stock prices is determined by the *attitudes* of investors to the future flow of profits, which are, in turn, determined to a large degree by the course of the business cycle, it would seem illogical at first to expect longer-term movements to be interrupted by what often prove to be very uncomfortable reactions (or in the case of a bear market, very deceptive rallies).

History shows that secondary reactions occur because of technical distortions, which arise in the market as a result of overoptimism (or overpessimism), and also because new factors emerge that suggest business conditions are not going to be as extreme as was originally anticipated, or even that they are going to materialize in the opposite direction. For example, after the first intermediate-term rally in a bull market for equities, a reaction may develop because investors, who had discounted a strong recovery, now see some chinks appearing that might even forecast an actual decline in business conditions. Such fears eventually prove ungrounded, but are sufficient to cause a countercyclical intermediate reaction. Another possibility might be a fear of rising interest rates, which could choke off the recovery. Since prices had discounted a strong recovery, this change in perception causes investors to pull back and prices to fall accordingly. At the same time, many investors get carried away during the rally phase and leverage themselves up. As prices begin to fall, this causes their equity to shrink and forces them to liquidate, which adds further fuel to the price decline.

A bear market rally for stocks generally takes place because of an improved outlook for business conditions over what was anticipated. A bear market rally for bonds develops under the opposite set of conditions.

Corrections in commodity and currency markets all have their roots in a changed, but incorrect, perception of the underlying (primary) economic trend. The catalyst for the rally is the rush by traders and investors to cover their short positions (for a definition and explanation of short selling, see the Glossary). It should be added that the *apparent* motivating force for the correction need not necessarily be directly linked to the outlook for business or interest rates.

> **Major Technical Principle** At any one time, there are four influences on prices. They are psychological, technical, economic, and monetary in nature.

Any of these influences could be the "excuse" for a countercyclical intermediate price movement. It could be linked to the anticipated resolution or worsening of a political or military problem, for example. Essentially, the change in anticipated conditions, combined with the unwinding of the technical distortions of the previous primary intermediate trend and its associated sharp price movement, are sufficient to confuse the majority. Only when business conditions are correctly expected to change from recovery to recession (or vice versa) is the primary trend of equities *likely* to reverse. Note the emphasis on the word "likely." Although equity prices fluctuate around perceived future economic conditions, there have been exceptions. For example, the economy moved out of recession at the end of 2001, yet stocks continued to decline into October 2002. In that case, it would appear that the unwinding of the tech bubble was a stronger influence than was improving economic activity. That sort of decoupling, though, is far more the exception than the rule.

In his excellent book *Profits in the Stock Market* (Lambert Gann Publishing, 1935), H. M. Gartley pointed out that in the 40 years ending in 1935, two-thirds of all bull market corrections in the U.S. stock market developed in two waves of liquidation separated by a minor rally that retraced between one-third and two-thirds of the first decline. Observation of such corrections since 1935 also bears out the finding that most intermediate corrections consist of two, rather than one or three, phases of liquidation. Unfortunately, intermediate corrections within a bear market cannot be so easily categorized since some are one-move affairs or consist of a rally out of a small base, while still others unfold as a very volatile sideways movement. Even though Gartley's observations were concerned with the equities, this form of correction applies to all financial markets.

Relationship Between Primary Intermediate Moves and Subsequent Reactions

In *Profits in the Stock Market,* Gartley published a series of diagrams using the classification of intermediate trends established by Robert Rhea. Gartley's conclusion was that the smaller in magnitude the primary intermediate-term movement was, the larger the retracement tended to be, and vice versa. He noted that this was just as valid for bull market reactions as for bear market rallies. Observations of the period since 1933 for virtually all markets appear to support this hypothesis. For example, the rally off the 1962 stock market low was only 18 percent, compared to the mean average of 30 percent between 1933 and 1982. This represented part of a double bottom formation and, therefore, the first primary intermediate rally. This relatively small advance was followed by a somewhat larger 71 percent retracement. However, the ensuing rally from late 1962 until mid-1963 was 32 percent and was followed by a small 25 percent retracement of the gain. Interested readers may wish to be satisfied that what goes up does not necessarily come down, and vice versa.

The 1976–1980 gold bull market was very powerful, but the intermediate corrections were quite brief. On the other hand, the rallies between 1982 and 1990 were far less strong, but were followed by corrections of much greater magnitude proportionally.

Using Intermediate Cycles to Identify Primary Reversals

Number of Intermediate Cycles

A primary movement may normally be expected to encompass two and a half intermediate cycles (see Figure 4.3). Unfortunately, not all primary movements correspond to the norm; an occasional primary movement may consist of one, two, three, or even four intermediate cycles. Furthermore, these intermediate cycles may be of very unequal length or magnitude, making their classification and identification possible only after

FIGURE 4.3 Intermediate Trends and Volume

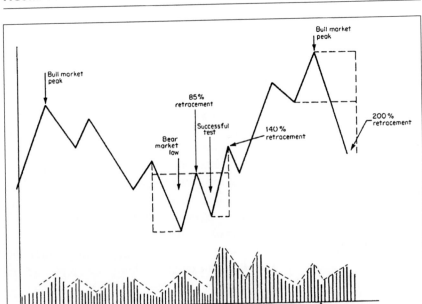

the event. Even so, intermediate-cycle analysis can still be used as a basis for identifying the maturity of the primary trend in most cases.

Whenever prices are well advanced in a primary intermediate trend following the complication of two intermediate cycles, technicians should be alerted to the fact that a reversal of the primary trend itself may be about to take place. Again, if only one intermediate cycle has been completed, the chances of prices reaching higher levels (lower levels in a bear market) are quite high.

Characteristics of the Final Intermediate Cycle in a Primary Trend

In addition to actually counting the number of intermediate cycles, it is possible to compare the characteristics of a particular cycle with those of a typical pivotal or reversal cycle of a primary trend. These characteristics are discussed in the following sections.

Reversal from Bull to Bear Market   Since volume leads price, the failure of volume to increase above the levels of the previous intermediate-cycle up phase is a bearish sign. Alternatively, if over a period of 3 to 4 weeks, volume expands on the intermediate rally close to the previous peak in volume but fails to move prices significantly, it represents churning and should also be treated bearishly. Coincidence of either of these characteristics with a downward crossover of a 40-week moving average (see Chapter 11) or a divergence in an intermediate-term momentum index (see Chapter 13) would be an additional reason for caution.

There are essentially two broad characteristics that suggest that the downward phase of an intermediate cycle could be the first downleg of a bear market. The first is a substantial increase in volume during the price decline. The second is a cancellation or retracement of 80 percent or more of the up phase of that same intermediate cycle. The greater the retracement, the greater the probability that the basic trend has reversed, especially because a retracement in excess of 100 percent means that any series of rising troughs has been broken, thereby placing the probabilities in favor of a change in the primary trend. Other signs would include the observation of a mega oversold or an extreme swing (see Chapter 13 on momentum for a full explanation of these terms).

Reversal from Bear to Bull Market　The first intermediate up phase of a bull market is usually accompanied by a substantial expansion in volume that is significantly greater than those of previous intermediate up phases. In other words, the first upleg in a bull market attracts noticeably more volume than any of the intermediate rallies in the previous bear market. Another sign of a basic reversal occurs when prices retrace at least 80 percent of the previous decline. Again, the greater the proportion of retracement, the greater the odds of a reversal in the basic trend. If the retracement is greater than 100 percent, the odds clearly indicate that a reversal in the downward trend has taken place because the series of declining peaks will have broken down.

Since volume normally expands substantially as the intermediate down phase during a bear market reaches a low, a shrinkage in volume during an intermediate decline could well be a warning that the bear market has run its course. This is especially true if the price does not reach a new low during this intermediate decline, since the series of declining intermediate cyclical lows, which is a characteristic of a bear market, may no longer be intact. An example of this is shown in Chart 8.12 where the overall peak in volume was seen in the June 1962 decline rather than the August–October sell-off.

A final sign might include a mega overbought condition or an extreme swing; again please refer to Chapter 13 for an explanation of these concepts.

Intermediate Trends in the U.S. Stock Market, 1897–1982

Amplitude and Duration of Primary Intermediate Upmoves

Between 1897 and 1933, Robert Rhea, the author of *Dow Theory,* classified 53 intermediate-trend advances within a primary bull market, which ranged in magnitude from 7 to 117 percent, as shown in Table 4.1.

I have classified 35 intermediate-term moves between 1933 and 1982, and the median averaged 22 percent from low to high. The results are shown in Table 4.2.

The median average primary intermediate advance since 1897 appears to be around 20 to 22 percent. The median primary intermediate upmove in the 1933–1982 period does not differ from that of the earlier period classified by Rhea. However, the median duration appears to have increased considerably, from 13 weeks in the 1897–1933 period to 24 weeks in the 1933–1982 period.

TABLE 4.1 Primary Intermediate Upmoves 1897–1933

Prorportion of Intermediate Moves	Price Magnitude
25	7–14
50	15–28
<u>25</u>	28–117
100	
Median 20	

TABLE 4.2 Primary Intermediate Upmoves 1933–1982

	Swings from Low to High, Percent	Duration, Weeks
Mean average	30	22
Median	22	24
Range	10–105	3–137

Amplitude and Duration of Primary Intermediate Downmoves

Using Rhea's classification, 39 cases of a primary intermediate decline developed between 1900 and 1932, as summarized in Table 4.3.

My research shows that between 1932 and 1982 there were 35 primary intermediate declines, with a median of 16 percent (the decline was measured as a percentage from the high). The results are summarized in Table 4.4.

The results in the 1932–1982 period did not differ appreciably from those in the 1897–1933 period. Rhea's median average swing was 18 percent, as compared to the more recent 16 percent, whereas, the median duration in the earlier period was 13 weeks, as compared to 14 weeks in the 1932–1982 period.

Amplitude, Duration, and Retracement of Bull Market Intermediate Corrections

Bull Market Secondary Reactions   Between 1898 and 1933, Rhea classified 43 cases of bull market secondaries. In terms of retracement of the previous primary intermediate upmove, they ranged from 12.4 to 180

TABLE 4.3 Primary Intermediate Downmoves 1900–1932

Proportion of Intermediate Moves	Price Magnitude
25	3–12
50	13–27
25	28–54
Median 18	

TABLE 4.4 Primary Intermediate Downmoves 1932–1982

	Swings from High	Duration (Weeks)
Mean average	18	17
Median	16	14
Range	7–40	3–43

percent, with a median of 56 percent. This compared with a range in the 1933–1982 period from 25 to 148 percent, with a median of 51 percent. The duration of the median in the earlier period was 5 weeks, as compared to 8 weeks between 1933 and 1982. The median percentage loss from the previous primary intermediate peak was 12 percent (the mean average was 13 percent) between 1933 and 1982.

Bear Market Rallies   Rhea estimated that the median bear market rally retraced 52 percent of the previous decline, which is comparable to my own median estimate of 61 percent in the 1932–1982 period. The two ranges were 30 and 116 percent and 26 and 99 percent, respectively. Median durations were 6 weeks in 1898–1933 and 7 weeks in 1932–1982. Rallies off the low averaged 12 and 10 percent for mean and median, respectively, for the 1933–1982 period.

Since 1982   Charts 4.1 and 4.2 show the S&P Composite between the end of 1982 and the opening of the twenty-first century.

The thick vertical lines approximate intermediate rally peaks and the thin ones intermediate troughs. The lower panel contains an intermediate oscillator, the intermediate Know Sure Thing (KST) (see Chapter 15 for an explanation), which roughly reflects the turning points. This period encompassed the secular bull market that began in 1982 and

CHART 4.1 S&P Composite 1982–1991 and an Intermediate KST

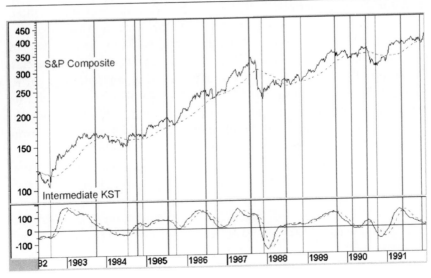

Source: From pring.com

CHART 4.2 S&P Composite 1991–2001 and an Intermediate KST

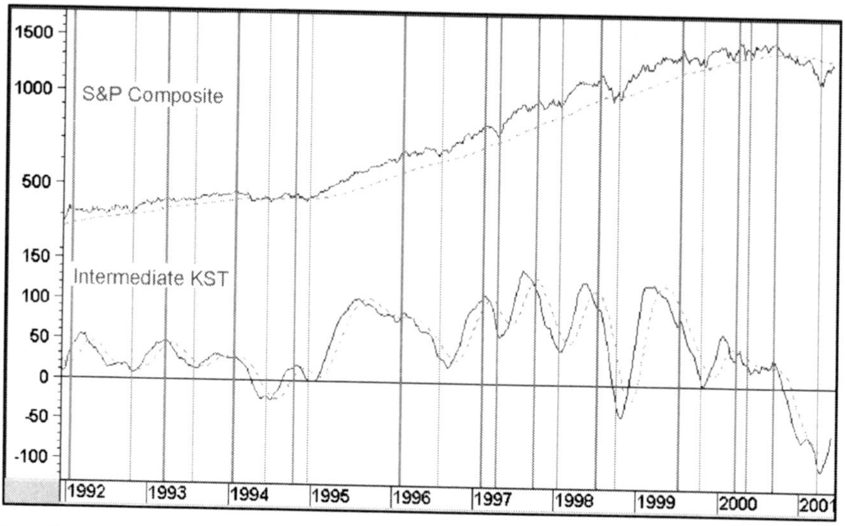

Source: From pring.com

ended at the turn of the century, as well as the subsequent secular bear. The classification of intermediate trends was particularly difficult compared to previous periods. I tried as much as possible to make the intermediate trends fit the swings in the oscillator. Because oscillators have a tendency to lead in bull markets, the actual peaks in the intermediate rallies usually lag those in the KST. The two charts show that the classification of these trends is far from a precise task, and confirms earlier research between 1897 and 1982, that the range of intermediate trends varies tremendously. In the period covered by Chart 4.1, for instance, the first intermediate rally in the bull market lasted well over a year, from August 1982 to October 1983. Even if I had taken the July 1983 top as a reference point, the rally would still have lasted for almost a year. Moreover, the whole year of 1995 was consumed by one complete intermediate advance.

Chart 4.3 fills in the balance of the picture until 2012. Note the particularly lengthy 2008 and 2009 trends, first on the downside and later on the upside.

CHART 4.3 S&P Composite 2001–2012 and an Intermediate KST

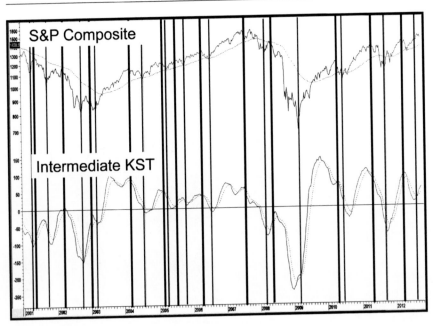

Source: From pring.com

Summary

1. The typical primary trend can be divided into two and a half primary intermediate cycles, each consisting of an upmove and a downmove. In a bull market, each successive up wave should reach a new cyclical high, and in a bear market, each successive down wave of the intermediate cycle should reach a new low. Breaking the pattern of rising lows and falling peaks is an important, but *not* unequivocal, warning of a reversal in the primary trend. For more conclusive proof, technicians should derive a similar conclusion from a consensus of indicators.

2. A secondary movement or reaction is that part of an intermediate cycle that runs counter to the main trend—a downward reaction in a bull market or a rally in a bear market. Secondary intermediate movements typically last from 3 weeks to 3 months and retrace between one-third and two-thirds of the previous primary intermediate price movement. Secondary price movements may also take the form of a line or horizontal trading pattern.

3. The character of intermediate cycles can be used to help identify primary trend reversals.
4. As an approximate rule, the stronger an intermediate rally, in a bull market the less the retracement is likely to be.

5

HOW TO IDENTIFY SUPPORT AND RESISTANCE ZONES

Support and resistance are two basic building blocks of the technical arsenal. They form a key role in price pattern analysis, which we will address later. A lot of people use the term *support* when they really mean resistance and use *resistance* when they really mean *support*. It's no wonder that there is a lot of confusion. Basically, these are points on a chart where the probabilities favor at least a temporary halt in the prevailing trend.

Support and Resistance

In their classic book *Technical Analysis of Stock Trends*, Edwards and Magee defined *support* as "buying (actual or potential) sufficient in volume to halt a downtrend in prices for an appreciable period," and *resistance* as "selling (actual or potential) sufficient in volume to satisfy all bids and hence stop prices from going higher for a time."

A support zone represents a *concentration of demand,* whereas resistance represents a *concentration of supply.* The word *concentration* is emphasized because supply and demand are always in balance. However, it is the relative enthusiasm of buyers as compared to sellers, or vice versa, that is important because that is what determines trends. If buyers are more enthusiastic than sellers, they will continually increase their bids until their purchasing demands have been satisfied. On the other hand, if sellers are the more anxious, then they will be willing to liquidate at lower

FIGURE 5.1 Support Violation

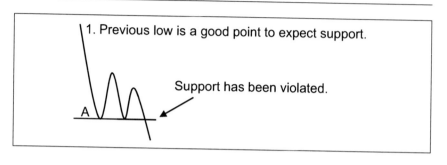

1. Previous low is a good point to expect support.

Support has been violated.

A

prices and the general price level will fall. If in doubt, think of support as a temporary floor for prices and resistance as a ceiling.

At the beginning of Figure 5.1, the price is declining. It finds a bottom at *A* and then moves up. The next time it falls to *A*, it again rallies, so *A* may now be said to be a support area.

This establishes our first principle of support/resistance analysis:

> **Major Technical Principle** A previous high or low is a potential resistance/support level.

The third time the price slips to *A*, it goes through or, as we say, it violates support. One of the first principles of identifying a potential support level, then, is to look for previous lows. In the case of potential resistance, this would be in the area of a previous high.

Figure 5.2 shows a more extended example. This time, the price found temporary support at *B*.

C also proves to be a support point, but note that the rallies are reversed at support level *B*. Thus, the second principle is:

> **Major Technical Principle** Support reverses its role to resistance on the way up.

Just think of it this way: A floor in a building acts as a support zone, but when you fall through it, the floor now becomes resistance, called a ceiling. The reason why support and resistance reverse their roles can be appreciated with an explanation of some elementary psychology. No one likes to take a loss, and while some people overcome this feeling by cutting their losses at an early stage,

FIGURE 5.2 Support and Resistance Reverse Their Roles

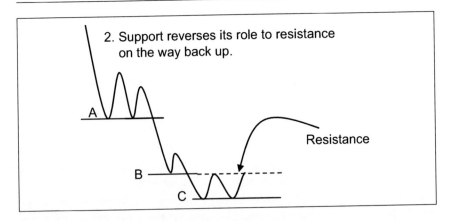

others hold on until the price comes back to where the security in question was originally bought. At that point, they are able to break even and sell, thereby creating a quantity of supply sufficient to temporarily halt the advance.

Finally, in Figure 5.3, we see the price rally through resistance at *B* and *A* (the former support level). The ensuing decline then finds support at *A* again. Thus, our third principle is:

Major Technical Principle Resistance reverses its role to support on the way down.

FIGURE 5.3 Support and Resistance Reverse Their Roles

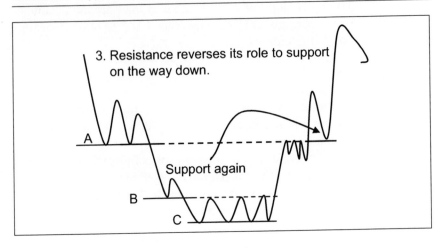

Rules for Determining Potential Support/Resistance Points

Previous Highs and Lows

We have already established that previous highs and lows are potential support or resistance levels. Highs are important because many market participants may have bought close to or at the actual high for a move. When prices decline, the normal human response is not to take a loss, but to hold on. That way, the pain of actually realizing a loss can be avoided. As a result, when the price returns to the old high, those who bought at that level have great motivation to sell in order to break even. Consequently, they liquidate. Also, those who bought at lower prices have a tendency to take profits at the old high, since that is the top of familiar ground. By the same token, any prices above the old high look expensive to potential buyers; consequently, there is less enthusiasm on their part, so they begin to pull away from the market.

When a price rallies and then falls back to the previous low, these bargain-basement prices appeal to potential buyers. After all, they missed the opportunity the first time prices retreated to this level, and they are therefore thankful to have another chance. For the same reason, sellers are reluctant to part with their securities as prices approach the previous low, since they saw them bounce before and naturally wonder why the same process should not be repeated.

Chart 5.1 shows the sugar price for a period spanning 2002–2003.

Note how previous highs and lows offer good support/resistance points for future trading. Unfortunately, there is no way of knowing whether a particular level will turn out to be support or resistance, or even whether it will be a pivotal point at all. That's why these are merely intelligent places for anticipating a temporary reversal. Resort to other indicators such as oscillators is therefore required.

At Round Numbers

Support and resistance zones have a habit of forming at round numbers. This is probably because numbers such as 10, 50, or 100 represent easy psychological points upon which traders and investors often base their decisions. In the 1970s, for example, the Dow Jones Industrials had a great deal of difficulty surpassing the 1,000 level. For gold in the 1980s and mid-1990s, the magic number was $400, and so forth. The guide for potential turning points, then, is to look for round numbers.

CHART 5.1 March 2003 Sugar Daily

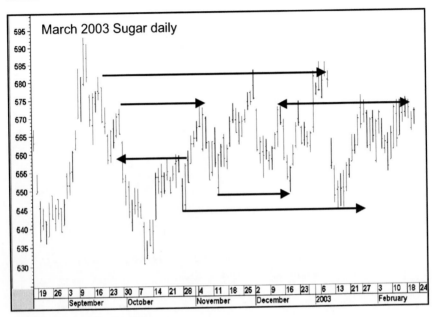

Source: Martin Pring's Weekly InfoMovie Report

Trendlines and Moving Averages Represent Dynamic Levels of Support and Resistance

Chapter 6 points out that a good trendline should reflect the underlying trend. One of the rules for assessing the significance of a line relates to how many times it has been touched or approached. The more, the merrier in this case. If a price falls back to a specific low on several occasions, this makes that particular price level a strong support zone. The same is true of trendlines and moving averages (MAs). Every time a price moves back to an up trendline or a rising MA and bounces, it is reinforced as a dynamic level of support. The same would be true in reverse for a declining trendline or moving average. Therefore, it makes sense to buy as the price falls to an up trendline (or rising MA) and to sell when it rises to a down trendline (or falling MA). A low-risk stop may then be placed just beyond the line or MA in case the support/resistance zone is violated.

Chart 5.2 shows a very good example of how a down trendline acted as resistance for Hewlett-Packard.

Note also that the interaction of a reliable MA, such as the 200-day MA featured in this chart, acts as reinforcement of the resistance zone.

CHART 5.2 Hewlett-Packard Daily

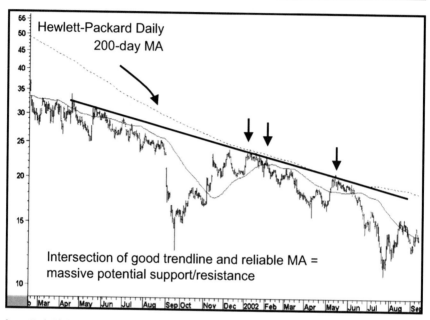

Source: Martin Pring's Weekly InfoMovie Report

This works in the same way as if we were building a house and doubled the thickness of the roof. The identical principle holds when a moving average and a trendline are at the same level; they double the strength of the resistance (or support in the case of an up trendline and MA intersection).

Emotional Points on a Chart Represent Potential Support/Resistance Levels

This concept will be covered in subsequent chapters when we consider gaps, extreme points of Pinocchio bars, two-bar reversals, key reversals, and so forth. For the moment, suffice it to say that most emotional points are those at which a price, following a persistent trend, experiences a strong extension of that trend. During the course of the bar's formation, it then abruptly reverses direction. It's the abruptness of the reversal that is the key since it tells us, depending on the direction, that either buyers or sellers are exhausted. When that point in the chart is again revisited, it often forms a barrier to further progress—in other words, a support or resistance level.

Gaps represent another example of emotional points. They are formed when buyers or sellers respond so emotionally to news that a blank

CHART 5.3 March 2003 Sugar Daily Resistance

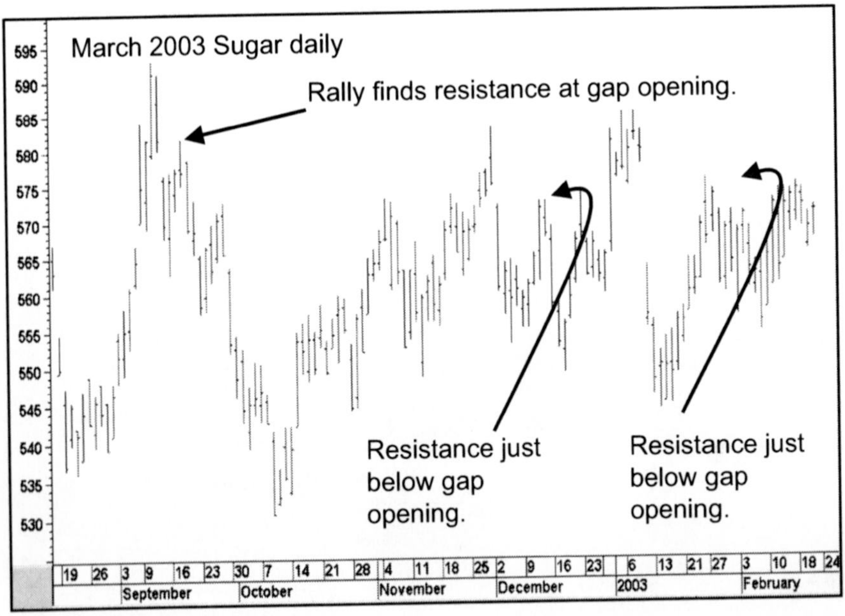

March 2003 Sugar daily

Rally finds resistance at gap opening.

Resistance just below gap opening.

Resistance just below gap opening.

Source: Martin Pring's Weekly InfoMovie Report

space, or gap, is left on the chart. In Chart 5.3, probably because of unexpected bad news, the sugar price experiences three downside gaps.

Later on, when emotions become more stable, the price rallies and tries to "close" each of the gaps. In the case of the gap on the left, resistance is found at its opening. In the other two examples, resistance forms at the lower part of the gap. Gaps are one of the most reliable technical concepts from the point of view of projecting potential support or resistance areas. We see some good examples in 2011 for the Market Vectors Coal exchange-traded fund (ETF) (Chart 5.4), where the small rectangles highlight the gaps and the horizontal lines represent the high and low for the gap, with their obvious support implications.

Chart 5.5 shows another emotional point for Boeing. This time, it's the bottom of a very wide bar in early 2002. Note that this low developed at a round number, $50.

Normally, this would have been a support level the next time the price fell to $50, but in the fall of 2002, the price went right through it. Even so, $50 did turn out to be a pivotal point the next time Boeing rallied. It goes to show that even if a support/resistance zone is violated once, it can still turn out to be a pivotal point in subsequent price action.

CHART 5.4 Market Vectors Coal ETF (KOL)

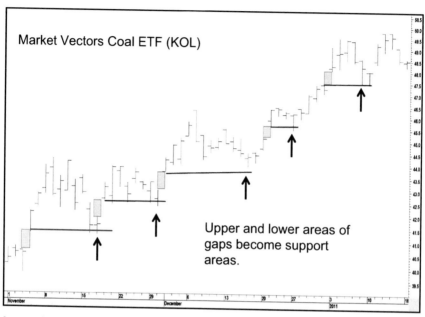

Source: Martin Pring's Weekly InfoMovie Report

Proportionate Moves, Retracements, and So On

The law of motion states that for every action, there is a reaction. Price trends established in financial markets are really the measurement of crowd psychology in motion, and are also subject to this law. These swings in sentiment often show up in proportionate price moves.

Perhaps the best-known principle of proportion is the *50 percent rule*. For instance, many bear markets, as measured by the Dow Jones Industrial Average (DJIA), have cut prices by half. As examples, the 1901–1903, 1907, 1919–1921, and 1937–1938 bear markets recorded declines of 46, 49, 47, and 50 percent, respectively. The first leg of the 1929–1932 bear market ended in October 1929 at 195, just over half the September high. The halfway mark in an advance sometimes represents the point of balance, often giving a clue to the ultimate extent of the move in question or, alternatively, indicating an important juncture point for the return move. Thus, between 1970 and 1973, the Dow advanced from 628 to 1,067. The halfway point in that rise was 848, or approximately the same level at which the first stage of the 1973–1974 bear market ended.

CHART 5.5 Boeing Weekly

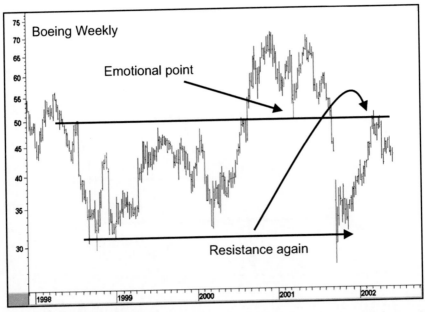

Source: Martin Pring's Weekly InfoMovie Report

By the same token, rising markets often find resistance after doubling from a low; the first rally from 40 to 81 in the 1932–1937 bull market was a double.

In effect, the 50 percent mark falls in the middle of the one-third to two-thirds retracement described in Chapter 2 in the discussion of peak-and-trough progression. These one-third and two-thirds proportions can be widely observed in all securities, and also serve as support or resistance zones.

Ratio-scale charts are helpful in determining such points, since moves of identical proportion can easily be projected up and down. Moreover, these swings occur with sufficient consistency to offer possible reversal points at both peaks and troughs. Remember, technical analysis deals with probabilities, which means that forecasts should not be made using this method in isolation.

In addition, when undertaking a projection based on the rules of proportion, it is always a good idea to see whether the price objective corresponds to a previous support or resistance point. If it does, the odds are much higher that this zone will represent a reversal point, or at least a temporary barrier. When a security price is reaching new all-time high ground,

CHART 5.6 PowerShares Dynamic Insurance ETF (PIC)

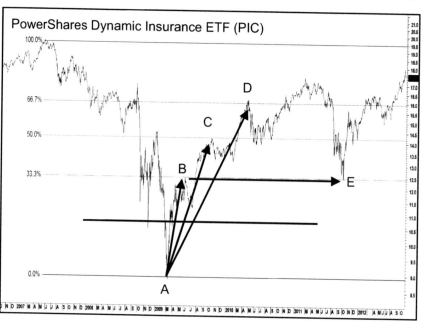

Source: Martin Pring's Weekly InfoMovie Report

another possibility is to try to extend up trendlines. The point at which the line intersects with the projection using the rules of proportion may well represent the time and place of an important reversal. Experimentation will show that each security has a character of its own, with some lending themselves more readily to this approach and others not at all.

Chart 5.6 shows an example using one-third, two-thirds, and 50 percent retracements for the PowerShares Dynamic Insurance ETF.

In this instance, the decline from the 100 percent line to the 0 percent line (*A*) is 100 percent of the move. If we want to establish possible resistance points for subsequent rebounds, then the intelligent places to monitor are these one-third, two-thirds, and 50 percent retracements. As you can see, the rally ending at *B*, *C*, and *D* represent a 33 percent, 50 percent, and 66 percent or two-thirds retracement, respectively. These pivot levels remain in force once surpassed. You can see this from the decline at *E*, which was halted at the 33 percent mark. While we do not know ahead of time when these retracement moves will halt at the one-third, 50 percent, or two-thirds pivotal points, we can certainly get some clues by examining some of the other technical indicators as the price approaches these junctures to see if things are, in fact, consistent with a turn.

Many technicians use a sequence of numbers discovered by Leonardo Fibonacci, a thirteenth-century Italian mathematician. The sequence has many properties, but a key one is that each new number is the sum of the two previous numbers in the series. Thus, 5 and 8 = 13, 8 and 13 = 21, and so on. The significance of this sequence for our purposes is that it offers some guidelines for proportionate moves. For example, each number in the sequence is 61.8 percent of the next number, 38.2 percent of the number after that, and so forth.

In this respect, Charts 5.7 and 5.8 show some possibilities for the silver ETF. The retracement moves are measured in exactly the same way as in the previous chart, except that Fibonacci numbers have been substituted.

In the case of Chart 5.7, the initial rally was halted at the 23.6 percent level, the next at 50 percent, and the third move up at a level just shy of 61.8 percent of the March to September 2008 decline. We can also see that an advance was held at the 50 percent mark at *E* and at the 61.8 percent level either side of *F*. In Chart 5.8, we see how the 38.25 level comes into play a couple of times and the value of a gap opening as two rallies were turned back at *B* and later at *D*. Note this very same level was reinforced as a pivotal point, not only because of its importance as a gap opening, but

CHART 5.7 Silver ETF

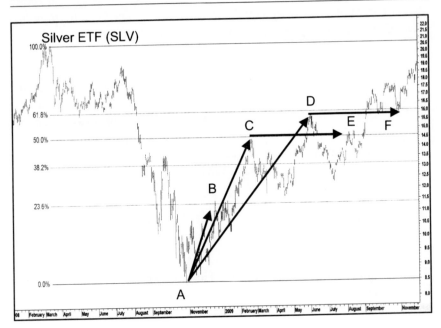

Source: Martin Pring's Weekly InfoMovie Report

CHART 5.8 Silver ETF

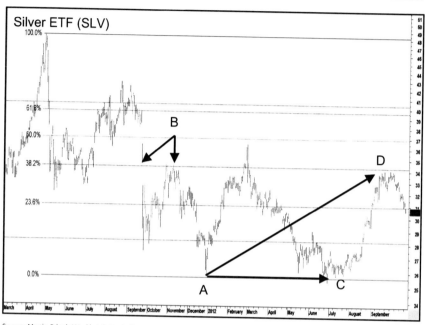

Source: Martin Pring's Weekly InfoMovie Report

also as a 38.2 percent retracement level, as we can see at *D*. Finally, previous lows as a support-generating principle came into their own at *C*.

Chart 5.9 shows the same principle applied to upside projections.

Once again, *AB* represents 100 percent of the decline and lines are drawn at upside Fibonacci proportions. In this case, the next higher number divided by the current number is 1.61, then 2.61, and so on. It is self-evident how the 161.8 percent and 261.8 percent proportions become key pivotal points in future price action. Once again, these levels are not guaranteed to become important pivotal points, but are intelligent places on the chart to anticipate that possibility.

Rules for Determining the Probable Significance of a Potential Support or Resistance Zone

At this point, you are probably asking, "How do I know how important each support and resistance level is likely to be?" Unfortunately, there is no hard-and-fast answer, but there are some general rules that can act as guidelines.

CHART 5.9 Palladium

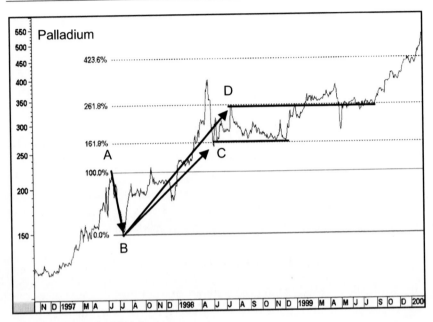

Source: Martin Pring's Weekly InfoMovie Report

The Amount of a Security that Changed Hands in a Specific Area—the Greater the Activity, the More Significant the Zone

This is fairly self-evident, for whenever you have a large number of people buying or selling at a particular price, they have a tendency to remember their own experiences. Buyers, as we have already established, like to break even. Sellers, on the other hand, may have bought lower down and recall that prices previously stalled at the resistance level. Their motivation for profit-taking becomes that much greater.

The Greater the Speed and Extent of the Previous Move, the More Significant a Support or Resistance Zone Is Likely to Be

The attempt to climb through the resistance level here can be compared to the efforts of a person who tries to crash through a door. If he attacks the door from, say, 10 or 12 feet away, he can propel himself with lots of momentum, and the door will probably give way. On the other hand, if he begins his attempt from 100 feet away, he will arrive at the door with less velocity and will probably fail in his attempt. In both cases, the door represented the exact same resistance, but it was the resistance relative to the velocity of the person that was important. The same principle can be applied to the market, in that a long, steep climb in price is similar to the 100-foot run, and the resistance level resembles the door. Consequently, the more overextended the previous price swing, the less the resistance or support that is required to halt it. Also, the faster a price moves on the upside, the more willing traders will be to take a quick profit. On the other hand, an abrupt move to the downside will make the price appear as that much more of a bargain than if it had slowly drifted lower.

Chart 5.10 features the gold price. Note how it makes a high in January 1986 and then falls away. The subsequent rally is quite steep; then the price runs out of steam and declines again.

Finally, in late July, it works its way higher in a fairly methodical manner. This time, the same level of resistance is easily overcome because buyers are not as exhausted as they were in their March attempt.

Examine the Amount of Time Elapsed

The third rule for establishing the potency of a support or resistance zone is to examine the amount of time that has elapsed between the formation

CHART 5.10 Gold

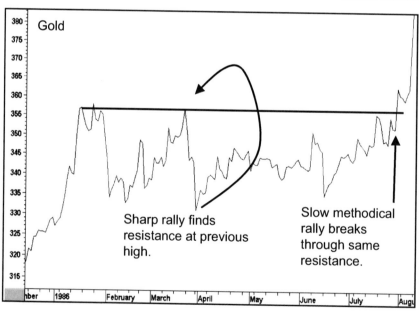

Source: Martin Pring's Weekly InfoMovie Report

of the original congestion and the nature of general market developments during that period. A supply that is 6 months old has greater potency than one established 10 or 20 years previously. Even so, it is almost uncanny how support and resistance levels remain effective time and time again, even when separated by many years.

Summary

1. Support and resistance represent a concentration of demand and supply sufficient to halt a price move, at least temporarily.
2. They are not signals to buy or sell, but intelligent places for anticipating a reversal and should always be used in conjunction with other indicators.
3. Potential support/resistance zones develop at previous highs and lows, round numbers, trendlines and MAs, emotional points on charts, and retracement points such as Fibonacci proportions.
4. The significance of a support or resistance zone depends upon the amount of an asset that previously changed hands in that area, the speed and extent of the previous price move, and the period of time that has elapsed since the zone was last encountered.

6

TRENDLINES

Trendlines are perhaps the simplest of the tools we use in the technical arsenal and are arguably one of the most effective. Since the construction of nearly all price patterns requires the use of trendlines, this concept is a fundamental building block of pattern identification and interpretation— the subject of Chapter 8. In this chapter, we will describe trendline characteristics and explain how the significance of individual lines can be determined.

A trendline is a straight line connecting either a series of ascending bottoms in a rising market or the tops of a descending series of rally peaks. Those joining the lows are called *up trendlines,* and those connecting the tops are referred to as *down trendlines.* It is also possible to construct horizontal trendlines joining a series of identical lows or identical highs. Typically, a down trendline is constructed by joining the final peak with the top of the first rally, as in Figure 6.1.

When the price breaks above the trendline, a trend change signal is given. The opposite is true for an up trendline (see Figure 6.2).

How to Draw Trendlines

In order for a line to be a true trendline, it must connect two or more peaks or troughs. Otherwise, it will be drawn in space and will have no significance. You will often see people constructing lines that only touch one point, as in Figure 6.3, or even no points at all, as in Figure 6.4.

Such lines have no meaning whatsoever, and are really worse than drawing nothing at all. This is because by simply appearing on the charts,

FIGURE 6.1 Down Trendline Connecting the Peaks

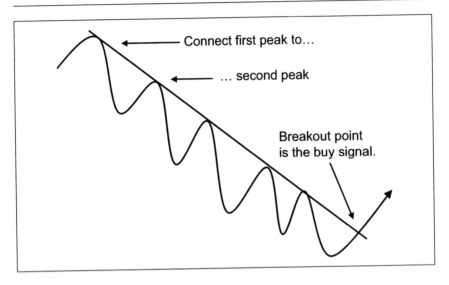

Connect first peak to...

... second peak

Breakout point is the buy signal.

FIGURE 6.2 Up Trendline Connecting the Troughs

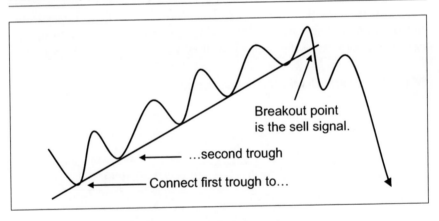

Breakout point is the sell signal.

...second trough

Connect first trough to...

such lines give the observer the impression that they actually have some significance. It's a fundamentally important point because

Major Technical Principle A true trendline is a graphic way of representing the underlying trend.

Consequently, if it only touches one point, it cannot be true trendline.

FIGURE 6.3 Incorrect Down Trendline Construction

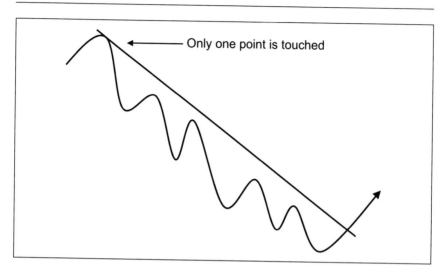

Only one point is touched

Ideally, an up trendline is constructed by connecting the final low with the first bottom in the rally, as line AD in Figure 6.5.

This is called the *primary trendline*. In the case of a primary trend, this would be the bear market low and the first intermediate bottom. The example shown here offers a fairly shallow angle of ascent. Unfortunately,

FIGURE 6.4 Incorrect Down Trendline Construction

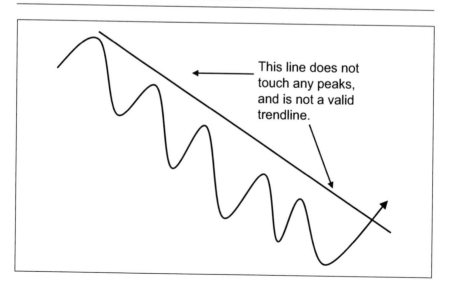

This line does not touch any peaks, and is not a valid trendline.

FIGURE 6.5 Primary and Secondary Up Trendlines

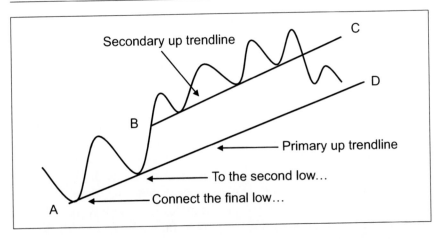

the price rallies sharply, which means that the violation develops well after the final peak. In such situations, it is better to redraw the line as the price moves up. In Figure 6.5, this is line BC, which is obviously a better reflection of the underlying trend. This is called a *secondary trendline*. Down trendlines are constructed using the same principles, but in reverse.

Since trends can be sideways, it follows that trendlines can also be drawn horizontally, which is often the case when we construct price patterns such as the neckline of a horizontal head-and-shoulders (H&S) pattern or the upper or lower boundaries rectangles (described in later chapters). In the case of price patterns, the penetration of these lines usually warns of a change in trend, as does the violation of rising or falling trendlines.

It's important to understand the following principle at this point.

Major Technical Principle   Drawing trendlines is more a matter of common sense rather than following a set of hard-and-fast rules.

Bar Versus Line or Close-Only Charts

Some charts are plotted with bars and others as line charts. The question naturally arises as to which form should be used for the purposes of trendline analysis. In most cases, bar charts offer more timely signals, whether it's a peak-and-trough progression, price pattern completion, or trendline violation. In technical analysis, timeliness comes with a price, and the price in this case is more whipsaws. With traditional daily or weekly charts, the closing price is very important because it sorts out the men, i.e., those who are willing to take home a position overnight or over a weekend, from the boys, i.e., those who are not. This has become less important as a factor for markets that trade for 24 hours, Sunday through Friday. However, since all markets are closed over the weekend, Friday closes continue to maintain their importance. Even so, *closing prices are, for the most part, more important chart points than highs or lows.* Also, since there is much excitement during the day as unexpected news breaks, highs and lows often represent random points on the chart. For this reason, it is often a better idea to construct trendlines using closing data. I am not going to say that's always the case, because some bar trendlines have greater significance than close-only ones, based on the rules outlined for significance described later in this chapter. Thus, it is always crucial to apply common sense as much as strict technical rules. The question you should be constantly asking is, "Which line better reflects the underlying trend?"

Trendline Breaks Can Be Followed by a Reversal or Consolidation

The completion of a price pattern can signify either: (1) a reversal in the previous trend—in this instance, it is known as a *reversal pattern*—or (2) a resumption of the previous trend, when it is called a *consolidation* or *continuation pattern.* Similarly, the penetration of a trendline will result in either a reversal of that trend or its continuation. Figure 6.6 illustrates this point from the aspect of a rising price trend.

FIGURE 6.6 Implication of a Trendline Break-Reversal

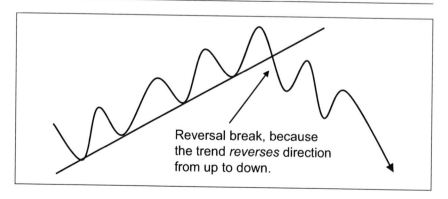

Reversal break, because the trend *reverses* direction from up to down.

FIGURE 6.7 Implication of a Trendline Break-Slowed Momentum

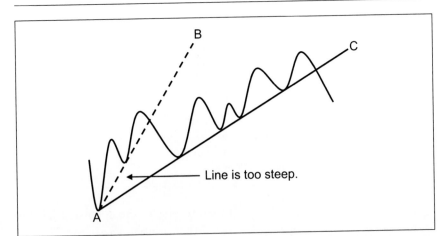

In this case, the trendline joining the series of troughs is eventually penetrated on the downside. The fourth peak represented the highest point in the bull trend, so the downward violation of the trendline signals that a bear move is under way.

The upward price trend and trendline penetration in Figure 6.7 are identical to those in Figure 6.6, but the action following this warning signal is entirely different.

This is because the trendline violation results in the advance continuing, but at a slower rate. A third alternative is that the price consolidates in a sideways trading range and then advances (Figure 6.8).

FIGURE 6.8 Implication of a Trendline Break-Continuation After Consolidation

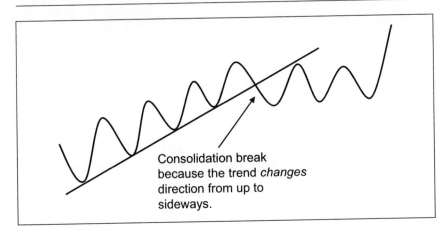

FIGURE 6.9 Implication of a Trendline Break-Reversal After Consolidation

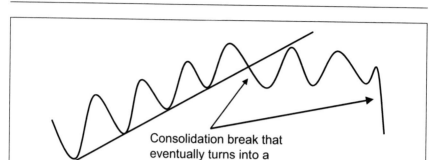

Consolidation break that eventually turns into a reversal break.

Finally, it may consolidate and then reverse to the downside. This is shown in Figure 6.9.

Thus, whenever a trendline is violated, the odds strongly favor a *change* in trend. That change can either be an actual reversal or a (sideways) trading range following an uptrend or downtrend.

In most instances, there is, unfortunately, no way of telling at the time of the violation which possibility will prove to be the outcome. Generally speaking though, the violation of trendlines with a sharp angle of ascent or descent is more likely to result in a consolidation. Also, valuable clues can be gleaned by applying other techniques described in subsequent chapters, and by evaluating the state of health of the market's overall technical structure (examined in Part II). Using the techniques discussed in Chapter 8 can also help. For example, in a rising market, a trendline penetration may occur at the time of, or just before, the successful completion of a reversal pattern. An example is shown in Figure 6.10.

FIGURE 6.10 Simultaneous Trendline and Price Pattern Breaks at Tops

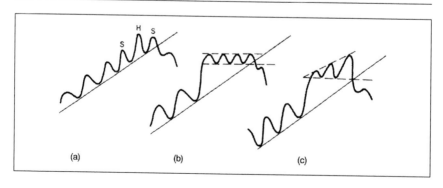

(a)   (b)   (c)

FIGURE 6.11 Simultaneous Trendline and Price Pattern Breaks at Bottoms

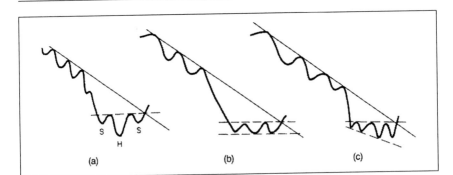

Figure 6.11 illustrates the same phenomenon from the aspect of a bear market reversal. If the violation occurs simultaneously with, or just after, the completion of a reversal pattern, the two breaks have the effect of reinforcing each other.

Sometimes, as in Figure 6.12, the trendline violation occurs *before* the completion of the pattern.

In such cases, the break should be regarded as a sign of an interruption of the prevailing movement rather than one of reversal, because a trend is assumed to continue until the weight of the evidence indicates otherwise. A couple of examples of this phenomenon appear in Chart 6.1 featuring Invesco Energy Fund.

This chart indicates two examples of where a trendline break and pattern completion develop close together. At the end of 1990, the Invesco Energy Fund violates a nice up trendline and shortly after, completes a right-angled broadening top. The end of the decline is signaled with another

FIGURE 6.12 Delayed Price Pattern Breaks at Tops and Bottoms

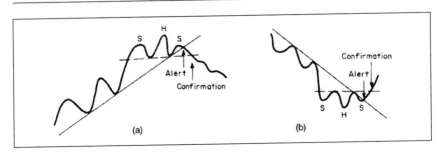

CHART 6.1 Invesco Energy Fund 1987–1993

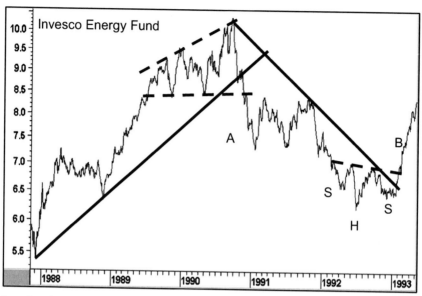

Source: From pring.com

down trendline break and the completion of a reverse head-and-shoulders pattern For a full description of these patterns please refer to Chapter 8.

Further clues to the significance of a specific trendline violation can be gleaned from volume characteristics, as described in the next chapter. For example, if a series of ascending peaks and troughs is accompanied by progressively lower volume, it is a sign that the advance is running out of steam (since volume is no longer going with the trend). In this instance, a trendline violation is likely to be of greater significance than if volume had continued to expand with each successive rally. It is not necessary for a downside penetration to be accompanied by high volume, but a violation that occurs as activity expands emphasizes the bearish undertone because of the obvious switch in the demand/supply balance in favor of sellers.

Major Technical Principle As a general rule, the violation of trendlines with a sharp angle of ascent or descent is more likely to result in a consolidation than a reversal.

Extended Trendlines

Most people observe the violation of a trendline, then assume that the trend has changed and forget about the line. This is a mistake because an extended line can become just as important as the previolated line itself. The difference is that an extended line reverses its role. Just as a return move often happens following a breakout from a price pattern, a similar move, known as a *throwback,* sometimes develops following a trendline penetration. Figure 6.13 shows a trendline reversing its previous role as support while the throwback move turns it into an area of resistance. Figure 6.14 shows the same situation for a declining market.

Chart 6.2 shows an up trendline break for the China ETF (FXI). The penetration of this line resulted in the extended line becoming resistance.

Later it was penetrated again, and a subsequent decline showed it to be a level of support. Finally, two trendlines converged in early March, and since they had just been violated on the downside, they reinforced each other as a resistance zone that quickly resulted in the price moving to the downside.

> **Major Technical Principle** An extended trendline reverses its support/resistance role.

FIGURE 6.13 Extended Up Trendline

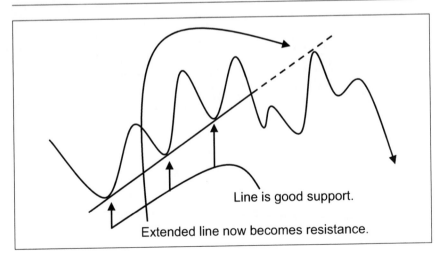

Line is good support.

Extended line now becomes resistance.

FIGURE 6.14 Extended Down Trendline

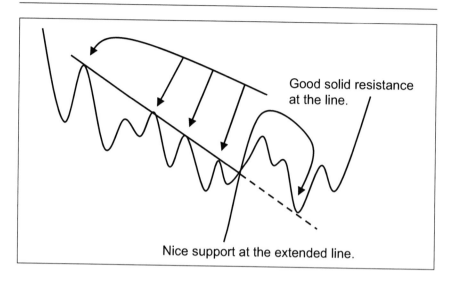

CHART 6.2 China Fund 2011–2012

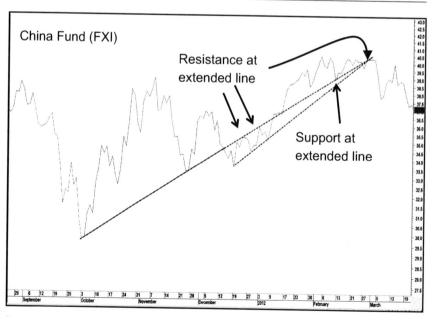

Source: From pring.com

Logarithmic (Ratio) vs. Arithmetic Scales

Scaling is an issue that is often overlooked in the technical community, but since it can have an important influence on how trendlines can be inter-preted, this is as good a place as any to introduce this concept. There are two axes on any market chart. The *x* axis, along the bottom, registers the date (except in point and figure charting), and the *y* axis, the price. There are two methods of plotting the *y* axis: arithmetic and logarithmic. Which one is chosen can have very important implications.

Arithmetic charts allocate a specific *point* or *dollar* amount to a given vertical distance. Thus, in Chart 6.3, each arrow has the same vertical distance and reflects approximately 250 points. That will be true at any price level.

A logarithmic scale, on the other hand, allocates a given *percentage* price move to a specific vertical distance. In Chart 6.4, each arrow repre-sents a move of approximately 100 percent, whether it is at lower prices or higher prices. There is very little noticeable difference between the scaling

CHART 6.3 S&P Composite 1870–2012 Arithmetic Scale

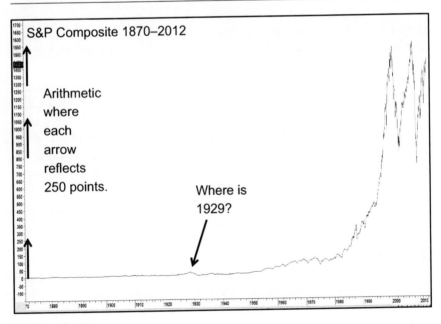

Source: From pring.com

CHART 6.4 S&P Composite 1870–2012 Logarithmic Scale

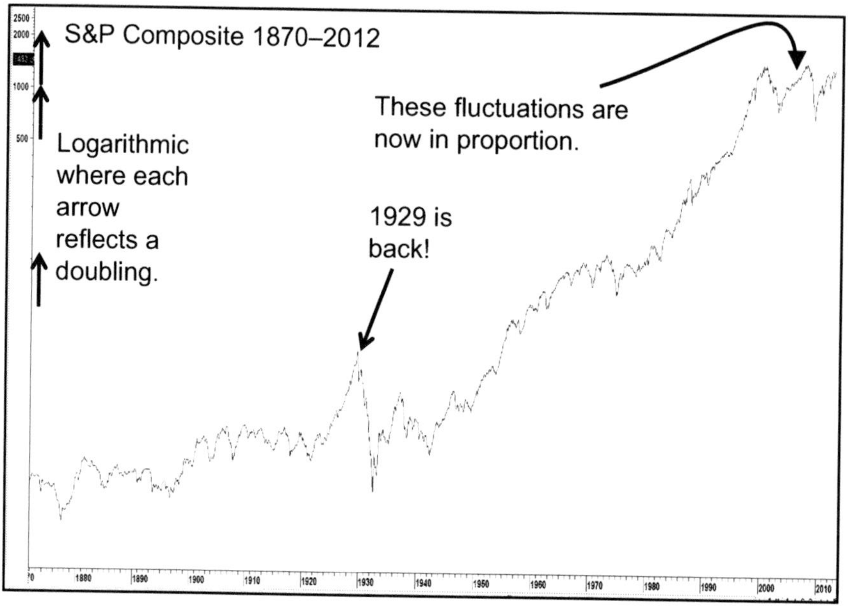

S&P Composite 1870–2012

Logarithmic where each arrow reflects a doubling.

These fluctuations are now in proportion.

1929 is back!

Source: From pring.com

methods when charts are plotted over short periods of time, where price fluctuations are relatively subdued. However, with large price fluctuations, there are considerable differences.

The arithmetic scale suppresses price fluctuations at low levels and exaggerates them at high points. Thus, the 85 percent 1929–1932 decline hardly shows up at all in Chart 6.3, but the 40 percent late-1990s–early 2000s retreat (no small decline) is greatly exaggerated. Chart 6.4 shows that the logarithmic scaling brings back 1929 and does not exaggerate the turn-of-the-century bear market. The media love to hype stories and news because that is what sells. You will find that charts featuring financial markets or economic numbers are almost always plotted on an arithmetic scale because this has the effect of exaggerating the most recent changes. Another hyping technique used by the media is to present the data for a short period using a very limited scale. The reader is then left with the sense of a dramatic move. This would not be the case if the data were displayed over a much longer period using a wider price scale.

As you can appreciate, I am very much in favor of using a logarithmic scale because it displays price trends in a proportionate way. Psychology tends to move proportionately as well, so it makes perfect rational sense to use logarithmic scaling. Having said that, when price fluctuations are relatively small—say, over a 3-month period—there is very little difference between the two scaling methods. As a purist, though, I still prefer the log scale at all times.

There is an even more important advantage of the logarithmic scale, which we shall learn when the concept of pattern price objectives is discussed later, but for now let's consider the implications for trendline interpretation.

The choice of scale is important for a timely and accurate use of trendline analysis, because at the end of a major movement, prices tend to accelerate in the direction of the prevailing trend; i.e., they rise faster at the end of a rising trend and decline more sharply at the termination of a bear market. In a bull market, prices rise slowly after an initial burst and then advance at a steeper and steeper angle as they approach the ultimate peak, looking rather like the left-hand cross-section of a mountain. Chart 6.5 shows an up trendline break for Intel based on a logarithmic scale.

CHART 6.5 Intel 2001–2002 Logarithmic Scale

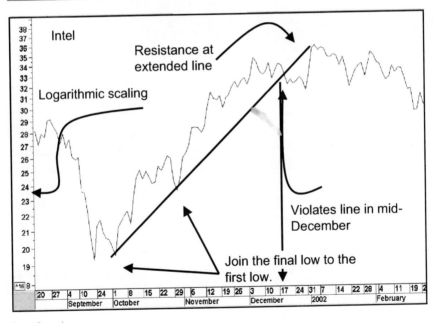

Source: From pring.com

CHART 6.6 Intel 2001–2002 Arithmetic Scale

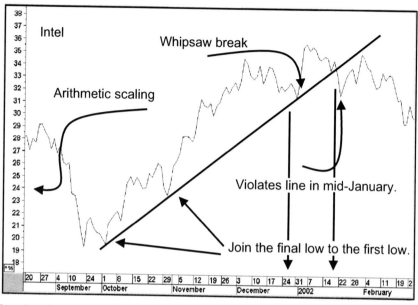

Source: From pring.com

Note that the downside penetration develops in mid-December. Chart 6.6 shows exactly the same period, but this time, the scaling is arithmetic.

The trendline break is entirely different, since it initially comes as a whipsaw in late December, followed by a valid break in mid-January. The downward-pointing arrow on the left marked the logarithmic break. Thus, it is apparent that up trendlines are violated more quickly on a logarithmic than on an arithmetic scale.

Conversely, down trendlines are violated sooner on an arithmetic scale. This can be seen from a comparison of Charts 6.7 and 6.8 for IBM.

Generally speaking, penetration of a logarithmically drawn trendline is more accurate in reflecting trend reversals than is penetration of an arithmetically drawn trendline; however, if the arithmetically constructed one is substantially more significant, based on the criteria listed next, then that would be the one to go with.

CHART 6.7 IBM 2001–2002 Arithmetic Scale

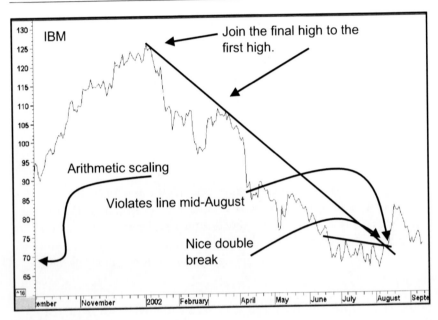

Source: From pring.com

CHART 6.8 IBM 2001–2002 Logarithmic Scale

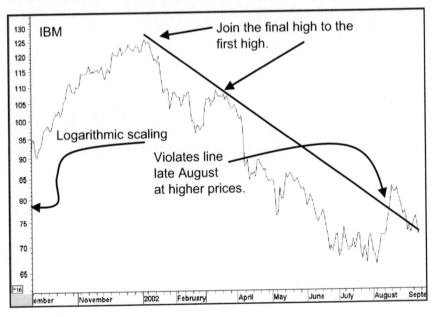

Source: From pring.com

Significance of Trendlines

It has been established that a break in trend caused by the penetration of a trendline results in either an actual trend reversal or a slowing in the pace of the trend. Although it may not always be possible to assess which of these alternatives will develop, it is still important to understand the significance of a trendline penetration; the following guidelines should help in evaluation.

Length of the Line

The size or length of a trend is an important factor, as with price patterns. If a series of ascending bottoms occurs over a 3- to 4-week span, the resulting trendline is only of minor importance. If the trend extends over a period of 1 to 3 years, however, its violation marks a significant juncture point. Just remember: Big trends result in big signals, small trends in small signals.

Number of Times the Trendline Has Been Touched or Approached

A trendline also derives its authority from the number of times it has been touched or approached; i.e., the larger the number, the greater the significance. This is true because a trendline represents a dynamic area of support or resistance. Each successive "test" of the line contributes to the importance of this support or resistance, and thus the authority of the line is a true reflection of the underlying trend. Just remember that a close encounter to the line (an approach) is almost as important as an actual touching because it still reflects the line's importance as a support or resistance area.

Also, if a line gains significance from the fact that it has been touched or approached, the extended line will become equally as important, but from a reverse point of view, since extended lines reverse their support/ resistance functions.

Angle of Ascent or Descent

A very sharp trend, as in Figure 6.15, is difficult to maintain and is liable to be broken rather easily, even by a short sideways movement.

All trends are eventually violated, but the steeper ones are likely to be ruptured more quickly. The violation of a particularly steep trend is not as

FIGURE 6.15 Steep Angles of Ascent

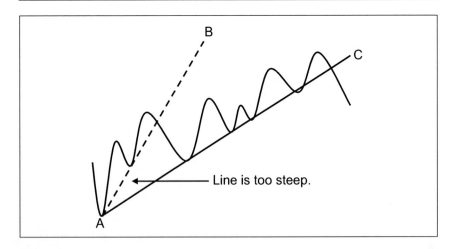

significant as that of a more gradual one. Penetration of a steep line usually results in a short corrective movement, following which, the trend resumes, but at a greatly reduced and more sustainable pace. Usually, the penetration of a steep trendline represents a continuation rather than a reversal break.

> **Major Technical Principle** The significance of a trendline is a function of its length, the number of times it has been touched, and the angle of ascent or descent.

Measuring Implication

Trendlines have measuring implications when they are broken, just as price patterns do. The maximum vertical distance between the peak in the price and the trendline is measured during a rising trend (see Figure 6.16).

This distance is then projected down from the point at which the violation occurs. The opposite for an up trendline violation is shown in Figure 6.17.

The term *price objective* is perhaps misleading. Objectives are usually reached when a trendline violation turns out to be a reversal, but because they are more often exceeded (as with price patterns), the objective becomes more of a minimum expectation. When prices move significantly through

FIGURE 6.16 Measuring Implications of Down Trendlines

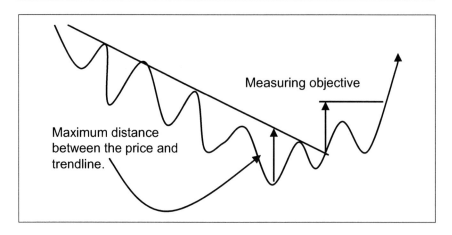

the objective, this area often becomes one of resistance to the next major rally, or support, for a subsequent reaction. Figures 6.18 and 6.19 show the some of these possibilities in both a down and up market.

Time and again, these price objective areas prove to be important support or resistance points. Unfortunately, there is no way to determine where the actual juncture point will be for any rally or reaction. This emphasizes a point made earlier: *that there is no known way of consistently determining the duration of a price movement.* It is only possible to speculate on the *probability* that a specific area will prove to be an important turning point.

FIGURE 6.17 Measuring Implications of Up Trendlines

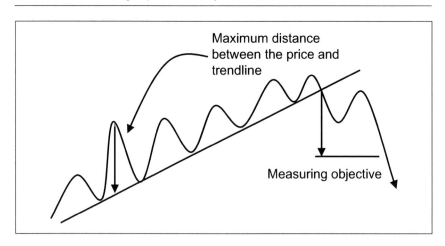

FIGURE 6.18 Downside Measuring Objectives

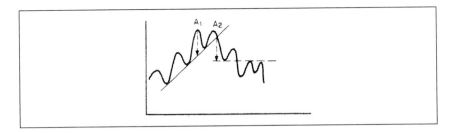

FIGURE 6.19 Upside Measuring Objectives

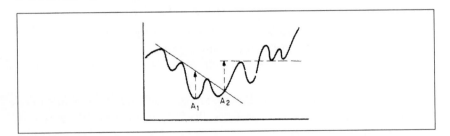

Corrective Fan Principle

At the beginning of a new primary bull market, the initial intermediate rally is often explosive, and so the rate of ascent is unsustainably steep. This happens because the advance is often a technical reaction to the previous overextended decline, as speculators who were caught short rush to cover their positions. As a result, the steep trendline constructed from the first minor reaction is quickly violated.

This is represented as line *AA* in Figure 6.20. A new trendline is then constructed, using the bottom of this first intermediate decline (*AB*).

The new line rises at a less rapid rate than the initial one. Finally, the process is repeated, resulting in construction of a third line, *AC*. These lines are known as *fan lines*. There is an established principle that once the third trendline has been violated, the end of the bull market is confirmed. In some respects, these three rally points and trendlines can be compared to the three stages of a bull or bear market, as outlined in Chapter 3. The fan principle is just as valid for downtrends, and can also be used for determining intermediate as well as cyclical movements.

FIGURE 6.20 The Fan Principle

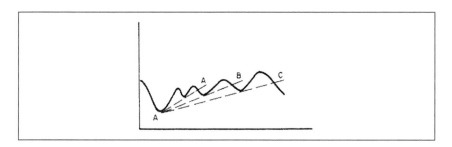

Trend Channels

So far, only the possibilities of drawing trendlines joining bottoms in rising markets and tops in declining ones have been examined. It is also useful to draw lines that are parallel to those basic trendlines, as shown in Figure 6.21.

In a rising market, the parallel line known as a *return trendline* joins the tops of rallies, and during declines, the return line joins the series of bottoms (see Figure 6.22). The area between these trend extremities is known as a *trend channel*.

The return line is useful from two points of view. First, it represents an area of support or resistance, depending on the direction of the trend. Second, and perhaps more important, penetration of the return trendline

FIGURE 6.21 Uptrend Channel

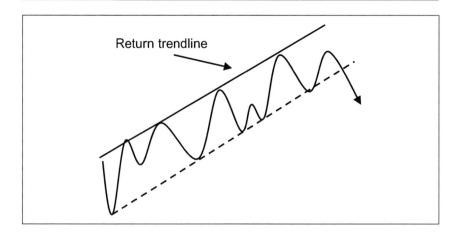

FIGURE 6.22 Downtrend Channel

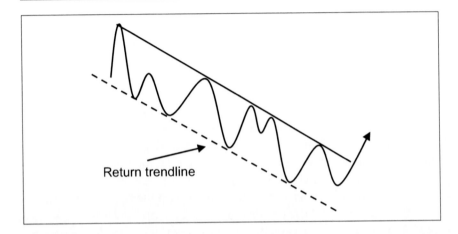

Return trendline

represents a signal that either the trend will accelerate or a reversal in the basic trend is about to take place, at least temporarily.

In Figure 6.23, the violation of the return line signifies that the price advance has begun to accelerate. In effect, the channel in Figure 6.23 represents a rising trading range, and the trendline violation is a breakout from it.

FIGURE 6.23 Breakout from Uptrend Channel

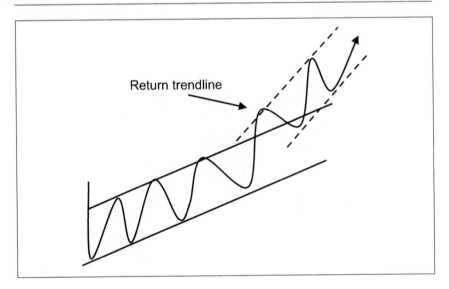

Return trendline

Exhaustion

On the other hand, if the angle of the trend channel is much steeper, as in Figures 6.24 and 6.25, the violation of the return line represents an exhaustion move.

The failure of the price to hold above (or below) the return line then signals an important reversal in trend. This is often the case if the break through the return line is accompanied by high volume.

Consider a situation in which a person is sawing a thick piece of wood. At first, the sawing strokes are slow but deliberate, but gradually, the person realizes that this task is going to take some time, becomes frustrated, and slowly increases the speed of the strokes. Finally, the person bursts into a frantic effort and is forced to give up the task, at least temporarily, because of complete exhaustion. The same principles hold true in a declining market. In this case, the expanding volume at the low represents a selling climax. As a general rule, the steeper the channel, the more likely it is that the breakout will turn out to be an exhaustion move.

Exhaustion also develops when a price rallies temporarily above a regular down trendline (or below an up trendline) and then breaks back below (or above) it. In the case of a down trendline, the situation is akin to someone jumping up and temporarily pushing through the ceiling. The person is able to pull their head through to the next floor for a few

FIGURE 6.24 Exhaustion Break from Downtrend Channel

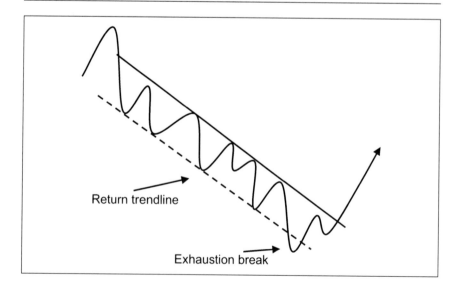

FIGURE 6.25 Exhaustion Break from Uptrend Channel

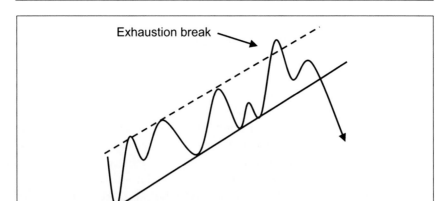

moments, but then falls sharply back to the floor below. At this point, he has used up all spare energy in the attempt to move to the next floor and is totally exhausted. Before he can make another attempt, he will need some time to gain some new energy. The same is true of the price, which makes an effort to rally above the trendline but is unable to maintain the breakout.

This temporary break often indicates that the prevailing trend has much further to run. It also raises a dilemma concerning the way in which a trendline should be constructed. In Figure 6.26, for instance, we see a false break above trendline *AB*.

FIGURE 6.26 Down Trendline Exhaustion Break

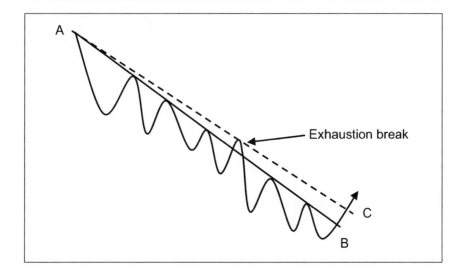

Should *AB* now be abandoned, or should the peak of the exhaustion break be connected to the rally high to form a new (dashed *AC*) trendline? Again, it's a matter of common sense. On the one hand, the top of the whipsaw break is technically the correct place to draw the line, but common sense suggests that the original line is a better reflection of the underlying trend. After all, at the time of the whipsaw, it had been touched three times. If a new line is then drawn to reflect the break, that line will have been touched only twice, once at the outset and once at the whipsaw peak. In a sense, the whipsaw is adding further credibility to the initial line because the price was unable to hold above it. If we had come upon this situation after the whipsaw break and tried to construct a line, it would have been even more obvious that line *AB* was far superior to line *AC* because it has been touched or approached on far more occasions.

Chart 6.9 shows that a resistance trendline joining the 1974 low and 1978 highs was temporarily violated. This proved to be an exhaustion move, since the S&P Composite was unable to hold above the line. This failure was followed by the 1987 crash. Not all exhaustion moves result in

CHART 6.9 S&P Composite 1973–1989

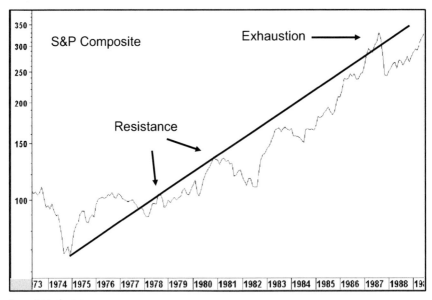

such dynamic consequences, but they certainly warn of potential trouble and should never be ignored.

The same principles are true in reverse for an up trendline. When you think about it, a whipsaw break actually adds credibility to the trendline. This is because the price is able to violate the line, but this line is so significant as a support/resistance area that the price is unable to hold the break. If it were not such a significant barrier, the break would have held and the whipsaw would have been avoided. Consequently, when the price is able to experience a valid break, the signal is that much stronger.

Chart 6.10 shows an example of a whipsaw downside break for Microsoft in 1998.

Major Technical Principle Exhaustion develops when a price rallies temporarily above a down trendline (or below an up trendline) and then breaks back below (or above) it.

CHART 6.10 Microsoft

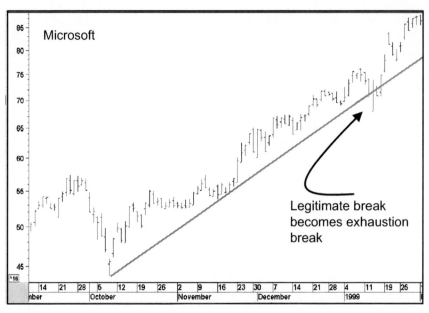

Source: pring.com

Summary

1. Trendlines are perhaps the easiest technical tool to understand, but considerable experimentation and practice are required before the art of interpreting them can be successfully mastered.
2. Trendline violations signal either a temporary interruption or a reversal in the prevailing trend. It is necessary to refer to other pieces of technical evidence to determine which is being signaled.
3. The significance of trendlines is a function of their length, the number of times they have been touched or approached, and the steepness of the angle of ascent or descent.
4. A good trendline reflects the underlying trend and represents an important support and resistance zone.
5. Extended trendlines are an important concept and should not be overlooked.
6. Exhaustion breaks often possess good predictive power.

7

BASIC CHARACTERISTICS OF VOLUME

Almost everything that technicians use in plotting a specific security involves either the price itself or a statistical variation on it. Volume can offer a new dynamic in our interpretation of crowd psychology. Therefore, analyzing volume trends gives us a better understanding of how and why price patterns work. In effect, the study of the characteristics of volume gives greater depth to the weight-of-the-evidence approach described earlier. Volume not only measures the enthusiasm of buyers and sellers, but also is a variable that is totally independent of price. In this chapter, we will discuss some general principles of volume interpretation, and in Chapter 26 some individual volume indicators. We are beginning our volume coverage at this point, as it is a basic building block of price patterns, in a similar way to the concepts of support and resistance, peak-and-trough analysis, and trendlines. At the end of this chapter all the basic building blocks will have been covered, leaving us prepared to tackle the subject of price patterns head on.

Benefits of Volume Studies

Volume studies offer three major benefits:

1. When price and volume patterns are compared, it is important to see whether they are in agreement. If so, the probabilities favor an extension of the trend.
2. If price and volume disagree, this tells us that the underlying trend is not as strong as it looks on the surface.

3. Occasionally, price action offers mild signs of an impending trend reversal, but volume can throw up characteristics of its own that literally shout this message. In such cases, a study that was limited to price action would fail to uncover a really good and obvious warning or opportunity.

Principles of Volume Interpretation

1. The first and most important principle is that *volume typically goes with the trend.* It is normal for activity to expand in a rising market and to contract in a declining one (see Figure 7.1). In this sense, volume is always interpreted in relation to the recent past.

   Comparing twenty-first-century 1 billion-plus share days on the New York Stock Exchange (NYSE) with early twentieth-century levels of 5 or 6 million is of little help. Such a comparison reflects institutional, not psychological, changes. Volume is higher today because of more companies being listed, the advent of derivatives, lower commissions, and so forth. On the other hand, a 3-billion-share day this week compared to a recent 1.5-billion-share day last month is relevant, because it shows a significant change in activity over a period in which major institutional changes will be nonexistent.

FIGURE 7.1 Volume Goes with the Trend

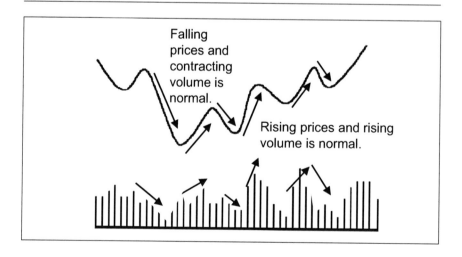

FIGURE 7.2 Volume Moves in Trends

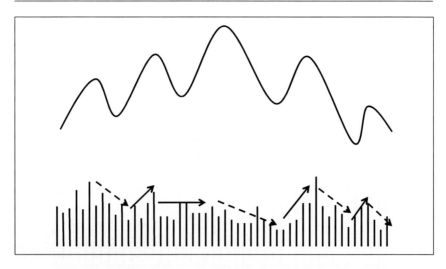

We know that when prices move in trends, this does not occur in a straight line. Instead, the price works its way up and down in a zig-zag fashion. Volume trends are similar. On the left side of Figure 7.2, for instance, the solid arrows indicate an expanding volume trend and the dashed ones declining trends.

It is apparent that the level of activity does not expand in every period. There are quiet periods and active ones, but the general thrust is up. It, too, is irregular. When we talk about volume rising or falling, we are usually referring to its trend. It is normal for such trends to be interrupted by aberrations in volume levels. Volume trends, like price trends, can be intraday, short, intermediate, or long, depending on the nature of the chart.

The amount of money flowing into a security must always equal the amount of money flowing out. This is true regardless of the level of volume. Consequently, it is the degree of enthusiasm of buyers or sellers that determines the course of prices. If buyers are bullish, they will raise their bids until their demands are satisfied. If sellers react to bad news, they may panic, pushing prices down sharply, but at all times, the amount of a security being sold is equal to that being purchased.

2. The combination of rising volume and rising price is normal. It indicates that things are in gear. Such a state of affairs has no forecasting value, except to imply that it is likely that a negative divergence between price and volume lies ahead.

3. Volume normally leads price during a bull move. A new high in price that is not confirmed by volume should be regarded as a red flag, warning that

FIGURE 7.3 Volume Leads Price in an Uptrend

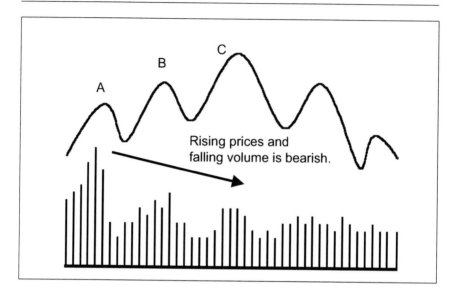

the prevailing trend may be about to reverse. In Figure 7.3 the price peaks at point *C*, yet the average volume reached its maximum around point *A*.

Such action is normal; the declining volume peaks warn of underlying technical weakness. Unfortunately, there are no hard-and-fast rules about how many divergences precede a peak. Generally speaking, though, the greater the number of negative divergences, the weaker the underlying technical picture. Also, the lower the peaks relative to each other, the less enthusiasm is being generated, and the more vulnerable the technical position becomes, once buying dries up or selling enthusiasm intensifies. A new high that is accompanied by virtually no volume is just as bearish as a new price high with virtually no upside momentum.

An example is shown in Chart 7.1 for Aligent Technology, where you can see that the volume clusters gradually become smaller as the price rallies. Eventually, this negative technical characteristic is confirmed as the price violates the 2010–2011 up trendline in early July 2011.

4. Rising prices accompanied by a trend of falling volume (Figure 7.4) is an abnormal situation. It indicates a weak and suspect rally and is a bear market characteristic.

When it is recognized, it can and should be used as a piece of evidence pointing to a primary bear market environment. Volume measures the relative enthusiasm of buyers and sellers. When it shrinks as prices rise,

CHART 7.1 Aligent Technology 2010–2011

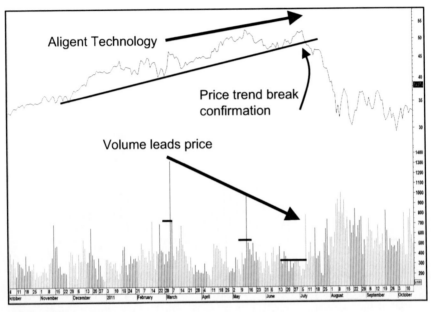

Source: From pring.com

FIGURE 7.4 Rising Prices and Falling Volume Is Bearish

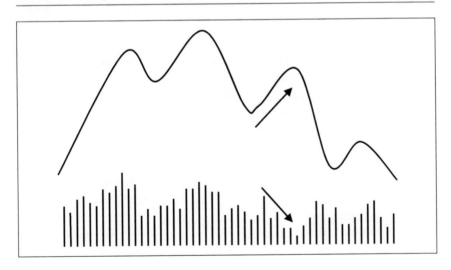

FIGURE 7.5 Falling Prices and Rising Volume Is Bearish

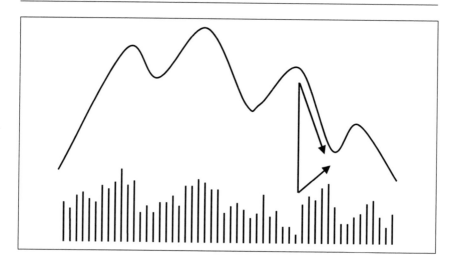

the advance occurs because of a lack of selling rather than because of sponsorship from buyers. Sooner or later, the trend will reach a point where sellers become more motivated. After that, prices will start to pick up on the downside. One clue is provided when activity increases noticeably as the price starts to decline. This is shown in Figure 7.5, where you can see that volume starts to pick up as the price starts a sell-off.

In such situations, it is not necessary for volume to expand throughout the decline, as it does in this example. It could be that it picks up for two or three bars just after the peak. In fact, this would be a more typical situation.

Figure 7.6 shows how the volume configurations change between a bull market and a bear market.

Chart 7.2 shows the final rally being accompanied by a trend of declining volume for Coors. When the lower trendline is violated, volume picks up noticeably. In this instance, we have one bearish volume configuration that is instantly followed by another.

Chart 7.3 shows several bear market rallies in which the rising price trend is accompanied by declining volume for Radio Shack.

5. Sometimes both price and volume expand slowly, gradually working into an exponential rise with a final blow-off stage. Following this development, both volume and price fall off equally sharply. This represents an exhaustion move and is characteristic of a trend reversal, especially when supported by a one- or two-bar price pattern (discussed in subsequent chapters). The significance of the reversal will depend upon the extent of

FIGURE 7.6 Volume Characteristics Change in Bull and Bear Markets

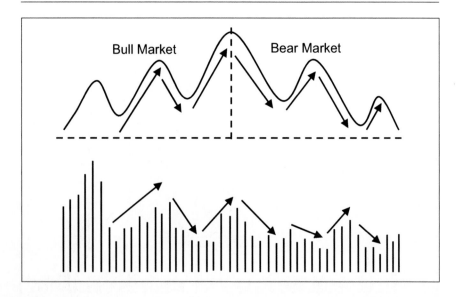

CHART 7.2 Coors 2000–2001

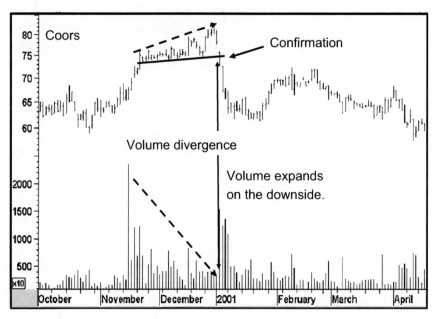

Source: From pring.com

CHART 7.3 Radio Shack 2000–2001

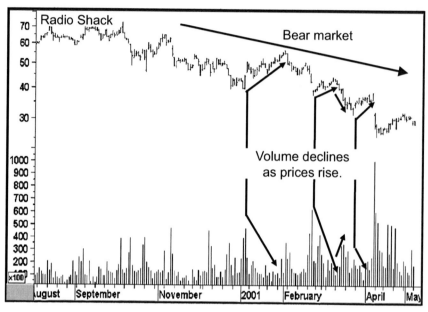

Source: From pring.com

the previous advance and the degree of volume expansion. Obviously, an exhaustion move that takes 4 to 5 days to develop will be nowhere near as significant as one that develops over a matter of weeks. This phenomenon is termed a *parabolic blow-off* and is featured in Figure 7.7.

Unfortunately, exhaustion, or blow-off, moves such as this are not easy to define in the sense that it is possible to construct clearly definable trendlines or price patterns. For this reason, it is usually not possible to spot the terminal phase until a period or so after volume and price have reached their crescendos. Furthermore, because of their nature, parabolic blow-offs are quite rare.

Chart 7.4 uses Newmont Mining to demonstrate a classic example of an exponential increase in both price and volume that ends in tears in the form of an abrupt reversal in late September 1987. We see another in Chart 7.5 featuring Amrep Ordinary.

6. A *selling climax* is the opposite of a parabolic blow-off. It occurs when prices fall for a considerable time at an accelerating pace, accompanied by expanding volume. Prices typically rise after a selling climax. The low that is established at the time of the climax is *unlikely* to be violated for a considerable time. I emphasized the word unlikely because there are no

FIGURE 7.7 Parabolic Blow-Off

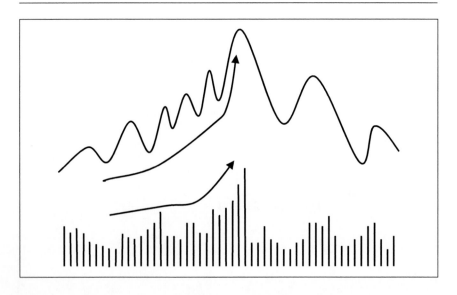

CHART 7.4 Newmont Mining 1986–1987

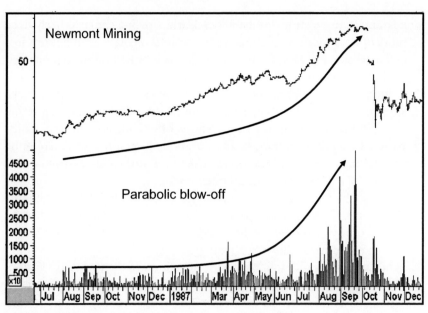

Source: From pring.com

CHART 7.5 Amrep Ordinary 2003–2009

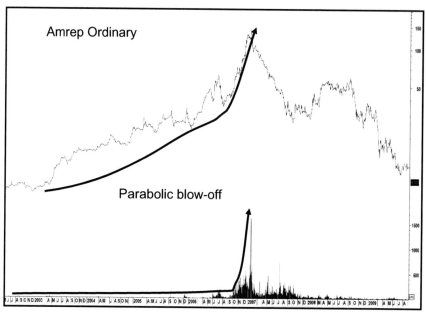

Source: From pring.com

guarantees, just a strong probability. Clearly, a selling climax is likely to be more of an indication of a final short- or intermediate-term bottom in a bull market. A price rise from a selling climax is by definition accompanied by declining volume. This is the only time when contracting volume and a rising price may be regarded as normal. Even so, it is important to make sure that volume expands on subsequent rallies, as indicated in Figure 7.8.

The termination of a bear trend is often, but not always, accompanied by a selling climax. Unlike parabolic blow-offs, which are quite rare, selling climaxes appear on the charts far more often and are, therefore, quite a common technical phenomenon.

In Chart 7.6, we see a selling climax develop in 2010 for Andarco Petroleum. This is then followed by a rally and a subsequent test on lower volume. Note how volume declines on the rally, a perfectly normal characteristic following a selling climax.

7. When prices advance following a long decline and then react to a level at, slightly above, or marginally below the previous trough, this is a bullish sign if the volume on the second trough is significantly lower than the volume on the first. There is an old saying on Wall Street, "Never short a dull market." This saying applies very much to this type of situation,

FIGURE 7.8 Selling Climax

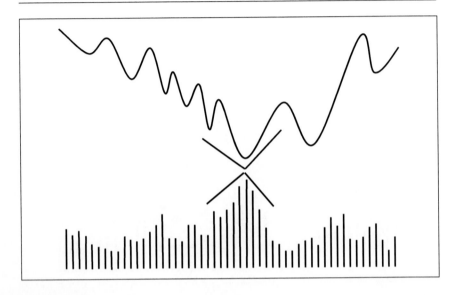

CHART 7.6 Andarco Petroleum Ordinary 2009–2012

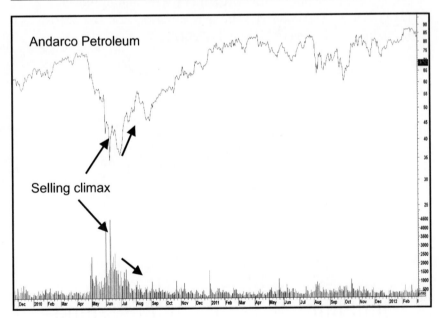

Andarco Petroleum

Selling climax

Source: From pring.com

FIGURE 7.9 Look for Low Volume when Testing Lows

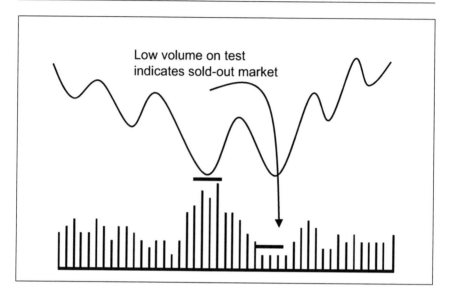

in which a previous low is being tested with very low volume. Such a situation indicates a complete lack of selling pressure (see Figure 7.9).

8. A downside breakout from a price pattern, trendline, or moving average (MA) that occurs on heavy volume is abnormal and is a bearish sign that confirms the reversal in trend (Figure 7.10).

FIGURE 7.10 Rising Volume on a Downside Breakout Is Bearish

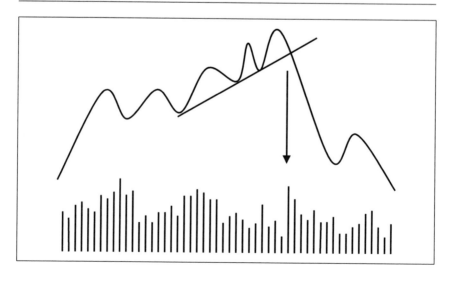

When prices decline, it is usually because of a lack of bids, so volume contracts. This is normal activity and does not give us much information. However, when volume expands on the downside, it is because sellers are more motivated, so the decline, other things being equal, is likely to be more severe.

9. When the price has been rising for many months, an anemic rally (Figure 7.11) accompanied by high volume indicates *churning* action and is a bearish factor.

    An example featuring Dresser Industries is shown in Chart 7.7.

10. Following a decline, heavy volume with little price change is indicative of accumulation and is normally a bullish factor (Figure 7.12).

11. Record volume coming off a major low is usually a very reliable signal that a significant bottom has been seen. This is because it indicates that an underlying change in psychology has taken place. Such reversals in sentiment are usually of a primary trend magnitude. Examples in the U.S. stock market developed in March 1978, August 1982 and 1984, and October 1998. A similar pattern also developed at the 1987 low in bonds and eurodollars. This is not an infallible indicator, though, because record volume was achieved in January 2001 for both the NYSE and NASDAQ, yet this did not turn out to be the final low for the bear market, which was achieved over a year later in October 2002.

12. When volume and price expand at a sharp pace, but short of a parabolic blow-off, and then contract slightly, this usually indicates a change in

FIGURE 7.11 Churning Is Bearish

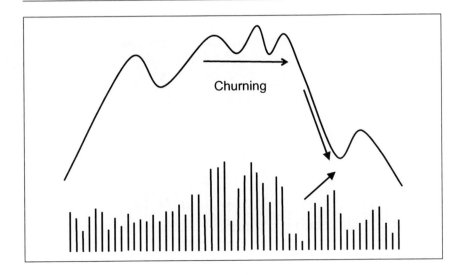

CHART 7.7 Dresser Industries Petroleum 2007–2009

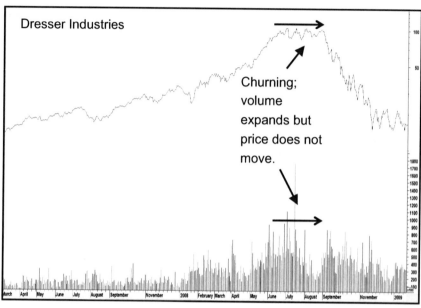

Source: From pring.com

FIGURE 7.12 Accumulation Is Bullish

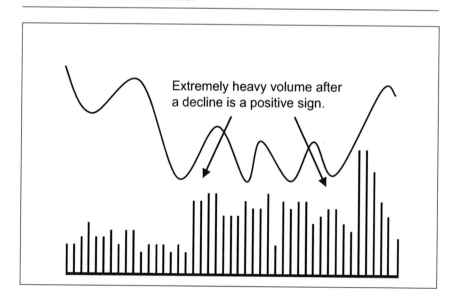

trend. Sometimes this is an actual reversal and at other times a consolidation. This phenomenon is featured in Figure 7.13 and represents
a temporary exhaustion of buying power.

It is associated with several one- and two-bar price patterns,
discussed in later chapters. The example shows the price eventually
selling off, but it could just as easily have risen. All the volume crescendo is telling us is that buyers are exhausted and we should expect
a pause. When that buying is exceptionally heavy, a more bullish
extreme in sentiment is indicated and is more likely to be followed by
an extended period of price erosion, as shown in Figure 7.13.

13. When the price experiences a small rounding top and volume experiences a rounding bottom, this is a doubly abnormal situation, since
price is rising and volume is falling as the peak is reached. After the
peak, volume expands as the price declines, which is also abnormal
and bearish. An example is shown in Figure 7.14. An example featuring
Microsoft is featured in Chart 7.8. Note how the letter *n* characterizes
the price action, whereas the volume configuration is closer to letter *u*.

14. When the price volatility shrinks to almost nothing and volume
does the same, this indicates total disinterest. When the situation is
eventually resolved, this is often followed by an above-average price
move. In Figure 7.15, for instance, price and volume fall to the kind

FIGURE 7.13 Extremely High Volume After a Sharp Advance Indicates Exhaustion

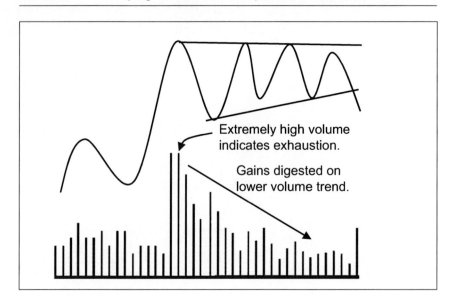

FIGURE 7.14 Watch Volume on Rallies and Reactions

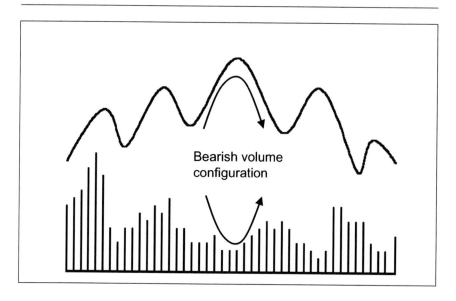

CHART 7.8 Microsoft 2007–2009

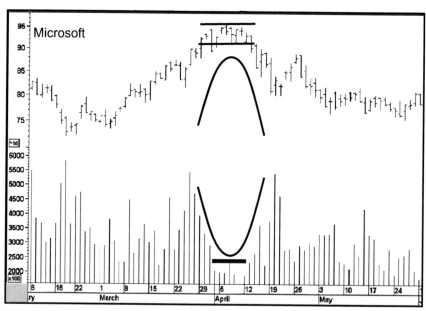

Source: From pring.com

FIGURE 7.15 Exceptionally Low Volume Is Very Bullish when Confirmed by Price and Expanding Volume

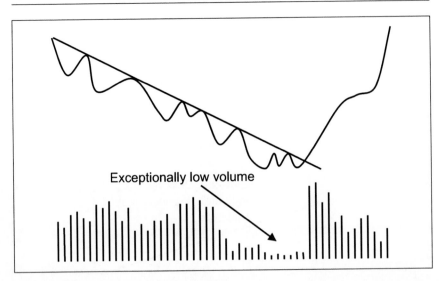

Exceptionally low volume

of levels where the slightest movement in either direction will signal a dramatic price movement.

In this case, the down trendline is violated on the upside and volume explodes; so, too, do prices. Generally speaking, the quieter the price and volume action relative to the preceding downtrend, the more explosive the *confirmed* subsequent rally is likely to be. In this case, "confirmed" means some kind of a price trend reversal accompanied by expanding volume.

A very narrow balance between buyers and sellers is certainly apparent in Chart 7.9, which features ICIC Bank.

Note the shrinking volatility of the price activity and the accompanying trend of lower and lower volume. The balance between buyers and sellers is extremely fine as we roll into early September. Then the price breaks to the downside and volume expands. That's the signal for an above-average price decline

None of the indicators used in the technical arsenal are guaranteed to work every time. This is certainly true of volume characteristics. However, when volume is used in combination with price characteristics in pattern interpretation, trendline violations and moving average crossovers it greatly enhances the probability that a specific setup or formation will "work." As we discuss specific price examples in subsequent chapters, the

CHART 7.9 ICIC Bank 2008

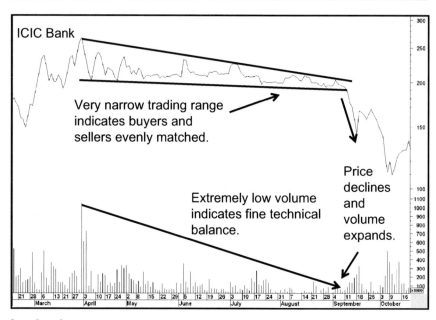

Source: From pring.com

basic volume principles described here will be expanded to suit individual cases.

You will also be able to appreciate at this point that most of the time volume as an indicator is not telling us very much. However, when it does speak and is confirmed by other indicators, a loud message is indeed given.

Summary

1. Volume is a totally independent variable from price.
2. It is normal for volume to go with the trend. When these characteristics are present, they have little forecasting value.
3. When volume trends are moving in a direction opposite to that of price, this is abnormal and either warns of an impending trend reversal or emphasizes the significance of any breakout.
4. Volume trends experience exhaustion phenomena. These are called parabolic blow-offs at tops and selling climaxes at lows.

8

CLASSIC PRICE PATTERNS

In earlier chapters we discussed the concepts of peak-and-trough progression, support and resistance, trendlines, and rudimentary volume characteristics. These are all basic building blocks of price pattern construction. Now it's time to put them all together to gain a better understanding of how we recognize, interpret, and appreciate the significance of specific formations. For a more complete, in-depth discussion of price patterns, their underlying psychology, and significance, please refer to *Martin Pring on Price Patterns* (McGraw-Hill, 2005).

The concept of price patterns is demonstrated in Figures 8.1 and 8.2. Figure 8.1 represents a typical market cycle in which there are three trends: up, sideways, and down. The sideways trend is essentially a horizontal or transitional one, which separates the two major market movements.

Sometimes, a highly emotional market can change without warning, as in Figure 8.2, but this rarely happens. Consider a fast-moving train, which takes a long time to slow down and then go into reverse; the same is normally true of financial markets.

To the market technician, the transitional phase has great significance because it marks the turning point between a rising and a falling market. If prices have been advancing, the enthusiasm of the buyers has outweighed the pessimism of sellers up to this point, and prices have risen accordingly. During the transition phase, the balance becomes more or less even until finally, for one reason or another, it is tipped in a new direction as the relative weight of selling pushes the trend (of prices) down. At the termination of a bear market, the reverse process occurs.

FIGURE 8.1 Top and Bottom Reversals

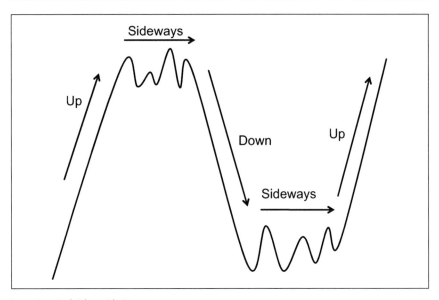

Source: From *Martin Pring on Price Patterns*

FIGURE 8.2 Reversal on a Dime

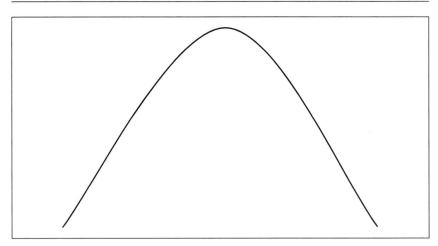

Source: From *Martin Pring on Price Patterns*

FIGURE 8.3 Trading Range Reversal

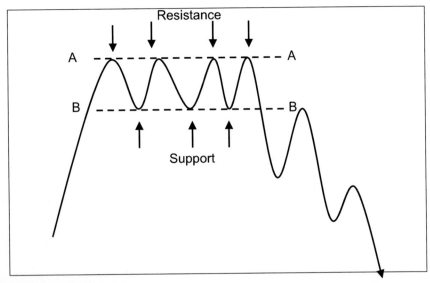

Source: From *Martin Pring on Price Patterns*

Major Technical Principle Transitions between a rising and a falling trend are often signaled by identifiable trading ranges known as price patterns.

These transition phases are almost invariably signaled by clearly definable price patterns or formations whose successful completion alerts the technician to the fact that a reversal in trend has taken place.

This phenomenon is illustrated in Figure 8.3, which shows the price action at the end of a long rising trend. As soon as the price rises above line *BB*, it is in the transitional area, although this is apparent only sometime after the picture has developed.

Once into the area, the price rises to line *AA*, which is a *resistance area*. The word "resistance" is used because at this point the price shows opposition to a further rise. When the demand/supply relationship comes into balance at *AA*, the market quickly turns in favor of the sellers because prices react. This temporary reversal may occur because buyers refuse to pay up for a security, or because the higher price attracts more sellers, or

FIGURE 8.4 Trench Warfare

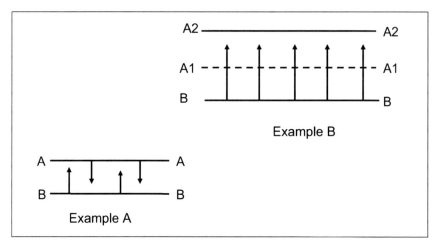

Source: From *Martin Pring on Price Patterns*

for a combination of these two reasons. The important fact is that the relationship between the two groups is temporarily reversed at this point.

Following the unsuccessful assault on *AA*, prices turn down until line *BB*, known as a *support level*, is reached. Just as the price level at *AA* reversed the balance in favor of the sellers, so the support level *BB* alters the balance again. This time, the trend moves in an upward direction, for at *BB*, prices become relatively attractive for buyers who missed the boat on the way up, while sellers who feel that the price will again reach *AA* hold off. For a while, there is a stand-off between buyers and sellers within the confines of the area bounded by lines *AA* and *BB*. Finally, the price falls below *BB*, and a major new (downward) trend is signaled.

To help explain this concept, the contest between buyers and sellers is like a battle fought by two armies engaged in trench warfare. In Figure 8.4, example *a*, armies A and B are facing off. Line *AA* represents army A's defense, and *BB* is army B's line of defense.

The arrows indicate the forays between the two lines as both armies fight their way to the opposing trench but are unable to penetrate the line of defense. In the second example, army B finally pushes through A's trench. Army A is then forced to retreat and make a stand at the second line of defense (line *AA2*). In the markets, line *AA* represents selling resistance, which, once overcome, signifies a change in the balance between buyers and sellers in favor of the buyers, so that prices will advance quickly until new resistance is met. The second line of defense, line *AA2*, represents resistance to a further advance.

On the other hand, army B might quite easily break through *AA2*, but the further it advances without time to consolidate its gains, the more likely it is to become overextended and the greater is the probability of its suffering a serious setback. At some point, therefore, it makes more sense for this successful force to wait and consolidate its gains.

If prices extend too far without time to digest their gains, they, too, are more likely to face a sharp and seemingly unexpected reversal.

Introducing the Rectangle

The transitional or horizontal phase separating rising and falling price trends discussed earlier is a pattern known as a *rectangle*. This corresponds to the "line" formation developed from Dow theory. The rectangle in Figure 8.5, marking the turning point between the bull and bear phases, is termed a *reversal* pattern.

FIGURE 8.5 Downside Breakout Signal

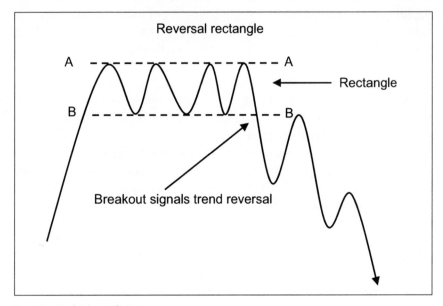

Source: From *Martin Pring on Price Patterns*

FIGURE 8.6 Upside Breakout Signal

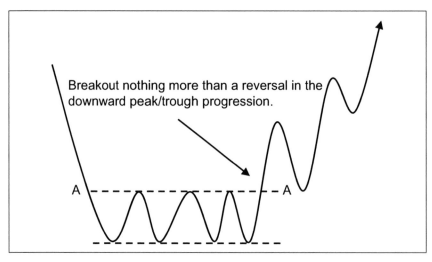

Source: From *Martin Pring on Price Patterns*

Reversal patterns at market tops are known as *distribution* areas or patterns (where the security is "distributed" from strong, informed participants to weak, uninformed ones), and those at market bottoms are called *accumulation* patterns (where the security passes from weak, uninformed participants to strong, informed ones. In Figure 8.6 we see a completed pattern with a victory for the buyers as the price pushed through line *AA*.

Note that as the price moves through *AA*, the series of declining peaks and troughs reverses to one of rising peaks and troughs. On the other hand, in Figure 8.7, the price breaks to the upside, reinforcing the series of rising peaks and troughs that precede the formation of the rectangle, thereby reaffirming the underlying trend.

In this case, the corrective phase associated with the formation of the rectangle would temporarily interrupt the bull market. Such formations are referred to as *consolidation* or *continuation* patterns. An example of a bearish continuation rectangle is shown in Chart 8.1 for the copper price and Chart 8.2 for the Dow Jones Rail Average.

During the period of formation, there is no way of knowing in advance which way the price will ultimately break; therefore, it should always be assumed that the *prevailing trend is in existence until it is proved to have been reversed.* Figure 8.8 shows an example of a continuation rectangle that develops in a downtrend.

FIGURE 8.7 Upside Continuation Breakout Signal

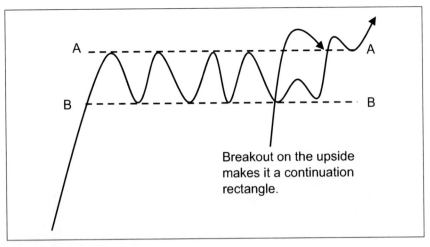

Breakout on the upside makes it a continuation rectangle.

Source: From *Martin Pring on Price Patterns*

CHART 8.1 Copper Featuring a Consolidation Rectangle

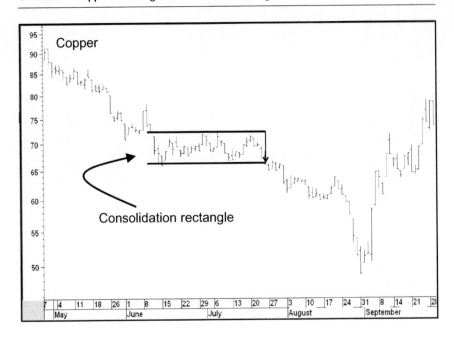

CHART 8.2 Dow Jones Rail Average 1946. This chart shows a classic rectangle as traced out by the Dow Jones Rail Average at the peak of the 1942–1946 bull market. Note the declining trend of volume as reflected by the declining dashed line during the formation of the rectangle. Worth special attention is the saucer-like formation of the volume during the late July to early August rally. The expansion of activity accompanying the downside breakout in late August signals the successful completion of this pattern.

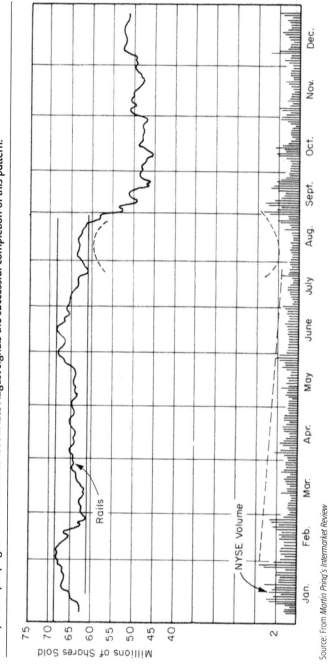

FIGURE 8.8 Downside Continuation Breakout Signal

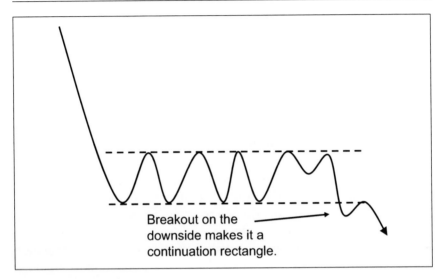

Source: From *Martin Pring on Price Patterns*

Size and Depth

The principles of price pattern construction and interpretation can be applied to any time frame, right from one-minute bars all the way through to monthly or even annual charts. However, the significance of a price formation is a direct function of its size and depth.

> **Major Technical Principle** The longer a pattern takes to complete, and the greater the price fluctuations within it, the more substantial the following move is likely to be.

Thus, a pattern that shows up on a monthly chart is likely to be far more significant than one plotted with intraday data and so forth. It is just as important to build a strong base from which prices can rise as it is to build a large, strong, deep foundation upon which to construct a skyscraper. In the case of financial market prices, the foundation is an accumulation pattern that represents an area of indecisive combat between buyers and sellers. The term "accumulation" is used because market bottoms always occur when the news is bad. In markets, such an environment stimulates sales by uninformed investors who were not expecting developments to improve. During an accumulation phase, more sophisticated investors and professionals would be positioning or accumulating the asset concerned in anticipation of improved conditions for the security in question six to nine months ahead. During this period, the security in question is moving from weak, uninformed traders or investors into strong and knowledgeable ones. At market tops, the process is reversed, as those who were accumulating at or near the bottom sell to less sophisticated market participants, who become more and more attracted as prices rise. For equities, this might develop because business conditions improve and forecasts for the economy are revised upward. Thus, the longer the period of accumulation, the greater the amount of a security that moves from weak into strong hands, and the larger is the base from which prices can rise. The reverse is true at market tops, where a substantial amount of distribution inevitably results in a protracted period of price erosion or base building.

Major Technical Principle   The longer the formation of any pattern takes and the more often it fails to break through its outer boundaries, the greater is the significance of the ultimate penetration.

The time taken to complete a formation is important because of the amount of an asset changing hands and also because a movement in price beyond the boundaries of a pattern means that the balance between buyers and sellers has altered. When the price action has been in a stalemate for a long time and investors have become used to buying at one price and selling at the other, a move beyond either limit represents a fundamental change, which has great psychological significance. A great example of a very long rectangle is shown in Chart 8.3 for the CRB Composite.

There was every probability that a breakout from such a pattern would be followed by a good move, but there was no indication that prices would rise so sharply over such a brief period of time.

The depth of a formation also determines its significance. Consider the trench warfare analogy once more. If the opposing trenches are very close together—say, within 100 yards—this means that the victorious assault, when it comes, will be less significant than if the armies are separated by several miles,

CHART 8.3 CRB Composite 1957–1982. This chart features a multiyear rectangle breakout that took place in 1972. There was no way of predicting the character of the rally, but the length of the rectangle indicated that something big was likely afoot.

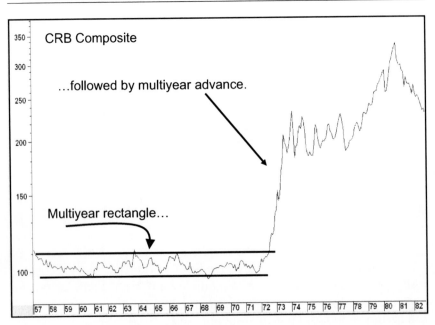

Source: From pring.com

for in that case, the battles will have been much more intense and the victory that much greater. The same is true in the financial markets. The breeching of a wide trading range has far greater psychological significance than does a narrow one.

Measuring Implications

Most of the results obtained with technical analysis procedures do not indicate the eventual magnitude of a trend. Price patterns are the exception, since their construction offers some limited forecasting possibilities. Pretty well all price patterns obtain measuring objectives from their depth. The rectangle is no exception. Figure 8.9 shows a rectangle that has formed and completed a (distribution) top.

The measuring implication of this formation is the vertical distance between its outer boundaries, i.e., the distance between lines *AA* and *BB* projected downward from line *BB*.

FIGURE 8.9 Rectangle Top Measuring Objective

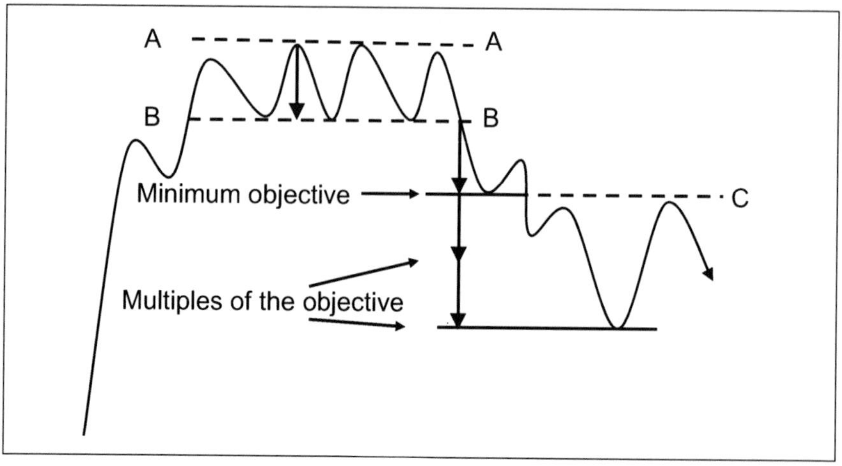

Source: From *Martin Pring on Price Patterns*

In many cases, the price trend will extend beyond the objective. In really strong moves, it will travel in multiples of it. We can take the process a step further by stating that the various multiples of the objective itself can become important potential support and resistance areas in their own right. Time and again, these price objective areas turn out to be important support or resistance points. Unfortunately, there is no way to determine where the actual juncture point will be for any rally or reaction. This emphasizes the principle that in technical analysis there is no known way of consistently determining the magnitude of a price movement. It is only possible to speculate on the *probability* that a specific area will prove to be a support or resistance zone. Consequently, while this measuring formula offers a rough guide, it is usually a *minimum* expectation.

Having established the fact that price patterns offer price objectives when completed, it is also important to revisit the options of arithmetic and logarithmic scaling covered earlier.

If you recall, arithmetic scaling involves using the same vertical distance for equal point amounts so that the difference in space between 2 and 4 is the same as that between 20 and 22. This compares to ratio or logarithmic scaling, where the same vertical distance plots the same proportionate move. Thus, for example, one inch might represent a 20 percent price move at whatever level it takes place.

The importance of using logarithmic scales whenever possible is shown in Figures 8.10 and 8.11. In Figure 8.10, the price traced out and

FIGURE 8.10 Measuring Implications Using an Arithmetic Scale

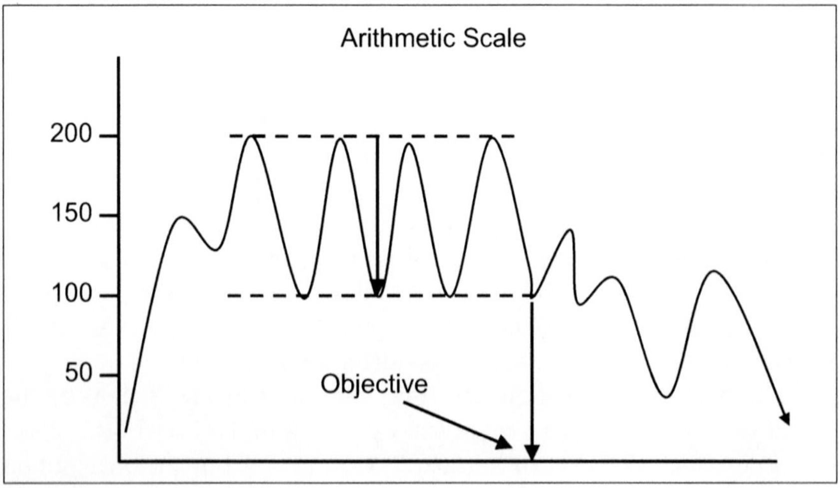

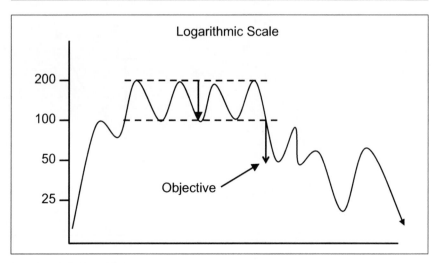

broke down from a rectangle. Projecting the vertical distance between 200 and 100 downward gives an objective of 0, clearly a very unlikely possibility.

On the other hand, Figure 8.11 uses the same projection based on a logarithmic scale. In this case, a more realistic objective of 50 is obtained.

FIGURE 8.11 Measuring Implications Using a Logarithmic Scale

It is important to remember that market prices are a function of psychological attitudes toward fundamental events. Since these attitudes have a tendency to move proportionately, it makes sense to plot them on a scale that reflects proportionate moves equally. Clearly, this distinction has little effect on very short-term (2 to 6 weeks) or intraday charts, but since you do not know exactly when it will, it's definitely a good idea to set your charting software to ratio as a default.

If a rectangle appears as a bottom reversal pattern, the measuring rules remain consistent with the example given for the distribution formation. The only difference is that we project the objective and multiples of the objective in an upward direction, not downward. The exact same principles also apply to continuation rectangles. Figure 8.12 shows an upside breakout from a rectangle that forms during a bullish trend.

Note in this case that the price does not immediately reach its upside objective, but does so after a small rally and reaction. This is why the objective is described by the term "ultimate." Most people buy the breakout on the assumption that they will make more or less instant profits as the price moves straight to the objective, but that is not necessarily the case.

Major Technical Principle   A measuring objective is a minimum ultimate objective.

FIGURE 8.12 Upside Continuation Rectangle Measuring Objective

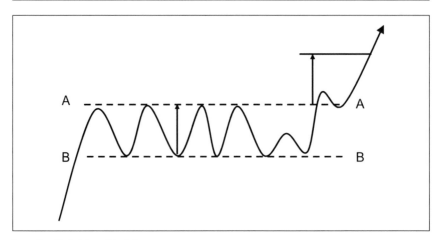

Source: From *Martin Pring on Price Patterns*

In many cases, the price will move beyond the objective. In really strong moves, it will move in multiples of the objective, where the various multiples or the objective itself become important support and resistance areas.

Confirmation of a Valid Breakout

Price

So far, it has been assumed that any move out of the price pattern, however small, constitutes a valid signal of a trend reversal (or resumption, if the pattern is one of consolidation). Quite often, misleading moves known as *whipsaws* occur, so it is helpful to establish certain criteria to minimize the possibility of misinterpretation. Conventional wisdom holds that you should wait for a 3 percent penetration of the boundaries before concluding that the breakout is valid. This filters out a substantial number of misleading moves, even though the resulting signals are less timely.

This approach was developed in the first part of the twentieth century when holding periods for market participants were much longer. Today, with the popularity of intraday charts, 3 percent could represent the complete move and then some! I have no basic objection to the 3 percent rule for longer-term price movements in which the fluctuations are much greater. However, the best approach is a common sense one based on experience and judgment in each particular case. It would be very convenient to be able to say that anything over a specific percentage amount represents a valid breakout, but unfortunately, a lot depends on the time frame being considered and the volatility of the specific security.

For example, electric utilities are very stable in their price action compared to mining stocks, where the volatility is far greater. Applying the same percentage breakout rule to both obviously doesn't make sense. What constitutes a decisive breakout, where the odds of a whipsaw are considerably reduced, is then very much a matter of personal judgment based on experience, trial, and error. This judgment should take into consideration such factors as the type of trend being monitored, the volatility of the security, volume, and momentum characteristics.

Another factor that can help early on in deciding if a breakout is valid is the fact that a good breakout should hold for several periods. For example, you may observe a decisive upside breakout from a rectangle on a daily chart, but if it cannot hold for more than one day above the breakout level, the signal is highly suspect. Often, the technical position is worse after such breakouts because breakouts that cannot hold indicate exhaustion and exhaustion moves are often followed by strong price trends in the opposite direction to that indicated by the (false) breakout.

On entering any trade or investment based on a price pattern breakout, it is important to decide ahead of time what type of price action would cause you to conclude that the breakout was a whipsaw. In effect, this will be below a support level for an upside breakout and below a resistance zone for a downward one. For this you can draw on the information contained in Chapter 5 on support and resistance. An example of a false upside breakout might be a penetration of a previous minor low, a decline below a predetermined level from the breakout point, or the rupture of a minor up trendline. Some possibilities are featured in Figure 8.13.

A stop should then be placed *below* the support level. In this way, you will have calculated the loss you are willing to undertake and the point where the original premise for the trade, i.e., the breakout, is no longer operative. Failure to make such a decision ahead of time will mean that your decision to sell is more likely to be based on emotion and kneejerk reactions to news events than on a logical preset plan.

FIGURE 8.13 Identifying a Whipsaw Breakout

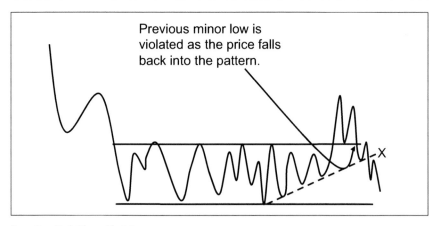

Source: From *Martin Pring on Price Patterns*

Retracement Moves   A great deal of the time, when the price breaks out from a pattern, the initial thrust is followed by a corrective move back to the upper or lower reaches of the formation, depending on the direction of the breakout. This is known as a *retracement* move, and it offers an additional entry point, often under substantially less emotional conditions. The retracement serves two functions. First, it helps to correct the excessive emotion associated with the breakout and brings people back to earth. From here, it is then possible for the new trend to extend on a sounder basis. Second, it acts as a test of the breakout. A downside retracement will find support at the breakout point and an upside retracement will find resistance in the lower boundary of the pattern as these two zones reverse their former roles.

Retracements, then, represent normal price behavior, and although they can be frustrating, are nothing to get concerned about. Indeed, the breakout itself is often a volatile illiquid affair, as one side or the other heads for the entrance or exit, depending on its direction. As a result, orders are often executed with horrendous fills. Price activity during the retracement process, on the other hand, is relatively quieter. This means that buying or selling can be undertaken in a much more controlled environment. Figure 8.14 shows that it is often a good idea to wait for a retracement in a rising trend and buy as the price signals that the retracement is over.

Cancellations   If the minimal objective proves to be the ultimate extension of the new trend, a substantial amount of accumulation or distribution,

FIGURE 8.14 Buy on the Retracement Breakout

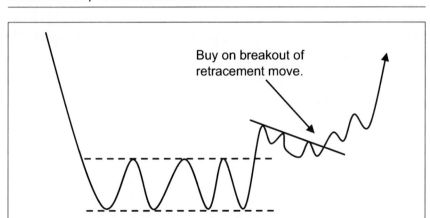

Buy on breakout of retracement move.

Source: From *Martin Pring on Price Patterns*

FIGURE 8.15 Cancellation

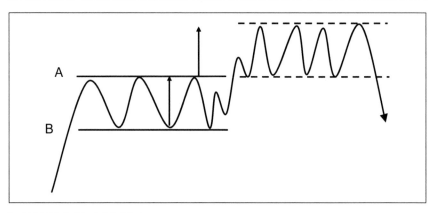

Source: From *Martin Pring on Price Patterns*

whichever is appropriate, will typically have to occur before prices can move in their previous direction. Thus, a 2-year rectangle might be completed and the downward price objective reached. Even though further price erosion does not take place, it is still *technically* necessary for a base (accumulation) of approximately the same size as the previous distribution (in this case, 2 years) to be formed before a valid uptrend can take place. An example is shown in Figure 8.15, where an upside breakout is cancelled by a downside one.

The word technically has been emphasized because that is not always the case, and there are lots of examples where large distribution formations have been cancelled by small ones and vice versa. That means if you can spot a cancellation, pay attention to the signal and look around at the other indicators to see if they agree. If so, go with the cancellation, as it's probably telling the truth.

Volume Considerations

So far, we have just considered price in our analysis, but volume is an important independent variable that can help us obtain a more accurate reflection of crowd psychology. To quickly recap, volume typically goes with the trend, i.e., it expands with a rising trend of prices and falls with a declining one. This is a normal relationship, and anything that diverges from it should be considered a warning sign that the prevailing price trend may be in the process of reversing. Volume is always measured in relation to the recent past. Thus, heavy volume relates to volume 20 to 30 bars or so ago, not to volume, say, 10 years ago, where institutional changes may have permanently increased the level of activity.

Major Technical Principle   Volume is always measured relative to its recent past.

In the case of the rectangle, and with most other patterns, it is normal for the trend of volume to contract as the formation develops. Activity may continue to fluctuate along with the price, but with the benefit of hindsight we would expect to see the various peaks and troughs of volume shrink as the pattern develops, along the lines of Figure 8.16. As it nears completion, disinterest prevails and volume often dries up.

The quality of an accumulation formation is certainly improved if volume expands on the upside break. Sometimes it is even possible to draw a trendline joining the lower volume peaks, as shown in Figure 8.16.

FIGURE 8.16 Volume Trend Shrinks as the Rectangle Is Being Formed

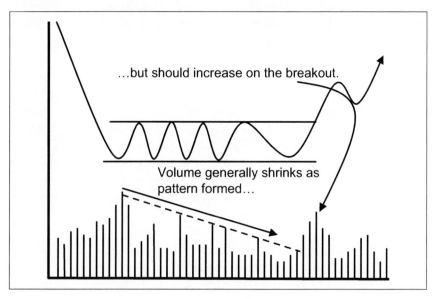

...but should increase on the breakout.

Volume generally shrinks as pattern formed...

Source: From *Martin Pring on Price Patterns*

FIGURE 8.17 Shrinking Volume on an Upside Breakout Is Bearish

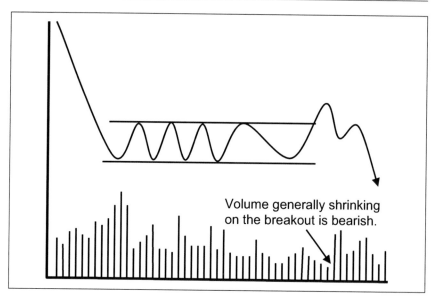

Volume generally shrinking on the breakout is bearish.

Source: From *Martin Pring on Price Patterns*

It is this upward surge in trading activity that confirms the validity of the breakout because it flags the enthusiasm of buyers. A similar move on low and declining volume would be suspect and would result in its failure to move with the trend. An example is shown in Figure 8.17.

In this instance, volume definitely declines as the price is breaking out. Such action typically signals that prices are advancing more on a lack of sellers than strong enthusiastic buyers. As the price starts to slip, volume picks up noticeably, suggesting that this is happening because of selling pressure. It is a definite sign that increases the possibility that the breakout is a whipsaw.

In many instances you will see charts where successful upside breakouts develop with no obvious change in activity, either on the upside or downside. Unfortunately, this is a fact of life. Thus, *a good volume expansion is a desirable, but not necessarily a mandatory, condition for a valid breakout.* It certainly increases the odds, but other indicators such as oscillators could also tip the balance. If volume declines on the breakout, as in Figure 8.17, this is more than a missing piece of positive evidence and is, actually, a negative factor. Figure 8.18 shows a downside breakout from a rectangle.

The same shrinking volume characteristics during the development of the pattern are present as for the bullish variety. However, volume characteristics

FIGURE 8.18 Expanding Volume on a Downside Breakout Is Bearish

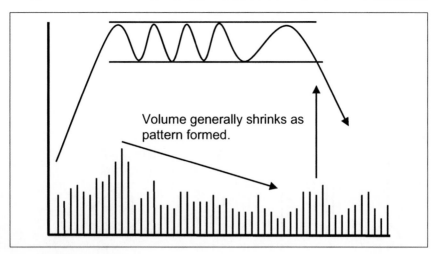

Source: From *Martin Pring on Price Patterns*

on the breakout are less critical. This is because it is normal for it to contract as prices decline. Thus, contracting volume on a breakdown is perfectly normal. What is not typical, though, is for it to expand on a downside move. This in itself suggests that sellers are more motivated and therefore adds a negative flavor to the pattern. More often than not, prices will reverse and put on a small recovery or retracement rally following the downside breakout (Figure 8.19).

This advance is invariably accompanied by declining volume, which itself reinforces the bearish indications. It is halted at the lower end of the rectangle, which now becomes an area of resistance. The same idea of declining volume should accompany a retracement move that follows an upside breakout. Figure 8.20 shows an example where both price volatility and volume shrink dramatically.

This combination indicates an extremely fine balance between buyers and sellers that takes place over an extended period. Normally, a price objective is determined by the depth of the formation. In this case, though, the finely balanced supply/demand situation is usually followed by a far greater and sharper move than that indicated by the normal measuring techniques. Figure 8.20 dramatizes a sharp downside breakout, but the principle of rapidly declining volume followed by a huge expansion applies equally as well to an upside breakout. In this instance, volume typically explodes as we move from a situation in which there is virtually no interest

FIGURE 8.19 Volume Should Shrink on the Retracement Rally

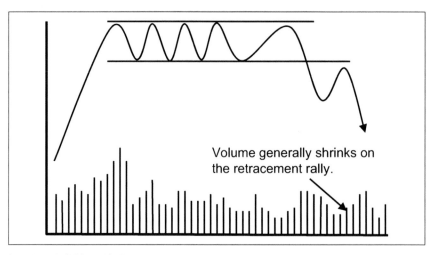

Volume generally shrinks on the retracement rally.

Source: From *Martin Pring on Price Patterns*

FIGURE 8.20 Narrow Rectangle and Nonexistent Volume Are Often Followed by a Sharp Move

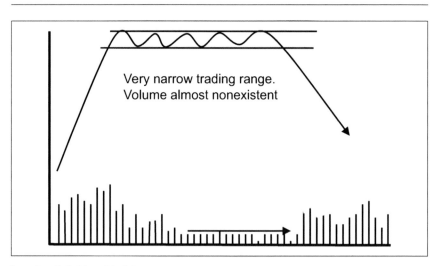

Very narrow trading range. Volume almost nonexistent

Source: From *Martin Pring on Price Patterns*

CHART 8.4 St. Jude Medical Featuring a Consolidation Rectangle

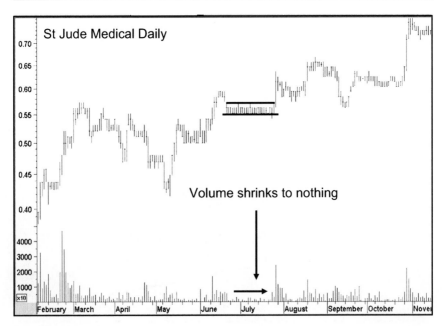

Source: Pring.com

by either party to one in which buyers cannot get enough of the security at any price. Such are the ingredients for the start of a dramatic rally. An example is shown in Chart 8.4 of the U.S.-traded St. Jude Medical, where a very narrow rectangle developed with a dramatic drop in volume. When activity expanded, a short but sharp rally followed.

Finally, Chart 8.5 features Moser Baer, an Indian stock, that shows the formation of a rectangle top. It meets the minimum requirement of trendline touches, so the lines as support or resistance areas are not that significant in themselves.

During the formation of the rectangle, the odd day experienced an expansion in volume, but the overall trend is a declining one. The fact that prices fell so sharply after the breakout is testament to the fact that volume does not necessarily have to expand on the downside. Prices can just as easily fall due to a lack of bids. Note also that while the price almost reached three times its objective, the level of the actual objective (A) became a resistance area on the way back up. Consequently, it's always a good idea to measure for these objectives at the outset because you can never be sure where prices might find timely reversal points.

CHART 8.5 Moser Baer 2006–2008 Rectangle Completion with Multiple Objectives

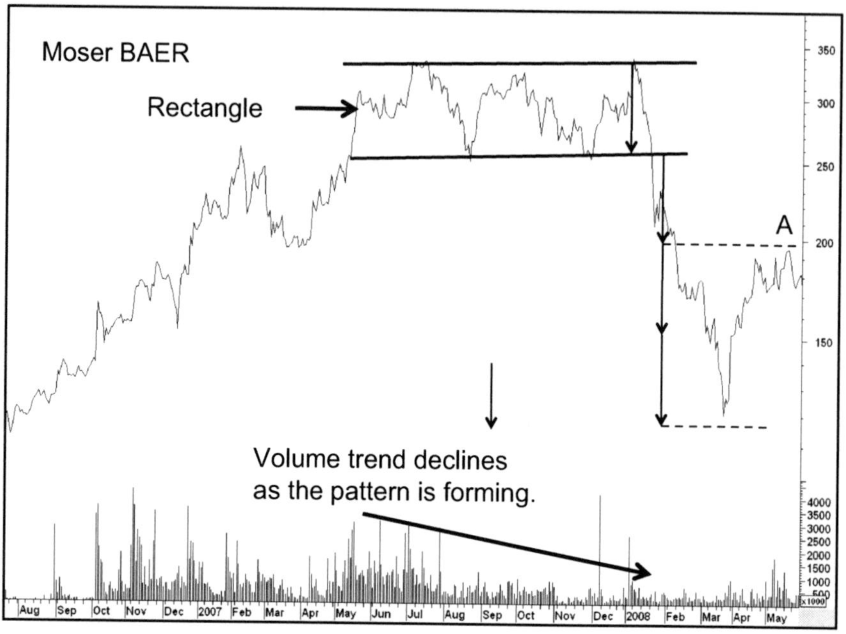

Source: From *Martin Pring's Intermarket Review*

A lot of the time, we find price moves following breakouts from consolidation patterns to be quite substantial, often more so than from reversal patterns. That's because reversal patterns need to build up some momentum, whereas momentum was already in place prior to the formation of the consolidation pattern.

Major Technical Principle   Volume usually leads price.

Head and Shoulders

Head and Shoulders as Reversal Patterns

At Tops   Head and shoulders (H&S) are probably the most reliable of all chart patterns. They occur at both market tops and market bottoms. Figure 8.21 shows a typical head-and-shoulders distribution pattern. (See also Chart 8.6.)

FIGURE 8.21 Classic H&S Top

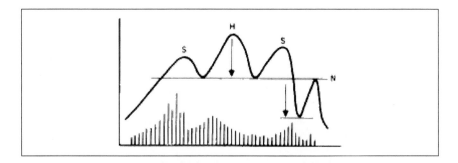

It consists of a final rally (the head) separating two smaller, although not necessarily identical, rallies (the shoulders). If the two shoulders were trends of intermediate duration, the first shoulder would be the penultimate advance in the bull market, and the second the first bear market rally. The head would, of course, represent the final intermediate rally in the bull market.

Volume characteristics are of critical importance in assessing the validity of these patterns. Activity is normally heaviest during the formation of the left shoulder and also tends to be quite heavy as prices approach the peak. The real tip-off that an H&S pattern is developing comes with the formation of the right shoulder, which is invariably accompanied by distinctly lower volume. Quite often, the level of volume contracts as the peak of the right shoulder is reached. The line joining the bottoms of the two shoulders is called the *neckline.*

If you look carefully at Figure 8.21, you will appreciate that the violation of the neckline also represents a signal that the previous series of rising peaks and troughs has now given way to at least one declining peak and trough. The right shoulder represents the first lower peak and the bottom of the move following the breakdown, a lower trough.

The measuring formula for this price formation is the distance between the head and the neckline projected downward from the neckline, as shown in Figure 8.21. It follows that the deeper the pattern, the greater its bearish significance once it has been completed. Sometimes, a head-and-shoulders completion will be followed by a fairly extensive downtrend; at other times, the negative effect of the pattern will be quickly cancelled by the completion of a base.

Often, traders will observe the formation of a head-and-shoulders top and anticipate a breakdown. This is an incorrect tactic based on this evidence alone because it is not known until later whether the prevailing trend will continue or if a reversal signal will be given with a decisive break below the neckline. Over the years, I have seen many analysts who should know better

CHART 8.6 *The New York Times* **Average, 1928.** This chart of the *New York Times* average of 50 railroad and industrial stocks shows the formation of an upward-sloping H&S during March, April, and May 1928. The minimum downside objective of about 182 was achieved fairly quickly, but a three-month period of base building commensurate with the H&S pattern was still necessary before the effect of the distribution was cancelled out and prices were able to resume their primary advance. Note the heavy volume on the left shoulder and head and the relatively low volume on the right shoulder. Also, activity declined substantially during the formation of the triangle, but began to expand during the breakout in September; a bullish expansion in such a volatile manner was a strong warning of the underlying weakness. A small right-angled broadening formation seemed to develop in July and August, but this would eventually prove to be the left shoulder of a 2½-month H&S pattern, the completion of which terminated the long bull market. Triangles and broadening formations are discussed later.

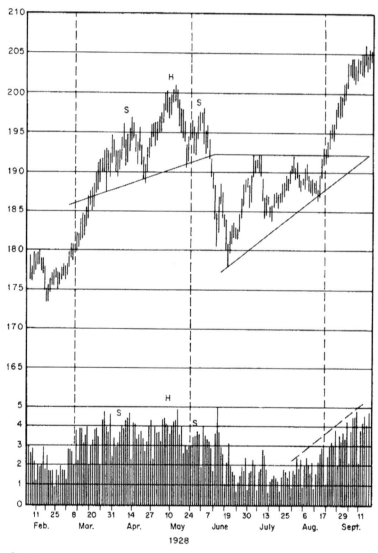

FIGURE 8.22 Complex H&S

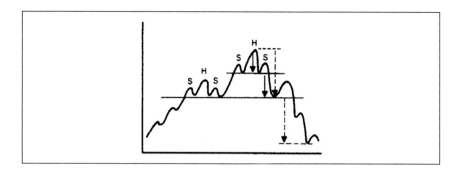

forecast a bearish trend based on an incomplete head-and-shoulders top. Remember, *in technical analysis, the prevailing trend is assumed to be in force until the weight of the evidence proves otherwise.* An incomplete head and shoulders is not evidence, just a possible scenario. Moreover, since a right shoulder rally should be accompanied by a trend of shrinking volume, one that develops under the context of heavy volume provides a clue that the "top" will fail.

H&S patterns can be formed in 10 to 15 minutes or can take decades to develop. Generally speaking, the longer the period, the greater the amount of distribution that has taken place, and, therefore, the longer the ensuing bear trend is likely to be. The larger H&S formations are often very complex and comprise several smaller ones, as shown in Figure 8.22.

The H&S patterns illustrated in Figures 8.21 and 8.22 have a horizontal neckline, but there are many other varieties (as Figure 8.23 shows), all of which possess the same bearish implications as the horizontal variety once they have been completed.

Chart 8.6 shows a classic H&S pattern that formed in the middle of 1928.

FIGURE 8.23 H&S Variations

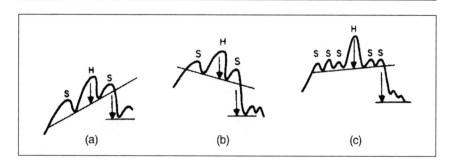

FIGURE 8.24 Classic Reverse H&S

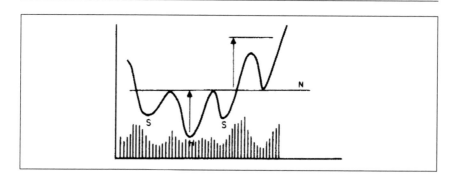

At Bottoms   Figure 8.24 shows an H&S pattern at a market bottom; this is usually called *an inverse H&S, a reverse H&S,* or an *H&S bottom.*

Normally, volume is relatively high at the bottom of the left shoulder and during the formation of the head. The major factor to watch for is activity on the right shoulder, which should contract during the decline to the trough and expand substantially on the breakout (see Chart 8.7).

CHART 8.7 DJIA 1898. This downward-sloping, inverse H&S pattern developed in the spring of 1898. Note that the April rally developed on very low volume. The subsequent reaction successfully tested the March low, and the ensuing breakout rally was accompanied by a bullish expansion of volume.

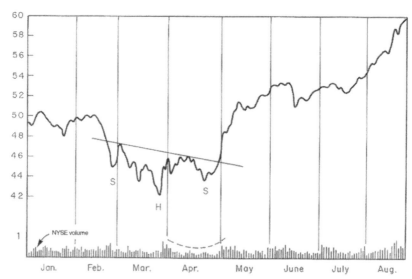

Source: Pring.com

FIGURE 8.25 Reverse H&S Variations

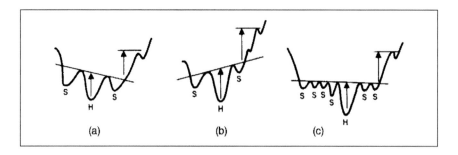

(a) (b) (c)

That's an ideal situation, but it is surprising how many successful breakouts develop under circumstances where the volume does not expand noticeably. If it contracts on the breakout rally, that is a definite no-no and is a strong sign that the breakout is likely to fail. Like the H&S distribution patterns, the inverse (accumulation) H&S can have a number of variations in trendline slope, number of shoulders, etc. Usually, the more complex the formation, the greater its significance. This goes back to the idea that price formations represent battles between buyers and sellers; the more battles that take place, i.e., the greater the complexity, the more significant the new trend once the battle has been resolved. Some of these reverse head-and-shoulders variations are shown in Figure 8.25.

H&S patterns are extremely reliable formations, and their successful completion usually gives an excellent indication of a trend reversal.

H&S Formations as Continuation Patterns

H&S and reverse H&S formations occasionally show up on the charts as continuation patterns. Measuring implications and volume characteristics are the same as for the reversal type. The only difference is that these patterns develop *during* a trend rather than at the end. Chart 8.8, featuring AEP Industries, shows a great example of a continuation reverse head and shoulders, complete with a huge expansion of volume just before and just after the breakout. Substantial markup phases such as this are not uncommon following these continuation formations.

Head-and-Shoulders Failures

We have already established that prices are determined by crowd psychology. Individuals can and do change their minds; so can crowds, and therefore,

CHART 8.8 AEP Industries 2011–2012 Featuring a Reverse Head and Shoulders

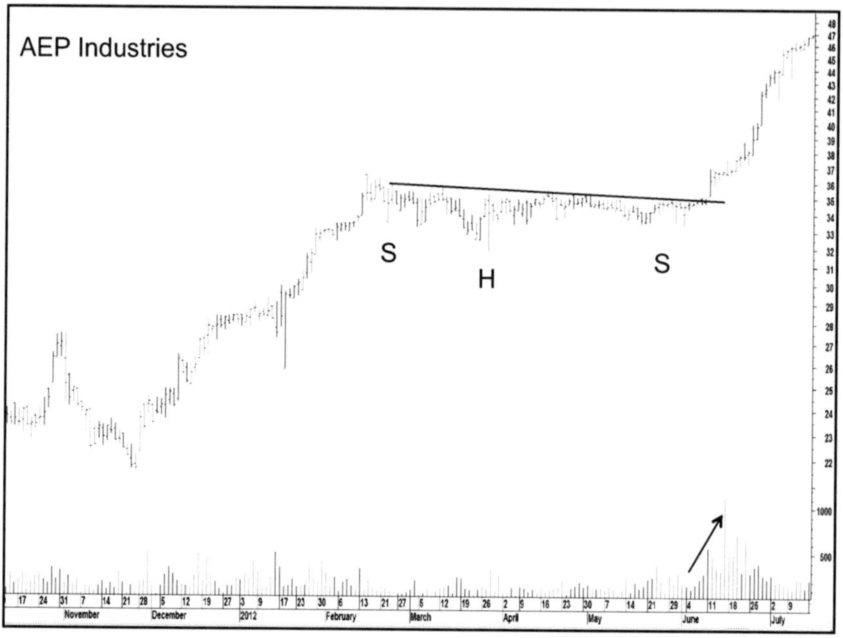

Source: From pring.com

markets. As a result, what might appear to be a perfectly valid head-and-shoulders breakout one day may well turn out to be a whipsaw the next. This is generally not the case, but any trader or investor who does not recognize the ability of markets to reverse otherwise perfectly legitimate signals is in a state of delusion.

The first step is to make sure that the pattern you are following is indeed a legitimate formation. For example, the price action may exhibit all the characteristics of an H&S distribution pattern, but the price refuses to penetrate the neckline. We have already established that until the formation is completed with a decisive break below the neckline, it is not a true pattern. This is because the neckline represents a support area, and support has not been violated. In the case of a horizontal formation, failure to penetrate the neckline also means that the series of rising peaks and troughs is still intact.

Chart 8.9 features a reverse head and shoulders for Albertson's that did not work. The price rallied up to the (solid) neckline for a final time in mid-2002, but was unable to push through.

CHART 8.9 Albertsons 1998–2003 Featuring a Failed Inverse Head-and-Shoulders Pattern

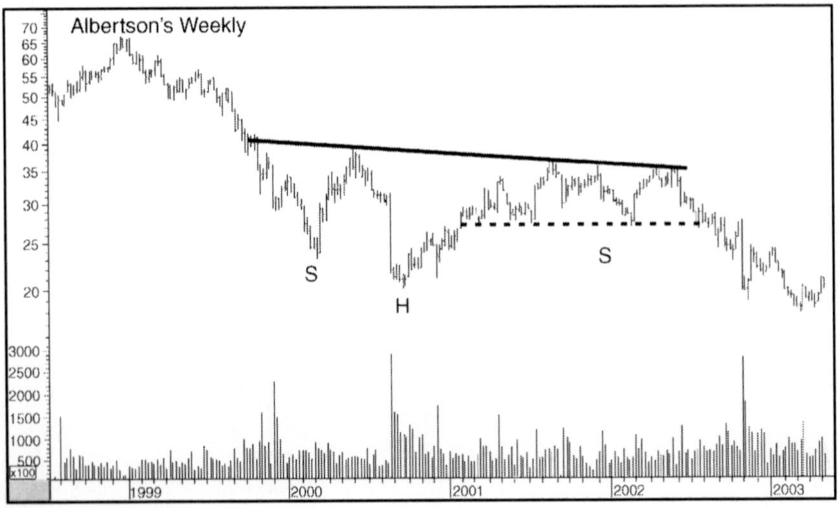

Source: From *Martin Pring on Price Patterns*

The dashed trendline is there to indicate that the final part of the head and the potential inverse right shoulder actually formed a head-and-shoulders top. Often, it is possible to spot these technical situations where the glass is half full or half empty. In this case, it was half empty, and the price declined.

Failures used to be fairly rare, but they now appear to be more common, which indicates the necessity of waiting for a decisive breakout on the downside (or the upside in the case of a reverse head and shoulders). They typically develop when the pattern suggests a break in the opposite direction to the then-prevailing trend. Obviously, if this is the actual top or bottom, the formation will be valid. However, when a head-and-shoulders top forms in a bull market and does not experience a meaningful decline, this will tend to be a countercyclical signal. In fact, the very failure of the pattern may be interpreted as a sign that the prevailing (dominant) trend probably is still in force.

There are several points in the chart where the probabilities of a valid signal sink below 50 percent and those of an outright failure start to increase. Figures 8.26 and 8.27 try to address these points. Point A in Figure 8.26 represents the bottom following the break below the neckline.

FIGURE 8.26 Identifying an H&S Failure

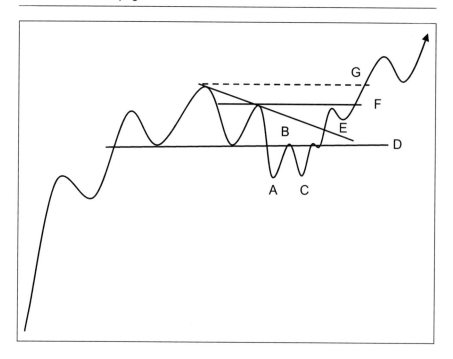

FIGURE 8.27 Identifying an Inverse Head-and-Shoulders Failure

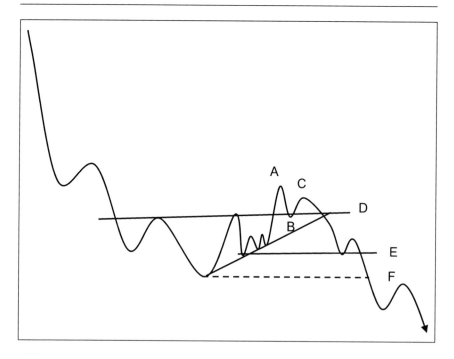

The next rally, which ends at *B*, is a perfectly typical development because retracements are a normal, and indeed healthy, phenomenon. The price then falls to *C* and something unexpected happens: Instead of following through on the downside, as would be expected from a head-and-shoulders top, the price rises back to the neckline again. This is the first sign that things may not work out as expected. When the price once again rallies back above the neckline (*D*), the odds of a failure increase. The balance tips more to the bullish side when the price moves above the down trendline joining the head with the right shoulder (*E*). This is probably the time to cover all shorts, since the reason for going short in the first place—i.e., the breakdown—no longer exists. The nature of the trendline will have a great deal to do with the change in probabilities. For example, if the line is steep and has been touched only twice, it will have nowhere near as much significance as it would if it were shallow and had been touched several times. A refresher on trendline interpretation in Chapter 6 would be a good idea at this point.

The next line of defense is the right shoulder. If the price can rally above this point (*F*), then in some cases, it will now be experiencing a series of rising peaks and troughs. Finally, when the price moves above the head, the pattern is cancelled beyond a reasonable doubt.

If action on the long side is contemplated, it should be taken either when the price breaks above the trendline joining the head and the right shoulder (line *E*) or when it breaks above the right shoulder (*F*) on heavy volume. Usually, such signals offer substantial profits in a very short period of time and are well worth acting on. Again, some common sense comes into play, for if the trendline joining the head and the right shoulder is unusually steep and has been touched only twice, it will not have the authority of a shallower trendline that has been touched or approached on numerous occasions.

Inverse H&S patterns can also fail, as we see from Figure 8.27.

Again, the failure is usually followed by a fairly lengthy decline as participants who bought in anticipation of an upward breakout are flushed out when the new bearish fundamentals become more widely known. Note that the line joining the head with the right shoulder is more significant in this example than that in Figure 8.26. That's because the line is shallower and has been touched on more occasions. The joint break with the neckline is also impressive and would greatly increase the odds of a failed pattern. The move below F obviously puts the issue beyond any reasonable doubt.

Chart 8.10 shows a failed head-and-shoulders top for Andrew Corp. This one developed during a very strong linear bull market.

CHART 8.10 Andrew Corp. 1993–1994 Featuring a Failed Head-and-Shoulders Top

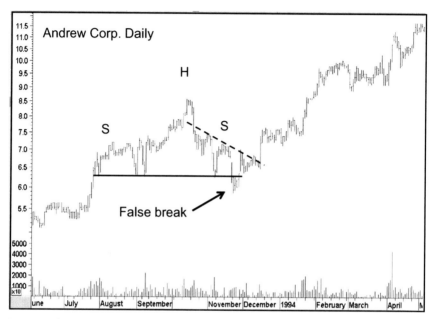

Source: From pring.com

The first indication of failure would have been given when the price broke back above the neckline after forming a small base. The clincher developed when the dashed trendline joining several rally peaks was bettered on the upside. Failed patterns are often followed by dynamic moves in the opposite direction to that indicated by the pattern. The rationale for this lies in the fact that market participants who bought or sold short, depending on the direction of the whipsaw, are caught on the wrong side of the market and are forced to liquidate. As a result, false moves should be viewed not with fear, but as an opportunity for profits. The degree of opportunity will depend on the strength of the signal and the closeness at which a realistic stop can be placed (the perceived risk). In this case, the trendline was a very strong one, and a stop could have been placed just below the low of the breakout day. Provided it was bought pretty close to the breakout point, this would have represented a very low-risk, potentially high-reward trade.

Major Technical Principle   If a technical signal is going to fail, it is often because it is taking place in the *opposite* direction to the main trend.

Double Tops and Bottoms

A double top consists of two peaks separated by a reaction or valley in prices. Its main characteristic is that the second top is formed with distinctly less volume than the first (see Figure 8.28 and Chart 8.11).

It is normal for both peaks to form at the same price level, but it is also possible for the second peak to slightly exceed the first or to top out just a little below it. Remember, this is not an exact science, but a common sense interpretation of a battle between buyers and sellers.

Minimum downside measuring implications for double tops, as shown in Figure 8.28, are similar to H&S patterns.

A double bottom is shown in Figure 8.29. This type of pattern is typically accompanied by high volume on the first bottom, very light volume on the second, and very heavy volume on the breakout.

Usually, the second bottom is formed above the first, but these formations are equally valid whether or not the second reaction reaches (or even *slightly* exceeds) the level of its predecessor.

"Double" patterns may extend to form triple tops or bottoms, or sometimes even quadruple or other complex formations. Some variations are shown in Figure 8.30.

In some instances, it may be difficult to differentiate between a head and shoulders, rectangle, or triple top and bottom. That is not important. What is important is the fact that such formations represent a battle between buyers and sellers. When one side or the other wins out with a reversal in the peak/trough progression or the violation of a trendline,

FIGURE 8.28 Double Top

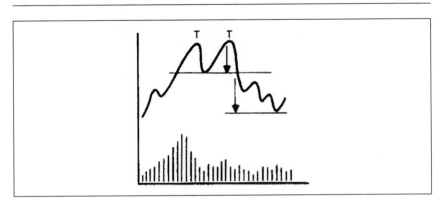

CHART 8.11 DJIA 1936-1937 Double Top. Following a substantial advance from 1932, the first post-Depression bull market ended in 1937. The chart shows a classic double top. Note that the volume during the July-to-August rally was substantially below that of the January-to-March peak.

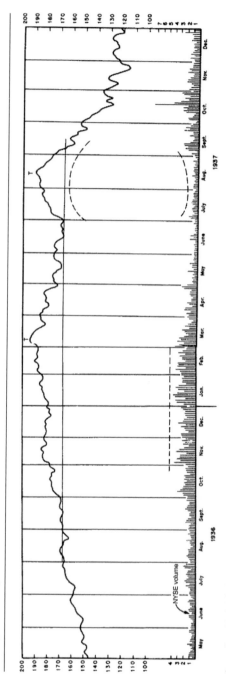

Source: From *Martin Pring's Intermarket Review*

FIGURE 8.29 Double Bottom

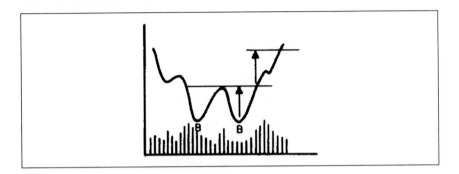

FIGURE 8.30 Triple Tops and Bottoms

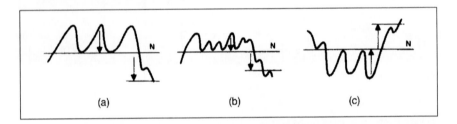

(a)　　　　　　　(b)　　　　　　　(c)

that's what is significant. Remember, we give these patterns specific names for identification purposes. If a formation, say, breaks in a bearish way, it does not matter what you call it—it's bearish and likely to lead to lower prices. That's really the lesson to take home.

> **Major Technical Principle** Ultimately, it does not matter what you call a pattern—the important thing is whether it has bullish or bearish characteristics.

The measuring implications of all these patterns are derived by calculating the distance between the peak (trough) and lower (upper) end of the pattern and projecting this distance from the neckline. Chart 8.12 Shows a classic double bottom in the DJIA in 1974 and 1962.

CHART 8.12 DJIA 1962. This chart depicts a classic double bottom in the DJIA, which formed during 1962. Note that the second one was accompanied by lower volume than the first. While volume expanded during the breakout, the increase in activity was not particularly spectacular.

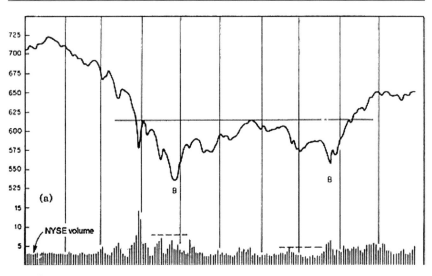

Source: pring.com

Broadening Formations

Broadening formations occur when a series of three or more price fluctuations widen out in size so that peaks and troughs can be connected with two diverging trendlines. The easiest types of broadening formations to detect are those with a "flattened" bottom or top, as shown in examples *a* and *b* in Figure 8.31.

The patterns in Figure 8.31 are sometimes referred to as a *right-angled broadening formation.* Since the whole concept of widening price swings suggests highly emotional activity, volume patterns are difficult to characterize, though at market tops, volume is usually heavy during the rally phases. The patterns at both bottoms and tops are similar to the H&S variety, except that the "head" in the broadening formation is always the last to be formed. A bear signal comes with a decisive downside breakout. Volume can be heavy or light, but additional negative emphasis arises if activity expands at this point.

Since a broadening formation with a flattened top is an accumulation pattern, volume expansion on the breakout is an important requirement, as

FIGURE 8.31 Right-Angled Broadening Formations

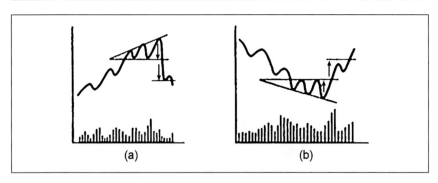

(a)   (b)

shown in example *b* in Figure 8.31. Examples of broadening formations are shown in Chart 8.13 for WW Grainger and Chart 8.14 for the copper price.

Notice how the bearish one exceeded its price objective by three times. That third multiple proved to be the end of the decline, following which a bullish broadening formation was formed. The power of these patterns

CHART 8-13 WW Grainger: A Right-Angled Broadening Formation. This chart shows that it is not always possible to draw the outer boundaries of the pattern so that they connect all the peaks and troughs exactly. The most important thing is to make sure that the bottoms diverge and that the tops form at roughly the same level. The concept is one of growing instability on the downside that is "unexpectedly" reversed to the upside.

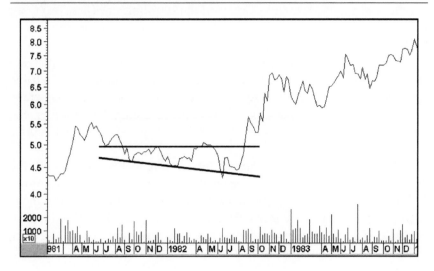

Source: From *Martin Pring's Intermarket Review*

CHART 8.14 Copper 2000–2002. It Features Two Broadening Formations

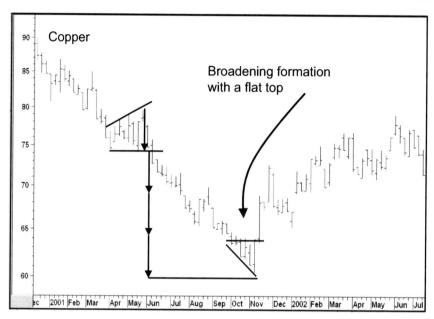

Source: From pring.com

can also be appreciated from Chart 8.14, which shows the formation of another right-angled pattern coming off the 2009 bottom. These two types of broadening formations can also develop as consolidation patterns. A bullish one is featured in Figure 8.32.

Broadening formations occasionally fail to work. Possibilities are shown in Figure 8.33. Unfortunately, there does not appear to be a reliable point beyond which it is safe to say that the pattern has failed to operate. The best defense in such cases is to extend the diverging trendlines, i.e., the dashed lines in Figure 8.33, and await a decisive penetration by the price as confirmation.

When completed, right-angled broadening formations of both the reversal and the continuation type result in a particularly dynamic move. It is almost as if they are aborted H&S formations in which the move is so powerful that there is not time to complete the right shoulder. An example of a bullish right-angled broadening formation, where the price objective was achieved multiple times, is shown in Chart 8.15 for Patni Computers.

FIGURE 8.32 Consolidation Right-Angled Broadening Formation

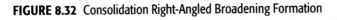

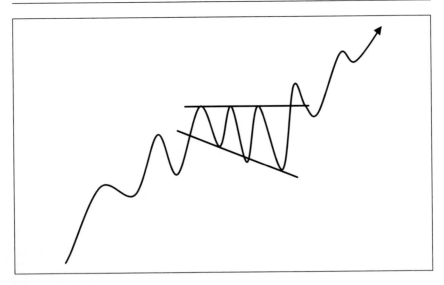

FIGURE 8.33 Broadening Formation Failures

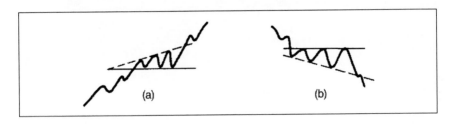

(a)   (b)

A variation on the right angled broadening formation is the broadening wedge. These patterns are similar in that they consist of two diverging trendlines, but instead of one of them being constructed at an angle of 90 degrees, it slopes up (or down in the case of a bullish pattern) but at a smaller angle of ascent (descent), as shown in Figures 8.34 and 8.35.

The measuring implications and other characteristics are identical to those of the right-angled variety.

The final type of broadening formation, known as an *orthodox broadening top*, is shown in Figure 8.36.

This pattern comprises three rallies, with each succeeding peak higher than its predecessor, and each peak separated by two bottoms, with

CHART 8.15 Patni Computers 2007–2008. Broadening Formation
with Multiple Price Objectives

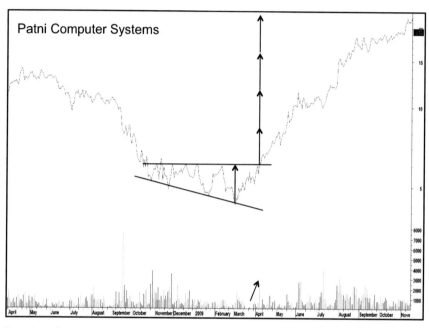

Source: From pring.com

FIGURE 8.34 Bearish Broadening Wedge

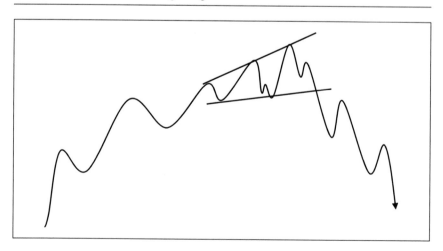

FIGURE 8.35 Bullish Broadening Wedge

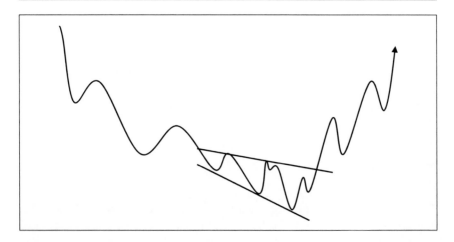

FIGURE 8.36 Orthodox Broadening Formation

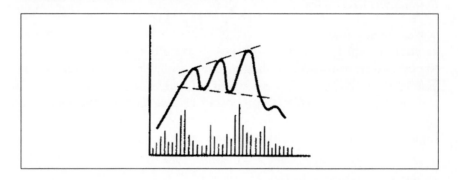

the second bottom lower than the first. Orthodox broadening formations are associated with market peaks rather than market troughs.

These patterns are extremely difficult to detect until some time after the final top has been formed, since there is no clearly definable level of support where the violation of which could serve as a benchmark. The violent and emotional nature of both price and volume swings further compounds the confusion and increases the complexity of defining these situations. Obviously, a breakout is difficult to pinpoint under such conditions, but if the formation is reasonably symmetrical, a decisive move below the descending trendline joining the two bottoms, or even a decisive move below the second bottom, usually serves as a timely warning that an even greater decline is in store.

Measuring implications are similarly difficult to determine, but normally, the volatile character of a broadening top formation implies the completion of a substantial amount of distribution. Consequently, price declines of considerable proportion usually follow the successful completion of such patterns. The problem is that they are quite rare and do not show up on the charts very often.

Triangles

Triangles, the most common of all the price patterns discussed in this chapter, are unfortunately the least reliable. They may be consolidation or reversal formations, and fall into two categories: symmetrical and right-angled.

Symmetrical Triangles

A symmetrical triangle is composed of a series of two or more rallies and reactions in which each succeeding peak is lower than its predecessor, and the bottom from each succeeding reaction is higher than its predecessor (see Figure 8.37).

A triangle is, therefore, the opposite of a broadening formation, since the trendlines joining peaks and troughs *converge,* unlike the (orthodox) broadening formation, in which they *diverge.*

FIGURE 8.37 Symmetrical Triangles

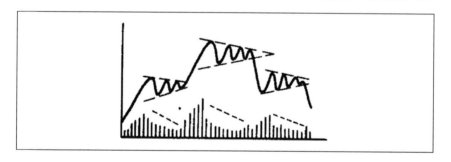

FIGURE 8.38 Classic Symmetrical Breakout

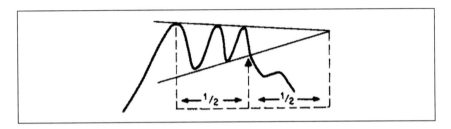

These patterns are also known as *coils,* because the fluctuation in price and volume diminishes as the pattern is completed. Finally, both price and (usually) volume react sharply, as if a coil spring had been wound tighter and tighter and then snapped free as prices broke out of the triangle. Generally speaking, triangles seem to work best when the breakout occurs somewhere between one-half and three-fourths of the distance between the widest peak and rally and the apex (as in Figure 8.38).

The volume rules used for other patterns are also appropriate for triangles. Another factor that affects reliability emanates from one of the principles of determining trendline significance. While a triangle can theoretically be constructed by joining four turning points, two for each line, it follows that *those lines will gain greater significance if touched or approached on more numerous occasions.* Consequently, when they are eventually violated, their more formidable role as a dynamic support/resistance zone will likely result in a more trustworthy signal.

Major Technical Principle   The more times the lines forming a triangle have been touched or approached, the greater the probability that their eventual violation will be valid.

Right-Angled Triangles

Right-angled triangles are really a special form of the symmetrical type, in that one of the two boundaries is formed at an angle of 90 degrees, i.e., horizontal to the vertical axis. An example is illustrated in Figure 8.39.

FIGURE 8.39 Right-Angled Triangles

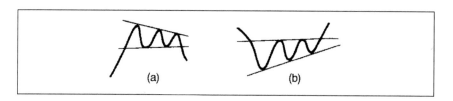

                      (a)   (b)

The symmetrical triangle does not give an indication of the direction in which it is ultimately likely to break, but the right-angled triangle does, with its implied level of support or resistance and contracting price fluctuations. One difficulty in interpreting these formations is that many rectangles begin as right-angled triangles. Consequently, a great deal of caution should be used when evaluating these elusive patterns. An example is shown in Figure 8.40, where a potential downward-sloping right-angled triangle in example *a,* develops into a rectangle in example *b.*

Traditionally, measuring objectives for triangles are obtained by drawing a line parallel to the base of the triangle through the peak of the first rally. This line (*BB* in Figure 8.41) represents the objective that prices may be expected to reach or exceed.

The reverse procedure at market tops is shown in Figure 8.41, examples *c* and *d.* The same technique is used to project prices when triangles are of the consolidation variety. However, in my own experience, I have not found this method to be particularly useful. I prefer, instead, to treat the triangle as with any other pattern by calculating its maximum depth and then projecting this distance at the breakout. An example of this alternative method is shown in Figure 8.42.

An example of a right-angled triangle followed by a bullish broadening formation is shown in Chart 8.16 featuring the DJIA.

FIGURE 8.40 Triangle Failures

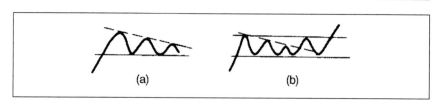

                      (a)   (b)

FIGURE 8.41 Triangle Measuring Implications

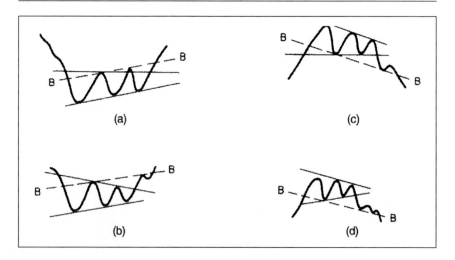

(a)

(c)

(b)

(d)

FIGURE 8.42 Alternative Triangle Measuring Implications

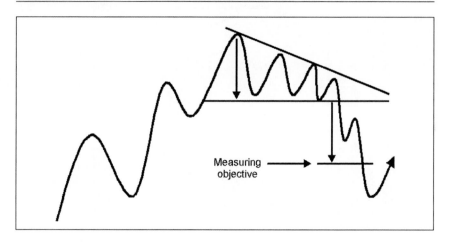

Measuring objective

Cup with a Handle

This pattern has been made famous by William O'Neil and is described in his *How to Make Money in Stocks* (McGraw-Hill, 1995). The pattern develops as a bullish one, usually in a continuation format. Figure 8.43 shows that it takes the form of a big U (the cup), followed by a rally and a

CHART 8.16 DJIA 1938. This excellent example of a right-angled triangle occurred at the bottom of the 1937–1938 bear market. Note the substantial volume that accompanied the upside breakout. Following the breakout, the average traced out a right-angled broadening formation with a flat top. Usually, breakouts from these consolidation patterns are followed by a dramatic rise. In this case, however, the 158 level in November was destined to become the high for the 1938–1939 bull market.

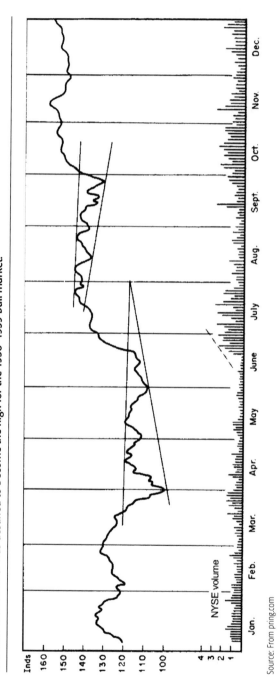

Source: From pring.com

FIGURE 8.43 Cup-and-Handle Formation

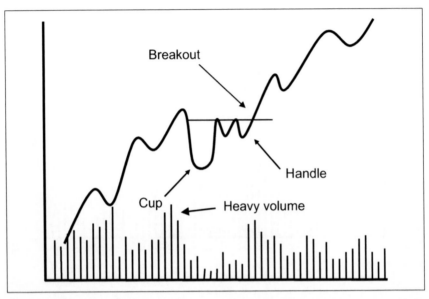

Source: From *Martin Pring on Price Patterns*

small rounding platform (the handle). The cup is typically preceded by a very strong rally, so the left side reflects aggressive profit-taking.

The left part of the cup usually marks the culmination of a strong rally and is often associated with heavy volume. The bottom of the cup can take the form of a rounding bottom, as in Figure 8.43, or some ranging action, as in Figure 8.44.

The next step in the development of this pattern is a rally on expanding volume, followed by a period of profit taking in which both volume and price go quiet. Finally, the handle is completed and prices explode to the upside.

If it is going to fail, the signal to look for is a break below the lower part of the handle. If the price eventually breaks above the upper level of the handle, the situation will again become bullish. Any breakouts that develop with shrinking volume, though, should be regarded with suspicion.

Chart 8.17 shows a cup with a handle formation for ADC Telecom. The breakout above the handle is not accompanied by much of an expansion in volume, but the price certainly doesn't suffer.

By its very nature, the cup with a handle is a consolidation formation. Since the breakout follows a shakeout move (the left part of the cup), it is often followed by a very strong rally.

FIGURE 8.44 Alternative Cup-and-Handle Formation

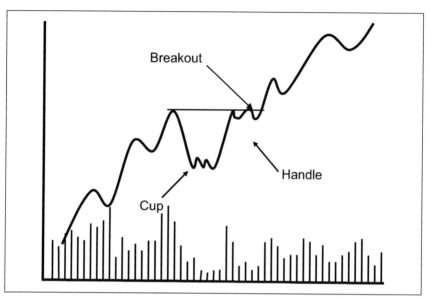

Source: From *Martin Pring on Price Patterns*

CHART 8.17 ADC Telecom 1990–1991 Cup-and-Handle Formation

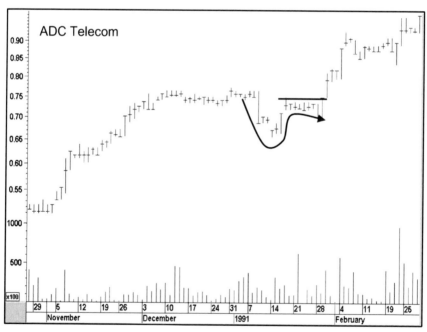

Source: From pring.com

Summary

1. Prices in financial markets move in trends. A reversal is characterized by a temporary period in which the enthusiasm of buyers and sellers is roughly in balance. This transitional process can usually be identified by clearly definable price patterns, which, when completed, offer good and reliable indications that a reversal in trend has taken place.
2. Until a pattern has been formed and completed, the assumption should be that the prevailing trend is still operative, i.e., that the pattern is one of consolidation or continuation. This principle is more important when the trend has been in existence for only a relatively short period, because the more mature it is, the greater the probability of an important reversal.
3. Price patterns can be formed over any time period. The longer the time required to form a pattern and the greater the price fluctuations within it, the more substantial the ensuing price movement is likely to be.
4. Measuring formulas can be derived for most types of patterns, but these are generally minimum objectives. Prices usually extend much further.
5. Price objectives represent the minimum ultimate target and are not normally achieved in one move. Usually, a series of rallies and reactions in an upside breakout is required, or reactions or retracements in a downside breakout, before the objective is reached.

9

SMALLER PRICE
PATTERNS AND GAPS

Most of the price patterns described in Chapter 8 can be observed in both reversal and continuation formations. The majority of the formations discussed in this chapter materialize during the course of a price trend and are, therefore, of the continuation variety. Since many of them are reflections of controlled profit-taking during an advance and controlled digestion of losses during a decline, these patterns, for the most part, take a much smaller time to form than those described in the previous chapter. They most commonly appear in the daily charts.

Flags

A *flag*, as the name implies, looks like a flag on the chart. It represents a quiet pause accompanied by a trend of declining volume, which interrupts a sharp, almost vertical rise or decline. As the flag is completed, prices break out in the same direction that they were moving in prior to its formation. Flags for both an up and a down market are shown in Figure 9.1.

Essentially, they take the form of a parallelogram in which the rally peaks and reaction lows can be connected by two parallel lines. The lines move in a countercyclical direction. In the case of a rising market, the flag is usually formed with a slight downtrend, but in a falling market, it has a slight upward bias. Flags may also be horizontal.

In a rising market, this type of pattern usually separates two halves of an almost-vertical rise. Volume is normally extremely heavy just before the point at which the flag formation begins. As it develops, volume gradually

FIGURE 9.1 Flags

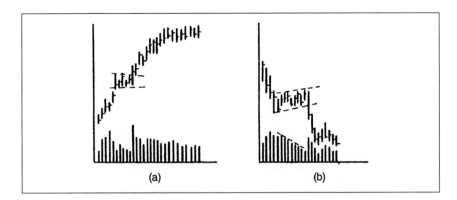

(a)   (b)

dries to almost nothing, only to explode as the price works its way out of the completed formation. Flags can form in a period as short as 5 days or as long as 3 to 5 weeks. Essentially, they represent a period of controlled profit-taking in a rising market.

The development of the flag in a downtrend is also accompanied by declining volume. This type of flag represents a formation with an upward bias in price, so the volume implication is bearish in nature, i.e., rising price with declining volume. When the price breaks down from the flag, the sharp slide continues. Volume tends to pick up as the price slips below the flag's lower boundary, but it need not be explosive. Only upside break-outs in bull markets require this characteristic.

It is important to make sure that the price and volume characteristics agree. For example, the price may consolidate following a sharp rise, in what appears to be a flag formation, but volume may fail to contract appreciably. In such cases, great care should be taken before coming to a bullish conclusion, since the price may well react on the downside. A flag that takes more than 4 weeks to develop should also be treated with cau-tion because these formations are, by definition, temporary interruptions of a sharp uptrend. A period in excess of 4 weeks represents an unduly long time for profit-taking and, therefore, holds a lower probability of being a true flag.

Flag formations are usually reliable patterns from a forecasting point of view, for not only is the direction of ultimate breakout indicated, but the ensuing move is also usually well worthwhile from a trading point of view. Flags seem to form at the halfway point of a move. Once the breakout has taken place, a useful method for setting a price objective is to estimate the

CHART 9.1 Adaptec Flag

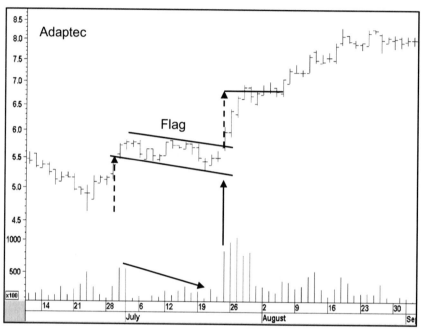

Source: From pring.com

size of the price move in the period immediately before the flag formation began and then to project this move in the direction of the breakout. In technical jargon, flags, in this sense, are said to fly at half-mast, i.e., half way up the move. Since flags take a relatively short period to develop, they do not show up on weekly or monthly charts.

Chart 9.1, featuring Adaptec, shows a flag together with the measuring implications, as shown with the two dashed arrows.

Pennants

A pennant develops under exactly the same circumstances as a flag, and has similar characteristics. The difference is that this type of consolidation formation is constructed from two converging trendlines, as shown in Figure 9.2.

In a sense, the flag corresponds to a rectangle, and the pennant to a triangle, because a pennant is, in effect, a very small triangle. The difference

FIGURE 9.2 Pennants

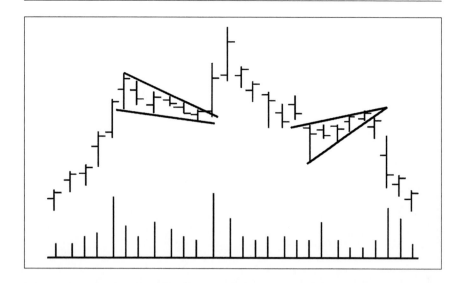

between them is that a triangle consists of a trading range bound by two converging trendlines that point in *different* directions. In the case of a pennant, they both move in the *same* direction. If anything, volume tends to contract even more during the formation of a pennant than during that of a flag. In every other way, however, pennants are identical to flags in terms of measuring implication, time taken to develop, volume character-istics, etc.

Chart 9.2 features a pennant for Adobe in an up market. Note how the volume shrinks during the formation of the pattern. It then expands on the breakout.

Wedges

A wedge is very similar to a triangle, in that two converging lines can be constructed from a series of peaks and troughs, as shown in Figure 9.3, but whereas a triangle consists of one rising and one falling line, or one horizontal line, the converging lines in a wedge both move in the same direction.

A falling wedge represents a temporary interruption of a rising trend, and a rising wedge is a temporary interruption of a falling trend.

CHART 9.2 Adobe Pennant

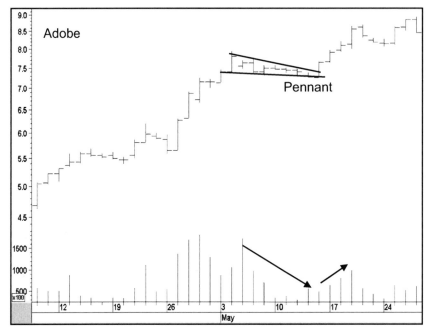

Source: From pring.com

FIGURE 9.3 Wedges

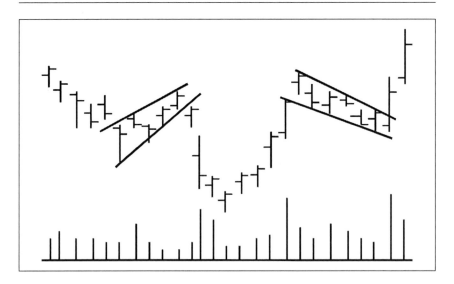

FIGURE 9.4 A Pennant vs. a Wedge

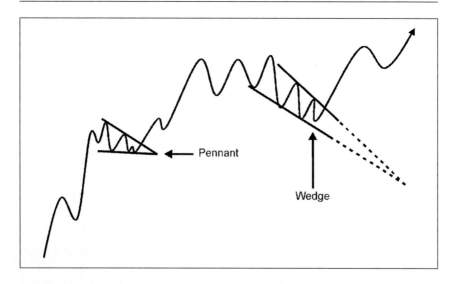

It is normal for volume to contract during the formation of both types of wedges. Since wedges can take anywhere from 2 to 8 weeks to complete, they sometimes occur on weekly charts, but are too brief to appear on monthly charts.

Rising wedges are fairly common as bear market rallies. Following their completion, prices usually break very sharply, especially if volume picks up noticeably on the downside.

The wedge and the pennant are very similar, since they both consist of converging trendlines that move in a contratrend direction. The difference is that the breakout point of a pennant forms very close to or even right at the apex. The two projected lines for the wedge, on the other hand, would meet way in the future—in many instances, literally off the charts. Figure 9.4 puts us straight on this one, as you can see that the projected dashed lines for the wedge meet well after the breakout point.

Compare this to the pennant, which is much more akin to a triangle. Sometimes, the difference between these two formations is hard to judge. If anything, wedges generally appear to take longer to form than pennants. As stated in the previous chapter, it really does not matter what we call these formations—the important question is whether their characteristics and volume configurations are bullish or bearish.

Chart 9.3 shows a bearish wedge for Yahoo!. Usually, such formations develop after a more protracted decline than that shown in the chart.

CHART 9.3 Yahoo! Wedge

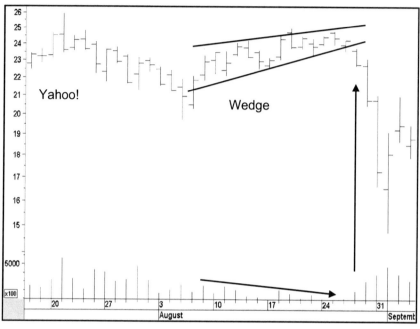

Source: From pring.com

However, there can be no mistaking the narrowing trading range as it was formed. The shrinking activity during the formation of the pattern and subsequent increase in volume on the breakout confirmed its bearish nature.

Saucers and Rounding Tops

Figure 9.5 shows the formation of a saucer and a rounding top. A saucer pattern occurs at a market bottom, while a rounding top develops at a market peak.

A saucer is constructed by drawing a circular line under the lows, which roughly approximates an elongated or saucer-shaped letter U. As the price drifts toward the low point of the saucer and investors lose interest, downward momentum dissipates. This lack of interest is also characterized by the volume level, which almost dries up at the time the price is reaching its low point. Gradually, both price and volume pick up until eventually each explodes into an almost exponential pattern.

FIGURE 9.5 Rounding (Saucer) Bottom

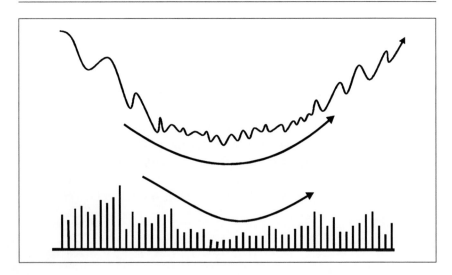

The price action of the rounded top is exactly opposite to that of the saucer pattern, but the volume characteristics are the same. As a result, if volume is plotted below the price, it is almost possible to draw a complete circle, as shown in Figure 9.6.

FIGURE 9.6 Rounding Top

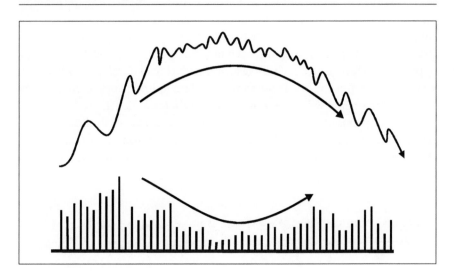

The tip-off to the bearish implication of the rounded top is the fact that volume shrinks as prices reach their highest levels and then expands as they fall. Both these characteristics are bearish and were discussed in greater detail in Chapter 7.

Rounding tops and bottoms are fine examples of a gradual change-over in the demand/supply balance that slowly picks up momentum in the direction opposite to that of the previous trend. Quite clearly, it is difficult to obtain breakout points for these patterns since they develop slowly and do not offer any clear support or resistance levels on which to establish a potential benchmark. Even so, it is worth trying to identify them, since they are usually followed by substantial moves. Rounding and saucer formations can also be observed as consolidation as well as reversal phenomena and can take as little as three weeks to as much as several years to complete.

Gaps

An upside gap occurs when the lowest price of a specific trading period is above the highest level of the previous trading period.

A downside gap develops when the highest price for a specific trading period is below the lowest price of the previous trading period.

On a daily bar chart, the trading period is regarded as a day, whereas on a weekly chart, it is a week, etc. By definition, gaps can occur only on bar charts on which intraday, weekly, or monthly prices are plotted. A gap is represented by an empty vertical space between one trading period and another. Daily gaps are far more common than weekly ones because a gap on a weekly chart can fall only between Friday's price range and Monday's price range; i.e., it has a one in five chance relative to a daily chart. Monthly gaps are even rarer, since such "holes" on the chart can develop only between monthly price ranges. The most common place to find gaps are on intraday charts at the open. I will have more to say on that point later.

A gap is closed, or "filled," when the price comes back and retraces the whole range of the gap. On daily charts, this process sometimes takes a few days, and at other times it takes a few weeks or months. In rare cases, the process is never completed.

Major Technical Principle There is an old saying that the market abhors a vacuum, which means that most gaps are eventually filled.

It is certainly true that almost all gaps are eventually filled, but this is not always the case. Because it can take months or even years to fill a gap, trading strategies should not be implemented solely on the assumption that the gap will be filled in the immediate future. In almost all cases, some kind of attempt is made to fill it, but quite often, a partial filling on a subsequent test is sufficient before the price again reverts to the direction of the prevailing trend. The reason why most gaps are closed is that they are emotional affairs and reflect traders who have strong psychological motivation—we could even say excess fear or greed, depending on the direction of the trend. Decisions to buy or sell at any cost are not objective ones, which means the odds of people having second thoughts when things have cooled down are pretty high. The second thoughts, in this case, are represented by the closing of the gap, or at least a good attempt at closing it.

Gaps should be treated with respect, but their importance should not be overemphasized. Those that occur during the formation of a price pattern, known as *common gaps,* or *area gaps,* are usually closed fairly quickly and do not have much technical significance. Another type of gap, which has little significance, is the one that results from a stock going ex-dividend.

There are three other types of gaps that are worthy of consideration: breakaway, runaway, and exhaustion gaps.

Breakaway Gaps

A breakaway gap is created when a price breaks out of a price pattern (as in Figures 9.7 and 9.8). Generally speaking, the presence of the gap emphasizes the bullishness or bearishness of the breakout, depending on which direction it takes. Even so, it is still important for an upside breakout to be accompanied by a relatively high level of volume. It should not be concluded that every gap breakout will be valid because the "sure thing" does not exist in technical analysis. However, a gap associated with a breakout is more likely to be valid than one that does not. Gap breakouts, which occur on the downside, are not required to be accompanied by heavy volume.

If a gap does turn out to be a whipsaw, then this will usually be signaled sooner rather than later. Since most gaps are filled, and there is rarely a reason why you have to buy, it could be argued that it is better to wait for the price to at least attempt to fill the gap before committing money. After all, if you miss out because the price does not experience a retracement, all you have lost is an opportunity. Certainly you will experience some frustration, but at least you will not have lost any capital. With markets, there is always another opportunity. If you have the patience and the discipline

FIGURE 9.7 Breakaway Gap

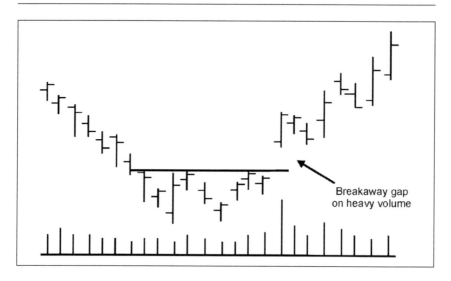

Breakaway gap
on heavy volume

to wait for that opportunity, you will be much better off in the long run. The problem, especially in this day and age of shrinking time spans, is that most of us are not blessed with the patience and discipline that we so badly require for successful trading and investing.

FIGURE 9.8 Three-Step Rule for Buying Breakaway Gaps

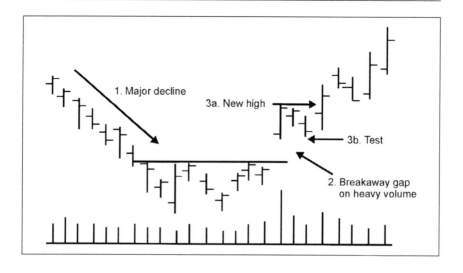

1. Major decline

3a. New high

3b. Test

2. Breakaway gap
on heavy volume

The danger of buying on a gap breakout is that you will get caught up in the emotions of the crowd. This buy-at-any-cost mentality is likely to result in discouragement when the price inevitably retraces to the downside as emotions calm down. The advice is not that you should never buy a gap breakout, but that you should think very carefully and mentally prepare yourself for the high probability that the price will correct, thereby placing your position temporarily under water.

Breakaway gaps that develop during the early stages of a primary bull market are more likely to be valid than those that develop after a long price advance. This is because young bull markets have a tremendous amount of upside momentum. Under such circumstances, there is less likelihood of indecisiveness being reflected in the charts in the form of retracement moves and trading ranges. On the other hand, breakaway gaps that develop at the end of a bull move are more likely to indicate emotional exhaustion, as the sold-out bulls literally give up on any possibility of being able to buy again at lower prices. The same principle in reverse applies to bear trends.

In *Technical Analysis of Stock Trends* (CRC Press, 2012) Edwards and Magee have a slightly different take. Their advice about whether to buy a breakaway gap rests on the volume configuration. They state that if volume is high just prior to the gap and shrinks as the price moves away from the upper part of the gap, then there is a 50-50 chance of a retracement. On the other hand, if volume expands at the upper part of the gap as prices move away from it, then the odds of a retracement or gap-closing effort are substantially less. Such characteristics, they imply, should be bought into.

I think this can be taken a little further by setting a three-step rule for buying breakout gaps. A theoretical example is shown in Figure 9.8. First, it's important for the gap to develop at the beginning of a move, which implies that it should be preceded by at least an intermediate decline. In other words, if a gap is to represent a sustainable change in psychology, it must have some pretty bearish psychology (as witnessed by the preceding decline) to reverse. Second, the gap day should be accompanied by exceptionally heavy volume. This again reflects a change in psychology because the bulls are very much in control. Third, an attempt to close the gap should be made within 2 to 4 days, and the price should take out the high of the day of the gap. If an attempt to close the gap fails, so much the better. The idea of the test is that market participants have had a chance to change their (bullish) minds and did not. The part of the rule about the new high is really a way of determining whether the market confirms the gap following the successful test.

CHART 9.4 Apple Breakaway Gap

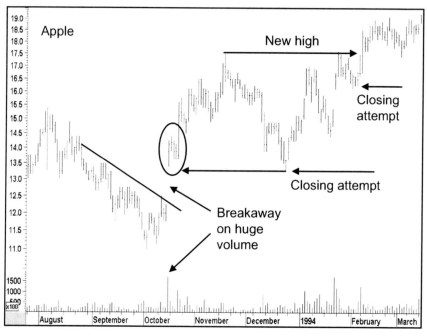

Source: From pring.com

Chart 9.4 offers two examples of this in October 1993 and, to a lesser extent, in February 1994.

Continuation or Runaway Gaps

Runaway gaps occur during a straight-line advance or decline when price quotations are moving rapidly and emotions are running high. Either they are closed very quickly, e.g., within a day or so, or they tend to remain open for much longer periods and are not generally closed until the market makes a major or intermediate swing in the opposite direction to the price movement that was responsible for the gap. This type of gap often occurs halfway between a previous breakout and the ultimate duration of the move. For this reason, continuation gaps are sometimes called *measuring gaps* (see Figure 9.9, examples *a* and *b*).

Chart 9.5 shows this concept in action as the measuring gap develops about halfway through the late August/September advance.

FIGURE 9.9 Runaway and Exhaustion Gaps

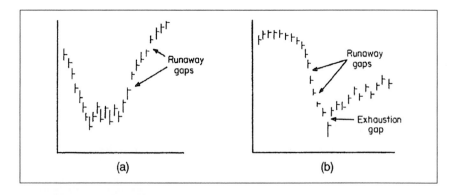

Exhaustion Gaps

A price move sometimes contains more than one runaway gap. This indicates that a very powerful trend is in force, but the presence of a second or third gap should also alert the technician to the fact that the move

CHART 9.5 Yahoo! Measuring Gap

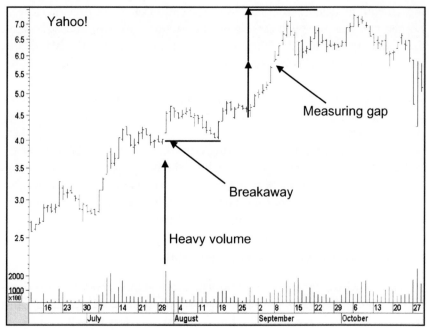

FIGURE 9.10 Island Reversal

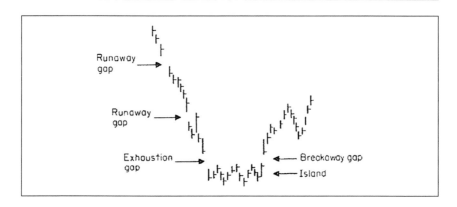

is likely to run out of steam soon. Hence, there is a possibility that a second or third runaway gap will be the final one. An exhaustion gap is, therefore, associated with the terminal phase of a rapid advance or decline and is the last in a series of runaway gaps (see Figure 9.9 example *b* and Figure 9.10).

One clue that an exhaustion gap may be forming is a level of volume that is unusually heavy in relation to the price change of that day. In such a case, volume usually works up to a crescendo well above previous levels. Sometimes, the price will close near the vacuum (or gap) and well away from its extreme reading. If the next day's trading creates an "island" on which the gap day is completely isolated by a vacuum from the previous day's trading, this is usually an excellent sign that the gap day was, in fact, the turning point. This indicates only temporary exhaustion, but should be a red flag that signals to highly leveraged traders that they should liquidate or cover their positions.

If the gap is the first one during a move, it is likely to be a runaway rather than a breakaway type, especially if the price objective called for by a price pattern has not yet been achieved. An exhaustion gap should not be regarded as a sign of a major reversal, but merely as a signal that, at the very least, some form of consolidation should be expected.

The Importance of Gaps as Emotional Points

The places where gaps start or terminate are potential pivotal points on a chart because they represent high emotion. If you have an argument with a friend and one of you shouts loudly at one point, you will both tend to remember that particular moment because it represents an emotional extreme. The same principle can be applied to technical analysis, since charts are really a reflection of psychological attitudes.

> **Major Technical Principle**   Gaps have the potential to become impor-
> tant support resistance levels that have the power to reverse short-term
> trends.

Just as people have a tendency to revisit their emotions after a heated debate, so do prices after an emotional gap move.

Gaps on Intraday Charts

There are really two types of opening gaps in intraday charts. The first develops as prices open beyond the trading parameters of the previous session, as in Chart 9.6. I'll call these "classic gaps" since these are the ones that also appear on the daily charts.

CHART 9.6 March 1997 Bonds 15-Minute Bar

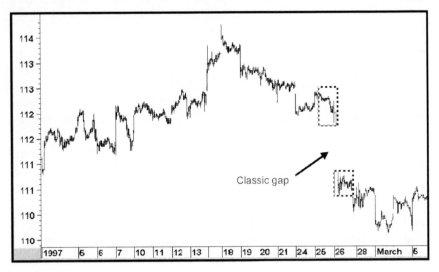

Source: From pring.com

CHART 9.7 March 1997 Bonds 15-Minute Bar

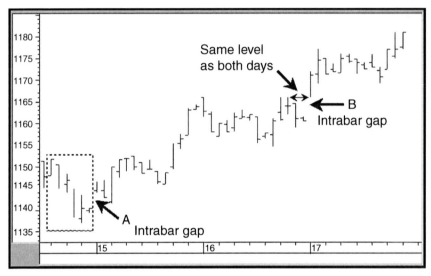

Source: From pring.com

The second, more common gap develops only on intraday charts as the opening price of a new day gaps well away from the previous session's closing bar. I'll call these gaps "intrabar gaps" because they only fall between two bars calculated on an intraday time frame. For example, in Chart 9.7, the price opened up higher and created a gap at A. However, if you look back you will see that the trading range of the previous day (contained within the box on the left) was not exceeded at the opening price, thus on a daily chart there would have been no gap.

If you are a trader with a 2- to 3-week time horizon using intraday charts, you should approach gaps in a different way than if you have a 1- or 2-day time horizon.

The first category should try to avoid initiating trades at the time the gap is created. This is because almost all gaps are eventually closed. Sometimes this happens within a couple of hours, and at other times it can take 2 or 3 weeks. Consequently, if you buy on an opening gap on the upside, as in this chart, you run the risk that it will soon be closed. The problem is that you do not know whether it will be 2 days or 4 weeks.

Intraday Opening Gaps

Intraday traders are also advised to step aside when the market opens sharply higher or lower. In the case of stocks, this is caused by an order imbalance. This means that the market makers are forced to go short so that they can satisfy the unfilled demand. They naturally try to get the price a little higher at the opening so that it will come down a little, enabling them to cover all or part of the short position. The process will be reversed in the case of a lower opening. The key, then, is to watch what happens to the price *after* the opening range. Normally, if prices work their way higher after an upside gap and opening trading range, this sets the tone of the market for at least the next few hours, often longer.

On the other hand, if the price starts to close the gap after a few bars, then the tone becomes a negative one. In Chart 9.8 featuring the now no longer listed Merrill Lynch, there is an opening gap on the Wednesday.

After a bit of backing and filling, the price gradually works its way lower throughout the day. The signal that the opening could be an aberration developed after the price slipped below trendline A. Note how the trendline proved to be resistance for the rest of the session. Thursday again sees an opening gap, but this time, there is very little in the way of

CHART 9.8 Merrill Lynch 7- to 5-Minute Bar

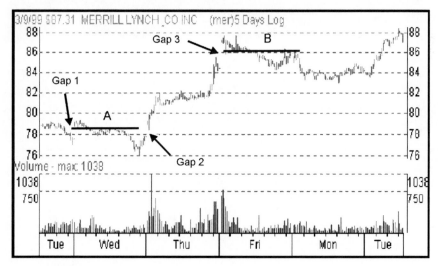

Source: From Telescan

a trading range since the price continues to climb. Again, the rally away from the opening bar set the tone for the rest of the day. Later, on Friday, another gap appears, but this time, the opening trading range is resolved on the downside as the price breaks below the $83 level flagged by the line. Once again, this proves to be resistance for the rest of the day.

Island Reversals

An island reversal is a compact trading range created at the end of a sustained move and isolated from previous price behavior by an exhaustion gap and a breakaway gap. A typical island reversal is shown in Figure 9.10 and Chart 9.9.

The island itself is not usually a pattern denoting a major reversal. However, islands often appear at the end of an intermediate or even a major move and form part of an overall price pattern, such as the top (or bottom) of a head-and-shoulders (H&S) pattern (or an inverse H&S pattern). Islands occasionally occur as 1-day phenomena, as is also shown in Chart 9.9.

CHART 9.9 Yahoo! Miscellaneous Concepts

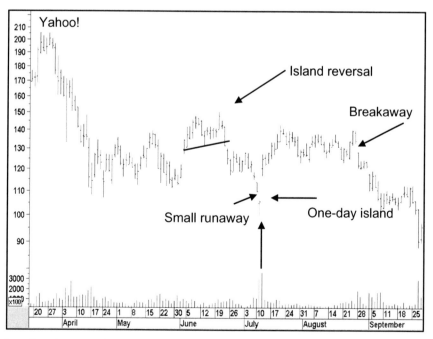

Source: From pring.com

Summary

1. Flags, pennants, and wedges are short-term price patterns that usually develop halfway along a sharp price movement. Their development is normally complete within 3 weeks, on a daily chart and they represent periods of quiet price movement and contracting volume. They are almost always continuation patterns.
2. Saucer formations and rounding tops are usually reversal patterns and are typically followed by substantial price movements. In both formations, volume contracts toward the center and is at its highest at either extremity.
3. A gap is essentially a vacuum or hole in a bar chart. Ex-dividend and area gaps have little significance. Breakaway gaps develop at the beginning of a move, runaway gaps in the middle of a move, and exhaustion gaps at the end.
4. The upper and lower areas of gaps represent potentially significant support and resistance areas.
5. Island reversals are small price patterns or congestion areas isolated from the main price trend by two gaps. They often signal the termination of an intermediate move.

10

ONE- AND TWO-BAR
PRICE PATTERNS

The price patterns we have considered so far take some time to complete, usually at least 20 bars. They all reflect changes in the relationship between buyers and sellers, which tells us that there has been a reversal in psychology.

Major Technical Principle   One- and two-bar patterns reflect changes in psychology that have a very short-term influence on prices.

Historically, the patterns described in this chapter were called 1- and 2-day patterns or 1- and 2-week patterns. With the advent of intraday charts, the title "inside days," "outside days," etc., is no longer a generic term. Therefore, I have chosen to use the term "bar" to refer to these patterns, since that term applies to all charts from 1-minute bars up to monthly ones. (For a more in-depth discussion on these fascinating patterns, please see *Martin Pring on Price Patterns* [McGraw-Hill, 2005].)

We have already established that a key factor influencing the significance of a pattern is its size. Since these one- and two-bar patterns do not take very long to form, they are, by definition, only of short-term significance. For example, a one-day pattern would only be expected under normal circumstances to affect the price over a 5- to 15-day period. A two-bar pattern created from 10-minute bars would influence the trend over the course of the next 50 minutes to an hour or so. Even so, the more I study these patterns, the more impressed I become with their ability to reliably signal short-term trend reversals.

Major Technical Principle One- and two-bar patterns should be interpreted as shades of gray rather than as black or white because some patterns offer stronger signs of exhaustion than others.

Therefore, not all are created equal. What we are doing is hunting for clues as to the degree of exhaustion being signaled by a particular reversal phenomenon. I could say the word "help," for example, but if I shout it from the rooftop, you will get the message far more clearly that I need help. The same principle operates in the marketplace. For example, if the outside bar encompasses the trading range of three or four bars, it is likely, other things being equal, to be more significant than if it barely encompasses one, and so forth.

There are some ground rules to bear in mind when interpreting these formations:

1. They generally reflect an exhaustion point. In the case of an uptrend, such patterns develop when buyers have temporarily pushed prices up too far and need a rest. In the case of downtrends, there is little, if any, supply because sellers have completed their liquidation. Such formations are almost always associated with a reversal in the prevailing trend.

2. In order for these phenomena to be effective, they must have something to reverse. This means that tops should be preceded by a meaningful rally and bottoms by a sharp sell-off.

3. It is important to interpret these patterns not so much from a black and white perspective, but as shades of gray, because not all of them are created equal. Some show all of the characteristics I will be describing later in a very strong way. Others will reflect just a few characteristics in a mild way. What we might call a five-star pattern, with all the characteristics, is more likely to result in a strong reversal than, say, a two-star pattern that has mild characteristics. It is, therefore, necessary to apply a certain degree of common sense to their interpretation rather than jumping to an immediate conclusion that the presence of one of these patterns guarantees a quick, profitable price reversal.

4. One- and two-bar formations may sometimes experience retracement moves in a similar way to classic price patterns. Since the extremities of most of these formations represent emotional (support/resistance) areas on the chart, retracements offer lower-risk entry points.

Outside Bars

Outside bars are those in which the trading range totally encompasses that of the previous bar. They develop after both down and up trends, and represent a strong signal of exhaustion. An example of a top reversal is shown in Figure 10.1, and a bottom in Figure 10.2. Note that example *b* shows what the bars would look like if they were displayed as rectangles, a smaller one followed by a longer one. Several subsequent figures reflect the same idea.

FIGURE 10.1 Bearish Outside Bars

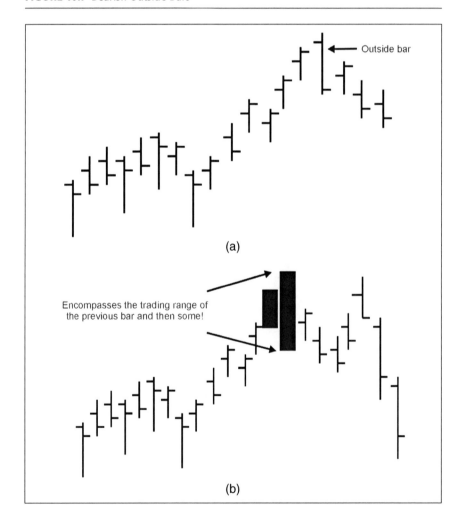

FIGURE 10.2 Bullish Outside Bars

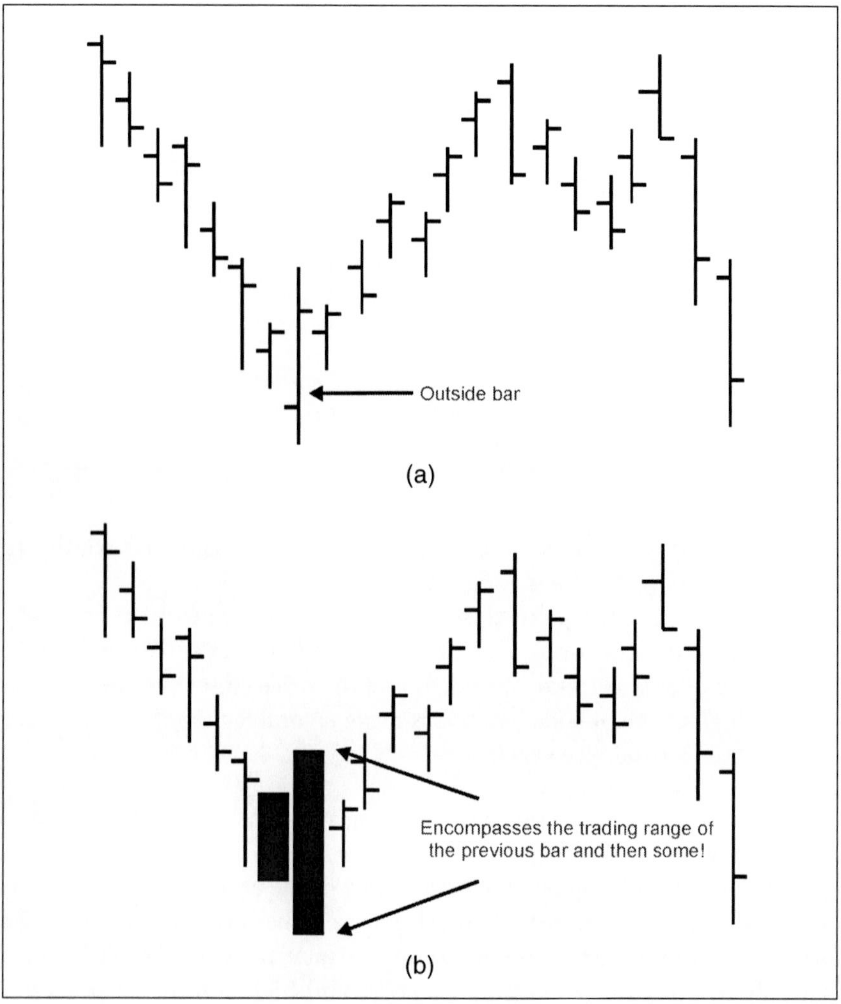

← Outside bar

(a)

Encompasses the trading range of
the previous bar and then some!

(b)

There are several guidelines for deciding on the potential significance of an outside bar. They are as follows:

1. The wider the outside bar relative to the preceding ones, the stronger the signal.
2. The sharper the rally (reaction) preceding the outside bar, the more significant the bar.
3. The more bars encompassed, the better the signal.

FIGURE 10.3 Outside Bars Showing Different Characteristics

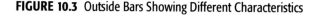

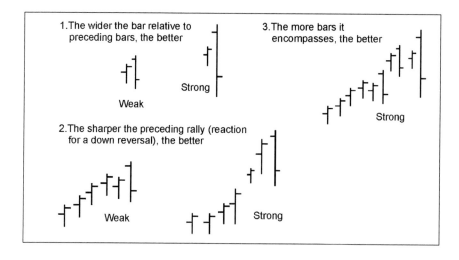

4. The greater the volume accompanying the outside bar relative to previous bars, the stronger the signal.
5. The closer the price closes to the extreme point of the bar away from the direction of the previous trend, the better. For example, if the previous trend was down and the price closes very near to the high of the outside bar, this is more favorable than if it closes near the low and vice versa.

Some comparative examples of strong and weak outside bars are featured in Figure 10.3.

When considering outside bars, or any of the other one- and two-bar price patterns, it is important to ask yourself the question "What is the price action of this bar telling me about the underlying psychology?" Wide bars, sharp preceding rallies or reactions, and high volume all suggest a change in the previous trend of sentiment.

Chart 10.1 features the summer 2012 price action for the Dow Jones Utility ETF. In this case, the signal was a strong one because the bar was extremely wide, encompassed the trading range of three previous sessions, and closed near its low.

Finally, the price rallied above the resistance trendline during the course of the day and closed well below it, thereby offering a classic signal of exhaustion. Also note that investors had a chance to revisit their emotions during the 2-day retracement move that took place in early August.

CHART 10.1 Dow Jones Utility ETF Outside Bar

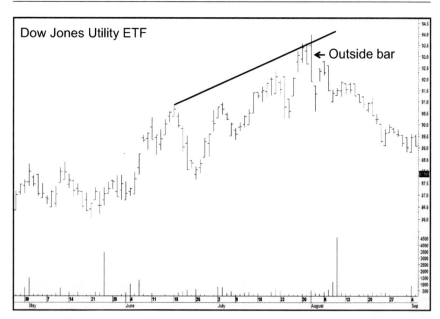

Source: From pring.com

Chart 10.2 shows a weekly outside bar for the cocoa price. This time, it's the third in a series of three outside bars. The effect is that they reinforce each other and produce a very strong signal.

In addition, notice that the final outside bar also closes above the support/resistance trendline joining several lows. This indicated that the downside break was a whipsaw, which added even more icing to the bullish cake.

Finally, Chart 10.3 features a daily chart of the NASDAQ 100. The outside bar on the left has a lot of the ingredients of a valid pattern. It is preceded by a good rally, and the bar itself is wide and encompasses several other bars. It also opened in the direction of the then-prevailing trend and closed on its low.

The question naturally arises as to why it failed. One explanation is that in really strong uptrends or downtrends, one- and two-bar pattern reversals represent contratrend signals, and contratrend signals often result in whipsaws. Note that in this case, the outside bar was the market's attempt to close a gap that had opened up several trading days earlier. The lower part of the bar, therefore, reached a support area.

In addition, it's important to remember that we are dealing in probabilities, not certainties, in technical analysis. Failures can and do exist.

CHART 10.2 Cocoa 1999–2000 Outside Bars

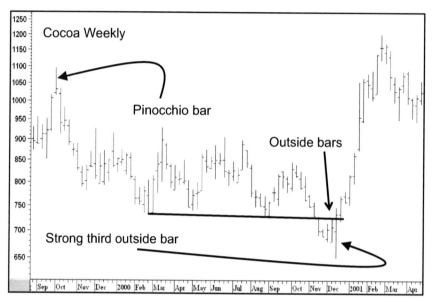

Source: From pring.com

CHART 10.3 NASADQ 100 Outside Bars

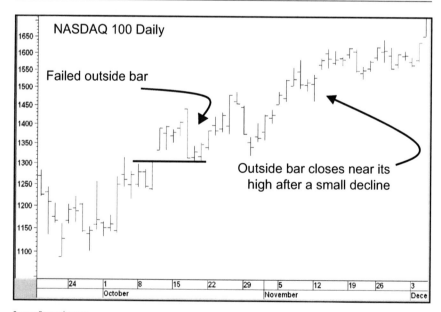

Source: From pring.com

That's why it is always necessary to look over your shoulder and mentally rehearse where you are going to get out should the low-probability losing scenario develop. In this case, the stop would be placed above the upper point of the outside day.

The second outside bar canceled out a bearish outside bar that had formed 2 days earlier. Usually, cancellations are followed by a pretty strong move, and this example was no exception as the price rallied sharply in mid to late November.

> **Major Technical Principle**   Not all one- and two-bar patterns are followed by a reversal in trend. Some, for example, may be followed by a change in trend.

Inside Bars

Inside bars are the opposite of outside bars, in that they form totally within the trading range of the preceding bar. An outside bar indicates a strong reversal in sentiment, but an inside one reflects a balance between buyers and sellers following a sharp up or down move, which is usually later resolved by a change in trend. During the period preceding the second bar of this formation, buyers or sellers have everything going their way, depending on the direction of the trend. Then a more even balance sets in during the formation of the inside bar, which then gives way to a trend in the opposite direction. Examples of inside bars are shown in Figures 10.4 and 10.5.

Guidelines for determining the significance of an inside bar are as follows:

1. The sharper the trend preceding the pattern, the better.
2. The wider the first bar and its immediate predecessors in relation to previous bars, the better. This brings the strong underlying momentum of the prevailing trend to a sort of climax.
3. The smaller the inside bar relative to the outside bar, the more dramatic the change in the buyer/seller balance and, therefore, the stronger the signal.
4. Volume on the inside bar should be noticeably smaller than that of the preceding bar since it indicates a more balanced situation.

FIGURE 10.4 Bearish Inside Bars

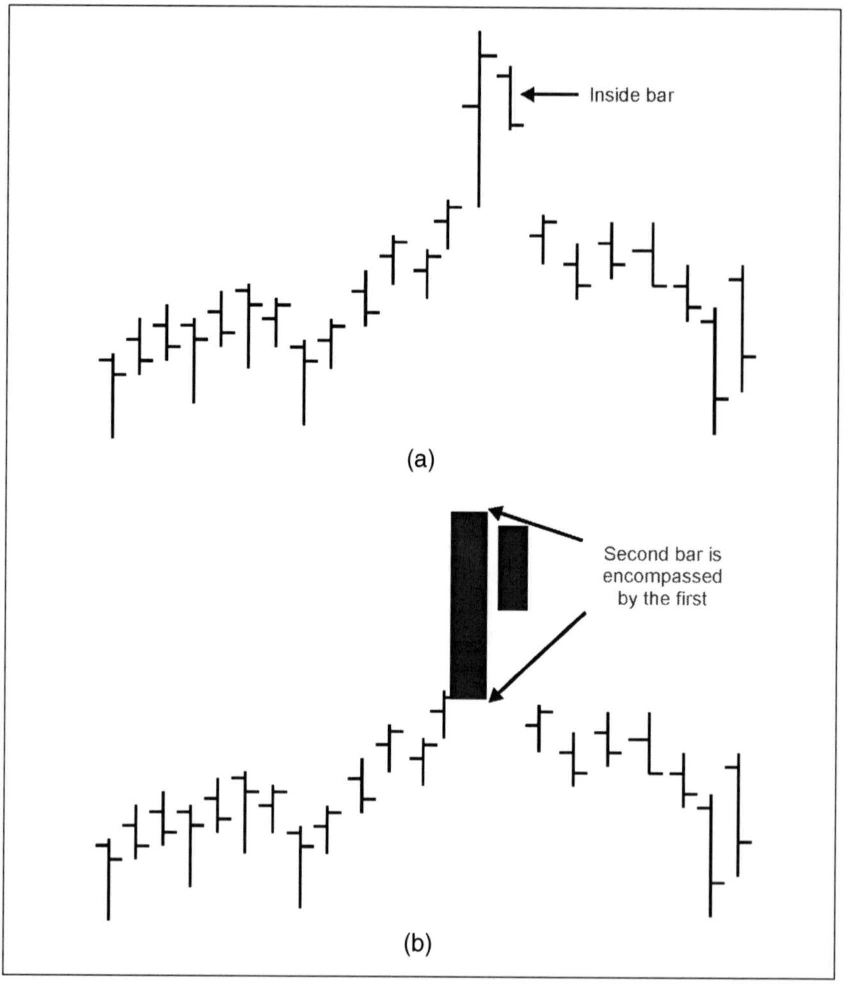

Chart 10.4 shows an example of an inside bar for Rockwell Collins. It is preceded by a very wide bar, which culminates the December 2011–January 2012 rally.

Normally, we would expect to see that wide bar experiencing a bigger difference between a relatively low opening and a much higher close, so the small difference between them hinted at a change in balance between buyers and sellers. That was confirmed by the inside bar for which volume and volatility were much reduced. Note also the two small outside bars that signaled the start and end of a small December rally. Chart 10.5 shows many technical events, including an inside bar just prior to the start of a major rally.

FIGURE 10.5 Bullish Inside Bar

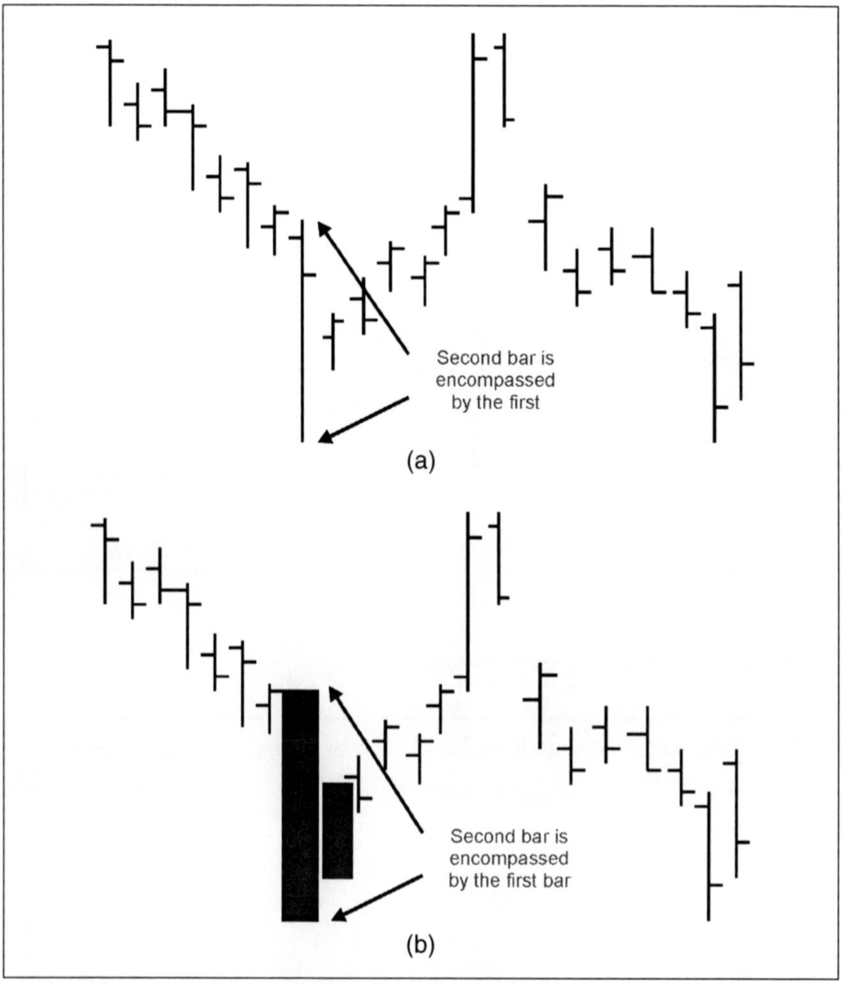

Second bar is
encompassed
by the first

(a)

Second bar is
encompassed
by the first bar

(b)

Sometimes these characteristics develop at a time when longer-term forces are poised for a major up thrust, and that was obviously the case here because there was no way to tell from the inside bar itself that such a robust advance would follow. Note also that the ranging action that preceded the inside bar was influenced by two outside bars at A and B. Remember these patterns are expected to have an effect for only 5 to 10 bars, so these, which triggered 3-day rallies, came up a little short. Finally, the bearish outside bar that developed in early March 2012 possessed very strong characteristics. First, it whipsawed above the trendline joining the two previous highs. Second, it encompassed many previous days of trading, and third, it closed near to its low.

CHART 10.4 Rockwell Collins Inside Bars

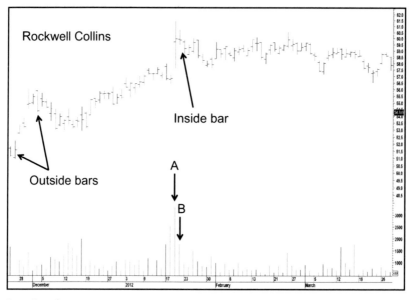

Source: From pring.com

CHART 10.5 Dow Jones UBS Commodity ETN Inside Bars

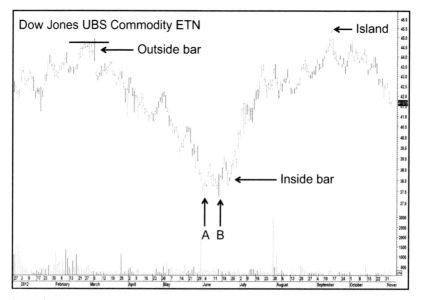

Source: pring.com

Two-Bar Reversal

A two-bar reversal is classic way in which the charts signal exhaustion. These patterns develop after a prolonged advance or decline. Examples are shown in Figures 10.6 to 10.8. The first bar of the formation develops strongly in the direction of the then-prevailing trend.

For a "five-star" signal in an uptrend, we need to see the close of the bar at, or very close to, its high. At the opening of the next period, buyers come in expecting more of the same.

This means the price should open very close to the high of the previous bar. However, the whole point of the two-bar reversal is that a change in psychology takes place as the bar closes slightly above or slightly below the low of the previous bar.

Hence, the high expectations of participants at the opening of the bar are totally dashed at the end of the period indicating a change in trend. To be effective, this has to be a climactic experience. This means that the two-bar reversal should contain as many of the following elements as possible:

1. It needs to be preceded by a persistent trend.
2. Both bars should stand out as having exceptionally wide trading ranges relative to previous bars.
3. The opening and closing of both bars should be close to their extremities.

FIGURE 10.6 Bearish Two-Bar Reversal

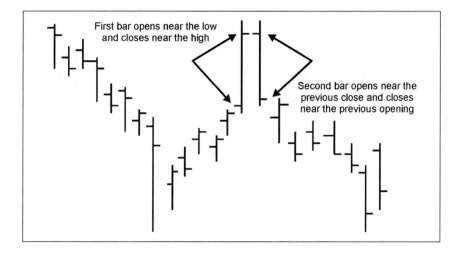

FIGURE 10.7 Bearish Two-Bar Reversal Comparing Trading Ranges

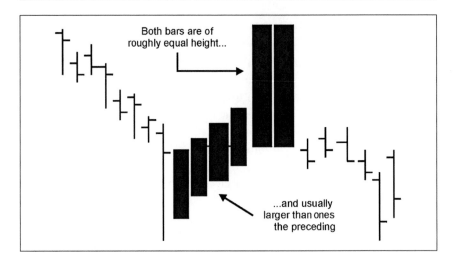

4. An expansion of volume on both bars enhances the concept of a change in sentiment.
5. Heavier volume on the second bar relative to the first emphasizes the preponderance of traders acting in the direction of the new trend.
6. Since a two-bar reversal ideally should indicate an abrupt change in sentiment, ideally they should not be followed by much in the way of a retracement move.

FIGURE 10.8 Bullish Two-Bar Reversal

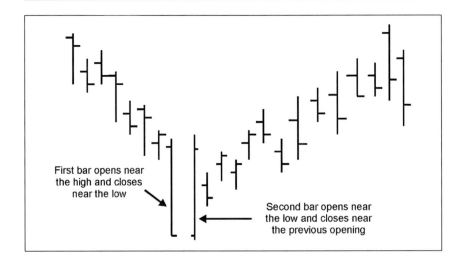

Chart 10.6 features a 5-minute bar for the S&P Composite, where we see a classic pattern, with the highs and lows falling at exactly the correct points following a good rally.

Note also that the second bar slightly exceeds the trading range of the first. This outside bar element adds a bearish factor to the pattern.

Chart 10.7 shows a two-bar reversal at the climax of a rally in U.S. Bancorp in the fall of 2000. Note how the volume expands dramatically.

Also, volume on the second day was slightly higher than that on the first, thereby providing an additional clue that the tide had turned in favor of the sellers.

Finally, Chart 10.8, featuring FX Energy, shows how two-bar reversals sometimes form as whipsaws, where the closing of the initial bar and the opening of the second one temporarily move through a support or resistance level.

In Chart 10.8, this happens to be resistance, as all those who went long during the formation of the two-bar reversal are trapped below the resistance trendline. This kind of situation is typically followed by an above-average decline and vice versa with a downside whipsaw.

These one- and two-bar price patterns generally have an effect for a very short period of time. They are not, therefore, suitable for long-term

CHART 10.6 S&P Composite Two-Bar Reversal

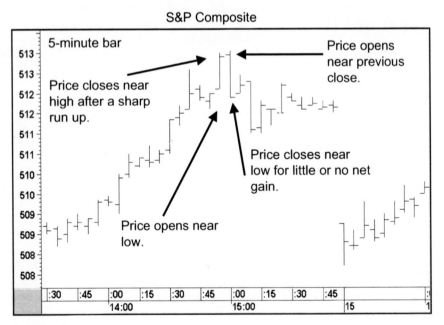

Source: From pring.com

CHART 10.7 U.S. Bancorp 2000 Two-Bar Reversal

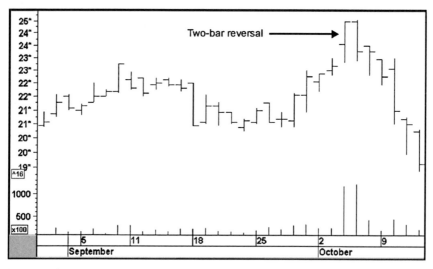

Source: From pring.com

CHART 10.8 FX Energy Two-Bar Reversals

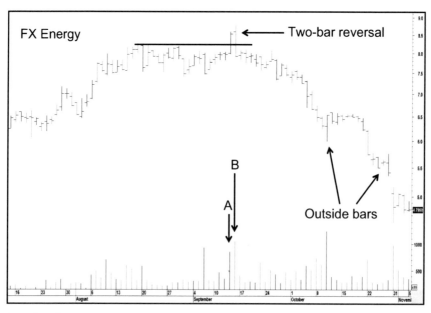

Source: From pring.com

investors. However, for traders who are looking for clear-cut entry and exit points, they can be of immense value.

Key Reversal Bars

A key reversal bar is one that develops after a prolonged rally or reaction. Often, the trend will be accelerating by the time the price experiences the key reversal bar. The classic pattern has the following characteristics:

1. The price opens strongly in the direction of the prevailing trend.
2. The trading range is very wide relative to the preceding bars.
3. The price closes near or below the previous close (or near or above the previous close in a downtrend reversal).
4. Volume, if available, should be climactic on the key reversal bar.

Examples of key reversal bars are featured in Figures 10.9, 10.10, and 10.11. In many cases, a retracement move follows a key reversal bar, especially if the initial reversal in trend is unduly sharp. Normally, the extreme point of the reversal bar is not exceeded.

Chart 10.9 shows a classic example in the left part of the chart, as the short-term rally is climaxed by an explosion of volume and a wide key reversal bar.

FIGURE 10.9 Bearish Key Reversal Bar

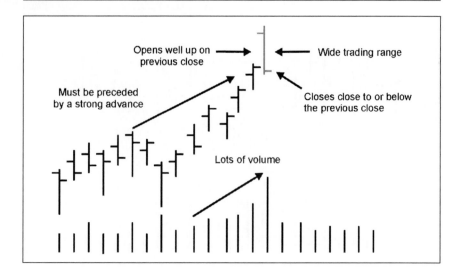

FIGURE 10.10 Bearish Key Reversal Bar Showing Retracement

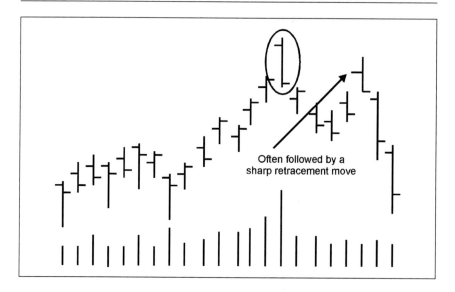

Quite often, a key reversal is followed by a sharp change in trend and a subsequent retracement. That is exactly what happened in this case as the price rallied in the fourth and fifth session following the key reversal. Note that the termination of this brief advance was signaled by an outside bar.

FIGURE 10.11 Bullish Key Reversal Bar

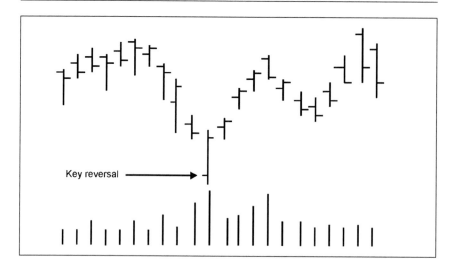

CHART 10.9 Barrick Gold 1999–2000 Key Reversal Bar

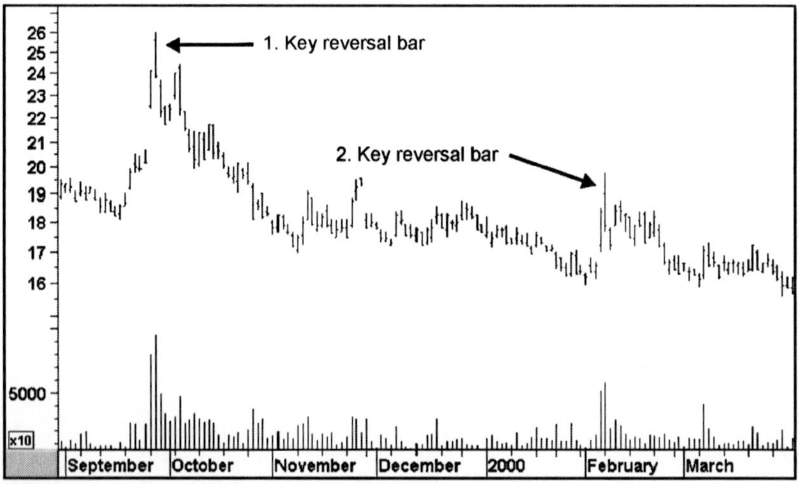

Source: From pring.com.

The second example of a key reversal to the right is also a good one, in that volume expands along with the trading range. However, it is not preceded by much of a rally and would not, therefore, earn as many stars as the first one.

Exhaustion Bars

Exhaustion bars develop after a really sharp up or down move. They are a form of key reversal but differ sufficiently enough to warrant their own category.

The requirements for an exhaustion bar are as follows:

1. The price opens with a large gap in the direction of the then-prevailing trend.
2. The bar is extremely wide relative to previous bars.
3. The opening price develops in the lower half of the bar in a downtrend and in the upper half in an uptrend.
4. The closing price should be both above the opening and in the top half of the bar in a downtrend, and in the lower half and below the opening in an uptrend.
5. The bar is completed with a gap to the left still in place.

Examples of exhaustion bars for both a top and bottom are featured in Figures 10.12 and 10.13.

FIGURE 10.12 Bullish Exhaustion Bar

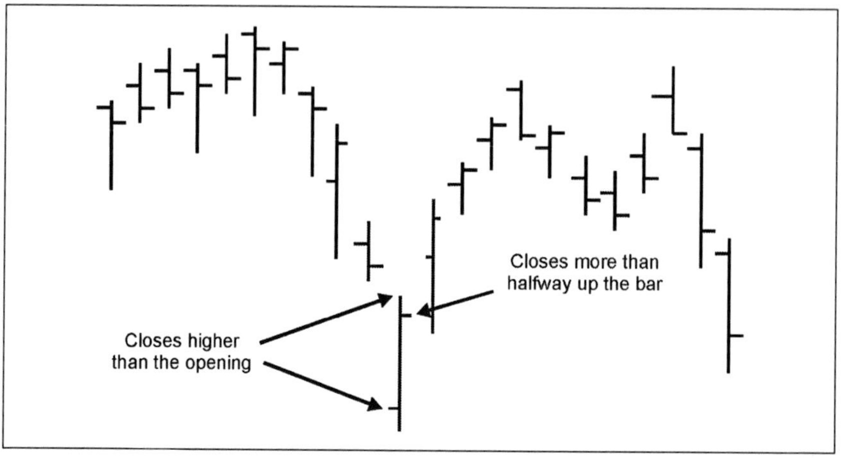

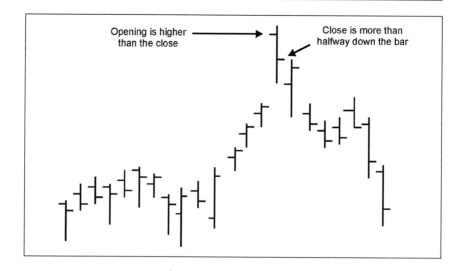

They differ from the one-bar island reversal, in that while there is a gap to the left of it, there is no gap between the exhaustion bar and its successor. Examples of one-bar island reversals are shown in Figure 10.14.

What we are looking for here is an extreme movement in the price that is preceded by an already strong move. The idea is that a bullish bar following a sharp decline opens with a huge gap, but closes above the opening and, ideally, more than halfway up the trading range. This reflects the concept of a reversal in psychology. The large gap and wide trading

FIGURE 10.13 Bearish Exhaustion Bar

FIGURE 10.14

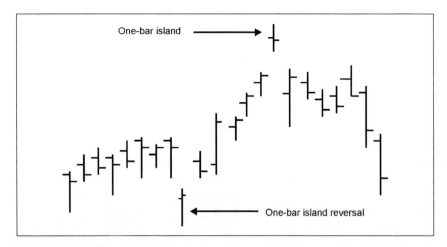

range also point up the kind of frenzied activity associated with a turn. The opposite set of conditions would be present for a bearish exhaustion bar.

Chart 10.10, featuring the 2012 price action of Ruby Tuesday, shows a classic exhaustion bar with the price gapping down sharply following a

CHART 10.10 Ruby Tuesday Exhaustion Bar

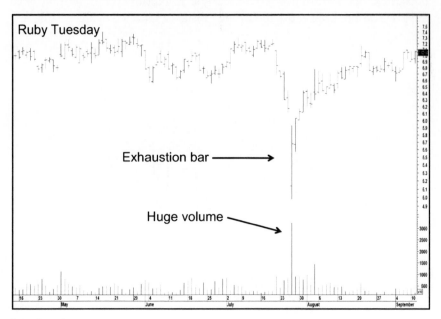

Source: From pring.com

waterfall decline. Then it closes well into the upper half of the bar, indicating that the sellers were no longer in control. The huge volume also contributed to the idea that an important change in sentiment had taken place.

You will find that gaps almost always develop on the intraday charts at the open due to some overnight change in psychology. This means that exhaustion bars tend to be more prevalent in these very short-term charts.

Pinocchio Bars

Exhaustion also shows itself in forms that are different from those we have so far considered. I call these "Pinocchio bars" because they temporarily give us a false sense of what is really going on. They are bars in which the bulk of the trading takes place beyond a support or resistance zone but the open and close do not. Often, this means the false move takes the price beyond a previous trading range, thereby giving a false impression of a breakout. The character Pinocchio tells us when he is lying because his nose gets bigger. In the case of our Pinocchio bar, it is the isolated part of the bar above the open and close (or below them for a bullish bar) that is the big nose that by the end of the bar signals a probable false move. Figures 10.15 and 10.16 offer two examples of false upside Pinocchio breaks. Figure 10.16 indicates that when a false break develops above a down trendline, this is indicative of exhaustion since the price cannot hold above the strong resistance reflected by the trendline.

FIGURE 10.15 Pinocchio Bars

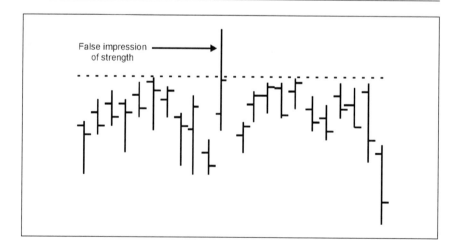

FIGURE 10.16 Pinocchio Bards and Down Trendlines

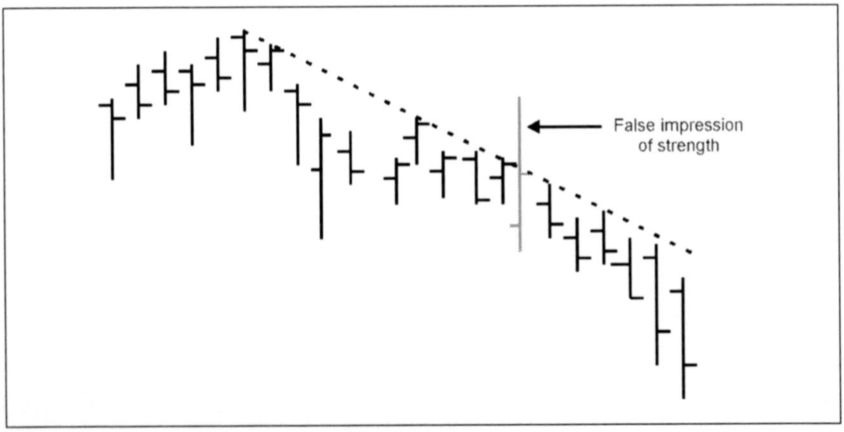

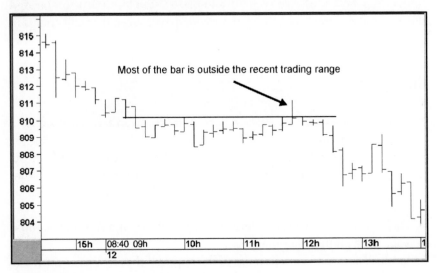

Marketplace examples of Pinocchio bars are featured in Charts 10.11 and 10.12. The first shows a break above the trading range, which was nullified by the time the bar closed.

The second shows a false break to the downside. As so often happens following whipsaws, the price moved in the opposite direction from that

CHART 10.11 S&P Composite Bearish Pinocchio Bar

CHART 10.12 S&P Composite Bullish Pinocchio Bar

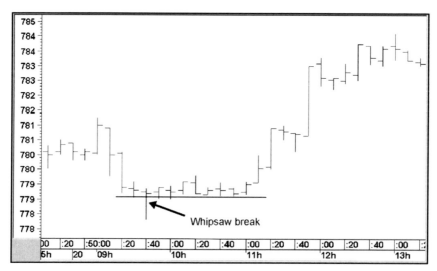

Source: From pring.com

indicated by the break. The outside bar in the left part of Chart 10.12 offers another form of Pinocchio bar.

One important fact about an exhaustion move is that the extremity of the move often proves to be an important support or resistance point. In that respect, it is often a good idea to place a stop loss a little bit beyond the extremity of the Pinocchio bar, provided, of course, that still results in a reasonable risk reward.

Summary

1. One- and two-bar reversals reflect exhaustion and usually signal a reversal in trend.
2. To be effective, these reversals must be preceded by a worthwhile move.
3. Their trend reversal significance is only of short-term duration. What constitutes as "short-term" will depend on the time span of the bar or bars in question.
4. Daily or weekly reversal patterns will be far more significant than those appearing on intraday chart.
5. Reversal bars that contain more of the required characteristics normally provide stronger signals than those that only have a few.

11

MOVING AVERAGES

It is evident that trends in prices for any freely traded entity can be very volatile, almost haphazard at times. One technique for dealing with this phenomenon is the moving average (MA). An MA attempts to tone down the fluctuations of stock prices into a smoothed trend so that distortions are reduced to a minimum. The three principal types of MAs used in technical analysis are simple, weighted, and exponential. When the terms "moving average or MAs" are used in this book, we are referring to the simple type. Exponential MAs (EMAs) and weighted MAs (WMAs) will always be specifically referenced. The construction and use of these averages are different; therefore, each type will be dealt with in turn. In the meantime, it's important to remember that MAs, like trendlines, should be considered as dynamic levels of support and resistance. They are dynamic because, unlike specific levels, which by definition remain constant, MAs keep changing their values. If a specific MA has not worked well in the past on a particular security, there are few grounds for suspecting that it will in the future and vice versa.

> **Major Technical Principle** Moving averages should be thought of as a dynamic level of support and resistance.

Simple MA

A simple MA (SMA) is, by far, the most widely used. It is constructed by totaling a set of data and dividing the sum by the number of observations. The resulting number is known as the *average* or *mean average.* In order

TABLE 11.1 Simple MA Calculation

Date		Index	10-Week Total	MA
Jan.	8	101		
	15	100		
	22	103		
	29	99		
Feb.	5	96		
	12	99		
	19	95		
	26	91		
Mar.	5	93		
	12	89	966	96.6
	19	90	955	95.5
	26	95	950	95.0
Apr.	2	103	950	95.0

to get the average to "move," a new item of data is added and the first subtracted. The new total is then divided by the number of observations, and the process is repeated.

For example, the calculation of a 10-week MA would follow the method shown in Table 11.1.

On March 12, the total of the 10 weeks ending on that date was 966, and 966 divided by 10 results in an average of 96.6. On March 19, the number 90 is added and the observation of 101 on January 8 is deleted. The new total of 955 is then divided by 10. The calculation of a 13-week MA would require totaling 13 weeks of data and dividing by 13. This process is then repeated in order to get the average to "move." Generally speaking, a rising MA indicates a rising trend (market strength), and a declining one denotes weakness.

A comparison of the price index with its 13-week MA (Chart 11.1) shows that the average changes direction well after the peak or trough in the price and is, therefore, "late" in changing direction. This is because the MA is plotted on the thirteenth week, whereas the average price of 13 weeks of observations actually occurs halfway through the week time span, i.e., in the seventh week.

CHART 11.1 NASDAQ 100 2011–2012 Centering an MA

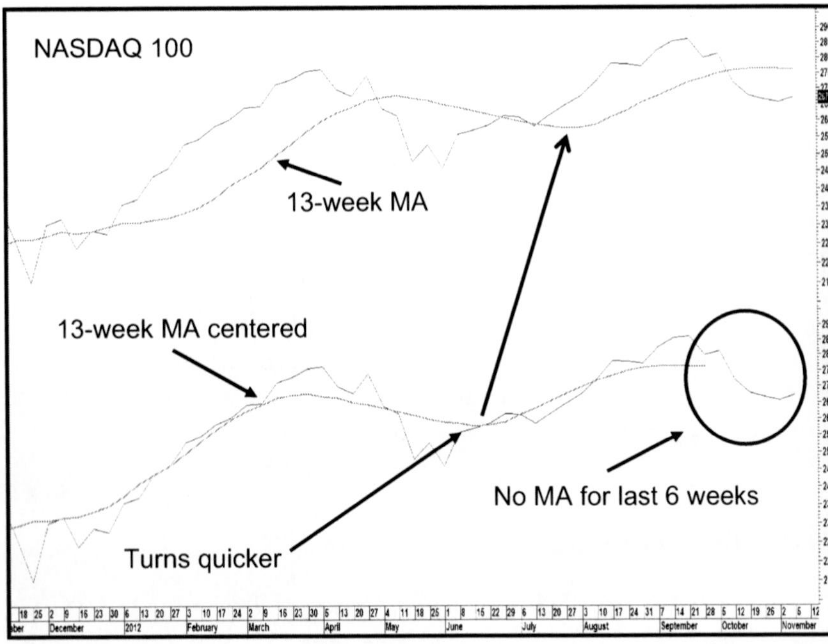

Source: From pring.com

> **Major Technical Principle** Changes in the price trend are identified by the price crossing the MA, not by a reversal in the direction of the MA.

If it is to reflect the underlying trend correctly, the latest MA should be centered, i.e., plotted on the seventh week, as shown in Chart 11.1 for the NASDAQ 100.

The chart in the lower panel shows an MA that has been centered. The good news is that it turns fairly closely to the turning point in the price. The bad news is that it is necessary to wait 6 weeks before it's possible to ascertain whether the average has changed direction. See how the centered MA plot ends 6 weeks prior to the end of the chart.

A time delay, though it is an irritant, is not particularly critical when analyzing other time series such as economic data. However, given the relatively rapid movement of prices in the financial markets and consequent loss of profit potential, a delay of this nature is totally unacceptable. Technicians have found that, for the purpose of identifying trend reversals, the best results are achieved by plotting the MA on the final week.

Changes in the price trend are identified, not by a reversal in direction of the MA, but by the price itself *crossing* its MA. A change from a rising to a declining market is signaled when the price moves below its MA. A bullish signal is triggered when the price rallies above the average. Since the use of MAs gives clear-cut buy and sell signals, it helps to eliminate some of the subjectivity associated with the construction and interpretation of trendlines.

More often than not, it pays to take action based on MA crossovers, but only if you can look back and see a fairly consistent relationship between the price and the MA. The degree of accuracy depends substantially on the choice of MA, as discussed later. First we need to examine some of the characteristics of MAs in greater detail.

Moving Average Characteristics

1. *An MA is a smoothed version of a trend, and the average itself is an area of dynamic support and resistance.* In a rising market, price reactions are often reversed as they find support in the area of the MA. If the rest of the evidence agrees, it's not a bad idea to wait for the price to reach its MA prior to making a purchase. After all, if the MA represents support, you can place a stop below support, i.e., the MA. Similarly, a rally in a declining market often meets resistance at an MA and turns down. The more times an MA has been touched, i.e., acts as a support or resistance area, the greater the significance when it is violated.

2. *A carefully chosen MA should reflect the underlying trend; its violation, therefore, warns that a change in trend may already have taken place.* If the MA is flat or has already changed direction, its violation is fairly conclusive proof that the previous trend has reversed.

3. *If the violation occurs while the MA is still proceeding in the direction of the prevailing trend, this development should be treated as a preliminary warning that a trend reversal has taken place.* Confirmation should await a flattening or a change in direction in the MA itself, or should be sought from alternative technical sources.

4. *Generally speaking, the longer the time span covered by an MA, the greater is the significance of a crossover signal.* For instance, the

violation of an 18-month MA is substantially more important than a crossover of a 30-day MA.

5. *Reversals in the direction of an MA are usually more reliable than a crossover.* In instances in which a change in direction occurs close to a market turning point, a very powerful and reliable signal is given. However, in most instances, an average reverses well after a new trend has begun and so is only useful as a confirmation.

In short, think of an average as a type of "moving trendline," which, like and actual trendline, obtains its significance from its length (time span), the number of times it has been touched or approached, and its angle of ascent or descent.

What Is a Valid Crossover?

A *crossover* is any penetration of an MA. However, close observation of any chart featuring an MA will usually reveal a number of whipsaw, or false, signals. How can we tell which ones are going to be valid? Unfortunately, there is no way of knowing for certain. Indeed, many whipsaws cannot be avoided and should be regarded as a fact of life. However, it is possible to avoid some of these close calls by using filtering techniques. The type of filter to be used depends on the time span in question, and is very much a matter of individual experimentation. For example, we may decide to take action on MA crossovers for which a 3 percent penetration takes place and to ignore all others. Violations of a 40-week MA might result in an average price move of 15 to 20 percent. In this instance, a 3 percent penetration would be a reasonable filter. On the other hand, since 3 percent would probably encompass the whole move signaled by a 10-hour MA crossover, this kind of filter would be of no use whatsoever.

Some analysts, recognizing that one-period whipsaws are quite common, require an MA crossover to hold for at least two periods. In the case of daily data, this approach would mean waiting for the second or third day before concluding that the average had been violated. A more sensible method is to use a combination of the period *and* percentage penetration for deciding whether a crossover is valid.

A useful tip is to wait for an MA crossover to take place at the same time a trendline is violated or a price pattern completed. Such signals strongly reinforce the trendline or price pattern signal and, therefore, need less in the form of a filter requirement. Two examples are shown in Chart 11.2 for the iShares MSCI Brazil ETF.

CHART 11.2 iShares Brazil 2011–2012 Joint Trendline/MA Violations

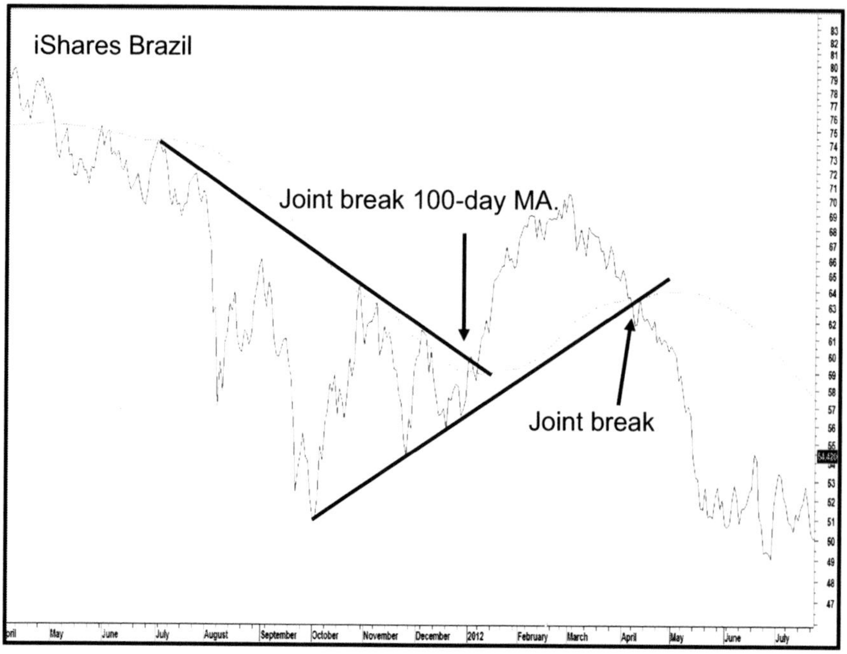

iShares Brazil

Joint break 100-day MA.

Joint break

Source: From pring.com

> **Major Technical Principle** If an MA crossover takes place at the same time a trendline is violated or a price pattern is completed, these signals strongly reinforce each other and, therefore, need less in the form of a filter requirement.

Sometimes, it's possible to see an MA crossover accompanied with exceptionally heavy volume. In such circumstances, you could lower your standards of what represented a decisive breakout since the expanding volume would emphasize enthusiasm by the buyers or fear by the sellers, depending on the direction of the break. We see this in Chart 11.3 for an early August 2012 downside break in the iShares MSCI Emerging Markets ETF.

The cross was accompanied by expanding volume and a trendline break. Two other breaks also developed on expanding activity, one of

CHART 11.3 MSCI Emerging Markets ETF 2010–2012 MA Crossovers and Volume Characteristics

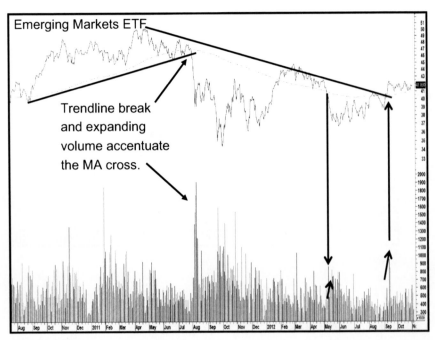

Source: From pring.com

which was an upside violation, which was also associated with a trendline break.

Chart 11.4 features the Eurotop Index together with a 40-week MA and two bands that have been plotted 3 percent above and below the average itself.

Buy signals are generated when the price crosses above the upper line and sell signals when it crosses below the lower one. This has the effect of filtering out some of the whipsaws, yet does not give up too much in terms of timing.

MAs are usually constructed from closing data. These are more reliable than intrasession prices because they reflect positions that investors are willing to carry overnight or, in the case of weekly charts, over the weekend. Moreover, bar charts are subject to intraday rumors and other random noise. It's certainly true that the bar charts are penetrated intraday and, therefore, offer more timely signals. However, there are also a far greater number of whipsaws or misleading signals. That's because the intraday trading can be subject to manipulation or distorted by kneejerk emotional reactions to news events. For this reason, it is usually best to

CHART 11.4 Eurotop 1993–2001 40-Week MA and 3 Percent Bands

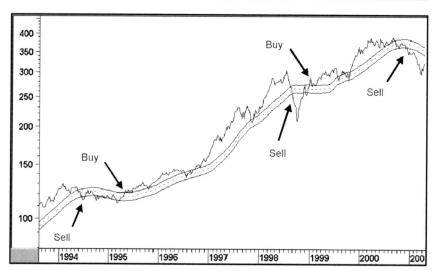

Source: From pring.com

wait for the closing price to penetrate the average before concluding that a crossover has taken place.

One exception to using close-only charts would be if the MA was touched or approached by the highs or lows of the bars on numerous occasions. In this instance, it would mean that the MA represented an unusually strong resistance or support level. Consequently, its penetration would have greater significance.

During a trading range, MA crossovers have a strong tendency to be counterproductive. Two examples are shown in Chart 11.5 for Asian Paints, an Indian stock. In these situations, it is usually best to use the outer ends of the trading range for the signal rather than the MA.

Obviously, no one rings a bell to say the price has entered a trading range, but after a couple of whipsaw signals, it becomes apparent. That is the time when a well-constructed trendline should be substituted for an MA crossover.

Choice of Time Span

MAs can be constructed for any time period, whether a few days, several weeks, many months, or even years. Optimal selection of length is very

CHART 11.5 Asian Paints MA 2002–2005 Crossovers and Trading Ranges

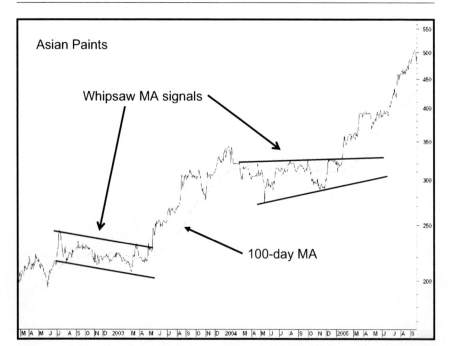

Source: From pring.com

important. For example, if it is assumed that a complete bull and bear cycle lasts for 4 years, an MA constructed over a time span longer than 48 months will not reflect the cycle at all. This is because it smoothes out all the fluctuations that take place during the period and will appear more or less as a straight line crossing through the middle of the data, unless there is a particularly sharp linear trend. On the other hand, a 5-day MA will catch every minor move in the stock cycle and will be useless for the purpose of identifying the actual top and bottom of the overall cycle. Even if the 48-month average were shortened to 24 months, using the crossover signals would still cause the 24-month average to give an agonizingly slow confirmation of a change in trend. The 4-week average would be so sensitive that it would continually give misleading or whipsaw signals. Only an MA that can catch the movement of the actual cycle will provide the optimum trade-off between lateness and oversensitivity, such as the 10-month MA in Figure 11.1.

The choice of MA depends on the type of market trend that is to be identified, i.e., short, intermediate, or primary. Because different markets

FIGURE 11.1 A Short- Versus a Longer-Term MA

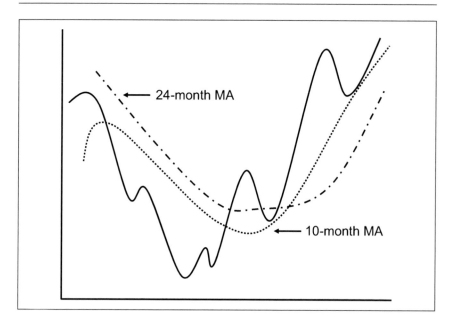

have different characteristics and the same markets go through different cyclic phenomena, there is no such thing as a "perfect" MA. In recent years, extensive computer research has been done on the optimum MA time span. The conclusion from all sources is that there is no one perfect time span.

What may work extremely well in one market over one specific period of time is unlikely to be duplicated in the future. When we talk about choice of time span, we are really trying to identify an MA that will work most of the time with a specific time frame, i.e., short, intermediate, or long.

Major Technical Principle   Try for consistency, never for perfection.

Perfection just does not exist in psychologically driven markets. Generally speaking, long-term time spans are less influenced by manipulation and kneejerk random reactions to unexpected news than are short-term ones. This is why long time spans usually give the best test results; both daily and weekly averages work best at or above a 40-period span. Research also shows that simple averages generally outperform

TABLE 11.2 Suggested Time Frames

Short-Term	Intermediate-Term	Long-Term
10-day	30-day	200-day/40-week/9-month*
15-day	10-week (50-day)	45-week[†]
20-day	13-week (65-day)	
25-day	20-week	12-month[‡]
30-day	26-week	18-month
	200-day	24-month

*Recommeneded by Willaim Gordon, *The Stock Market Indicators*, Investors Press, Palisades Park, NJ, 1968.
[†]Reported by Robert W. Colby and Thomas A. Meyers in *The Encyclopedia of Technical Market Indicators*, Dow Jones-Irwin: Homewood, IL, 1988, to be the best average for the U.S. stock market using weekly data.
[‡]Ibid. Colby and Meyers. Reported to be the best average for the U.S. stock market using monthly data.

weighted and exponential ones.[1] Recognizing these limitations, the time spans in Table 11.2 are suggested.

The important thing to remember is that an MA is *one* tool in the technical arsenal, which is used with other techniques as part of the *art* of identifying trend reversals. Again, it's important to remember that we are looking for a time span that works reasonably well over most securities, i.e., the idea of consistency over perfection. After all, it's always possible to find the perfect time span with back-testing and fitting the data accordingly. However, we are interested in the past only in so far that it can reliably point us in the right direction in the future, and deliberately fixing past results does not help us in this task—quite the reverse.

Advancing a Simple Moving Average

A technique that has a lot of potential, but is not widely used, is to advance an MA. In the case of a 25-day MA, for example, the actual plot would not be made on the twenty-fifth day, but advanced to the twenty-eighth or thirtieth, and so forth. The advantage of this approach is that it delays the crossover and filters out occasional whipsaws or false signals. In *Profits in the Stock Market* (Lambert Gann Publishing, 1935), H. M. Gartley calculated that during the period 1919–1933, which covered almost all kinds of market situations, use

---

[1]Arthur Skarlew, *Techniques of a Professional Commodity Chart Analyst,* Commodity Research Bureau: New York, 1980.

of a simple 25-day MA crossover netted 446 Dow points (slightly better than 433 points for the 30-day MA and far better than 316 and 216 for 40- and 15-day MAs, respectively). However, when the 25-day average was plotted on the twenty-eighth day, crossovers resulted in an increase of 231 points to 677. The 30-day MA, when advanced 3 days, also produced superior results, with an additional gain of 204 points for a total of 637.

Although the 25-day MA advanced 3 days may not ultimately prove to be the best combination, the technique of advancing an MA is clearly one that could be usefully incorporated into the technical approach. It is always difficult to know how much to advance an MA. Experimentation is the answer. One possibility is to advance the average by the square root of the time span; e.g., a 36-week MA would be advanced by 6 days (the square root of 36 = 6).[3]

In that spirit, Chart 11.6 features the iShares MSCI Hong Kong ETF with both a 25-day MA and a 25-day MA that has been advanced by 5 days.

Note how the regular (dashed) MA experiences whipsaws as flagged by the solid arrows, whereas the advanced (solid) MA does not. The dashed arrows indicate where both MAs are penetrated on a whipsaw basis. This

CHART 11.6 iShares Hong Kong 2008–2009 Advancing MAs

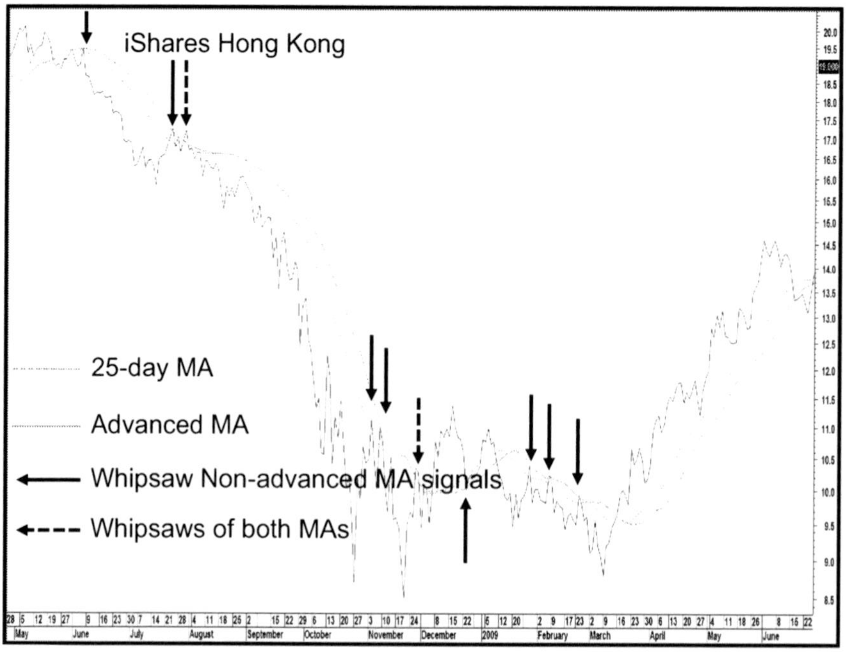

Source: From pring.com

approach appears to come into its own after a strong trend, such as when the regular average was temporarily penetrated by two small back rallies that developed in November 2008. It is in situations such as this that the delaying effect of advancing the MA avoids the whipsaw. Of course, there is a trade-off and that comes in the form of delayed signals, but in most situations, the loss of timing is offset by fewer misleading signals.

Convergence of Averages

A sharp price move is often preceded by a gradually narrowing trading range. In effect, decreasing price fluctuations reflect a very fine balance between buyers and sellers. When the balance is tipped one way or the other, the price is then free to embark upon a major move. This kind of situation can often be identified by plotting several MAs and observing when they are all at approximately the same point. Chart 11.7, for example, shows the daily price for cash euroyen. Note how the three MAs almost completely converge just before the price embarks on a sharp decline.

CHART 11.7 Cash Euroyen 1999–2000 Multiple MAs

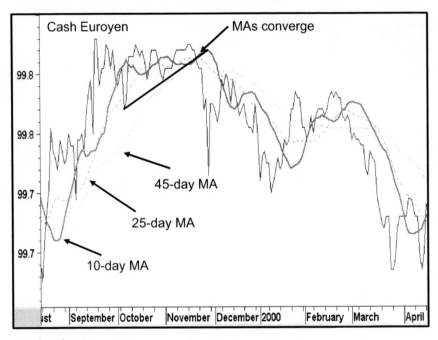

Source: From pring.com

The convergence of the averages warns that a major move is likely, but the actual signal comes from the violation of the trendline.

Multiple Simple MAs

Some techniques of trend determination involve more than one MA. Signals are given by a shorter-term MA crossing above or below a longer one. This procedure has the advantage of smoothing the data twice, which reduces the possibility of a whipsaw, yet it warns of trend changes fairly quickly after they have taken place. In this respect, Chart 11.8 features the iShares MSCI Italian ETF. Two averages that have traditionally been used for identifying primary trend moves are the 10- and 30-week spans.

Signals are given when the (dashed) 10-week average moves below the 30-week average. Some technicians prefer to wait until the 30-week series is moving in the direction of the cross, so a negative cross would require a declining 30-week MA. Negative signals of either variety warn that the major trend is down. It is not assumed to have reversed until either the 10-week MA moves higher than the 30-week MA or it does so when

CHART 11.8 MSCI Italian ETF 2006–2012 Two MAs

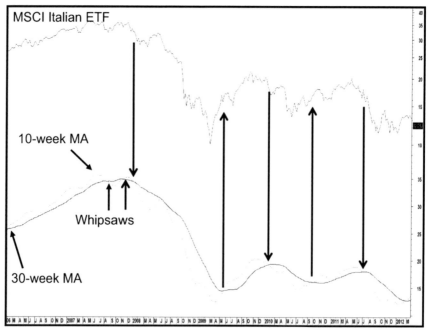

Source: From pring.com

both are rising simultaneously. By definition, either methodology results in signals being triggered after the ultimate price peak or trough. Therefore, they serve as a *confirmation* of a change in trend rather than as actual juncture points in themselves. If the signal develops close to the final turning point, then it can be acted upon in a timely and practical way. On the other hand, if it is triggered some distance from the previous peak or trough, then it can merely be used as confirmation. Even that information can be useful because if you are going to run into trouble, it will usually be when you act on a contratrend signal. A clearer understanding of the direction of the main trend through this double moving average approach will offer less of a chance that contratrend trades will be executed.

An alternative approach is to use two averages of similar or identical time spans and advance the plot of one of them along the lines discussed earlier. Chart 11.9, which again features the Italian ETF, shows such a setup for a 25-week MA and a 25-week MA advanced by 5 weeks.

The advantage of this method is that it appears to generate fewer whipsaws; the disadvantage is that the signals have a tendency to be less timely. These two multiple moving averages are not offered as the Holy Grail, but more as

CHART 11.9 MSCI Italian ETF 2006–2012 Two MAs, with One Advanced

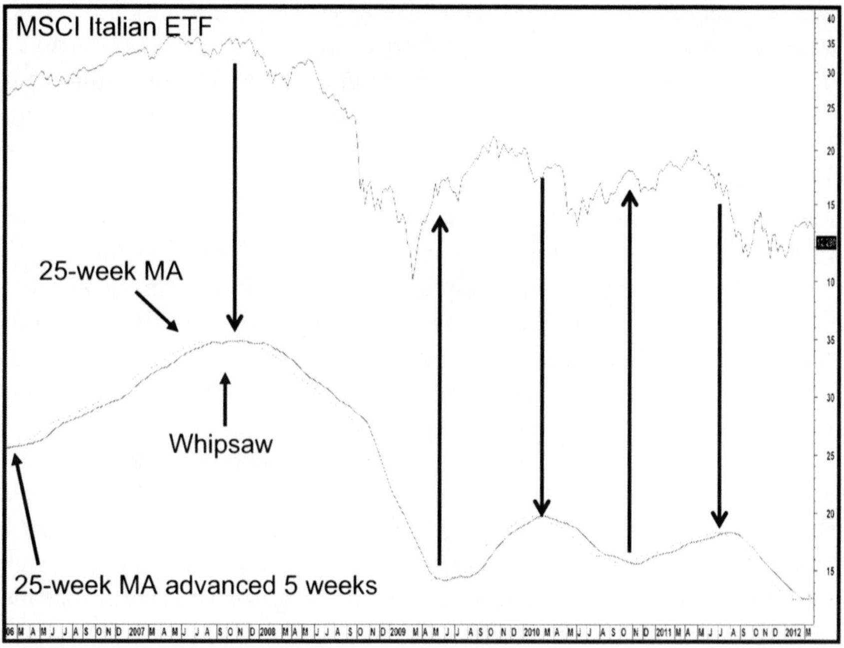

FIGURE 11.2 A Moving Average in a Trading Range

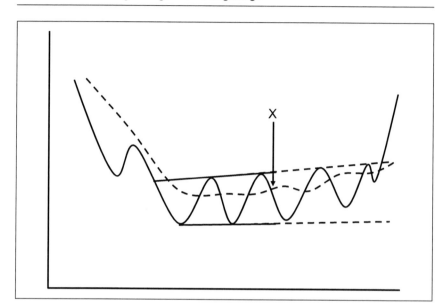

a starting point because I am sure that the resourceful reader could come up with a better combination. Just remember in such experimentation that consistency is much preferred over perfection, which does not exist, of course.

MAs should *always* be used in conjunction with other indicators. This is because prices occasionally fluctuate in a broad sideways pattern for an extended period of time, resulting in a series of misleading signals. The good news is that such frustrating trading-range action is often followed by an extremely strong trend in which the losses incurred from the trendless period of whipsaw signals are more than made up for. This is because the whipsaws indicate confusion between buyers and sellers, and this implies a big battle. When one or the other wins out, the victorious side is then able to push prices in a much stronger way.

Figure 11.2 shows an example of an MA offering numerous whipsaw signals as it moves through a trading range.

At first, it is not obvious that the price action is a trading range. However, at point X, when the price crosses below the MA again, it is possible to construct two trendlines that reflect this ranging action. At such a time it makes much better sense to await the verdict by acting on a trendline break rather than an MA crossover, since there is no reason to suspect that the next crossover after X will not turn out to be a whipsaw.

Weighted MAs

A simple moving average (SMA) can only correctly represent a trend from a statistical point of view if it is centered, but centering an average delays the signal, as discussed earlier. One technique that attempts to overcome this problem is to weight the data in favor of the most recent observations.

An MA constructed in this manner (WMA) is able to "turn" or reverse direction much more quickly than a simple MA, which is calculated by treating all the data equally.

There are countless ways in which data can be weighted, but the most widely used method is a technique whereby the first period of data is multiplied by 1, the second by 2, the third by 3, and so on until the most recent one. The calculations for each period are then totaled. The divisor for a simple MA is the number of periods, but for this form of weighted average, the divisor is the sum of the weights; i.e., $1 + 2 + 3 + 4 + 5 + 6 = 21$. For a 10-week weighted MA, the sum of the weights would be $1 + 2 + 3 + 4 + 5 + 6 + 7 + 8 + 9 + 10 = 55$. Table 11.3 illustrates how the calculations are made.

Another method is to calculate a simple MA, but in doing so, use the most recent observation twice, which doubles its weight.

The interpretation of a weighted average is different from that of a simple average because the weighted average is more sensitive. A warning of a trend reversal is given by a change in direction of the average rather than by a crossover.

Exponential Moving Averages

Weighted MAs are helpful for the purpose of identifying trend reversals. In the past, the time-consuming calculations required to construct and maintain such averages greatly detracted from their usefulness. The widespread use of computers in the last few decades has largely overcome this drawback. An exponential moving average (EMA) is a shortcut to obtaining a form of weighted MA. A calculation for a 20-week EMA is shown in Table 11.4.

In order to construct a 20-week EMA, it is necessary to calculate a simple 20-week MA first, i.e., the total of 20 weeks of observations divided by 20. In Table 11.4, this has been done for the 20 weeks ending January 1, and the result appears as 99.00 in column 6.

The 20-week average becomes the starting point for the EMA. It is transferred to column 2 for the following week. Next, the entry for the twenty-first week (January 8 in the earlier example) is compared with the

TABLE 11.3 Weighted Moving Average Calculation

Date		Index (1)	6 x Col. 1 (2)	5 × Col. 1 1 Week Ago (3)	4 × Col. 1 2 Weeks Ago (4)	3 × Col. 1 3 Weeks Ago (5)	2 × Col. 1 4 Weeks Ago (6)	1 × Col. 1 5 Weeks Ago (7)	Total Cols. 2-7 (8)	Col. 8 ÷ 21 (9)
Jan.	8	101								
	15	100								
	22	103								
	29	99								
Feb.	5	96								
	12	99	594	480	396	309	200	101	2080	99.1
	19	95	570	495	384	297	206	100	2052	97.7
	26	91	546	475	396	288	198	103	2006	95.5
Mar.	5	93	558	455	380	297	192	99	1981	94.3
	12	89	534	465	364	285	198	96	1924	92.5

TABLE 11.4 EMA Calculation

Date	Price (1)	EMA for Previous Week (2)	Difference (col. 1 − col. 2) (3)	Exponent (4)	Col. 3 × Col. 4 ±/− (5)	Col. 2 + Col. 5 EMA (6)
Jan. 1	...	...	...	...	...	99.00
8	100.00	99.00	1.00	0.1	+0.10	99.10
15	103.00	99.10	3.90	0.1	+0.39	99.49
22	102.00	99.49	2.51	0.1	+0.25	99.74
29	99.00	99.64	(0.64)	0.1	−0.06	99.68

EMA, and the difference is added or subtracted and posted in column 3; i.e., 100 − 99 = 1.00. This difference is then multiplied by the exponent, which for a 20-week EMA is 0.1. This exponentially treated difference, 1.00 × 0.1, is then added to the previous week's EMA, and the calculation is repeated each succeeding week. In the example, the exponentially treated difference for January 8 is 0.1, which is added to the previous week's average, 99.00, to obtain an EMA for January 8 of 99.10. This figure in column 6 is then plotted.

If the difference between the new weekly observation and the previous week's EMA is negative, as in the reading 99.00 versus 99.64 for January 29, the exponentially treated difference is subtracted from the previous week's EMA.

The exponent used varies with the time span of the MA. The correct exponents for various time spans are shown in Table 11.5, where the time periods have been described as weekly.

In effect, however, the exponent 0.1 can be used for any measure of 20 days, weeks, months, years, or an even longer period.

TABLE 11.5 Exponential Factors for Various Time Frames

Number of Weeks	Exponent
5	0.4
10	0.2
15	0.13
20	0.1
40	0.05
80	0.25

Exponents for time periods other than those shown in the table can easily be calculated by dividing 2 by the time span. For example, a 5-week average will need to be twice as sensitive as a 10-week average; thus, 2 divided by 5 gives an exponent of 0.4. On the other hand, since a 20-week average should be half as sensitive as for a 10-week period (0.2), its exponent is halved to 0.1.

If an EMA proves to be too sensitive for the trend being monitored, one solution is to extend its time period. Another is to smooth the EMA by another EMA. This method uses an EMA, as calculated earlier, and repeats the process using a further exponent. There is no reason why a third or fourth smoothing could not be tried, but the resulting EMA, while smoother, would be far less sensitive.

> **Major Technical Principle**   All forms of MAs represent a compromise between timeliness and sensitivity.

By definition, EMA crossovers and reversals occur simultaneously. Buy and sell signals are, therefore, triggered by crossovers just like a simple moving average.

Types of MA Compared

Chart 11.10 shows the three types of calculations plotted on the same chart of the popular Indian market index, the Nifty.

You can see that at essentially all times the weighted (WMA) average is the most sensitive since it hugs the turning points more closely. The simple (SMA) and exponential (EMA) alternate, depending on how the data falls. My experience is that in most situations the SMA works best, though I have to admit that unless I am relying on a longer-term time span, such as a 200-day/ 9-month average, I rarely place much emphasis on the crossovers unless other evidence, such as a trendline break, suggests that the trend has reversed.

Useful MA Time Spans

Table 11.2 has already listed some suggested time frames for simple moving averages. This section will expand the discussion a bit by applying some of these ideas to the markets.

CHART 11.10 The Indian Nifty's Three Types of MA

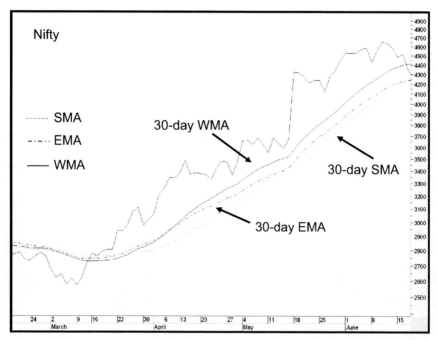

Source: From pring.com

We discussed the importance of the primary trend and the need to identify its direction earlier. That brings us to the subject of the 12-month SMA. This time span has been very useful for identifying reversals in such trends, as has the 9-month (200-day/39-week) one. It really does not matter too much which you choose, although the 12-month span is preferred since it contains all the months of the calendar year and is therefore seasonally adjusted. Chart 11.11 shows the Morgan Stanley Capital International (MSCI) World Stock Index.

If you are going to monitor primary trends, a 12-month MA for this global equity series is not a bad place to start. The solid arrows indicate where the 12-month MA has acted as a good support/resistance zone. The dashed ones show a couple of whipsaw signals, which emphasize the point that we are going for consistency over perfection. Most of the period under consideration experienced primary bull markets, but the shaded areas indicate primary bears, as defined by the relationship between the index and its MA.

CHART 11.11 MSCI World Stock Index 1987–2008 12-Month MA

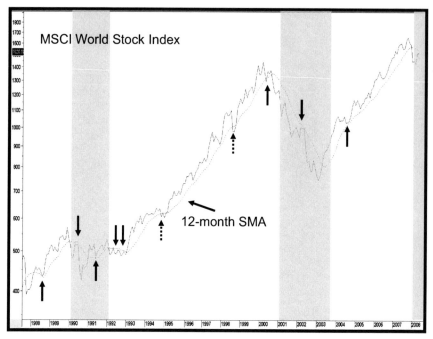

Source: From pring.com

Chart 11.12 features a 200-day SMA for the (dollar-based) gold price. Once again, it gets its share of whipsaw signals, but by and large, it works reasonably well.

It further underlies the point that MA crossovers should not be used in isolation, but in conjunction with other indicators to form a weight-of-the-evidence approach.

Finally, Chart 11.13 shows a 65-week EMA for the Canadian dollar/U.S. dollar cross. This time span appears to be very useful for incorporation with longer-term charts. The solid arrows note the places where the average serves as an effective support/resistance zone, whereas the dashed ones point up some whipsaws.

You should not expect all markets to behave this well, but if it's possible to look back at several years of data and see such a good relationship, then it's reasonable to expect it to work reasonably well in the future. If not, then lower the importance of the average in your analysis.

You may be wondering why we have not included many short-term MAs in our explanation. The reason is that the briefer the time frame

CHART 11.12 Spot Gold 2003–2008 200-Day MA

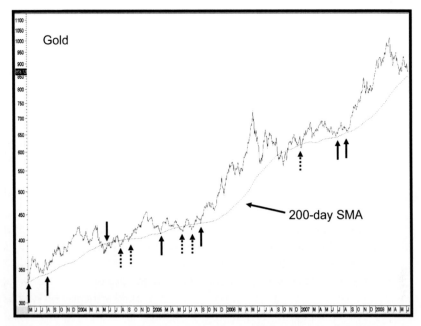

Gold

200-day SMA

CHART 11.13 Canadian Dollar 1997–2008 65-Week EMA

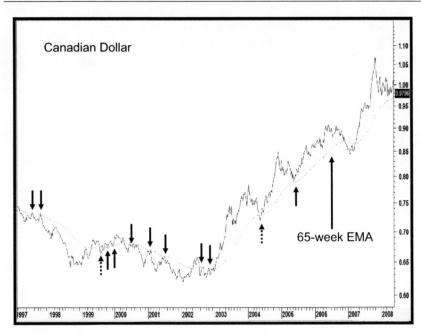

Canadian Dollar

65-week EMA

under consideration, the greater the effect of random noise and the less reliable the MA crossover technique becomes.

Summary

1. One of the basic assumptions of technical analysis is that stocks move in trends. Since major trends comprise many minor fluctuations in prices, an MA is constructed to help smooth out the data so that the underlying trend will be more clearly visible.
2. Ideally, a simple MA (SMA) should be plotted at the halfway point of the time period being monitored (a process known as centering), but since this would involve a time lag during which stock prices could change rapidly and lose much of the potential profit of a move, it is plotted at the end of the period in question.
3. This drawback has been largely overcome by the use of MA crossovers, which provide warnings of a reversal in trend, and by the use of WMAs or EMAs, which are more sensitive to changes in the prevailing trend since they weight data in favor of the most recent periods.
4. There is no such thing as a perfect average. The choice of time span always represents a trade-off between timeliness—catching the trend at an early stage—and sensitivity—catching the trend turn too early and causing an undue amount of whipsaws. For short-term trends, 30- and 50-day spans are suggested, but for longer-term time spans, 40- and 45-week averages are recommended. A helpful time span using monthly data is 12 months.

12

ENVELOPES AND
BOLLINGER BANDS

Envelopes

It has already been established that moving averages (MAs) can act as important juncture points in their role as support and resistance areas. In this respect, the longer the time span, the greater the significance of MAs. This support and resistance principle can be taken one step further by constructing symmetrical lines parallel to an MA of any variety, called *envelopes* (see Figure 12.1).

This technique is based on the principle that stock prices fluctuate around a given trend in cyclical movements of reasonably similar proportion. In other words, just as the MA serves as an important juncture point, so do certain lines drawn parallel to that MA. Looked at in this way, the MA is really the center of the trend, and the envelope consists of the points of maximum and minimum divergence from it. Just as a leash pulls an unruly dog back to its owner and then allows him to run off in the opposite direction until the leash stops him, prices act in a similar manner. The leash in this case is the two envelopes, or more if we choose to draw them.

There is no hard-and-fast rule about the exact position at which the envelope should be constructed. That can be discovered only on a trial-and-error basis with regard to the volatility of the price being monitored and the time span of the MA. This process can be expanded, as in Figure 12.2, to include four or more envelopes (i.e., two above and two below the MA).

FIGURE 12.1 An MA with a + and − 10% Envelope

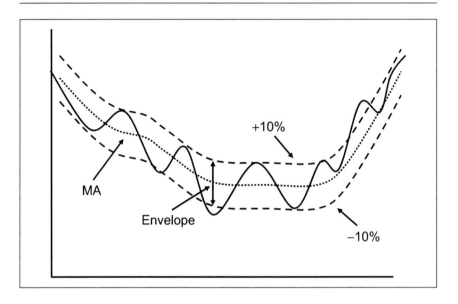

FIGURE 12.2 An MA and Four Envelopes

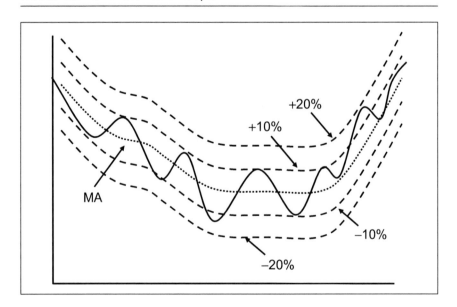

Each is drawn at an identical proportional distance from its predecessor. In this example, the envelopes have been plotted at 10 percent intervals. If the MA is at 100, for example, the envelopes should be plotted at 90, 110, etc. Since prices are determined by psychology, and psychology tends to move in proportion,

Major Technical Principle   Envelopes are best calculated using proportionate as opposed to point or dollar amounts.

For example, 10 percent above and below the MA as opposed to 10 points etc.

Chart 12.1, which features the Indian market average, the Nifty, shows that the envelope technique can be helpful from two aspects: (1) developing a "feel" for the overall trend and (2) discerning when a rally or reaction is overextended.

CHART 12.1 The Nifty 2004–2009 and Two 10 Percent Envelopes

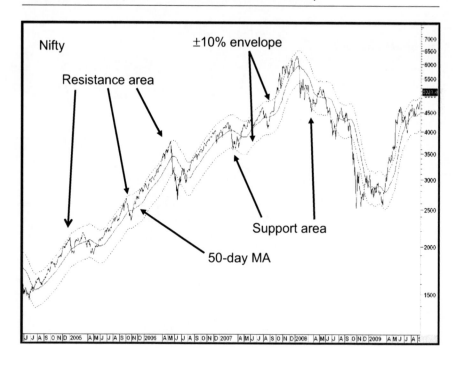

The disadvantage is that there is no certainty that the envelope will prove to be the eventual turning point. This method, like all techniques that attempt to forecast the duration of a move, should be used on the basis that if the index reaches a particular envelope, there is a good probability that it will reverse course at that juncture, provided of course, that the envelope has had a reasonable record of acting as a support/resistance point in the past. The actual trading or investment decision should be determined after assessing a number of characteristics, of which envelope analysis is one ingredient. In Chart 12.1, you can see that the upper band consistently acted as a good resistance zone during the 2004–2008 bull market. However, the advance in 2009 was so strong that reaching the upper envelope really had no technical meaning whatsoever. As for the downside, there were a couple of times the price reversed at the –10 percent level, but either it never reached it, as in the 2004–2006 period, or it greatly exceeded it, as in 2008. Clearly, if this technique is to be employed with any degree of certainty, it is very important to make a careful study of the relationship between the price and a specific envelope ahead of time to establish its reliability. In this respect, Chart 12.2 shows the iShares Biotech ETF

CHART 12.2 iShares Biotech 2007–2012 and Two 10 Percent Envelopes

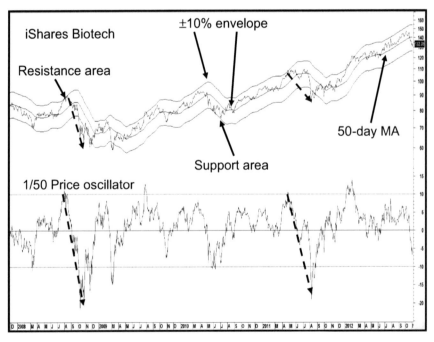

CHART 12.3 Bovespa 1995–2009 and Two 35 Percent Envelopes

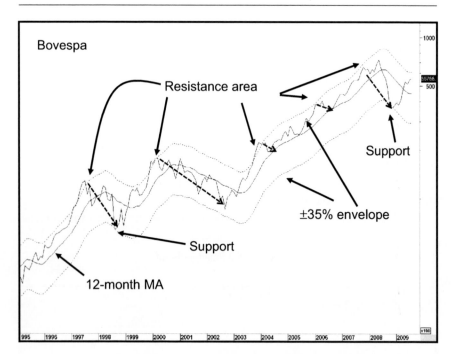

with a 10 percent envelope. The lower panel shows the data displayed in a different manner, with the MA at zero and the upper and lower envelopes being represented by the dashed horizontal lines at +10 percent and –10 percent. Note how the envelopes often serve as support and resistance areas and that the price occasionally swings from one envelope to the other, just as the oscillator swings like a pendulum from an overbought to oversold condition.

Chart 12.3 goes through a similar exercise for the Brazilian Bovespa Index, but this time the envelope has been expanded to 35 percent to suit the characteristic of the market. Once again, the touching of the envelope suggests the direction of the primary trend, upper envelope touches being a bull market characteristic and vice versa. That does not mean that touching the outer band is a prerequisite for a bull market. Just as it's possible to have winter without snow, it's also possible to experience a primary trend where the outer envelope is not touched or penetrated. The dashed arrows show that the recrossing of the envelope is usually followed by an important decline of some kind. The early 2004 signal was an obvious exception to this rule. My suggestion is to experiment with many different combinations of MAs and envelopes because each security has its own personal characteristics. Some will work quite well for you, but never expect perfection—it doesn't exist.

Bollinger Bands

The Concept

Bollinger bands (Chart 12.4) operate in a similar way, except that the envelopes, or bands, are calculated using standard deviations.[1] For those of you who, like me, are not mathematically oriented, a simple explanation is that the bands contract or expand, depending on the level of volatility. The greater the volatility, the wider the bands, and vice versa.

CHART 12.4 NASDAQ 100 2011–2012 and a Bollinger Band

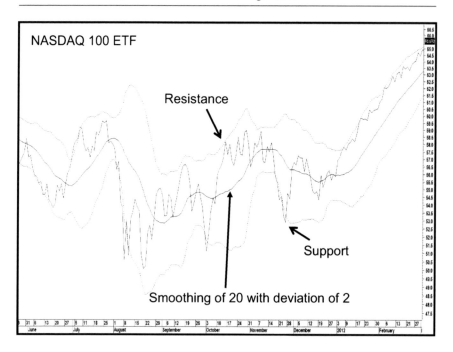

---

[1]John Bollinger, Bollinger Capital Management, P.O. Box 3358, Manhattan Beach, CA (www.bollingerbands.com)

CHART 12.5 NASDAQ 100 2011–2012 Comparing Bollinger Smoothing Parameters

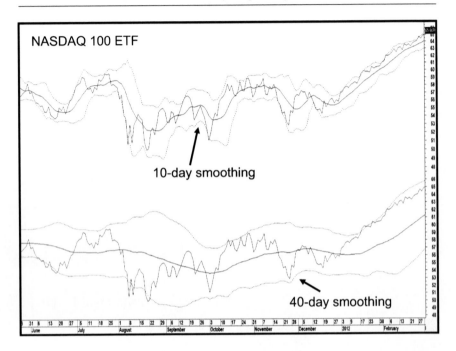

The first requirement in plotting a Bollinger band is a time span, as with a moving average. The longer the span, the smoother, but less sensitive, are the fluctuations. Chart 12.4, featuring the NASDAQ 100 ETF, plots both bands with the standard or default time span of 20 periods and a deviation of 2.

Chart 12.5 compares the difference with different smoothings. The plot in the upper window shows one of 10 days and the lower one a smoothing of 40 days. It is pretty obvious that the 40-bar span is far smoother and is plotted further away from the price action.

The second parameter for plotting a Bollinger band is the amount of deviation. In this respect, the bands in the upper window of Chart 12.6, again featuring the NASDAQ 100 ETF, are calculated with a value of 4. The lower panel takes it to the other extreme with a deviation of 1 percent. It is fairly evident from this comparison that the smaller the deviation, the tighter the band and vice versa. The tight band in the lower panel is touched so many times, it is not at all useful. Alternatively, a larger deviation factor returns a band that is rarely, if ever, touched. Think of

CHART 12.6 NASDAQ 100 2011–2012 Comparing Bollinger Standard Deviation Parameters

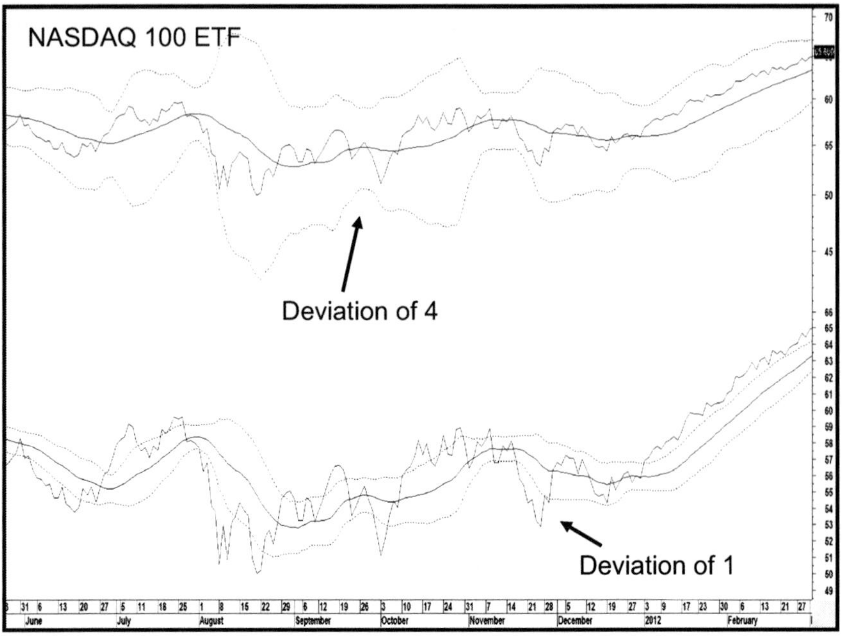

the deviation as a parameter that corresponds with an overbought/oversold level.

John Bollinger, the creator of this technique, recommends a factor of 20 for the time span and 2 for the deviation. Those are the parameters used for the remainder of charts in this chapter.

Rules for Interpretation

Rule 1. When the bands narrow, there is a tendency for sharp price changes to follow.

> This, of course, is another way of saying that when prices trade in a narrow range and lose volatility, demand and supply are in a fine state of balance and its resolution will trigger a sharp price move. In this context, a narrowing of the bands is always relative to the recent past. That's where Bollinger bands can help visually by showing the narrowing process. They also give us some indication of when a breakout might materialize because the bands start to diverge once the price begins to take off. Two examples are shown

CHART 12.7 Oneok 2000–2001 and Bollinger Bands

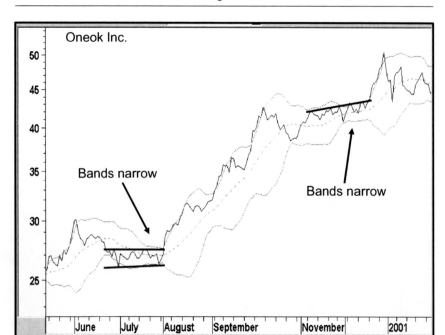

in Chart 12.7, where it is also possible to construct some trendlines marking the breakout points.

Rule 2. If the price exceeds a band, the trend is expected to continue.

This is really another way of saying that if the price moves above the band, upside momentum is strong enough to support higher ultimate prices, and vice versa. This is a common experience at the start of a bull market and vice versa for a downward penetration. After both breakouts in Chart 12.7, we see the price immediately move outside the band. The re-crossover of the Bollinger band usually indicates short-term exhaustion, and it quickly pulls back again. However, this is just a process of pausing for breath until the trend is then able to extend again. By now, you will have noticed that the price often crosses the band several times before the trend reverses. The obvious question at this point is: How do you know when it has been crossed for the last time? In other words, how do you know how to spot the bottom and top of a move? The answer lies in the next rule.

CHART 12.8 NYSE Composite Intraday Chart and Bollinger Bands

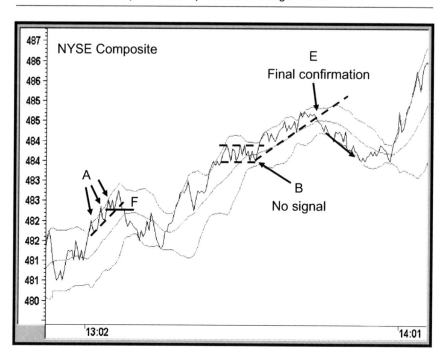

Rule 3. When the price traces out a reversal formation after it has crossed outside a band, expect a trend reversal.

In Chart 12.8, featuring the New York Stock Exchange (NYSE) Composite, we see a series of three rallies that touch or exceed the upper band (range A). The first two show no sign of exhaustion. However, after the final attempt, the up trendline is violated. Then the price falls below the previous minor low to complete a small top at point F.

Later, the price touches the outer band again just prior to the trading range at B, but there is no signal since it manages to hold above the lower portion of the trading range. Finally, a nice up trendline is violated and a sell signal is triggered at point E, following a temporary penetration of the outer band. What we are seeing is a series of overstretched readings, which is what a price touching the band really is. It finally confirms the overbought reading. If there is no signal, the implication is that following a brief correction,

CHART 12.9 NYSE Composite Intraday Chart and Bollinger Bands

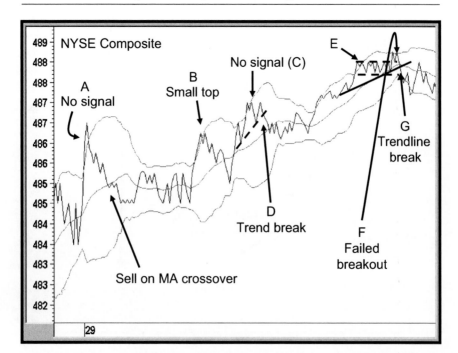

the price will then go on to register a new high or low for the move, depending on its direction. That is not always the case because there is no such word as *always* when working with technical indicators. For instance, Chart 12.9, also featuring the NYSE Composite, shows where the price crosses below the upper band (point A), yet it does not go on to make a new high until a worthwhile decline has taken place. In such instances, the best place to liquidate a long position is when the price crosses below the moving average.

Later on, at point B, you can see a small double top as the price tries for a second time to break above the band. At the next attempt (point C), there is no signal, but after the subsequent penetration, a trendline is violated (point D). Then we see a series of lows (range E). But this support was not broken, so there was no reason to sell. Finally, the price tries to break out from the trading range, but is held back by the upper band (point F). A subsequent trendline break (point G) is the signal to liquidate. In retrospect, what we see is a failed breakout, which just adds to the bearishness, once the series of lows is penetrated on the downside.

Sometimes it is possible to combine Bollinger band analysis with the Know Sure Thing (KST). This indicator is discussed at length in

CHART 12.10 Vijaya Bank 2006–2007 and Bollinger Bands

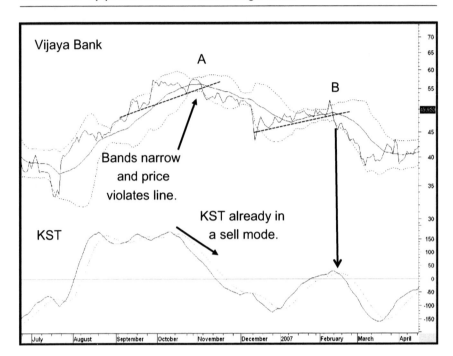

Chapter 15; for now, just think of it as a smoothed momentum indicator that triggers buy and sell momentum indications when it crosses above or below its moving average. In Chart 12.10 featuring Vijaya Bank, an Indian stock, the bands narrow in the late October period as the price experiences a sideways correction.

The question is: Which way will the price break? A vital clue can sometimes be gleaned by looking at an oscillator. In this chart, I am using the KST, but it could easily be the moving-average convergence divergence (MACD), stochastic, relative strength indicator (RSI), and so forth. The idea is that the KST is already declining and therefore telling us that short-term momentum is trending down. Since the price soon confirms the violation of the dashed trendline, it is not surprising that the narrowing bands, i.e., finely balanced supply/demand situations, are resolved in a negative way. Later on at point B, we see a similar setup with the narrowing bands. This time, the KST falls below its MA at around the same time that the trendline is violated.

Summary

1. Envelopes are moving averages that are plotted at equidistant levels above and below a specific moving average.
2. They provide useful support/resistance points that often halt rallies and reactions.
3. Occasionally, it is a good idea to plot several series of envelopes around the moving average.
4. Bollinger bands are a form of envelope that is constructed from standard deviations. These expand and narrow, depending on pricing volatility.
5. When Bollinger bands narrow, the subsequent widening of the bands is often followed by a sharp price move.
6. When the price breaks through one of the bands, this is a sign of strong momentum and we should expect the trend to continue.
7. When the price returns through the band, expect a pause in the trend, unless this crossover is associated with a trendline break, in which case the crossover probably represents exhaustion.

13

MOMENTUM I:
BASIC PRINCIPLES

The methods of trend determination considered so far have been concerned with analysis of the movement of the price itself through trendlines, price patterns, and moving-average (MA) analysis. These techniques are extremely useful, but they identify a change in trend only *after it has taken place*. The use of momentum indicators can warn of latent strengths or weaknesses in the indicator or price being monitored, often well ahead of the final turning point.

This chapter will examine the general principles of momentum interpretation that apply in some degree or another to all such oscillator type indicators. Rate of change will be used as a case study. The subsequent two chapters will discuss other specific momentum indicators.

Introduction

The concept of upside momentum is illustrated in the following example. When a ball is thrown into the air, it begins its trajectory at a very fast pace; i.e., it possesses strong momentum. The speed at which the ball rises gradually diminishes, until it finally comes to a temporary standstill. The force of gravity then causes it to reverse course. This slowing-down process, known as a *loss of upward momentum*, is a phenomenon that is also experienced in financial markets. The flight of a ball can be equated to a market price. The price's rate of advance begins to slow down noticeably before the ultimate peak in prices is reached.

On the other hand, if a ball is thrown inside a room and hits the ceiling while its momentum is still rising, the ball and the momentum will reverse at the same time. Unfortunately, momentum indicators in the marketplace are not dissimilar. This is because there are occasions on which momentum and price peak simultaneously, either because a ceiling of selling resistance is met or because buying power is temporarily exhausted. Under such conditions, the *level* of momentum is often as helpful as its *direction* in assessing the quality of a price trend.

Major Technical Principle The use of momentum indicators can warn of latent strengths or weaknesses in the indicator or price being monitored, often well ahead of the final turning point.

The idea of downward momentum may be better understood by comparing it to a car that is pushed over the top of a hill. The car begins to roll downhill and, as the gradient of the hill steepens, to accelerate; at the bottom, it reaches maximum velocity. Although its speed then begins to decrease, the car continues to travel, but finally it comes to a halt. Market prices act in a similar fashion: The rate of decline (or loss of momentum) often slows ahead of the final low. This is not always the case, however, since momentum and price sometimes (as at peaks) turn together as prices meet a major level of support (resistance). Nevertheless, momentum leads price often enough to warn of a potential trend reversal in the indicator or market average that is being monitored.

Momentum is a generic term. Just as "fruit" describes apples, oranges, grapes, etc., so "momentum" embraces many different indicators. Examples include rate of change (ROC), the relative strength indicator (RSI), moving-average convergence divergence (MACD), breadth oscillators, and diffusion indexes.

There are essentially two broad ways of looking at momentum. The first uses price data for an individual series, such as a currency, commodity, stock, or market average, and manipulates it in a statistical form that is plotted as an oscillator. We will call this *price momentum* (although volume can be manipulated in the same way). The second is also plotted as an oscillator, but is based on statistical manipulation of a number of market components, such as the percentage of New York Stock Exchange (NYSE) stocks above a 30-week MA. This measure is referred to as *breadth momentum* and is discussed in Chapter 27. Price momentum can be constructed for any price series, but breadth momentum can be calculated only for a series that can be broken down into various components.

> **Major Technical Principle** The principles or characteristics of momentum interpretation are the same for all indicators, but some are specially constructed to bring out a particular characteristic.

This chapter outlines the eight basic principles. (For further study please refer to *The Definitive Guide to Market Momentum,* Martin J. Pring, 2009, Traders Press or the momentum module at the online technical analysis course at Pring.com.) We will be using ROC as an example, but you should remember that it is only *one* type of price momentum indicator. Chapters 14, 15, 26, and 27 will discuss other individual indicators for price and breadth momentum, respectively.

It should be noted that the type of trend reversal signaled by a momentum indicator depends upon the time span over which it has been calculated. It is accepted practice to use daily data for identifying short-term trends, weekly data for intermediate trends, and monthly data for primary trends.

It is very important to note that the use of momentum indicators assumes that markets or stocks are experiencing a normal cyclic rhythm, which is expressed in price action by rallies and reactions. However, in some instances, countercyclical reactions are almost nonexistent. Price movement is then reflected as a linear uptrend or downtrend. This is an unusual phenomenon, and when it develops, momentum indicators fail to work.

> **Major Technical Principle** It is of paramount importance to use momentum analysis in conjunction with some kind of trend-reversal signal in the price series itself.

Momentum Interpretation

Rate of Change

The simplest way of measuring momentum is to calculate the rate at which a security price changes over a given period of time. This is known as a rate of change (ROC) indicator. If it is desired, for example, to construct an ROC using a 10-week time span, the current price is divided by the price

10 weeks ago. If the latest price is 100 and that one 10 weeks ago was 105, the ROC or momentum indicator will read 95.2, that is, 100 divided by 105. The subsequent reading in the indicator will be calculated by dividing next week's price by the price 9 weeks ago (see Table 13.1); the result is a series that oscillates around a central reference point.

This horizontal equilibrium line represents the level at which the price is unchanged from its reading 10 weeks ago (Figure 13.1). If an ROC calculation were made for a price that remained unchanged, its momentum index would be represented by a straight line.

When an ROC indicator is above the reference line, the market price that it is measuring is higher than its level 10 weeks ago. If the ROC indicator is also rising, the difference between the current reading of the price and its level 10 weeks ago is growing. If an ROC indicator is above the

TABLE 13.1 10-Week ROC Calculation

Date	DJIA (1)	DJIA 10 Weeks Ago (2)	10-Week Rate of Change (col. 1 divided by col. 2) (3)
Jan. 1	985		
8	980		
15	972		
22	975		
29	965		
Feb. 5	967		
12	972		
19	965		
26	974		
Mar. 5	980		
12	965	985	98.0
19	960	980	98.0
26	950	972	97.7
Apr. 2	960	975	98.5
9	965	965	100.0
16	970	967	100.3
23	974	972	100.2
30	980	965	101.6
May 7	985	974	101.1

FIGURE 13.1 ROC Using Percentage Scaling

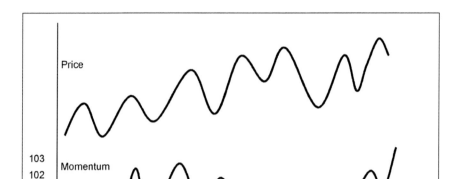

central line but is declining, the price is still above its level 10 weeks ago, but the difference between the two readings is shrinking. When the ROC indicator is below its central line and falling, the price is below its level 10 weeks ago, and the difference between the two is growing. If the indicator is below its central line but rising, the price is still lower than its level 10 weeks ago, but its rate of decline is slowing.

In short, a rising ROC indicator implies expanding velocity, and a falling one implies a loss of momentum. Rising momentum should be interpreted as a bullish factor, and declining momentum as a bearish one.

There are two methods of scaling an ROC chart. Since the choice does not affect the trend or level of the index, the method used is not important, but a brief explanation is in order because the two alternatives can be confusing. The first method is the one described earlier and shown in Figure 13.1, where 100 becomes the central reference point. In the example, 100 (this week's observation) divided by 99 (the observation 10 weeks ago) is plotted as 101, 100 divided by 98 as 102, 100 divided by 102 as 98, and so on.

The alternative is to take the difference between the indicator and the 100 level and plot the result as a positive or negative number, using a reference line of 0. In this case, 101 is plotted as +1, 102 as +2, 98 as −2, and so on (see Figure 13.2).

FIGURE 13.2 ROC Using Plus and Minus Scaling

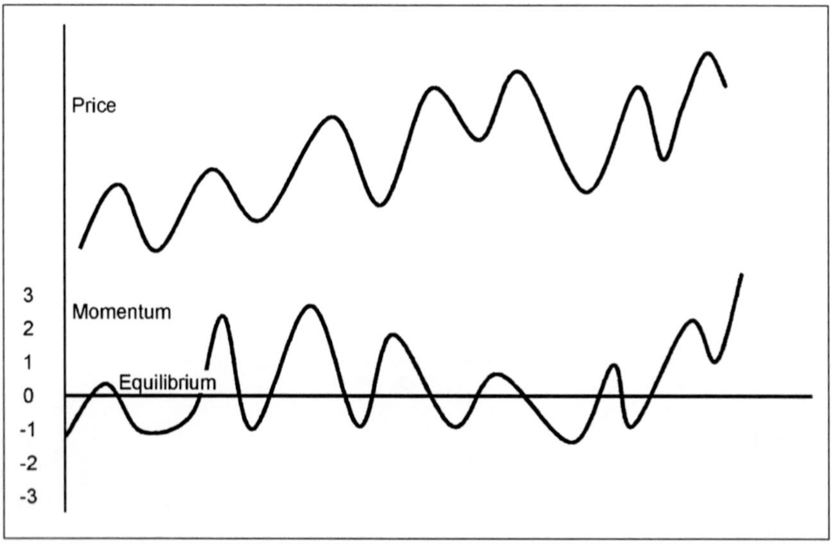

Selection of Time Span

Choosing the correct time span is important. For longer-term trends, a 12-month or 52-week momentum is generally the most reliable, although a 24- or 18-month period can also prove useful. For intermediate trends, a 9-month, 26-week (6-month), or 13-week (3-month) momentum works well. Price movements of even shorter duration are often reflected by a 10-, 20-, 25-, or 30-day span. Reliable short/intermediate movements are often reflected with a 45-day (9-week) span.

> **Major Technical Principle** The analysis of any technical situation will be enhanced by the calculation of several momentum indicators, each based on a different time span.

In this way, trendlines, price patterns, or divergences, which may not be apparent in one period, are more apparent in another. The discovery of signs of a trend reversal in several indicators constructed from different time spans adds further fuel to the weight of the evidence. An example

CHART 13.1 iShares MSCI World Stock ETF 2002–20012 Multiple Momentum Trend Breaks

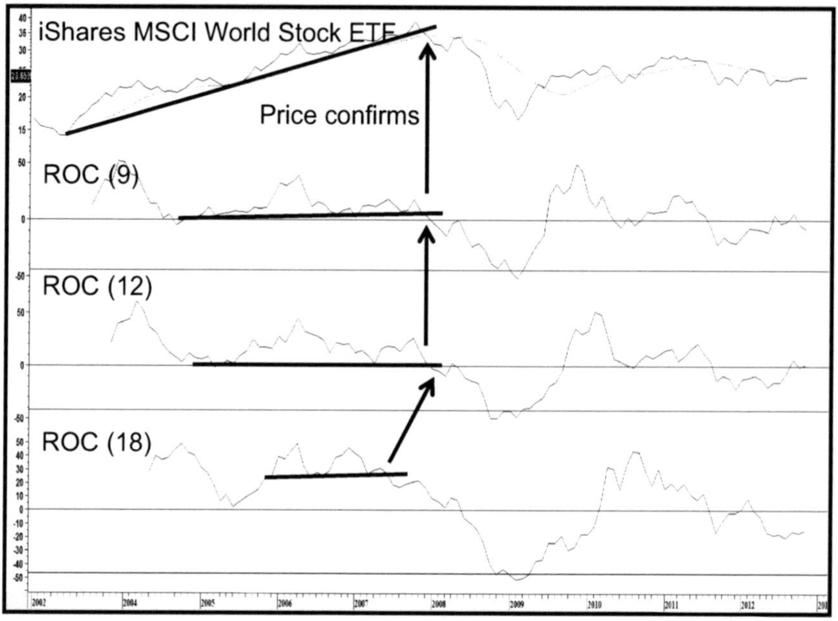

Source: From pring.com

of this is featured in Chart 13.1 for the iShares MSCI World Stock ETF (symbol ACWI) just prior to the 2007–2009 bear market. Note that the trendline for the price was violated more or less simultaneously with the 12-month MA for a stronger signal than just the trendline on its own.

Principles and Applications of Momentum Indicators

The following description of the principles and use of momentum indicators applies to all forms of oscillators, whether constructed from an individual price series or from an index that measures internal market momentum, such as those described in Chapter 27.

These principles can be roughly divided into two broad categories.

1. *Those that deal with overbought conditions, oversold conditions, divergences, and the like.* I will call these *momentum characteristics*. If you study momentum indicators or oscillators, you'll find that they have certain characteristics that are associated with subsurface strengths or weaknesses in the underlying price trend. It's rather like

looking under the hood of an engine. Quite a lot of the time you can identify mechanical trouble before it becomes self-evident. Momentum and sentiment are closely allied, and the relationship between them is discussed in Chapter 29.

2. *The identification of trend reversals in the momentum indicator itself.* I will call these *momentum trend reversal techniques.* In this case, we are making the assumption that when a trend in momentum is reversed, prices will sooner or later follow.

Trend-determining techniques, such as trendline violations, moving-average crossovers, etc., when applied to momentum, are just as valid as when utilized with price. The difference, and it is an important one, is that a trend reversal in momentum is just that—a reversal in momentum. Momentum typically reverses along with price, often with a small lead, but just because oscillators change direction, doesn't always mean that prices will too. Normally, a reversal in the momentum trend acts as confirming evidence of a price trend reversal signal. In effect, this momentum signal performs the act of supplementary "witness" in our weight-of-the-evidence approach. I will have more to say on this one a little later, but for now, take special note of the fact that actual buy and sell signals can only come from a reversal in trend of the actual price, not the momentum series.

Momentum Characteristics

1. Overbought and Oversold Levels   Perhaps the most widely used method of momentum interpretation is the evaluation of overbought and oversold levels. This concept can be compared to a person taking an unruly dog for a walk on a leash. The leash is continually being pulled from one side of the person to the other as the dog struggles to get free. Despite all its activity, however, the dog can move no farther away than the length of the leash.

The same principle holds true for momentum indicators in the marketplace, except that the market's "leash" should be thought of as made of rubber, so that it is possible for particularly strong or weak price trends to extend beyond the normal limits, known as *overbought* and *oversold* levels. These areas are drawn on a chart at some distance above and below the equilibrium level, as in Figure 13.3. The actual boundaries will depend on the volatility of the price being monitored and the time period over which the momentum indicator has been constructed, For example, an ROC indicator has a tendency to move to wider extremes over a longer period than over a shorter one. It is highly unlikely that a price will move

FIGURE 13.3 Overbought and Oversold Zones

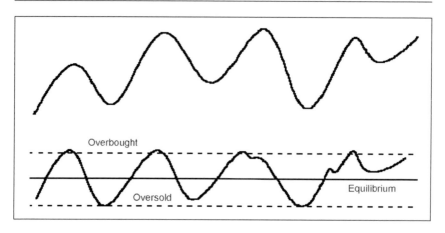

10 percent over a 10-day period; yet, over the course of a primary bull market extending over a 12-month period, a 25 percent increase would not be uncommon. Some indicators, such as the RSI and stochastic, have been specially constructed to move within definite predetermined boundaries.

When a price reaches an overbought or oversold extreme, the probabilities favor but, by no means guarantee, a reversal. An overbought reading is a time to be thinking about selling, and an oversold one warns that the current technical position may warrant a purchase. In many cases, when a price reaches an overbought extreme, the news is good, participants are optimistic, and human nature tells us to buy. Unfortunately, the opposite is more likely to be the case. On the other hand, an oversold reading is usually associated with a negative news background. The last thing we want to do is raise our shaking hand, pick up the phone, and call our friendly broker or nervously click online, but that is often a reasonable time to do it, provided the overall technical position is favorable.

In view of the variability of indicators such as ROC, there is no hard-and-fast rule about where the overbought and oversold lines should be drawn. This can be determined only by studying the history and characteristics of the security being monitored. They should be drawn such that they will act as pivotal points, which, when touched or slightly exceeded, are followed by a reversal in the oscillator. When a particularly sharp price movement takes place, these boundaries will become totally ineffective. Unfortunately, this is a fact of life, but by and large, it is usually possible to construct overbought and oversold benchmarks that are price-sensitive. Again, the market "leash" is made of rubber and can remain in overbought or oversold territory for long periods. Consequently, it is essential to get confirmation from a reversal in the trend of the price itself before taking any drastic action.

2. Oscillator Characteristics in Primary Bull and Bear Markets   I mentioned earlier that the character of an oscillator alters according to the price environment. In a bull market, oscillators tend to move into an overbought condition very quickly and stay there for a long time. In a bear market, they can and do remain in an oversold condition for a long time. In effect, an oscillator is not unlike a migrating bird in the Northern Hemisphere. I've divided the price action in Figure 13.4 into a bear market, followed by a bull, and finally another bear market. As we enter the bear phase, the true range of the oscillator shifts to the south, in a similar way to a bird in the Northern Hemisphere migrates south to escape the cold northerly winter. Then, when the bull market starts, the oscillator's trading pattern migrates north again. As a new bear market begins, just like the bird the oscillator finally shifts south again.

   This is useful information in itself, for if it's possible to draw parallel horizontal lines like these against an oscillator, it provides a valuable clue as to whether the prevailing primary trend is bullish or bearish.

> **Major Technical Principle**   Oscillators behave in different ways, depending on the direction of the primary trend.

FIGURE 13.4 Changes in Momentum Characteristics in Bull and Bear Markets

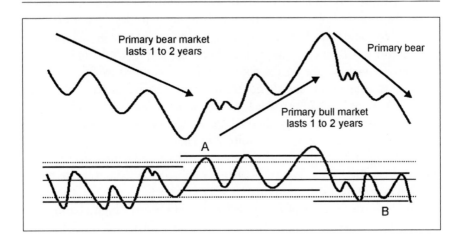

The second point is that if you have an idea of the direction of the primary trend, you can anticipate what price action might follow from a specific overbought or oversold reading. In a bull market, the price is extremely sensitive to an oversold condition. That means that when you are lucky enough to see one, look around for some confirming signals that the price is about to rally. An example might be the violation of a down trendline, etc. The reason for this sensitivity lies in the fact that the oversold reading very likely reflects an extreme in short-term sentiment. Market participants are focusing on the latest bad news and using that as an excuse to sell. Since this is a bull market, they would be better served by remembering the positive long-term fundamentals that will soon emerge and using this weakness as an opportunity to buy.

The same thing happens in reverse during a bear market. Traders are focused on bad news, which sends the price down. Then, some unexpectedly good news hits the wires and the price rallies. However, when it is fully digested, most people realize that things really haven't changed at all and the price declines again. Thus, the overbought reading more often than not will correspond with the top of a bear market rally.

Looking at it from another perspective, during a bull market, the price will be far less sensitive to an overbought condition. Often, it will be followed by a small decline or even a trading range, as at point A in Figure 13.4. The rule, then, is don't count on a short-term overbought condition to trigger a big decline because the odds do not favor it.

Finally, people often point to an oversold condition and use that as their rationale for a rally. Your favorite financial columnist might say "Analysts point out that the market is deeply oversold and a snapback rally is expected." Once again, it very much depends on the environment. In a bull market, that's true, but the columnist is more likely to say that "despite a short-term oversold condition, analysts are expecting lower prices because …" and then the columnist will go on to list a load of bearish factors justifying his or her position. Remember the media tend to reflect the crowd, which is usually wrong at turning points and do not make accurate forecasts, especially when quoting "experts." In a bear market, though, a market or stock is far less sensitive to an oversold reading, often failing to signal a rally, or possibly being followed by a trading range, as at point B in Figure 13.4.

The maturity of the trend, whether primary or intermediate, often has an effect on the limits that an oscillator might reach. For example, when a bull market has just begun, there is a far greater tendency for it to move quickly into overbought territory and to remain at very high readings for a considerable period of time. In such cases, the overbought readings tend to give premature warnings of declines. During the early phases of the bull cycle, when the market possesses strong momentum, reactions to the oversold level are much more responsive to price reversals, and such readings, therefore, offer more reliable signals. *It is only when a bull trend is maturing, or during bear phases, that overbought levels can be relied upon to signal that a rally is shortly to be aborted.* The very fact that an indicator is unable to remain at, or even to achieve, an overbought reading for long is itself a signal that the advance is losing momentum. The opposite is true for a bear trend.

3. Overbought/Oversold Re-crossovers   In most cases, excellent buy and sell alerts are generated when the momentum indicator exceeds its extended overbought or oversold boundary and then re-crosses back through the boundary on its way to zero. Figure 13.5 demonstrates this possibility. This approach filters out a lot of premature buy and sell signals generated as the indicator just reaches its overextended boundary, but one should still wait for a trend reversal in the price itself before taking action.

4. Mega Overboughts and Oversolds   As discussed in Chapter 29, there is a close connection between market sentiment indicators and the characteristics of oscillators. Since market sentiment differs widely during a bull and bear market, it follows that such variations are occasionally reflected in

FIGURE 13.5 Overbought and Oversold Re-crossovers

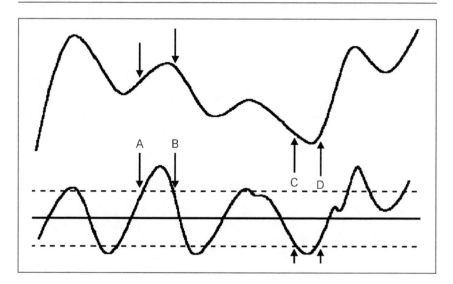

changing characteristics of momentum indicators. I have termed one of these phenomena "mega overboughts and oversolds." A mega overbought is the initial thrust in a bull market following the final low. It's a reading in the momentum indicator that takes it well beyond the normal overbought condition witnessed in either a preceding bull or bear market. It should, for example, represent a multiyear high for the oscillator concerned—perhaps even a record overbought reading. Such conditions are usually a sign of a very young and vibrant bull market. The very fact that an oscillator is able to even rise to such a level can be used, along with other trend-reversal evidence, to signal that a new bull market has begun. It represents a sign that the balance between buyers and sellers has unequivocally shifted in favor of buyers. It's something like a person using all his strength to crash through a locked door. It takes a tremendous amount of energy to achieve, but once the door is finally shoved open, there is nothing to hold that person back any longer. In the same way, a mega overbought removes the price from its bear market constraints, leaving it free to experience a new bull market. An example is shown in Figure 13.6.

This is about the only instance when opening a long position from an overbought condition can be justified. Even so, it can only be ratio-nalized by someone with a longer-term time horizon. This is due to the fact that whenever an oscillator experiences a mega overbought, higher prices almost always follow after a short-term setback or consolidation

FIGURE 13.6 Mega Overbought

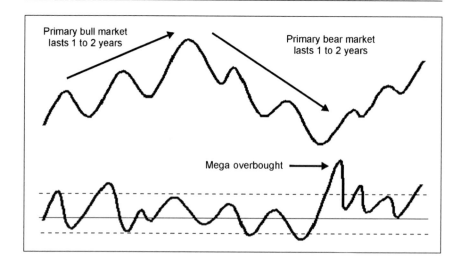

has taken place. A highly leveraged trader may not be able to withstand the financial pressure from the contratrend move, whereas the long-term investor can. In most instances, you will probably find that the correction following the mega overbought is a sideways rather than a downward one, but there are just enough exceptions to cause the over-leveraged trader a lot of sleepless nights. Since a mega overbought is associated with the first rally in a bull market, it's a good idea to check and see if volume is also expanding rapidly. If it takes the form of record volume for that particular security, the signal is far louder because record volume coming after a major decline is typically a reliable signal of a new bull market. Expanding volume is a more or less necessary condition since it is consistent with the idea that buyers now have the upper hand and that the psychology has totally reversed.

Having said that, there are occasions when a mega overbought is followed not by a reversal, but by a change in trend. In other words, the previous bear market emerges into a multiyear trading range rather than a full-fledged bull market. The point here is that that the low that precedes the mega overbought is not normally decisively violated for many years.

The same concept also appears in reverse for oversold extremes. Consequently, when a price decline following a bull market high pushes a momentum indicator to a new extreme low, well beyond anything witnessed either during the previous bull market or for many years prior to that, the implication is that sellers now have the upper hand. The fact that it is possible for the momentum indicator to fall so sharply and so deeply is in itself a sign that the character of the market has changed. When you see this type of action, you should, at the very least, question the bull market scenario. Look for telltale signs that a new bear market may be underway. What are the volume configurations on the subsequent rally? Does volume now trend lower as the price rises compared to previous rallies that were associated with trends of rising volume? And so forth. The same possibilities of a change, as opposed to a reversal in trend, also apply in the sense that a mega oversold is typically the first decline in a bear market, but occasionally, it can also signal a change in trend from a primary bull market to a multiyear trading range. An example of a mega oversold is shown in Figure 13.7. Both mega conditions are usually best observed in short-term oscillators with a time span ranging from 10 to as many as 30 days. On weekly charts, it's also possible to go out as much as 13 weeks, though obviously such signals are less timely than those derived from shorter-term time spans. They never develop from indicators whose construction constrains their fluctuations between 0 and 100, such as the RSI and stochastic.

FIGURE 13.7 Mega Oversold

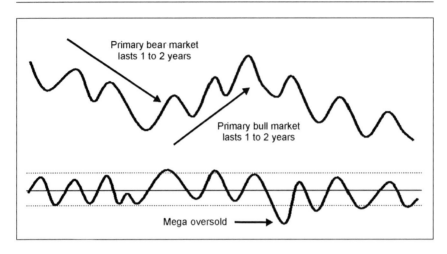

Chart 13.2 features the Spider Technology ETF (symbol XLK) at the 2009 primary bear market low. See how the high reading in the 10-day ROC exceeds anything seen prior for a classic mega overbought signal. This is quite remarkable when you remember that the first sign of a primary trend reversal is given within 10 days of the bear market low. This is not sufficient evidence to call a turn, but certainly enough to alert the observant analyst to be looking around for confirming evidence, such as a break above the horizontal trendline flagging the completion of a double bottom.

5. Extreme Swings The extreme swing is another phenomenon that signals a dramatic shift in psychology. It reflects the idea that some primary trend reversals are signaled by a swing from unbelievable exuberance as the bull market reaches its peak, to one of complete despondency and depression as the first bear market setback gets underway. The opposite is true of a transition from a primary bear to a primary bull market. In order for an extreme swing to develop, it is necessary to experience a prolonged uptrend or downtrend. The extreme swing then appears in a momentum indicator by an especially strong move in the direction of the then-prevailing trend, as shown in Figure 13.8. This is then followed by an extreme reading in the opposite direction. In Figure 13.8 we see a blow-off to the bull move as the oscillator reaches a highly overbought reading. This is subsequently followed by a price decline that pushes it to the other extreme. Such action indicates a dramatic shift in sentiment as market participants change from a mood

CHART 13.2 Spider Technology ETF 2005–2009 Mega Overbought

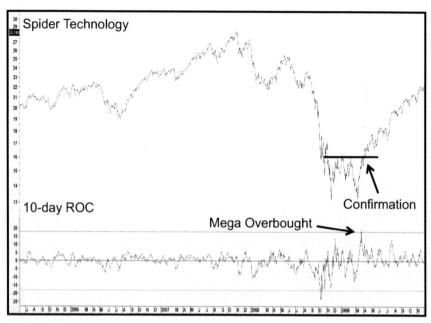

Source: From pring.com

FIGURE 13.8 Bearish Extreme Swing

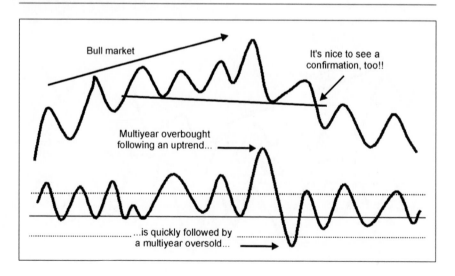

of euphoria to one of despondency as the market eventually reacts in the opposite direction to that originally expected.

In order to qualify for an extreme swing, the first swing must represent the strongest move in several years, certainly the strongest since the initial thrust from the previous bear market bottom. It is really a climax move for the bull market. The second swing to the downside should really be a mega oversold, though in some cases, an extreme oversold will suffice.

This phenomenon undoubtedly occurs because the first swing encourages participants who have been right about the prevailing trend and discourages those who have been wrong. In the case of a bull market, the final rally also squeezes out all of the remaining shorts, so when the trend reverses, there is virtually no buying activity from speculators covering short positions. The preceding sharp advance also encouraged buyers who could see that there was only one way prices could go, and that was up. As a result, decisions on the buy side are made carelessly and without thought for the fact that prices may move the other way. When they do, such individuals are flushed out of the market with no quarter given. Since there are few short sellers able to pick up the pieces, the price drops ferociously.

Extreme swings also develop between a bear and bull primary trend, as featured in Figure 13.9. In this case, though, the mood swing is from total despondency and depression as the bear market squeezes out the last of the bulls to one of disbelief as the market reverses to the upside. At market bottoms, it is the shorts who gain confidence from the sharp and persistent downtrend. Even the strongest bulls are forced to capitulate,

FIGURE 13.9 Bullish Extreme Swing

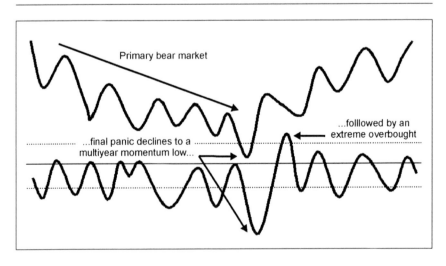

CHART 13.3 iShares FTSE China 25 ETF 2005–2009 Extreme Swing

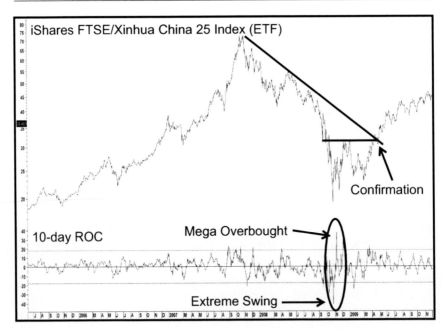

Source: From pring.com

and eventually there is no one left to sell. Then, during the rally phase, the shorts are forced to cover and new buying comes in because of the perceived improvement in the fundamentals. Since there is virtually no one left to sell, prices shoot up and a mega or extreme overbought is registered.

Needless to say, extreme swings are quite unusual, but when you can spot them, it really pays to follow their lead since a new trend invariably results.

Chart 13.3 shows an example of a bullish extreme swing for the China iShare (symbol FXI), at the 2007–2009 primary bear market low. Note that in this case the bullish part of the pattern was also a mega overbought condition. It barely qualified, though, because although it was a multiyear overbought following a bear market, that decline was only a few months longer than our minimum requirement of 9 months for one of these phenomena.

> **Major Technical Principle** Mega and extreme conditions represent preliminary signals of a primary trend reversal. Confirmation by the price usually puts the issue beyond reasonable doubt.

FIGURE 13.10 Momentum and Divergences

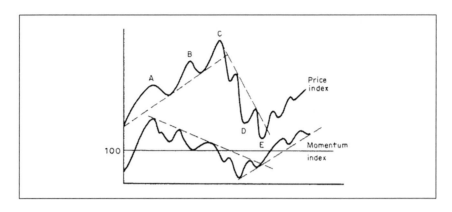

6. Divergences The ball example used at the beginning of the chapter showed that maximum velocity was obtained fairly close to the point at which the ball leaves the hand. Similarly, prices in financial markets usually reach their maximum level of momentum ahead of the final peak in prices. In Figure 13.10, this is shown at point A.

If the price makes a new high, which is confirmed by the momentum index, no indication of technical weakness arises. On the other hand, if momentum fails to confirm (point B), a *negative* divergence is set up between the two series, and a warning of a weakening technical structure is given. Such discrepancies normally indicate that the price will undergo a corrective process. It can take the form of either a sideways or a horizontal trading range, or (more likely) a downward one. However, the price will sometimes continue upward to a third top and be accompanied by even greater weakness in the momentum index (point C). Occasionally, the third peak in the momentum index may be higher than the second but lower than the first. Either circumstance requires some degree of caution, since this characteristic is a distinct warning of a sharp reversal in price or a long corrective period.

Figure 13.10 also shows a *positive divergence*. In this instance, the price makes its low at point E, but this was preceded by the oscillator, which bottomed at D.

> **Major Technical Principle** It is extremely important to note that divergences only warn of a weakening or strengthening market condition and do not represent actual buy and sell signals.

FIGURE 13.11 Extreme Bearish Divergence

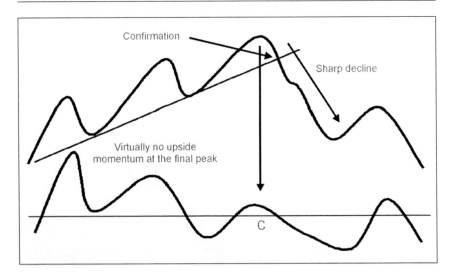

Whenever any divergence between momentum and price occurs, it is essential to wait for a confirmation from the price itself that its trend has also been reversed. This confirmation can be achieved by: (1) the violation of a simple trendline, as shown in Figures 13.10 and 11: (2) the crossover of a moving average (MA); or (3) the completion of a price pattern. This form of insurance is well worth taking, since it is not unknown for an index to continually lose and regain momentum without suffering a break in trend during a long cyclical advance. Examples of this phenomenon occurred during the 1962–1966 bull market in U.S. stocks, and in Japanese stocks between 1982 and 1990.

Major Technical Principle   As a general rule, the greater the number of negative divergences, the weaker the underlying structure.

A good example can be seen in Chart 13.4, which shows the Nikkei Index violating an important 3½-year secondary trendline after the 13-week ROC indicator had negatively diverged several times with the index. As a result, the final rally was accompanied by very little in the way of upside momentum. It would have been a mistake to sell on any of the prior divergences, but a very timely sell signal was generated by waiting for

CHART 13.4 Nikkei 1995–1990 Negative Divergences

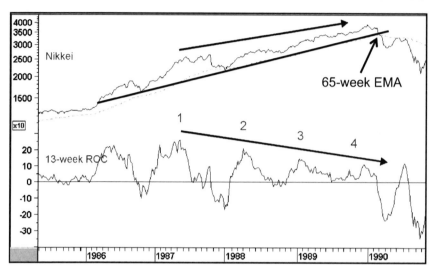

Source: From pring.com

a confirmation in the form of a trend break in the index itself through a negative 65-week EMA crossover.

> **Major Technical Principle**   A divergence that develops close to the equilibrium line is often followed by a sharp price move when confirmed by the price.

At point C in Figure 13.11, the price moves to a significant new high, but the momentum indicator is barely able to remain above the equilibrium line. Such a situation demands the utmost caution *when accompanied by a trend break,* for it is usually a sign of extreme technical weakness and is often, though certainly not always, followed by a very sharp decline. The opposite type of situation (Figure 13.12) in a bear market should be viewed as a very positive characteristic, especially if the upward trend break in price is accompanied by high volume. The more explosive the volume, the more reliable the signal is likely to be.

In a sense, it is possible to equate momentum divergences and price trend breaks with dark clouds and rain. If you look up at the sky and observe dark clouds, common sense tells you that it will probably rain, but you do

FIGURE 13.12 Extreme Bullish Divergence

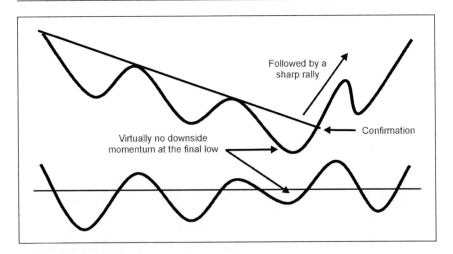

not know for sure until you can hold out your hand and actually feel rain falling. In other words, the clouds (like the divergences) warn of the deteriorating weather (technical condition), but the change is signaled only by the first raindrop (reversal in the price). It is possible to take the analogy a step further by concluding that the darker the clouds (the greater the number of divergences), the heavier the rainstorm (the sharper the price decline) will be.

7. Price Discrepancy Divergence   A further indication of subtle strength or weakness is given when the momentum series moves strongly in one direction, but the accompanying move in the price index is a much smaller one. Such a development suggests that the price index is tired of moving in the direction of the prevailing trend, for despite a strong push of energy from the momentum index, prices are unable to respond. This unusual, but powerful, phenomenon is illustrated for both tops and bottoms in Figures 13.13 and 13.14. The mid-1990 rally in the 13-week ROC for the Nikkei in Chart 13.4 represents good example. Note also how the price was turned back a couple of times by the 65-week EMA.

8. Complex Divergences   It is widely recognized that price movements are simultaneously influenced by several cyclic phenomena. Because a single momentum indicator can monitor only one of these cycles, it is always a good idea to compare several different momentum indicators based on differing time spans.

One approach is to plot two momentum indicators of differing time spans on the same chart, as shown in Figure 13.15. Since this method tries

FIGURE 13.13 Bullish Price Discrepancy Divergence

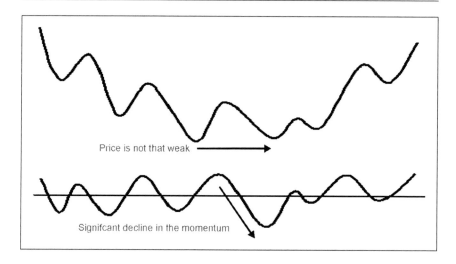

FIGURE 13.14 Bearish Price Discrepancy Divergence

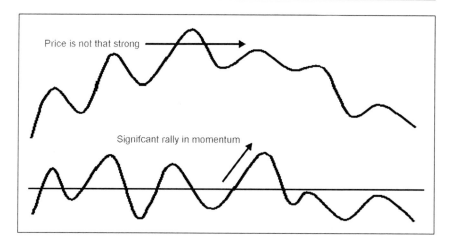

to monitor two separate cycles, it is wise to choose two widely different time spans. For example, not much could be gained from the comparison of a 12- and a 13-week ROC since they would move very closely together. On the other hand, a combination of 13- and 26-week spans would clearly reflect different cycles.

Most of the time, the two indicators are moving in gear, so this study does not give us much information. On the other hand, when the longer-term

FIGURE 13.15 Complex Divergence

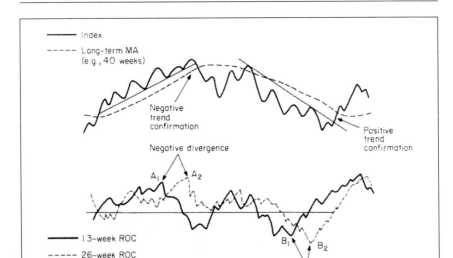

indicator reaches a new peak and the shorter one is at or close to the equilibrium line, they are clearly in disagreement or out of gear (point A_2, Figure 13.15). This normally, but not necessarily, indicates that a reversal in trend will take place, and it is usually an important one. Even so, it is very important to make sure that any such divergence is confirmed by a reversal in the price trend itself. In Figure 13.15, a trend break does occur, but in Figure 13.16, no reversal took place and the price continued on upward.

Complex divergences also occur in a positive combination, as indicated later on at point B_1 in Figure 13.15, but again, it is mandatory to wait for that trend-reversal signal in the price itself.

An example in Chart 13.5 features the United States Oil ETF. Note that it offers a good example of a positive and negative complex divergence, together with a confirmation. Generally speaking, the wider the divergent time spans within reason, the more likely you will be to spot these interesting characteristics.

Momentum Trend Reversal Techniques

1. Trendline Violations Occasionally, it is possible to construct a trendline on the momentum indicator by connecting a series of peaks or troughs.

FIGURE 13.16 Complex Divergence with Nonconfirmation

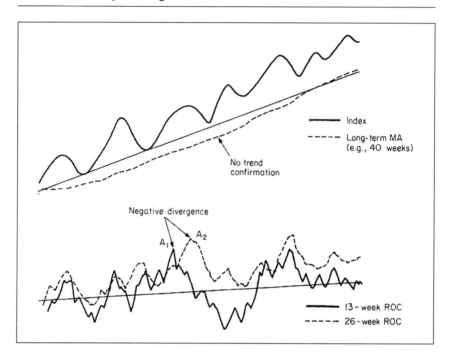

CHART 13.5 U.S. Oil ETF Complex Divergences

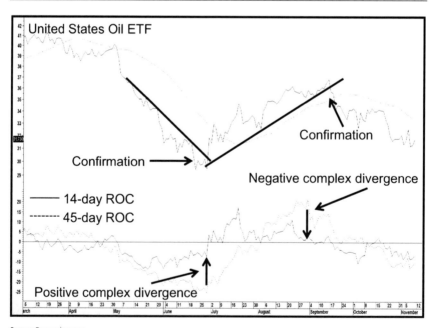

FIGURE 13.17 Bearish Momentum Trend Break

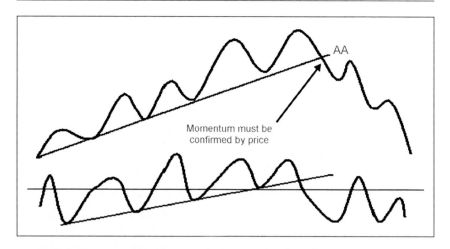

An example for an uptrend reversal is shown in Figure 13.17. When the line is violated, a trend reversal signal for the oscillator is generated.

The construction and significance of the break should be based on the principles outlined in Chapter 6. This type of momentum weakness must be regarded as an alert, and action should be taken only when confirmed by a break in the price trend itself (indicated at point AA in Figure 13.17). In effect, the momentum trend break is reinforcing the price trend break, and it offers an additional piece of evidence that the trend has reversed.

An example signaling a new uptrend is featured in Figure 13.18. It is possible for the momentum trend break to precede that of the price by some time, yet it does not generally lose its potency because of this.

Major Technical Principle As a general rule, it does appear that if both lines are violated more or less simultaneously, the or if the price trend is violated first, strength of the signal is enhanced.

It should also be noted that momentum trendline breaks can be confirmed by any legitimate trend-reversal technique in the price, be it a moving average crossover, price pattern, peak-trough progression reversal, etc.

FIGURE 13.18 Bullish Momentum Trend Break

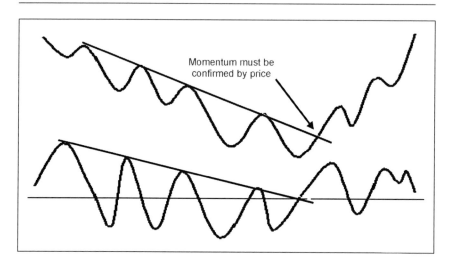

2. Momentum Price Patterns Momentum indicators are also capable of tracing out price patterns. Because of the shorter lead times normally associated with reversals of falling momentum, a breakout from an accumulation pattern, when accompanied by a reversal in the downward trend of the price itself, is usually a highly reliable indication that a worthwhile move has just begun. An example is shown in Figure 13.19.

It is important to use a little common sense in interpreting momentum price patterns. Figure 13.20, for example, shows a breakout from a reverse head-and-shoulders (H&S) pattern that takes place from an overbought condition. This is not to say that such signals will never be valid, but it stands to reason that a breakout from an extreme level is very unlikely to

FIGURE 13.19 Momentum Price Pattern Completion

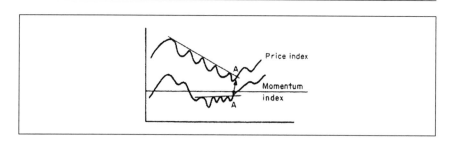

FIGURE 13.20 Overbought Momentum Pattern Completion

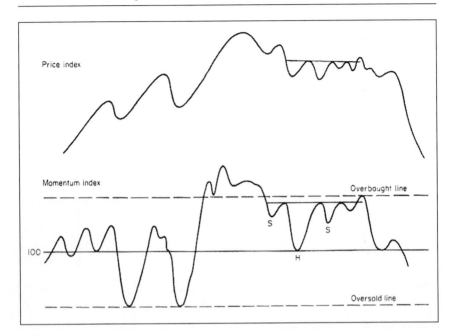

result in a sustainable price move. Remember, technical analysis deals with probabilities, and the odds of a favorable outcome in this case are low. If you want a tip-off, this type of failure typically develops in a contratrend way as a false upward breakout in a primary bear market or false downside move in a primary bull market.

Chart 13.6 is rich in examples of momentum trendline breaks and price pattern completions. The September 2012 break of the dashed up trendline is a classic example of why it is important to wait for some price confirmation, as the failure of the price to do this was followed by a really good rally.

3. Equilibrium Crossovers   Some technicians have devised indicators that offer buy and sell signals when the momentum indicator crosses above and below its equilibrium or zero line. Many markets do not lend themselves to this approach, so its implementation depends very much on a trial-and-error basis through experimentation. In any event, it is always a good idea to use this method in conjunction with a reversal in the price itself. Chart 13.7 shows how zero crossovers used in conjunction with 12-month ROC crossovers have consistently given reliable buy signals for

CHART 13.6 Barclays iPath India ETF Momentum and Price Patterns

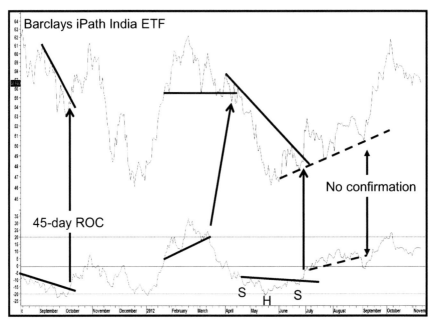

Source: From pring.com

CHART 13.7 Economist Commodity Index 1969–2000 Equilibrium Crossovers

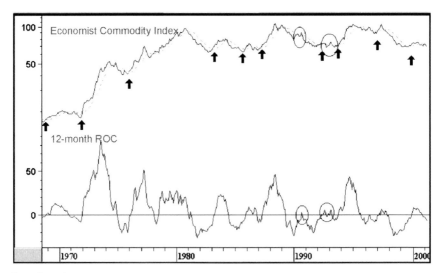

Source: From pring.com

the Economist All Items Commodity Index. The two sets of ellipses point up a couple of whipsaw signals.

4. Momentum and Moving Averages   By now, it is apparent that all the trend-determining techniques used for price are also applicable to momentum. Interpretation of momentum indicators, as described earlier, depends to a considerable extent on judgment. One method of reducing this subjectivity is to smooth the ROC index by using an MA. Warnings of a probable trend reversal in the price being monitored are offered by momentum moving average crossovers, as indicated in Figure 13.21.

One of the problems associated with this approach is that the momentum indicator is often much more jagged than the price index that it is trying to measure, causing the generation of an unacceptable number of whipsaw signals. It is possible to filter out some of these whipsaws by using a combination of two MAs, as shown in Figure 13.22. Buy and sell alerts are given when the shorter-term MA crosses above or below its longer-term counterpart.

This interpretation of momentum is explained in greater detail in the next chapter, since momentum forms the basis of the trend deviation and MACD indicators.

FIGURE 13.21 MA Crossovers

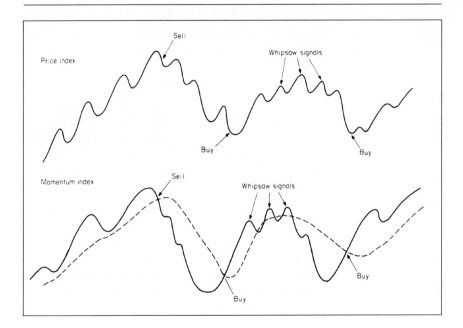

FIGURE 13.22 MA Crossovers Smoothed

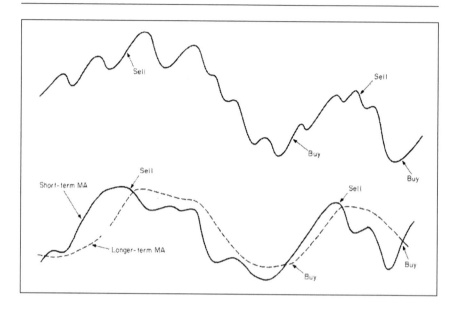

Smoothed Momentum Indicators

Another way of incorporating MAs into momentum studies is to smooth the momentum indicator by a long-term MA. The meaning of "long-term" in this case will depend on the type of trend being monitored. For example, a 20- to 30-day time span would be suitable for a short-term price movement, but a 6-, 9-, 12-month or even longer smoothing is more appropriate for a primary trend. Warnings of a probable trend reversal in the price would be offered by a reversal in the smoothed momentum index itself, as shown in Figure 13.23, example *a*, or by a penetration of the MA through a designated overbought or oversold level, as in example *b*. The level of the dashed overbought and oversold barrier would be determined on a trial-and-error basis, with reference to a historical study of the relationship between the price and the momentum curve.

   If the momentum series is found to be unduly volatile, it is always possible to smooth out fluctuations by calculating an even longer-term MA, or by smoothing the MA itself with an additional calculation.

   Another possibility is to construct an oscillator by combining the MAs of three or four ROCs and weighting them according to their time span. This possibility is discussed at length in Chapter 15.

FIGURE 13.23 (a) Directional Changes of Smoothed Momentum MAs. (b) Overbought/Oversold Re-crossovers of Smoothed Momentum MAs

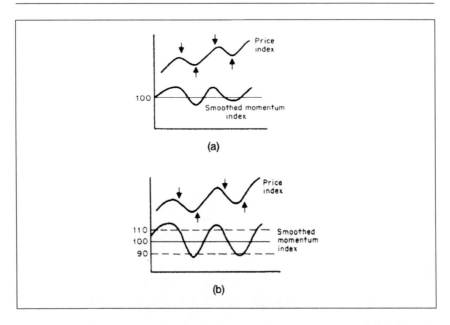

Chart 13.8 shows the effectiveness of combining two ROC indicators and smoothing them. In this case, the smoothing is a 10-month weighted average of 11- and 14-month rates of change of the S&P Composite monthly closing prices.

This was an approach devised by E. S. C. Coppock. Since this indicator has been found useful for market bottoms rather than tops, the momentum curve is significant only when it falls below the zero reference line and then rises. The arrows show that bull market signals between 1982 and 2012 were particularly timely. I have traced this indicator back to 1900 and found that only 3 signals out of 29, in 1913, 1941, and 2002, were premature. Clearly an excellent track record. Even these signals could have been filtered by requiring a positive 12-month MA crossover. Please note that this indicator can be just as easily applied to other markets or relationships.

The lower panel shows how it is possible to also incorporate trendline violations and price pattern completions using the raw data, i.e., the sum of the two ROCs.

A further variation on construction of a smoothed momentum index is to take the ROC of an MA of a price index itself. This method reverses the process described earlier, for instead of constructing an ROC and then

CHART 13.8 S&P Composite 1980–2012 Coppock Indicator

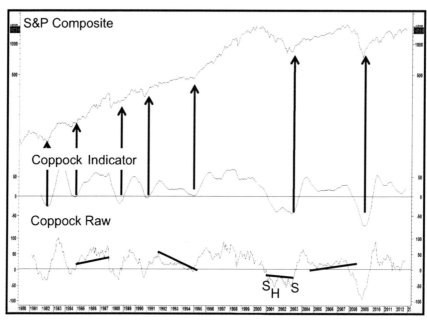

Source: From pring.com

smoothing the resulting momentum index, the price index itself is first smoothed with an MA and an ROC is taken of that smoothing.

Summary

1. Momentum is a generic term embracing many different types of oscillators.
2. Momentum measures the rate at which prices rise or fall. It gives useful indications of latent strengths or weakness in a price trend. This is because prices usually rise at their fastest pace well ahead of their peak and normally decline at their greatest speed before their ultimate low.
3. Since markets generally spend more time in a rising than a falling phase, the lead characteristic of momentum indicators is normally greater during rallies than during reactions.
4. Oscillators reflect market sentiment and have different characters in primary bull and bear markets.
5. There are two basic methods of interpreting momentum: momentum characteristics and momentum trend reversals.
6. Momentum signals should *always* be used in conjunction with a trend-reversal signal by the actual price.

14

MOMENTUM II: INDIVIDUAL INDICATORS

It is recommended that you study all of the momentum indicators described in this and the next chapter, subsequently selecting the two or three with which you feel intuitively comfortable with. Following too many indicators will likely lead to confusion. If you wish to find a more in-depth explanation of these and many other momentum indicators, please refer to my *Definitive Guide to Momentum Indicators* (Marketplace Books, 2009) or the momentum module in my online audio/visual course at Pring.com.

The RSI

The Formula

The relative strength indicator (RSI) was developed by Wells Wilder.[1] It is a momentum indicator, or oscillator, that measures the relative internal strength of a stock or market against *itself*, instead of comparing one asset with another, or a stock with a market. The formula for the RSI is as follows:

$$RSI = 100 - \frac{[100]}{1 + RS}$$

where RS = the average *of x* days' up closes divided by the average *of x* days' down closes. The indicator's design aims to overcome two problems involved in construction of a momentum indicator: (1) erratic movements and (2) the need for a constant trading band for comparison purposes.

Erratic movements are caused by sharp alterations in the values, which are dropped off in the calculation. For example, in a 20-day rate-of-change (ROC) indicator, a sharp decline or advance 20 days in the past can cause sudden shifts in the momentum line even if the current price is little changed. The RSI attempts to smooth out such distortions.

The RSI formula not only provides this smoothing characteristic, but also results in an indicator that fluctuates in a constant range between 0 and 100. The default time span recommended by Wilder is 14 days, which he justified on the basis that it was half of the 28-day lunar cycle. Unfortunately, the lunar cycle includes weekends and, therefore, has more than 14 trading days. Nonetheless, this default time span works quite well in reality, and that's what really counts.

The RSI Is Useful for Making Comparisons Between Securities

The nature of the RSI calculation allows the accurate comparison of different securities on the same chart. In Chart 14.1 there are two series:

CHART 14.1 ROC versus RSI Characteristics

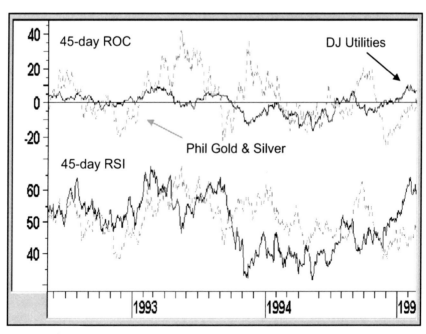

the Dow Jones Utilities and the Philadelphia Gold and Silver Share Index. The upper panel plots a 45-day ROC, and the lower one a 45-day RSI. With the ROC, it is not possible to easily compare the two because the Utilities are far less volatile. On the other hand, you can see that the divergence in volatility is far less in the lower panel featuring the RSI.

Constructing Overbought/Oversold Lines

Because of this, it is much easier to establish universal standards for the overbought and oversold benchmarks. Using the 14-day default, they are traditionally set at 30 for oversold and 70 for overbought. In an article entitled "How RSI Behaves,"[2] Peter W. Aan argued that the average value of an RSI top and bottom occurred close to the 72 and 32 levels, respectively. This research would indicate that the 70 and 30 levels recommended by Wilder should be moved further apart to better reflect the average overbought and oversold value.

It is important to note that the magnitude of the oscillations of the RSI is inverse to that of most other momentum series. For example, the ROC indicator is subject to wider fluctuations as the time span becomes longer. It works in an opposite way for the RSI. For the RSI, equilibrium is the halfway point, which in this case is the 50 level. It is, therefore, traditional to place the overbought oversold lines equidistant from this point. We should remember that longer time spans in the RSI calculation result in shallower swings and vice versa. Consequently, the 70/30 combination is inappropriate when the time span differs appreciably in either direction from the standard 14-day period. Chart 14.2, for example, features a 9-day RSI for the Hang Seng Index in Hong Kong, where an 80/20 combination gives a much better feel for the overbought/oversold extreme than the 70/30 default value. This is due to the fact that shorter time spans result in wider RSI oscillations. The lower panel features a 65-day RSI where the narrower swings result in a more appropriate 62.5/37.5 combination. In this instance, neither of the default 70/30 values is reached at any time.

The terms "long" and "short" with regard to time spans refer to the type of data under consideration in a relative sense. For example, a 60-day RSI would represent a long span for daily data, but for monthly numbers, a 60-day, i.e., 2-month, span would be very short. Some consideration should therefore be given to this factor when choosing a specific RSI time span. Chart 14.3 plots two RSIs for identical time periods (60 days or 2 months). However, the overbought/oversold lines are drawn

CHART 14.2 Hang Seng, RSI 1999–2010 Overbought/Oversold Time Span Comparisons

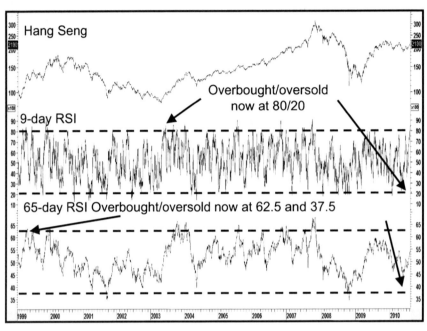

Source: From pring.com

CHART 14.3 Procter & Gamble 40-day versus 2-month RSI

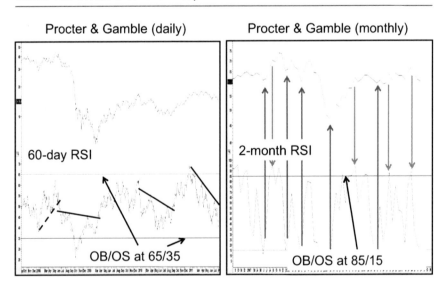

Source: From pring.com

at different levels because one calculation is based on daily and the other on monthly data.

Because RSIs based on shorter-term time spans are more volatile, they are more suitable for pointing out overbought and oversold conditions. On the other hand, longer-term spans are more stable in their trajectories and therefore lend themselves better for the purpose of constructing trendlines and price patterns.

Time Spans

The RSI can be plotted for any time span. In his book *The New Commodity Trading Systems and Methods* (Wiley, 1987). Perry Kaufman questions the exclusivity of the 14-day time span (the default) selection. He points out that maximum divergence occurs when the moving average is exactly half the time span of the dominant cycle. In other words, if you make the assumption that the primary trend of the stock market revolves around the 4-year business cycle, a moving average of 24 months will give you the greatest divergence between the high and low points of the cycle. In the case of the 28-day cycle, 14 days is the correct choice, but it is important to understand that there are many other cycles. Working on this assumption, for example, would mean that a 14-hour RSI would be inappropriate if the dominant cycle was something other than 28 hours. The same would be true for weekly and monthly data.

In practice, a 14-day time span works quite well, but only for shorter periods. I also use 9-, 25-, 30-, and 45-day spans. For weekly data, the calendar quarters operate effectively, so 13-, 26-, 39-, and 52-week spans are adopted. As for monthly charts, the same spans for the ROC are recommended, i.e., 9, 12, 18, and 24 months. For longer-term charts, covering perhaps two years of weekly data, a time span of about 8 weeks offers enough information to identify intermediate-term turning points. A 26-week RSI results in a momentum series that oscillates in a narrower range, but, nevertheless, usually lends itself to trendline construction. Very long-term charts, going back 10 to 20 years, seem to respond well to a 12-month time span. Crossovers of the 30 percent oversold and 70 percent overbought barriers give a very good idea of major long-term buying and selling points. When the RSI pushes through these extremes and then crosses back toward the 50 level, it often warns of a reversal in the primary trend. Remember, these suggested spans tend to work *consistently* well, but never *perfectly* well. If you are looking for perfection, technical analysis is probably not your best analytical choice!

CHART 14.4 S&P Composite, 1898–2012 12-Month RSI

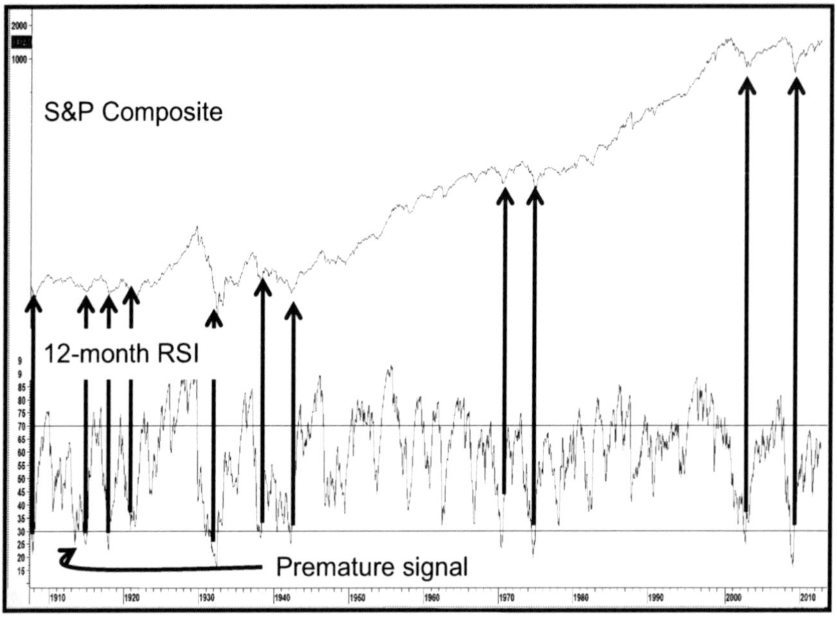

Source: From pring.com

To isolate major buy candidates, it is important to remember that the best opportunities lie where long-term momentum, such as a 12-month RSI, is oversold. In this respect, Chart 14.4 shows that an oversold reversal for the S&P using a 12-month RSI has triggered some very prescient signals in the last 100 years. As with all indicators, this one is not perfect, as you can see from the premature buy signal in the early part of the twentieth century. More care is needed in identifying tops, as equities have a natural tendency to take longer to build than to tear down. Consequently, overbought reversals have a habit of being premature, especially when the secular trend is a positive one.

Returning to buying opportunities, if you can also identify an intermediate-and a short-term oversold condition, all three trends—primary, intermediate-term, and short-term—are then in a classic position to give a high-probability buy signal.

RSI Interpretation

Some of the principal methods used to interpret the RSI are as follows.

Extreme Readings and Failure Swings   Any time an RSI moves above its overbought or below its oversold zone, it indicates the security in question is ripe for a turn. The significance depends upon the time. For example, the 45-hour RSI shown in Chart 14.7 is nowhere near as significant as an RSI constructed with a 12-month time span, as in Chart 14.4. An overbought or oversold reading merely indicates that, in terms of probabilities, a counter-reaction is overdone or overdue. It presents an opportunity to consider liquidation or acquisition, but not an actual buy or sell signal.

More often than not, the RSI traces out a divergence, as in Figure 14.1. In this case, the second crossover of the extreme level at points A and B usually offers good buy and sell alerts. These divergences are often called *failure swings*.

We see a bearish failure swing at the end of 2011 at point A in Chart 14.5 featuring a smoothed version of a 9-day RSI.

Trendline Violations and Pattern Completions   The RSI can also be used in conjunction with trendline violations. Generally speaking, the longer the time span for any particular period, i.e., daily, weekly, or monthly, the better the opportunity for trendline construction. Important buy and sell signals are generated when trendlines for both price and the RSI are violated within

FIGURE 14.1 RSI Failure Swing

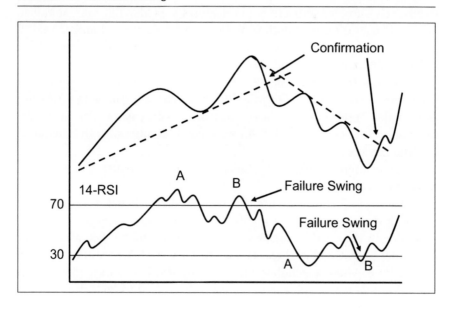

CHART 14.5 Molex, 2009–2011 Smoothed RSI

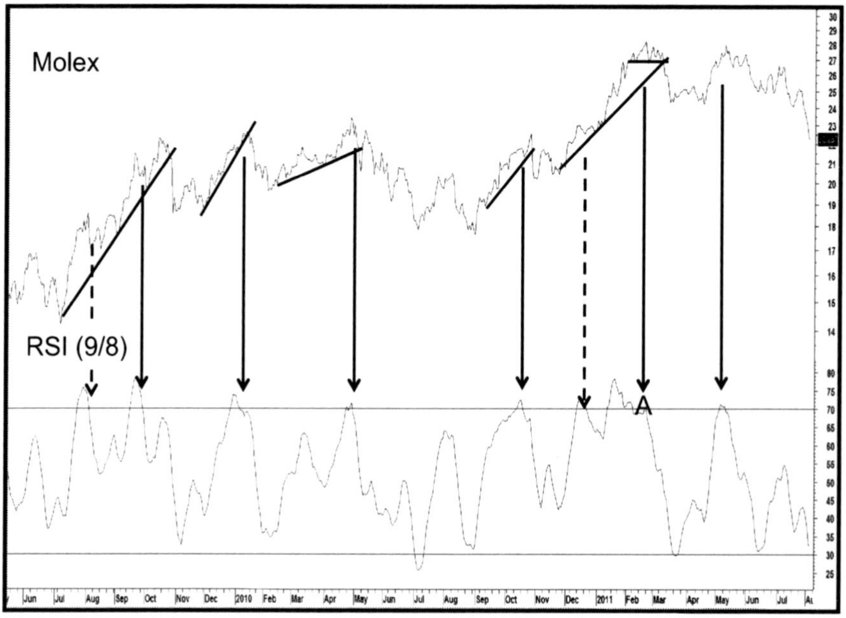

a relatively short period. Chart 14.6 features a 14-day RSI for Caterpillar. The RSI starts off after a decline by forming a reverse head-and-shoulders pattern, which is more or less simultaneously confirmed by the price. After a good rally materializes, the RSI violates this up trendline. Note how the extended line becomes resistance for the final rally. We can also construct a trendline for the price. Finally, the RSI completes a broadening formation with a flat bottom, and a nasty downside break ensues. The next rally peak also experiences a small RSI top, which is confirmed with a trendline violation by the price.

An example of the RSI's ability to form price patterns is shown in Charts 14.6 and 14.7.

Chart 14.7 shows an hourly chart for Intel. It has a 45-hour RSI in the lower panel, which roughly corresponds to a week of trading. I have drawn the overbought/oversold lines at 62 and 38. See what a nice combination of trendline breaks we get in April 2011. We see another setup in late June, where a trendline break on the RSI is confirmed by one on the price. It's even possible to observe a right-angled triangle. If you study

CHART 14.6 Caterpillar, 2009–2010 RSI and Price Patterns

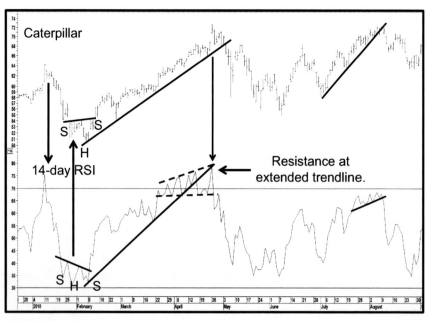

Source: From pring.com

CHART 14.7 Intel and a 45-Hour RSI Featuring Price Patterns

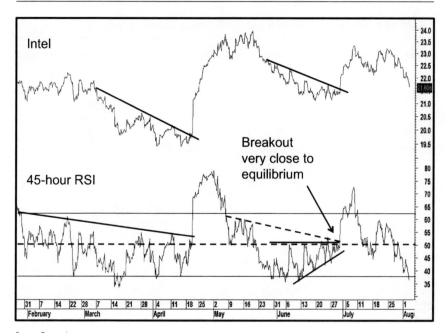

Source: From pring.com

the equilibrium line at 50, it's apparent that the strong late June breakout develops slightly above this critical point of balance.

Smoothing the RSI   It is a perfectly legitimate technique to smooth the RSI. One of my favorite approaches is to smooth a 9-day RSI with an 8-day moving average (MA). Because the fluctuations are not as great as the raw data, the overbought/oversold lines are drawn at 70 and 30, not my usual default of 80/20 for a 9-day span.

Chart 14.5, featuring Molex, contains a 9-day RSI smoothed with an 8-day MA. The downward-pointing arrows flag all of the overbought reversals. The solid ones show confirmed reversals with varying degrees of success. The dashed arrows indicate overbought reversals where it was not possible to construct a meaningful trendline. Needless to say, they were all failures.

RSI and Peak-and-Trough Progression   The RSI often traces out a series of rising or falling peaks and troughs, which, when reversed, offer important buy or sell alerts. Chart 14.8 shows that the 14-day RSI for Suntrust Banks experienced two peak and trough reversals, each of which was confirmed by a price trend break. These are flagged by the arrows.

CHART 14.8 Sun Trust Banks, 1997 RSI and Peak-and-Trough Analysis

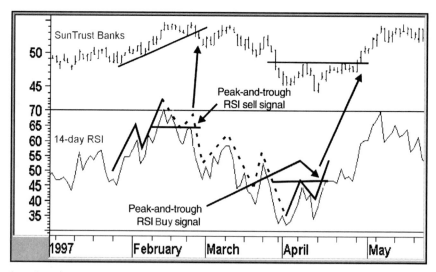

Source: From pring.com

Two Variations on the RSI

Chande Momentum Oscillator

The Chande Momentum Oscillator (CMO), named after its inventor Dr. Tushar Chande, is a variation on the RSI, yet is uniquely different. It has three characteristics:

1. The calculations are based on data that have not been smoothed. This means that extreme short-term movements are not hidden, so the indicator reaches overbought/oversold extremes more often, but not enough to result in too many signals.
2. The scale is confined within the –100 to +100 range. This means that the zero level becomes the equilibrium point. With the RSI, the 50 level is the equilibrium point, and is not always readily identifiable. With zero as the pivotal point, it is easier to see those periods when momentum is positive and those when it is negative. The zero equilibrium, therefore, makes comparisons between different securities that much easier as well.
3. The formula uses both up and down days in the calculation.

Interpretation   Chart 14.9 compares a 14-day RSI with a 14-day CMO. The first thing to notice is that the CMO reaches an overbought/oversold extreme more times than the RSI—in February and June of 2000 and January of 2001, for instance. Sometimes it is possible to construct timelier and better trendlines for the CMO, though occasionally it works the other way. The March 2000 break, for instance, came off a better trendline for the CMO than the RSI; so, too, did the breaks from trendline AB and CD. The two trendlines in the summer of 2000 were slightly better for the RSI. Note also that both series experienced positive divergences at the October 2000 low, but that for the CMO was a much stronger signal, since the September bottom was well above that of mid-October. It doesn't always work in favor of the CMO, but I prefer it because of the more numerous overbought/oversold readings and the plus and minus scaling, which makes it easier to spot positive and negative readings.

One approach that I have found helpful is to plot a 20-day CMO and smooth it with a 10-day MA, such as that plotted in Chart 14.10. I then take a smoothing of this indicator—in this case, a 10-day simple moving average. That's the dashed line that hugs close to the CMO, using the crossovers to generate buy and sell alerts. However, since there are a lot

CHART 14.9 FTSE, 2000–2001 Comparing the RSI with the CMO

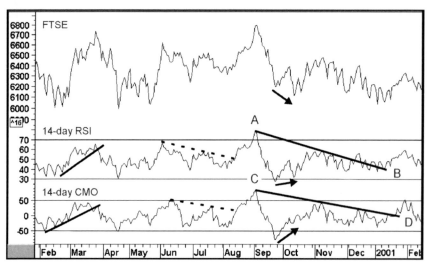

Source: From pring.com

CHART 14.10 Heng Seng, 1998–2000 Smoothed CMO

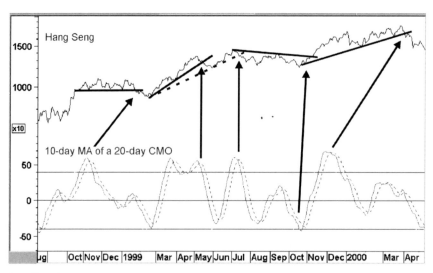

Source: From pring.com

of moving-average crossovers, it's important to try to filter out those that are not likely to work out. That's done by taking crossovers that develop at an extreme level more seriously, since they tend to be more accurate. Then make sure that this is confirmed by a trend break in the price. Some examples are shown in the chart.

Relative Momentum Index

The relative momentum index, or RMI, is another variation on the RSI. When calculating the RMI, the standard RSI formula is modified to allow for a momentum factor. The actual formula by Roger Altman was published in the February 1993 *Stocks and Commodities* magazine article.

This modification has two effects. First, it smooths the indicator, and second, it accentuates the degree of the fluctuation. The result is a less jagged oscillator that experiences more overbought/oversold readings. The RMI requires two parameters: the time frame and the momentum factor.

If the RMI has a momentum factor of 1, the indicator is identical to the RSI. It is only when the momentum factor is greater than 1 that the two series diverge. Chart 14.11 shows two variations on the RMI. The middle panel features a 14-day span with an 8-day momentum factor, and the lower

CHART 14.11 ATT 1996–2001 Two RMI Variations

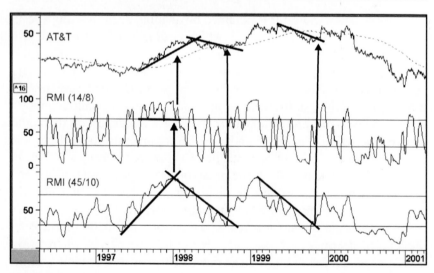

Source: From pring.com

one a 45-day span with a 10-day momentum factor. Since it is an RSI-based indicator, longer-term spans involve less volatility. Note that the fluctuations in the 45-day series are much less pronounced than the 14-day RMI.

Generally speaking, the longer-term span offers slower and more deliberate movements that lend themselves more easily to trendline construction. Several examples are shown in Chart 14.11, but I particularly like the late 1998 signal since it is confirmed by a simultaneous breakout above the trendline and the 200-day MA. Whenever a price crosses above a trendline and reliable moving average simultaneously, it emphasizes the strength of the signal since they reinforce each other as dynamic resistance areas.

RSI Conclusion

Most of the time, the RSI and its two variations, like all oscillators, are not telling us very much. It can be really useful when it triggers divergences, complete price patterns, or violate trendlines. When such characteristics are also confirmed by a trend-reversal signal in the price itself, it is usually a wise policy to pay attention because the RSI has a good record of reliability.

Trend Deviation (Price Oscillator)

A trend-deviation indicator is obtained by dividing or subtracting a security's price by a measure of trend, which is usually a form of MA. It is also possible to base a trend deviation using linear regression techniques. However, we will concentrate on the moving-average technique here. This approach is also called a "price oscillator" in some charting packages. Of the two approaches, subtraction or division, division is preferred since it is more reflective of proportionate moves. For a discussion on this topic, you are referred to Chapters 6 and 8, which compare the logarithmic and arithmetic scales. Chart 14.12 plots the two approaches using a 1/10 price oscillator. The "1" and "10" in the price oscillator legend refer to the fact that a 1-day MA (i.e., the close) is divided by a 10-day MA. Note how the volatility becomes exaggerated as the point movements in the gold price become greater in the last few years. The division calculation returns far more rational swings in the indicator. For short-term charts, where prices do not experience large percentage movements between the low and the high, this is not an important distinction. However, when prices are being

CHART 14.12 Spot Gold, 1985–2011 Comparing Price Oscillator Comparing Subtraction and Division Calculations

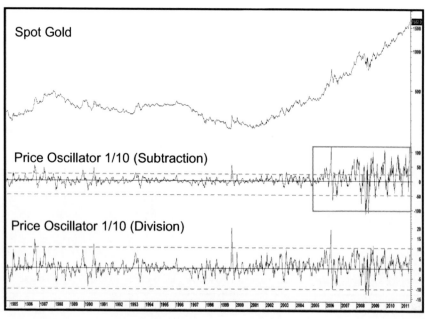

Source: From pring.com

compared over many years and there is a substantial net loss or gain over that period, it is wiser to adopt the division approach.

Since the average represents the trend being monitored, the momentum indicator shows how fast the price is advancing or declining in relation to that trend. An oscillator based on a trend-deviation calculation is, in fact, a horizontal representation of the envelope analysis discussed in Chapter 12, but it also shows subtle changes of underlying technical strengths and weaknesses. The top panel of Chart 14.13 shows the price of Brookline Bancorp and its 50-day MA. Two bands at +10 and −10 percent of the 50-day MA have been plotted above and below it. The bottom panel represents the same data but expressed in momentum (price oscillator) format. Therefore, the MA appears as the equilibrium line at zero and the two bands as overbought and oversold levels at +10 and −10 percent. In this way a negative zero crossover is the same as a negative 50-day crossover and so forth.

The interpretation of a trend-deviation indicator is based on the same principles described in Chapter 13. This method can be used to identify divergences and overbought and oversold zones, but it appears to come

CHART 14.13 Brookline Bancorp, 2010–2011 Price Oscillator Interpretation

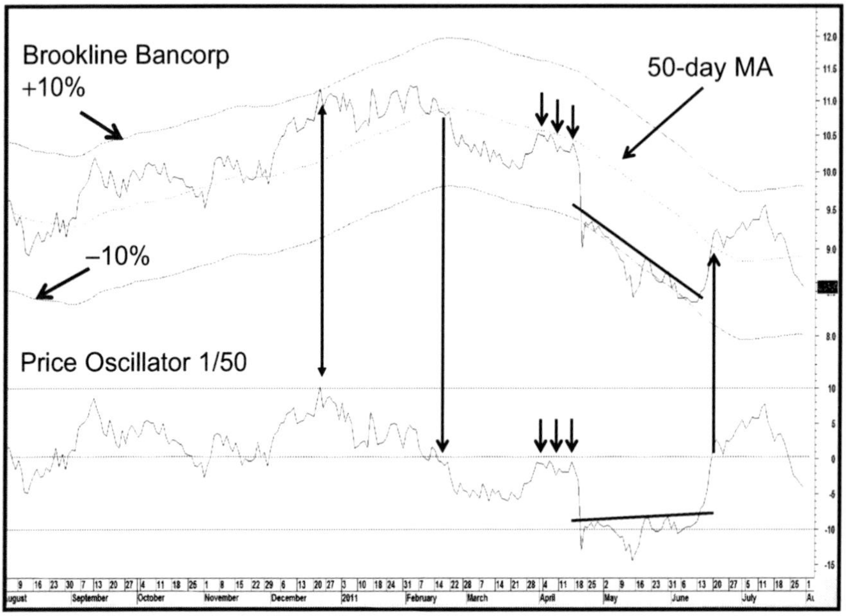

Source: From pring.com

into its own when used in conjunction with trendline construction and MA crossovers.

Trendline Construction

Chart 14.14 shows the crude oil price together with a trend deviation calculated from a close divided by a 45-day MA. This is a fairly jagged indicator and lends itself to overbought/oversold, trendline, and price pattern analysis. We see a good example of a descending triangle break along with a price confirmation in May 2011. Later on, there is barely any upside momentum at point A, and the price and oscillator both subsequently violate trendlines. Most of the time it's not possible to forecast the character of a price move following a technical event. In this case, though, the very weak positive momentum at A indicated the vulnerability of the situation. Later on, in June 2012, we see an unconfirmed reverse head and shoulders in the oscillator. I say "unconfirmed" because it was not really possible to construct a meaningful down trendline on the price. Finally, a

CHART 14.14 Light Crude, 2011–2012 Price Oscillator Interpretation

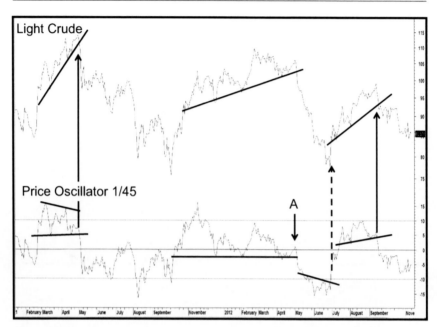

Source: From pring.com

price pattern completion for the oscillator and a trendline violation for the price leave the chart with a confirmed short-term downtrend.

Trend Deviation and MAs

An alternative approach with trend deviation indicators is to smooth out unwanted volatility with the aid of two MAs, as shown in Chart 14.15. The actual trend-deviation series is calculated by taking a 26-week MA of the closing price divided by a 52-week MA. The second series is simply a 10-week MA of the first. Buy and sell alerts are then triggered as the smoothed trend-deviation indicator crosses above or below its 10-week MA. Then look for a confirmation from the price itself. Two examples are shown in Chart 14.15, one for a top and the other for a bottom. This is very much a guerilla approach because the buy alert indicated by the dashed arrow was signaled almost at the top of the rally. This example demonstrates the importance of picking and choosing between signals, only selecting those that develop close to a turning point. If this filtering

CHART 14.15 S&P Airlines, 1995–2001, and a Smoothed Trend-Deviation Indicator

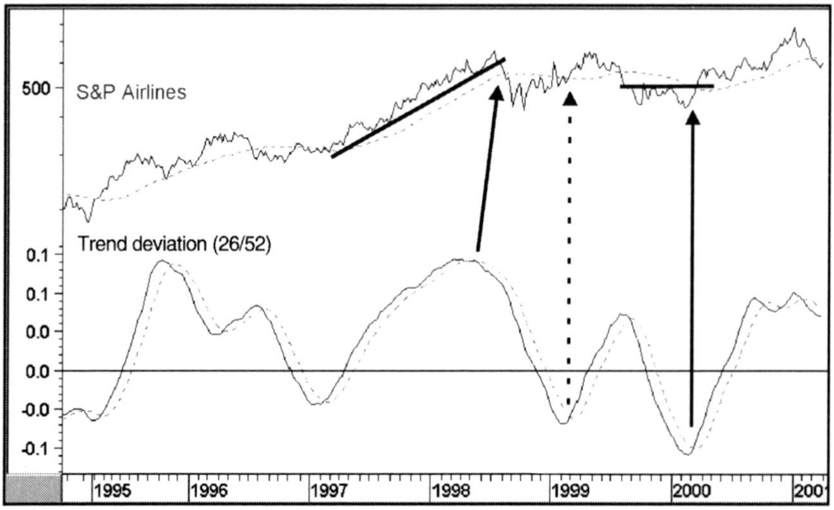

Source: From pring.com

approach is not taken, then there is considerable risk that action will be taken close to the end of the trend.

A useful method that greatly reduces such whipsaw activity but still offers timely signals is to lag the 52-week MA by 10 weeks when the trend-deviation calculation is being made. This means that each weekly close is divided by the 52-week MA as it appeared 10 weeks before. This new calculation has been plotted in the center panel of Chart 14.16.

In this example, the whipsaw in late 2000 was filtered out since the trend-deviation indicator fails to cross decisively below its MA. I am not suggesting this is the only legitimate combination for weekly charts, but it is one that appears to operate quite well. There is always a trade-off when you try to make signals less sensitive, and in this case, we find that there is occasionally a small delay compared to the nonlagged 52-week MA. The most obvious one on this chart developed at the beginning of 1997, where the lagged series in the center panel crossed its MA at a slightly higher price. In most instances though, this is a small price to pay if a costly whipsaw can be avoided.

MACD

The moving-average convergence divergence (MACD) trading method is form of trend-deviation indicator using two exponential moving averages,

CHART 14.16 S&P Airlines, 1995–2001, and Two Smoothed Trend-Dev

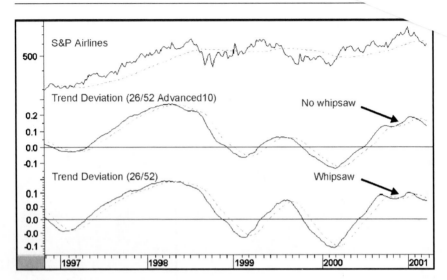

Source: From pring.com

the shorter being subtracted from the longer. The two MAs are usually calculated on an exponential basis in which more recent periods are more heavily weighted than in the case of a simple MA. It is normal for the MACD to then be smoothed by a third exponential moving average (EMA), which is plotted separately on the chart. This average is known as the "signal line," the crossovers of which generate buy and sell signals. It obtains its name from the fact that the two EMAs are continually converging and then diverging from each other. The MACD has gained great popularity over the years, but in effect, it is really just another variation on a trend-deviation indicator that employs two EMAs as its method of deviation. A visual of its construction is therefore very similar to Chart 14.13.

MACDs can be used in an infinite number of time periods. Gerald Appel of Signalert,[3] who has done a considerable amount of research on the subject, recommends that buy signals on a daily chart be constructed from a combination of 8, 17, and 9 exponential MAs, but he feels that sell signals are more reliable when triggered on the basis of a 12, 25, and 9 combination. On the other hand, the popular MetaStock program plots the default values as 12 and 26 with the signal line at 9.

Chart 14.17 shows Microsoft in 2011 and 2012. The dotted arrows indicate whipsaw signals, and the long arrows indicate those signals that were confirmed with a trendline break of some kind.

CHART 14.17 Microsoft, 2010–2011 MACD Interpretation

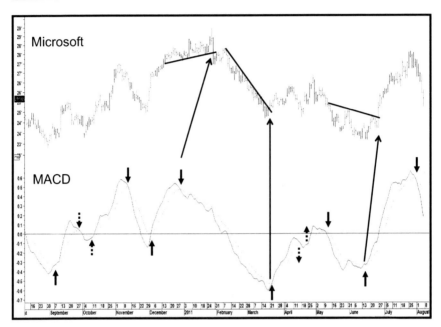

Source: From pring.com

General Electric is shown with an MACD indicator in Chart 14.18. Another technique is to construct overbought/oversold lines, trendlines, and price patterns and to look for divergences. In Chart 14.18, for instance, both series complete head-and-shoulders patterns at the end of the year 2000. The MACD also experiences a negative divergence. Note how the divergence, flagged by the right shoulder, is barely able to rally above zero. The result is an above-average decline. Note also that the indicator remained below the equilibrium point and touched its oversold level several times during the balance of the period covered by the chart. This type of action reflects bear market activity.

The MACD often works well with monthly data. In this respect, we look at the CRB Spot Raw Industrial Commodity Index in Chart 14.19, where the solid arrows indicate good primary-trend momentum buy signals. The two dashed ones indicate smaller rallies, which fall into the failure category.

The MACD is often plotted in a histogram format and the signal line against it, as in Chart 14.20 featuring Homestake Mining. The chart shows a classic head-and-shoulders pattern. Note that the MACD

CHART 14.18 General Electric and an MACD Indicator

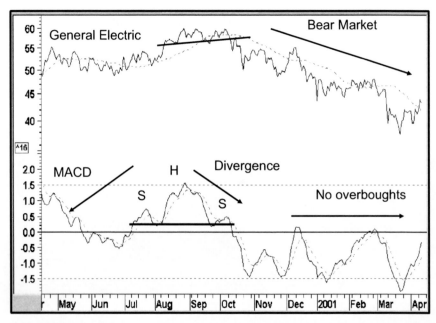

Source: From pring.com

CHART 14.19 CRB Spot Raw Industrials, 1977–2012 Long-Term MACD Buy Signals

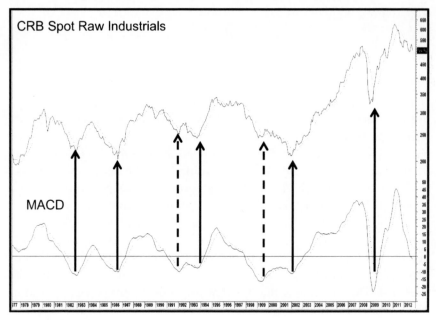

Source: From pring.com

CHART 14.20 Homestake Mining and an MACD in Histogram Format

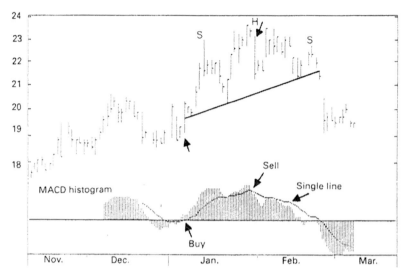

histogram gradually became weaker as the pattern progressed. This was only a short-term sell signal, but the price eventually fell below the signal level.

Stochastics

The stochastic indicator has also gained a great deal of popularity among futures traders, with the result that the standard formula uses very short-term time spans. The theory behind the indicator, which was invented by George Lane,[4] is that prices tend to close near the upper end of a trading range during an uptrend. As the trend matures, the tendency for prices to close away from the high of the session becomes pronounced. In a downward-moving market, the reverse conditions hold true.

The stochastic indicator, therefore, attempts to measure the points in a rising trend at which the closing prices tend to cluster around the lows for the period in question, and vice versa, since these are the conditions that signal trend reversals. It is plotted as two lines: the %K line and the %D line. The %D line is the one that provides the major signals and is, therefore, more important.

The formula for calculation of %K is:

$$\%K = 100[(C - L_5\text{close})/(H_5 - L_5)]$$

where C is the most recent close, L_5 is the lowest low for the last five trading periods, and H_5 is the highest high for the same five trading periods. Remember that the calculation of stochastic indicators differs from that of most other momentum indicators in that it requires high, low, and closing data for the calculation.

The stochastic formula is similar to the RSI in that the plots can never exceed 0 or 100, but in this case, it measures the closing price in relation to the total price range for a selected number of periods. A very high reading in excess of 80 would put the closing price for the period near the top of the range, while a low reading under 20 would put it near the bottom of the range.

The second line, %D, is a smoothed version of the %K line. The normal value is three periods. The %D formula is as follows:

$$\%D = 100 \times (H_3/L_3)$$

where H_3 is the three-period sum of $(C - L_5)$ and L_3 is the three-period sum of $(H_5 - L_5)$.

The momentum indicator that results from these calculations is two lines that fluctuate between 0 and 100. The %K line is usually plotted as a solid line, while the slower %D line is usually plotted as a dashed line.

The popularity of the stochastic indicator can no doubt be explained by the smooth manner in which it moves from an overbought to an oversold condition, lulling a trader into feeling that price trends are much more orderly than would appear from an observation of an RSI or an ROC indicator.

Longer-term time frames, used on monthly and weekly charts, appear to work much better than the shorter-term stochastics used on daily futures charts. Colby and Meyers, in *The Encyclopedia of Technical Market Indicators* (McGraw-Hill, 2002),[5] noted that the stochastic indicator tested very poorly relative to MA crossovers and other momentum indicators.

Overbought and oversold bands for the stochastic are usually plotted in the 75 to 85 percent area on the upside and in the 15 to 25 percent area on the downside, depending on the time span in question. An overbought indication is given when the %D line crosses the extreme band, but an actual sell alert is not indicated until the %K line crosses below it. When the two lines cross, they behave very similarly to a dual MA system. If you wait for the penetration, you can avoid getting trapped into shorting a strongly bullish move or buying an extremely negative one.

The behavior of the indicator will depend very much on the selected time frames. Since the %K and %D can be thought of as moving averages, it follows that the longer the time span, the smoother the resultant indicator. The upper panel of Chart 14.21 shows a very volatile 5/5 combination, whereas the lower window contains a 30/100 combination. Note that the %K is much less volatile than that in the upper window. The same is true for the 100 parameter used in the %D. However, it is so flat that it is essentially useless from the point of view of reflecting the cyclic rhythms. In reality, one would never use such a combination.

Slowed Stochastic

It is also possible (and desirable) to extend the calculation in order to invoke a slowed version of the stochastic. In this instance, the %K line is replaced with the %D line, and another MA is calculated for the %D. Many technicians argue that this modified stochastic version gives more accurate signals. It certainly results in a more deliberate action. A comparison between a regular and a slowed stochastic is featured in Chart 14.22.

CHART 14.21 S&P Composite, 2010–2011 Comparing Two Stochastic Time Spans

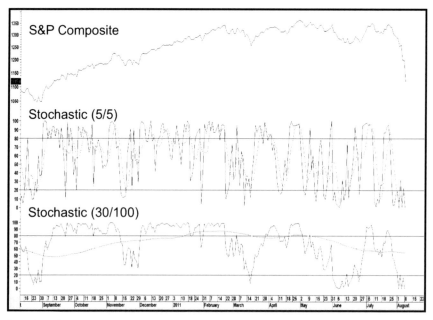

Source: From pring.com

CHART 14.22 S&P Composite, 2010–2011 Comparing a Stochastic with a Slowed Stochastic

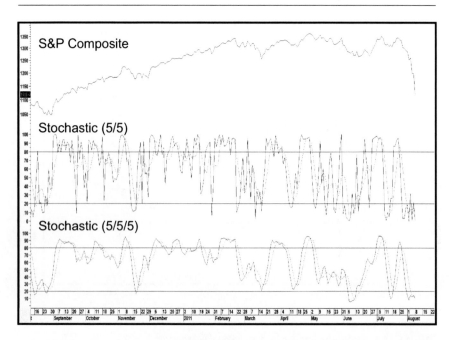

The 5/5 in the upper window legend refers to a 5 period for the %K and D, respectively. The 5 in the middle of the lower window legend refers to the slowing factor.

Chart 14.22 compares a regular stochastic to a slowed one.

General Interpretation

Crossovers   Normally, the faster %K line changes direction sooner than the %D line. This means that the crossover will occur before the %D line has reversed direction, as in Figure 14.2.

Divergences   Figure 14.3 shows examples of where the %K fails to confirm a new high or low in the price, thereby setting up a divergence, which when confirmed, signals a change in trend.

Divergence Failure   An important indication of a possible change in trend arises when the %K line crosses the %D line, moves back to test its extreme level, and fails to cross the %D line, as in Figure 14.4.

FIGURE 14.2 Stochastic Crossovers

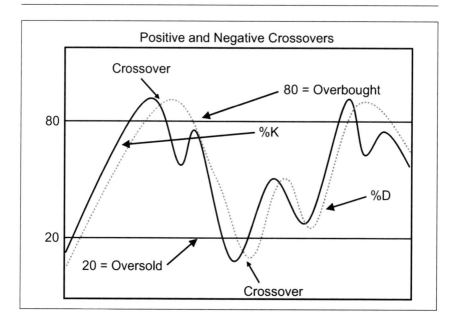

FIGURE 14.3 Stochastic Positive and Negative Divergences

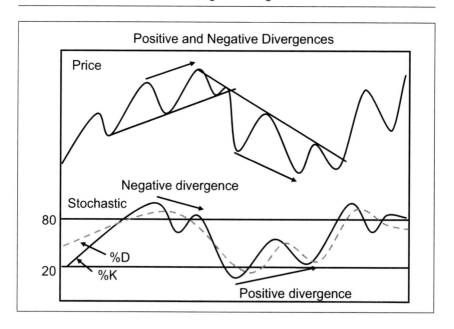

FIGURE 14.4 Stochastic Divergence Failure

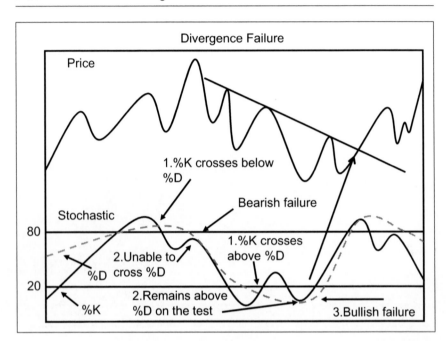

Once again, it is always important to see some price confirmation, and that is given with the break above the down trendline in the right side of the diagram.

Chart 14.23 shows some examples of divergence failures: two confirmed bearish ones and one unconfirmed bullish one

Reverse Divergence   Occasionally during an uptrend, the %D line will make a lower low, which is associated with a higher low in the price, as shown in Figure 14.5.

This is a bearish omen, and conventional wisdom suggests looking for a selling opportunity on the next rally. This condition is sometimes referred to as a *bear setup*. A positive reverse divergence is featured in Figure 14.6.

Extremes   Occasionally the %K value reaches the extreme of 100 or 0. This indicates that a very powerful move is under way, since the price is consistently closing near its high or low. If a successful test of this extreme occurs following a pullback, it is usually an excellent entry point.

CHART 14.23 Microsoft and Divergence Failures

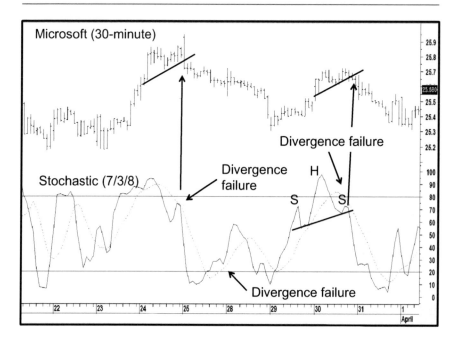

FIGURE 14.5 Stochastic Negative Reverse Divergence

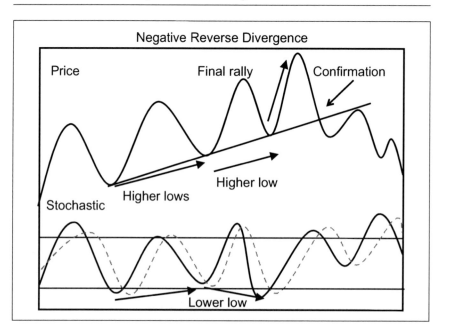

FIGURE 14.6 Stochastic Positive Reverse Divergence

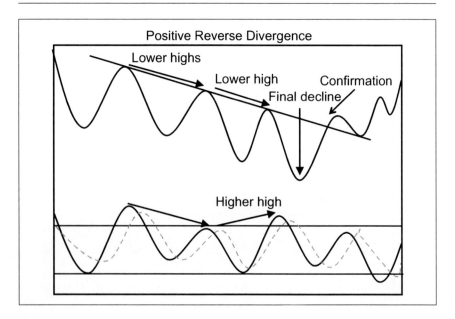

Hinge   When either the %K line or the %D line experiences a slowdown in velocity, indicated by a flattening line, the indication is usually that a reversal will take place in the next period. Examples are shown in Figure 14.7 and Chart 14.24 in the form of a 10-minute chart for Pfizer.

Slowing It Down for Better Signals

It is often a useful idea to tweak the parameters to obtain a slower-moving indicator where %K and %D crossovers can be used to good effect. Chart 14.25, featuring the S&P Composite, shows a 20/20/20 and a 20/10/10 combination. Both show divergences, but the smoother series experiences just one whipsaw, whereas the 20/10/10 variety experiences three. The trade-off is that the more volatile series triggers crossovers on a timelier basis.

Finally, we move up to the monthly charts where the 24/15/10 combination in Chart 14.26 really comes into its own. This combination, in most cases, will reflect primary trend swings in a fairly good way. For example, there is a positive stochastic crossover at the end of the 2000–2002 bear market confirmed with a nice trendline violation.

FIGURE 14.7 Stochastic Hinges

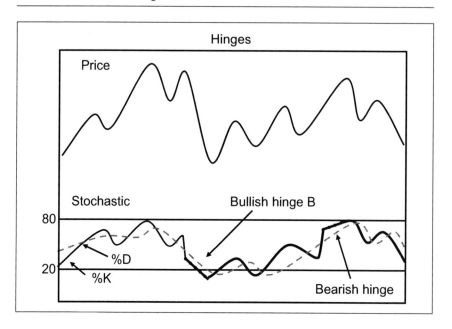

CHART 14.24 Pfizer and Two Hinges

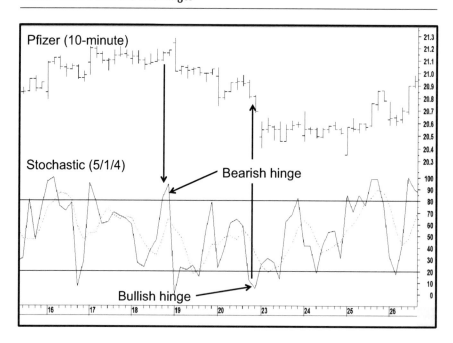

CHART 14.25 S&P Composite, 2010–2011 Negative Divergences

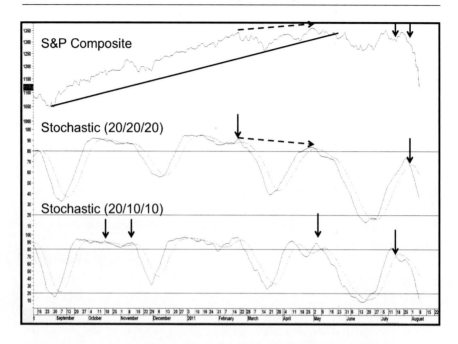

CHART 14.26 Echostar, 1998–2011 Stochastic with Long-Term Crossover Signals

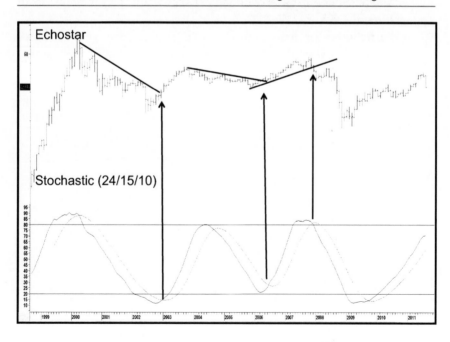

There was another buy signal confirmed in 2006. Finally, a sell signal in late 2007 was essentially confirmed simultaneously with a trendline penetration.

Summary

1. The RSI is bounded by 0 and 100. Overbought and oversold lines should be wider as the time span gets shorter.
2. The RSI lends itself more easily to comparing the momentum of different securities than does the ROC.
3. The RSI can be used in conjunction with overbought and oversold lines, divergences, price patterns, trendlines, and smoothings.
4. Trend-deviation indicators are calculated by dividing the close or a short-term MA by a longer-term one.
5. Trend-deviation indicators can be used with trendlines, price patterns, and MAs. They also lend themselves to overbought/oversold and divergence analysis.
6. The MACD is a form of trend-deviation indicator.
7. The stochastic indicator assumes that prices close near the low at the end of a rally and near their highs at the end of a downtrend.
8. The stochastic indicator is confined between 0 and 100 and consists of two lines, the %K and the %D.
9. Stochastic indicators lend themselves to crossovers, divergences, hinges, extremes, and reverse divergences and are usually plotted in their slowed version.

15

MOMENTUM III: INDIVIDUAL INDICATORS

Summed ROC: "Know Sure Thing" (KST)

The Long-Term KST

We are going to start off this KST explanation by discussing an indicator suitable for price swings associated with primary trends or those that revolve around the so-called 4-year business cycle, subsequently turning to its application for intermediate- and short-term trends.

Chapter 13 explained that rate of change (ROC) measures the speed of an advance or decline over a specific time span, and is calculated by dividing the price in the current period by the price N periods ago. The longer the time span under consideration, the greater the significance of the trend being measured. Movements in a 10-day ROC are far less meaningful than those calculated over a 12- or 24-month time span and so forth.

The use of an ROC indicator helps to explain some of the cyclical movements in markets, often giving advance warning of a reversal in the prevailing trend, but *a specific time frame used in an ROC calculation reflects only one cycle*. If that particular cycle is not operating, is dominated by another one, or is influenced by a combination of cycles, it will be of little value.

> **Major Technical Principle** At any one time, price is determined by the interaction of many different time cycles. An indicator that takes this into consideration is likely to be timelier without losing too much in the way of sensitivity.

CHART 15.1 S&P Composite, 1978–1988 Three Rates of Change

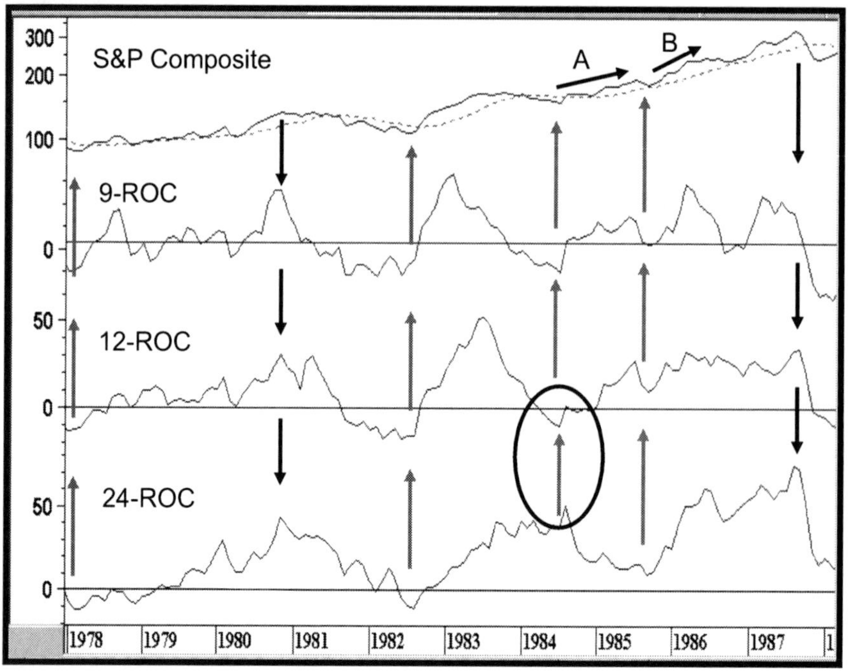

Source: From pring.com

This point is illustrated in Chart 15.1, which shows three ROC indicators of different time spans: 9 months, 12 months, and 24 months.

The 9-month ROC tends to reflect all of the intermediate moves, and the 24-month series sets the scene for the major swings. The arrows flag the important turning points in this period. They show that, for the most part, all three ROCs are moving in the same direction once the new trend gets under way. A major exception occurred at the 1984 bottom. Here we see the price rise, but immediately after, the 24-month ROC declines while the others continue on up. During the period covered by arrow A, the speed of the advance is curtailed because of the conflict between the three cycles. Later on, though, all three ROCs get back in gear on the upside, and the rally approximated by arrow B is much steeper. In effect, major turning points tend to occur when several cycles are in agreement, and speedy advances and declines develop when more cycles are operating in the same direction. Even this is a fairly limited view because there are far more than three cycles operating at any one point in time.

CHART 15.2 S&P Composite, 1980–2012 and a Smoothed 24-Month ROC

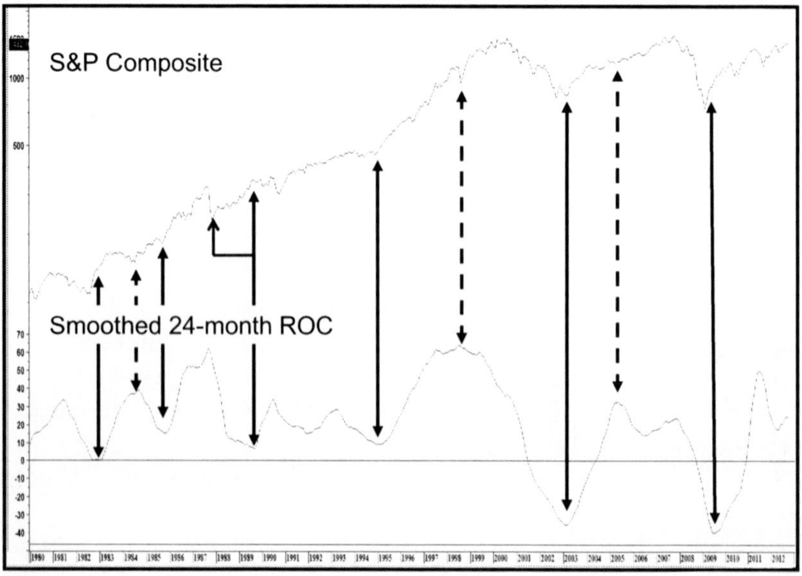

Source: From pring.com

Clearly, one ROC time span taken on its own does not give us a complete picture. This was one of the factors considered in the design phase of the KST. Another requirement was an indicator that fairly closely reflected the major price swings over the time period under consideration, primary trends for monthly charts, short-term trends for daily charts, and so forth.

Chart 15.2 shows the S&P during the 1980–2012 period.

The oscillator is a 24-month ROC smoothed with a 9-month MA. This series certainly reflects all of the primary trend swings during this period. However, if we use the indicator's changes in direction as signals, close examination shows that there is a lot to be desired. For example, the 1984 low is signaled with a peak in the oscillator. Similarly, the 1989 bottom in the momentum series develops almost at the rally peak. Also, the 1998 low was signaled with a peak in the oscillator, and the 2005 momentum peak was clearly premature. What is needed, then, is an indicator that reflects the major trend, yet is sensitive enough to reverse fairly closely to the turning points in the price. We are never going to achieve perfection in this task, but a good way of moving toward these goals is to construct an indicator that includes several ROCs of differing time spans. The function of longer time frames is to reflect the primary swings, while the inclusion of the shorter ones helps to speed up the turning points. The formula for the KST is as follows:

TABLE 15.1 Formula for Time Frames Used in the Long-Term KST

Time Frame	Smoothing		Weight
9-month	6-MA	×	1
12-month	6-MA	×	2
18-month	6-MA	×	3
24-month	9-MA	×	4

Since the most important thing is for the indicator to reflect the primary swings, the formula is weighted so that the longer, more dominant time spans have a larger influence.

Chart 15.3 compares the performance of the smoothed 24-month ROC to the long-term KST between 1974 and 1990. It is fairly self-evident that the KST reflects all of the major swings being experienced by the smoothed

CHART 15.3 S&P Composite, 1974–1991 The KST Compared to a 24-Month Smoothed ROC

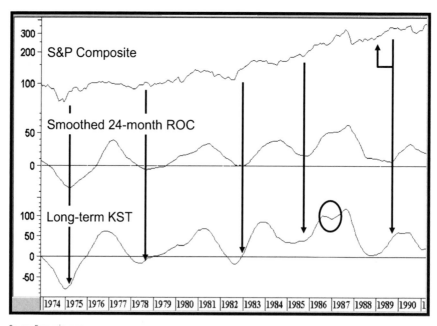

24-month ROC. However, the KST turning points develop sooner than those of the ROC. The vertical arrows slice through the ROC as it bottoms out. In every instance, the KST turns ahead of the arrow, the lead time varying with each particular cycle. Note how in 1988 the KST turns well after the 1987 bottom, but just at the time when the market begins to take off on the upside. The ROC reverses direction much later. There is one period when the KST underperformed, and that is contained within the 1986–1987 ellipse where the KST gave a false signal of weakness, unlike the ROC, which continued on up.

The dominant time frame in the KST's construction is a 24-month period, which is half of the so-called 4-year business cycle. This means that it will work best when the security in question is experiencing a primary uptrend and downtrend based on the business cycle. For example, Chart 15.4 shows the KST during the 1960s and 1970s, where the S&P was in a clearly defined business cycle–type trading range. Periods of accumulation and distribution occur between the time when the KST

CHART 15.4 S&P Composite, 1963–1979 Long-Term KST in a Volatile Cyclical Environment

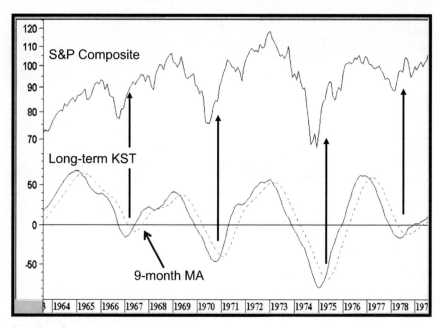

Source: From pring.com

and its moving average (MA) change direction. There are really three levels of signaling. The first occurs when the indicator itself changes direction, the second when it crosses its 9-month MA, and the third when the MA itself reverses direction. In most cases, the MA crossover offers the best combination of timely signals with a minimum of whipsaws. Changes in the direction of the 9-month MA offer the most reliable signals, but these usually develop well after the turning point. The timeliest and most reliable signals thereby develop in those situations where the MA reverses close to a turning point. If it does not, this event should merely be interpreted as a confirmation of a move that is already in progress.

For the most part, the KST has been reasonably reliable, but like any other technical approach, it is by no means perfect. For instance, the same calculation is shown in Chart 15.5, but this time, for the Nikkei. During periods of a secular or linear uptrend (as occurred for Japanese equities in the 1970s and 1980s), this type of approach is counterproductive since many false bear signals are triggered. However, in the vast majority of

CHART 15.5 Nikkei, 1975–1992 KST Operating in a Linear Trend Environment

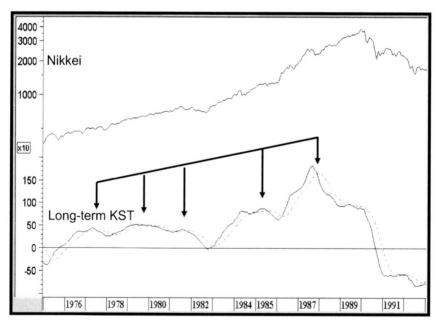

Source: From pring.com

situations, prices do not experience such linear trends, but are sensitive to the business cycle. It is for this reason that I call this indicator the KST. The letters stand for "know sure thing" (KST). Most of the time, the indicator is reliable, but you "know" that it's not a "sure thing."

> **Major Technical Principle**   The KST should always be used in conjunction with other indicators.

The principles of interpreting the long-term KST are the same as any other oscillator, though its "default" technique is to observe positive and negative MA crossovers. Occasionally, it's possible to construct trendlines and even observe price patterns, as well as conduct overbought/oversold analysis.

Short- and Intermediate-Term KSTs

The KST concept was originally derived for long-term trends, but the idea of four smoothed and summed ROCs can just as easily be applied to short-term, intermediate, and even intraday price swings. Formulas for various time frames are presented in Table 15.2. These are by no means the last word and are suggested merely as good starting points for further analysis.

TABLE 15.2 Suggested KST Formulas*

	ROC	MA	Weight	ROC	MA	Weight	ROC	MA	Weight	ROC	MA	Weight
Short-term[†]	10	10	1	15	10	2	20	10	3	30	15	4
Short-term[‡]	3	3[¶]	1	4	4[¶]	2	6	6[¶]	3	10	8[¶]	4
Intermediate-term[‡]	10	10	1	13	13	2	15	15	3	20	20	4
Intermediate-term[‡]	10	10[¶]	1	13	13[¶]	2	15	15[¶]	3	20	20[¶]	4
Long-term[§]	9	6	1	12	6	2	18	6	3	24	9	4
Long-term[§]	39	26[¶]	1	52	26[¶]	2	78	26[¶]	3	104	39[¶]	4

*It is possible to program all KST formulas into MetaStock, Wealth Lab, Trade Station, AmiBroker, Esignal, and several other software packages.
[†]Based on daily data.
[‡]Based on weekly data.
[§]Based on monthly data.
[¶]EMA

CHART 15.6 U.S. Dollar Index, 2006–2012 and an Intermediate KST

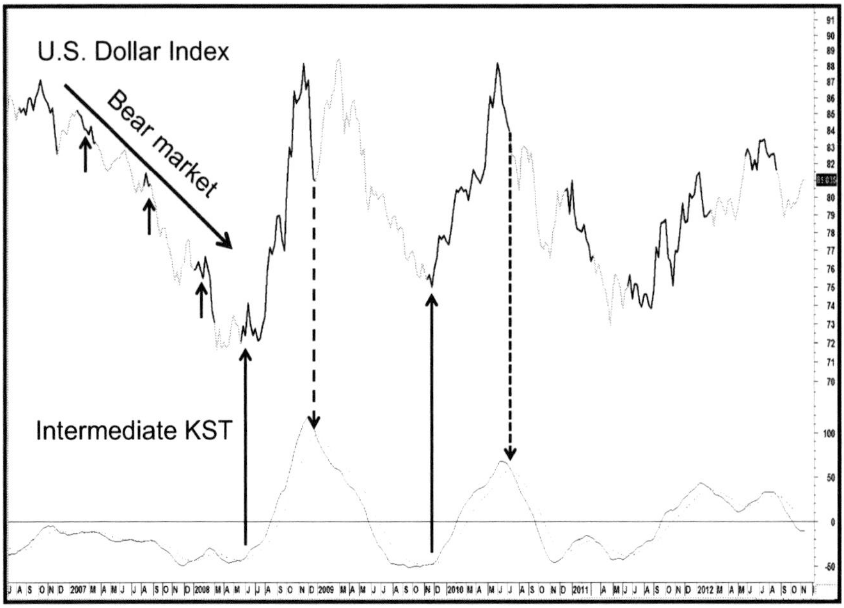

Source: From pring.com

Readers may experiment with different formulas for any of the time frames and may well come up with superior results. When experimenting, strive for consistency, never perfection, for there is no such thing in technical analysis.

Chart 15.6 shows an intermediate KST for the U.S. Dollar Index. The dark highlights indicate when the KST is above its 10-week exponential moving average (EMA), and the lighter plots when it is below. Two round-trip signals have been flagged with the arrows to demonstrate this. The principle of countercyclical trends being weak and the danger of trading them can also be appreciated from this chart. The three small arrows in the 2007–2008 period indicate bullish signals that ran counter to the main trend, which was negative. All three were short-lived and lost money.

Chart 15.7 features the London copper price. One of the things I like about the indicator, especially in its short-term and intermediate varieties, is its flexibility of interpretation. Nearly all of the interpretive techniques discussed in Chapter 13 can be applied. In Chart 15.7, for example, we see an overbought crossover at the tail end of 1994. It did not amount to any-thing because it was not possible to come up with any trend-reversal signals

CHART 15.7 Cash Copper, 1993–2001 Intermediate KST Interpretation

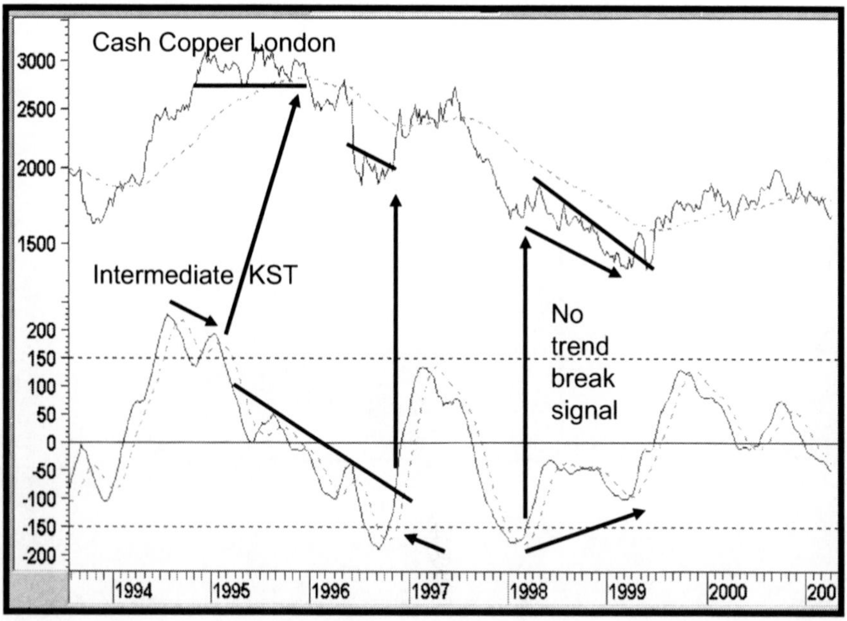

Source: From pring.com

in the price. Later on, though, in early 1995, we see a negative divergence, and at the end of the year an overbought crossover, a 65-week EMA crossover, and a head-and-shoulders top in the price—classic stuff. There were a couple of false buy signals on the way down, but the rally peaks in the KST lent themselves to the construction of a nice down trendline. The violation of the line, the oversold crossover, and the completion of the base in the price combined together to offer a nice buy signal in late 1996. The next time the KST crossed its oversold level in 1998, there was no good place to observe a trend-reversal signal in the price. That was not true in early 1999, where a positive divergence, EMA crossover by the KST, and a trendline break in the price offered a good timely entry point. Note that after the price broke above the down trendline it subsequently found support at the extended line.

Chart 15.8 features the Global X FTSE Columbia ETF with a daily KST. It demonstrates the fact that this series has the occasional ability to trace out price patterns, as it does in late 2010. Note also the bear market that began late in that year and the inability of the KST to rally much above the equilibrium level.

CHART 15.8 Global X Columbia ETF, 2009–2012 and a Daily Short-Term KST

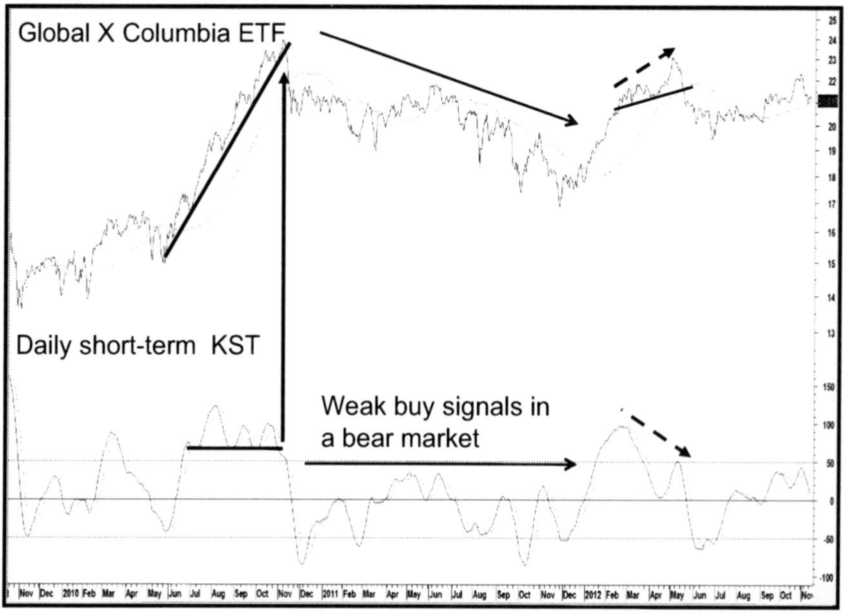

Source: From pring.com

> **Major Technical Principle** Sometimes, a study of the characteristics of an oscillator can be helpful in identifying the direction of the primary trend. Weak rallies indicate bear markets, and weak reactions indicate primary uptrends.

Note also the ability of the KST to signal divergences, such as the negative discrepancy in early 2012. Chart 15.9 shows the same information as its predecessor, but this time the solid arrows flag positive and negative overbought/oversold crossovers that were confirmed by the price. The failed (dashed) arrows show the value of waiting for such signals to be confirmed by the price.

> **Major Technical Principle** The first rule in using the short-term KST is to try to get a fix on the direction and maturity of the primary trend and never trade against it.

CHART 15.9 Global X Columbia ETF, 2009–2012 Daily Short-Term KST Interpretation

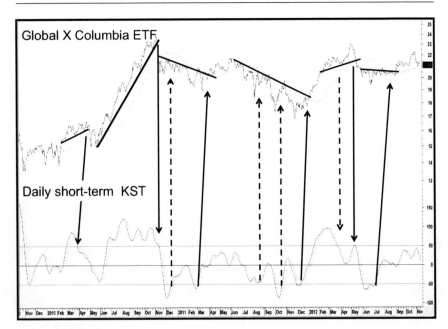

Source: From pring.com

Identifying the direction of the main trend is easier said than done. However, if you pay attention to the price relative to its 65-week or 12-month MA and the level and direction of the long-term KST, or Special K (explained later in this chapter), you will at least have an objective measure of the primary trend environment.

Chart 15.10, featuring Indian Hotels, again brings out the concept of constructing overbought and oversold lines and seeing what happens when the KST reverses from such levels. In this exercise, I am not concentrating on confirmations, but in qualifying the distinction between the generation of pro- and contratrend signals. The solid arrows indicate protrend signals, and the dashed ones indicate contratrend signals.

Using the KST in the Market Cycle Model

Three Main Trends Earlier chapters explained that there are several trends operating in the market at any particular time. They range from intraday, hourly trends right through to very long-term or secular trends that evolve over a 19- or 30-year period. For investment purposes, the

CHART 15.10 Indian Hotels, 1998–2003 and a Weekly Short-Term KST

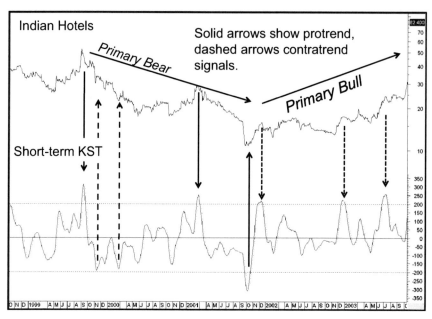

Source: From pring.com

most widely recognized trends are short-term, intermediate-term, and long-term. Short-term trends are usually monitored with daily prices, intermediate-term with weekly prices, and long-term with monthly prices. A hypothetical bell-shaped curve incorporating all three trends is shown in Figure 1.1.

From an investment point of view, it is important to understand the direction of the main, or primary, trend. This makes it possible to gain some perspective on the current position of the overall cycle. The construction of a long-term KST is a useful starting point from which to identify major market cycle junctures. The introduction of short-term and intermediate series then allows us to replicate the market cycle model.

The best investments are made when the primary trend is in a rising mode and the intermediate and short-term market movements are bottoming out. During a primary bear market, the best selling opportunities occur when intermediate and short-term trends are peaking and the long-term series is declining.

In a sense, any investments made during the early and middle stages of a bull market are bailed out by the fact that the primary trend is rising,

CHART 15.11 S&P Europe ETF 350, 2006–2011 and Three KSTs

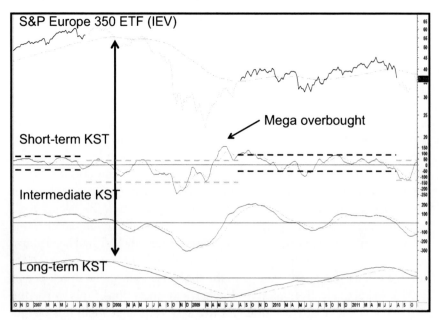

Source: From pring.com

whereas investors have to be much more agile during a bear market in order to capitalize on the rising intermediate-term swings.

Combining the Three Trends   Ideally, it would be very helpful to track the KST for monthly, weekly, and daily data on the same chart, but plotting constraints do not easily permit this. It is possible, though, to simulate these three trends by using different time spans based on weekly data, shown for the S&P European 350 ETF in Chart 15.11.

Note that the formula for the short-term KST differs from its daily counterpart in that the time spans (see Table 15.2) are longer and the formula, like all three included on the chart, uses EMAs rather than the simple moving average. This arrangement facilitates identification of both the direction and the maturity of the primary trend (shown at the bottom), as well as the interrelationship between the short-term and the intermediate trends. The dark plot shows when the long-term KST is above its 26-week EMA and the lighter plot when it is below. Sometimes, KST primary trend signals coincide with the price itself crossing its 65-week EMA, as was the case in December 2007 and August 2009. The chart also shows the approximate trading bands for the short-term KST in bull and bear markets as defined by the long-term KST EMA crossover approach. Note how it rarely moves to the oversold zone during the bullish environments and rarely to the overbought zone when the main trend is down.

The best buying opportunities seem to occur either when the long-term index is in the terminal phase of a decline, or when it is in an uptrend but has not yet reached an overextended position.

Quite often, the long-term series stabilizes but does not reverse direction, thereby leaving the observer in doubt as to its true intention. Vital clues can often be gleaned from the action of the short-term and intermediate series in conjunction with the price action itself. For example, it is unusual for the intermediate series to remain above or below equilibrium for an extended period—say, more than 9 months to a year. Consequently, when it falls below zero after a lengthy period of being above it, this argues for a bearish resolution to a flat long-term series and vice versa. A sell signal of this nature was triggered in early 2008 after the intermediate KST had been above zero for over 4 years, although you can't see all of that from this chart. Note also the mega overbought reading in the short-term series that developed in 2009. It was actually the highest reading since the inception of this ETF in the year 2000. The KST can be plotted for free at www.pring.com in this market cycle format for any Yahoo! symbol, whether U.S. or international.

The KST and Relative Action

The KST can also be adapted to relative strength lines and is especially useful for long-term (primary trend) analysis when applied to industry groups or individual stocks. This is because sector rotation develops around the business cycle as different groups are coming in and out of fashion. As a result, linear uptrends and downtrends are far less likely to develop than with absolute price data. For a fuller discussion on these matters and KST applications, see Chapters 19 and 22.

Are There KST Substitutes?

The KST is not the only answer to our smoothed momentum problems, since it is also possible to substitute the moving-average convergence divergence (MACD) using the default parameters, or the stochastic using a 24/15/10 combination, in the likely event that your charting software does not carry the KST or the ability to replicate it. Those same parameters for the stochastic appear to work for all three time frames. Chart 15.12

CHART 15.12 S&P Aluminum Index, 1992–2012 Comparing Long-Term Momentum Indicators

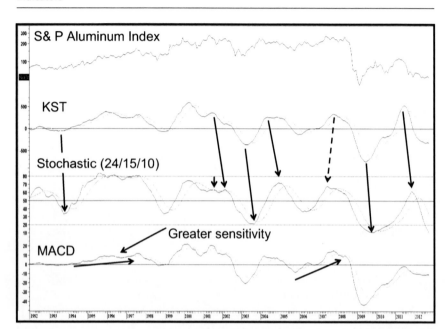

Source: From pring.com

compares the three indicators using monthly data. Note that in most cases, the KST coincides with or leads turning points in the stochastic. The dashed arrow indicates when the stochastic led. Alternatively, the more sensitive MACD often gives false impressions of trend reversals that either turn out to be false or are reversed before a crossover of the signal line takes place. For these reasons, I prefer the KST for all trends, not just long-term ones. It may well be possible to come up with superior parameters for both indicators, and the reader is certainly encouraged to make an attempt to do so.

The Special K

An alternative method of charting the KST comes when all three of them are combined into one indicator, which I call the "Special K." This gives us true summed cyclicality where the short-, intermediate-, and long-term trends are combined into one super one. The calculation is made by adding the daily KST formula to that of the intermediate and long-term series based on daily data. Thus, say the 12-month time span used in the

TABLE 15.3 Special K Formula

ROC	SMA	Times	Weight	Equals	Total
10	10	×	1	=	10
15	10	×	2	=	20
20	10	×	3	=	30
30	15	×	4	=	60
50	50	×	1	=	50
65	65	×	2	=	130
75	75	×	3	=	225
100	100	×	4	=	400
195	130	×	1	=	130
265	130	×	2	=	260
390	130	×	3	=	390
530	195	×	4	=	780
Special K					2485

long-term KST calculation is replaced by 265 days as an approximation for the trading days in a calendar year. Table 15.3 contains the formula, and Figure 15.1 features the concept in a visual format. It is really a practical adaptation of the dashed line (short-term trend) in Figure 15.1. It also

FIGURE 15.1 The Special K versus the Long-Term Trend

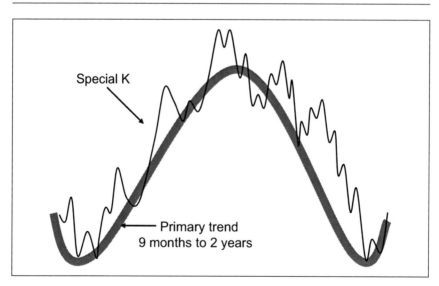

contrasts the slow, deliberate path of the long-term KST with the more jagged trajectory of the Special K. In an ideal world, the Special K ought to peak and trough more or less simultaneously with the price at bull and bear market turning points. In most situations, that actually happens. When it does, the trick is being able to identify these turning points as quickly as possible. The usual caveat with premature momentum turning points developing in linear uptrends or downtrends still applies.

The prime function of the Special K, then, is to identify primary trend turning points. Since this indicator also includes short-term data in its calculation, a subsidiary benefit lies in identifying smaller trends and putting that in context with the direction and maturity of the primary trend.

Using the Special K to Identify Long-Term Price Movements

The following are some of the Special K characteristics:

1. The Special K is a curve that reflects the dominant long-term KST, but is not as smooth, since it also contains data that reflect short-term and intermediate price movements.
2. Primary trend peaks and troughs in the price itself often coincide simultaneously with those of the Special K. Where linear uptrends or downtrends are present, the Special K (SPK) leads such turning points and sets up a divergence. The arrows on Chart 15.13 show some of these turning points for the S&P Composite. Note that in 1998 the SPK peaked prematurely due to the presence of a secular uptrend in U.S. equities. There are even more examples in Chart 15.14 of the CRB Composite. Of the 12 peaks and troughs between 1983 and 2012, only one did not develop simultaneously with the SPK.
3. This indicator lends itself to trendline construction. Usually, when lines greater than 9 months in duration are penetrated, there is a high probability that the primary trend has reversed. This is demonstrated in Chart 15.15 for the S&P Composite, where we see several SPK trendline penetrations confirmed by a similar action by the price. Occasionally, the trend is so steep that it is impossible to construct a meaningful trendline. In such cases, joint moving-average crossovers between the price and SPK that develop within a short time of each other usually serve as timely signals. A joint MA crossover takes place at A along with some trendline violations, but the rally off the 2009 bottom would have been signaled with the MA cross approach. The MA for the price has a 200-day span, and the one for the SPK has a 100-day span smoothed by an additional 100-day MA.

CHART 15.13 S&P Composite versus the Special K, 1995–2011

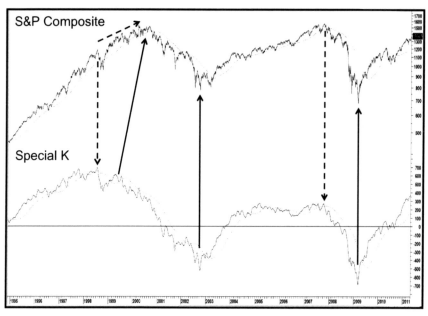

Source: From pring.com

CHART 15.14 CRB Composite versus the Special K, 1983–2012

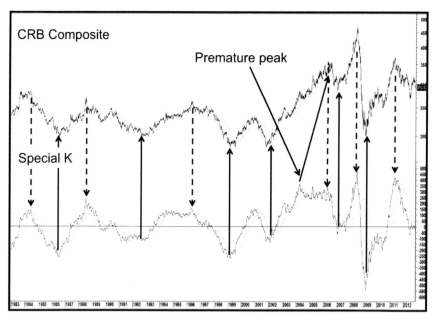

Source: From pring.com

CHART 15.15 S&P Composite versus the Special K, 1995–2011 Trendline Interpretation

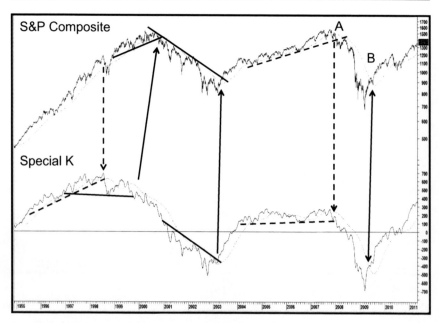

Source: From pring.com

Chart 15.16 also shows some joint MA breaks at points A, B, and C, as well as numerous trendline combinations. Note that occasionally the SPK will trace out a small trading range, and when this has been completed, reversal signals are triggered. The 2007 and 2010 lows offer two examples of this phenomenon.

4. Peak-and-trough reversals often show up at primary trend turning points. We see three instances in Chart 15.17 for the Bombay Stock Exchange FMGC Index at points X, Y, and Z. Not all turning points are signaled in this way, just as it's not always possible to construct a meaningful trendline. However, if we see a trend break and an obvious peak/trough reversal, the odds of a primary trend reversal are greatly enhanced.

Using the Special K to Identify Short-Term Price Movements

If you compare movements in the daily KST in Chart 15.18 with those of the Special K, you will see that they are very close indeed, which means that we really do get the summed cyclicality of that dashed short-term trend curve in our original market cycle diagram (Figure 1.1).

CHART 15.16 CRB Composite versus the Special K, 1999–2012 Trendline Interpretation

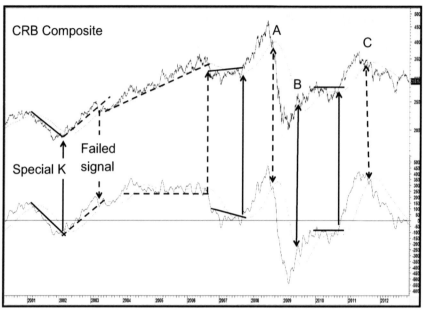

Source: From pring.com

CHART 15.17 BSE FMG Index, 2001–2009 Special K Interpretation

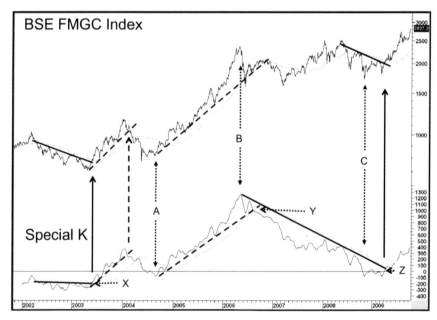

Source: From pring.com

CHART 15.18 S&P Composite, 2004–2008 the Special K versus the Daily Short-Term KST

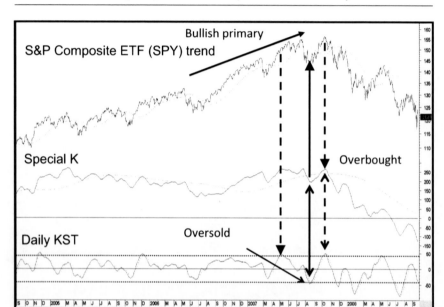

Source: From pring.com

That means we can use its gyrations to help identify short-term reversals in the Special K. For example, if the KST is overbought and reversing, as in October 2007, it is more likely to result in an imminent reversal in the trajectory of the Special K and, therefore, the price. The oversold reading that preceded it in August 2007 also worked quite well. However, during May 2007 we get another KST overbought reversal. The Special K also reverses, but there is no immediate decline. The reason? It's because this sell signal was a contratrend one, as the prevailing primary trend was bullish.

Chart 15.19, featuring the CRB Composite, also displays the daily KST in the bottom window.

We see an overbought KST with a reversing Special K in May 2000, and this is followed by a 3-month correction. However, there is more to it than that. Most of the time when the KST reverses direction, the Special K does as well. However, when the KST reverses to the upside, for example, and there is very little or no Special K response, the chances are that bearish intermediate and long-term forces are dominating, thereby putting substantial downward pressure on the Special K. Under such circumstances,

CHART 15.19 CRB Composite, 2000–2003 Using the KST Special K Relationship for Interpretation

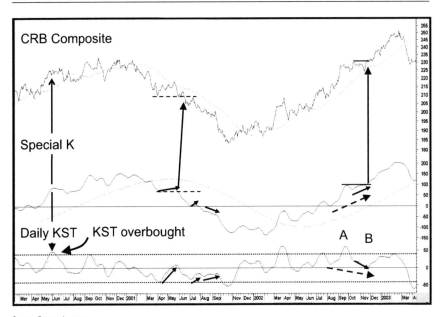

Source: From pring.com

the Special K is most likely going to move lower once the daily KST rally is over, thereby confirming that the main trend remains bearish. Several examples of this phenomenon are seen in the chart, the most glaring of which developed in the August/September 2001 period when the KST experienced a gentle rally but the Special K continued in its decline with no sign of strength whatsoever. This weakness was not apparent by observing the action of the daily KST, but by comparing it to the weak action of the Special K, it was possible to appreciate the downside pressure being applied by the intermediate and long-term cycles. Another small discrepancy developed in July 2001, where the Special K was hardly able to rally at all. The April/May 2001 period also shows a strong KST rally but a very weak Special K advance.

Bullish divergences develop when the KST declines but the dominant longer-term cycles used in the Special K calculation propel it upward. A good example developed in November 2002 and January 2003, as indicated by the two solid arrows. The idea of rising peaks and troughs for the Special K is especially important, because it indicates strength in the dominant intermediate and primary trend cycles. For example, look at the two dashed arrows. The one for the KST shows a lower low in November 2002 and that for the Special K shows a higher trough, if you can call it that, at B.

Finally, there is another way in which the near-term movements can help in deciding whether a specific short-term KST buy or sell signal is going to work or not. Note the horizontal dashed line marking the short-term low in the Special K in May 2001. When the indicator violates this level, it signals that a new low in the price itself is likely. In the case of the May 2001 example, the Special K took out its low just about 2 weeks before the CRB itself did.

The reverse situation developed in November 2002, where the Special K moved to a new high. In this case, there was no lead by the momentum indicator, as the price broke out more or less simultaneously with it.

Major Technical Principle If the Special K registers a new high or low for the move, the price usually follows.

How the Special K Generates Short-Term Buy and Sell Signals

One of the most important things for short-term traders to grasp is the fact that

Major Technical Principle Trades executed in the direction of the main trend are much more likely to be successful than those generated in a countercyclical way.

One starting point that helps us arrive at an objective way of determining the direction of the primary trend is to use the SPK. Obviously, we can easily tell with the benefit of hindsight where the actual SPK peaks and troughs formed, but in real time, we do not have this luxury. One solution is to determine its position vis-à-vis its 100-day MA smoothed with a 100-day MA. Positive readings would indicate a primary bull market and vice versa.

Chart 15.20 shows such a system for the Dow Jones UBS Commodity Index. The shaded areas represent bear markets as defined by the SPK/MA relationships. No signals are generated during this type of environment. The dark highlights indicate when the SPK crosses above its 10-day MA and

CHART 15.20 Dow Jones UBS Commodity Index, 2009–2012 Generating Pro-Trend Short-Term Buys and Sell Signals

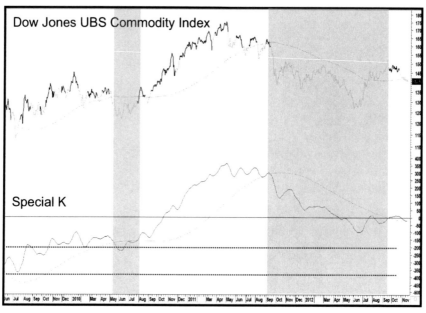

Source: From pring.com

when the primary bull/bear model is bullish. This approach is far from perfect because there are points when the model is bullish but the price has already reversed and so forth. Rather than blindly using this approach as a mechanical system, I think it better to use pro-trend signals as an alert and to then use other indicators as a filter in a weight-of-the-evidence approach.

Self-generated charts and templates for these SPK systems are included in an add-in package for MetaStock, which is available at www .pring.com

Special K Drawbacks and Benefits

Like all momentum indicators, the SPK does come with drawbacks. The most noticeable derives from the fact that the indicator's construction assumes that the price series in question is revolving around the typical business cycle. Consequently, it reverses prematurely during linear trends and will lag when the cycle is unusually brief. That is, of course, a drawback with any long-term momentum indicator.

However, in the few years I have been working with it, I have grown more and more impressed with its ability to identify numerous primary trend turning points where other indicators have failed.

The Directional Movement System

The objective of the directional movement system, designed by Welles Wilder, is to determine whether a market is likely to experience a trending or trading range environment. The distinction is important because a trending market will be better signaled by the adoption of trend-following indicators, such as moving averages, whereas a trading range environment is more suitable for oscillators. In practice, I am not impressed with the ability of the directional movement system to accomplish this objective, other than to identify a change in trend. On the other hand, there are, I find, several other ways in which this indicator can be usefully applied.

The Calculation

The calculation of the directional movement system is quite involved, and time does not permit a full discussion here. For that readers are referred to Wilder's *New Concepts in Technical Trading Systems* (Trend Research, 1978), to my own *Definitive Guide to Momentum Indicators* book and CD-ROM tutorial (Marketplace Books, 2009), or to my online audio-visual technical analysis course at Pring.com.

To simplify matters, the directional movement indicator is plotted by calculating the maximum range that the price has moved, either during the period under consideration (day, week, 10-minute bar, etc.) or from the previous period's close to the extreme point reached during the period. In effect, the system tries to measure directional movement. Since there are two directions in which prices can move, there are two directional movement indicators. They are called +DI and −DI. The resultant series is unduly volatile, so each is calculated as an average over a specific time period and then plotted. Normally, these series are overlaid in the same chart panel, as shown in Chart 15.21 for the euro using the standard, or default, time span of 14 periods.

There is one other important indicator incorporated in this system, and that is the average directional movement (ADX). The ADX is simply an average of the + and −DIs over a specific period. In effect, it subtracts the days

CHART 15.21 Euro, 2011–2012 Featuring a +DI and –DI

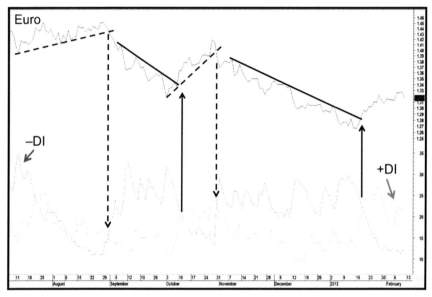

Source: From pring.com

of negative directional movement from the positive ones. However, when the –DI is greater than the +DI, the negative sign is ignored. This means that the *ADX only tells us whether the security in question is experiencing directional movement or not.* Again, the normal default time span is 14 days.

The ADX is calculated in such a way that the plot is always contained within the scale of 0 to 100. High readings indicate that the security is in a trending mode, i.e., it has a lot of directional movement, and low readings indicate a lack of directional movement and are more indicative of trading range markets.

> **Major Technical Principle** The ADX tells us nothing about the direction in which a price is moving, only its trending or nontrending characteristics.

The Two DIs

In Chart 15.21, buy alerts are signaled when the +DI crosses above the –DI (solid arrows) and vice versa (dashed arrows). In this example, there

CHART 15.22 Gold Trust ETF, 2011–2012 Comparing "Raw" with Smoothed DIs

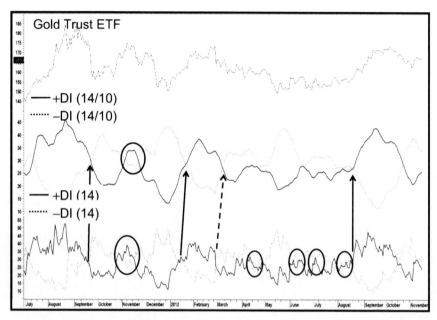

Source: From pring.com

are several occasions when it is possible to confirm such crossovers with a trendline violation in the price. Moving-average crossovers or price patterns could just as easily be substituted. These DI crossovers are fairly accurate and not subject to whipsaws.

Unfortunately, things do not always work out as well, which you can see from the whipsaw signals in the five ellipses in the bottom window of Chart 15.22. That's one reason why it is important to make sure that these crossovers are confirmed by the price. Another way around this is to smooth the two DIs as I have done in the middle panel of Chart 15.22 using a 10-day MA. This certainly eliminates a lot of the whipsaws, as you can see from the ellipses, but there is a trade-off in that the signals are occasionally delayed because this approach is less sensitive. In this instance, I have placed arrows at some of the key points where the smoothed series cross each other. Again, it's important to remember that these are momentum signals and should be confirmed by the price. In addition, this approach, like most others, should be used where you decide to fight the battle. That means that if the price has already moved a long way by the time the signal has been triggered, it is probably best to ignore it for new positions.

The ADX

A high ADX reading does not tell us that that the market is overbought and about to go down. Instead, it measures the intensity of the move from a directional point of view. Consequently, when it reaches a high reading and starts to reverse, a warning is given that the prevailing trend has probably run its course. From here on in we should expect it to *change*. This is different from a *reversal* in trend, since a change in trend could also be from up to sideways or down to sideways. In Chart 15.23, a 14-day ADX has been plotted against the Gold Trust ETF, the GLD. Note how reversals from high readings signal turning points at both tops and bottoms. Since the upward and downward trajectories are fairly deliberate, negative 10-day MA crossovers at high ADX readings act as good confirmation that a peak has been seen. The indicator in the bottom panel is simply the differential between a 10-day MA of a 14-day +DI and a –DI, as shown in the center panel of Chart 15.22. By comparing the position of the ADX to the differential, it is fairly obvious whether a high-end reversal is coming from an overbought or oversold level. When the ADX reverses in such a manner, it's then a good idea to obtain some kind of price confirmation.

CHART 15.23 Gold Trust ETF, 2011–2012 the ADX versus a DI Differential Indicator

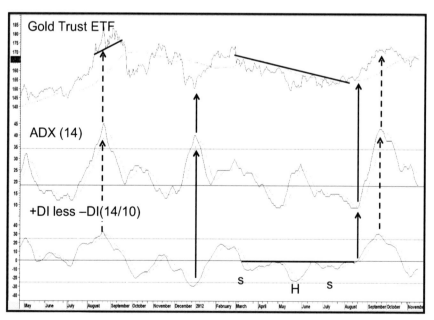

Source: From pring.com

Of the three instances in this chart, only the first in September 2011 was confirmed.

Low readings in the ADX indicate a lack of directional movement. These these can be helpful as well when it is fairly clear that a new rising trend of directional movement from such a benign level is under way. In this respect, the differential indicator traced out a reverse head and shoulders in the late summer of 2012 just as the ADX was crossing above its MA from a subdued level. The low ADX reading told you there was no directional movement and to be prepared for some. In addition, the breakout from the base in the differential and trendline violation in the price said it would be an upward one.

Summary

1. The KST can be constructed for any time frame, from intraday to primary.
2. It is calculated from the smoothed ROC of four time spans, each of which is weighted according to the length of its time span.
3. Long-term, short-term, and intermediate KSTs can be combined into one chart to reflect the market cycle model.
4. The KST lends itself to numerous momentum interpretive techniques.
5. The KST can successfully be applied to relative strength analysis.
6. The Special K is a summation of the short-term, intermediate, and long-term KSTs and can be useful for identifying short-term and long-term trend reversals.
7. In most situations, the Special K peaks and troughs very closely to primary-trend turning points.
8. Trend reversals in the Special K are signaled by trendline violations, moving-average crossovers, and peak/trough progression reversals.
9. The +DI and –DI measure positive and negative short-term direction. They can be smoothed to eliminate whipsaws and can be differentiated to result in a timely oscillator.
10. When the raw or smoothed DIs cross, they trigger buy and sell momentum signals.
11. The ADX measures the directional movement of a trend.
12. A rising ADX indicates an increase in directional movement and vice versa.
13. When the ADX reverses direction from a high reading, the prevailing trend is likely to change.

16

CANDLESTICK
CHARTING

Candle Construction

The candlestick form of charting began to gain popularity in the 1990s.[1] This method originated in Japan several centuries ago and basically offers the same information as bar charts. The difference is that candlestick charts can often make it easier to spot certain technical phenomena not readily apparent with a quick glance at a bar chart. Bar and candlestick charts are compared in Figures 16.1 and 16.2. Although candlesticks can be plotted for any period, from minute to monthly, I will use the term "daily" as a generic reference in this chapter to eliminate repetition.

Candlestick charts can only be plotted for markets in which opening prices as well as closes, highs, and lows are known. One disadvantage is that they take up a lot of horizontal space, which limits the amount of data that can be physically displayed. Fortunately, trend-reversal signals tend to be very short term in nature, with their effects generally lasting for a few days and rarely more than three weeks. Candlestick charts offer indications of both reversal and continuation phenomena, just as bar charts do. Some examples in this chapter demonstrate these phenomena in candlestick formations. They really come into their own in the identification of shorter-term reversals and continuation situations.

---

[1]Steve Nison, *Japanese Candlestick Charting Techniques,* New York: New York Institute of Finance, 1991.

FIGURE 16.1 Bar versus Candle Charts

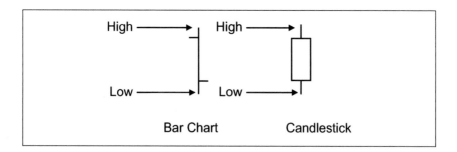

FIGURE 16.2 Bar versus Candle Charts

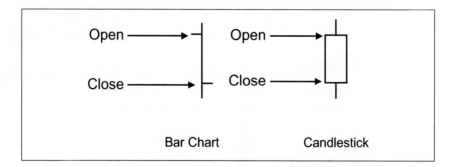

Candlesticks are certainly no magic wand, but they are unquestionably a useful technical tool for short-term traders. They consist of a vertical rectangle with two lines spiking up and down. The vertical rectangle is known as the *real body* and encompasses the trading activity between the opening and closing prices (Figure 16.3).

For example, if the opening price is higher than the closing price, it will be recorded at the top of the real body and the closing price at the bottom. The vertical line above the real body measures the distance between the high of the day and the higher of the opening or closing price. The lower line represents the distance between the low of the day and the lower of the opening or closing price. Days when the close is higher than the opening are represented by transparent (white) real bodies; days when the opening is higher than the close are displayed by a solid (black) real body (Figure 16.4). Even though candlesticks can be plotted for any period in

FIGURE 16.3 Candle Construction

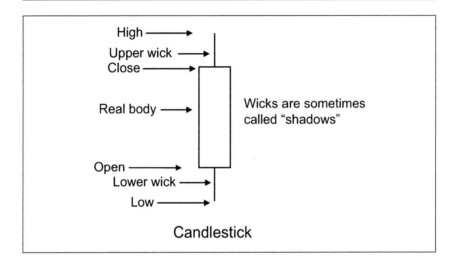

FIGURE 16.4 Real Bodies

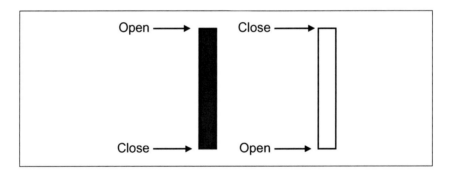

which information is available, I use days in the example because daily candlestick charts are the most common.

> **Major Technical Principle** In candlestick charting, the greatest emphasis is given to the opening and closing prices and the trading range between them.

The thin vertical lines that protrude from the real body reflect the high and low for the day. These are known as upper and lower *shadows* or *wicks*. Since the closing and opening prices can be identical, or identical with the

FIGURE 16.5 Selected Candle Formats

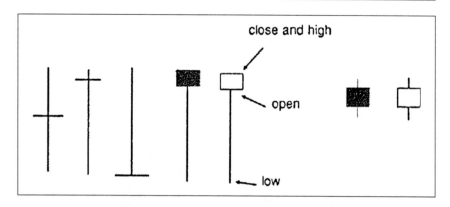

high or low, a number of possible combinations need to be represented. Some of them are shown in Figure 16.5. Candlesticks provide essentially the same information as bar charts, but their more pronounced visual representation of the material enables technicians to identify characteristics that are less obvious on bar charts. Certain phenomena illustrated in bar charts have been given their own names, such as "key reversal days" or "island reversal days." Likewise, with candlestick charts, because of the large number of potential variations for both individual days and price formations encompassing several days, it has been common practice to give exotic names to the various possibilities.

Basic Candlestick Pattern Building Blocks

The candlestick patterns in Figure 16.6 are among the most essential individual candlestick lines for building candlestick patterns. A *doji* is a trading session where the opening and closing prices either are the same or very close to each other. When dojis appear in trading ranges, they reflect an environment where buyers and sellers are temporarily in balance and are, therefore, of little significance. However, when they develop after an advance or decline, the appearance of a more balanced state between supply and demand is a vital clue that the trend may be about to change, since this state of implied balance follows a period in which either buyers (rally) or sellers (decline) were previously in control.

Finally, there is a *spinning top*. Small real bodies characterize them, where the shadows can be short or long. It is the size of the real body, rather than the shadow's size, that is important in identifying a spinning top. Spinning tops are not important when they appear in trading ranges,

FIGURE 16.6 Spinning Tops

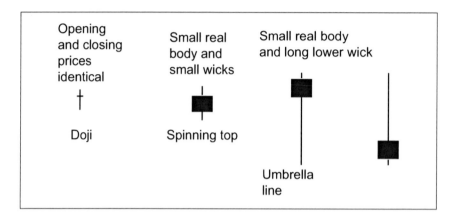

but they are significant when they develop as part of a price pattern, since they represent a battle between the bulls and the bears. Spinning tops indicate indecision, where participants cannot agree on whether prices should rally or react. When they appear after a prolonged rally or reaction, it is a sign that upside or downside momentum is dissipating. Putting it another way, we could say that in previous sessions, buyers or sellers had the upper hand, but the spinning top tells us the fight is more evenly matched. Thus, another small change in the balance between supply and demand could tip the price trend the other way. This is why a spinning top is an initial sign a trend may be in the process of reversing. Only when this is confirmed by other price action, which we shall get into later, should you take action.

Figure 16.6 includes an *umbrella line.* The concept behind umbrella lines is that the opening and closing prices develop close to the high of the day. The real body in this case more closely resembles a square than a rectangle. Umbrellas tend to be bullish after a decline and bearish following an advance. If they develop within the confines of a trading range, they have no real significance.

Belt-Hold Lines (Yorikiri)

A bullish belt hold (long white line in Figure 16.7*a*) is a one-candlestick pattern consisting of a long white candlestick in which the price opens on the session low and then works its way higher throughout the session. The price does not have to close at the high, but the longer the real body, the more

FIGURE 16.7 Belt Holds (Long White/Black Lines)

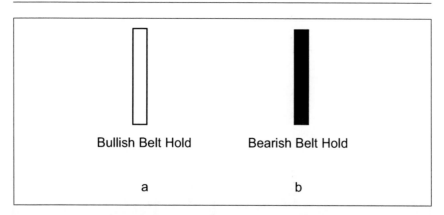

Bullish Belt Hold   Bearish Belt Hold

a   b

positive the candlestick. Also, if a belt hold has not appeared on the chart for quite a while, it is an unusual phenomenon, so, it gains in importance when it does appear. This is because traders are making a very strong statement about their feelings toward the market with a belt hold, compared to the smaller candlesticks that were previously the norm. Just think of a crowd murmuring and then a loud voice comes from within the crowd. It is obviously a person who wants to be heard. The belt hold following a long period of smaller candlesticks amounts to the same thing—it's a 1-day pattern that says loudly, "Listen to me because I am telling you the short-term trend has changed."

A bearish belt hold (the long black line in Figure 16.7*b*) is the opposite. It is a long black candlestick in which the price opens at the high and then works its way lower as the session progresses. Belt holds are often important pivotal days, since the high and low occasionally act as support and resistance areas in subsequent price action. The halfway point of the real body of a belt hold also should be monitored for a possible price reversal during later price swings.

The upper and lower areas of belt holds are potential future support/resistance levels. An example is shown in Chart 16.1.

Candlestick patterns basically fall into two broad categories, reversal and continuation, so we will split our discussion into these respective parts, starting with the more interesting reversal phenomena. Candlesticks can be applied to any time frame, though when they appear on intraday charts they do not have as much significance as on daily or weekly charts. Their effect, like that of bar charts, should only be expected to last for between 5 and 10 candles. Thus, it would be reasonable to expect a candlestick pattern on an hourly chart to last for 5 to 10 hours and on a monthly chart for 5 to 10 months and so forth.

CHART 16.1 Ciena

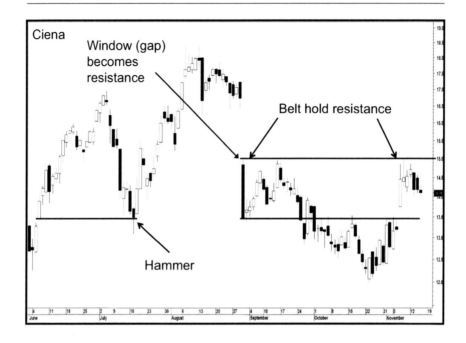

Reversal Phenomena

Hammers and Hanging Men (Takuri and Kubitsuri)

These formations (Figures 16.8 and 16.9) have probably gained more notoriety than all the others because of their imposing titles. A "hanging man" is an umbrella line that develops after a rally. The shadow should be at least twice the size of the real body. It looks rather like the body of a man with dangling legs and, as its name implies, is a bearish pattern. If a hanging man appears after a prolonged up move, it should be treated with respect, especially if it occurs after a gap. A hanging man can be identified by the fact that the shadow, or wick, is at least twice the height of the real body. The color of the body is not important.

A "hammer" is identical to a hanging man but occurs after a market decline, when it is a bullish sign. It gets its name from the idea that the price is "hammering out" a bottom. In effect, it represents the kind of trading day when the price temporarily slips quite sharply, for there is a "run" on the selling stops. Nevertheless, the technical position is sufficiently constructive to cause buyers to come into the market and push the price back up toward or

FIGURE 16.8 Hanging Man

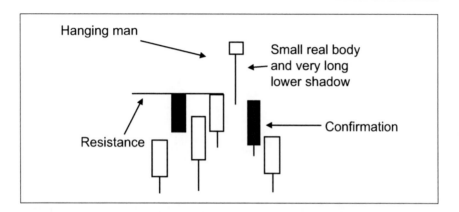

FIGURE 16.9 Hammer

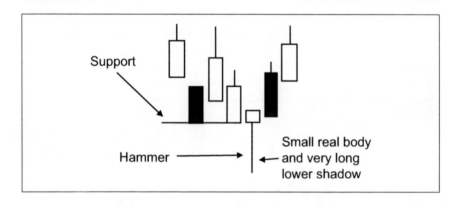

above the opening level. It is always better to see some confirmation. In the case of a hanging man, this confirmation could take the form of a long, black candlestick, as indicated in Figure 16.8. An example of a hammer is shown in Chart 16.1 for Ciena. Note how the open and the close develop well above the day's low, thereby indicating seller exhaustion following a sharp setback.

Dark Cloud Cover (Kabuse)

In real life, dark clouds (Figure 16.10) hint at the possibility of rain, so a "dark cloud" candlestick formation implies lower prices. Its bearish connotations are most pronounced during an uptrend or in the upper part

FIGURE 16.10 Dark Cloud Cover

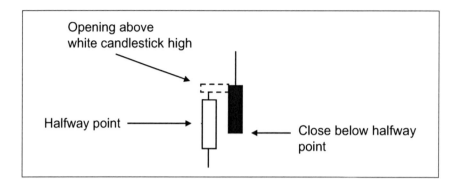

of a congestion zone. It is a form of key reversal, since the price closes down on the day after a gap higher opening. It consists of 2 days' price action. The first is a strong, white real body, and the second is a black body in which the open develops above the upper wick of the white candlestick and the close occurs in the lower half of the previous white real body. An example is shown in Chart 16.2. Normally these patterns develop after a

CHART 16.2 S&P ETF

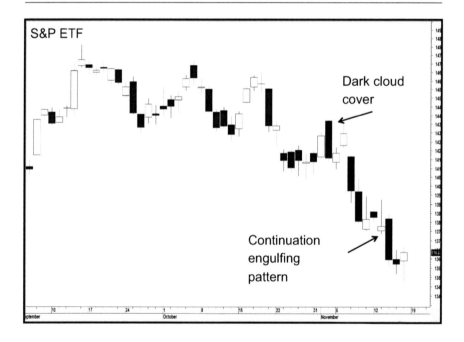

FIGURE 16.11 Piercing White Line

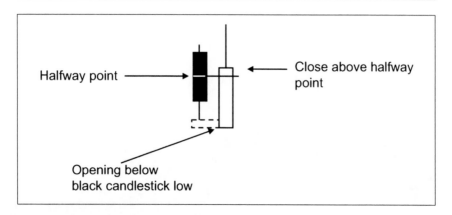

sharp rally where there are plenty of traders willing to take profits. This one also qualifies as an engulfing pattern (described later).

Piercing Line (Kirikorni)

This pattern (Figure 16.11) would be more aptly named "sunny sky" because it is the exact opposite of the dark cloud and is, therefore, bullish. It is important to note whether the second day's white body closes more than halfway above the previous body, with an opening price that traded below the lower wick of the previous black candlestick. Chart 16.3 shows a classic example at the October 2011 low in the S&P ETF, the SPY. We also see another example earlier that barely qualifies under the rule that states that the black candlestick should close more than halfway below the real body of the previous white candle. Chart 16.4 also shows a couple more instances of piercing white lines.

Engulfing Pattern (Tsutsumi)

This formation (Figures 16.12 and 16.13) develops significance after a prolonged price move. It is characterized by two consecutive, relatively shadowless, real bodies in which the real body of the second day "engulfs" that of the first. It is bullish in a downtrend, when the second day is a white body, and bearish in an uptrend, when it appears as a black one. We are treated to a bearish engulfing pattern for the Global X Silver Mine ETF

CHART 16.3 S&P ETF

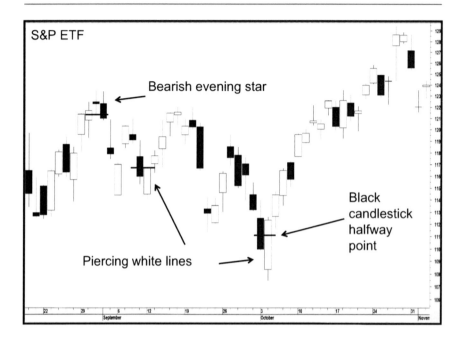

CHART 16.4 Global X Silver Miners ETF, 2011–2012

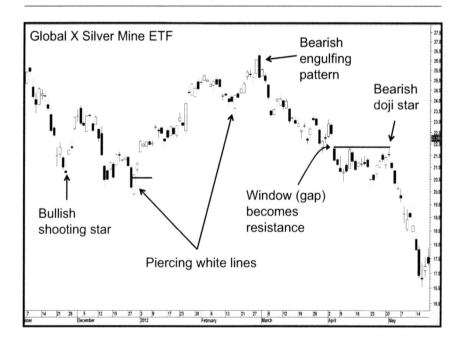

FIGURE 16.12 Bullish Engulfing Pattern

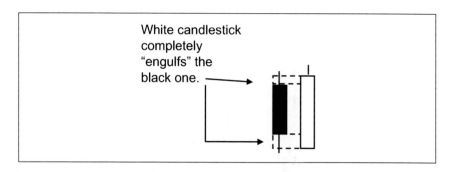

White candlestick
completely
"engulfs" the
black one. ——→

FIGURE 16.13 Bearish Engulfing Pattern

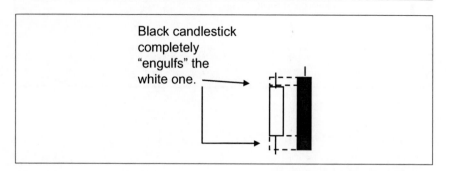

Black candlestick
completely
"engulfs" the
white one. ——→

in Chart 16.4. Even though this was a classic pattern, there was no way to forecast the enormity of the ensuing decline. A bullish engulfing pattern appears in Chart 16.5.

Stars (Hoshi)

Stars are common phenomena in candlestick charts and come in four different reversal varieties. They are combinations of wide real bodies and spinning tops. The morning star (Figure 16.14) heralds a new day (up move) and is bullish.

It consists of two long real bodies separated by a spinning top. The star is represented by the spinning top, which is made on a gap. The third body should be white and should result in a closing price being more than

CHART 16.5 Echostar Communications

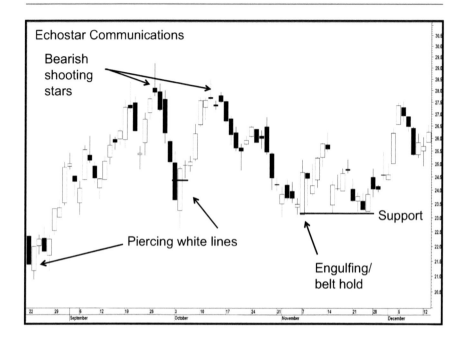

FIGURE 16.14 Bullish Morning Star

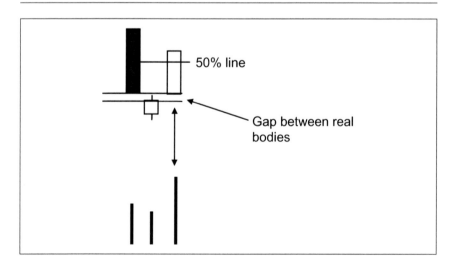

FIGURE 16.15 Bearish Evening Star

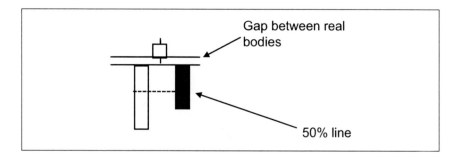

halfway up the body of the first. The *evening star* (Figure 16.15) is a precursor of night. It has the opposite characteristics and implications of a morning star.

An example appears in Chart 16.3 for the S&P ETF in September 2012. Ideally, I would have liked to see a larger white real body as the first candlestick in the pattern, but it worked nevertheless. Candlestick patterns, like all technical phenomena, can and do fail from time to time, and stars are no exception. In this respect, Figure 16.16 shows a failed bearish evening star, as the white candlestick to the right takes the price above the spinning top. A cancellation of a morning star would develop in exactly the opposite way, with a black real body taking the price below the spinning top.

A bearish evening *doji star* (Figure 16.17) bullish occurs after a lengthy rally. It consists of a gap and a doji line. An example appears in Chart 16.4 and a bullish morning doji star in Figure 16.18.

FIGURE 16.16 Cancelled Evening Star

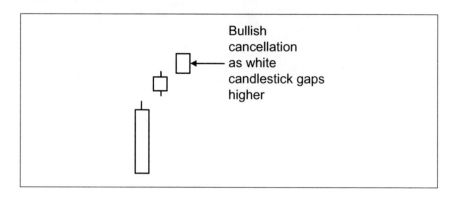

FIGURE 16.17 Bearish Evening Doji Star

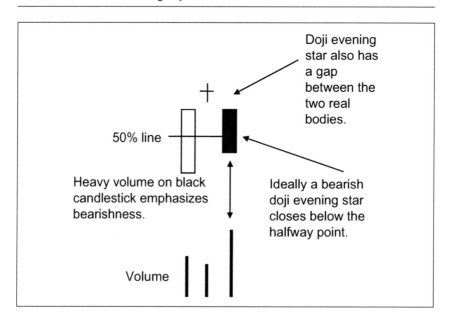

Doji evening star also has a gap between the two real bodies.

50% line

Heavy volume on black candlestick emphasizes bearishness.

Ideally a bearish doji evening star closes below the halfway point.

Volume

FIGURE 16.18 Bullish Morning Doji Star

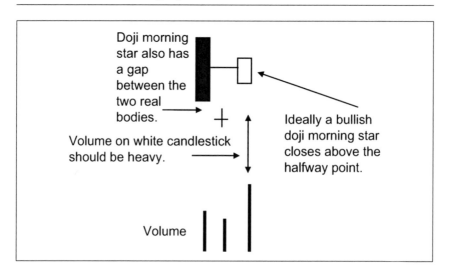

Doji morning star also has a gap between the two real bodies.

Volume on white candlestick should be heavy.

Ideally a bullish doji morning star closes above the halfway point.

Volume

FIGURE 16.19 Long-Legged Doji

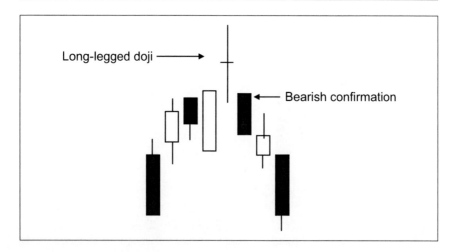

A particularly wide trading range, where the opening and closing are more or less identical, is known as a long-legged doji. An example is shown in Figure 16.19

Where it appears after a long white candlestick, it can be quite ominous.

A *shooting star* (Figures 16.20 and 16.21) is like a short-term top. The daily price action experiences a small gap, where the real body appears at the end of a long wick or upper shadow. We see a couple of examples of bearish shooting stars in Chart 16.5. Late September 2011 witnessed a classic shooting star, with two relatively large real bodies sandwiching a

FIGURE 16.20 Bearish Shooting Star

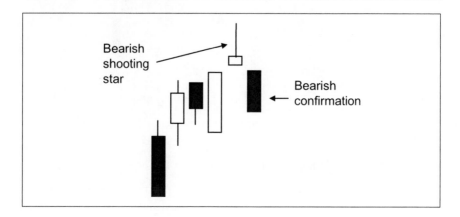

FIGURE 16.21 Bullish Shooting Star (Inverted Hammer)

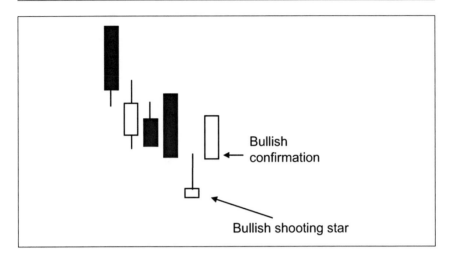

much smaller one. The October pattern, on the other hand, saw two relatively small real bodies surround an even smaller one, and represents a bit of a stretch. The same comments could be applied to the shooting star in Chart 16.4. A bullish shooting star is also featured in Chart 16.6.

CHART 16.6 Oracle Corp

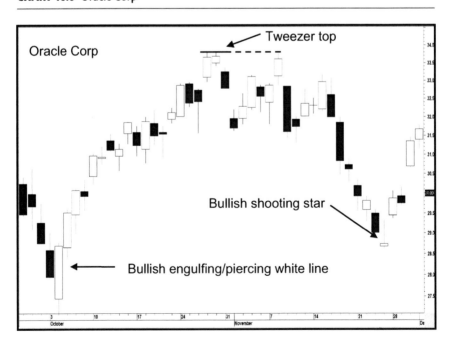

FIGURE 16.22 Upside Gap Two Crows

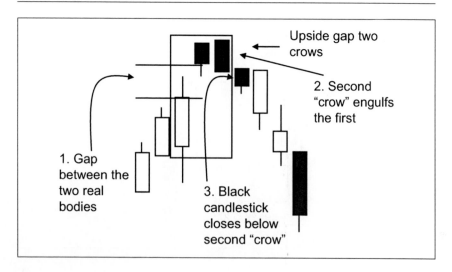

Upside Gap Two Crows (Narabi Kuro)

This bearish formation (Figure 16.22) consists of a long white line followed by two black lines. The first black line gaps to the upside. The third
day often closes the gap, but because it is a black line where the close is
below the open, its implication is bearish.

Three Black Crows (Sanba Garasu)

The three black crows pattern (Figure 16.23) consists of three declining
black candlesticks, which form after an advance and indicate lower prices.
Each candlestick should close at or near its session low. You can see that
none of them have a lower wick and each of the three real bodies opens
within the range or right at the bottom of the previous session's real body.
A good example is featured in Chart 16.7 for Aseer Trading, Tourism and
Manufacturing, a Middle Eastern stock. The first crow was a kind of shooting star, which in itself suggested that buyers had spent all their investment
funds.

Tweezer Tops and Bottoms (Kenuki)

If you hold a tweezer upside down, you will see that the two points are at
identical levels (Figure 16.24). The same is true of a tweezer top, which

FIGURE 16.23 Three Black Crows

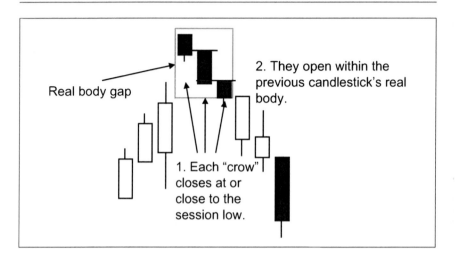

Real body gap

2. They open within the previous candlestick's real body.

1. Each "crow" closes at or close to the session low.

CHART 16.7 Aseer Trading Tourism and Manufacturing

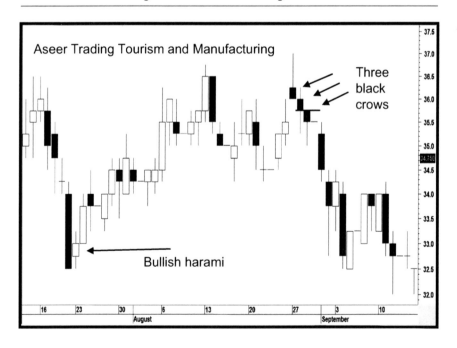

Aseer Trading Tourism and Manufacturing

Three black crows

Bullish harami

FIGURE 16.24 Tweezer Top and Bottom

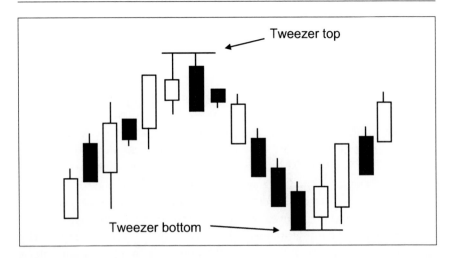

consists of two candlesticks, for which the high of the day is identical. Actually, it's possible for a tweezer to consist of more than 2 days with an identical top. Make no mistake about it—we are talking about the high, which can be a shadow or real-body close or open. This pattern is short-term bearish because the first day's high acts as resistance, so when the second day is unable to punch through the horizontal line (which marks the area of the top), it indicates a loss of upside momentum. In this example, the second day is also an engulfing pattern, which is an important point, since a tweezer often contains a price pattern as part of its formation.

A tweezer bottom occurs when, after a decline, two or more candlesticks make an identical low. This again indicates a loss of downside momentum since the price finds support in the area of the low. In this figure, we see a tweezer literally hammered out because the second low to touch the horizontal line is a part of a hammer candlestick.

One factor that will increase the significance of a tweezer is the nature of the pattern being formed. For example, if the second day of a tweezer top is a hanging man, we would have two pieces of evidence that the trend may be about to reverse: the tweezer and the hanging man. If the top of a tweezer temporarily pushes through resistance, such as a meaningful trendline, this would emphasize the significance since it would indicate exhaustion. The same would apply to the temporary violation of a support trendline. You can see an example of a tweezer top in Chart 16.6. Note how the tweezer resistance later on proved to be a barrier to a subsequent advance. That same chart also shows an example of a piercing white line, or is it a bullish engulfing pattern? It really does not matter what we call it because this is a bullish formation, and that's all that matters!

Counterattack or Meeting Lines (Deai Sen/Gyakushu Sen)

A bullish counterattack line (Figure 16.25) develops when, after a decline, a black candlestick is followed by a white candlestick and both close, or "meet," at the same level. This is why this 2-day pattern is sometimes referred to as a *meeting line*. The first day is usually a long black candlestick. The second day opens sharply lower, leading most traders to believe prices will continue to give way. However, by the end of the day, the price has regained everything lost (a counterattack by the buyers) and closes unchanged. The meeting line, therefore, indicates that the downside momentum has probably dissipated and a reversal in trend is likely.

A bearish counterattack, or meeting line (Figure 16.26), is formed when, after an advance, a white candlestick is followed by a black candlestick and both close at the same level. The psychology behind this one is fairly evident. The sharply higher opening on the second day has the bulls in a

FIGURE 16.25 Bullish Counterattack Line (Meeting Line)

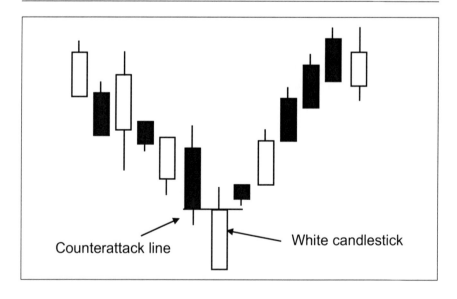

FIGURE 16.26 Bearish Counterattack Line (Meeting Line)

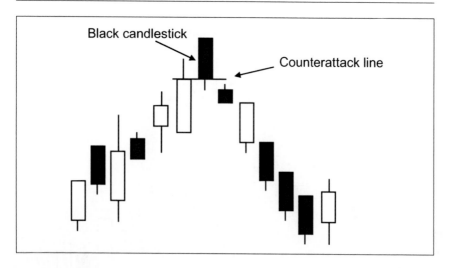

euphoric mood since these new gains come on top of an already sharp rally. However, euphoria turns to disappointment as the price unexpectedly returns to the unchanged level.

More specific rules for identifying these patterns are as follows:

1. The first day is colored in the direction of the prevailing trend, and the second day forms in the opposite color (white/black for tops and black/white for bottoms).
2. Both real bodies extend the prevailing trend and are long.
3. The closes are identical.

These patterns do not appear that often on the charts, but when they do, the sharp contrast between two long real bodies of differing colors touching each other after a prolonged trend should not be underestimated.

Tower Tops and Bottoms

A tower top consists of a rally cumulating in a long white candlestick. This is then followed by a trading range in which the price gradually works its way higher and then lower in a kind of reverse-saucer format, as in Figure 16.27.

The pattern is completed with a long black day that opens roughly where the long white day closed (the two pillars of the "tower").

FIGURE 16.27 Tower Top

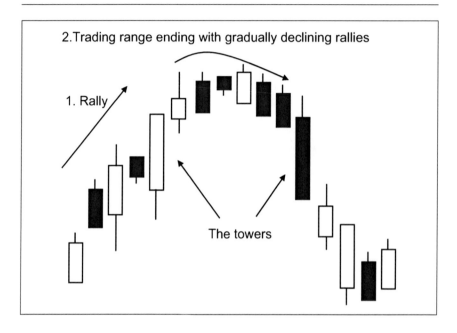

The tower bottom is exactly the opposite, as shown in Figure 16.28. Ideally, the two pillars of the towers form at the same level, though this is not a prerequisite.

Harami Lines (Yose)

Chapter 6 offered the idea that trendline violations are followed by either a reversal or a temporary consolidation. The harami is similar to the consolidation trendline break in that it indicates a loss of momentum. The main difference is that harami are of much shorter duration and consist of 2 days' price action. The harami forms a real body that is sufficiently small so that it is engulfed by the prior day's long real body. If it is also a doji, it is called a "harami cross." These patterns often warn of an impending trend change, especially if they follow a series of strong white or black candlesticks. If we imagine a short-term rally where the buyers are in control, the harami indicates a point of balance between both sides, as neither can push prices on a closing or opening basis beyond the limits of the previous candlestick. Sometimes this results in an actual price reversal, and at other times a harami is followed by a consolidation. Figures 16.29 and 16.30

FIGURE 16.28 Tower Bottom

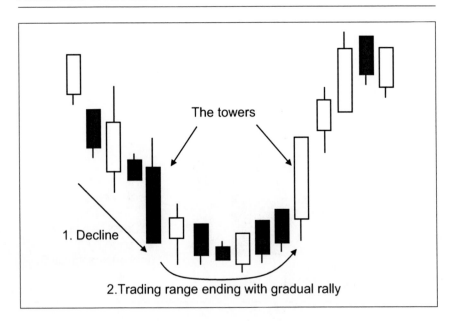

FIGURE 16.29 Bearish Harami

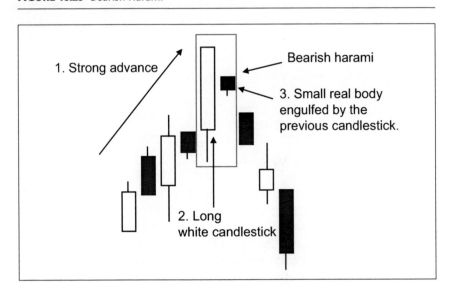

FIGURE 16.30 Bullish Harami

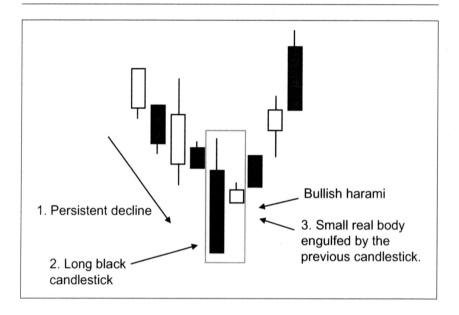

1. Persistent decline

2. Long black candlestick

Bullish harami

3. Small real body engulfed by the previous candlestick.

show examples of a harami where it is a reversal pattern. If, after a decline, the second candlestick forms around the lower area of the first, it is expected that a consolidation rather than a reversal will follow and vice versa for a harami that develops after a rally. The color of the second candlestick is immaterial to the outcome; rather, it's the idea of a balance between buyers and sellers that takes precedence. Chart 16.7 offers a nice example of a bullish harami, where we see a sharp decline culminating in a long, black real body. Finally, there is a very small real body in contrast.

Continuation Formations

Rising and Falling Three Methods

These formations are very similar in concept to a flag in bar charts, except that they take only a few days, not weeks, to develop. The rising method (Figure 16.31) is a bullish pattern and consists of a powerful white line followed by a series of three or four declining small black lines.

These declining candles should be accompanied by a noticeable contraction in volume, which indicates that a very fine balance is devel-

FIGURE 16.31 Rising Three Methods

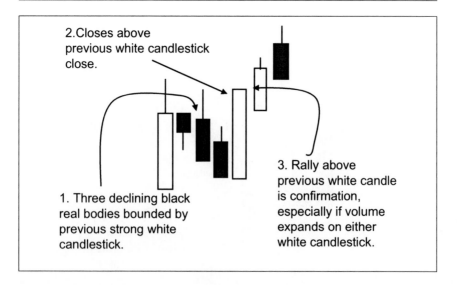

2. Closes above previous white candlestick close.

1. Three declining black real bodies bounded by previous strong white candlestick.

3. Rally above previous white candle is confirmation, especially if volume expands on either white candlestick.

oping between buyers and sellers. The final part of the pattern is a very strong white line that takes the price to a new closing high. If volume data are available, this final day should record a significant increase in activity. The bearish falling three methods (Figure 16.32) is exactly the opposite, except that volume characteristics are of no significance on the last day.

Windows (Ku)

Japanese chartists refer to gaps as "windows" (Figures 16.33 and 16.34). Whereas gaps are said to be "filled" in traditional bar charts, windows are "closed" in candlestick charts. Windows, therefore, have the same technical implications as gaps. Chart 16.4 shows examples of where the opening and closing levels of windows acted as support and resistance for subsequent price action.

Upside and Downside Gaps (Tasuki)

A tasuki gap (Figure 16.34) occurs after an advance. The requirement is an upside white-line gap (window) followed by a black line *that does not close it.*

FIGURE 16.32 Falling Three Methods

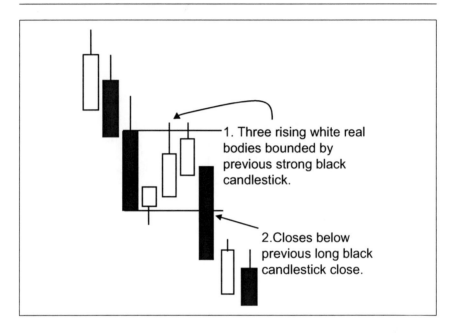

1. Three rising white real bodies bounded by previous strong black candlestick.

2. Closes below previous long black candlestick close.

FIGURE 16.33 Windows

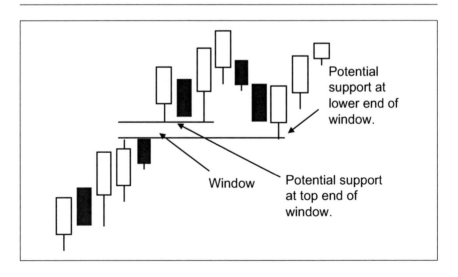

Potential support at lower end of window.

Window

Potential support at top end of window.

FIGURE 16.34 Upside Gap Tasuki

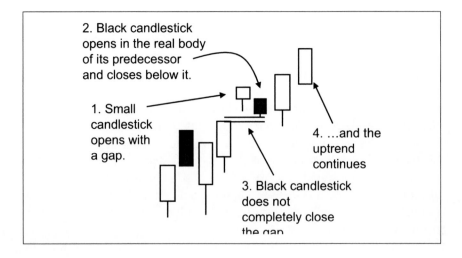

This type of pattern is usually followed by higher prices. However, if the gap is filled, the formation deteriorates into an upside gap with one crow and, therefore, loses its bullish portent. The downside gap is exactly the opposite and is featured in Figure 16.35.

FIGURE 16.35 Downside Gap Tasuki

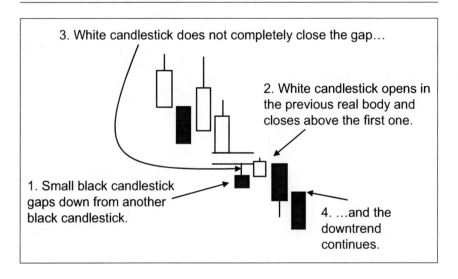

Candlestick Charts and Western Techniques

There is a tendency among many technicians to look at candlesticks in isolation. My preference, remembering the weight-of-the-evidence approach discussed earlier, is to combine selected Western charting techniques with candlesticks. This involves, among other things, the inclusion of price patterns, trendlines, and oscillators into the analysis.

Chart 16.8 for instance, shows a head-and-shoulders top for Microsoft that was completed in November 2000. Note that the sell-off during the right shoulder was an identical three-crow pattern. Later on, we see a double bottom. The rally from the second low consisted of a bullish belt hold, which in itself indicated that prices were headed higher. This bottom was also associated with a reverse head and shoulders in the relative strength indicator (RSI). Finally, the head-and-shoulders top in the RSI was confirmed with a harami.

One important question concerns where to draw the trendlines. Should they touch the wicks, real bodies, or a combination of both? The answer lies in our usual commonsense approach. Since the opening

CHART 16.8 Microsoft, 2000–2001

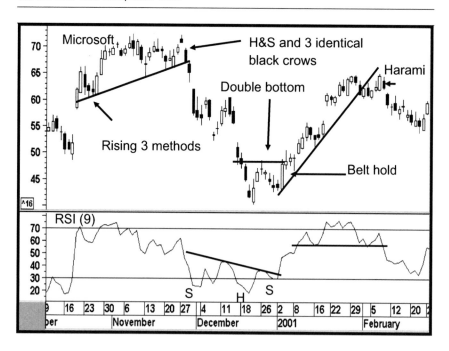

and closing prices are generally more important than the high and low lines that exclusively touch, real bodies will generally be more significant than those only touching the wicks. However, a longer line that has been touched on more occasions that only touches the wicks will probably be more significant than a line that is relatively short and only touches two real bodies.

Candlestick Volume Charts

Candlestick volume charts are the same as regular candlestick charts with one important difference. The width of the real bodies varies with the level of volume during that particular session. The greater the volume, the wider the real body and vice versa. This is shown in Figure 16.36.

It can be a very useful way of presenting the data because the signals from the regular candlesticks are preserved, yet the width of the real bodies offers a quick and simple overview of the volume pattern. Examples of how bullish and bearish volume patterns would show up on candlestick volume charts are shown in Figures 16.37 and 16.38.

Chart 16.9 shows a candlestick volume chart for Walmart, the world's largest retailer.

Notice how the early November window following the bullish engulf-ing pattern was closed soon after. However, the very thin candlesticks that were involved in the retracement move indicated a lack of volume, which is precisely the type of thing that is required in a pull-back of this nature. Heavy volume in such a situation would indicate selling pressure, as opposed to the situation here, where prices were clearly falling because of a lack of buying interest.

FIGURE 16.36 Candle Volume Configurations

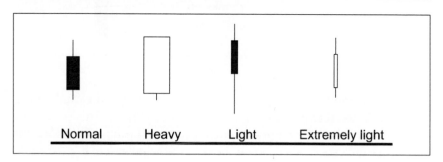

| Normal | Heavy | Light | Extremely light |

FIGURE 16.37 Normal Volume Characteristics

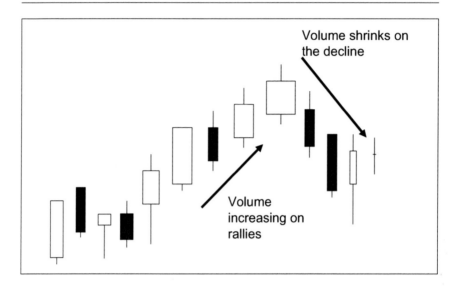

FIGURE 16.38 Bearish Volume Characteristics

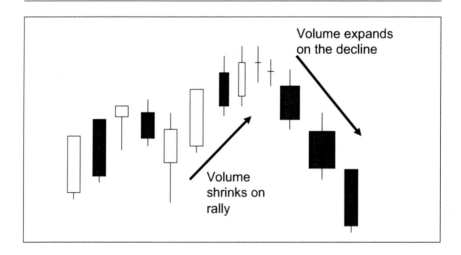

The previous rally experienced a series of very thin candlesticks, which indicated that prices were rising on lower volume. This is opposite to the norm, where rising prices and volume are healthy. Therefore, the very thin candlesticks warned that the days of the rally were numbered.

CHART 16.9 Walmart, 2000–2001 Candle Volume

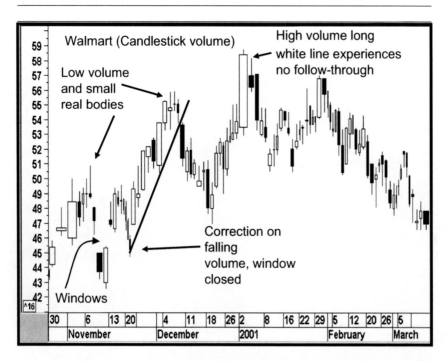

The late November–early December rally was associated with wider candlesticks, which was a good sign. However, as we reach the week of the fourth, the candlesticks move sideways but are very thin. This indicated that the balance between buyers and sellers was more evenly matched. The doji on the day of the high also reflects this even balance. This type of characteristic is often followed by a trend reversal, especially if volume picks up on the downside. That's precisely what happened here as the up trendline is violated and the candlesticks thicken up.

The long, white line that developed at the very end of December looked good at the time since this candlestick was a pretty wide one, indicating heavy volume. However, there was no follow-through on the upside, which indicated that the long, white line was a buying climax. This was confirmed first with the establishment of a harami on the subsequent day and by a long, black candlestick that retraced all of the ground gained by the long, white line.

Chart 16.10 shows an engulfing pattern for the March 2011 top for Broadvision. While there wasn't a lot of "engulfing" going on, the width

CHART 16.10 Broadvision

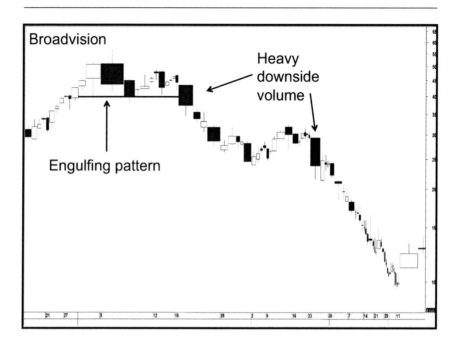

of the second bar indicated huge motivation by sellers to get out. Later on, we see another wide bar, which succeeded in violating support, as evidenced by the penetration of the horizontal trendline. The downtrend was resumed in late April by another long, wide, black real body.

Summary

1. Candlestick charts can be constructed only from data that include opening prices, and therefore, the technique is not one that can be applied to all markets.
2. Candlestick charts provide a unique visual effect that emphasizes certain market characteristics not easily identifiable from bar or closing charts.
3. Candlestick patterns form as reversal and continuation types.
4. Candlesticks can be used in conjunction with Western techniques in a weight-of-the-evidence approach.
5. Adding volume to the formula often brings out actionable technical characteristics that are not always apparent when volume and price are plotted separately.

17

POINT AND FIGURE
CHARTING

Point and Figure Charts versus Bar Charts

Point and figure charts differ from bar charts in two important ways. First, bar charts are plotted at specific time intervals regardless of whether there is any change in price. A new plot on a point and figure chart, on the other hand, is made only when the price changes by a given amount. Point and figure charts are only concerned with measuring price, whereas bar charts measure both price (on the vertical axis) and time (on the horizontal axis).

The second major difference is that bar charts record every change in price for the period they are measuring, but point and figure charts ignore all price movements that are smaller than a specified amount. For example, if a box is set at price movements of 5 points for the *Dow Jones Industrial Average* (DJIA), only price changes in excess of 5 points will be recorded, and smaller fluctuations will not appear.

Construction of Point and Figure Charts

Point and figure charts are constructed using combinations of X's and O's, known as boxes. The X shows that prices are moving up, the O that they are moving down. Once the amount of historical data to be plotted has been established, there are two important decisions to be made before a chart can be constructed.

First, the size of each box must be determined. For individual stocks, it is common practice to use a l-point unit or box for issues trading above $20 and a ½-point unit for lower-priced stocks. However, for very long term charts or for averages consisting of much higher numbers, it is more convenient to use 5-, 10-, or even 20-point boxes. As the box size is decreased, the detail of price movement graphically displayed is increased, and vice versa. In following the price action of a stock or market over many years, it is more convenient to use a relatively large box since small boxes will make the chart unduly large and unmanageable. Often, it is a good idea to maintain two or three different versions, just as daily, weekly, and monthly bar charts may be plotted.

The second decision is whether to use a regular point and figure formula or to use a reversal chart (which should not be confused with a reversal pattern). The straight point and figure chart is plotted just as the data are recorded. If the price moves from 64 to 65, five X's will be plotted on a 20¢-point chart, as in Fig. 17.1(a). If the price reverses from 67 to 66, five O's will be posted. Reversal charts, on the other hand, follow a predetermined rule:

FIGURE 17.1a 20¢-Point Chart

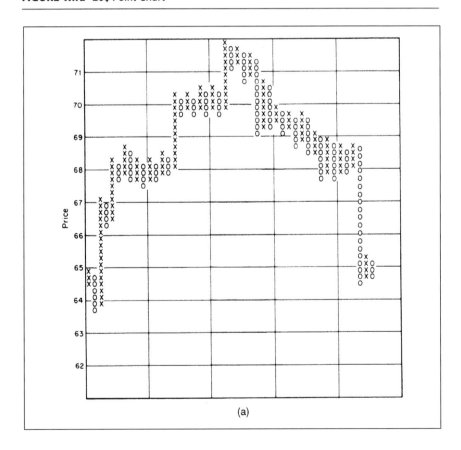

(a)

FIGURE 17.1*b* Closing Prices (Line Chart)

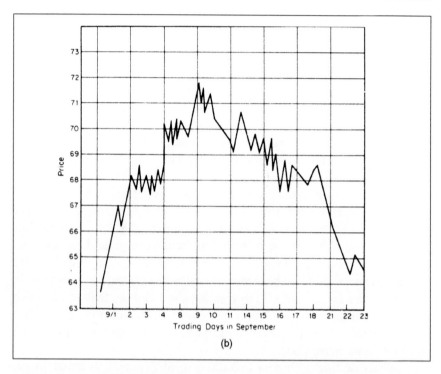

(b)

A new series of X's or 0's cannot begin until prices have moved by a speci-fied amount in the opposite direction to the prevailing trend. The use of the reversal technique therefore helps to reduce misleading or whipsaw sig-nals and to greatly compress the size of the chart so that more data can be plotted. Figure 17.1(*b*) shows the same data plotted as a line chart.

The construction of ½-point, 5-point, or 10-point charts, or charts by any other measure, is identical to the previous method except that a new box can be posted only when the price has moved by the degree specified, that is, by ½ point, 5 points, or 10 points, respectively. Since only price is recorded, it could take several days or even weeks before a new box is plotted. Hence, a common practice is to record dates either at the foot of the chart or in the boxes at the appropriate points. A combination of both date locations is used for longer-term charts. For example, the year is recorded at the bottom of the chart against the column that the first posting of that year was made for, and the beginning of each month is recorded in a box using the number of the month, 1 for January, 2 for February, and so on.

The decision about unit size (and thus the degree of price change required to trigger a new column of O's or X's) is essentially based on personal judgment. It is determined by the price range and degree of volatility of the indicator, stock, or market under consideration. Reducing the size of the units (figures) increases the detail of the price movement portrayed. Making the unit larger expands the base of data, that can be included, but this limits the number of fluctuations that can be illustrated (see Chart 17.1). Following a market with bar or line charts on a daily, weekly, or monthly basis corresponds to keeping several point and figure charts using various unit sizes.

Point and figure charts are plotted on an arithmetic scale. If drawn on paper, they would have traditionally been constructed with 8, 10, or 12 squares to the inch. Occasionally, point and figure charts are plotted on a semilogarithmic or ratio scale, though this is not the norm, because price objectives are calculated in a different way than those on regular charts with a time scale.

Data published in the financial press covering the high, low, and close for specific stocks are not suitable for accurate point and figure charts. For example, if a $15 stock has an intraday price range of $1½, it is impossible to know for point and figure purposes the actual course of the stock from 14½ to 16. It could have risen from 14½ to 16 in one move, which for a ½-point chart would have been represented by three rising X's. Alternatively, it might have moved from 14½ to 15½, back to 14½, and then to 16, which would have resulted in two X's, two O's, and then a column of three X's. The character of the rally has a very important bearing on the appearance of a point and figure chart.

When dealing with data published in this form, it is better to use larger units so that intraday fluctuations do not distort the chart unduly. If more detail is required, the data should be purchased from a source that publishes intraday price movements. Charting packages featuring intraday data that have point and figure options are not affected by this problem.

Accepted rules for plotting point and figure data where the actual prices on the tape are not known are as follows:

- If the opening price is closer to the high than the low, assume that the course of prices is open, high, low, and close.
- If the opening price is closer to the low, assume open, low, high, and close.
- If the opening price is also the high, assume open, high, low, and close.
- If the opening price is also the low, assume open, low, high, and close.
- If the opening price is the low and the closing price is the high, assume open, low, close, and high.
- If the opening price is the high for the day and the close is the lowest price, assume open, high, close, and low.

CHART 17.1 Gold Price $5 and $2 Reversals. These two charts show the gold price plotted on $5 and $2 reversals. The trendlines are self-explanatory. Note that the $5 chart captures 10 years of history very concisely. On the other hand, the 2-point reversal chart, which covers March to November 1982, offers far better detail.

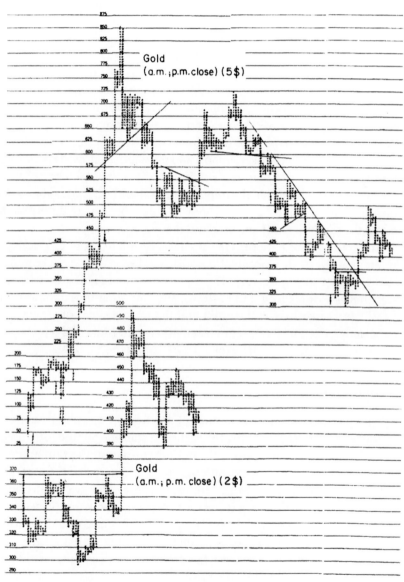

Source: From Chart Analysis London.

Interpreting Point and Figure Charts

General

Since point and figure charts do not include volume, moving averages (MAs), or time, price action is the only element to be examined. In this respect, the basic principles of bar chart analysis are applied. There are certain disadvantages to using point and figure charts; for example, key reversal days, islands, gaps, and other such formations do not show up. On the other hand, if properly constructed, these charts represent all important price swings, even on an intraday basis. They effectively emphasize important support and resistance areas. For example, on a weekly bar chart, a single bar representing a weekly price action can take up only one line. However, if there was considerable volatility during the week in which support and resistance were each tested three or four times, this would most likely show up on a point and figure chart as a congestion area. As a result, the importance of these levels would be drawn to the attention of the technician, who would then be in a good position to interpret the significance of any breakout that might develop.

Point and figure patterns are similar in nature to those of price patterns and may be of the continuation or reversal type. The most common ones are shown in Figure 17.2. Head-and-shoulders (H&S) and inverse H&S patterns, double tops and bottoms, and rounding tops and bottoms can easily be recognized as the point and figure equivalent of regular bar or close-only price formations, discussed previously. Most of the price patterns shown in Figure 17.2 are explained in Chapter 5.

The Count Method

Chapter 5 pointed out that the minimum downside projection from an H&S top is derived by projecting the vertical distance from the top of the head to the neckline downward at the point of breakout. In point and figure charting, the *width* of the pattern is used to determine the measuring objective, which is again projected from the breakout point. No one to my knowledge has thus far satisfactorily explained why this principle appears to work. It seems to be based on the idea that lateral and vertical movements are proportional to each other on a point and figure chart. In other words, the more times a price has undergone price swings within two given levels (as dictated by the price pattern), the greater the *ultimate* move is likely to be once the breakout has taken place. On a point and figure chart, the dimensions of the consolidation or reversal pattern can

FIGURE 17.2 Point and Figure Price Patterns (Study Helps in Point and Figure Techniques)

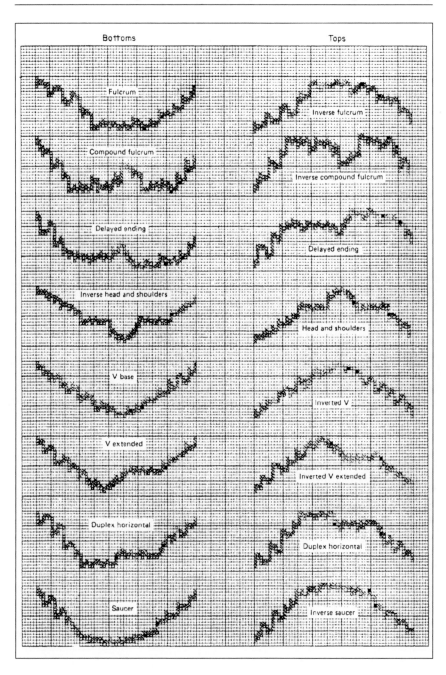

be easily discerned by adding up the number of boxes and projecting the number downward or upward, depending on which way prices break out.

The problem with the count method is that formations with irregular outlines can generate confusion about where the count should begin. The best approach is to select an important horizontal line in the formation, measure across it, and add (or subtract) the number of boxes in the line to (or from) the level of the line.

Price projections for point and figure formations are by no means 100 percent accurate in all situations. In general, upside projections are likely to be exceeded in bull markets, and downside projections surpassed in bear markets. Projections that are made counter to the prevailing trend have a tendency not to be achieved, such as a downside projection in a bull market. Chart 17.2 shows a couple of examples of the count method in action.

CHART 17.2 Honeywell (.50 × 1). This chart features a number of price formations for Honeywell using a .50 × 1 combination. Note that the measuring objective from the base on the left was reached almost to the dollar. The H&S top that followed offered a nice sell signal as the neckline was penetrated. The objective in this case called for the price to fall back to its previous low. As it turned out, this was exceeded. Note how the subsequent rally found resistance in approximately the same area as the objective. Finally, we see a nice trendline break in the right-hand side of the chart.

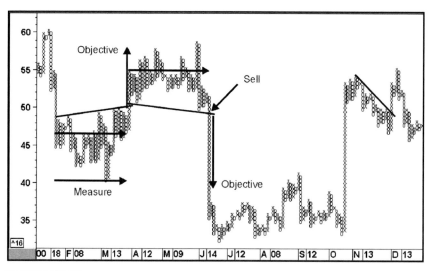

Source: From pring.com

Trendlines on Point and Figure Charts

It is possible to construct trendlines on point and figure charts by joining a series of declining peaks. Up trendlines are drawn by connecting a series of rising lows, and horizontal trendlines are created by joining identical support or resistance levels. The same principles of interpretation discussed in Chapter 8 apply to trendlines drawn on point and figure charts. The trendline takes its significance from a combination of length, the angle of descent or ascent, and the number of times it has been touched. Misleading or whipsaw signals occur occasionally. However, if a carefully chosen reversal amount is used as a filter in the construction of the chart, such whipsaws can be kept to a minimum. Another possibility would be to draw a parallel line one box above (or below) the actual trendline as a filter and use this as the signal to buy (or sell). Although some timeliness is clearly lost with this type of approach, it does offer some protection from misleading price moves.

Major Technical Principle   The fundamental difference between price projections based on point and figure charts and those based on bar or close-only charts is that the measuring formula of point and figure charts is derived from a horizontal rather than a vertical count.

It is also possible to construct oscillators and plot them underneath point and figure charts. Since time is ignored in the point and figure charts, oscillators will appear differently than on regular charts where the time scale is plotted for each unit (hour, day, week, and so on). An example using a 14-period relative strength indicator (RSI) is shown in Chart 17.3.

CHART 17.3 Boeing (1 × 1) and an RSI. This chart of Boeing shows that it is possible to combine an oscillator with a point and figure chart. The joint breakout by the price and RSI offered a timely buy signal on June 16.

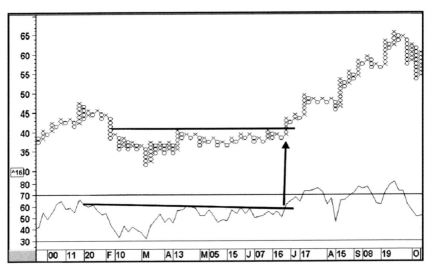

Source: From pring.com

Summary

- Point and figure charts measure only one dimension: price.
- Point and figure charts are constructed from columns of X's and O's, known as figures, which represent a specified, predetermined price movement.
- Point and figure charts often point up support/resistance zones better than bar charts because they emphasize the number of price swings that take place within a given congestion area.
- Point and figure charts are interpreted similarly to bar charts, the main exception being the measuring formula, which is achieved by the principle of the count.

18

MISCELLANEOUS TECHNIQUES FOR DETERMINING TRENDS

We are going to start off with the concept of proportion, which is concerned with offering some ideas on the *possible* magnitude of a price move. I deliberately emphasize the word possible because there is no known technique that can consistently forecast magnitude or duration. These techniques should be used only as an indication of the *probable* extent of the move, not as the basis of an actual forecast. Perhaps the simplest way to explain the principle of proportion is to say that crowd psychology, as reflected in market prices, has a tendency to move in specific proportional amounts that have a habit of repeating, but unfortunately not in a predictable pattern. Thus, we could say that stock prices have a habit of doubling and that may have happened three times in the last 20 years. However, there is no guarantee that they will do so in the current cycle. All we can do is observe when this happens and say that this is a good place to anticipate a reversal. Our decision, though, must be based on a consensus of indicators of which the principle of proportion is one. In this instance, the doubling would be an alert to look more closely at the balance of the evidence.

Proportion

The law of motion states that for every action, there is a reaction. Price trends in financial markets are really a reflection of changes in crowd psychology. The measuring implications of price patterns, trendlines, moving averages (MAs), and envelopes, which were discussed earlier, are examples of proportion in practice.

Support and resistance levels can help offer some ideas of just where a price trend may be temporarily halted or reversed. The principles of proportion can do the same thing, but they go much further.

For example, when a security price is exploring new, all-time-high ground, there is no indication of where a resistance level may occur because no transactions have taken place there. In such cases, the concept of proportion offers a clue to potential juncture points.

Perhaps the best-known principle of proportion is the *50 percent rule.* For instance, many bear markets, as measured by the Dow Jones Industrial Average (DJIA), have cut prices by half. For instance, the 1901–1903, 1907, 1919–1921, and 1937–1938 bear markets recorded declines of 46, 49, 47, and 50 percent, respectively. The first leg of the 1929–1932 bear market ended in October 1929 at 195, just over half the September high. Sometimes, the halfway mark in an advance represents the point of balance, often giving a clue as to the ultimate extent of the move in question or, alternatively, indicating an important juncture point for the return move. Thus, between 1970 and 1973, the market advanced from 628 to 1,067. The halfway point in that rise was 848, or approximately the same level at which the first stage of the 1973–1974 bear market ended.

By the same token, rising markets often find resistance after doubling from a low; the first rally from 40 to 81 in the 1932–1937 bull market was a double.

The 50 percent mark falls halfway between the one-third and two-thirds retracement described in the discussion of Dow theory. These one-third and two-thirds proportions can be widely observed in all financial markets, and also serve as support or resistance zones. Ratio scale charts are helpful in determining such points, since moves of identical proportion can easily be projected up and down.

Chart 18.1 shows the 2000–2002 bear market. Note how the March 2001 rally retraced 50 percent of the bear market's first downleg. The next advance retraced a little more than 33 percent of the primary trend drop up to that point. Finally, you can see how the area of the 9/11 low proved to be resistance for the July/August 2002 advance.

It is not possible to project which proportion will result from a specific move. However, these swings occur with sufficient consistency to offer possible reversal points at both peaks and troughs. If general market conditions and additional technical analysis of the price are consistent, there is a good chance that the projections based on this approach may prove accurate.

CHART 18.1 S&P Composite, 1999–2003 Retracement Moves

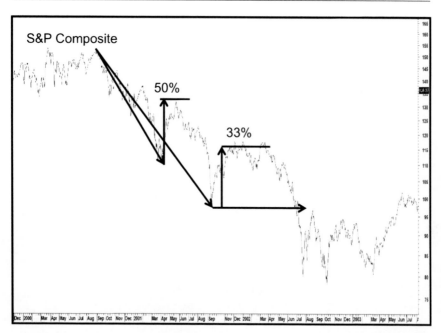

Source: From pring.com

Remember, technical analysis deals with probabilities, which means that forecasts solely based on this method should never be undertaken. If you are making a projection based on the rules of proportion, it is always a good idea to see whether the projection corresponds to a previous support or resistance point. If so, the odds will be much higher that this zone will represent a reversal point, or at least a temporary barrier. When a market is reaching new, all-time-high ground, another possibility is to try to extend up trendlines. The point at which the line intersects with the projection using the rules of proportion may well represent the time and place of an important reversal. Experimentation will show that each market, stock, or commodity has a character of its own, some lending themselves more readily to this approach, others not at all.

Chart 18.2, featuring Amazon, shows some retracement moves and does some 50 percent projections into new high territory. The full decline between 1999 and 2002 flagged by the thick arrow sports a 0 percent because at that point there is no retracement. The 50 percent mark halts the initial rally and forms support in 2008. The 150 percent level becomes a pivotal point, not as a resistance, but as support for subsequent declines.

CHART 18.2 Amazon, 1998–2012 Retracement Moves

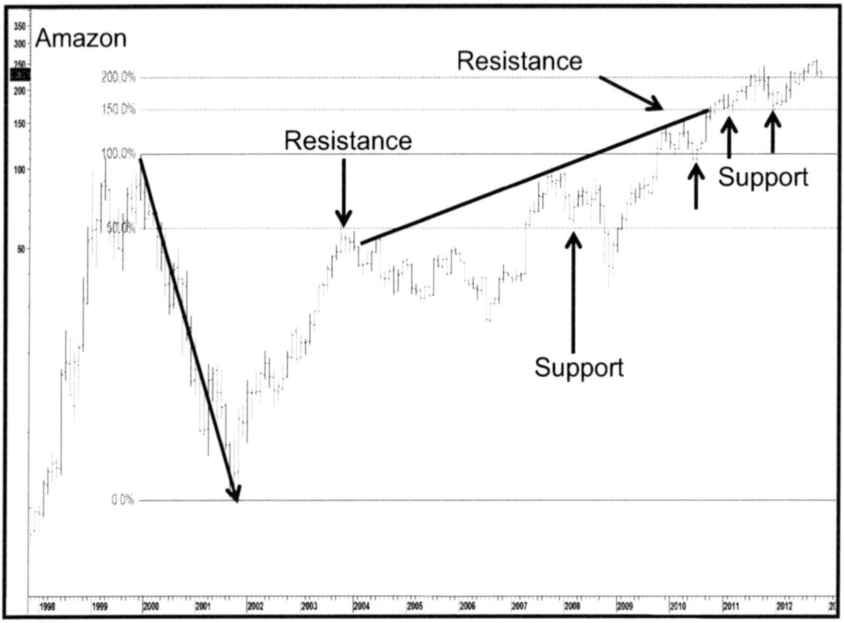

Source: From pring.com

Major Technical Principle Always use projections using the principles of proportion in conjunction with other indicators.

Speed Resistance Lines

This concept incorporates the one-third and two-thirds proportions, but instead of incorporating them as a base for a probable price objective, uses them in conjunction with the speed of an advance or a decline. This concept was developed by the late, great Edson Gould, one of the finest technical minds of all time.

During a downward reaction, a price may be expected to find support when it reaches a line that is advancing at either two-thirds or one-third of the rate of advance from the previous trough to the previous peak. This is illustrated in Figure 18.1.

FIGURE 18.1 Speed Resistance Line (Bull Retracement)

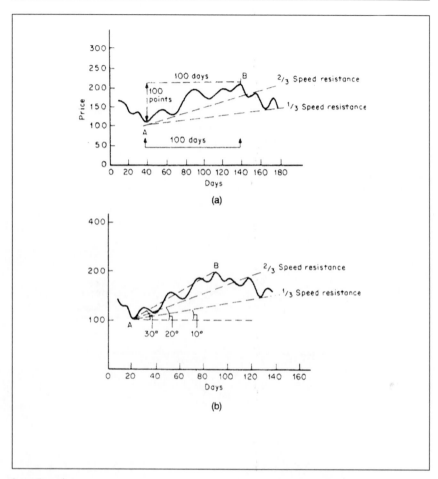

Source: From pring.com

In examples *a* and *b*, A marks the trough and B the peak. The advance from A to B is 100 points and takes 100 days, so the speed of the advance is 1 point per day. A one-third speed resistance line will advance at one-third of that rate (that is, a third of a point per day), and a two-thirds line will move at two-thirds of a point per day.

A rally or decline is measured from the extreme intraday high or low and not the closing price. In order to construct a one-third speed resistance line from example *a*, it is necessary to add 33 points (i.e., one-third of the 100-point advance) to the price at A and plot this point directly under B.

In this case, A is 100 points, and so a plot is made at 133 under B. This point is then joined to A and the line extended to the right-hand portion of the graph. Similarly, the two-thirds line joins A and the 166 level on the same date as B. If the chart were plotted on a ratio scale, the task would be much easier. All that would be required would be a line joining A and B (this is shown in example b). The angle of ascent—in this case, 30 degrees—would then be recorded. Two lines at one-third (10 degrees) and two-thirds (20 degrees) of this angle are then drawn. Figure 18.2 illustrates the same process for a declining market. Once constructed, the speed resistance lines act as important support and resistance areas.

FIGURE 18.2 Speed Resistance Line (Bear Retracement)

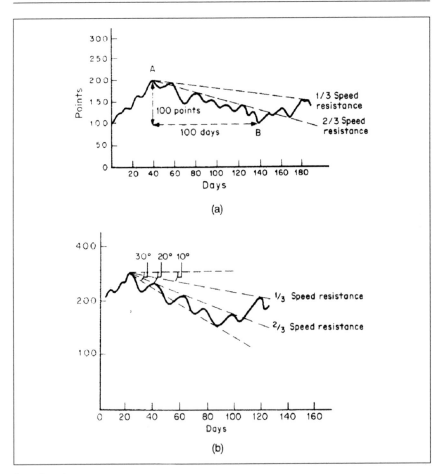

More specifically, the application of these lines is based on the following rules:

1. A reaction following a rally will find support at the two-thirds speed resistance line. If this line is violated, the support should be found at the one-third speed resistance line. If the price falls below its one-third line, the probabilities indicate that the rising move has been completed and that it will decline to a new low, possibly below that upon which the speed resistance lines were based.
2. If the price holds at the one-third line, a resistance to a further advance may be expected at the two-thirds line. If it moves above the two-thirds line, a new high is likely to be recorded.
3. If the price violates its one-third line and then rallies again, it will find resistance to that rally at the one-third line.
4. Rules 1 through 3 apply in reverse for a declining market.

Chart 18.3 shows the application of these rules in the marketplace, where A and B mark the points at which the lines are anchored, since these

CHART 18.3 NASDAQ 100, 2007–2012 Speed Resistance Lines

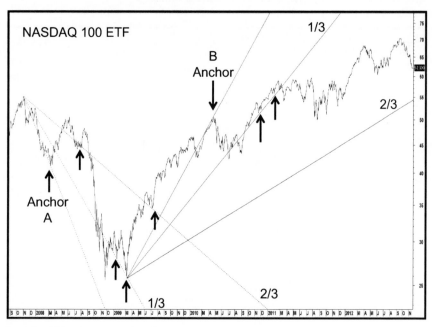

Source: From pring.com

represent the first intermediate turning points in their respective bear and bull markets. Obviously, with the benefit of hindsight, it is easy to spot these turning points, but in reality, it is likely to be several weeks before they could be identified. Only then would it be possible to use the lines as potential support/resistance levels. These are flagged with the small arrows. It would have been possible to come up with examples where the lines served more often as pivotal points, but the situation in Chart 18.3 is, unfortunately, more the rule than the exception.

Fibonacci Fans

Fibonacci fan lines are displayed by first drawing a line between two extreme points: a high and low (vice versa in a declining market). An invisible vertical line is drawn through the second extreme point. Three lines are then constructed from the first extreme point (the low) passing through the invisible vertical line with their slopes at the Fibonacci levels, usually 38.2 percent, 50.0 percent, and 61.8 percent. These lines indicate potential areas of support and resistance. In Chart 18.4, the thick arrow joins the 2009

CHART 18.4 S&P Composite, 2009–2012 Fibonacci Fan Lines

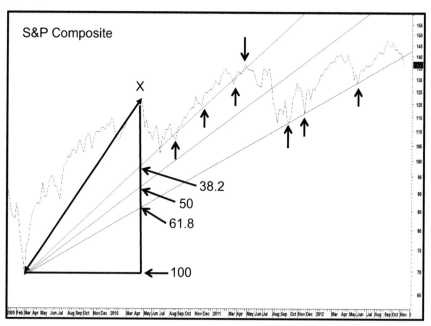

Source: From pring.com

low in the S&P Composite to its first intermediate high. The Fibonacci fan lines at 38.2, 50, and 61.8 percent flag the three retracement levels, as at the vertical line. It is once again very important to emphasize that such pivotal points do not always appear as conveniently as in the chart. This emphasizes the idea already put forward that one should always use these techniques along with other indicators. They should never be used on their own to make a prediction because of their lack of reliability.

Gann Fans

Gann lines are named for the early twentieth-century commodity trader W. D. Gann. They come in three forms: Gann lines, fans, and grids. The most practical appears to be the fan approach. The concept and application are very similar to the speed resistance lines discussed earlier. Gann's idea was that specific geometric patterns and angles had unique characteristics for the prediction of price turning points. Essential to this approach was a balance between time and price. Thus, a 45-degree angle offered a perfect balance between price and time. That could only be achieved if the distance on the chart is the same for price and time, thus mandating an arithmetic scaling on the price axis. An example is shown in Chart 18.5, where the nine Gann recommended angles are plotted.

CHART 18.5 Advanced Micro Circuit, 2000 Gann Fan Lines

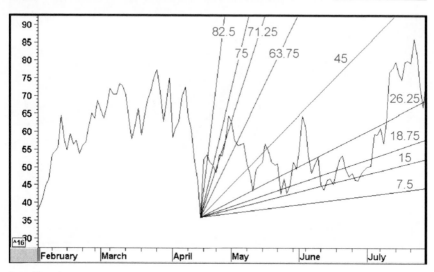

Source: From pring.com

The following table reflects the rise (price increase) over run (time difference). As way of explanation 12 × 1 rise run means that the price increases twice as fast compared to the time taken for a run of 1, and so forth.

1 × 8	82.5 degrees
1 × 4	75 degrees
1 × 3	71.25 degrees
1 × 2	63.75 degrees
1 × 1	45 degrees
2 × 1	26.25 degrees
3 × 1	18.75 degrees
4 × 1	15 degrees
8 × 1	7.5 degrees

Source: Steve Achelis, *Technical Analysis A to Z*, Probus, 1995, p. 148.

Chart 18.6 shows Gann fans. In this instance, the central line connects the high with the December low and the rise/run proportions are the same; the center line reflects a 1 × 1, the upper line reflects an 8 × 1, and so forth.

CHART 18.6 Advanced Micro Circuit, 2000–2001 Gann Fan Lines

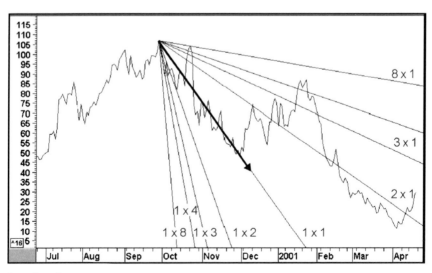

Source: From pring.com

However, because the time and price distances are not the same, the lines are at different angles. The principles of interpretation are similar, in that it is assumed that when one line is penetrated, the price will find resistance at the next one if it is rising, or support in the case of a decline. Thus, the lines are continually reversing their support/resistance functions. See how the initial rally finds resistance at the 2 × 1 line. This line is subsequently penetrated on the way up, but acts as support for the next two reactions. Once again, there are far more exceptions than those reversal points that make up the rules. This means, of course, that Gann fans should be used as a place for anticipating a reversal, depending on what the other indicators are saying.

Ichimoku Cloud Charts

The Components

A relatively recent introduction to the Japanese technical arsenal is the Ichimoku cloud, also known as Ichimoku Kinko Hyo. Literally translated, it means "at one glance balance bar chart." The cloud and its ancillary indicators provide trading signals through the ability to identify trend direction, as well as indicating potential support and resistance areas. Goichi Hosoda, the creator of this approach, argues that traders adopting it can immediately identify the trend and isolate potential signals within it. At first glance, the cloud approach appears complicated, almost intimidating, but when explained, its interpretation is relatively straightforward.

The first thing to understand is that the relationship between the price and the cloud identifies basic uptrends and downtrends, and the relationship between two other indicators in the system generates short-term buy and sell signals under that context.

Altogether, there are five moving parts to the system. They have been labeled in Chart 18.7.

To simplify the explanation, we start off in Chart 18.8 by focusing on two indicators: the conversion line (also called the turning line) and the base line (also called the standard line). The conversion line is calculated as the midpoint of the 9-day high-low range. The default setting is nine periods, and the formula would be (9-period high + 9-period low)/2. The base line uses the same approach, but this time, the high over 26 periods is added to the low over that same period. The total is once again divided by two. The Japanese term for the conversion line is *Tenkan-sen* and for the base line, it is

CHART 18.7 Microsoft 2012 Ichimoku Cloud

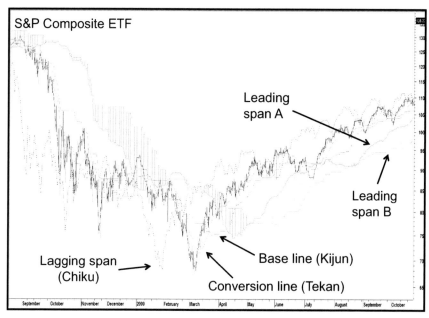

Source: From Pring.com

CHART 18.8 S&P Composite ETF, 2011–2012 Ichimoku Conversion and Base Line with Lagging Span

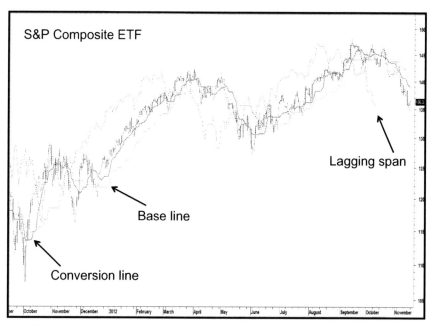

Source: From pring.com

CHART 18.9 S&P Composite ETF, 2011–2012 Ichimoku Leading Spans

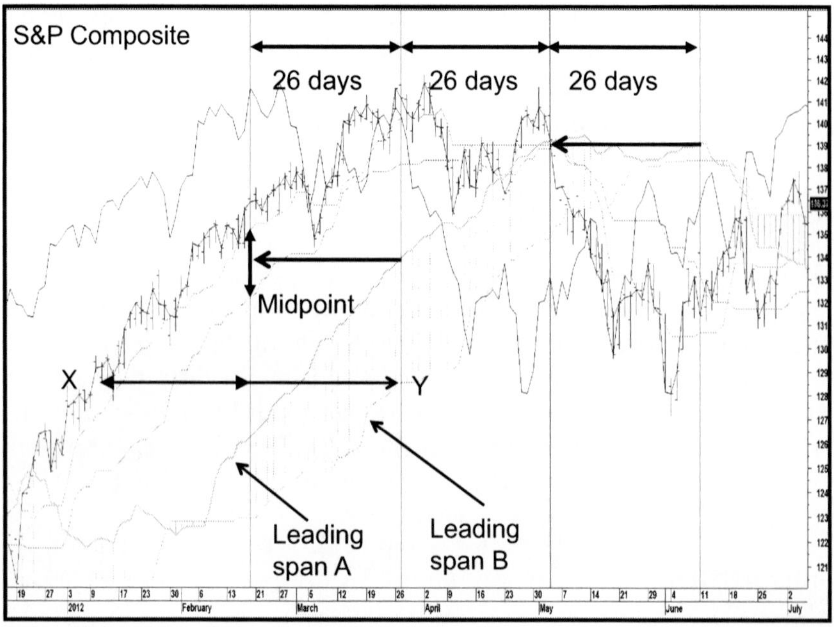

Source: From pring.com

Kijun-sen. The relationship between these two indicators forms the basis for short-term buy and sell signals, as well as the faster of the two cloud boundaries. Let's consider the cloud first and then talk about the signals.

The boundary derived from the conversion and base line relationship is the cloud (leading) span A or 1 (*senkou span A*). This indicator is calculated by adding the value of the conversion line to that of the base line and dividing by two. It uses the word *leading* in its description because the result is plotted 26 periods into the future as shown in Chart 18.9.

The second cloud border, cloud (leading) span B or 2 (*senkou span B*) is calculated by adding the 52-period high to the 52-period low and dividing by two. The result is also plotted 26 periods in advance. In Chart 18.9, the 52-period high/low is calculated at point X and the result is plotted at point Y. Since the high/low calculation returned a low number at X, cloud span B was plotted at quite a distance below the prevailing price at Y in late March 2012 because the actual price was much higher. The fifth moving part is the lagging line, which is the closing price shifted back 26 days. In the vast majority of situations, this series crosses the cloud after the price and represents a confirming signal that the trend has changed.

The parameters outlined earlier are the recommended default ones, but there is no reason why others cannot be adopted. Also, the charts in this chapter feature daily data, but this approach can be applied to any time period.

Since cloud span A, the thicker line, is derived from the shorter-term conversion and standard lines, it moves faster than span B, which relies on its construction from a longer 52-period average high/low relationship.

Time Frames

As with any other form of technical methodology, it's often a good idea to try to gain some understanding of the direction of the longer-term and more dominant trend than that being plotted. In this chapter, we have focused on daily charts and short-term and intermediate time frames. However, it also makes sense to explore the clouds being formed on the more dominant weekly and monthly charts. Traders with a very near-term horizon are encouraged to experiment with intraday time periods.

Interpretation

The Major Trend Since the cloud is constructed from price action and this action is projected 26 days into the future, it indicates future support/resistance zones. An example is shown in Chart 18.10. It also shows that when the price is above the cloud, the cloud acts as a natural support area and vice versa. It's also a characteristic that prices interact with the outer and inner edges of the cloud.

The trend is up when the price is above the cloud and down when it is under it. It is considered neutral when the price is actually in the cloud. However, some analysts believe that the direction from which the price entered the cloud determines the direction of the trend. That would mean that if, for example, in a bull market the price drops into the cloud, the prevailing positive trend is still considered to be in force. Only when the price falls completely through the cloud is the trend deemed bearish. A compromise approach would say that when the price enters the cloud from above, this reduces the strength of the uptrend. At that time, the consensus of other indicators is then used to come to a meaningful conclusion as to the true state of the trend.

The quality of the uptrend is strengthened when the leading span A (thick cloud border) is rising and is above the leading span B (thin cloud border). This situation produces a light cloud (normally green when colors are available) on the chart. Conversely, a downtrend, when the price is below

CHART 18.10 Microsoft 2012 Ichimoku Cloud Resistance Points

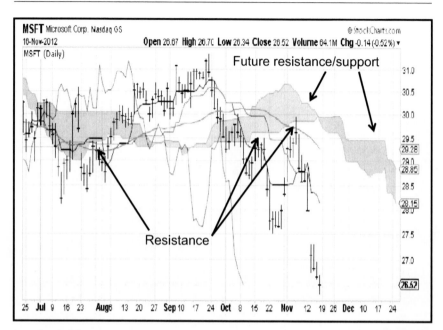

Source: From Stock Charts.com

the cloud, is reinforced when the leading span A (normally green cloud line) is below the leading span B (normally red cloud line). Chart 18. 11 just features the cloud.

The bullish and bearish periods are indicated with the arrows, and at point A the cloud span crosses above B for a stronger trend signal. At B1 and B2, the price slips into the cloud itself and the trend is then defined as being flat. At just after B1, it moves back above the cloud again and is bullish.

Chart 18.12 also flags bullish and bearish signals. Coming into the chart, the trend is bullish even though the price is declining. At A, it falls into the cloud, generating a neutral signal. As it rises through the (thick) span A, a bullish trend is again signaled. Unfortunately, the bottom building process results in another whipsaw at C. This is quickly resolved with a bullish signal at D. The trend remains positive all the way through until G. However, the A span cloud border (thick) line crosses below the B (thin) line at E. This tells us that upside momentum is dissipating and takes the positive trend down a notch. Note at E how the cloud changes temporarily from a light (normally green) to a dark (normally red) highlight. We quickly see a regaining of momentum at F as the lines revert to their

CHART 18.11 Amazon, Ichimoku Cloud Bullish and Bearish Signals

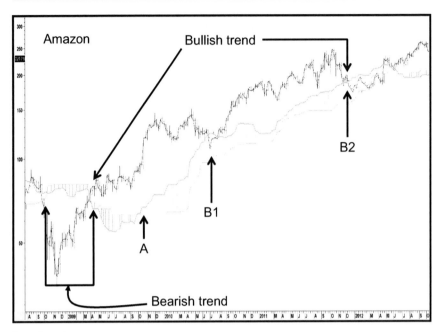

Source: From pring.com

CHART 18.12 S&P Composite ETF

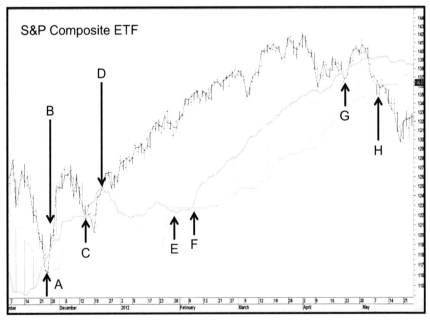

Source: Pring.com

former status. After a false break to the downside at G and a subsequent small rally, a downtrend is signaled at H as the price slips below the lower boundary of the cloud.

Chart 18.10 shows how the cloud served as a resistance level for the Microsoft price in 2012. When the cloud is extended, as it is in this chart, it is helpful in that it indicates future potential levels of support or resistance.

Shorter-Term Signals

The relationship between the price and the conversion and base lines can be used to identify faster, and more frequent, signals. In conjunction with the idea that pro-trend signals are generally stronger than contratrend signals, positive conversion/base line crossovers are reinforced when prices are above the cloud and the cloud has a light (green) shading. Bearish signals are reinforced when prices are below the cloud and the cloud has a (red) dark highlight. Conversely, signals that are counter to the existing trend are deemed weaker.

CHART 18.13 iShares Germany ETF, 2011–2012 Ichimoku Cloud Short-Term Buy and Sell Signals

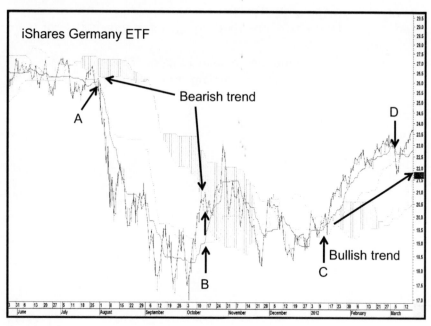

Source: From pring.com

Chart 18.13 features the iShares Germany ETF, the EWG, with the clouds and lines, but excluding the lagging line to reduce the clutter. The period marked by the arrows on the left indicates when the price is below the cloud and, therefore, identifies when the trend is bearish. The thick conversion line crosses below the dashed base line at point A, and the short-term system stays bearish until it crosses back above it at B. The period between B and C experienced ranging action, a trading characteristic not suitable for cloud analysis. Then at C we see another buy signal, but when it was generated, the price was slightly below the cloud, thereby flagging a bear trend. It would have been possible to enter the trade when the price crossed above the cloud because it had not moved much by this point and would not have been overbought. In this instance, a good profit would have been earned by the time the sell signal was triggered at D.

Summary

1. Price often moves in proportions, the most common of which are one-half, one-third, and two-thirds.
2. Speed resistance lines, Fibonacci fans, and Gann fans offer potential support/resistance pivotal points.
3. Ichimoku cloud charts offer both longer-term and short-term trend signals.
4. Future cloud action indicates potential support/resistance areas.
5. Cloud charts can be plotted for any time frame, from intraday to monthly.

19

THE CONCEPT OF RELATIVE STRENGTH

The Concept

Relative strength (RS) is a technical concept that measures the relationship between two securities. It's important to note that *relative strength* as we will be using it here has nothing to do with Welles Wilder's relative strength indicator (RSI), which is discussed in Chapter 14.

The concept explained here is comparative relative strength, where the price of one security is divided by that of another. The result is then plotted as a continuous line whose trend is then analyzed. There are several ways in which relative strength can be used:

1. To compare one asset class to another in order to decide which one to buy, or to better understand an intermarket relationship. For example, we might compare gold to bonds to see which was in a rising trend. If the relationship was in an uptrend, it would indicate that on a price basis, gold was outperforming bonds and that it was, therefore, the preferred asset. It would also tell us that the market was anticipating an inflationary environment since gold is largely purchased as an inflation hedge, whereas credit-worthy bonds typically do better in deflationary times.

   Another possibility might arise when a review of the technical position indicates that both the U.S. and Japanese stock markets are in a bullish trend. Analyzing the trend of the relationship between them indicates which market is likely to outperform.

2. In commodity trading, a spread is a form of relative strength. A spread involves the relationship between one commodity and another, such as corn to hogs. Alternatively, a spread captures the relationship between a distant contract and a nearby one. In this instance, traders are attempting to discover relationships that have diverged from the norm and riding on the spread until the two contracts come back into line. Moreover, changes in these relationships also warn of emerging surplus or shortage conditions that help in supply/demand analysis relative to current and future conditions.

3. A currency is really a relative relationship. For example, there is no such thing as *the U.S. dollar* in an external sense, because it consists of a number of cross-rates: dollar-yen, euro-dollar, Canadian-U.S.dollar, and so forth. Each currency is merely a relationship between itself and other currencies.

4. Sometimes the relative action between two entities reflects confidence and can be used for the purpose of analyzing the market itself. For example, we may find that the ratio between the technology and consumer staple sectors is falling. Technology reflects hot money that flows when confidence is high, and consumer staples are defensive issues that investors buy when they are apprehensive. A declining trend in this relationship would therefore reflect declining confidence and represent a bearish factor. This is a different type of relative relationship, which is covered in greater detail in Chapter 28.

5. The most common and important use of relative strength is to compare the price of a security to an index corresponding to its universe. The most common example would be a stock to a market average. For example, we might compare the performance of Facebook to the S&P Composite. If the resultant RS line is rising, it would mean that Facebook was outperforming the market and vice versa.

It is this concept of comparing an individual security to a market average that we will be concentrating on in this chapter. Please note that unless otherwise stated, all relative strength comparisons are calculated against the S&P Composite.

Major Technical Principle Relative strength is a very powerful concept that facilitates individual stock selection.

Construction of an RS Line

An RS line is obtained by dividing the price of one item by another. The numerator is usually a stock, and the denominator a measurement of "the market," for example, the NASDAQ or the S&P 500. Outside the US it would be a stock price compared to a specific country average such as the DAX in Germany, the Nifty in India and so forth. In later chapters we will also look at the relative relationships between sectors and industry groups against the market, as this represents a shortcut method of stock selection. For example, it is quicker to study the RS lines for 12 sectors and then study the components of the selected area than to review 3,000 to 5,000 individual stocks.

The relative strength concept can also be expanded to the commodity area. This is achieved by comparing the price of an individual commodity, such as corn, to a commodity index, such as the Thompson Reuters Commodity Research Board (CRB) Composite or the Dow Jones UBS Commodity Index. Our examples will focus on individual stocks relative to the market, but this and other concepts are equally acceptable. In this respect, Figure 19.1 shows the closing price of the stock in the upper panel and its RS in the lower one.

When the line is rising, it means that the stock is outperforming the market. In this case, the denominator is the S&P Composite, so

FIGURE 19.1 RS and Price

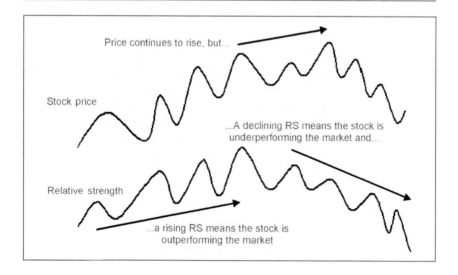

a rising line means that the stock is outperforming the S&P. Later on, it continues to rally, but the RS line peaks out. This means that the stock is now underperforming the market. Another possibility might involve the comparison of an individual country's stock or index to a global indicator, such as the Morgan Stanley World Stock Index. As long as the appropriate currency adjustments are made, the concepts are the same.

The interpretation of relative trends is subject to exactly the same principles as the price itself. It is important to note that an RS indicator is just what the name implies: *relative.* A rising line does not mean that an item, such as a stock, is advancing in price—merely that it is outperforming the market, or rising *relative* to the market average. For example, the market as measured by the S&P Composite may have fallen by 20 percent and the stock by 10 percent. Both have lost value, but the RS line would be rising because the stock retreated less than the market.

> **Major Technical Principle**   Relative strength moves in trends, just like the absolute price.

RS Interpretation

Because the RS line moves in trends, it lends itself to trend-reversal techniques such as price patterns, trendlines, and moving-average (MA) crossovers. Momentum indicators may also be calculated from relative relationships.

Relative trends can be interpreted in similar ways to trends in absolute prices. However, the introduction of relative analysis into the equation presents an additional dynamic. This arises from a comparison of the two series that often throws up subtle differences in much the same way as a comparison between the price and an oscillator.

Since RS trends tend to experience more random noise than absolute price trends, we generally find that charts based on weekly and monthly data tend to be more reliable than those constructed from daily RS data. This same principle is true for the absolute price, but more so, I believe, for relative action.

Positive and Negative RS Divergences

When both the price and the RS are rising, they are said to be "in gear." Important trends usually begin with both series acting in concert, but eventually,

FIGURE 19.2 RS and a Negative Divergence

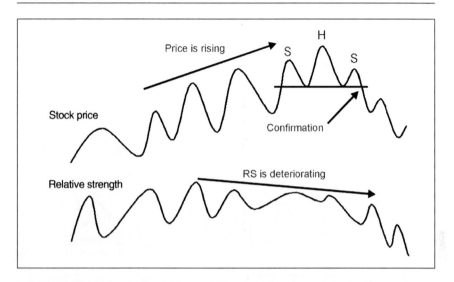

the RS line fails to confirm new highs being set by the price itself. This type of situation indicates that the odds favor the stock beginning a period of underperformance against the market. However, weakness in RS is not an absolute sell signal, i.e., one indicating that the price itself will go down; it is merely a relative signal, i.e., one implying a switch from an issue that has started to become out of favor to one that is coming into favor.

Quite often, though, *a divergence or series of divergences between the price and RS represents an early warning sign of trouble*, which is later confirmed by a trend-reversal signal in the price itself. In Figure 19.2 the two are in gear at the start, but later on, the RS line diverges negatively with the price on three occasions. Finally, the price itself completes a top and declines.

The opposite set of circumstances holds true in a declining market, in which *an improvement in RS ahead of price is regarded as a positive sign.* An example is shown in Figure 19.3. This time, the confirmation comes from a trendline break in the price.

Trend-Reversal Techniques

1. Moving-Average Crossovers   Sometimes it's a good idea to run a moving average through the price using the crossovers as legitimate signals of a change in trend. It's also possible to do the same thing for a relative strength line, but because the RS line tends to be much more volatile, this technique

FIGURE 19.3 RS and a Positive Divergence

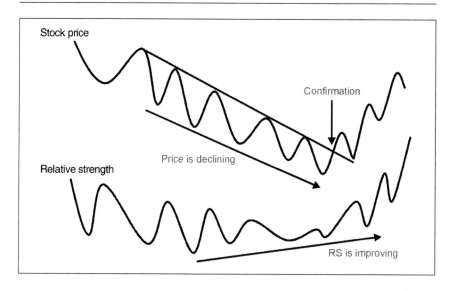

often proves unprofitable because of the numerous whipsaws that are generated. This is especially true for short-term trends, but even long-term moving
averages, such as a 40-week simple or 65-week exponential, often result in
more whipsaw signals than we might like. Figure 19.4 offers an alternative.
It involves plotting two moving averages, a short-term and a longer-term

FIGURE 19.4 RS and MAs

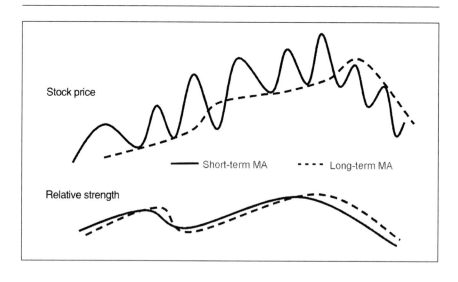

CHART 19.1 General Motors, 1993–2001 and RS MA Crossovers

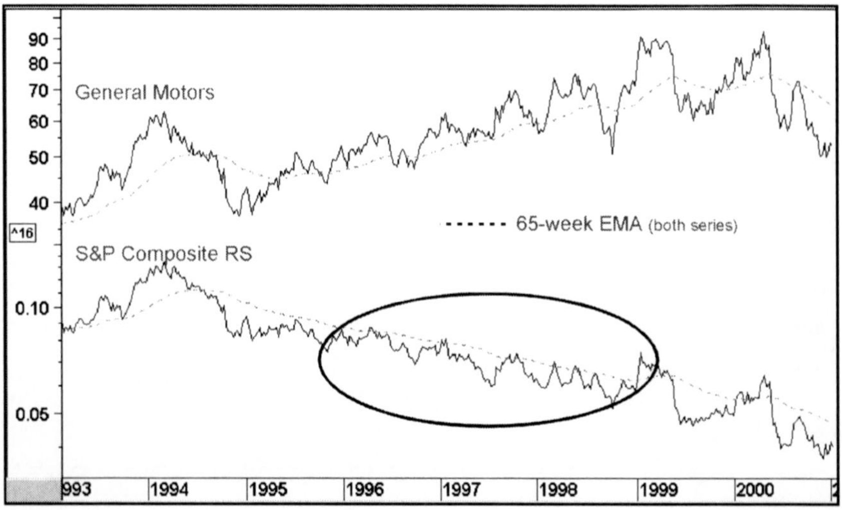

Source: From pring.com

average, using the crossovers for signaling trend reversals. This approach definitely eliminates whipsaws, but the trade-off is that several signals are less timely.

An example is shown in Chart 19.1 for General Motors. Note the numerous whipsaws for the 65-week exponential moving average (EMA) being flagged by the ellipse.

Chart 19.2 shows an alternative where the 65-week EMA is used with its 10-week EMA as a method of signaling trend changes. Note that nearly all of the 1996–1998 whipsaws have been eliminated. We are still left with a couple, but the 1996–1998 pounding is totally avoided as the 65-week red line remains below the solid blue line during the whole period. It is a good idea when you have settled on a time span that makes sense to take a look back historically to make sure it has worked consistently in the past. This should include as much historical data as possible so that its performance during a variety of market conditions can be assessed. For example, a chart plotted with weekly data should ideally cover at least 8 years (two complete cycles) of data.

2. Trendline Violations In my view, a better alternative to the moving-average approach is to construct trendlines against the relative strength line. The concept is to construct a trendline for the RS line and when that is violated to look around for a legitimate trend-reversal signal in the price itself. In that way we can see that the price is responding to the relative

CHART 19.2 General Motors, 1995–2000, and RS MA Crossovers

Source: From pring.com

strength or weakness. Figure 19.5 shows an example of a reversal from an uptrend to a downtrend.

Figure 19.6 shows that this is also a useful way to identify "buy" candidates. The first thing to do is wait for a violation of the RS line.

FIGURE 19.5 RS and Up Trendlines

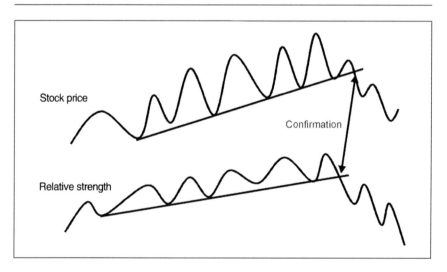

FIGURE 19.6 RS and Down Trendlines

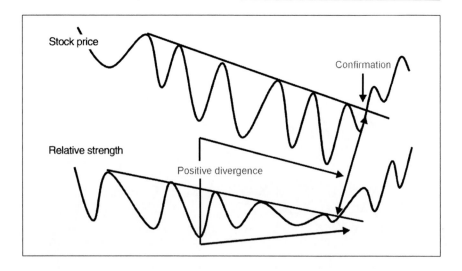

Then, when the price also confirms with a trend-reversal signal, you can take some action. These joint violations don't occur that often, but when they do, it's usually a signal of an important reversal. In this case, the strength of the signal has been enhanced because it was preceded by a positive divergence. The divergence did not represent a signal to buy, but it did set the scene for some positive action later on by indicating that the technical position is improving. Incidentally, the confirmation by the absolute price does not have to be a trendline break—it could be a price pattern completion, a reliable, (and I emphasize the word "reliable") moving-average crossover, or even a reversal to a series of rising peaks and troughs. Remember at all times that the size of the new trend will depend principally on the time frame being charted and the length of the lines. Intraday breaks, for example, reflect small trends and will have nowhere near the significance of trendline violations on the monthly charts.

3. Price Patterns   Price patterns can also be employed to analyze trends in relative strength. In Figure 19.7 the RS line completed a head-and-shoulders top.

This certainly indicates that the RS trend has reversed and provides enough evidence to justify a switch from this stock in favor of one where the RS trend was emerging in a positive way. However, it does not signal that the price itself is going to decline, though in many instances, that will prove to be the case. In this particular example, the absolute trend reversal

FIGURE 19.7 RS and Price Patterns

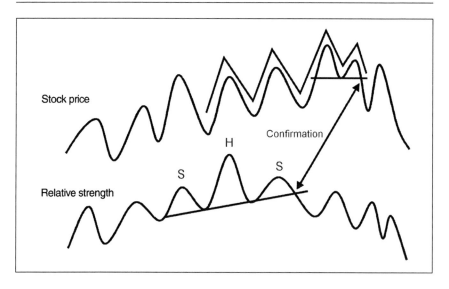

is signaled when the short-term low flagged by the small horizontal trend-line is violated, because this confirms that the series of rising bottoms and tops has now been reversed. Note that even though the price subsequently rallies back through the line, this does nothing to reverse the peak/trough progression to the upside, so the trend is still regarded as negative.

Figure 19.8 features a reversal from a downtrend to an uptrend. First, the RS line diverges positively with the price. This is our initial indication that both trends may be about to reverse. Then the RS line traces out a rectangle and breaks to the upside, later to be followed by the price completing a broadening formation with a flatish top.

Divergences and Trend Signals   Sometimes a study of the relationship between the price and RS line can be quite revealing. Chart 19.3, for example, featuring Stanley Works, shows the price reaching a new high in April 2006 but the RS line fails to confirm. This provided some advance warning that the technical structure was not as positive under the hood. When both trendlines were violated later on, this confirmed the weakness and lower prices ensued. Later on, the price began to rally and everything was in gear until June 2007. This was the warning that when both trendlines were penetrated that price weakness would continue.

Chart 19.4 shows another RS example. This time, it was the Turkish Akbank versus the Turkish Index. At the start of 2005, the divergence

FIGURE 19.8 RS and Price Patterns

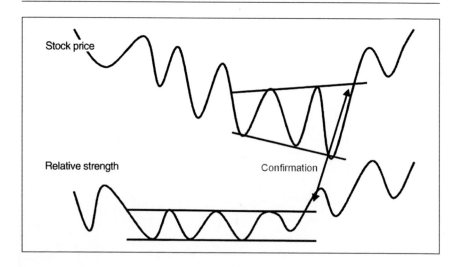

CHART 19.3 Stanley Works, 2005–2007 RS, Divergences and Price Confirmation

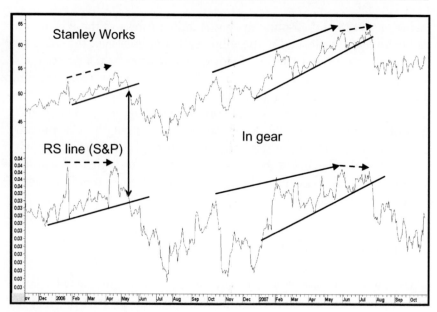

Source: From pring.com

CHART 19.4 Akbank, 2004–2005 RS, Divergences and Price Confirmation

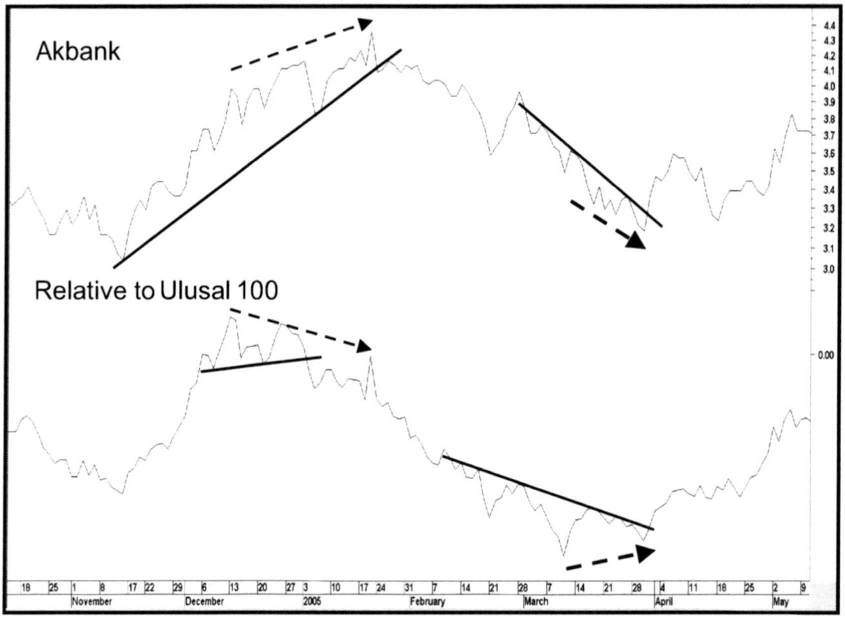

Source: From pring.com

between the RS and absolute price was quite serious, as the RS line was falling quickly. It violated its trendline early on, but when the price followed suit, a very nasty decline followed. Quite often, when we see a discrepancy as large as this, the weakening RS line is offering a loud warning that despite what we see on the surface (rising absolute prices), the technical picture is really quite weak. The price is being dragged up by the market and when it finally turns, the deteriorating relative strength chickens come home to roost. Later on, we see a positive RS divergence as the RS line bottomed in early March, but the subsequent late-March higher low was not confirmed by the price. Later, both series violated down trendlines and a rally was confirmed.

Long-Term Relative Strength

Chart 19.5 features a monthly close of the S&P Domestic Oil relative strength line. This is a very long-term chart that encompasses much of the twentieth century. It is useful in that it demonstrates that the RS line lends

CHART 19.5 S&P Domestic Oil Index, 1960–2012 Long-Term RS Trend Analysis

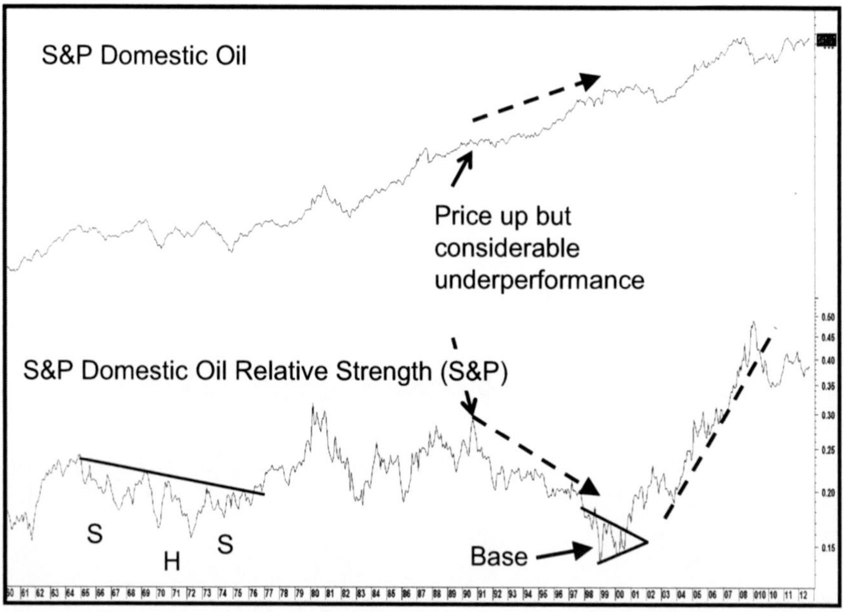

Source: From pring.com

itself to price pattern and trendline construction. These formations are not completed very often, but they are usually followed by a relative price move that lasts for many years. It's important to bear this in mind because most of the patterns look small on the chart but actually extend over considerable periods of time. Their completion, therefore, signals a change in the environment that typically lasts for many years, even decades. For example, it traces out a 12-year reverse head-and-shoulders top in the 1970s. A break of this magnitude signals a change in sentiment for a very long time. Indeed, a huge rally took the RS line to its secular peak in 1980.

Note the fact that the Oil Index itself experienced a substantial rally between 1980 and the end of the century. Does this mean that oils would have been a good place to invest in this 20-year period? Hardly, because the persistent decline in the RS line indicated that they were consistent underperformers. Only in the next decade did the relative action come into its own as it broke out from a triangle base, resulting in a rally by both series. In 2008, this strong relative rally was halted as the 2003–2008 up trendline was violated.

Obviously, we would not make a practice of studying these long-term charts every week or so, but say, once a quarter, it does make sense to review the bigger picture to see whether any major trends might be emerging.

Major Technical Principle   It is the longer-term trends that dominate the characteristics of their shorter-term brethren.

On a more regular basis, we would look at monthly charts covering shorter periods of time, later moving down to the weekly and daily ones.

Individual Stocks and Relative Strength Analysis

Chart 19.6 features a daily chart of Hewlett-Packard. It starts off in early 2005 with the simultaneous completion of two inverse head-and-shoulder patterns.

CHART 19.6 Hewlett-Packard, 2003–2012 Long-Term RS Analysis

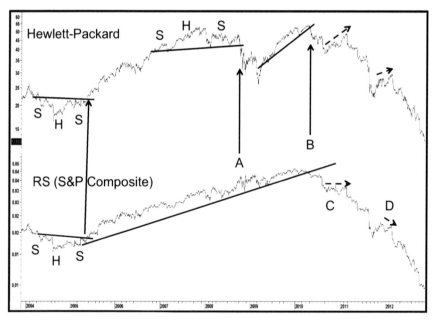

Source: From pring.com

In 2007 and some of 2008, the absolute price traces out a head-and-shoulders top, and at the breakdown point at A, the RS line is close to a high. The actual price starts to fall like a stone but the RS line continues its upward march. This shows that Hewlett-Packard was a *relatively* safe place to be. Its recovery bounce into 2010 continued to indicate that the price had weathered the storm and was likely headed higher. However, both series violated trendlines at B. The RS trendline was far more significant because it was much longer—6 years—and had been touched or approached on eight occasions. This indeed was a serious break, and anyone who had confidence in the stock because it had weathered the previous bear market quite well should have paid attention to this very serious break. In the following three years, the bottom literally fell out of the market. Even during the two small rallies at C and D, the relative performance continued to deteriorate.

> **Major Technical Principle**   It's always better to avoid a stock when it tries to rally during a downtrend but the RS line does not.

On the other hand, an improving RS line is often an early clue that a turn may be at hand. In such cases, the clincher is the eventual confirmation by the price.

Relative Strength and Momentum

Long-Term Trends

Since classic trend-determining techniques can be applied to RS lines, it is a small step to expand the analysis to embrace momentum indicators derived from relative strength lines. While it is certainly practical to apply oscillators to short-term momentum derived from RS lines, by far, the best use of momentum in relative work, I believe, is to use oscillators based on long-term spans, especially if they have been carefully smoothed to limit unwanted fluctuations.

Chart 19.7 features the relative strength line of the Dow Jones Oil and Gas Sector ETF together with a long-term Know Sure Thing (KST) of relative strength. The waves against the RS line reflect those in the KST. Peaks in the KST roughly correspond with its peaks and troughs. As we shall

CHART 19.7 Dow Jones Oil and Gas RS, 2005–2012 and Long-Term RS Momentum

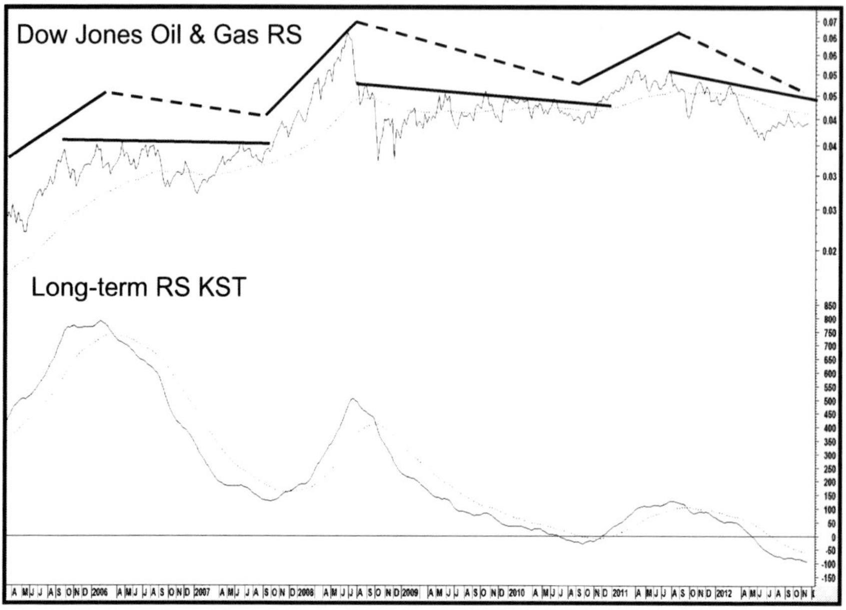

Source: From pring.com

learn in a later chapter on group rotation (see Chapter 22), RS lines are far more cyclical in their patterns than absolute prices. This makes the use of smoothed long-term oscillators such as the KST far more accurate in their reflection of the primary trend. Remember, absolute prices can be subject to strong linear trends, which means that even the best-designed smoothed long-term momentum indicator will offer premature buy and sell signals. We cannot say this will never happen with a long-term momentum indicator constructed from relative action, but it is certainly a lot less likely.

The principal objective is to identify a security when its long-term KST is below zero and starting to poke above its 26-week EMA. Incidentally, the average plotted against the RS line itself is a 65-week EMA. Note that even with a substantial time span such as this there were still numerous whipsaws, especially after the late-2008 bottom. This is one of the reasons why I prefer to use trendline violations of the RS line in conjunction with long-term RS KST reversals. They are certainly not perfect, but tend to be relatively more reliable, as demonstrated by three of them in this chart. This example used a KST, but it is possible to substitute any smoothed long-term momentum indicator. The KST just happens to be my preference. Alternatives could be a stochastic, a moving-average convergence divergence (MACD), or other trend deviation indicator. The basic idea is to use one that closely resembles the primary up and down waves yet turns reasonably close to the turning points. When experimenting, always try for consistency over a number of securities in different time periods; never aim for perfection because it just doesn't exist.

Once the direction and maturity of the long-term trend of the RS has been established, it is then time to move to the shorter-term charts.

Short-Term Trends

Chart 19.8 features the relative action of the Spider Metal and Mining ETF (symbol XME) together with two rates of change (ROCs). The 10-day series registered a post-1989 (limit of my database) high. The 45-day ROC also traced out an extreme swing and broke out from a small base a little later on. The price eventually confirmed with the completion of a

CHART 19.8 Spider Metal and Mining ETF RS, 2004–2010 RS and Momentum Interpretation

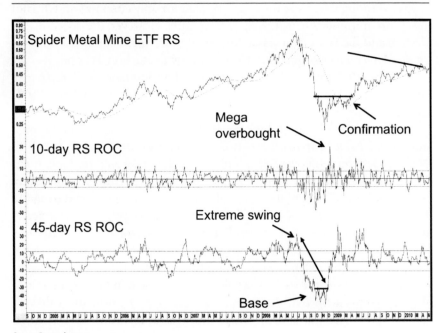

Source: From pring.com

CHART 19.9 Abbott Labs RS, 1998–2001 and Short-Term RS Momentum

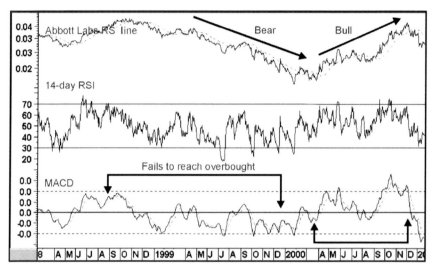

Source: From pring.com

small-platform, double-bottom formation. In a strict sense, this was not a mega overbought because the price declined for only 6 months and did not reach my minimum benchmark of 9 months. However, the speed of the decline and the fact that it was a post-1989 overbought condition that was *confirmed by the price* qualifies it as one in my poetic license book.

Chart 19.9 features the relative action of Abbott Labs in the top panel, followed by a 14-day RSI of the RS line, and in the lower panel an MACD of the RS line.

It is fairly evident by looking at the chart that there are two main environments: a bear market between the end of 1999 and the start of 2000. This is then followed by a bull move. Now take a closer look at the MACD. During the bear market, it fails to reach an overbought condition, yet oversold readings fail to signal rallies. The opposite is true during the bull phase. This is typical of oscillators since they change their characteristics in primary bull markets. Just like birds in the Northern Hemisphere, they migrate to the south during the winter (or the bear market) and to the north in the summer (or the bull market). Whenever you can spot a situation where an oversold oscillator fails to trigger much in the way of a rally, this represents a tip that the prevailing trend may be bearish. It doesn't happen every time, of course, but in most cases, this rule will work out. In this case, the failure of the January 1999 MACD oversold condition to

CHART 19.10 Abbott Labs RS, 1998–2001 and Short-Term RS Momentum

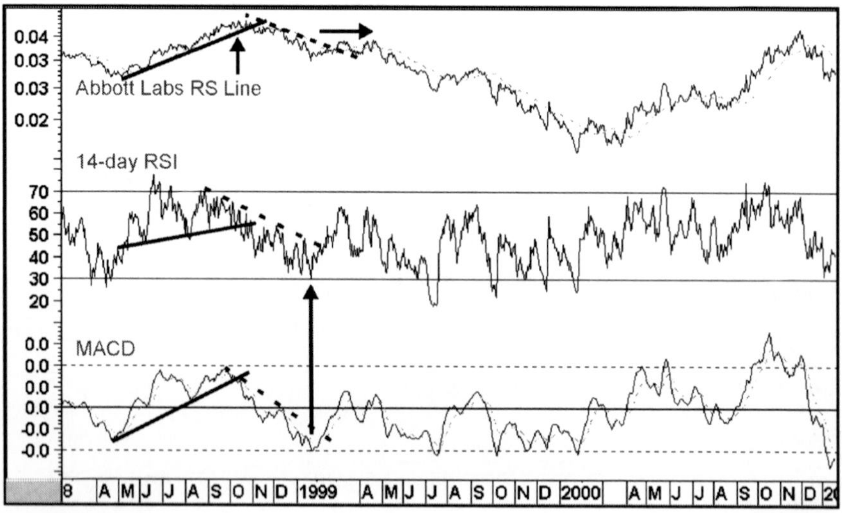

Source: From pring.com

generate a rally and its failure to register an overbought reading a little bit later pointed to a bear market environment.

A sign that a bull market was starting did not come when the MACD reached an overbought reading, which, after all, is still possible in a bear market. Instead, it came when the May decline in the oscillator did not fall back to an oversold reading but was held just above zero. Such action indicated that the underlying character of the MACD had probably changed for the better.

Chart 19.10 shows an analysis of the relative action in greater detail starting with the October top. Signs of weakness started to appear as both the RSI and the MACD of relative strength violated up trendlines. This was then confirmed by the RS line itself violating one of its own. This joint action was not important enough to signal a bear market, but it definitely indicated that the uptrend would likely be stalled for several months. In effect, Abbott Labs was probably underperforming the market during that period. If you look carefully, you can see that the RSI trendline was, in fact, the neckline of a head-and-shoulders top.

As we move on, the price action becomes progressively disappointing. The January oversold condition merely triggers a sideways trading range after which the relative downtrend is resumed. Also, look at the three dashed down trendline breaks. They should have been followed by a good rally but they were not—this type of action is often indicative of a bear market.

CHART 19.11 Abbott Labs RS, 1998–1999 and Short-Term RS Momentum

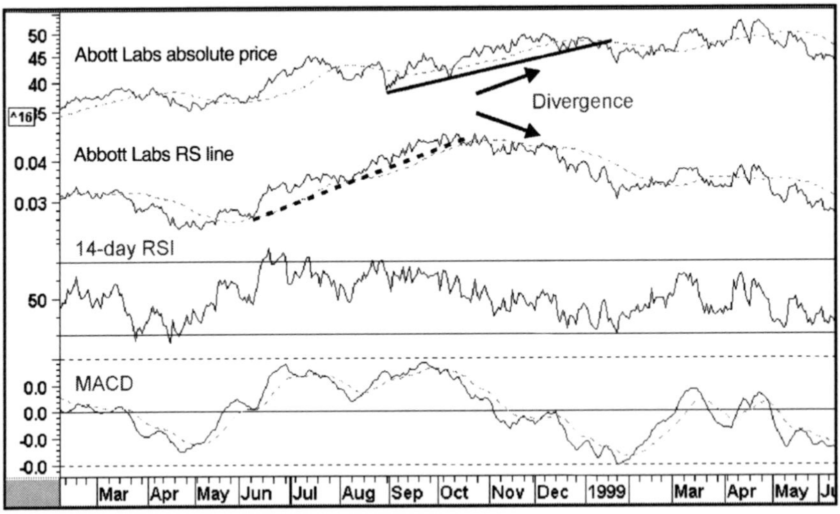

Source: From pring.com

Chart 19.11 shows the same period but also includes the actual price. The dashed up trendline marks the approximate point where the relative sell signal was triggered, but note that the absolute price continued to extend its rally. It then diverged negatively with the RS line, indicating underlying technical weakness. However, it remained above its solid up trendline until January 1999. If the sell signals in the RS line that had developed previously were not sufficient evidence to justify liquidation, the violation of this trendline in the absolute price certainly was.

Chart 19.12 shows a close-up of the bullish period featured in Chart 19.9. Remember, coming into this period the RS line had been in a strong bear market where the momentum indicators had been triggering false signals. However, in March 2000 some positive action by both momentum series starts to develop, since they barely fell below the equilibrium level at the time the RS line was reaching its second low in the top panel. Also, the MACD moved above its previous high, indicating a probable change in character more suitable for a bull than a bear market.

Finally, the RS line confirmed by breaking above the horizontal line, marking the top of a double-bottom formation. At the same time, it confirmed that a series of rising peaks and troughs was now under way. Throughout the bear market, each rally high was lower than its predecessor; likewise with the bottoms.

CHART 19.12 Abbott Labs RS, 1999–2000 and Short-Term RS Momentum

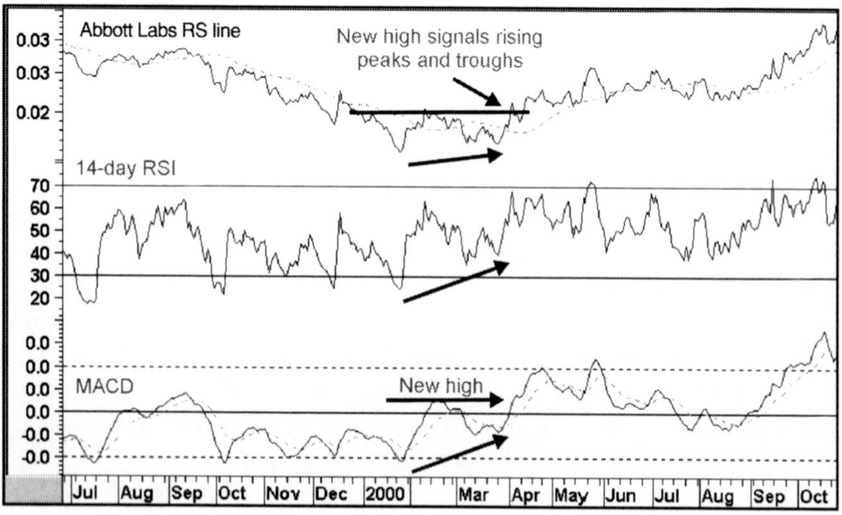

Source: From pring.com

Spreads

RS is widely used in the futures markets under the heading "spread trading," in which market participants try to take advantage of market distortions. These discrepancies arise because of unusual fundamental developments that temporarily affect normal relationships. Spreads are often calculated by subtracting the numerator from the denominator rather than dividing. I prefer the division method because it presents the idea of proportionality. However, if a spread is calculated over a relatively short period (for example, less than 6 months), it is not important whether subtraction or division is used.

Spread relationships arise because of six principal factors:

- *Product relationships,* such as soybeans versus soybean oil or meal, oil versus gasoline or heating oil
- *Usage,* such as hogs, cattle, or broilers to corn
- *Substitutes,* such as wheat versus corn or cattle versus hogs
- *Geographic factors,* such as copper in London versus copper in New York or sugar in Canada versus sugar in New York

- *Carrying cost,* such as when a specific delivery month is out of line with the rest
- *Quality spreads,* such as T-bills versus eurodollars or S&P versus Value Line

Some of these relative relationships, such as London versus New York copper, really represent arbitrage activity and are not suitable for the individual investor or trader.

On the other hand, the so-called TED Spread, which measures the relationship between high-quality T-bills and lower-quality eurodollars, is a popular trading vehicle.

In some cases, spreads move to what was previously an extreme and proceed to an even greater distortion. For this reason, it is always important to wait for some kind of trend-reversal signal before taking a position. While the risk associated with such transactions is by no means eliminated, it will certainly be reduced.

Other relationships between various asset categories are further analyzed in subsequent chapters. These relationships may be used for different purposes, but all are subject to trend reversals that can be identified by the techniques already described.

Summary

1. Comparative relative strength compares one security with another. The result is plotted as a continuous line.
2. The most common application is to compare a stock or sector with a market average. When the line is rising, it means that the security in question is outperforming the market and vice versa.
3. Divergences between the absolute price and relative strength warn of latent strengths and weaknesses and can help in identifying potential trend reversals.
4. Relative strength moves in trends. Any legitimate trend-determining technique can be applied to a relative line.
5. Joint trendline breaks in both the absolute price and the RS line usually result in reliable trend-reversal signals.
6. One of the most useful techniques for analyzing the primary trend of relative action is the use of smoothed long-term oscillators, especially the KST.

20

PUTTING THE INDICATORS TOGETHER: THE DJ TRANSPORTS 1990–2001

It is now time to combine the indicators that we have covered so far into an analysis of the long-term picture. For this purpose I've chosen the Dow Jones transportation average between 1990 and 2001. Chart 20.1 shows the average together with its 9-month MA. This was one of the best testing averages derived by optimizing from 1931 through to the year 2000.

The upward and downward pointing arrows indicate the principal turning points in this period. The 1990 bottom was not an easy one to recognize because the average virtually reversed on a dime. Chart 20.2 shows that the 18-month rate of change (ROC) violated a sharp down trendline just before the price.

The relative strength (RS) line, in the center panel of Chart 20.3 actually broke its bear market trendline ahead of the absolute price. This indicated that the DJ Transports were likely to outperform the market during the early stages of the new bull market.

The vertical line in Chart 20.4 shows that this was one of the few occasions in which all three oscillators were simultaneously oversold. This chart also offered the strongest buy signal because the down trendline for the price was violated at approximately the same time as the 65-week exponential moving average (EMA). Also, the 39-week CMO completed a base. By February 1991, several positive signs had therefore developed, all of which indicated that downside momentum had probably dissipated

CHART 20.1 Dow Jones Transports, 1989–2001, and Turning Points

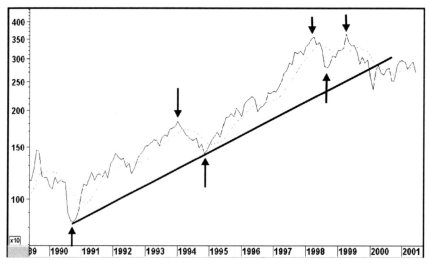

Source: From pring.com

CHART 20.2 Dow Jones Transports, 1989–2001, and Long-Term Momentum

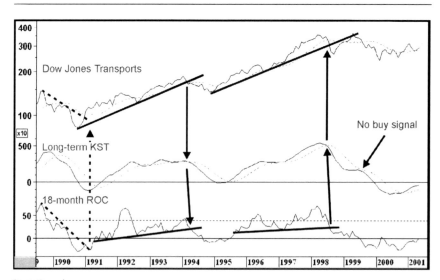

Source: From pring.com

CHART 20.3 Dow Jones Transports, 1989–2001, and Relative Strength

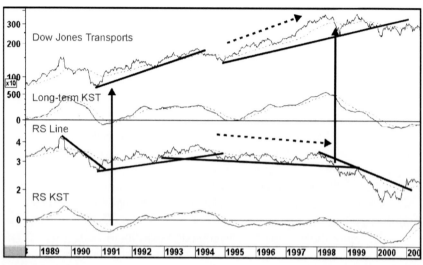

Source: From pring.com

CHART 20.4 Dow Jones Transports, 1989–2001, and Three Weekly CMOs

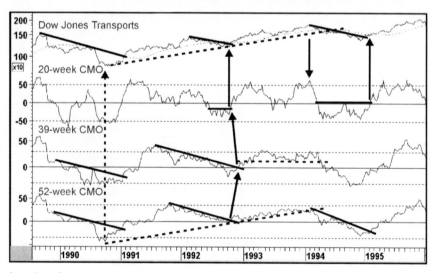

Source: From pring.com

sufficiently to allow the long-term know sure things (KSTs) to reverse to the upside.

The next major event was the intermediate peak in 1992. The average briefly crossed below its 12-month (Chart 20.2) and 65-week EMAs (Chart 20.3), and the long-term KST also triggered a negative whipsaw signal. These events could certainly have justified the conclusion that the Transports had begun a bear market. However, once the average and the long-term KST (Chart 20.2) had crossed back above their respective moving averages (MAs), there was little reason to maintain a bearish stance.

Unfortunately, this whipsaw type activity occasionally develops from an intermediate correction. Under such circumstances it is important to keep an open mind on the indicators. In this case, Chart 20.4 shows that the 20-week Chande momentum oscillator (CMO) broke out from a base and several down trendlines were broken, so there was plenty of evidence that the tide had turned.

The top of the bull market developed 2 years later in early 1994. Signs of a major top were quite widespread. In Chart 20.2 the Transports simultaneously violated a 4-year up trendline and the 12-month MA. The KST gave a decisive sell signal, and the 18-month ROC completed a head-and-shoulders (H&S) top. In the whole 11 years covered by the chart, there were only two completed chart patterns for this indicator, so the early 1994 breakdown was very significant.

Chart 20.4 was equally significant in its bearish entrails. The 39- and 52-week CMOs diverged negatively with the price, and both series completed a top or experienced a major trendline violation. At the peak itself, the 20-week CMO was actually overbought. The chart shows that, except for the strongest of up- or downtrends, the overbought and oversold conditions were often associated with intermediate-type reversals. Later in the year something more ominous started to happen, and this was a trendline break in the RS line. For the first time since the bull market in RS began the long-term RS, KST (shown in Chart 20.3) triggered a decisive sell signal. Although it was not apparent at this point, the transports had begun a long period of underperformance.

Because the ensuing bear market was relatively mild, the bottom in early 1995 was only signaled on the weekly charts. Once again, Chart 20.4 holds the key, as the down trendline in the 52-week CMO was violated and a base in the 20-week series completed. The Transports themselves more or less simultaneously broke above their bear market down trendline and 65-week EMA. The long-term KST in Chart 20.3 also turned positive around the same time.

The average remained above its 65-week EMA for the next 4 years and the series of rising peaks and troughs continued. Then, some extremely serious trend breaks developed. First, the average itself crossed below its 12-month MA and violated its bull market trendline (Chart 20.2). The KST also triggered a sell signal and the 18-month ROC completed a top.

Chart 20.5 shows that the Transports also completed and broke down from an upward-sloping H&S top and crossed below its 65-week EMA more or less at the same time. Notice how the 39- and 52-week CMOs were actually below zero at the time the average was forming the right shoulder. This distinct lack of upside momentum was a very bearish sign. Not surprisingly, the Transports experienced a pretty sharp decline into the fall of 1998.

The most serious technical damage of all came from Chart 20.3 in the form of a major breakdown in the RS line below a 6-year support trendline. This happened as the absolute price was crossing below its 65-week EMA. Trouble on the RS front had been signaled long before this, because it had utterly and completely failed to confirm the bull market in the absolute price. By the time of the 1998 peak in the Transports themselves, the RS line had experienced a major negative divergence. When the RS line moved to a new post-1993 low at the end of 1996, this should have been warning enough that there were far better places for exposure than transportation stocks.

CHART 20.5 Dow Jones Transports, 1995–2001, and Three Weekly CMOs

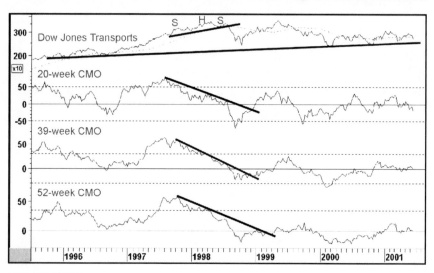

Source: From pring.com

The 1998 bottom, like that of 1990, was an elusive affair, but more so because the turn was so sharp. All three CMOs in Chart 20.5 violated down trendlines, but the average itself did not cross above its average until it had rallied a long way from the bottom. No down trendlines could be drawn against the price, so it was not really possible to build a timely and convincing bullish case. In cases where the evidence of a trend reversal is incomplete, it is always better to avoid the security in question. In any event, the overriding factor should have been the early 1998 breakdown in the RS line, as this set the scene for the next several years of trading action.

Indeed, as it turned out, the 1998–1999 advance was really an above-average reflex rally since all the price was able to do was to rally back to resistance in the form of its 1998 high and the extended bull market trend-line. During this whole period the KST failed to give a buy signal and the RS line in Chart 20.3 never crossed back above its 65-week EMA.

Finally, the average violated its 1990–2000 up trendline at the start of the new century. This was not a great trendline, for, although it was quite long, it had only been touched on two occasions and was not therefore a great reflection of the underlying trend. However, it did result in a sideways trading range over the ensuing 2 years. The critical point after this would be the trendline joining a series of lows between 1996 and 2001. A break below it, not with standing other evidence, would be a serious technical blow.

Summary

This has been a brief account of the technical position of the Transports between 1990 and 2000. Although it was not possible to include too many indicators, it has enabled us to describe how trend indicators for price, momentum, and RS can be combined to help identify major turning points.

Part II

MARKET STRUCTURE

21

PRICE: THE MAJOR AVERAGES

In previous editions, our central theme focused on technical principles, with a primary objective of analyzing the U.S. stock market. In the early 1980s, when the United States was far more dominant in the global financial scene, that approach had some merit. In the second decade of the twenty-first century and beyond, the attention of technicians has become far more diverse, having broadened to international stock markets, bonds, commodities, and currencies. While our coverage will be broadened in this edition, it is not possible to cover all of the market averages and indexes that have been developed for these various entities in one small chapter.

Another important financial market development in the twenty-first century has been the rapid expansion and burgeoning popularity of exchange-traded funds (ETFs) and, to a lesser extent, exchange-traded notes (ETNs). Previously, the purchase of an index involved the acquisition of its individual components, but with ETFs, it was now possible to buy the index just like a stock. That's because the ETF is a basket of stocks whose management objective is to replicate a stated index. To give you an idea of their growth, I stated in my book *The Investor's Guide to Active Asset Allocation* (McGraw-Hill, 2006) that there were then 160 listed ETFs. In mid-2013, that number was closer to 1,500 and still growing. One personally important introduction was the Pring Turner Business Cycle ETF, in December 2012 (symbol DBIZ). The fund adopts an active approach based on the business cycle and technical strategies outlined in this book.

In this chapter we are going to examine some of the principal U.S. indexes and expand the discussion to cover some of the ETFs that reflect major global equity, bond, and commodity indexes.

U.S. Equities

There is no ideal index that represents the movement of "the market." It's true that the majority of stocks move together in the same direction most of the time, but there is rarely a period when specific stocks or several industry groups are not moving contrary to the general direction of the trend. The general level of stock prices is basically measured in two principal ways. The first, known as an *unweighted index*, takes a mean average of the prices of a wide base of stocks; the second also takes an average of the prices of a number of stocks, but in this case, they are weighted by the capitalization of each company (i.e., the number of shares outstanding multiplied by their price). The first method monitors the movement of the vast majority of listed stocks, but since the second gives a greater weight to larger companies, movements in a market average constructed in this way more fairly represent changes in the value of investor portfolios. For this reason, weighted averages are usually used as the best proxy for "the market." These averages are compiled from stocks representing public participation, market leadership, and industry importance.

Several price indexes have been developed that measure various segments of the market. Their interrelationship offers useful clues about the market's overall technical condition. Chapter 3 discussed in detail the relationship between the Dow Jones Industrial Average (DJIA) and the Dow Jones Transportation Average, but there are many other useful indexes, such as the Dow Jones Utility Average, unweighted indexes, and a few bellwether stocks groups. They are examined in this chapter in the context of their contribution to the U.S. market's overall technical structure.

Composite Market Indexes

The DJIA is the most widely followed stock market index in the world. It is a price-weighted average and is constructed by totaling the prices of 30 stocks and dividing the total by a divisor. The divisor, which is published regularly in *The Wall Street Journal* and *Barron's*, is changed from time to time because of stock splits, stock dividends, and changes in the composition of the average. In recent decades, its makeup has expanded from its industrial base to include consumer goods financials and other sectors. However, strictly speaking, it is not a "composite" index, since it does not include such industries as transportation or utilities. Yet, the capitalization of the DJIA is still equivalent to a substantial percentage of the outstanding capitalization on the New York Stock Exchange (NYSE), and it has normally proved to be a reliable indicator of general market movements. The original reason for including a relatively small number of stocks in an average was convenience. Years ago, the averages had to be laboriously calculated by hand. With the advent of the computer, the inclusion of a more comprehensive sample became much easier.

One of the drawbacks of the method used in the construction of the DJIA is that if a stock increases in price and is not split, its influence on the average will become substantially greater, especially if many of the other Dow stocks are growing and splitting at the same time. In spite of this and other drawbacks, however, the Dow has, over the years, acted fairly consistently with many of the more widely capitalized market averages. The ETF that represents the DJIA is the SPDR Dow Jones Industrial Average ETF (symbol DIA).

The Standard & Poor's (S&P) Composite, which comprises 500 stocks representing well over 90 percent of the NYSE market value, is another widely followed bellwether average. Its ETF is the SPDR S&P 500 (symbol SPY). The index is calculated by multiplying the price of each share by the number outstanding, totaling the value of each company, and reducing the answer to an index number.

Over the years, the S&P 500 has become the benchmark against which professional money managers are judged. It is also the most widely traded equity futures contract.

Most of the time, the DJIA and S&P 500 move in the same direction, but there are times when a new high or low is achieved in one index but not the other. Generally speaking, the greater the divergence, the greater the next move in the opposite direction is likely to be. Chart 21.1 shows that in late 1968 the S&P 500 reached a new all-time high, unlike the DJIA, which was not able to

CHART 21.1 Key Market Averages, 1964–1978

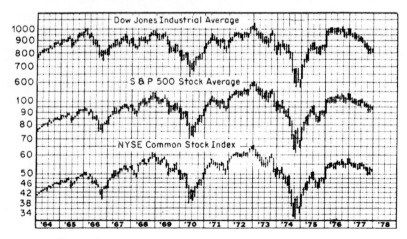

Source: From Securities Research.

CHART 21.2 The DJIA versus the S&P Composite, 1998–2001 and Divergences

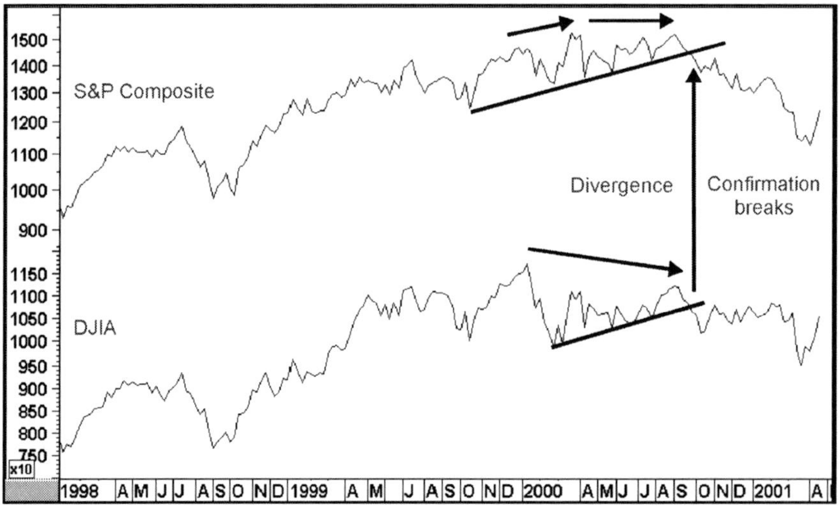

Source: From pring.com

surpass its 1966 peak. This development helped to signal a bear market that wiped nearly 40 percent off the value of both averages. On the other hand, the 1973–1974 bear market was completed with a double bottom. In the case of the DJIA, the second bottom in December 1974 was lower than the October one, yet the S&P 500 failed to confirm the new low in the DJIA. In the space of the next two years, the DJIA rose by some 80 percent. This is also shown in Chart 21.1.

Chart 21.2 compares the DJIA to the S&P Composite for the turn of the century. For most of the 1990s, both series were in gear. However, the DJIA made its peak in January 2000, and the S&P topped out in March and September of that year. This indicated that both averages were out of gear with each other. The confirmation of a bear trend came later in the year when both averages violated important up trendlines. Do not get the impression that the lack of a divergence means a healthy market, because there was no discrepancy at the next bull market peak in 2007, and this was followed by one of the worst bear markets in history.

The NASDAQ Composite is a capitalization-weighted index consisting of all the stocks listed on the NASDAQ. Since it contains most of the technology heavyweights, it is very much a technology-driven index. However, when it comes to ETFs, the NASDAQ 100 (symbol QQQ) is the preferred vehicle. This index/ETF is constructed from the 100 NASDAQ issues with the largest capitalization.

The NYSE compiles an all-encompassing index called the NYSE Composite. In a sense, it represents the ideal average, since its value is based on the capitalization of all shares on the exchange. Its movements are very similar to those of the DJIA and the S&P 500. Nevertheless, divergences between the trends of these three averages offer additional confirmation of changes in the overall technical structure.

The most comprehensive indicator of all is the Wilshire 5000 Equity Index, which represents the value-weighted total, in billions of dollars, of all actively traded common stocks in the United States. Conceptually, this is the indicator that should be used for monitoring trends of the overall market, but because of the lethargy of the investment community and the obvious vested interest of the sponsors of the other popular averages, it has not received the widespread recognition that it justly deserves.

Value Line has published the Value Line Arithmetic, an equally weighted price index that reflects the broad market. Since its construction emphasizes smaller stocks, it occasionally differs in its trajectory with, say, the Wilshire 5000 in a significant way. Chart 21.3 compares the two.

CHART 21.3 Wilshire 5,000 versus the Value Line Arithmetic 1998–2012 and Divergences

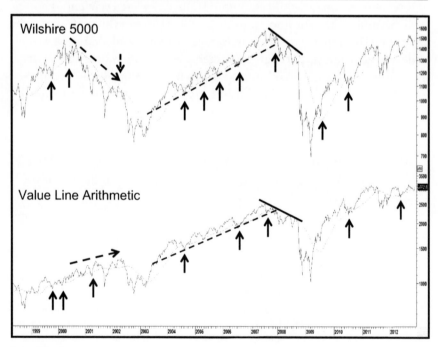

Source: From pring.com

Note how there was a huge discrepancy between them just after the 2000 stock market peak. That was undoubtedly due to the unwinding of the tech bubble since tech stocks had fought their way to huge weightings in the cap-weighted indexes. Generally speaking, any form of discrepancy whichever index leads is a sign of weakness in the prevailing trend that, when confirmed by price, usually results in a worthwhile reversal. You can see a small divergence at the 2007 peak, which was confirmed by two trendline breaks.

The Market Averages and MAs

When experimenting with a moving average (MA) from the point of view of trend determination, it is first necessary to assess the type of cycle to be considered. The 4-year stock market cycle has corresponded to the U.S. business cycle for many decades. Since the stock market is greatly influenced by business cycle developments, this 4-year (or, to place it more exactly, 41-month) cycle is of great significance in trend determination. Consequently, the choice of an MA to detect such swings is limited to anything less than the full period, i.e., 41 months, since an MA covering this whole time span would smooth out the complete cycle and theoretically become a straight line. In practice, the MA does fluctuate, since the cycle is rarely limited exactly to its average 41 months and varies in magnitude of price change. Through computer research[1] it has been found that a 12-month MA for the S&P Composite was the most reliable between 1910 and the early 1990s. Between then and 2012, there were only four whipsaw signals.

> **Major Technical Principle** When choosing a time span for a moving average, go for consistency over a number of securities rather than perfection.

---

[1]Robert W. Colby and Thomas A. Meyers, *The Encyclopedia of Technical Market Indicators,* Homewood, IL: Dow Jones-Irwin, 1988.

[2]Investors Press, Palisades, NJ, 1968. The actual rule used for buy signals was as follows: "If the 200-day (40-week) average line flattens out following a previous decline, or is advancing and the price of the stock penetrates that average line on the upside, this comprises a major buying signal."

In his book *The Stock Market Indicators* (Investors Press, 1968), William Gordon calculated that a 40-week crossover gave 29 buy and sell signals for the DJIA between 1897 and 1967. The average gain for all bull signals (i.e., between the buy and sell signals) was 27 percent, and the average change from sell signals was 4 percent. For investors using the buy signals to purchase stocks, nine resulted in losses, although none greater than 7 percent, while gains were significantly higher. This approach has worked reasonably well since 1967, though it is important to note that 40-week MA crossovers of the S&P Composite resulted in many whipsaws in the late 1970s. As so often happens after a number of whipsaws, the 1982 buy signal was superb. It captured most of the initial advance of the 1982–1987 bull market, while the second, in late 1984, would have kept investors in the market until the Friday before the 1987 crash.

The arrows in Chart 21.4 show whipsaw 40-week MA crossovers for the S&P Composite between 1996 and 2012. They may look plentiful on the chart, but developed, on average, about once every 18 months or so.

CHART 21.4 S&P Composite, 1996–2012 versus a 1/40 Price Oscillator

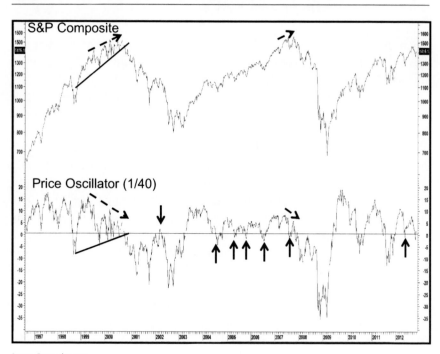

Source: From pring.com

There were also quite a lot of occasions when the average acted as a support or resistance area by turning back advances and declines. When combined with the valid crossover signals, it can be argued that the 40-week MA acts as a fairly reliable benchmark, but as always, keep the following principle in mind.

> **Major Technical Principle**   Moving averages should always be used in conjunction with other indicators to obtain a weight-of-the-evidence approach.

For intermediate swings, crossovers of 13- and 10-week (50-day) averages have proved to be useful benchmarks, but naturally, an MA covering such a brief time span can result in many misleading whipsaws and is, therefore, less reliable than the 40-week average. For even shorter swings, a 30-day (6-week) MA works well, although some technicians prefer a 25-day average.

The Major Averages and ROCs

There are many ways in which the techniques described in previous chapters can be adapted to the major averages. In Charts 21.5 and 21.6, for instance, the S&P Composite is featured with a 9-month rate of change (ROC).

It seems that an excellent signal of an intermediate to primary trend bottom develops when the ROC either re-crosses above its oversold line at −20 percent or touches the −20 percent level and then reverses. Alternatively, a re-crossing of the +20 percent level appears to be a reasonably reliable intermediate peak or bear market signal. Obviously, this is not a perfect indicator, but for the most part, it works with a high degree of statistical reliability. Some of the most glaring errors are flagged by the ellipses. The first, in 1929–1930, which was obviously premature, and the second in the late 1990s, where several signals of weakness completely failed. Chart 21.7 shows the same exercise for more recent times, but in this instance, the S&P has been adjusted by the Consumer Price Index (CPI). Note that in a secular bull market there is a slight tendency for the sell signals to fail, whereas the opposite is true in the secular bear between 2000 and 2012.

Another technique is to construct an up trendline joining the bear market low with the first intermediate bottom. This is then combined with a 12-month ROC where a similar trendline is constructed or a price pattern,

CHART 21.5 S&P Composite, 1900–1950 versus a 9-Month ROC

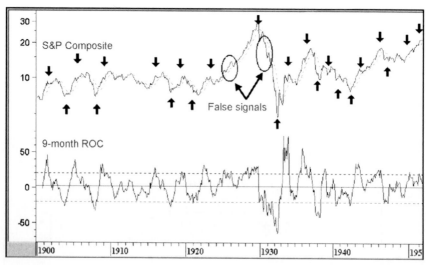

Source: From pring.com

CHART 21.6 S&P Composite, 1950–2001 versus a 9-Month ROC

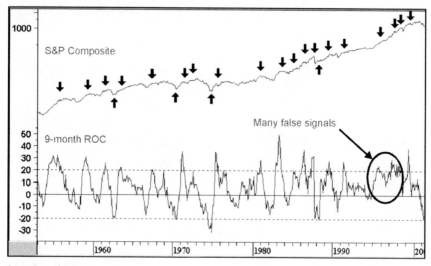

Source: From pring.com

CHART 21.7 CPI Adjusted S&P Composite, 1979–2012 versus a 9-Month ROC

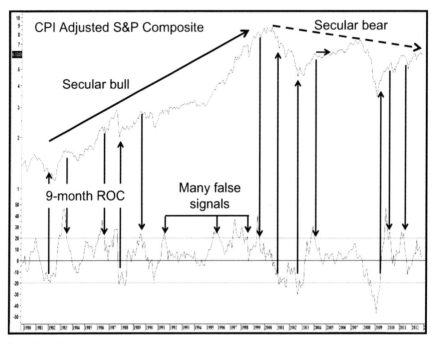

Source: From pring.com

if available, flagged. That is the idea behind most of the trendlines drawn in Charts 21.8 and 21.9. Sometimes it is not possible to construct such lines and we are left with the alternative of a secondary trendline. When both are violated, this is usually a good sign that the bull move is over. Most of the time, the signals come fairly close to the bull market peak.

> **Major Technical Principle** In cases where it is obvious that trendlines are going to be violated well after the turning point, it is usually best to disregard them and rely on other evidence.

Chart 21.10 shows the trendline break technique with a 65-week ROC of the Dow Industrials. With a time span of this length, signals tend to be few in number. Sometimes the ROC offers a useful trendline break, such as

CHART 21.8 S&P Composite, 1966–1983 and Trendlines

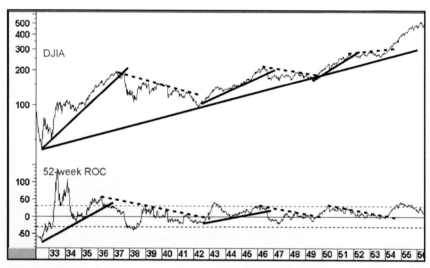

Source: From pring.com

CHART 21.9 S&P Composite, 1989–2012 and Trendlines

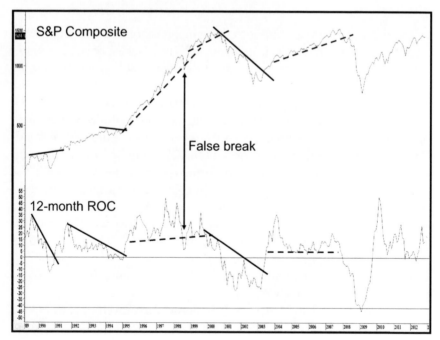

Source: From pring.com

CHART 21.10 DJIA, 2000–1012 and Trendlines

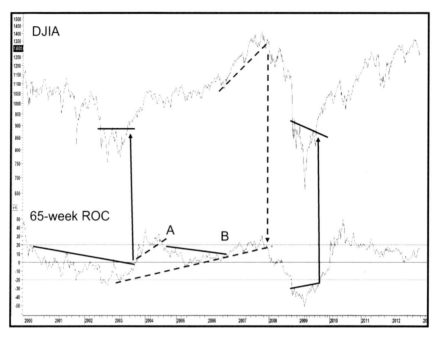

Source: From pring.com

at A and B, but the price trend is so sharp that it is not possible to construct a meaningful trendline. That, unfortunately, is a fact of life and is better ignored than forced, i.e., drawing a sharp trendline just to make the data fit.

A simpler technique for identifying intermediate trends is to use reversals in the trend of a 13-week ROC of a market average, such as the S&P Composite, in conjunction with a reversal in the trend in the level of the average itself. The technique used in Chart 21.11 involves the drawing of trendlines for both the weekly closing price of the DJIA and its 13-week momentum. When a break in one index is confirmed by the other, a reversal in the prevailing trend usually takes place. Such signals are illustrated in the chart by the arrows. This type of analysis should be supported where appropriate with price pattern analysis for the S&P, and with other techniques utilizing the momentum principles described in Chapter 13. This method does not always give a signal, but whenever there are clearly definable violations of trendlines that have been touched three or more times, the conclusions drawn are usually extremely reliable.

In Chart 21.12 the letters A–E indicate where overbought/oversold crossovers are not confirmed by the price. In the cases of B and D, these

CHART 21.11 DJIA, 1970–1975 and a 13-Week ROC

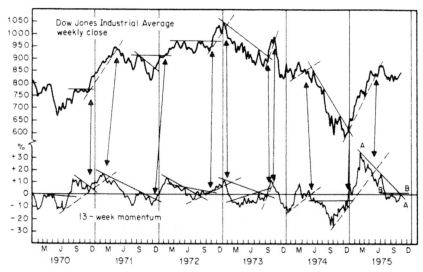

Source: From pring.com

CHART 21.12 DJIA, 2001–2011 and a 13-Week ROC

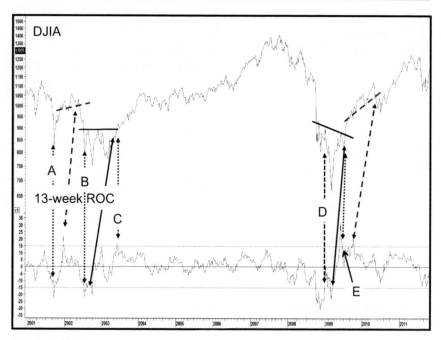

Source: From pring.com

were preliminary signals, where a subsequent oversold decline was eventually confirmed. A, C, and E were never confirmed.

The Dow Jones Transportation Average

In the last part of the nineteenth century and the early part of the twentieth century, rail was the dominant form of transportation and, therefore, an average composed solely of rails represented a good proxy for transportation stocks. In 1970, the Rail Average was expanded to embrace other transportation segments, and the index was renamed the Dow Jones Transportation Average.

The Transportation Average is basically affected by two factors: volume of business and changes in interest rates. First, when a business recovery gets under way, inventories are low and raw materials are needed to initiate production. Transportation volume picks up, and investors, anticipating such a trend, bid up the price of transportation shares. At business cycle peaks, companies typically overbuild their stocks; the result is that when sales start to fall, their requirements for raw materials are reduced. Transportation volume then falls sharply, and the stocks react accordingly. Second, transport companies tend to be more heavily financed with debt than industrials. Because of the leverage of this heavy debt structure, their earnings are also more sensitive to changes in interest rates and business conditions than those of most industrial companies. As a result, the Transportation Average quite often leads the Industrial Average at important juncture points. Indeed, recently conducted research data since the mid-1950s confirmed that the Transportation sector outperformed the market during the early primary bull phase and underperformed during the latter stages of the cycle. (Note: See my book *The Investor's Guide to Active Asset Allocation*.)

The significance of the Dow theory rule requiring confirmation of both the Industrials and Transportations should now be more obvious, since a move by the producer stocks (the Industrials) really has to be associated with an increased volume of transportation, which should be reflected by a similar move in the Transportation stocks. In a similar vein, increased business for the Transportation stocks is likely to be of temporary significance if the industrial companies fail to follow through with a rise in sales and production levels. The longer-term cycles of the Transportation Average and the Industrial Average are more or less the same as a result of their close association with business conditions. The techniques and

CHART 21.13 DJ Transports, 1996–1998 and Three Indicators

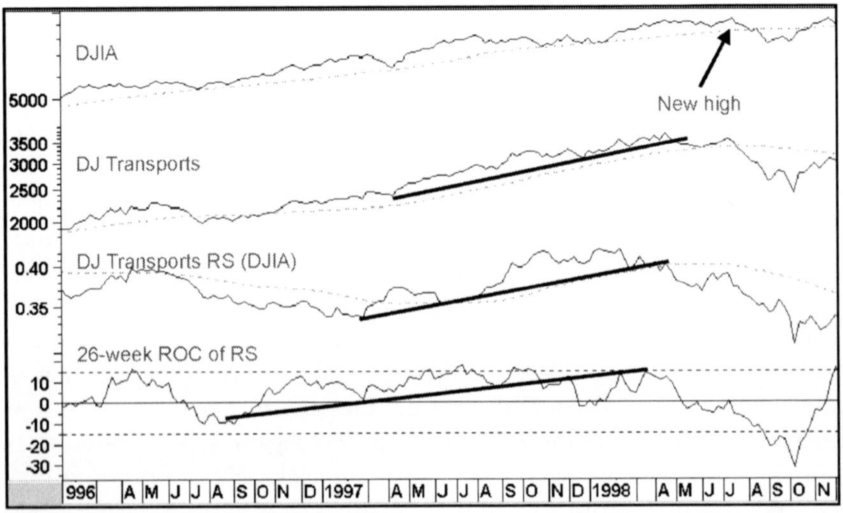

Source: From pring.com

choice of time spans for MAs, ROCs, etc., are, therefore, similar to those described earlier for the Industrials.

One principle that is not normally used for the Industrials but that can be applied to the Transportations is that of relative strength (RS). This technique is particularly useful during periods of nonconfirmation between the two averages, when RS can offer a useful clue as to how the discrepancy will be resolved. One such example occurred in the summer of 1998 when the DJIA made a marginal new high. Chart 21.13 shows that the Transports remained above their 40-week MA but the average had already violated a secondary uptrend, thereby indicating potential weakness. As it turned out, when the Industrials reached their new high, the Transports rallied back to the extended trendline that they had previously violated. However, the real tip-off that the Transports were unlikely to confirm the Industrials came from the fact that the RS line had crossed below its MA and secondary up trendline in April 1998. The 26-week ROC of relative strength also violated an up trendline. Thus, at the time when the Industrials were making a new high in July, the Transport RS line was declining and well below its MA. Finally, the ROC was unable to rally above zero, which represented an additional sign of vulnerability.

The Dow Jones Utility Average

The Dow Jones Utility Average comprises 15 utility stocks drawn from electric utilities, gas pipelines, telephone companies, etc. This average has historically proved to be one of the most reliable barometers of the Industrials. This is because utility stocks are extremely sensitive to changes in interest rates and interest rates generally lead the overall stock market. Interest rate changes are important to utility stocks for two reasons. First, utility companies require substantial amounts of capital because they are usually highly financed with debt relative to equity. As interest rates rise, the cost of renewing existing debt and raising additional money puts pressure on profits. When interest rates fall, these conditions are reversed and profits rise. Second, utility companies generally pay out their earnings in the form of dividends so that these equities are normally bought just as much for their yield as for their potential capital gain. When interest rates rise, bonds, which are also bought for their yield, fall in price and thus become relatively more attractive than utilities. As a result, investors are tempted to sell utility stocks and buy bonds. When interest rates fall, the money returns once again to utility stocks, which then rise in price.

Major Technical Principle   Since changes in the trend of interest rates usually occur ahead of reversals in the stock market, the Utility Average more often than not leads the DJIA at both market tops and market bottoms.

Generally speaking, when the Utility Average flattens out after an advance or moves down while the Industrials continue to advance, it is usually a sign of an imminent change in trend for the Industrials. Thus, the Utilities led the Industrials at the 1937, 1946, 1953, 1966, 1968, 1973, and 1987 bull market peaks. Conversely, at the 1942, 1949, 1953, 1962, 1966, 1974, and 1982 bottoms, the Utilities made their bear market lows ahead of the Industrials. At most major juncture points, the Utilities coincided with the Industrials, and occasionally, as at the 1970 bottom and the 1976 top, the Utilities lagged. Chart 21.14 shows that for the most part since the 1970s they have led, but lagged at the 2000 peaks and very slightly at the 2007 top.

The relationship between the Utilities and the Industrials is often overlooked because they usually give their loudest message when other market activity is at its most exciting. It is normal behavior at market tops for the Utility Average to quietly decline while investors, analysts, and the

CHART 21.14 DJIA versus DJ Utilities 1980–2013

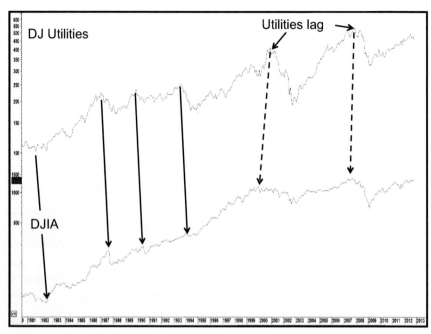

Source: From pring.com

media are excited about huge price advances yet to be seen. Chart 21.14 shows a classic example in 1987. In August, the Industrials were at an all-time high, but the Utility Average was already in a well-established bear market. At market bottoms, fear, depression, and sometimes panic reign while the Utility Average is very quietly in the process of turning up.

The Unweighted Indexes

An unweighted index is calculated by adding the prices of a universe of stocks and dividing the total by that number. The resulting average is then weighted by price rather than capitalization. The most widely followed is the Value Line Arithmetic.

Unweighted indexes are useful because they closely represent the price of the "average" stock often found in individual portfolios, as opposed to the blue chips, to which institutional investment is more oriented. Unweighted indexes are also helpful in gaining an understanding of the market's technical structure since they have a tendency to lead the market (i.e., the DJIA) at market tops. When a persistent divergence of this nature between the DJIA and the Value Line develops, it almost always results in the Dow being dragged down as well. Once a divergence starts, a cautious approach should be maintained until both the DJIA and the Value Line break out from price patterns or declining trendlines, etc.

A show of good RS by the unweighted indexes at a time of sustained weakness in the major averages often indicates that a significant rally will follow when the decline is over. This occurred in 1978, when the Value Line Composite Index made its low in late 1977, several months ahead of the DJIA.

Chart 21.15 shows the Value Line Arithmetic against the S&P Composite between 1984 and 1990. In late 1985, the Value Line made a lower low than it did at the beginning of the year, but the S&P made a higher low. This out-of-gear situation was a negative sign but was never confirmed by the S&P violating its 40-week EMA. We see a similar type of situation in 1986, but again, this potentially negative discrepancy was not confirmed by a negative S&P MA crossover. The situation in 1990 was different because the S&P not only penetrated its MA but violated a major up trendline as well. This reaffirms an important principle—that of confirmation. There are countless situations where we can compare two indicators or averages and

CHART 21.15 Value Line Arithmetic versus S&P Composite, 1984–1990

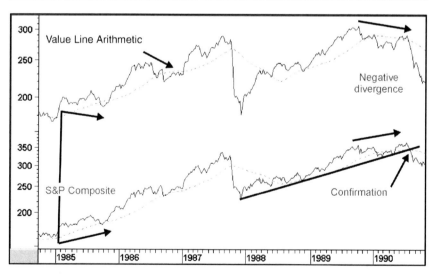

observe disagreements. However, just as divergences in oscillators should be confirmed by price, so these disagreements, whether they are positive or negative in nature, must be confirmed before we can come to a conclusion that the trend has reversed.

The NASDAQ

The technology boom of the 1990s brought the NASDAQ Composite into a kind of prominence that it had never experienced before. This capitalization-weighted index is dominated by large technology companies and has become a proxy for the technology sector. The NASDAQ has no consistent leading characteristics like the Utilities, probably because several technology sectors, such as semiconductors, have lagging tendencies. However, it can be used with relative strength analysis. Chart 21.16 features the NASDAQ together with its RS line against the S&P Composite. Note how a joint trendline break in 1991 signaled a major rally. Later on, another down trendline break in the RS line was confirmed. This time, it was a solid break

CHART 21.16 NASDAQ Composite, 1983–2000 versus NASDAQ RS

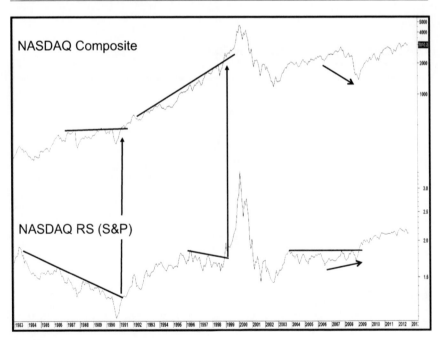

Source: From pring.com

above a resistance trendline, the violation of which resulted in an acceleration in the speed of the bull market.

Also worthy of note is the fact that the RS line diverged positively with the NASDAQ Composite Index at the 2009 low. This was quite different from the previous bear market where the NASDAQ Composite outperformed on the downside. While there was a nice breakout above a trendline on the RS line, there was no such possibility for the price itself, which literally reversed on a dime.

The Russell Indexes

The Frank Russell Organization, among other things, publishes three important indexes: The Russell 3000, 2000 and 1000. The Russell 1000 is a composite capitalization-based series containing the 1,000 largest stocks in the country. The Russell 2000 represents the next 2,000 issues based on capitalization. Finally, the Russell 3000 is a composite index of the other two. It represents in excess of 95 percent of the investable U.S. equity

CHART 21.17 Three Russell Indexes 1999–2000

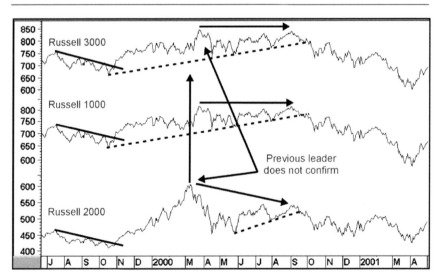

market. These indexes are plotted in Chart 21.17. Normally, they move in gear with each other. It is when they disagree that the discrepancies can sometimes be very revealing. In October 1999, all three succeeded in violating important down trendlines, and the joint break indicated a rally lay ahead. On the other hand, the Russell 2000, which is often used as a proxy for the low-cap sector, experienced a sharp rally going into February 2000. All three indexes then retreated, but the Russell 2000 was unable to rally to a new high, unlike the other two. Thus, we have what had previously been the leader no longer leading. Such leadership failures are often a sign that the prevailing trend is running out of steam and throws up a definite red flag.

> **Major Technical Principle** When several closely related securities are being led by one of the group and that leader fails to signal a new high (or low in the case of a declining trend), this is usually a sign of exhaustion and is followed by a trend reversal.

In this case, the April rally proved to be the top of the bull market. Finally, we see that the Russell 1000 rallied back to its spring high in September 2000 but the Russell 2000 was unable to confirm. When all three violate their (dashed) up trendlines a little later, the divergences were confirmed and a major decline followed.

The relationship between the Russell 2000 (low cap) and Russell 1000 (blue chip/high cap) can also be helpful because it can provide a clue as to which category investors should favor. Chart 21.18 shows that the relationship can be quite cyclical in nature. This can be seen from the long-term Know Sure Thing (KST). Sometimes it is possible to augment KST MA crossovers with trendline breaks in the ratio itself.

This was the case in 1991 and 1995, but the drop was too steep in the late 1990s to construct a line. The next breakout, flagged by the dashed arrow, developed with the sharp rise in 2000, which turned out to be a whipsaw. The reason was the dramatic first-quarter run up in the technology sector, which temporarily dominated the Russell 2000. Later on, if one was prepared to ignore this false move, it was possible to observe a subsequent breakout from the extended base at the end of 2000.

The KST peaked in 2002, fully three years before the 2005 top, which was confirmed with the violation of a dashed up trendline. Even that followed a second lower KST peak. A small decline followed, and the next upleg in the secular bull market of this relationship was signaled by the

CHART 21.18 Russell 2000/1000 Ratio, 1987–2012 and Long-Term Momentum

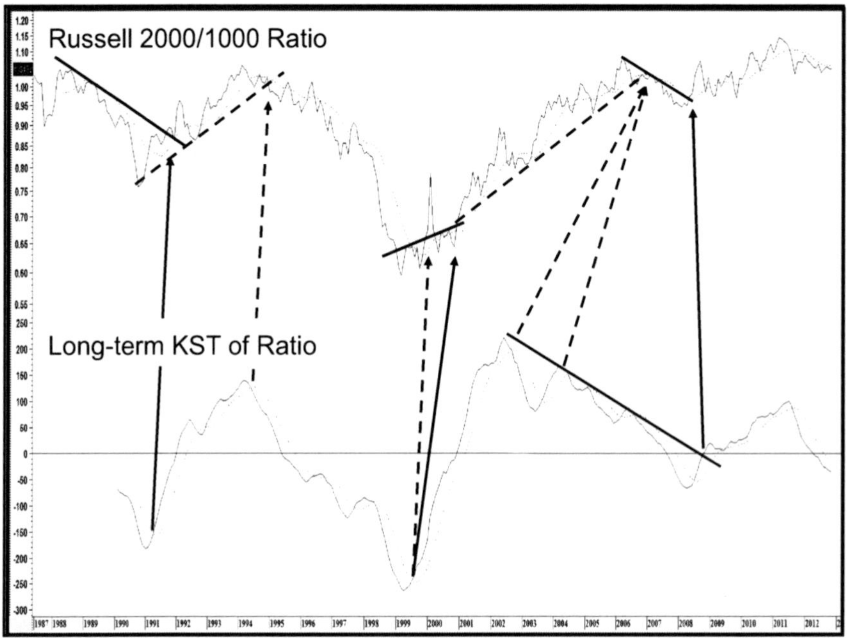

Source: From pring.com

price violating the solid down trendline in 2008. The KST followed with a lag, which is unusual, and the ratio continued to rally into early 2011.

Global Equity Indexes

MSCI, Dow Jones, and FTSE are the leading index providers for international equity indexes, but since the vast majority of widely traded international ETFs fall under the Morgan Stanley Capital International (MSCI) banner, we will focus on two of their offerings. The MSCI World Stock Index has been available since the mid-1960s and includes over 6,000 stocks from developed countries. A related index, the MSCI All Country World Index, incorporates both developed and emerging countries. It is the tracking index for an ETF (symbol ACWI), and is used here as a proxy for global equities.

There are also many regional and individual country indexes that are too numerous to mention. However, the MSCI Europe Australasia

Far East Index does deserve mention, since for all intents and purposes, it represents 22 developed countries, excluding its biggest component, the United States. Canada is also excluded. In effect, it reflects the rest of the non-U.S. world. This ETF carries the symbol EFA and is useful when calculated as a ratio between the SPY and itself. A rising ratio trend then indicates that the United States is outperforming the rest of the world and vice versa.

Global Bond Indexes

The most comprehensive U.S. bond ETF is the Barclay's Aggregate Bond (symbol AGG). AGG holds bonds across the spectrum: Treasury notes, Treasury bonds, corporate bonds, utilities, U.S. agencies, and more. About 40 percent of its holdings at the end of 2012 were invested in bonds with a maturity greater than 5 years. It serves as a proxy for the overall U.S. credit market. A good proxy for long-term U.S. government bonds is the Barclay's 20+-year Treasury bond ETF (symbol TLT).

Internationally, the Barclay's Capital Global Treasury Ex-U.S. Capped Index is a useful benchmark for the world, with the exception of the United States. It includes government bonds issued by investment-grade countries outside the United States, in local currencies, that have a remaining maturity of 1 year or more. Since the tracking index for this fund includes a large group of countries, it could be adversely affected by questionable sovereign debt. The symbol for this ETF is BWX.

Commodity Indexes

The commodity index that you will find used a lot in this book is the CRB Spot Raw Industrials published at CRBtrader.com. This series is constructed from 18 raw industrial commodities, none of which except cotton are traded on the major exchanges. This series is very useful for intermarket and interasset analysis since it is not driven by weather, but by economic developments. Therefore, it better reflects true inflationary conditions as they arise in the commodity markets thereby affecting bond yields and equity prices.

There are two principal commodity funds based on tracking indexes. The first is the DB Commodity Fund, which tracks the DB Commodity

Index. At the end of 2012, this index comprised just over 50 percent energy with 22 percent in grains and the balance in metals. The weightings are determined by the liquidity of the various contracts rather than by their economic importance. The second is the Dow Jones UBS Commodity ETN, the DJP, which tracks the Dow Jones UBS Commodity Index. The rough commodity sector ratings in December 2012 were energy 30 percent, agriculture 32 percent, industrial and precious metals 32 percent, and a small 6 percent in livestock. Of the two funds, the DBC is the more liquid.

Summary

1. There is no perfect index or average that consistently and truly represents "the market."
2. There are two principal methods of calculating market averages: those that use capitalization and those that incorporate an unweighted formula.
3. The technical indicators described elsewhere in this book can be applied to market averages.
4. Most of the time, market indexes move in gear with each other. It is when discrepancies develop and are confirmed that reversals in trend are signaled.

22

PRICE: SECTOR ROTATION

Chapter 2 discussed the relationship between the three key asset classes—debt, equity, and commodities—and the business cycle. It was established that there are certain periods when they move in concert, but more often, their trends diverge. The combination depends on the maturity of the business cycle. The most important point to remember is that deflationary forces predominate during the early stages of the cycle, whereas inflationary pressures come to the fore as the recovery matures. No business cycle ever repeats itself exactly, and the leads and lags between the peaks and troughs of the various financial markets differ from cycle to cycle. In spite of this drawback, the concept of the chronological development of the debt, equity, and commodity cycles works quite well in practice.

This chapter takes a description of this process one step further by pointing out that specific industry groups are sensitive to different types of economic conditions, in effect categorizing them according to their sensitivity to deflationary or inflationary forces, i.e., leading or lagging characteristics. Since the cycle itself is continually moving from deflationary to inflationary conditions and back again, it follows that the various industry groups also undergo a rotation. Unfortunately, this categorization is far from an exact process. First, many industries do not conveniently fall into an inflationary or a deflationary category. Second, equities rise and fall in reaction to the outlook for profits and, also, what is more important, in response to investor attitudes to those profits. Because interest rates are a significant, but not necessarily dominant, influence on the profits of interest-sensitive stocks, it follows that the price performance of certain interest-sensitive issues may, from time to time, become unlatched from or independent of the price movements in the credit markets. For example, savings and loan stocks declined in 1989 because of a financial crisis in the industry. Normally, they would have been expected to rise because interest rates fell during most of that year.

In spite of such drawbacks, the theory of sector rotation serves two useful functions. First, it can provide a framework within which to assess the maturity of a primary trend. For example, if there is technical evidence that the stock market is deeply oversold when the primary trend signals a reversal from bearish to bullish, it would be very useful to know that some of the groups that normally lead market turns have failed to confirm new lows made by the market averages or have established an uptrend in relative strength. On the other hand, in a situation in which the technical picture is indicating the possibility of a market top, it would be helpful to know that leading industry groups had made their highs some weeks or months earlier, and that stronger relative performance was concentrated in industry groups that typically lag the stock market cycle.

Second, the sector rotation theory is helpful in determining which groups, and, therefore, which stocks, should be purchased or pared back. This aspect is discussed in greater detail in Chapter 32.

The comments in this chapter refer to the U.S. stock market, but the concept of sector rotation can be extended in principle to other stock markets. Every country experiences business cycles, and there is no reason why Italian or Japanese utilities should not respond to changes in interest rates just as U.S. equities do. Indeed, it is possible to take this concept one step further by saying that markets heavily weighted to the resource area, such as Canada, Australia, and South Africa, ought to perform best at the tail end of the global economic cycle, and in most cases, they do.

Major Technical Principle A bull market is an extended period, usually lasting between 9 months and 2 years, in which most stocks move up most of the time. A bear market is an extended period between 9 months and 2 years in which most stocks decline most of the time.

The Concept of Sector Rotation

In Chapter 2 we established the fact that the stock market in the form of the S&P Composite discounts the economy and peaks and troughs with the economic growth path. That's the theory, but the reality is closer to that set out in Chart 22.1. The lower panel features my Master Economic Indicator,

CHART 22.1 S&P versus the Master Economic Indicator, 1966–2010

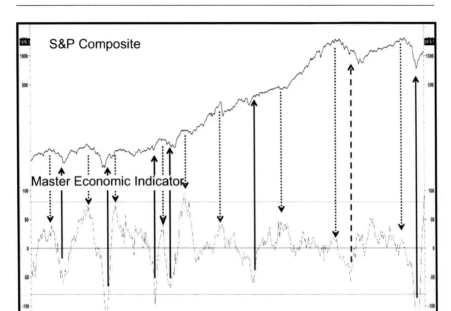

Source: From pring.com

which is constructed from the momentum of several forward-looking economic indicators. Equity market lows are consistently identified with the growth path of the economy bottoming out. Most tops are as well, but those at 2000 and 2007 were preceded by a series of declining peaks in the economy's growth path. Nevertheless, the chart's message is that there is a definite relationship between equity prices and business activity in most cycles.

Since the economy can be divided into sectors that experience a chronological sequence as the cycle unfolds, it follows that equity sectors should, like the S&P, discount their sectors of the economy in a rotational way. Chart 22.2, for example, compares the S&P Homebuilders Index with national housing starts data.

There is not a lot that can be gained from such a raw comparison. However, Chart 22.3 shows the Know Sure Thing (KST) for both series. The dashed line reflects the homebuilders, and the solid one housing starts. There is no question that the dashed homebuilder line leads the solid housing start momentum line. The relationship is not exact and, of course, the magnitude and lead times vary from cycle to cycle. However, there can be

CHART 22.2 Homebuilders versus Housing Starts, 1966–2012

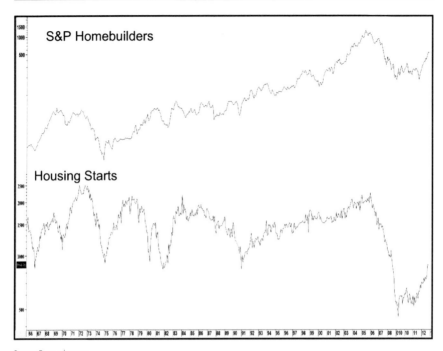

S&P Homebuilders

Housing Starts

Source: From pring.com

CHART 22.3 Homebuilder Momentum versus Housing Start Momentum, 1989–2012

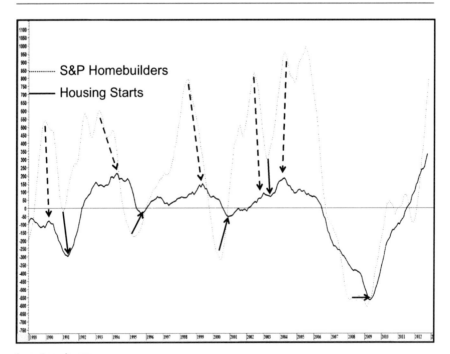

········· S&P Homebuilders

—— Housing Starts

Source: From pring.com

no disputing the fact that homebuilding stocks lead their industry. The same principle can be applied to other stock groups and industries, and the result is sector rotation. In this scheme of things, the S&P Composite or some other aggregate market measure represents a coincident indicator for the stock market as a whole, just as gross domestic product (GDP) is for the economy. If the S&P is a coincident indicator, it follows that there are sectors that typically lead it and those that bring up the rear.

For example, Chart 22.4 shows a key intermarket relationship—that between brokers and the stock market. It is based on the idea that the profits of these companies expand as the market rises. That happens because rising prices mean more customer profits and when customers are making money, they trade more, thereby generating greater commissions. Higher prices also attract companies planning on going public, so the number of underwritings rise along with the fees they generate and so forth. Since brokerage stocks anticipate brokerage profits and typically rise and fall with market prices, it follows that brokerage stocks have a tendency to lead the overall market.

CHART 22.4 S&P Composite versus Amex Brokers Index, 1978–2012

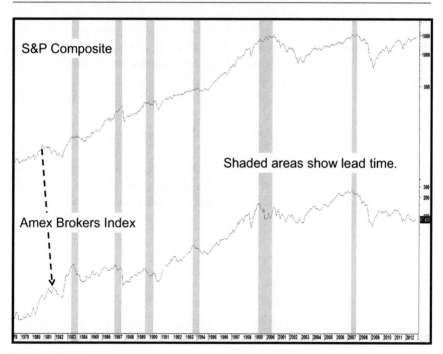

Source: From pring.com

The key point that I am leading up to is that if the economy goes through a rotational process starting with housing and ending with capital spending, the same thing should be true of the various stock sectors, each of which is discounting its own portion of "the" economy—hence, the sector rotation process. As we examine the various sectors, two things will become evident. The first is that there is a definite order to the way things can be expected to unfold as the cycle progresses. Second, while this is true most of the time, there are enough exceptions to keep us on our toes. These exceptions most often develop because of special circumstances that specific industries may be going through that change the way in which that particular stock sector fits into the normal business cycle progression.

Since the majority of stocks are rallying most of the time during a bull market, it follows that most record their bear market lows about the same time as the averages. When utilities are described here as a leading group and steels as a lagging group, the implication is not necessarily that utilities reach their lows ahead of the low in the S&P Composite, although they do in most instances. What is more likely to happen is that utilities, being interest-sensitive, will put on their best performance *relative to the market* around the beginning of the cycle. Similarly, steels might advance with the averages during the early stages of the bull market, but their best relative performance has a *tendency* to occur during the later stages of a bull market or the early phases of a bear market. Notice that I have emphasized the word "tendency" because that is really what we are talking about— tendencies and probabilities, never certainties.

The overall market consists of sectors, which are a reflection of the companies making up the various segments of the economy. The economy, as defined by an aggregate measure, such as gross domestic product (GDP), is either rising or falling at any given time. However, there are very few periods in which all segments advance or decline simultaneously. This is because the economy is not one homogeneous unit, but an aggregate of a number of different parts. Some industries respond better to deflationary conditions and the early stages of the productive cycle; others are more prosperous under inflationary conditions, which predominate at the tail end of the business cycle.

Major Technical Principle The stock market discounts the economy, but stock sectors discount their sector of the economy. Since the economy experiences a set series of economic events, so, too, do stock sectors. The process is called sector rotation.

Economic recoveries are typically led by consumer spending, which is spearheaded by the housing industry. As interest rates fall during a recession, demand for housing gradually picks up. Hence, home building and some building and construction stocks can be considered leading groups. In the same way, the lumber price, a key housing ingredient, has had a consistent (though not perfect) record of leading industrial commodity prices in general.

Because they anticipate a consumer spending improvement, retail stores, restaurants, cosmetics, tobacco, and so forth also show leading tendencies, as do certain interest-sensitive areas, such as telephone and electric utilities, insurance, savings and loans, and consumer finance companies. As the recovery continues, inventories, which were cut dramatically during the recession, become depleted. Manufacturing industry groups, which might be classified as coincident, then respond by improving in price or relative strength (RS). Finally, as manufacturing productive capacity is used up during the last stages of the recovery, these companies seek to expand by investing in new plant and equipment. Consequently, stock groups associated with capital spending, such as steels, some chemicals, and mines, have a tendency to then emerge as market leaders.

Confidence is another influence on the group rotation cycle. During the initial stage of a bull market, emphasis is placed on prudence because investors have lost a considerable amount of money and the news is usually very bad. Stocks with good balance sheets and high yields begin a period of superior RS. As the cycle progresses, stock prices rise, the news gets better, and confidence improves. Eventually, the rotation turns to more speculative issues of little intrinsic value. Even though the peak in speculative issues usually leads that of the major averages, their most rapid and volatile period of advance typically occurs in the final or third leg of a bull market.

Some groups are not readily classifiable in terms of the productive process. Air transport, which goes through sharp cyclical swings, is a case in point. This industry average either coincides with or lags slightly at bear market lows, but is almost always one of the first groups to turn down before a peak. This could be because these companies are sensitive to interest rates and energy prices, both of which have a tendency to rise at the end of the business cycle. Drug stocks as a group, on the other hand, have a distinct tendency to present their best relative performance at the tail end of the bull market and in this respect should be regarded as a lagging group. They are likely also to lag in terms of RS at market bottoms, although this tendency is far less pronounced than their tendency to lag at market tops.

It is also worth noting that the sector rotation process has a tendency to work during intermediate-term rallies and reactions as well as primary ones.

What Are Sectors and Industry Groups?

When we talk of sectors, we are referring to broad categories of equities that contain a number of individual industry groups. Each sector is, in turn, broken down into industry groups. There are 10 or 11 generally accepted sectors, depending on your point of view, and 80-plus industry groups. The following list of sectors is arranged in *rough* proximity to their performance around the business cycle, starting with utilities, an early leader, through to energy. The word "rough" has been italicized because the cycle rarely, if ever, unfolds in exactly the manner expected.

Sectors

Utilities
Financials
Transportation
Telecommunications
Consumer Staples (nondurables)
Consumer Discretionary (durables)
Health Care
Technology
Industrials
Materials
Energy

This list of sectors is based on the Dow Jones methodology. S&P, an alternative provider categorizes transports, a leading sector, under the "industrial" (lagging) banner.

If we take the Utility sector, examples of individual industry groups would include electric, gas, and water utilities. Technology embraces, among other things, semiconductor manufacturers, software companies, Internet companies, electronic instruments, and so forth.

Sector Rotation and Global Equity Markets

In this book, we are principally concerned with the United States. However, it is helpful to know that as the world becomes a smaller place with greater corporate integration, the interaction between companies

CHART 22.5 Relative Momentum of S&P Metals versus BSE Metals, 2006–2008

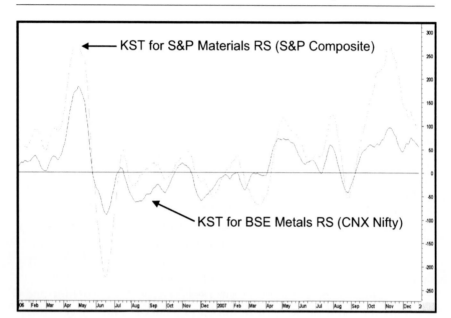

Source: From pring.com

engaged in the same industry in different parts of the globe is also becoming closer. Thus, when the chemical industry is doing well in the United States, it is also usually prospering in Europe. The only reason why these two regional sectors would act differently would be due to currency changes and discrepancies in local laws, costs, or economic conditions.

In this respect, Chart 22.5 compares the relative strength momentum of the metals sector for the United States and India. It is certainly not a tick-by-tick perfect correlation, but it is fairly evident that when metals are doing well or poorly compared to the Indian market (The Nifty), metals in the United States, for the most part, are moving in a similar way.

There is a growing base of international-sector exchange-traded funds (ETFs) being listed by such sponsors as Global X and Guggenheim that adds to the plethora of issues already established using the Dow Jones and S&P tracking indexes. The S&P also has a family of global-sector ETFs that add some diversification, although most of them have a predominant weighting in U.S. companies.

Splitting the Cycle into Inflationary and Deflationary Parts

Putting the group rotation theory into practice is not an easy matter because the character of each cycle is different. In a rough sense, the business cycle can be split into a deflationary part and an inflationary part. A useful starting point is to obtain an inflation/deflation indicator in order to determine that a falling trend in this indicator is deflationary and a rising one inflationary.

One way would be to compare the price of a specific deflation-sensitive stock, such as a utility, with an inflation-sensitive one, such as a mining company. The problem with this approach is that one of them may be affected by internal conditions totally unrelated to the business cycle. The same drawback might be true of a comparison of two industry groups, such as utilities versus gold. For instance, the utility group could be suffering from aggressive government regulation, whereas the gold group may be unduly stimulated because of a mining strike in South Africa. Neither event would be associated with the business cycle, but both would strongly influence the trend and level of an inflation/deflation ratio.

A better solution is obtained by constructing an inflation indicator from several inflation-sensitive groups and a deflation indicator from deflation-sensitive industry indexes. Thus, if one particular industry is influenced by noncyclical forces, it will not unduly distort the total result. A comparison of an inflation- and deflation-sensitive index of S&P groups does not tell us a lot. However, when a ratio is constructed between them, a very useful inflation/deflation gauge is returned.

The Inflation Group Index is constructed from a simple average of the S&P Gold, Domestic Oil, Miscellaneous Metal, and Aluminum, and the Deflation Group Index from Electric Utilities, Banks, and Property and Casualty Companies.

Chart 22.6 shows the ratio and its KST as well as the KST of the ultimate inflation/deflation indicator: the commodity (CRB Spot Raw Industrials) bond (Barclays 20+ Government Bond ETF, symbol TLT) ratio. The important thing to notice is the closeness of their trajectories, yet they are constructed from totally different components. At one glance, you can appreciate how the internals of the stock market reflect inflationary and deflationary forces as they unfold in a typical business cycle. Unfortunately, we do not have a consistent established leader, as both KSTs alternate in that role.

CHART 22.6 Inflation/Deflation Ratio versus Two Momentum Series, 1959–2012

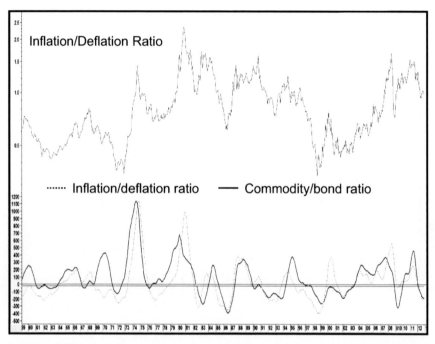

Source: From pring.com

Chart 22.7 takes this a step further by comparing trends in the inflation/deflation ratio to that of industrial commodity prices. These series do not move in exactly the same direction all the time, but there is a definite correlation between them. The arrows show those periods when the 18-month rate of change (ROC) of the ratio moves above the +50 percent level and either crosses below its moving average (MA) or the overbought zone, whichever comes first. As you can see, they generally offer great sell signals for the commodity index, but even more timely ones for the ratio itself. The relationship is so consistent that when a sell signal is triggered, the odds of a new cyclical trend favoring deflation-sensitive equities are extremely high.

Before we leave the inflation/deflation relationship, it is worth pointing out that there is a simpler way to achieve an inflation/deflation ratio, and that is to divide the Goldman Sachs Natural Resource by the Spider Consumer Staples ETF, or the IGE by the XLP. The IGE is our proxy for inflation-sensitive areas, and the defensive XLP is our proxy for early cycle leaders. Chart 22.8 shows that the trajectories of the two series are

CHART 22.7 Inflation/Deflation Ratio versus CRB Spot Raw Industrials, 1971–2012

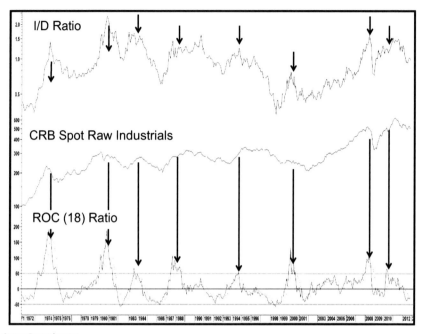

Source: From pring.com

CHART 22.8 IGE/XLP Ratio versus the Inflation/Deflation Ratio, 2002–2012

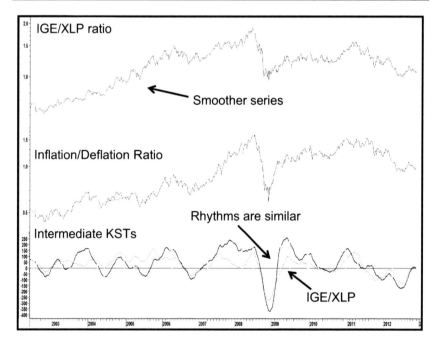

reasonably similar. The disadvantage is that the history of their relationship only goes back to the turn of the century, compared to several decades for the original inflation/deflation ratio.

Relative Paths of Leading and Lagging Groups Usually Diverge

Chart 22.9 shows the relationship between financials, a leading sector, and computers, a lagging one. Some observers believe that technology is a leading sector. However, this chart and research presented in *The Investor's Guide to Asset Allocation* (McGraw-Hill, 2006) shows that it has a tendency to lag. That point can be appreciated from the chart because both series diverge in their trajectories, offering different opportunities at different times. You can see how, during the last couple of years of the 1982–2000 secular bull market, financials underperformed greatly because of the tech leadership. During the first year or so of the ensuing bear market, these roles were reversed.

CHART 22.9 Computer versus Financial Relative Sector Momentum, 1986–2012

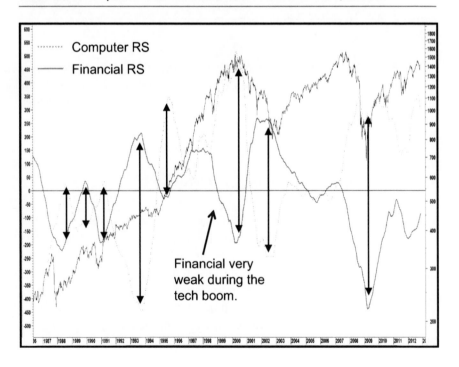

CHART 22.10 S&P Composite versus Financial Sector Relative Momentum, 1981–2012

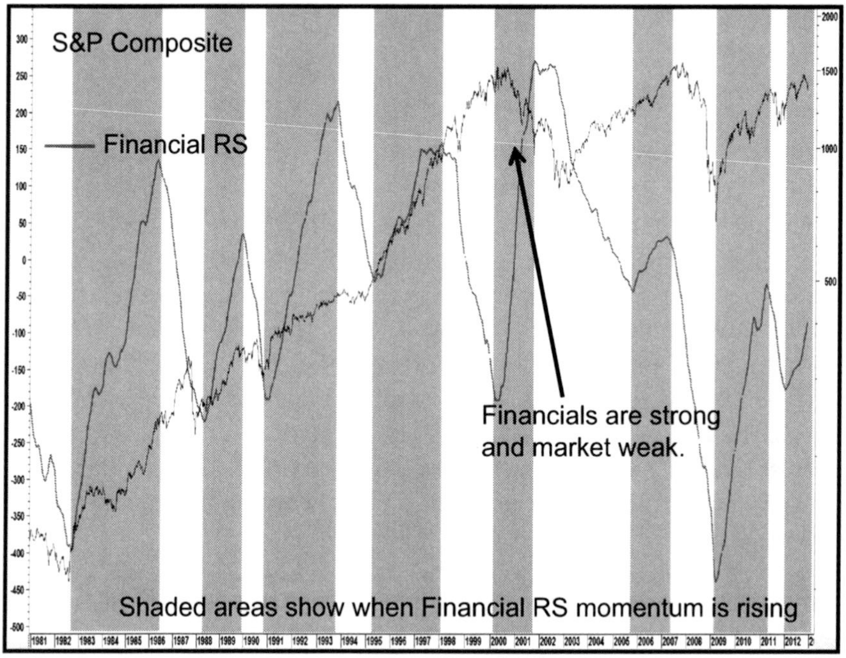

Source: From pring.com

Chart 22.10 features the relative long-term KST for the financials in order to demonstrate that when they are outperforming the S&P, the market is usually rising. These periods have been flagged by the shaded areas. Note the one exception developed during parts of the 2000–2002 bear market.

Leading, Middle, and Lagging Groups

Finally, you may be under the impression that all inflation- or deflation-sensitive sectors move in tandem, but that is not the case. In this respect, Chart 22.11 features the relative long-term KST for lagging sectors—gold, metals, mining, and energy. Some of the time they do move in tandem, but there are a lot of situations when one or more of them do not. The point here is that when other indicators are demonstrating that the cycle has reached an inflationary phase, it's important to check individual sectors or industry groups to make sure that they are acting in sympathy with the macro environment.

CHART 22.11 Selected Lagging Group Relative Momentum, 1995–2012

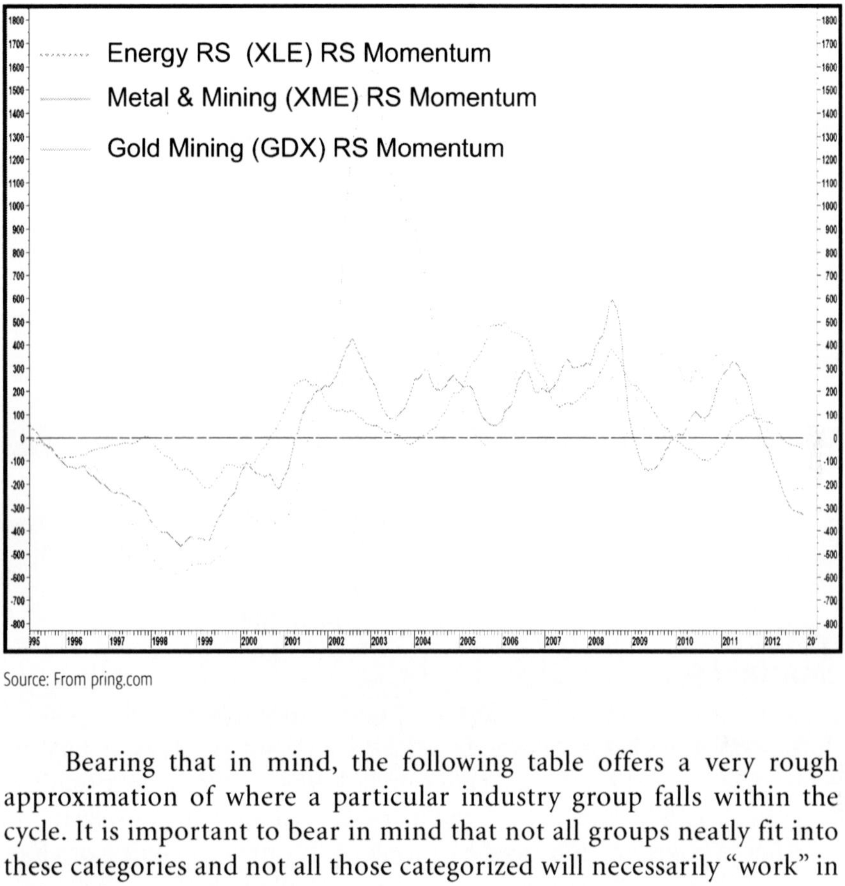

Source: From pring.com

Bearing that in mind, the following table offers a very rough approximation of where a particular industry group falls within the cycle. It is important to bear in mind that not all groups neatly fit into these categories and not all those categorized will necessarily "work" in each cycle.

Leading (Liquidity Driven)

Utilities
   Electric
   Telephone
   Natural Gas
Financials
   Brokers
   Banks
   Insurance Companies
   S&L's

REITs
   Homebuilders
   Containers and Packaging
   Consumer Nondurables
      Beverages
      Household Goods and Housewares
      Tobacco
      Personal Care
      Foods

Restaurants	Airlines
footwear	Truckers
Textile Manufacturers	Railroads
Transports	Air Freight

Middle

Retailers

Manufacturers

Health Care

Consumer Durables

   Autos and Parts

   Furniture and Appliances

Building Materials

Containers Metal and Glass

Leisure and Entertainment

Hotels

Waste Management

Late Cycle leaders (Earnings Driven)

Energy

   Oil

   Coal

   Drillers

   Mining

Basic Industry

   Papers

   Chemicals

   Steels

   Heavy Machinery

Most Technology

   Computer Manufacturers

   Electronics

   Semiconductors

Summary

1. The stock market cycle experiences a distinct pattern of sector rotation because of the chronological nature of the business cycle. Interest-sensitive groups have a tendency to lead at peaks and troughs. Corporations, whose profits are enhanced by increases in capital spending or commodity price inflation, generally lag the overall market.
2. Sometimes significant changes in the fundamentals of an industry will cause a group to be uncharacteristically strong or weak during a specific cycle. Therefore, it is better to monitor a spectrum of groups rather than a specific one as a proxy for the rotation process.
3. An understanding of the industry group rotation cycle is helpful both in assessing the maturity of a primary trend and for the purpose of stock selection.
4. In a broad sense, it is possible to divide equity market sectors into inflation and deflation beneficiaries.
5. Sector rotation is not limited to the United States, but is a global concept.

23

TIME: ANALYZING SECULAR TRENDS FOR STOCKS, BONDS, AND COMMODITIES

Our discussion of these long-term trends will begin with a quick review of the Kondratieff long wave, later moving on to consider what constitutes secular trends and how they come about. Finally, it will be helpful to look at some ways by which we can identify reversals in this all-important price movement.

Major Technical Principle Secular trends exist for bonds, stocks, and commodities and average 15 to 20 years, sometimes longer but rarely shorter.

The Long (Kondratieff) Wave

In the 1970s, a school of thought (this author included) rationalized long-term trends in equity prices through an explanation of the Kondratieff wave. Nikolai Kondratieff, a Russian economist, observed that the U.S. economy had undergone three complete waves between its inception and the time he made his study in the 1920s. Interestingly, E. H. Phelps Brown and Sheila Hopkins of the London School of Economics wrote about the recurrence of a regular 50- to 52-year cycle in UK wheat prices between 1271 and 1954.

Kondratieff used wholesale prices as a central part of his theory, but since movements in commodity prices and interest rates are usually so closely interwoven, they could just as easily have been used.

Using U.S. economic data between the 1780s and the 1920s, Kondratieff observed that the economy had traversed through three very long-term structural cycles, each lasting approximately 50 to 54 years in length. It consists of three parts: an up wave, which is inflationary; a down wave, which is deflationary; and a transitional period that separates the two. The up and down waves vary in time, but typically take between 15 and 25 years to play out. The transition, or *plateau period,* exists for around 7 to 10 years.

Figure 23.1 uses the trend of wholesale (commodity) prices to reflect the cycle. The up wave is associated with rising interest rates and commodity prices. The transition, or plateau period, is accompanied by stable rates and prices, and the down wave with declining rates and prices.

The cycle begins with the start of the up wave, which gets underway when the structural overbuilding of the previous cycle has been substantially worked off. The overbuilding phase involves an excessive accumulation of debt, so cleaner balance sheets are another sign that a new cycle is underway. Kondratieff also noticed that each of the major turning points were associated with a war. Those that developed around the end of the down wave he termed *trough wars.* They acted as a catalyst to use capacity and get the inflationary process underway again. At some time during the early phase of the up wave, new technology is adopted, and that grows from seeds that were planted in the previous cycle. As the wave progresses, recessions become fewer and less severe and entrepreneurs become more emboldened. Growing confidence results in a progressively higher number of careless decisions being made. Throughout this period, price inflation is building in intensity, culminating in a peak war that sucks up excess capacity with a consequential explosion in commodity prices.

The up wave then culminates in a sharp recession as the price structure reverts toward equilibrium and the careless, overextended nature of many business decisions results in a substantial number of bankruptcies as the economy contracts sharply.

Thus begins the transitional phase, called the plateau period because commodity prices experience a flat or ranging action not much below the up-wave peak. Equity investors love the predictability of this stable phase. Consequently, the plateau period is associated with very strong equity bull markets, such as the roaring 1920s. During the plateau period, the excesses of the previous boom are never unwound and typically new ones develop. It's really the eye of the Kondratieff storm. As an example of

FIGURE 23.1 The Kondratieff Wave 1789–2000

The Kondratieff Wave 1789–2000

Legend:
— U.S. Wholesale Prices
— Idealized Kondratieff Wave

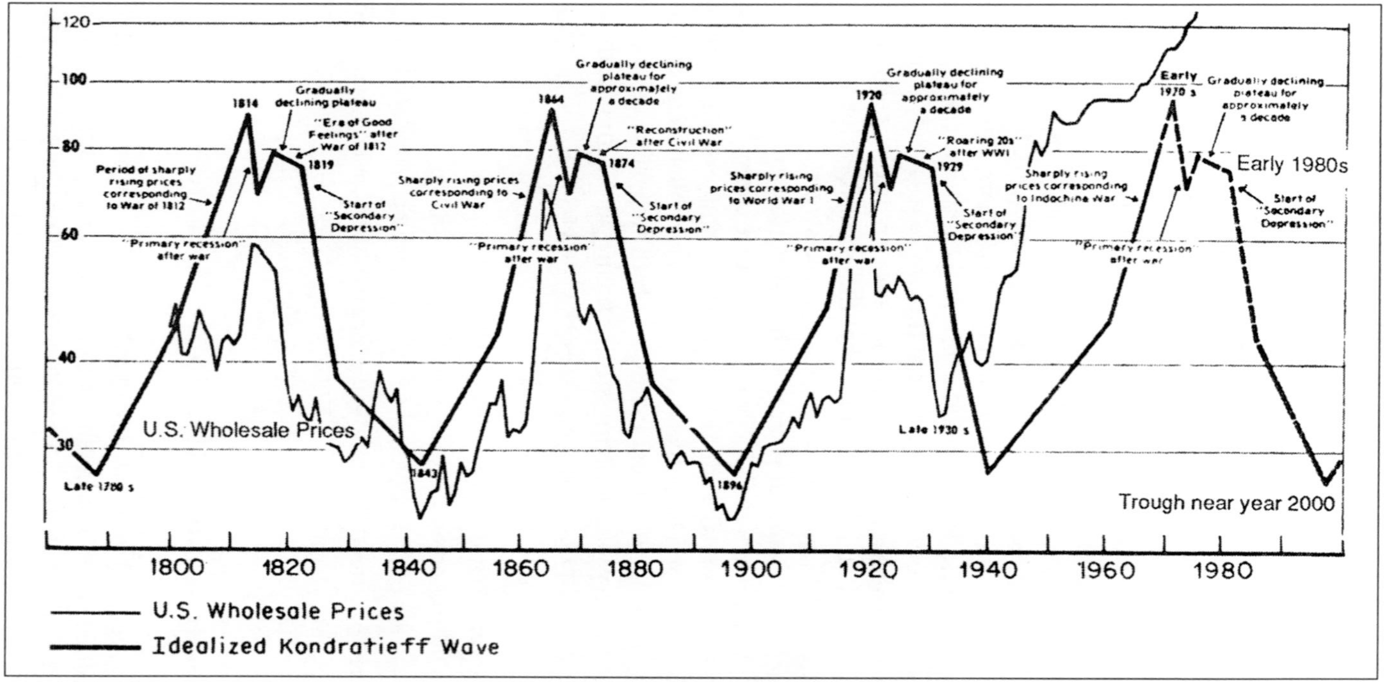

plateau-oriented excesses, 1929 saw the U.S. auto industry with the capacity to produce 6.4 million cars, yet the best previous sales year had been 4.5 million.

The next phase is the down wave in which deflationary forces take over and the system painfully corrects its excesses. Once this cathartic process has run its course, it's possible for a new cycle to get underway.

There is no question that the very long-term structural and psychological trends observed by Kondratieff continue to operate today. However, as a rigid forecasting tool, it leaves a lot to be desired. For example the idealized cycle shown in Figure 23.1 called for a trough low around the year 2000, yet we know with the benefit of hindsight that this turned out to be a secular *peak* as far as stock prices were concerned. Bond yields, instead of bottoming, continued lower for the next 12 years. Commodity prices, true to form, did trough around the turn of the century. The idea of peak-and-trough wars suddenly emerging at the two key turning points at first glance appears to be irrational, in that they are a predetermined part of the wave. However, when it is considered that these wars develop at times when the cycle is at its most structurally unbalanced stages, it is not hard to see how domestic economic unrest can transform into a military conflict.

What is not disputable is the fact that commodity prices, real stock prices, and bonds continue to experience secular or very long-term trends of their own and that secular trends between inflationary and deflationary forces do exist. It is these trends on which we will focus since they set the scene for very long-term investment themes and dominate the characteristics of primary or business cycle–associated trends.

> **Major Technical Principle** The best approach to analyzing secular trend movements is to assume that they form over a long but indeterminate period, as opposed to a predetermined period, and are subject to the same trend-determining techniques used in identifying reversals in any other trend.

Secular Trends in the Equity Market

In earlier chapters, we discussed the concept of the secular trend, an extended price movement that embraces many different business cycles and averages between 15 and 20 years. In this chapter, the very long-term or secular trend will be examined in greater detail because it dominates everything, whatever the asset class—bonds, stocks, or commodities. The calendar year goes through four seasons—spring, summer, winter, and fall—and various phenomena are associated with each season, such as winter being the coldest. However, the seasons are not the same in all parts of the world. That's because the weather is ultimately dominated by the climate. In the Dakotas, winter is extremely cold and long and summers are short, but in Florida, winter is hardly felt and summers are hot and extended. Both areas of the country receive the same seasons, but their climates dictate the *nature* of those seasons. The same is true for the business cycle, since each one undergoes the same chronological sequence of events, whatever the direction of the secular trend. However, the *characteristics* of each individual cycle differ, depending on the direction and maturity of the secular trend. Figure 23.2 overlays the secular trend on the cyclical.

Chart 23.1 shows that since 1900 the U.S. equity market has alternated between bullish and bearish secular trends, which have averaged 14 and 18.5 years, respectively.

We will be concentrating on the secular equity bears here because of their challenging nature, secular bulls being a largely buy-and-hold environment. You may be saying to yourself that the 1900–1920 and 1966–1982 periods were really trading ranges and, therefore, not bear markets.

FIGURE 23.2 Secular versus Primary Trends

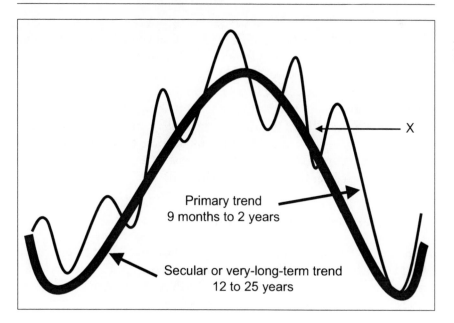

CHART 23.1 U.S. Stock Prices, 1900–2012 Showing Secular Trends

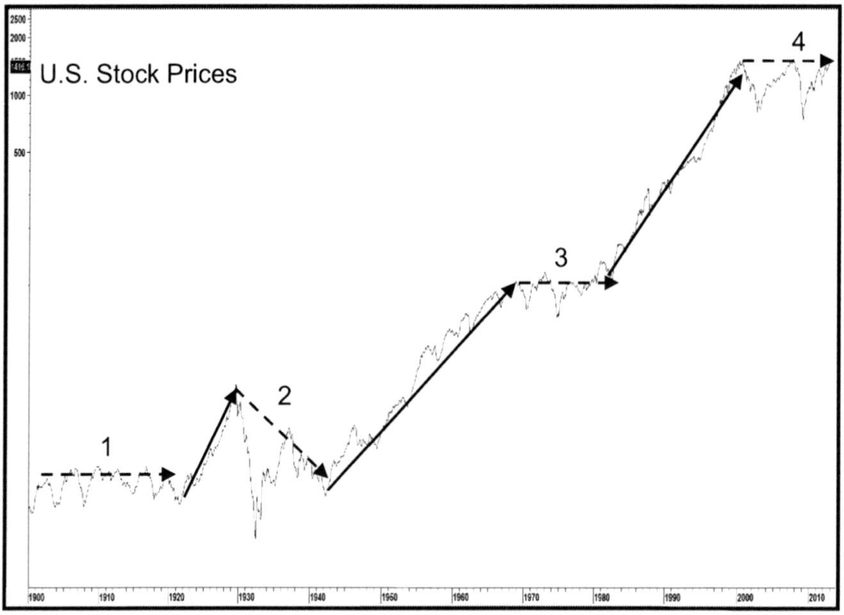

Source: From pring.com

However, we are only looking at part of the picture. For example, it's possible to buy a stock at $10 and sell it for $20. That would imply a doubling of the original investment, but the real question should be what the purchasing power of the proceeds is when the stock is sold compared to when it was purchased. If the cost of living had doubled, there would be no gain. Chart 23.2 puts this in perspective because it shows the S&P deflated by the Consumer Price Index (CPI). Now the *trading ranges* reflect their true bear market status. Two questions that might come to mind at this point are: What are the root causes of these secular bear trends? and How can the birth of a new secular bull market be identified?

Causes of Secular Equity Bear Markets

There are three primary reasons why secular bear markets take place, and they have their roots in psychology, structural economic problems, and unusual volatility of commodity prices. The third factor is, to some extent, an offshoot of the second. Let's consider them in turn.

CHART 23.2 Inflation-Adjusted Equities and the Shiller P/E 1899–2012

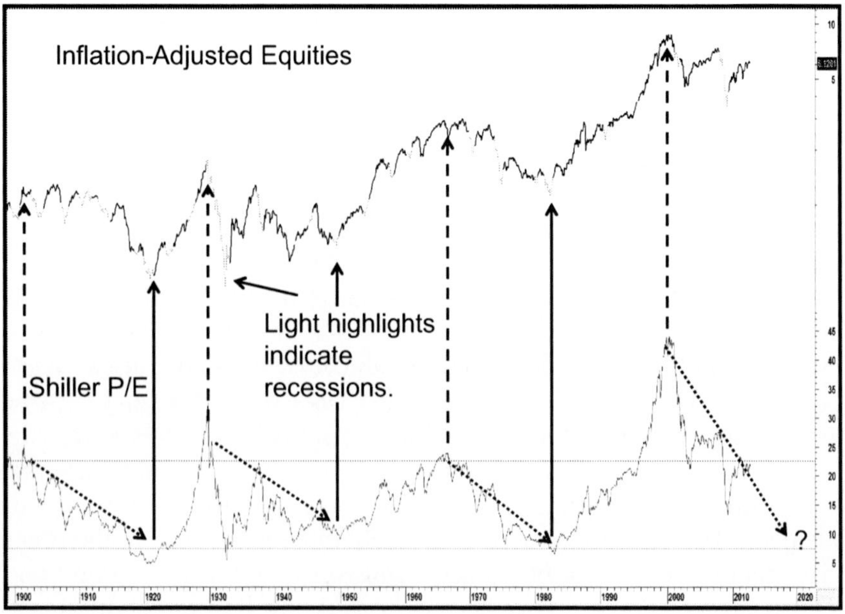

Source: From pring.com

Psychological Causes If you refer to Chart 23.2 again, you will see the Shiller Price Earnings Ratio in the bottom panel. This series uses a 10-year average of earnings adjusted for inflation in order to iron out cyclical fluctuations. You may be wondering why we are featuring what is essentially a fundamental indicator in a technical book. The answer is that the price/earnings (P/E) ratio is treated here as a measure of sentiment. For example, why were investors prepared to pay a very high P/E for stocks in 1929? The answer was that they were projecting previous years of upward multiple revisions. Such a level of overvaluation clearly indicated that investors were unusually optimistic. The P/E declined during successive secular bear markets to a low reading in the 7 to 8 area. Why? Because investors had watched inflation-adjusted stocks decline for a couple of decades, expected more of the same, and wanted be paid handsomely for the excessive risk that was generally perceived. In effect, sentiment typically reverses from exceptional optimism reflected by a high P/E to panic and despair at the secular low. The chart shows that the psychological pendulum is continually swinging from one extreme to the other. It also demonstrates that a prerequisite for a sustainable new secular bull is a once-in-a-generation mood of despondency and despair. Please note that although the actual low developed in 1932, it was not until 1949 that the P/E ratio was able to rally away from its oversold zone on a sustainable basis. That is a principal reason why that particular secular bear is dated in such a way. These psychological swings associated with giant earnings contraction and expansion cycles are not just limited to P/E ratios. They also extend to other methods of valuation, such as swings in the dividend yield on the S&P Composite, from 2 to 3 percent at peaks, to an average of 6 to 7 percent at secular lows. Replacement value for the whole stock market, as measured by the Tobin Q Ratio, moves from $1.00 to $1.15 at peaks to average a discounted 30 cents on the dollar at secular lows. The same principles hold true. High valuations, whichever method is used, reflect optimism and careless decisions, and low ones reflect fear and extreme pessimism, where investors demand to be paid handsomely for what the crowd thinks is a very risky environment.

Ironically, the actual level of inflation-adjusted earnings, when calculated as a 10-year moving average, actually rose during each of the twentieth-century secular bear markets. Consequently, the more important influence on equity prices over long periods of time is investors' attitude to those earnings rather than the earnings themselves.

> **Major Technical Principle**   It's the attitude of investors to earnings that is more influential on equity prices than the earnings themselves.

To understand the nature of secular price movements in equities, we need to take into consideration the fact that the longer a specific trend or condition exists, the more mentally ingrained it becomes. Investors are cautious at the start of a secular bull market because they are mindful of the previous bear market. Eventually, they gain confidence, as each successive primary-trend bull market rewards them. This process extends as investors gradually lower their guard, sooner or later falling victim to careless decisions as they are sucked in by their own success and egged on by an ever more optimistic crowd around them. In addition, due to the passage of time, new, younger market participants arrive on the scene, investors who had no experience of the previous secular bear and, therefore, no fear of another one. A common mantra—"this time, it's different"—typically comes to the fore.

Structural Causes The second cause of secular bear markets is structural in nature. The secular peak is preceded by a decade or so in which a specific industry or economic sector gains in popularity. This results in a misallocation of capital as everyone wants a piece of the action and overbuilding results in substantial excess capacity. In the early part of the nineteenth century, the culprit was canals; in the 1870s, it was railroads. Recently, we saw the dot-com and later the housing bubbles. Such excesses usually take at least a couple of business cycles to unwind, but the pain that that involves gets the attention of governments whose solutions compound the problem and drag out the secular bear. For example, the natural response to the 1930 downturn was to slap on tariffs to protect an overbuilt U.S. manufacturing industry. Other governments around the world followed suit in retaliation. It was worse than a zero-sum game because international trade spiraled on the downside, so everyone lost. In the twenty-first century, the problems are compounded by demographic trends as fewer workers have the burden of supporting greater numbers of older nonworkers. Government response to this reality has been to run huge, mathematically unsustainable deficits, which, not understandably, will become a burden on future growth.

If evidence of structural deficiencies during secular downtrends is required, look no further than Table 23.1, which sets out their characteristics. The third column catalogues the number of recessions experienced in previous secular bears. They number between four and six, which compares to two in the 1949–1966 secular bull and one in the 1982–2000 period. An economy that is continually experiencing periods of negative growth is clearly one cursed with structural challenges. Also, the repeated experience of recessionary behavior adds to the mood of psychological despair at the secular bear market low.

TABLE 23.1 Comparing Secular Bear Characteristics
It may take two or more business cycles for valuations to reach historic secular lows.

	Time Frame	Duration	No. of Recessions	Starting P/E	Finishing P/E	Decline (Inf.-Adj.)
1	1901–1920	19 Yrs 6 Months	6	25.2	5.1	269%
2	1929–1949	19 Yrs 9 Months	4	32.6	9.1	267%
3	1966–1982	16 Yrs 6 Months	4	24.1	6.6	262%
	Average	18 Yrs 7 Months	4.7	27.3	6.9	266%
4	2000–Dec. 2011	11 Yrs 4 Months	2	44.2	20.8	237%

Source: http://www.econ.yale.edu/~shiller/data.htm; Pring Turner Capital Group

Unstable Commodity Trends It could be argued that unstable commodity prices are a symptom of structural problems rather than a root cause of secular equity bears. However, there can be no doubt that these secular environments are characterized by unstable commodity prices on the upside as well as occasional pockets of sharp, but mercifully brief, waterfall declines. The drop between 1929 and 1932 was a prime example, though the briefer 1920–1921, 1974–1975, 1980, and 2008 declines remind us that equities do not like unstable commodity prices whichever direction they develop.

Chart 23.3 compares the Inflation Adjusted S&P Composite (spliced to the Cowles Commission Index prior to 1926) to the CRB Spot Raw Industrials (spliced to U.S. wholesale prices prior to 1948). The chart flags secular bear markets with the dashed arrows. It is fairly evident that all of them, with the exception of the pockets of deflation outlined earlier, have been associated with a background of rising commodity prices. The relationship is not an exact tick-by-tick correlation, but the chart clearly demonstrates that a sustained trend of rising commodity prices sooner or later results in the demise of equities.

CHART 23.3 Inflation-Adjusted Equities and Commodity Prices, 1850–2012

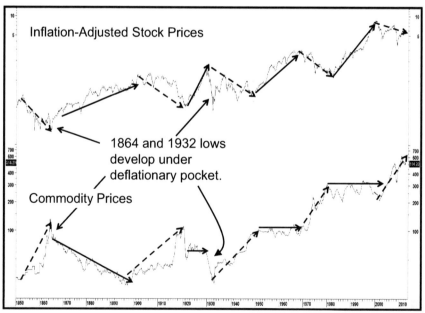

The thick solid arrows show that a sustained trend of falling or stable commodity prices is positive for equities as all secular bulls developed under such an environment. This point is also underscored by the opening decade of the last century. It is labeled a secular bear, but real equity prices were initially quite stable, as they were able to shrug off the gentle rise in commodities. Only when commodity prices accelerated to the upside a few years later did inflation-adjusted stock prices sell off sharply.

A useful approach for identifying a secular peak in commodity prices, and usually a secular low in equities, is to calculate a price oscillator or trend-deviation measure. In this case, the parameters used in Chart 23.4 are a 60-month (5-year) simple moving average divided by a 360-month (30-year) average.

The downward-pointing arrows indicating reversals from an over-extended position have offered four reliable buy signals for equities in the last 150 years or so. If nothing else, the chart demonstrates that dissipating long-term inflationary pressures are very positive for equities.

CHART 23.4 Inflation-Adjusted Equities versus Long-Term Commodity Momentum, 1829–2012

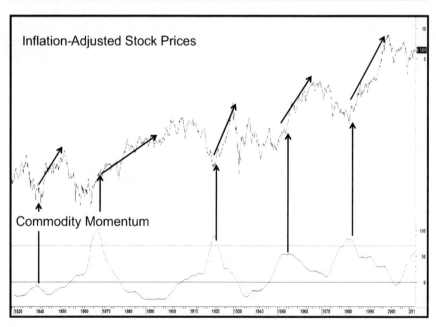

Source: From pring.com

Secular Trends of Commodity Prices

In the previous section we established the fact that secular trends develop in commodity prices and that their direction greatly influences long-term trends in equities. It's difficult to pinpoint a specific cause of secular commodity bull markets, as they appear to emanate from a combination of structural imbalances, wars, and liquidity provided by central banks to offset these problems. Long-term uptrends in commodity prices also embolden producers to expand capacity, leading to overbuilding at or just after secular peaks. Secular bear markets, then, evolve as this oversupply situation is gradually worked off. Psychology also plays a part in that monetary velocity greatly affects the inflationary ability of any given dollar of liquidity in the system. Suffice it to say that these factors integrate in such a way that it is possible to observe clear-cut secular trends in commodity prices. Chart 23.5 shows a historical perspective back to the early nineteenth century. You can see that, excluding the rising trend that began in 2001, the average secular bull market lasted 19 years and the average

CHART 23.5 U.S. Commodity Prices, 1840–2012 Highlighting Secular Trends

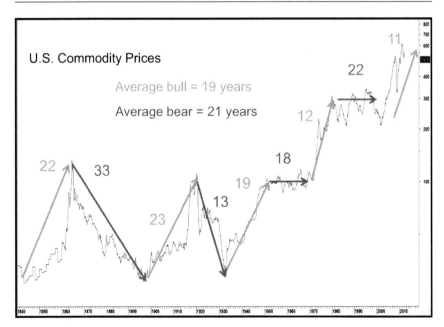

Source: From pring.com

bear 21 years, for an overall average of 20 years. Some of these "bear" markets were really trading ranges, as the 1950s and 1960s and the 1980–2001 periods testify.

Secular Trends in Bond Yields and Prices

Chart 23.6 shows the long-term history for bond yields. It is fairly evident that their trends are much better behaved than their volatile commodity counterparts, which makes secular reversals relatively easier to identify. The arrows show the five secular trends since 1870. The two completed bear markets for bond prices (bull markets in yields) averaged 30 years, and the bull markets for bond prices (bear markets in yields) averaged 25 years, for an average of 27.5 years. U.S. bond yields had been in a secular downtrend (bull market for bond prices) since 1981, or for about 31 years at the end of 2012. This favorable bond trend is long in the tooth in terms of time served, which makes it likely

CHART 23.6 U.S. Government Bond Yields, 1865–2012 Highlighting Secular Trends

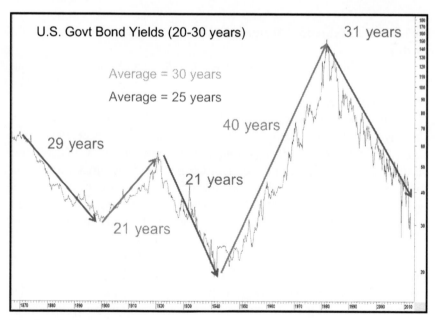

Source: From pring.com

CHART 23.7 U.S. Government Bond Yields versus Commodity Prices, 1860–2012

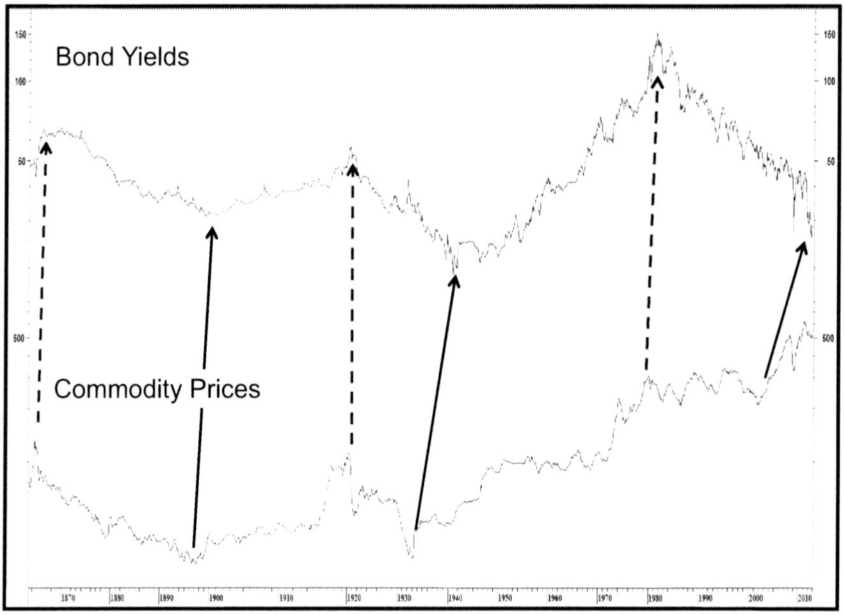

Source: From pring.com

that it will not extend that much into the second decade of the current century.

Arguably the biggest driver of secular trends in bond yields is inflation in the form of industrial commodity prices. In this respect, Chart 23.7 compares bond yields to commodity prices.

The relatively close, but certainly not perfect, correlation between them is self-evident. What is striking is that commodity prices led yields in four of the five secular turning points shown on the chart. In 1920, the two reversed more or less simultaneously. Clearly, the lead times varied, and one could certainly argue the point that the mid-1990s commodity peak was higher than that of 1980. Nevertheless, the record shows that commodities lead interest rates at *secular* as well as at *cyclical* turning points. Unfortunately, the leads for each turning point are varied, starting from the simultaneous reversal in 1920 to a 10-year lead time in the 1932–1946 period. Even so, the strong secular commodity rally in the 2001–2011 period, coming after a 31-year decline in yields, suggests that a secular reversal in favor of inflation may well be in the cards as we approach the middle part of the decade.

Techniques That Help Determine the Direction of Secular Trends

Background

When we are trying to spot changes in primary trends associated with the business cycle, it is occasionally possible to identify reversal signals that take place within a matter of a couple of months of the final turning point. Secular trends extend over many business cycles and, therefore, are much longer in duration. This means that it may take many years, or indeed several business cycles, before a reversal signal can be identified. However, the patience and discipline required to track down these changes are well worth the trouble. First, such signals do not develop very often and are likely to remain in force for one or more decades. Second, the direction of the secular trend has a huge influence on the character of the primary trend. Bull markets in uptrends last, on average, much longer than bull markets in downtrends and so forth. Understanding the direction of the secular trend can, therefore, put us ahead in the process of allocating assets around the business cycle.

The explanation that follows does not offer all the answers we might like, but it does represent a starting point.

One of the problems we face is that the recorded history of U.S. financial markets does not go back very far when we consider that a secular trend often extends for 25 years or more. This means that there are not that many turning points to consider. All we can do is apply some of the trend-following principles and tools that might be used for identifying reversals in short-term trends and see how well they work. Specifically, I have found that momentum offers the most accurate and timely signals when confirmed by trendline breaks, whereas moving-average analysis plays a less substantive role. Let's start our analysis with stocks.

Identifying Secular Equity Trend Reversals

The average secular equity bull market since 1900 has lasted 12 years, whereas 18.5 years is the number for bear markets. If the 1921–1929 bull market outlier is ignored, the average length of just over 17 years is more in line with the average secular bear. Once a new secular trend has been identified, one starting point is to relate the time that has already elapsed to the average in order to see how much that trend may be expected

CHART 23.8 Secular Bear Markets Are Deeply Cyclical Affairs, 1900–2011

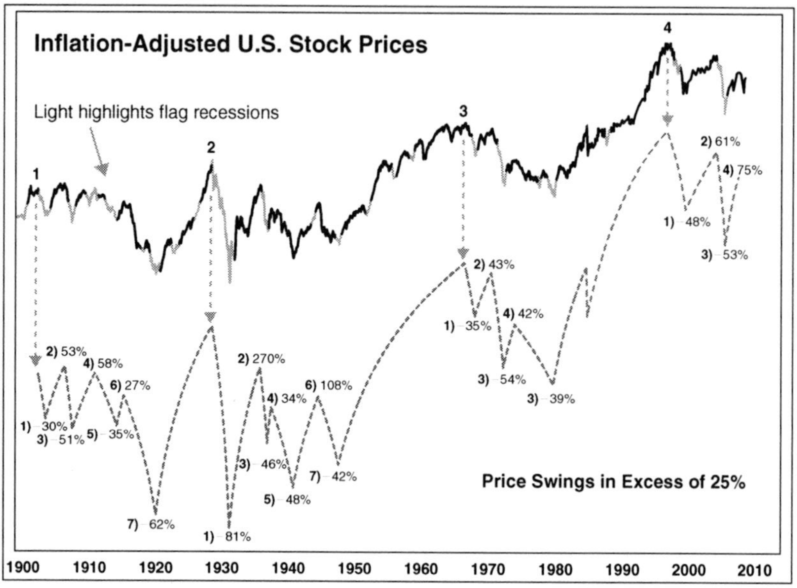

Source: From pringturner.com

to extend into the future. Another benchmark would be the Shiller P/E Ratio to see where it stands relative to its 22 times to 5 to 7 times extreme benchmarks. Chart 23.8 shows that previous secular bears have undergone five to seven price swings in excess of 25 percent. Working on the assumption that all secular bears will be subject to a similar experience, that, too, could be used as a benchmark for discerning the maturity of any existing decline.

Secular bulls are completely different, as primary-trend bear markets that develop under their context rarely experience declines in excess of 25 percent. The 1920–1929 and 1950–1966 inflation-adjusted bulls averaged around 400 percent, and the 1982–2000 experience was close to 700 percent.

Charts 23.9 and 23.10 compare the U.S. stock prices to a price oscillator using a 3-year moving average (MA) divided by a 12-year span. Since annual data are being used, precise timing should not be expected, but the peaks and troughs in this indicator nevertheless do offer some useful benchmarks of the market's long-term temperature. Secular accumulation points are indicated in Chart 23.9 when the oscillator bottoms out from at

CHART 23.9 U.S. Stock Prices and a Trend Deviation Indicator 1800–2012 Showing Peaks

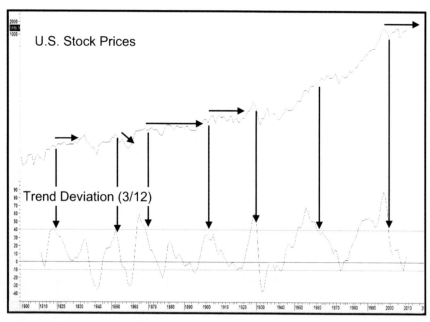

Source: From pring.com

CHART 23.10 U.S. Stock Prices and a Trend Deviation Indicator 1800–2012 Showing Bottoms

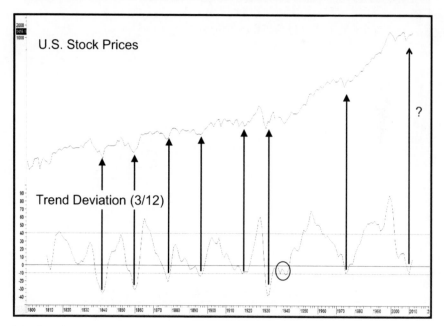

Source: From pring.com

or below the −10 percent level. Only one of the seven signals since 1800 has proved to be a whipsaw and that was the one given in the late 1930s. It will be interesting to see whether the 2012 signal will turn out to be a valid one or more of an accumulation indication as it was in the 1930s and 1940s. Since markets spend more time rising than falling, the negative-signaling benchmark has been raised from 10 percent to 40 percent. In this exercise, peaks are signaled when the oscillator crosses below the +40 percent level. They have been flagged with the downward-pointing arrows. Often, the actual market peak is signaled when the oscillator reverses direction, so the negative overbought crossover is a more conservative approach. In some instances, these peaks are followed by multiyear trading ranges rather than actual declines, but in all instances, nominal prices had a hard time advancing for many years after the signal was given.

Trendlines are often a very useful secular identification tool. Chart 23.11 shows how trendline violations or price pattern completions have reliably signaled major reversals over the last 100 years or so. The problem, of course, is that it is not always possible to construct lines against

CHART 23.11 Inflation-Adjusted Equity Prices 1890–2012 Showing Trendline Applications

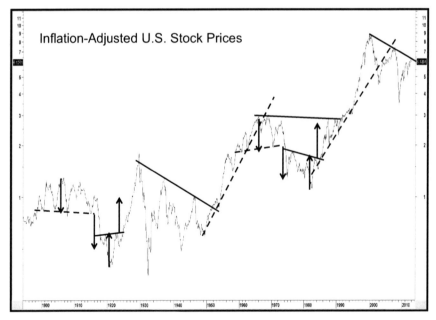

CHART 23.12 Inflation-Adjusted Equity Prices 1890–2012 Showing Oscillator Signals

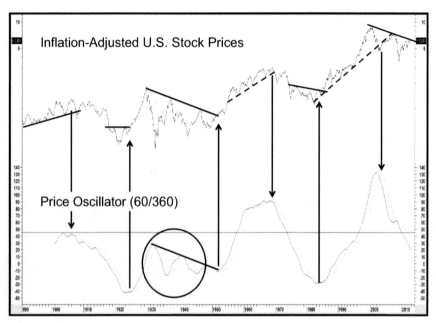

Source: From pring.com

fast markets, such as the 1929–1932 drop. Alternatively, lines can be constructed but their violation comes well after the turning point. That does not happen to any of the lines drawn on Chart 23.11, but would have for, say, the one joining the 1911 to the 1915 top had it been included.

An alternative is to combine trendline violations with an oscillator. In this case, a useful secular span is to divide a 60-month (5-year) by a 360-month (30-year) moving average, as shown in Chart 23.12. Apart from the disastrous 1930s signal contained in the ellipse, when every signal developed completely out of kilter with the price, this approach worked well in the 1900–2013 period.

Identifying Secular Commodity Trend Reversals

One method is to run a long-term moving average through the data. The problem is that we need to extend the time frame to eliminate whipsaws, but the signals often develop well after the new trend is under way.

CHART 23.13 U.S. Commodity Prices, 1800–2012 and a Rate of Change Indicator

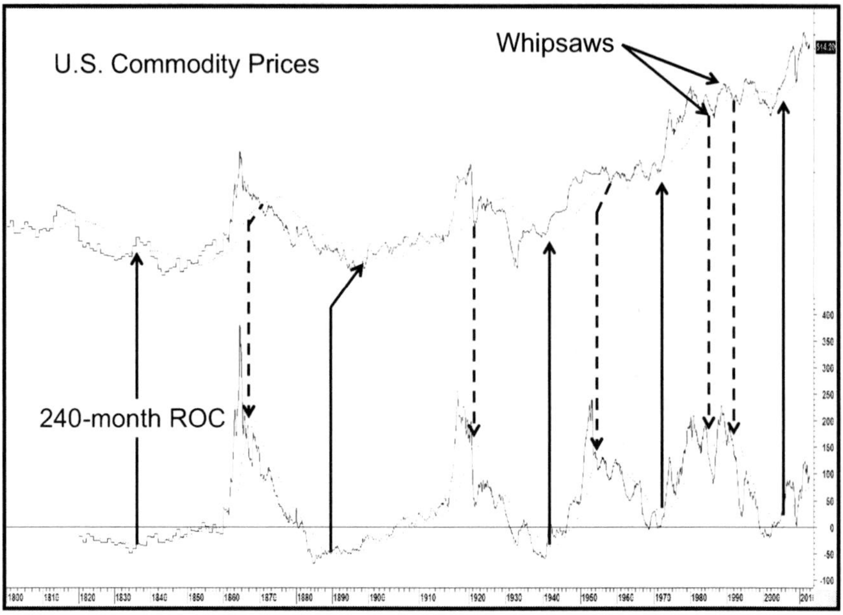

Source: From pring.com

Chart 23.13 shows a 156-month (13-year) MA for U.S. commodities. It works reasonably well, and crossovers are reliable enough to provide a hint of a reversal, but certainly not enough on which to bet the mortgage. Note that prior to 1860, annual prices are used in the commodity index.

The chart also includes a momentum indicator—in this case, a 240-month (20-year) rate of change (ROC). The smoothing is a 72-month (6-year) MA, which is very good at identifying parabolic tops. Reversals in the smoothing often give reliable signals at bottoms. In that respect, the up-pointing (solid) arrows show when the moving average of the momentum series reverses to the upside. Often, these signals develop some time ahead of the final turning point in commodity prices, so some of the arrows slant to the right to indicate when the price series confirms with a moving-average crossover. The downward-pointing (dashed) arrows indicate secular peaks. In this case, the signals develop when the ROC crosses below its 72-month moving average, *not when the*

CHART 23.14 U.S. Commodity Prices, 1800–2012 and a Price Oscillator

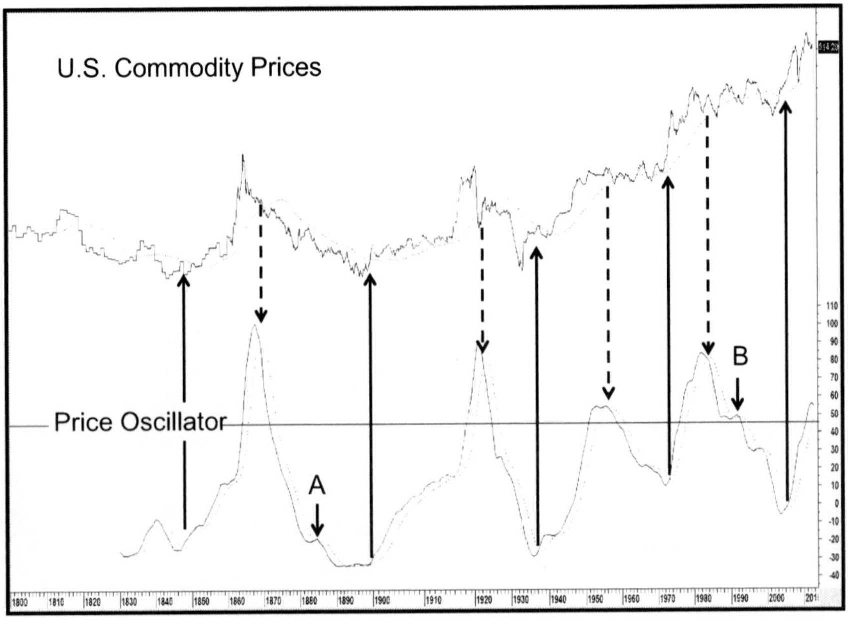

Source: From pring.com

average reverses direction. This is because bottoms tend to be rounded affairs, whereas peaks typically take the form of a spike. Note the two whipsaw signals that developed in the 1980–2001 trading range. At the end of 2005, the moving average for the ROC moved back above its 156-month moving average. This was the fifth confirmed buy signal in almost 150 years of data.

Another useful technique is to adopt the 60-month/360-month price oscillator approach used earlier for stocks. This is shown in Chart 23.14, where 48-month MA crossovers of the oscillator are used as momentum buy/sell alerts. Notice the two arrows at A and B, which indicate the only whipsaws in nearly 200 years of history—okay, a couple of the signals were late, but not a bad overall performance.

Trendline analysis can also be adopted for commodity prices. Some examples are shown in Chart 23.15. Note the dashed up trendline that has its roots in the 1930s. If it is ever violated, expect to see a major commodity decline or extended trading range follow.

CHART 23.15 U.S. Commodity Prices, 1800–2012 and Trendline Application

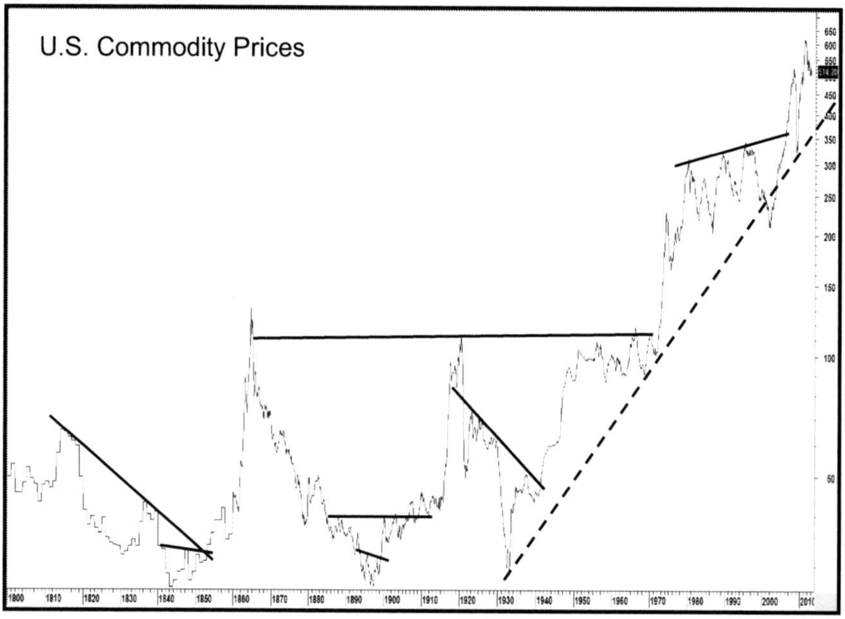

Source: From pring.com

Identifying Secular Bond Yield Reversals

Many of the same techniques used in commodity analysis can be adopted for bond yields. For example, Chart 23.16 shows that the 240 ROC/trend-line combination works quite well. The series in question uses the 30-year yield since its inception in the 1990s but is also spliced to the 20-year government yield prior to that.

The path of bond yields tends to be smoother than that of stocks and commodities, so a useful combination is to compare a 9-month exponential moving average (EMA) with that of a 96-month series. This is shown in Chart 23.17.

The small arrows show the very few whipsaws that have taken place in the last 150 years or so. Note that the yield remained below its 96-month MA for most of the course of the post-1981 secular bear. Since the MA and trendline are in the same vicinity and the line has been touched or approached on numerous occasions, their joint penetration should prove to be a very reliable secular trend-reversal signal whenever that comes.

CHART 23.16 U.S. Bond Yields, 1865–2012 and a Rate of Change

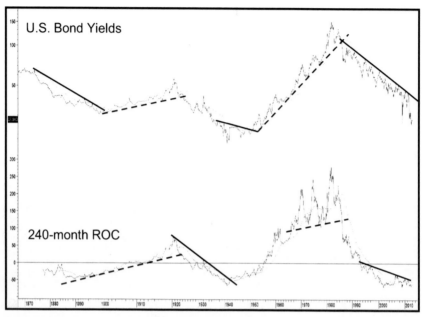

Source: From pring.com

CHART 23.17 U.S. Bond Yields, 1865–2012 and Two Moving Averages

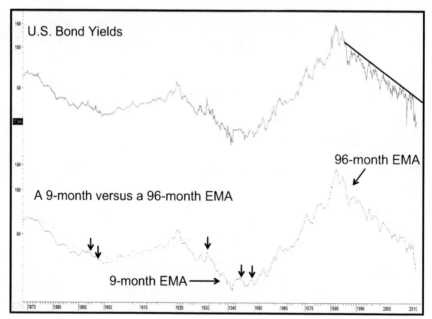

Source: From pring.com

CHART 23.18 U.S. Bond Yields, 1928–2012 and Trendline and Peak-and-Trough Analysis

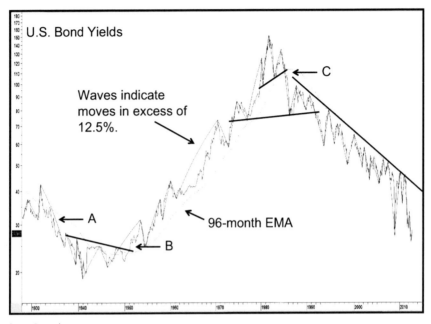

Source: From pring.com

Chart 23.18 shows a more recent history. Note how the 96-month EMA and trendline were almost indistinguishable between 1990 and 2013, thereby reinforcing each one as a resistance barrier. Note also that the yield did not reverse on a dime at either of the two secular turning points shown on the chart. Instead, it experienced an extended trading range in both instances.

Peak-Trough Progression

Peak-trough progression is another technique that can be applied to the process of identifying secular reversals in bonds yields. It is not a perfect approach, but seems to work on a timelier basis than most. The idea is that a valid uptrend develops when each successive peak is higher than its predecessor, as is each successive trough. In this instance, a *peak* is a rally high associated with a specific business cycle and a *low* is a low associated with the contraction or slowdown. When the series of rising peaks and troughs gives way to one of lower peaks and troughs, a trend-reversal signal is given by this technique. The magnitude and duration of the new trend, however, are not indicated.

That would be nice to know, but a warning on the direction is not to be sneezed at. Downtrend reversals are signaled in exactly the opposite way, with a series of rising peaks and troughs replacing a declining trend. It should not be assumed that this technique will work in every situation, but it is surprising how effective it can be, especially when used in conjunction with moving-average crossovers and trendline violations, etc.

The solid wave forms represent movements in excess of 12.5 percent and are used as a basis for objectively measuring what constitutes a legitimate peak or trough. The first signal at A is actually a reconfirmation of the secular downtrend that began in 1920. The series of declining peaks and troughs had been interrupted in early 1932 with a higher high. Since the 1931 low was slightly below its predecessor, the declining troughs were still intact. The break below it at A reconfirmed the secular downtrend. Point B shows the reversal of this decline in the late 1940s. The yield then continued to trace out a series of rising peaks and troughs until point C in the early 1980s. As the chart closes in 2012, the downward peak tough progression continues.

Secular Trends Dominate the Characteristics of Primary Trends

In an earlier chapter, we learned that the primary trend determines the characteristics of shorter-term price movements. During a bull market, short-term uptrends have greater magnitude than short-term uptrends that develop in a primary bear market and vice versa. The same is also true for the relationship between the secular and business cycle (primary) associated trend. This is fairly self-evident if you look at Chart 23.2. You can see that primary-trend bear markets that developed, say, in the 1949–1966 or 1982–2000 secular bull market are far more benign those that developed in the secular bearish periods between 1966 and 1982 or 2000 and 2012. An understanding of the direction of the secular trend clearly puts you in a very powerful position. For example, if you correctly conclude that equities are in a secular bull market, it is likely that prices will be much more sensitive to an oversold reading. On the other hand, if the very long-term trend is a downward one, oversold readings would have far less power. Moreover, it is very probable that the magnitude and duration of a primary trend rally will be less in a secular bear market and more likely to run into resistance rather than register a sustainable new all-time high.

There is an old saying that surprises come in the direction of the main trend. Since the secular trend is really the more dominant, this means that during the secular uptrend, any surprises are likely to come on the inflationary side. Commodity prices rise much faster and further than most people expect. The same would be true of bond yields. The opposite set of surprises develops during a deflationary secular trend. Having said that, these "surprises" typically occur as the trend is in a more mature phase. When it is starting off, commodity prices and interest rates often experience a trading range or transitional period lasting around 5 to 10 years. It is only toward the end of the up wave, when distortions are beginning to evolve, that scary and unexpected rises in commodity prices and yields materialize.

Tables 23.2 to 23.5 show the actual movements during the 1946–1981 up phase and the 1981–201?down phase for Moody's Corporate AAA yields.

We have noted that 2012 was the low for the secular trend, but in early 2013, there is insufficient evidence to draw a firm conclusion on this, even though several indicators were suggesting that that could be the case.

During the secular rise in yields, the average bull part of the cycle lasted around 30 months and took yields approximately just under 40 percent higher; bear markets in yields were shorter, at 19 months, and smaller, as they averaged 13 percent. During the down wave between 1981 and 2012, the bear markets lasted much longer, at 42 months, and took yields down an average 29 percent. Bull markets were shorter, averaging 15 months, but

TABLE 23.2 Cyclical Yield Rise in a Secular Uptrend

Date	Time in Months	Rise %
4/46–12/47	20	16
1/50–6/53	41	25
4/54–9/57	41	44
5/58–1/60	20	29
2/63–9/66	43	31
2/67–6/70	40	68
12/72–10/74	22	31
9/77–3/80	30	64
6/80–9/81	15	46
Average	30.2	39.3

TABLE 23.3 Cyclical Yield Decline in a Secular Uptrend

Date Range	Time in Months	Decline %
12/47–1/50	25	10
6/53–4/54	10	16
9/57–5/58	8	13
1/60–2/63	37	9
9/66–2/67	5	8
6/70–12/72	30	16
10/74–9/77	35	15
3/80–6/80	3	18
Average	19.1	13.1

TABLE 23.4 Cyclical Yield Decline in a Secular Downtrend

Date Range	Time in Months	Decline %
9/81–5/83	20	9
6/84–2/87	32	38
9/87–9/93	60	36
11/94–1/99	62	30
5/2000–7/2003	38	33
Average	42.4	29.4

TABLE 23.5 Cyclical Yield Rise in a Secular Downtrend

Date Range	Time in Months	Rise %
5/83–6/84	24	18
2/87–9/87	7	23
9/93–11/94	14	31
1/99–5/2000	16	29
Average	15.25	25.25

still took the yield up an average of 25 percent. Not every bull move in a secular advance is greater than every bull move in a secular decline and vice versa. However, the average figures indicate that if you can make a correct interpretation about the direction of the secular trend, you have already come a long way in the investment battle.

Summary

1. The Kondratieff wave describes the long-term interaction between inflation and deflationary forces, but its rigid, almost predetermined, interpretation has meant that many financial events have not transpired as expected.
2. Since the nineteenth century, stocks, commodities, and bonds have alternated between secular bull and bear markets, generally lasting about 15 to 20 years.
3. Secular bear markets for stocks are determined by long-term psychological swings. They are influenced by structural economic problems and unusually volatile commodity prices.
4. Secular trends can be analyzed with regular technical tools such as momentum, trendline, and moving-average analysis.
5. Surprises typically come in the direction of the secular trend, which determines the characteristics of the primary or business cycle–associated trends.

24

TIME: CYCLES AND SEASONAL PATTERNS

Basic Principles

Time is represented on the horizontal axis of most technical charts. It is normally used in conjunction with price, volume, and breadth, the other three dimensions of psychology involved in determining trends in the stock market. These latter three, though, are measured on the vertical axis. Time can also be assessed independently through the analysis of cycles.

Discussions of the importance of time have, so far, been limited to the idea that the significance of a reversal in trend depends upon the length of time needed for a distribution or accumulation to complete. The longer the period, the greater the magnitude and duration of the next move are likely to be. Removing the speculative excesses of a trend requires a commensurately large corrective movement, just as the discipline of a long period of accumulation provides a sound base from which a substantial and lengthy advance can take place. The very long (8-year) bull market between 1921 and 1929 was interrupted by corrective reactions, but the substantial increase in stock prices during this period resulted in a considerable amount of excess confidence and speculative excesses, which were only erased by a sharp and lengthy decline.

Similarly, the 1966 stock market peak was preceded by 24 years of basically rising prices followed by a long period of consolidation involving widely swinging stock prices. When adjusted for inflation, stock prices peaked in 1965, subsequently experiencing an extremely severe secular bear market, which was comparable to the 1929–1932 debacle.

Another example comes from the big bull market in gold, which started in 1968 at $32 and ran up to $850 in January 1980. While the price decline was not as severe as the 1929 crash, the next 20 years were spent in a frustrating sideways trading range at prices well under half their peak value. Once that cathartic process had been completed, prices were free to more than double from their 1980 peak.

> **Major Technical Principle** Time is concerned with adjustment because the longer a trend takes to complete, the greater its psychological acceptance and the greater the necessity for prices to move in the opposite direction and adjust accordingly.

Investors become accustomed to rising prices in a bull market, with each reaction being viewed as temporary. When the trend finally has reversed and the first bear market rally takes place, the majority are still convinced that this, too, is a temporary reaction and that the bull trend is being renewed. The initial response is always disbelief, as reflected in the attitude "It's bound to come back" or "It's a good company; I am in it for the long-term." As prices work their way lower in a bear market, the adjustment takes a less optimistic form because the majority of investors forsake their expectations of a rising market and look for them to move sideways for a time. The psychological pendulum finally swings completely to the other (bearish) side, as investors watch prices slip even further and become overly pessimistic. At this point, sufficient time and downside price action have elapsed to complete the adjustment process, and the market in question is then in a position to embark on a new bull cycle.

Time has been viewed here in an emotional context, since it is required for investors to adjust from their unrealized expectations. Both traders and investors should realize that time is deeply bound up with the business cycle. This is due to the fact that a strong and lengthy recovery, like those between 1921–1929 and 1990–2000 breed confidence among investors and businesspeople. As a result they tend to become inefficient, careless, and overextended due to this long period of prosperity. The subsequent contraction in business conditions needed to wipe out these distortions is thus more severe. Equity prices suffer the double influence of: (1) losing their intrinsic value due to the decline in business conditions and (2) being revalued downward from the unrealistically high levels that prevailed during the period of prosperity. The reverse set of circumstances applies following a long market decline.

Major Technical Principle The idea of a reaction commensurate with the previous action is known as the principle of proportionality.

Measuring time as an independent variable is a complicated process, since prices move in periodic fluctuations known as *cycles.* Cycles can operate for periods ranging from a few days to many decades. At any given moment, a number of cycles are operating simultaneously, and since they are exerting different forces at different times, the interaction of their changing relationships often has the effect of distorting the timing of a particular cycle.

The most dominant of the longer ones is the so-called 4-year cycle, in which there is a nominal or average length between troughs of 41 months. Since several other cycles are operating at the same time but with different influences, the length of the 4-year variety can vary either way by 6 months or so.

Cycles are shown on a chart in the form of a sine wave, as in Figure 24.1. These curves are usually based on a rate of change (ROC) or trend-deviation calculation, which is then smoothed to iron out misleading fluctuations. Since it occurs only rarely that two cycles are of identical length, an average, or *nominal,* period is calculated. This theoretical time span is used as a basis for forecasting.

Major Technical Principle Since it occurs only rarely that two cycles are of identical length, an average, or nominal, period is calculated. This theoretical time span is used as a basis for forecasting.

FIGURE 24.1 Typical Cycle

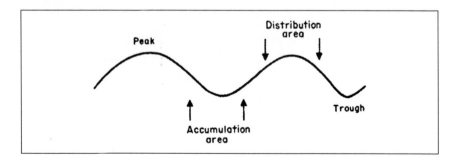

FIGURE 24.2 Typical versus Idealized Cycle

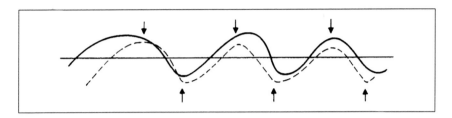

In Figure 24.2, this idealized cycle is represented by the dashed line and the actual cycle by the solid one. The arrows indicate the peaks and troughs of the idealized cycle: In actual fact, price trends rarely reverse exactly at theoretical points, especially at peaks, where there is often a long lead time. Nevertheless, the theoretical points provide a useful guide. Three other important principles are concerned with cycle analysis in addition to those of proportionality and nominality. The first is the *principle of commonality,* which states that cyclicality of similar duration exists in the price action of all stocks, indexes, and markets. This means that a 4-year cycle exists not only for the U.S. stock, bond, and commodity markets, but also for each individual stock and for international markets as well.

> **Major Technical Principle**   The greater the number of markets, stocks, or commodities in a universe that are moving in the same direction, the stronger that trend is likely to be.

For example, if two food stocks are experiencing breakouts, the trend for food stocks is likely to be less significant than if, say, 10 stocks are experiencing similar breakouts. The old adage "strength in numbers" certainly come to mind on this point.

> **Major Technical Principle**   The principle of variation states that while stocks go through similar cycles, the price magnitudes and durations of these nominal cycles will be different because of fundamental and psychological considerations.

In other words, all stocks, indexes, and markets go through a similar cycle, but the timing of both their peaks and their troughs differs, and so

FIGURE 24.3 Leading versus Lagging Sectors

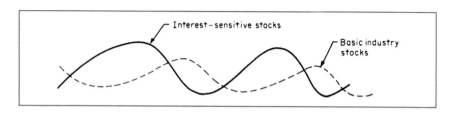

does the size of their price fluctuations. For example, the interest-sensitive and cyclical (basic industry) stocks go through the similar cycle, but because interest-sensitive stocks, such as utilities, lead the market, cyclicals, such as steel groups, generally lag behind them. This is shown in Figure 24.3. Similarly, the interest-sensitive issues may rise by 80 percent from the trough to the peak of their cycle, while the cyclicals might advance by only 20 percent, and vice versa.

Chart 24.1 also illustrates this principle, and shows the interaction of financial series during a typical business cycle. The rising part usually consists of three stages, which correspond to the three phases described in Dow theory. It is normal for prices to reach a new high as each stage unfolds, but sometimes this does not happen. This is known as a *magnitude*

CHART 24.1 Typical Cycles with Financial Series in Percentage of Their Averages. A Mechanistic Approach to Business Cycle Conditions

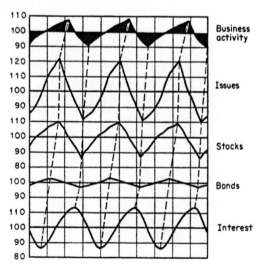

Source: From L. Ayres, Cleveland Trust, 1939.

failure, and is a distinct sign of weakness. A magnitude failure occurs because of very poor underlying fundamentals. In effect, the cycle misses a beat. Magnitude failures are a characteristic of a contratrend price movement such as a short-term rally in a primary bear market, a primary trend advance that develops under the context of a secular bear, and so forth.

The opposite can also occur; exceptionally strong fundamentals (or the perception of them) can give rise to a fourth stage, in which prices undergo an additional upward leg. For equity markets, this final upward surge is often associated with an extended period of declining interest rates. Such strong underlying conditions normally develop when the 4-year cycle occurs in conjunction with the peak of longer-term cycles, such as that associated with secular trends.

In cases in which the cyclic turning points of a number of components of a particular market converge, the magnitude of the next move will be much greater. For example, the turning points of individual stock markets around the world can occur at different times. However, in the summer of 1982, most of their cyclical lows coincided. The resulting rally in virtually all markets was explosive.

The third principle is *summation.*

> **Major Technical Principle**   The principle of summation occurs when several cycles are combined into the calculation of a specific indicator.

It is really the combination of a number of cycles into one and is the concept behind the Know Sure Thing (KST) market cycle model discussed in Chapter 15. If the result were plotted as one idealized cycle, it would be represented by a curve similar to the Special K indicator, also discussed in the same chapter.

There are four influences affecting a time series trend at any one time: secular, cyclical, seasonal, and random. The cyclical trend is the starting point for the purpose of analyzing primary bull and bear markets. Specifically, this is the 4-year, or *Kitchin, cycle.* The secular influence is a very long-term one that embraces several 4-year cycles. From the point of view of a stock, bond, or commodity market, the most dominant secular cycle" is *ranges from 30 to 50 years between troughs.* Two other important cycles in excess of 4 years are the 9.2-year and 18⅓-year cycles.

Figure 24.4, adapted from *Business Cycles* by Joseph Schumpeter (McGraw-Hill, 1939), combines the effect of three observable business cycles into one curve. In effect, it shows the summation principle using

FIGURE 24.4a Schumpeter's Model of Nineteenth-Century Business Cycles. (*From Joseph Schumpeter,* Business Cycles, *McGraw-Hill, New York, 1939.*)

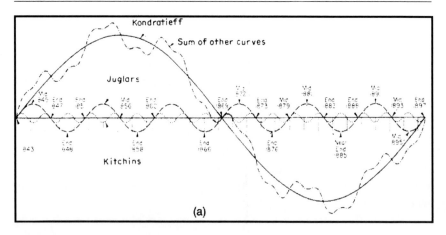

(a)

FIGURE 24.4b Twentieth-Century Business Cycle and Crisis Points (Calculated Path).

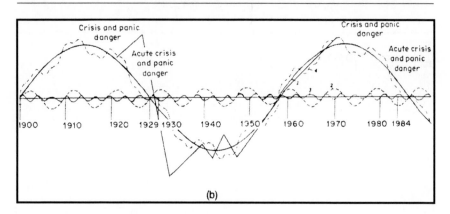

(b)

three longer-term cycles: the 50- to 54-year (Kondratieff), the 9.2-year, and the 41-month (Kitchin) cycles. The model is not intended to be an exact prediction of business conditions and stock prices, but rather to indicate the interaction of the shorter cycles with the longer ones. Even so, it is worth noting that the long-term curve crossed below the zero line in 1987. Projecting the down wave from that point forward to its expected positive equilibrium crossover 20 to 25 years later certainly brings us into the ballpark for the secular low in commodity prices, which actually took place in 2001. A more detailed description of the long wave was presented in Chapter 23. For now, we will concentrate on a few cycles of relatively shorter duration.

The 18-Year Cycle

Normally, the amplitude of a cycle is a function of its duration; i.e., the longer the cycle, the bigger the swing.

The 18-year or, more accurately, the 18⅓-year cycle, has occurred fairly reliably in stock market prices since the beginning of the nineteenth century, but its recent performance is questionable. Even so, this cycle gains credibility because it operates in other areas, such as real estate activity, loans and discounts, and financial panics.

The smoothed line in Chart 24.2 is a 3-year centered moving average (MA) of common-stock prices from 1835 to 2012. This average helps to smooth the trend and isolate the long-term picture more clearly. The beginning of the 18-year cycle at major market bottoms is self-evident when the vertical lines are referenced.

While the average cycle lasts 18⅓ years, actual cyclical lows can vary 2 to 3 years either way. The increase in government interference in the

CHART 24.2 S&P Composite, 1835–2012 the 18 ⅓-Year Cycle

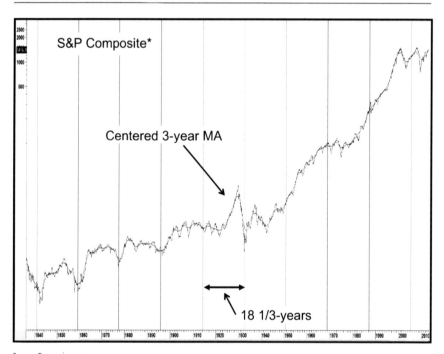

Source: From pring.com
* The history of this index only goes back to 1926, so it has been spliced to other series.

economy resulting from the Keynesian revolution has had the effect of bias-ing the cycle to the upside to the extent that there is a question of whether it is still operating. For example, the conceptual low in the 1987–1988 period did not coincide with a bottom associated with a business cycle. Note that the early 1950s and 1987–1988 lows developed during the course of a secular bull market as defined in the previous chapter. In such cases, we would not expect to find much in the way of downside cyclicality, but those juncture points, like regular cyclic lows, still qualified as a long-term buying opportunity.

On balance, since 1840, the 18-year cycle has operated fairly consis-tently. However, the erratic nature of the last two cycles leads us to ques-tion whether this 18-year periodicity is still continuing to operate, and is another reason why cycles, just like any other technique, need to be aug-mented with other indicators.

The 17.5-Year Cycle

A slight variation on the 18-year cycle is its 17.5 counterpart. This is fea-tured in Chart 24.3, where you can see that it has embraced many signifi-cant bottoms as well as tops. Secular turning points, such as 1929, 1949, 1966, 1982, and 2000, all developed close to expected bottoms or inver-sions. Unfortunately, this cycle does not distinguish between tops and bot-toms—there again, momentum indicators are required for this process.

The 9.2-Year Cycle

Chart 24.4 shows the 9.2-year cycle in stock prices from 1830 to 1946. The dashed lines represent the ideal cycle, which reversed exactly on schedule, and the solid line shows the actual annual average as a percentage of its 9-year MA trend.

The cycle occurred 14 times during the 1930–1946 period, and according to the Bartels test of probability, it could not occur by chance more than once in 5,000 times. Further evidence of the significance of this cycle is given by observation of the 9.2-year periodicity in other phenom-ena as unrelated as pig iron prices and the thickness of tree rings.

One problem with using the technique illustrated in the chart is that the annual average is expressed as a percentage of a centered 9-year MA. This means that the trend is not known until 4 years after the fact, so there is always a 4-year lag in learning whether the 9.2-year cycle is still operat-ing. Nevertheless, if the theoretical crest in 1965 is used as a base and the

CHART 24.3 S&P Composite, 1840–2012 the 17.5-Year Cycle

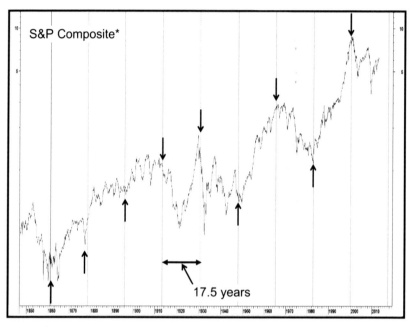

Source: From pring.com
*The history of this index only goes back to 1926, so it has been spliced to other series.

CHART 24.4 The 9.2-Year Cycle in Stock Prices 1830–1946

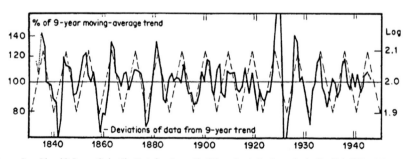

Source: From Edward R. Dewey, *Cycles: The Mysterious Forces That Trigger Events.* Hawthorne Books, New York, 1971, p. 119.

9.2 years are subtracted back to 1919, the peaks of the 9.2-year cycle correspond fairly closely to major stock market tops.

The vertical lines in Chart 24.5 show the 9-year cycle theoretical lows using the 1932 bottom as a centering device. The small black arrows show how the actual low diverged from the theoretical low or became an inverted

CHART 24.5 S&P Composite, 1900–2012 the 9.2-Year Cycle

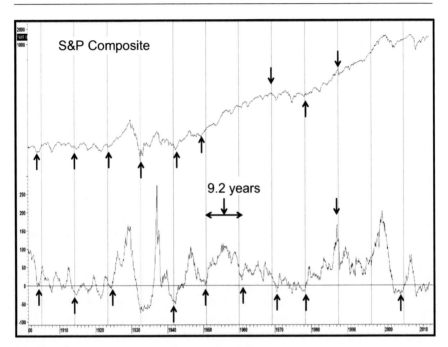

Source: From pring.com

high. Those against the 55-month ROC (half the time span of the cycle) point up when the cycle turning point corresponded with an important ROC reversal or the start of a more accelerated trend.

The cycle worked well until the 1990s—after that, the lows represented good buying points but developed halfway up the rallies. The fact that this cycle completely missed the lows of 2002 and 2009 suggest it may not still be operating.

The Decennial Pattern

This pattern was first noted by Edgar Lawrence Smith in his book *Tides and the Affairs of Men* (Macmillan, 1932).[1] Smith researched equity prices back to 1880 and came to the conclusion that a 10-year pattern, or cycle, of stock price movements had more or less reproduced itself over that 58-year period. He professed no knowledge as to why the 10-year pattern seemed to recur, although he was later able to correlate the decennial stock patterns with

---

[1] From Smith, *Tides and the Affairs of Men*, p. 55ff.

rainfall and temperature differentials. Even though the cycle is a relatively reliable one, there has been to date no rational explanation as to why it works.

Smith used the final digit of each year's date to identify the year in his calculations. The years 1881, 1891, 1901, etc., are the first years; 1882, 1892, etc., are the second; and so forth. Inspired by the research of Dr. Elsworth Huntington and Stanley Jevons,[2] who both emphasized the 9- to 10-year periods of recurrence in natural phenomena, Smith experimented by cutting a stock market chart into 10-year segments and placing them above each other for comparison, as shown in Chart 24.6. He concluded from this data that a typical decade consists of three cycles, each lasting approximately 40 months.

The late Edson Gould, who came into prominence in the mid-1970s because of his uncannily accurate stock forecasts, used the decennial cycle as a cornerstone for his research. In his 1974 stock market forecast Gould wrote, "In the 35 years that have passed since Mr. Smith's book was published—35 years of wars, inflation, and vast changes in our economic monetary set-up and background—the action of the stock market has, much of the time, fitted unusually well with the 10-year pattern."[3] Smith's discovery has stood the test of time.

The stock series in Chart 24.7 represents a simple average of the decennial pattern from 1900 to 2009, giving equal weight to the proportional movements of each period. It starts off with years ending in zero and ends with those terminating with nine. You can see that the trajectories are very similar during secular bull and bear markets even though they represent different years. The chart also brings out the fact that secular bull years are easier to make money in than secular bears, a fairly obvious observation but nonetheless a very important one.

The pattern is plotted together with a 12-month ROC in Chart 24.8. The swings in the ROC show four down phases and an equal number of advances, as flagged by the solid lines.

The decennial pattern can be of greater value if it is used to identify where the strong and weak points usually occur and then to see whether other technical phenomena are consistent. For example, in the middle of year 9, the 12-month ROC indicator for the average cycle is highly overbought, which is consistent with a decline or consolidation, starting at the end of that year and following through to the year ending in zero. In 1949, the 12-month ROC was highly oversold and was inconsistent with its normal position in the decennial pattern. Instead of declining into 1950, the market actually rose. This experience is a good example of why the decennial approach should be used with other technical indicators and not in isolation.

---

[2] The cycle was also noted by Professor William Stanley Jevons, an English economist, in the second half of the nineteenth century.

[3] From Smith, *Tides and the Affairs of Men*.

CHART 24.6 The Decennial Pattern of Industrial Stock Prices

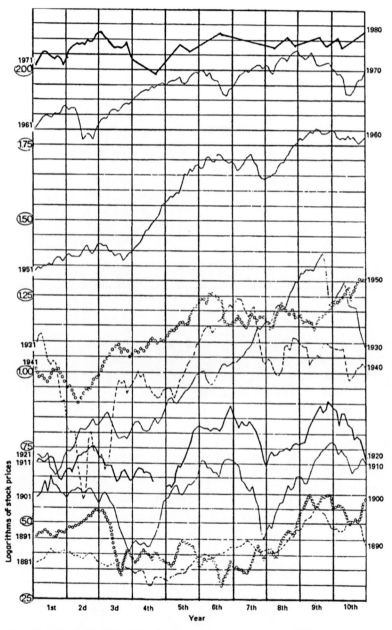

Source: Adapted from Edson Gould's 1974 Stock Market Forecast. The years 1974–1980 are represented by our own approximations for major waveforms in the DJIA.

CHART 24.7 Decennial Cycle 1900–2009 Distinguishing between Secular Bull and Bear Markets

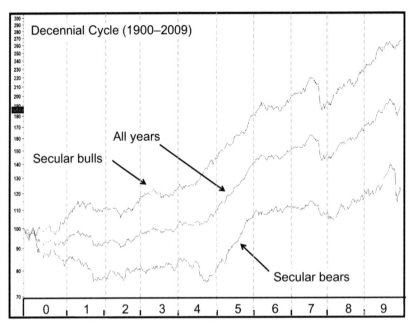

CHART 24.8 Decennial Cycle 1900–2009 and a Momentum Indicator

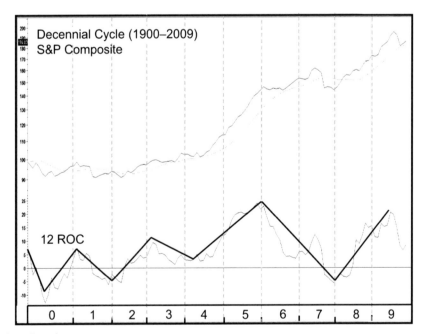

Important Years

The strongest period in the cycle is centered on years ending in a five and extends until the early part of the seventh year. There is a distinct upward bias beginning at the tail end of the seventh or the middle of the eighth year, which runs through to the third quarter of the ninth. Indeed, Table 24.1 shows that 9 years rallied 10 times from a total of 13, only being eclipsed by the super 5 years, which have a 12-1 rally advantage. That exception developed in 2005, but would not be an exception had we used the S&P Composite in our calculation. The weakest years are those ending in a seven or a zero.

Chart 24.9 compares the average cycle with the S&P Composite in the opening decade of the current century. By and large, the trajectories were quite similar until the 2008 financial crisis began to unfold and the market

TABLE 24.1 The 10-Year Stock Market Cycle

	Annual Percent Change in Dow Jones Industrial Average Year of Decade									
Decades	**1st**	**2nd**	**3rd**	**4th**	**5th**	**6th**	**7th**	**8th**	**9th**	**10th**
1881–1890*	3.0	−2.9	−8.5	−18.8	20.1	12.4	−8.4	4.8	5.5	−14.1
1891–1900	17.6	−6.6	−24.6	−0.6	2.3	−1.7	21.3	22.5	9.2	7.0
1901–1910	−8.7	−0.4	−23.6	41.7	38.2	−1.9	−37.7	46.6	15.0	−18.0
1911–1920	0.5	7.6	−10.3	−5.1	81.7	−4.2	−21.7	10.5	30.5	−32.9
1921–1930	12.7	21.7	−3.3	26.2	30.0	0.3	28.8	48.2	−17.2	−33.8
1931–1940	−52.7	−23.1	66.7	4.1	38.5	24.8	−32.8	28.1	−2.9	−12.7
1941–1950	−15.4	7.6	13.8	12.1	26.6	−8.1	2.2	−2.1	12.9	17.6
1951–1960	14.4	8.4	−3.8	44.0	20.8	2.3	−12.8	34.0	16.4	−9.3
1961–1970	18.7	−10.8	17.0	14.6	10.9	−18.9	15.2	4.3	−15.2	4.8
1971–1980	6.1	14.6	−16.6	−27.6	38.3	17.9	−17.3	−3.1	4.2	14.9
1981–1990	−9.2	19.6	20.3	−3.7	27.7	22.6	2.3	11.8	27.0	−4.3
1991–2000	20.3	4.2	13.7	2.1	33.5	26.0	22.6	16.1	25.2	
Total % Change	7%	40%	41%	89%	369%	74%	38%	222%	111%	81%
Up years	8	7	5	7	12	7	6	10	9	4
Down years	4	5	7	5	0	5	6	2	3	7

*Based on annual close
Cowles Indices 1881–1885

CHART 24.9 S&P Composite versus the Decennial Pattern 2000–2009

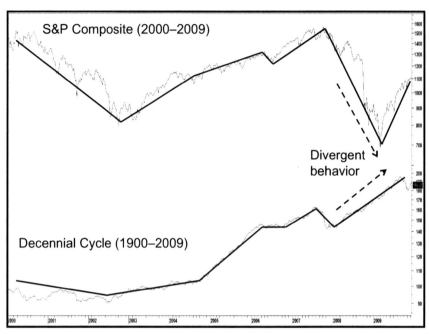

Source: From pring.com

sold off sharply instead of rising. This discrepancy once again offers a timely warning that however promising a historical pattern or relationship may be, it is mandatory to form a weight-of-the-evidence conclusion because in the world of financial forecasting nothing is predetermined except the recurring cycle of fear and greed! Moreover when using these types of cyclical patterns and the cycles themselves for analysis greater emphasis should be placed on *direction* rather than *magnitude*.

The 41-Month (4-Year) Cycle

The so-called 4-year cycle is a 40.68-month (41-month) cycle. It has been observed to operate in stock prices since 1871. Around 1923, Professor Joseph Kitchin was also able to show a cycle of 41 months in bank clearings, wholesale prices, and interest rates in the United States and United Kingdom. This cycle has since carried his name.

The Kitchin cycle as applied to stock prices is illustrated in Charts 24.10*a* and *b*. Between 1871 and 1946 it has occurred 22 times with almost uncanny

CHART 24.10a The 41-Month Rhythm in Stock Prices, 1868–1945

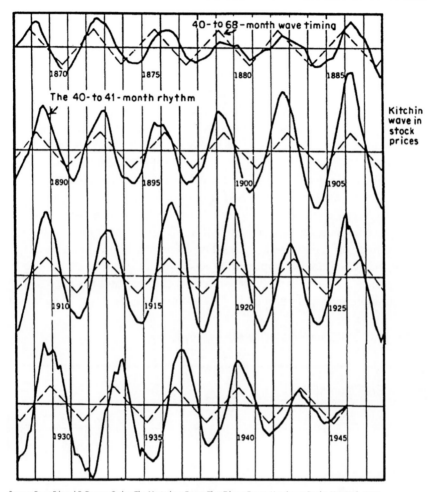

Source: From Edward E. Dewey, *Cycles: The Mysterious Forces That Trigger Events.* Hawthorne Books, New York, 1971.

CHART 24.10b The 41-Month Rhythm in Stock Prices Reversed, 1946–1968

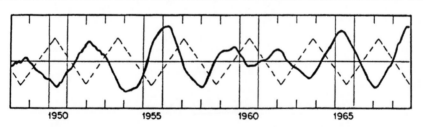

Source: From Edward E. Dewey, *Cycles: The Mysterious Forces That Trigger Events.* Hawthorne Books, New York, 1971.

consistency. Then in 1946, as Edward Dewey describes it, "Almost as if some giant hand had reached down and pushed it, the cycle stumbled, and by the time it had regained its equilibrium, it was marching completely out of step from the ideal cadence it had maintained for so many years."[4]

The 4-year cycle can also be observed by looking for a major buying opportunity every 4 years, and in this way is arguably the most reliable of the cycles described here. Charts 24.11 and 24.12 show that this usually develops after a decline, such as in 1962, 1966, 1970, 1974, 1978, 1982, 1990, 1994, 1998, and 2002. Sometimes, as in 1986 and 2006, the market is very strong and the buying opportunity develops after a sideways consolidation. The 4-year cycle year of 2010 also developed a buying opportunity, but this time it came after an intermediate decline in the middle of the year. The charts center the cycle in 1921 and 1974, respectively, so that the vertical lines represent the idealized lows. The important thing to notice is that the actual buying opportunity lows develop close to either side of these points. Many of them closely intersect the vertical lines as well. The most notable failure developed in 1930 about halfway down the greatest

CHART 24.11 S&P Composite, 1910–1958, 4-Year Cycle

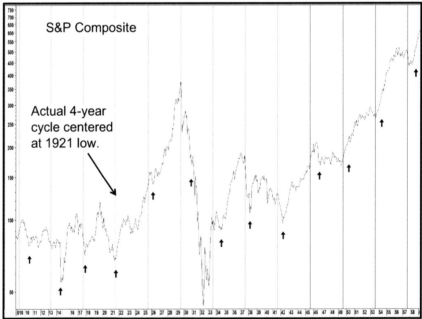

Source: From pring.com

---

[4]*Cycles: The Mysterious Forces That Trigger Events,* Hawthorne Books, New York, 1971, p.121.

CHART 24.12 S&P Composite, 1959–2018, 4-Year Cycle

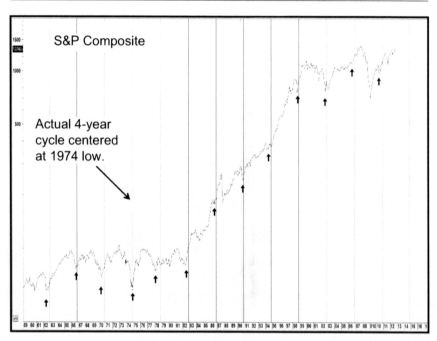

Source: From pring.com

bear market in history. Once again, this anomaly indicates the fact that a particular indicator or cycle that has operated successfully in the past is no guarantee that it will continue to do so in the future.

Presidential Cycle

The presidential cycle is closely allied to its 4-year counterpart but is more of a pattern than an actual cycle with two lows separated by a cyclic high. The presidential cycle can be split into 4 separate years like the presidential term. In the first year, presidents like to do some economic housecleaning to prepare for better times as the subsequent election approaches. Wars also tend to develop in the first half of the term. The most recent example was the Iraq invasion, which began in late 2003, although strictly speaking, that took place very early in the second half of the term. The Afghanistan surge by President Obama was advertised in December 2009 less than 1 year into his presidency. The point here is that the first year of the cycle

CHART 24.13 Presidential Cycle, 1833–2011, Annual Returns

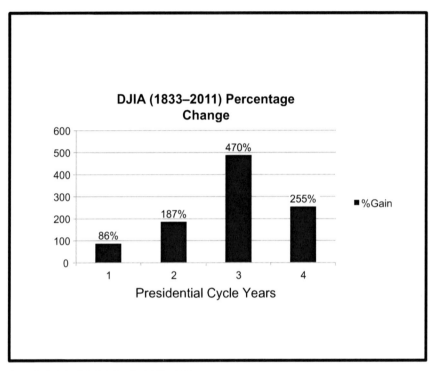

Source: *Stock Market Cycles* by Jeffrey Hirsch (Wiley, 2002).

involves economic pain and stress and is a drag on equity prices. In *Stock Market Cycles* (Wiley, 2002), Jeffrey Hirsch lays out the fact that between 1833 and 2011 the market gained 724 percent in the last 2 years of the presidential cycle compared to 273.1 percent for the first two. By way of contrast to the austerity of the first 2 years, the pre-election and election years are characterized by pump priming. The percentage return for each of the 4 years in the cycle is shown in Chart 24.13. Returning to the first year we find that a number of bear markets begin at such times. Examples include 1929, 1937, 1957, 1969, 1973, 1981, and 2001, although in the case of the latter the actual high was registered in 2000.

Chart 24.13 also shows that the third year of the cycle is by far the best. Indeed, there has not been a down year in the third year of a presidential election year since the outbreak of World War II in 1939, when the Dow Jones Industrial Average (DJIA) lost 3 percent.

Chart 24.14 lays out the average performance for each year of the cycle. Here it is evident that the period that starts at the end of the mid-term

CHART 24.14 Composite Presidential Cycle, 1900–2010

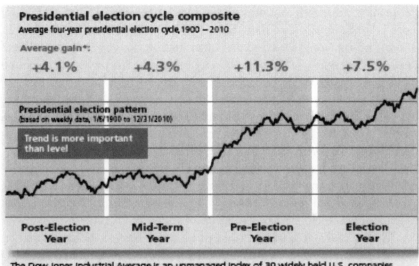

Presidential election cycle composite
Average four-year presidential election cycle, 1900 – 2010

Average gain*:

+4.1%   +4.3%   +11.3%   +7.5%

Presidential election pattern
(based on weekly data, 1/6/1900 to 12/31/2010)

Trend is more important
than level

| Post-Election | Mid-Term | Pre-Election | Election |
| Year | Year | Year | Year |

The Dow Jones Industrial Average is an unmanaged index of 30 widely held U.S. companies
commonly used to measure stock market performance.
* The S&P 500 is an unmanaged index of 500 widely traded common stocks. It is not possible to
invest directly in an index. Past performance is no guarantee of future results.

year and ends toward the final quarter of the pre-election year is statistically the strongest. When combined with the strongest year in the decennial cycle (1915, 1935, 1955, 1975, and 1995), an explosive rally typically develops every 20 years. The manuscript for this book is being prepared in early 2013, so it will be interesting to observe how the next fifth decennial third presidential combination due in 2015 will behave.

Seasonal Patterns

There is a distinct seasonal pattern of stock prices that tends to repeat year after year. Equities seem to have a spring rise, a late-second-quarter decline, a summer rally, and a fall decline. Apart from seasonal changes in the weather that affect economic activity and investor psychology, there are also some seasonal patterns in financial activities. For example, July and January are heavy months for dividend disbursement, retail trade around the year's end (Christmas) period is the strongest of the year, and so on.

Stocks purchased in October have a high probability of appreciating if held for a 3- or 6-month period, as that month ends the worst-performing

6 months of the year. It has also posted more bear market lows than any other month. Not surprisingly, the November–January period offers the best-performing consecutive months of the year (S&P average gain of 4.3 percent since 1950). Failure to do well in this part of the year is often a sign of trouble. The late Edson Gould observed that "if the market does not rally, as it should during bullish seasonal periods, it is a sign that other forces are stronger and that when the seasonal period ends those forces will really have their say."

Close to the center of this 3-month bullish seasonal is the period surrounding Christmas marked by the last five trading days of the old year and embracing the first two of the new year. This is the so-called Santa Claus rally, which according to Jeffrey Hirsch in *Stock Market Cycles*, has averaged 1.5 percent since 1953. Yale Hirsch, Jeffrey's father, coined the expression "If Santa Claus should fail to call, bears may come to Broad and Wall." Examples include 1968, 1981, 2000, and 2008, all of which were followed by bear markets. This, of course is a great example of Edson Gould's failed seasonal principle outlined above.

Chart 24.15 represents the seasonal tendency of the stock market to rise in any given month. The probabilities were calculated over the twentieth century by Tim Hayes at Ned Davis Research (see Table 24.2). All movements are relative, since a month with a strong tendency will be

CHART 24.15 The Seasonal Pattern in the Stock Market

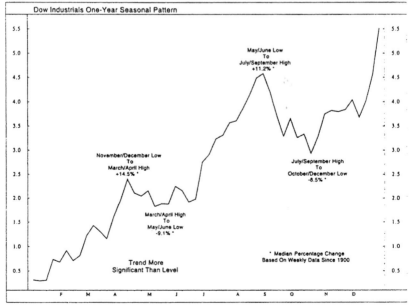

Source: From *The Research Driven Investor* by Timothy Hayes (McGraw-Hill, New York, 2000).

TABLE 24.2 DJIA Monthly Performance Since 1900

Jan.	Feb.	March	April	May	June	July	Aug.	Sept.	Oct.	Nov.	Dec.
Average rise/fall											
1.1%	−.1%	.7%	1.1%	−.1%	.5%	1.4%	1.1%	−1%	0%	.9%	1.5%
Percentage of months in which the market gained											
64	50	61	55	52	52	61	65	42	55	62	73

Source: Ned Davis Research.

accentuated in a bull market, and vice versa. It is also important to note that the direction of the trend is more important than the level.

The January Barometer was originally devised by Yale Hirsch in 1972. Simply stated, the indicator adheres to the maxim that "as goes the S&P in January, so does the whole year" (Jeffrey Hirsch, *Stock Market Cycles*, p. 143). According to Hirsch, the barometer has an 88.7 percent accuracy.

One final comment on seasonality derives from the fact that the May to October period has the worst track record. "Sell in May and go away" has some statistical merit on its side. For instance, Jeffrey Hirsch calculates that a hypothetical $10,000 investment in the DJIA compounded to $674,074 for the November–April period, compared to a $1,024 loss over a 62-year period. That does not mean that every May–October period lost money, nor that every November–April one made money, but it does indicate a strongly positive bias toward the November–April period.

My friend Sam Stovall at S&P Capital IQ takes it one step further. He points out that two good performing sectors in the negative May–November period are the defensive consumer staples and health care. Alternatively, the higher beta materials and industrials outperform in the bullish November–May period.

End of the Month Bullish Seasonal

The year-end effect of superior returns also seems to apply to the month's end. Data covering the 89-year period ending in 1986 show that returns from the last trading day of a month (day 1 in Figure 24.5) to the end of the third trading day of the new month are consistently good. The rationale for this effect may well come from higher month-end cash flows, such as salaries, dividends, etc.

Indeed, these four trading days average 0.118 percent, versus 0.015 percent for all trading days. Turn-of-the-month returns can be said to account for all the positive capital gain returns generated by the market. In an article entitled "Calendar Anomalies,"[5] Bruce Jacobs and Kenneth

---

[5]*MTA Journal*, winter 1989–1990.

FIGURE 24.5 Turn of the Month (Average Daily Returns)

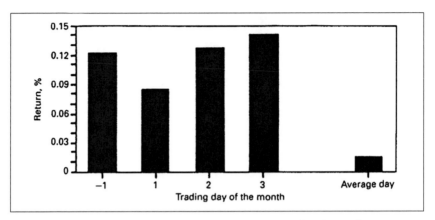

Data from J. Lakonishok and S. Smidt, "Are seasonal abnormalities real? A ninety year perspective," Johnson working paper 80–07, Cornell University, Ithaca, 1987.

Levy point out that this effect was less prevalent in the 1980s, which goes to show that it is not a wise policy to follow one indicator exclusively. In the 2001 edition of the *Stock Traders Almanac*, a must-read for the seasonally oriented trader, Yale Hirsch points out that this seasonal indicator shifted between 1981 and 2000 to the last 4 and first 5 trading days of the new month. The most bullish day of all appears to be the first day of the month, according to the Almanac's 2013 edition, as the editors point out that in the previous 15 years the DJIA gained more points on that day than all the others combined.

However, it does make sense to integrate this reliable long-term seasonal effect with short-term oscillators. Clearly, the potential for the market to advance at this time will be much greater if it is oversold going into the last (presumably) bullish day of the month.

Days of the Week

The term "blue Monday" is very much justified. The influence of weak Mondays originated during the 1929–1932 crash. During the Depression, the market advanced, on average, every day of the week except Mondays. It could be said that the entire market decline took place over weekends during the periods from Saturdays to closings on Mondays.

Figure 24.6 shows the average return for each day from 1928 to 1982. Monday is the only down day. Remembering that this takes into account "black Thursday" in 1929 but does not include the 500-point drop that occurred on "black Monday" in 1987, it just goes to emphasize the point.

FIGURE 24.6 The Day-of-the-Week Effect (Average Daily Returns)

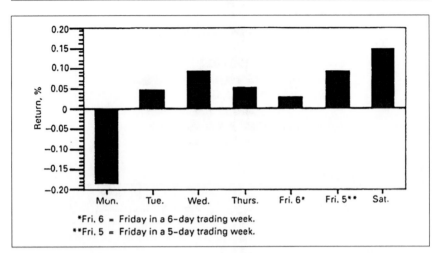

*Fri. 6 = Friday in a 6-day trading week.
**Fri. 5 = Friday in a 5-day trading week.

Source: Data from D. Klein and R. Stambaugh," A Further Investigation of the Weekend Effect in Stock Returns," *Journal of Finance*, July 1984, pp. 819–837.

There does not appear to be any acceptable rationale for this effect, which also occurs in non-U.S. equity markets, debt instruments, and even orange juice.

Pre-Holiday Advances

The day preceding holidays is statistically a bullish period. This is indicated in Figure 24.7, which covers the period between 1963 and 1982. With the exception of Presidents' Day, all these (average) pre-holiday trading sessions handsomely beat the average day.

Time of Day

Recent studies[6] have indicated that there is a definite time-of-day effect, as shown in Figure 24.8. There is little difference in the activity from day to day, except for Monday mornings. All days, however, show an upward bias going into the last half-hour. The study showed that this rallying effect was emphasized even to the closing bell, with the average return of the last trade equal to 0.05 percent, or 0.6 cents per share. The nearer the return took place to the closing bell, the higher it was. Trades after 3:55 P.M. averaged 0.12 percent returns, or 1.75 cents per share. That upbeat note is a good place to close this chapter.

[6]Harris, "How to Profit from Intradaily Stock Returns," *Journal of Portfolio Management*, winter 1986.

FIGURE 24.7 The Holiday Effect (Average Pre-Holiday Returns)

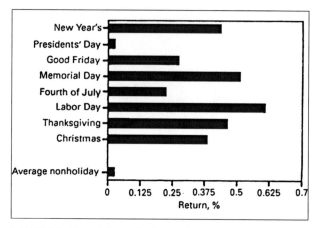

Source: Data from R. Ariel, "High Stock Returns before Holidays," Sloan working paper, MIT, Cambridge, MA, 1984.

FIGURE 24.8 Time-of-the-Day Effect

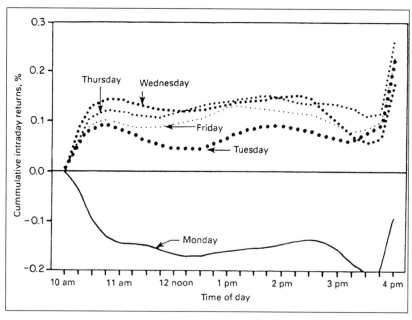

Source: Data from L. Harris, "A Transactions Data Study of Weekly and Intradaily Patterns of Stock Returns," *Journal of Financial Economics*, vol. 16, 1986, pp. 99–117.

25

PRACTICAL IDENTIFICATION OF CYCLES

This chapter discusses some of the basic principles of cyclic analysis and uses examples to illustrate some simple techniques that help in their identification.

Cycles Defined

A *cycle* is a recognizable price pattern or movement that occurs with some degree of regularity in a specific time period. A market, stock, or indicator that has a relatively consistent price low at 6-week intervals is said to have a 6-week cycle. That successive lows are higher or lower than their predecessor is of no importance in identifying the cycle. What is significant is that there is a clearly definable "low" point every 6 weeks, separated from its predecessor by a high point known as the *cycle high*. Figure 25.1 shows some possible examples.

Figure 25.1 also shows that while cycle lows occur at approximately 6-week intervals, cycle highs can vary. Occasionally, they arrive early, as at point A; sometimes, they occur in the middle of the cycle, as at point B; but, they may also appear late, as at point C. Generally, when the cycle high develops shortly after the cycle low, the implications are that the upward part of the cycle is weak and that its overall strength lies on the downside. In this situation, each cycle low is normally below that of its predecessor. Similarly, a cycle high that is "late" in arriving, i.e., that arrives well after the halfway period, usually indicates a strong cycle, with the implication that

FIGURE 25.1 Cycle Highs and Lows

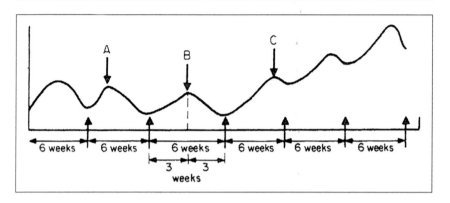

the low will be above the low of the previous cycle. A number of different cycles can be observed for any market or stock, some long and some short in duration. The task of the technician is not to identify as many as possible, but to isolate the most dominant and reliable ones.

Principles

There are several principles:

1. The longer the cycle, the greater the amplitude in price is likely to be; e.g., a 10-week cycle will have far greater trading significance than a 10-hour cycle.
2. It follows from item 1 that the larger the cycle, the greater the significance of the low.
3. The larger the number of cycles reaching a low at around the same time, the stronger the ensuing price movement is likely to be.
4. In a rising trend, the cycle high has a tendency to "translate to the right," i.e., to occur after the halfway point of the cycle. The same principle holds in reverse for bear markets; i.e., there is a tendency for the cycle high to translate to the left.
5. It is possible to observe cyclic highs that occur at regular time intervals.
6. A projected cyclic high or low may develop in the opposite way to that anticipated. In such cases, the cycle is said to be "inverted."

Methods of Detection

Many mathematical techniques have been used to identify cycles. Fourier analysis, for example, isolates the existence of various cycles by length, amplitude, phases, etc. Systematic reconnaissance is a technique that tests for periods requested. The result is a period gram that shows the most dominant cycles. Although such techniques can be useful, they tend to make technical analysis look as if it is an exact science, which it very definitely is not. This chapter will be confined to three methods of cycle identification: deviation from trend, momentum, and simple observation.

Deviation from Trend

This method takes a series of data and divides each item by a moving average (MA). The period under observation represents the deviation, and the MA represents the trend.

Chapter 11 explained that since an MA is designed to reflect the underlying price trend, ideally it should be plotted halfway along its span. This is because the "average" price occurs halfway through the time span, e.g., in the seventh week for a 14-week MA. However, changes in direction of the MA usually occur far too late to offer timely signals for the purpose of identifying trend reversals. For this reason, technicians normally use an MA crossover for generating signals. Since only historical data are used in cycle identification, this disadvantage is not important. The MA deviation is, therefore, calculated by dividing the period in question by the midpoint of the MA. The price observation for February 27 is divided by a 13-week MA, as calculated on April 18; i.e., the MA is "moved" back 7 weeks. The result is then plotted as an oscillator, which isolates the cyclical high and low points.

It is then a relatively simple task to see whether any consistent time periods separate these points. One method is to note down the time differences between all the cycle lows and highs in order to determine which ones come up most frequently. Since MAs smooth out all cycles within their time span, it is important to experiment with several averages in order to identify as many cycles as possible. The more reliable ones should then be used in the analysis.

Momentum

A simpler method is to calculate a momentum series and smooth it by an appropriate MA, as determined by trial and error. This approach will bring out the underlying rhythm in the price movement, just as a deviation-from-trend calculation does. It is doubtful whether the momentum approach alone can be successfully used for cycle identification, but it can prove to be an invaluable confirmation of cyclical reliability when used in conjunction with the technique of simple price observation discussed later.

The position of a momentum indicator can also be useful in warning of potential cyclic inversions, i.e., when a projected cyclic low might turn out to be a cyclic high, and vice versa. For example, a cyclic inversion may occur when the observed data project that a cyclic low is likely to develop around a specific date, while the momentum indicator used in conjunction with this study is at, or coming down from, an overbought level. A good example is shown in Chart 24.5 featuring the S&P Composite. In 1987, the 9.2-year cycle appeared to reach its peak, as measured by the 55-month rate of change (ROC) at exactly the time when a low should have been recorded.

Simple Observation

Chart 25.1 shows the Philadelphia Gold and Silver Share Index. The solid line represents an 82-week cycle of lows and the dashed line a 126-week

CHART 25.1 Philadelphia Gold and Silver Share Index and a 41-Week ROC, 1995–2002

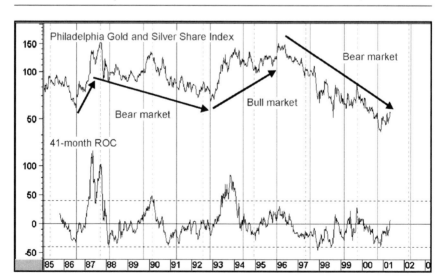

Source: From pring.com

cycle of highs. The ROC has a time span of 41 weeks, i.e., half the 82-week cycle. Neither of these cycles is perfect but they do, for the most part, explain most of the turning points in the period under consideration. These two cycles were isolated on a trial-and-error basis using the cycle line tool in the MetaStock program.

If you do not have access to a package such as this and wish to accomplish this task manually, the easiest method of identifying cycles is to start by observing on a price chart two or three major lows that appear to be relatively equidistant. The next step is to pencil in the projections for that particular cycle. If a substantial proportion of those projections result in either highs or lows, it is a good idea to mark them with a colored pencil. If most projections result in failure, the cycle should be abandoned and a new one sought. A cycle high occurring at any of these points should be treated as a successful projection, since the first objective of cycle analysis is to determine potential turning points. Once a reliable cycle has been established, the analyst should look at all the important cycle lows that are "unexplained" by the first cycle and try to "explain" them by discovering another cycle. The chances are that the second cycle will not only fit some of the unexplained lows, but will also occur at or near some of the cycle lows previously established. This is very important because a basic principle of cycle analysis is that the greater the number of cycles making a low around a certain time, the stronger the ensuing move is likely to be. Such knowledge *must* be used in conjunction with other technical evidence, but if that, too, offers a green light, the odds that a significant up wave will occur are increased.

The next step in the method is discussed in the following section.

Combining Cycle Highs and Lows

The vertical lines in Chart 25.1 point up a fairly reliable pattern for both cycle highs and lows. One of the most important points that comes out of this exercise is the fact that the various turning points derive their significance from the direction of the main or primary trend. In this respect, the arrows on the chart flag the various bull and bear market environments. Note how the cycle tops tend to have greater magnitude in a bear market, such as the 1987 and 1990 tops. Conversely, the 1986 and late-1992 lows developed in a bull market and experienced far greater magnitude than the 1997 and 1999 signals, which developed in a bear market.

One of the advantages of combining high and low cycles is that this approach makes it possible to obtain some idea of how long a rally or reaction might last. This arises from the proximity of the high and low. For example, the late-1992 low developed just after the high. The ensuing decline was quite brief. The reverse was true at the end of 1999, where the low was very close to the early 1990 high. The rally in this instance was short. The position of the ROC can often provide a clue as to whether a particular cyclical turning point will "work." For example, the strong peaks in 1987, 1990, and late 1999 all developed when the ROC was at or close to an overbought condition. Similarly, the 1986 and 1988 lows were associated with moderately oversold conditions that failed to materialize.

Not all examples work out quite as accurately as that shown in Chart 25.1. Readers are cautioned not to try to make a cycle "work." If it does not fit naturally and easily, the chances are that it either does not exist or is likely to be highly unreliable and therefore should not be used. In any event, *such analysis should always be used in conjunction with other indicators.*

Summary

1. Recurring cycles, both of low points and high points, can be observed from charts of financial markets.
2. A cycle turning point is significant both for the time interval between cycles and for the number of cycles that are turning at the same time.
3. Cyclic analysis should always be used in conjunction with other indicators.
4. Suspected cycles that do not easily fall into a consistently recurring pattern should not be made to "work" and should be discarded.

26

VOLUME II: VOLUME INDICATORS

Chapter 7 outlined some basic principles for interpreting volume. Now we will explore several volume indicators that can be applied to any security, finishing up the discussion with volume indicators that are more suitable for analyzing markets as a whole.

Rate of Change (ROC) of Volume

Normally, volume is displayed as a histogram underneath the price. A quick glance at any chart often reveals a noticeable increase in the size of the volume bars that are associated with breakouts, selling climaxes, and so forth. This is all well and good, but occasionally there are subtle shifts in the level of activity that are not easily detectable by this method. By massaging the volume data with an ROC calculation, it is possible to observe some new insights into the dynamics of volume interpretation.

Chart 26.1 shows a 10-day ROC of volume together with a regular volume histogram for Northern Trust. I am using a 10-day ROC here, but, of course, it is possible to use any time span you wish. The price peak at A looks quite normal under the histogram method, but the ROC technique indicates a dramatic surge commensurate with an exhaustion move.

Peaks in the ROC indicator can often signal exhaustion that is not readily apparent with the histogram. In Chart 26.2 featuring T. Rowe Price, the initial peak at A is well signaled by the ROC, but not by the histogram in the bottom panel. The peak at B is indicated by an expansion in the histogram levels, but the rise is nowhere near that of the volume ROC, which was close

CHART 26.1 Northern Trust, 2000–2001

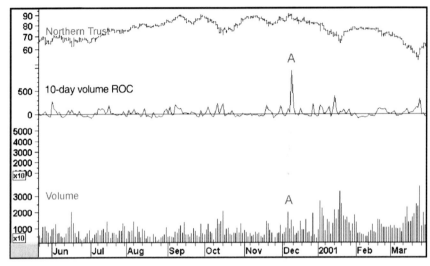

Source: From pring.com

CHART 26.2 T. Rowe Price, 1999–2001

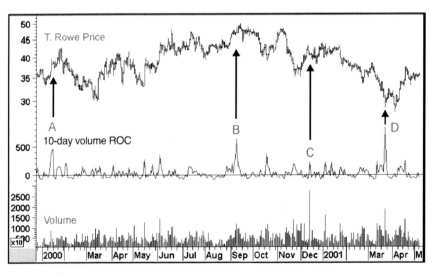

Source: From pring.com

to a record for the period covered in the chart. At C, the histogram rallies to a record level, but this is not picked up by the ROC. In this instance, the high volume followed the initial peak by 2 days and appears to be an isolated affair totally unimportant from an analytical point of view. Finally, at D, both series

CHART 26.3 Stanley Works, 1999–2000 and a Volume ROC

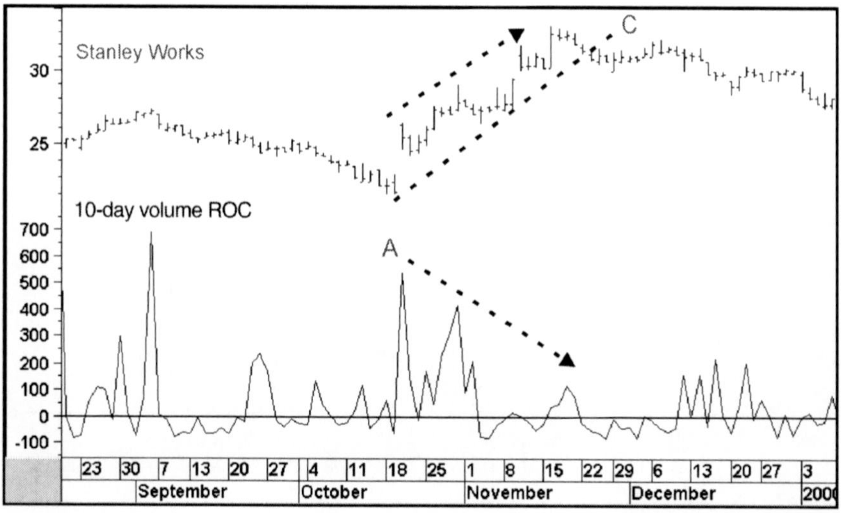

Source: From pring.com

flag the selling climax at the first bottom but the comparison is far more dramatic for the ROC.

The ROC sometimes flags divergences. In Chart 26.3 featuring Stanley Works, for instance, the two dashed arrows point up the series of declining momentum peaks and rising price highs. This indicated serious potential weakness, and sure enough, the price did experience a decline once it had confirmed by violating its up trendline.

In Chart 26.4 we see a situation at A where it is possible to observe a down trendline break in volume, which is also confirmed by a similar break in the price. Later on at B, the volume ROC traces out a small inverse head-and-shoulders pattern, which indicated a short-term trend of higher activity. This time, though, the price violated a trendline on the downside. This indicated an expansion of volume on the downside, which is a bearish sign. Sometimes, short-term trades can take advantage of overbought readings since they often flag short-term turning points.

It is fairly evident by now that a simple ROC of volume can be a pretty jagged indicator suitable only for pointing up exhaustion moves, divergences, and on a limited basis, constructing trendlines. Consequently, it makes sense to run a moving average through a volume rate of change because it smooths out the jagged nature of the raw data.

In Chart 26.5 this has been taken one step further by calculating a 10-day moving average of a 25-day volume ROC.

CHART 26.4 Stanley Works, 1999–2000 and a Volume ROC

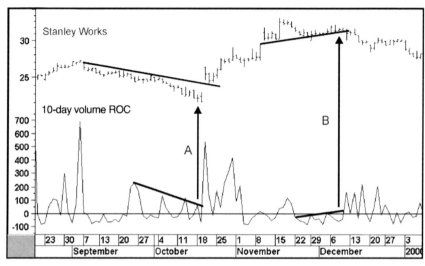

Source: From pring.com

This series is a lot smoother than those we have been looking at so far. It is fairly evident that this approach lends itself more readily to price pattern and trendline analysis. First note that the overbought and oversold lines are not drawn on an equidistant basis. This is because the

CHART 26.5 Snap-on Inc, 1992–1994 and a Volume ROC

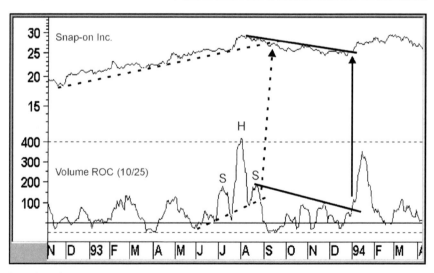

Source: From pring.com

calculation treats the ROC as a percentage. Volume can expand, even on a smoothed basis, by 200 percent or 300 percent quite easily, yet can only fall by 100 percent. This means that downside action is far more limited than upside potential. Later on we will look at some alternative form of calculating a smoothed ROC of volume. There are two principal events on the chart. The first is a head-and-shoulders top. The head represented a buying crescendo, which indicated a change of trend. Once the neckline had been violated, this merely represented a confirmation that the volume trend was down. Since the price also violated an up trendline, both price and volume were now in gear on the downside, and it was reasonable to expect an extended correction.

The end of the sell-off was signaled as both the price and volume violated important downtrend lines. Since they were now in gear on the upside, this provided a nice confirmation that the uptrend was healthy. The down trendline for volume actually represents the neckline of a reverse head-and-shoulders pattern. I did not display the H and S letters on the chart because the left shoulder was also the right shoulder of the previous upward-sloping head-and-shoulders top, and this would have complicated things.

Volume ROC: The Percent Calculation

We discovered earlier that the volume ROC indicator, when calculated with a percent method, does not lend itself to pointing up oversold volume conditions very well. A solution is to calculate the ROC using a subtraction method, as I have done in the lower panel of Chart 26.6. An oversold condition is signaled at A for the subtraction method, but not for the division calculation. The disadvantage of the subtraction calculation is that volume momentum cannot be compared over long periods of time if the security being monitored experiences a substantial increase in average daily volume. For charts that span less than 2 years of data, the subtraction technique is probably a better approach, though it's important to remember that because the volume level for individual stocks and markets can vary tremendously, the overbought and oversold lines will have to be adjusted accordingly. In Chart 26.6 the upper dashed horizontal lines represent an overbought reading in both volume indicators. Since the price had been declining, the high level at B signaled a selling climax. The subtraction-based oscillator was deeply oversold at A, the next slightly lower bottom. This indicated a classic double-bottom characteristic. It is also apparent, if it was not before now, that a high overextended reading in a volume oscillator does not necessarily mean that the price is overbought—merely that volume is overextended. A high reading in volume oscillators can mean a top or a bottom, depend-

CHART 26.6 Snap-on Inc, 1994–1995 and Two Volume ROC Calculations

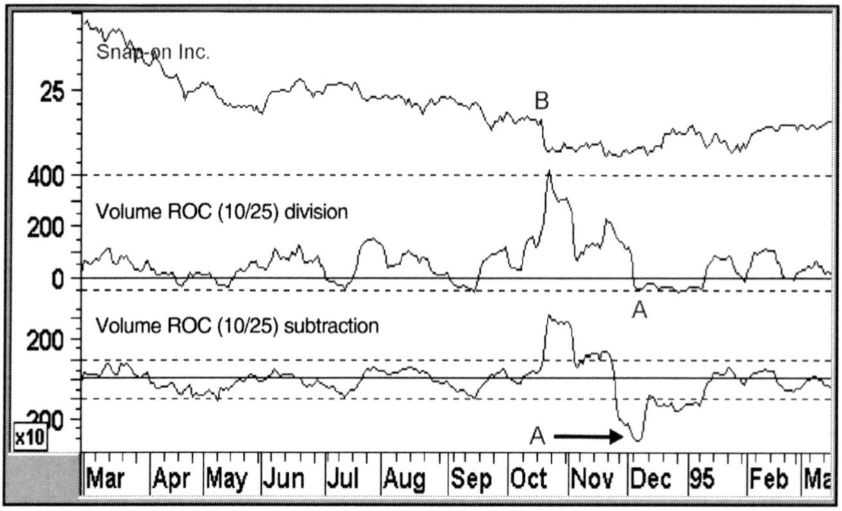

Source: From pring.com

ing on the previous price action. I'll have more to say on that point a little later.

> **Major Technical Principle**   A high overextended reading in a volume indicator does not necessarily mean that the price is overbought—merely that volume is overextended. A high reading can mean a top or a bottom, depending on the direction of the previous trend. A reversal from a high reading may also indicate a change as opposed to a reversal in trend.

Primary-Trend Volume ROC

Annual (12-month) ROCs are a useful way of measuring primary-trend price momentum, but since volume trends are more random, such indicators tend to be quite jagged in nature. Chart 26.7 shows the annual ROC price for the Standard & Poor's (S&P) Composite and New York Stock Exchange (NYSE) Volume. However, in order to overcome the jagged nature of the volume data, both series have been smoothed with a 6-month moving average (MA). When used together, the two series can be extremely instructive.

CHART 26.7 Price versus Volume Momentum, 1969–1990

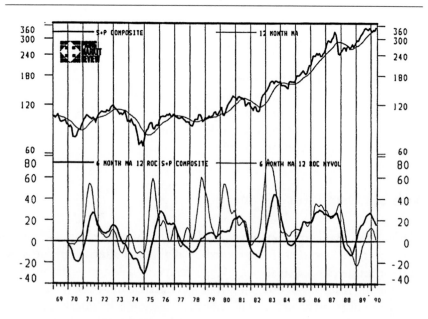

Several observations can be made:

1. The volume curve has an almost consistent tendency to peak out ahead of price during both bull and bear phases.
2. In most instances, fairly reliable indications of a *potential* trend reversal can be obtained when the volume momentum crosses price.
3. When the price index is above its zero reference line and is falling but volume is rising (e.g., 1953, early and late 1976, 1981, and late 1987; the experience in early 1964 appeared to be an exception), the expanding activity represents distribution and should be interpreted as a very bearish factor once the rally has terminated.
4. A reversal in volume at a market bottom should be confirmed by a reversal in price momentum.
5. Very high readings in the volume indicator are usually followed by strong bull markets.
6. When volume crosses below zero, it is normally, but not always, a negative sign. The most bearish situations seem to arise when the price indicator is well above zero. In 1988, for instance, price momentum was well below zero when volume moved into negative territory but the market rallied. On the other hand, in 1969, 1973, and 1977 volume

crossed below zero just after price momentum had started to roll over from an overbought level, and this was followed by a major decline.

7. During the initial stages of a bull move, volume momentum is always above price. (The 1988–1989 rally represents the *only* exception.)

Chart 26.7 shows that a reversal in one curve unaccompanied by a reversal in the other at market bottoms tends to give a premature signal. For example, volume turned up ahead of price at the end of 1973 and 1977. Consequently, it is wiser to await a signal from both, even though it may occur at a slightly higher price level.

Volume Oscillator

The volume oscillator is an alternative method of presenting volume in a momentum format. It is calculated by dividing a short-term measure of the volume trend, usually a moving average, by a longer-term one and plotting the result as an oscillator. It is also possible to divide the close by a measure of trend as well. In effect, the calculation is identical as that for price under the trend deviation section in Chapter 14. The only difference is that volume is substituted for price. An example is shown in Figure 26.1 The resulting indicator is an oscillator that revolves around a zero reference line. A zero reading in the indicator occurs when both MAs are at identical levels. Positive readings develop when the shorter-term (10-day in the figure) MA is above its longer-term (25-day) counterpart, and vice versa. At points A and B the two moving averages cross and the indicator also moves through zero. On the other hand, C and D represent overbought and oversold readings, respectively, where the distance between the two averages is greatest. Ten- and 25-day time spans have been used in the example, but any widely separated spans could be used instead.

An example is shown in Chart 26.8 featuring Humana. Here we can see that the volume oscillator breaks above a small down trendline in March 1999. This upside breakout merely indicated that the trend of volume was likely to be up. It said nothing about the course of prices. In this instance, the price violated a horizontal trendline, which indicated a bearish combination of declining prices and expanding volume. This was then followed by an overbought reading in the oscillator, a sign of a selling climax. That could have proved to be the final bottom. However, the oscillator broke above a trendline in July 2000 and the price violated one on the downside, indicating an almost exact replay of the 1999 price action.

FIGURE 26.1 Calculating a Volume Oscillator

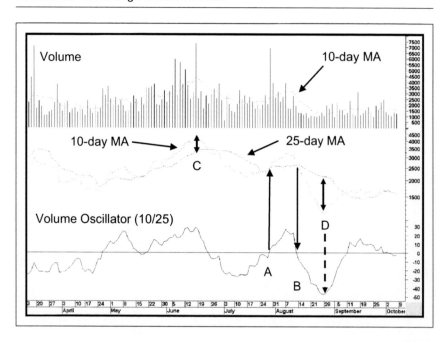

CHART 26.8 Humana, 1998–1999, and a Volume Oscillator

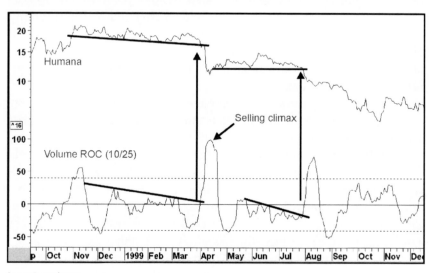

Source: From pring.com

CHART 26.9 Advent Claymore, 2011–2012, and a 10/25 Volume Oscillator

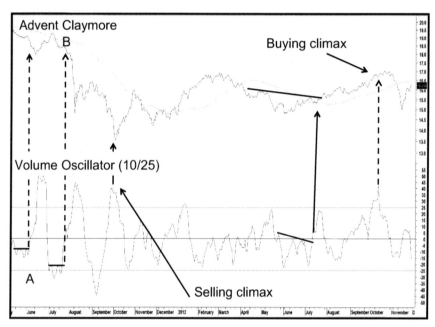

Source: From pring.com

Chart 26.9 features Advent Claymore, where we can see that oscillator breakouts at A and B signified a new trend of rising volume. We can also see a selling and buying climax in October 2011 and 2012, respectively. A joint trendline break in July 2012 also signaled a nice rally. The volume breakout indicated that the advance would take place under a background of rising activity, which clearly added strength to its validity until the bearish October buying climax.

Chart 26.10 features a 15/45 volume oscillator for Columbia Energy. This longer-term interrelationship offers more deliberate and less jagged price action. The most obvious thing to note is the late-1999 summer reverse head and shoulders in the oscillator. Once again, an increase in volume was indicated, but this time the price broke to the upside. We see another example later on in November. It is rare when these oscillators are able to trace out price patterns, but when they do, the signals tend to be very reliable. The chart also shows a buying climax in early November, which was later confirmed by a trend break in the price itself, then a selling climax in the following March.

It is fairly obvious by now that volume oscillators move between bands of extremes just as price momentum does, but with one important difference.

CHART 26.10 Columbia Energy, 1999–2000, and a Volume Oscillator

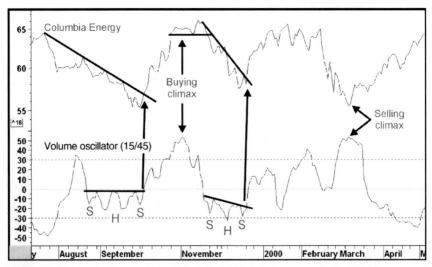

Source: From pring.com

When a price index is overextended on the upside, it usually indicates an overbought market, with the implication that a reversal to the downside is due. An unusual rise in activity is also associated with an imminent trend reversal, but it is essential to relate the movement of the volume oscillator to the prevailing movement in price.

Apart from this important difference, volume oscillators should be interpreted in the same way as price oscillators. One of the strong points of the volume oscillator is that reversals from overbought readings often signal exhaustion, either from the buy or sell side. Other indicators should then be consulted to make sure that the volume action is being confirmed.

One possibility is the use of volume with a price oscillator. This relationship is not always exact. If volume and price changes are not closely related for the stock or market being followed, this approach should not be used.

Chart 26.11 shows the Brazilian Index, the Bovespa.

At point A we see the higher price preceded by a series of declining volume peaks. These indicated vulnerability, which was finally confirmed when the price violated its dashed up trendline. I would have expected to see a more prolonged decline, but a selling climax developed at point B as an oversold price oscillator combined with an overbought volume oscillator. The price oscillator is not telling us much at point C, but the volume series is, as it violates a very significant down trendline.

CHART 26.11 The Brazilian Bovespa 2006–2008, a Price versus Volume Oscillator

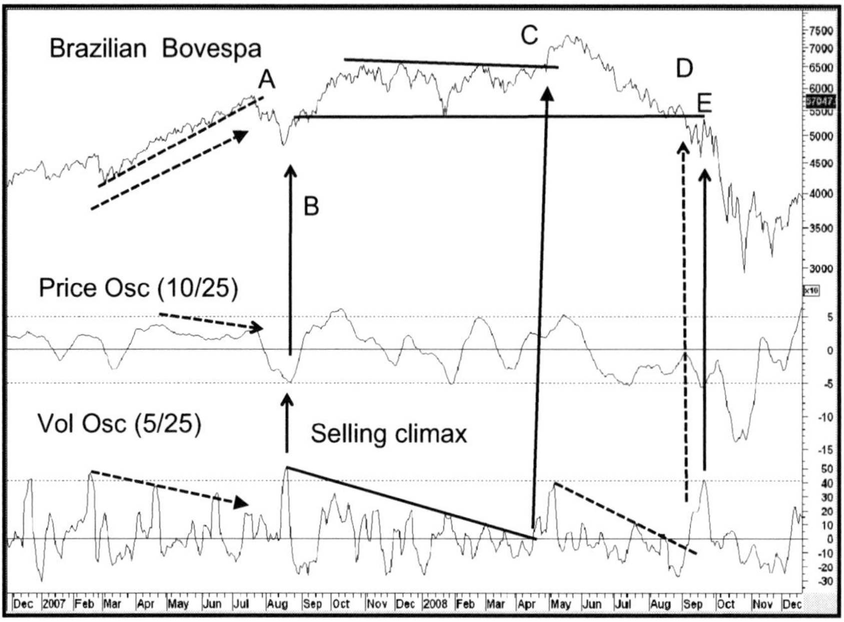

Source: From pring.com

Since the price breaks to the upside, this turns out to be a bullish period as the index rallies to its final bull market peak. Things get a bit complicated in early September 2008 as the volume oscillator rallies above a down trendline. This indicated that volume was going to expand, and since the price broke below the horizontal support trendline at D, that indicated weaker prices. However, volume soon expanded to selling climax proportions at E and that should have been bullish. In fact, the price fell below the low of the selling climax very quickly and that meant that a lot of people were trapped at higher prices. While a selling climax does not necessarily mark the final bottom, there is usually an interregnum before prices register a new low. In this case, that did not happen and therefore provided a clue that things would get much worse.

The following are the main rules for interpreting the volume oscillator:

1. When the oscillator reaches an extreme and starts to reverse, it is indicating the potential for a reversal of the prevailing trend.
2. Volume oscillators occasionally lend themselves to trendline and pattern construction.

3. Expansion in price associated with a contraction in the volume oscillator is bearish.
4. An expansion in the oscillator associated with a contraction in price is bearish, except when volume reaches an extreme, in which case, a selling climax is usually signaled.
5. The volume oscillator usually leads the price oscillator.

Remember, this is by no means a perfect indicator; therefore, you should first make sure that it is acting consistently with the price trend being measured, and also that there is corroborating evidence from other indicators.

The Demand Index

The Demand Index was developed by Jim Sibbet as a method of simulating upside and downside volume for markets and stocks where such data are not generally available. It combines price and volume into one indicator with the objective of leading market turning points. The Demand Index is based on the premise that volume leads price, and is included in many charting packages. Unlike the volume ROC and volume oscillator, the Demand Index always moves in the same direction as the price, in that high readings indicate overbought conditions and vice versa. I find this to be a very useful indicator when used in the following ways:

1. A divergence between the indicator and the price points up an underlying strength or weakness, depending on whether it is a positive or negative one.
2. Overbought and oversold crossovers often generate good buy and sell signals. Since the level of the Demand Index is affected by the volatility of the security being monitored, optimum places to plot overbought and oversold levels will vary and should be determined on a case-by-case approach. That said, the + and −25 levels appear to be a good compromise for most markets.
3. The index sometimes forms price patterns and trendline violations, which normally represent a reliable *advance* warning of an impending price trend reversal.

Chart 26.12 featuring Citrix shows some interesting features. First, at A, both the price and demand index break trendlines for a good sell signal. Later on, the process is reversed as the Demand Index completes a base along with the price. The resulting rally can only be described as a whipsaw. Does this

CHART 26.12 Citrix Systems, 2000–2001, and a Demand Index

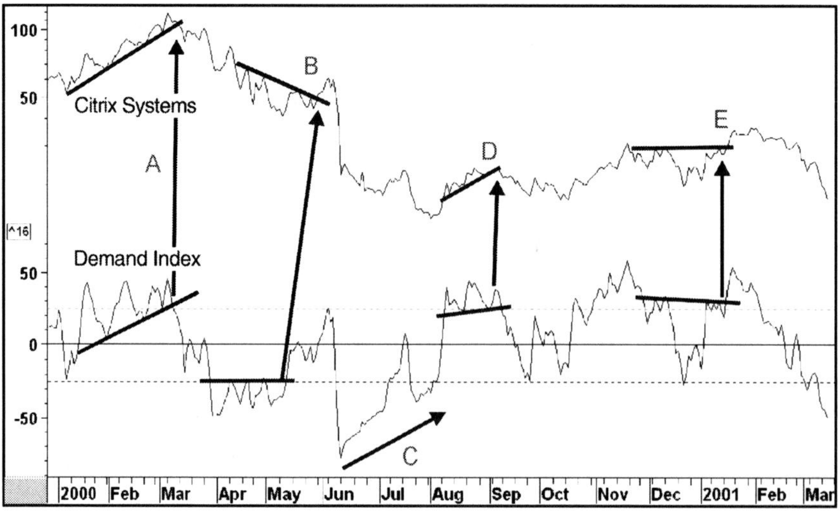

Source: From pring.com

mean that the Demand Index is no good? No, this is a normal phenomenon in a bear market. What looks to be a very valid breakout turns out to be a whipsaw—it can happen with any indicator. The remedy is to try to get a fix on the direction of the main trend before any short-term analysis is attempted. Point C shows a positive divergence between the Demand Index and the price, and point D a small double trendline break. Finally, at E we see a breakout by the Demand Index from a reverse head-and-shoulders pattern, but it fails. Once again we need to use some common sense because the breakout came from an overbought condition. As we learned in the momentum section, breakouts from such high levels typically result in whipsaws.

Chaikin Money Flow

The Chaikin Money Flow (CMF) indicator is based on the principle that rising prices should be accompanied by expanding volume and vice versa. The formula is as follows:

$$CMF = SUM\ (AD, n)\ /\ SUM(VOL, n)$$

where n = period

$$AD = VOL * (CL - OP)\ /\ (HI - LO)$$

where AD stands for accumulation distribution.

The formula emphasizes the fact that market strength is usually accompanied by prices closing in the upper half of their daily range with increasing volume. Likewise, market weakness is usually accompanied by prices closing in the lower half of their daily range with increasing volume. This indicator can be calculated with any time span—the longer the period, the more deliberate the swings. Money flow indicators calculated with a short-term time frame, such as 10 periods, are, therefore, much more volatile.

When prices consistently close in the upper half of their daily high/low range on increased volume for the period under consideration, then the indicator will be positive (i.e., above the zero line). Conversely, if prices consistently close in the lower half of their daily high/low range on increased volume, then the indicator will be negative (i.e., below the zero line).

It's possible to construct overbought and oversold lines and use these as buy and sell alerts, but the indicator really comes into its own with divergence analysis. In Chart 26.13 featuring National Semiconductor we can see some good examples in practice. In early 1994, the Chaikin was falling sharply as the price ran up to its final peak, and at the time of the actual high was barely above the equilibrium line. This showed that the quality of the last few weeks of the rally left a lot to be desired. At the end of 1995, the divergence was more blatant since the indicator was barely able to rise above the zero line at a time when the price was making a new high. Both these examples were followed by long downtrends.

CHART 26.13 National Semiconductor, 1993–1997, and a CMF

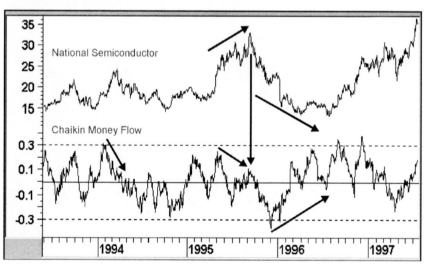

Positive divergences also work quite well, as we can appreciate from observing the mid 1996 bottom. See how the price makes a marginal new low but the oscillator is hardly below zero. This compares to the late-1995 bottom, where it was at an extremely oversold condition. Of course, this is merely a positive momentum characteristic—we still need to witness some kind of trend reversal in price to confirm this event. Divergences are not uncommon in momentum indicators. What sets the money flow indicator apart from the rest is that the divergences are usually far more blatant than, say, the relative strength indicator (RSI) or ROC series. As a result, it can provide clues of probable trend reversals that may not be apparent elsewhere.

One of the ways in which I like to use the indicator is to study trading ranges and then compare the price action to the oscillator to see if it is giving a clue as to the direction of the eventual breakout. Chart 26.14 shows American Business Products with a 20-period CMF. The price was experiencing a sideways trading range in 1987. During the formation of the rectangle, the money flow indicator violated an up trendline and diverged very negatively with the price in the September/October period. This combination indicated vulnerability, so it was not surprising that the price experienced a nasty decline.

Later on, the price traced out another trading range, but this time the CMF rallied the moment the trading range started.

Choice of time span also influences the character of the indicator. A short one, such as 10 days, returns a volatile series, whereas the 45-day span

CHART 26.14 American Business Products, 1986–1991, and a CMF

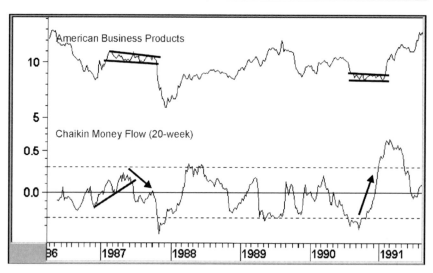

CHART 26.15 Reliance Communications, 2006–2009, and a CMF

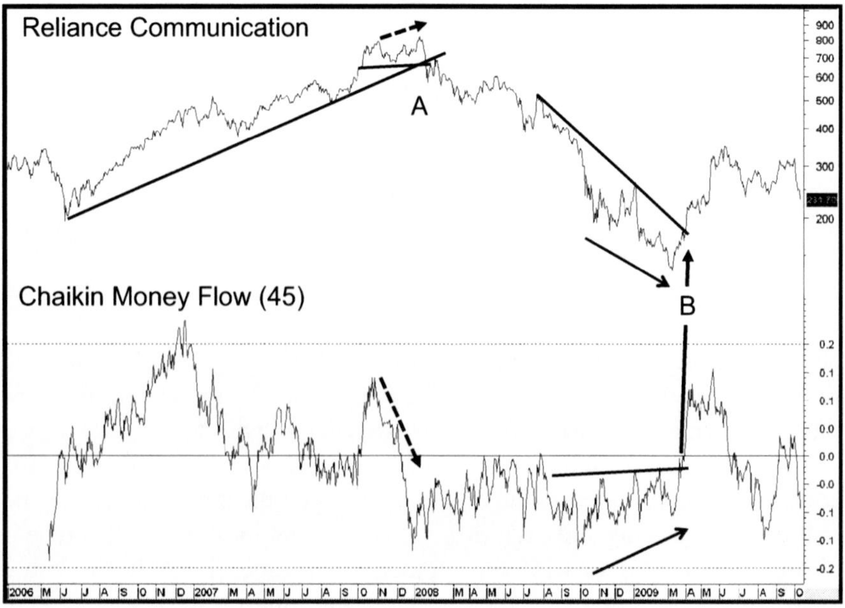

used in Chart 26.15 for Reliance Communications, an Indian stock, offers a more deliberate path. In this instance, you can see how the indicator deteriorated substantially as the price peaked at A.

Note the final few sessions formed a kind of trading range even though the price moved slightly higher. However, the Chaikin was deteriorating throughout this period until the price confirmed with a double trendline break. The opposite was true at B, where we see a series of positive divergences culminating with a joint trendline break to the upside.

Volume in the Stock Market

Upside/Downside Volume

Measures of upside/downside volume try to separate the volume in advancing and declining stocks. Using this technique makes it possible to determine in a subtle way whether distribution or accumulation is taking place. The concept sounds good, but in practice, volume momentum based on ROC or trend-deviation data appears to be more reliable.

TABLE 26.1 Calculation of the Upside/Downside Volume Line

Date	Volume of Advancing Stocks, in Millions	Volume of Declining Stocks, in Millions	Difference	Upside/Downside Line
Jan. 1	101	51	+50	5050
2	120	60	+60	5110
3	155	155	0	5110
4	150	100	+50	5160
5	111	120	−9	5151

The upside/downside volume data is published daily in *The Wall Street Journal* and weekly in *Barron's* and provided by many data services. Upside/downside volume is measured basically in two ways.

The first is an index known as an *upside/downside volume line.* It is constructed by cumulating the difference between the daily plurality of the volume of advancing and declining stocks. Since an indicator of this type is always started from an arbitrary number, it is a good idea to begin with a fairly large one; otherwise, if the market declines sharply for a period, there is the possibility that the upside/downside line will move into negative territory, which unduly complicates the calculation. If a starting total of 5,000 million shares is assumed, the line will be constructed as shown in Table 26.1.

These statistics are not published on a weekly or monthly basis, so longer-term analysis should be undertaken by recording the value of the line at the end of each Friday, or taking an average of Friday readings for a monthly plot. The appropriate MA can then be constructed from these weekly and monthly observations.

It is normal for the upside/downside line to rise during market advances and to fall during declines. When the line fails to confirm a new high (or low) in the price index, it warns of a potential trend reversal. The basic principles of trend determination discussed in Part I may be applied to the upside/downside line.

When a market is advancing in an irregular fashion, with successively higher rallies interrupted by a series of rising troughs, the upside/downside line should be doing the same. Such action indicates that the volume of advancing issues is expanding on rallies and contracting during declines. When this trend of the normal price/volume relationship is broken, a warning is given that one of two things is happening. Either upside volume is failing to expand sufficiently or volume during the decline has begun to expand excessively on the downside. Both are bearish factors. The upside/downside line is particularly useful when prices may be rising to new highs and overall volume is expanding. In such a case, if the volume of declining stocks is rising in relation to that of advancing stocks, it will show up either as a slower rate of advance in the upside/downside line or as an actual decline.

The upside/downside line from 1986 to 1987 is shown in Chart 26.16 together with its 200-day MA. For most of this period, the line remained above its MA despite some fairly large short-term corrections in the S&P Composite. In mid October it fell below its 200-day MA just before the crash. An important up trendline was violated earlier for both the price and the upside/downside volume line which had the effect of emphasizing the bearish signal.

Also worth noting were the positive divergences that occurred in October 1986, when the S&P made a new short-term low, which was not confirmed by the cumulative upside/downside line.

Chart 26.17 compares the line to the S&P between 2010 and 2012.

The dashed arrows represent negative divergences, where the line failed to confirm new S&P highs, and the dashed lines represent joint confirmation. There were no noticeable positive divergences during this period. Chart 26.18 shows the same period, but this time both series are plotted with a 100-day MA. Note how the most reliable crossovers, flagged with the large arrows, develop when both series confirm. The arrows at A, B, and C indicate

CHART 26.16 S&P Composite, 1985–1987, and an Upside/Downside Volume Line

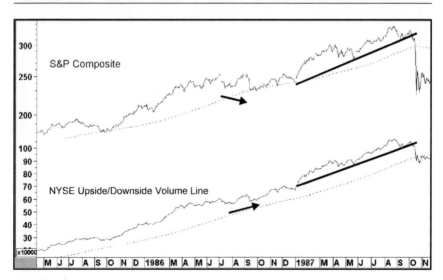

Source: From pring.com

CHART 26.17 S&P Composite, 2010–2012, and an Upside/Downside Volume Line

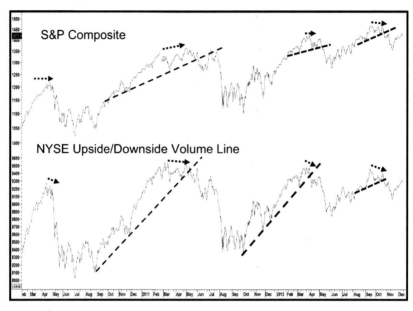

Source: From pring.com

CHART 26.18 S&P Composite, 2010–2012, and an Upside/Downside Volume Line

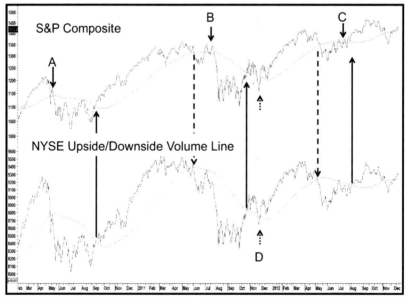

Source: From pring.com

where the S&P break was unconfirmed by the upside/downside line. C was a complete failure of this system as both series whipsawed.

There are several ways to construct oscillators of this data. One possibility is to use the following formula:

$$\text{Oscillator} = M\,(U - D)/(U + D)$$

In this case, U = upside volume, D = downside volume, and M is the MA time span. This formula is plotted in the bottom panel of Chart 26.19 using a 30-day MA.

Notice how this setup allows negative divergences and, more importantly, joint trendline breaks that signal both buy and sell signals. In Chart 26.20 we see a 30-day MA of the oscillator in the previous chart together with its 12-day MA plotted as a dashed line. This series comes more into its own as it reverses from an overextended level. The solid arrows flag successful signals, and the three dashed ones the two failed sells, as well as the failed buys signal in August 2011.

Another possibility is to plot an oscillator of up and down volume and overlay them. Chart 26.21 features such an exercise using two daily

CHART 26.19 NYSE Composite, 2010–2012, and an Upside/Downside Volume Oscillator

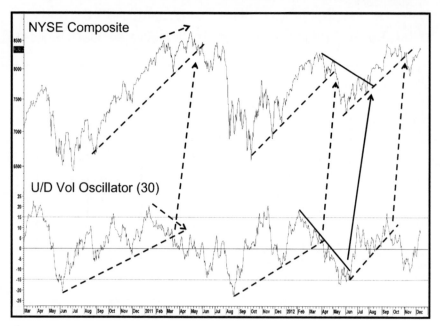

CHART 26.20 NYSE Composite, 2010–2012, and a Smoothed Upside/Downside Volume Oscillator

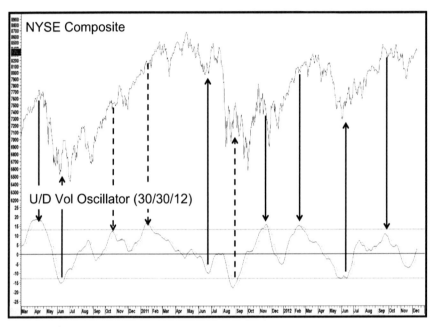

Source: From pring.com

CHART 26.21 S&P Composite, 2000–2001, and Two Upside/Downside Volume Oscillators

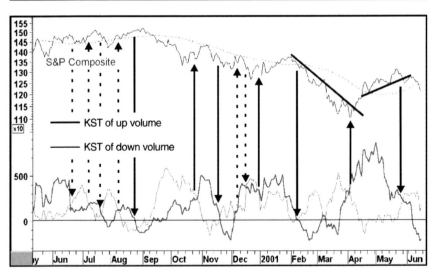

Source: From pring.com

Know Sure Things (KSTs), but a stochastic, smoothed RSI, etc., could have served the purpose equally as well. The idea is that when the KST of upside volume crosses that for downside volume, a buy signal is triggered and vice versa. The various signals have been flagged in the chart by the up and down arrows. The dashed arrows indicate whipsaw signals. As usual, there is no way of knowing whether a signal will be accurate or not, and that is the reason why we need to monitor the price action for some kind of confirmation, as well as base the decision on the position of other indicators.

Major Technical Principle   When the upside/downside volume line fails to confirm a new high (or low) in the price index, it warns of a potential trend reversal.

The Arms Index

This indicator was developed by Richard Arms and is constructed from breadth and upside/downside volume data. It is sometimes referred to as the TRIN or MKDS. It is calculated by dividing the ratio of advancing and declining stocks by the ratio of volume in advancing issues over volume in declining issues. In almost all cases, daily data are used, but there is no reason why a weekly or even monthly series could not be constructed. Normally, the Arms Index is used in conjunction with NYSE data, but its principles can be applied to any market situation, such as the NASDAQ, where upside/downside volume and breadth data are available. There is one important thing to note, and that is that movements in the Arms Index are inverse to those of the market. This means that oversold conditions appear as peaks and overbought conditions as valleys. Since this is contrary to virtually all other indicators described in this book, the chart examples are presented inversely in order to be consistent with the other indicators.

The concept behind this indicator is to monitor the relative power of the volume associated with advancing issues to that of declining ones. Ideally, it is important to see a healthy amount of volume moving into rising issues relative to that associated with declining stocks. If this is not the case, the indicator will diverge negatively with the market average and vice versa.

This momentum series can be calculated for any period. For example, the quote services and the number appearing on the CNBC ticker represent an instant in time and are based on the volume and number of issues experiencing an up or down tick. Unless you are fortunate enough to be able to chart this indicator on a continuous basis through a real-time service, isolated quotes of this nature are limited to gauging whether the market is *intraday* overbought or oversold. In this respect, 120 or higher is regarded as oversold and 50 or below overbought (remember, these numbers are inverse to the other momentum indicators).

The Arms Index can also be used with a moving average where the 10-day (open TRIN) time span is the most widely followed. It is interpreted in much the same way as the 10-day A/D ratio discussed earlier in this chapter. Most of the time, these two series move in a consistent manner, but from time to time the Arms Index gives some subtle indications that the prevailing trend is about to reverse. Generally speaking, when the 10-day Arms rises above 150, this signals a major low. Sometimes this happens right away; at other times there is a delay of 10 to 20 days before the final bottom is seen. Between 1968 and 2001 there were no exceptions to this rule. Chart 26.22 shows three different versions of the Arms Index with a 10-, 25-, and 45-day time span. The rationale for including three indicators in the chart was explained in Chapter 13. The arrows indicate those points when at least two of these inversely plotted series are at an extreme and have begun to reverse, since tops tend to be rolling affairs where volume leads price. The Arms Index often reaches its extreme ahead of the market average, whereas selling climax conditions seen at bottoms are usually far more coincident in nature.

CHART 26.22 S&P Composite, 1997–2001, and Three Arms Indicators

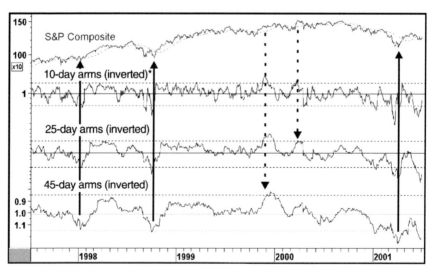

Source: From pring.com

On Balance Volume

On Balance Volume (OBV) was discovered by Joe Granville and published in his book *Granville's New Key to Stock Market Profits* (Literary Licensing, 2011). The indicator is plotted as a continuous, cumulative line. It begins with an arbitrary number, which rises and falls depending on what the price does. The volume for the day is added in when the price rises, and is subtracted when it falls. If intraday charts are being used, volume units would be added and subtracted based on the time frame of the bars. For weekly charts, the basis would be the week and so forth. OBV, therefore, offers a rough approximation for buying and selling pressure and has become a very popular indicator. It is interpreted by comparing the line to the price, using divergences, trendline breaks, price patterns, and MA crossovers to point up underlying strengths or weaknesses.

Chart 26.23, featuring RF Micro Devices, shows a few OBV characteristics. We see a negative divergence right at the beginning of 2011 and this is later confirmed at A, where both series make new lows. A positive

CHART 26.23 RF Micro, 2010–2011, and an On Balance Volume Line

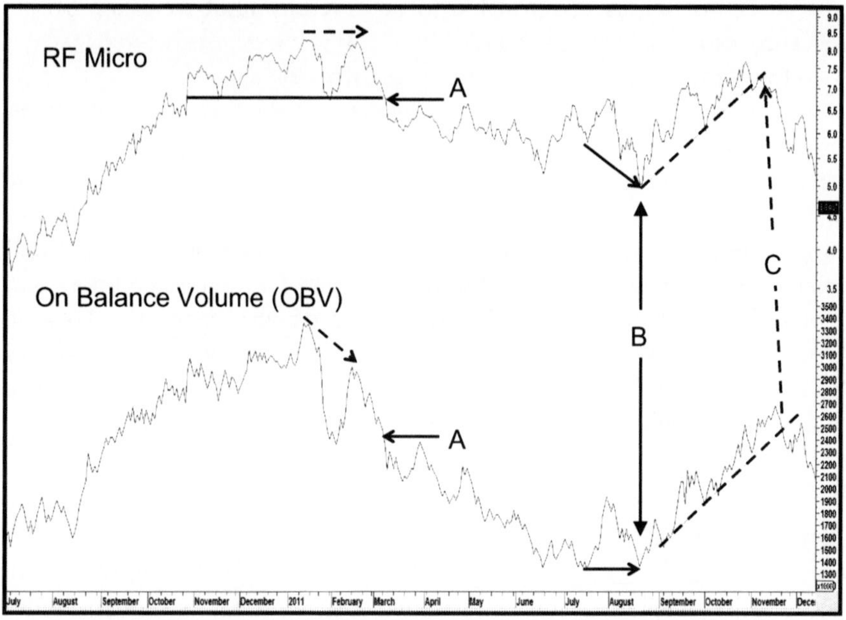

CHART 26.24 Alergan, 1998–2000, and OBV

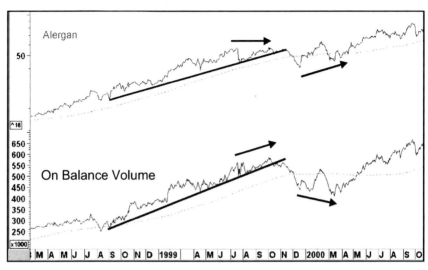

Source: From pring.com

divergence, where the price makes a new low but the OBV does not, develops at B, but it was not possible to observe any joint trendline breaks because the action was too volatile. Finally, at C it was possible to construct two trendlines, both of which were eventually violated.

I do not find the OBV indicator to be as accurate as this in most situations. Indeed, its warnings are often as misleading as the valid signals. My advice, therefore, is to tread carefully with this indicator and make sure its signals are backed up with other approaches. This is especially true for positive and negative divergences, but not so much with the joint trendline break, which I find to be more accurate. Chart 26.24 featuring Alergan, for instance, shows a situation at the end of 1999 when OBV was pointing to higher prices, but they went down; in early 2000, weaknesses in the OBV pointed to lower prices, but they went up! Note that in both charts the joint trendline technique worked, which as mentioned earlier, is probably the best way to interpret this indicator.

Equivolume

Equivolume is a plotting concept developed by Dick Arms (www.armsinsider .com). It is similar to the candlestick volume approach discussed earlier. Bars are plotted in different widths depending on the level of volume for that particular period. The greater the volume, the wider the bar. The top and bottom of the bar represent the high and low for that period. This is a very useful approach because it graphically shows in one series whether prices are rising or falling on light or heavy volume. The width of the box is controlled by a normalized volume value. The volume for an individual box is normalized by dividing the actual volume for the period by the total of all volume displayed on the chart. Therefore, the width of each equivolume box is based on a percentage of total volume, with the total of all percentages equaling 100.

The resulting charts represent an important departure from all other analytical methods, in that *time becomes less important than volume* in analyzing price moves. It suggests that each movement is a function of the number of shares or contracts changing hands rather than the amount of time elapsed.

Because of this, the dates on the x axis are not equidistant from each other, as is normally the case. They instead depend on the volume patterns for their location. Chart 26.25 shows an equivolume arrangement for MMM Company. At A the price breaks out with a couple of thick bars, indicating very heavy volume. In effect, this is a classic buy signal. At B the rally is associated with very narrow equivolume bars, which tells us that there is a distinct lack of upside volume. Thus, a warning of an impending trend reversal is given.

In Chart 26.26 for Aditya Birla Nuvo, you can see the trading range in November 2007 is associated with extremely low volume (narrow bars).

CHART 26.25 MMM, 2000–2001, and Equivolume

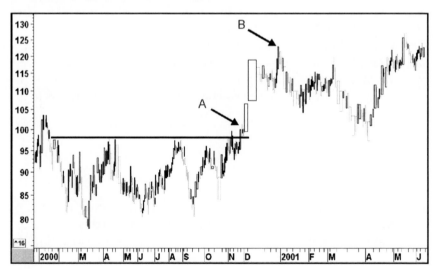

CHART 26.26 Aditya Birla Nuvo, 2007–2008, and Equivolume

Source: From pring.com

Then the price breaks to the upside with a wider (high-volume bar). Just after the January 2008 peak the bars widen again and the falling price/expanding volume combination results in a sharp drop. The tail end of the May and August rallies is also accompanied by a bearish shrinkage in volume. Note how the August rally runs into resistance at the two previous very wide bars at the two dashed lines at X. At the August high, nearly anyone who had bought since April was coming home with a loss, and that meant some oversupply pressuring the price. When the price fell to the line at Y, it took it below the heavy volume bar in July, thereby adding even more unhappy traders to the already high total.

Summary

1. The ROC of volume often gives signs of subtle changes in the level of activity that are not apparent from volume data represented as a histogram.
2. The ROC of volume can be expressed as a percentage or in a subtraction format.

3. Volume ROCs and oscillators can be used with overbought/oversold crossovers, trendline analysis, and price patterns.

4. Overbought readings in the volume ROC can be followed by declining or rising prices, depending on the nature of the previous trend.

5. The Demand Index is constructed from volume and price; moves in the same direction as a regular price oscillator; and is best used with divergence and overbought/oversold analysis, trendline, and price pattern construction.

6. The Chaikin Money Flow is constructed from volume and price data and moves in the same direction as a regular price oscillator. It is best used with divergence analysis.

7. Upside/downside volume measures the volume in advancing and declining stocks. It can be used as a continuous line or in oscillator format.

8. The Arms Index is constructed from advancing and declining stocks and their respective volume. It is usually calculated over a 10-day span. Readings in excess of 150 signal major bottoms.

9. OBV is constructed as a continuous line and used with divergence analysis. Joint trendline breaks between the OBV line and the price offer a more accurate method of interpretation.

10. Equivolume is a form of charting that plots the thickness of each bar according to the volume experienced during its formation. The thicker the bar, the higher the level of activity and vice versa.

27

MARKET BREADTH

Breadth indicators measure the degree to which the vast majority of issues are participating in a market move and, therefore, monitor the extent of a market trend. Generally speaking, the fewer the number of issues that are moving in the direction of the major averages, the greater the probability of an imminent reversal in trend. Breadth indicators were originally developed to monitor trends in the stock market, but in recent years, they have been expanded to embrace any market that can conveniently be subdivided into components. Even though most of the comments in this chapter refer to U.S. equities, it should be remembered that breadth can just as validly be extended to other markets around the world. For example, experiments with Indian, Brazilian, and several Middle Eastern markets have shown they are susceptible to such analysis, and I see no reason why other countries would not also lend themselves to this approach.

Breadth analysis can be applied to any sector or market that can be broken down into a basket of securities that are reflective of an overall index. An example might include a selection of commodities being compared to a commodity index or a series of currencies to an overall currency index such as the Dollar Index and so forth. The main thing to bear in mind is that the principles of interpretation remain constant.

The concept of breadth can probably be best explained using a military analogy. In Figure 27.1, lines AA and BB indicate military lines of defense drawn up during a battle. It might be possible for a few units to cross over from AA to BB, but the chances are that the BB line will hold unless an all-out effort is made. In example *a,* the two units represented by the arrows are quickly repulsed. In example *b,* on the other hand, the assault is successful since many units are taking part, and army B is forced to retreat to a new line of defense at B_1.

FIGURE 27.1 Trench Warfare

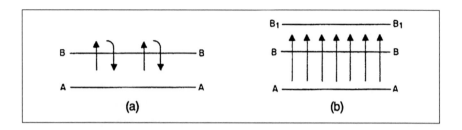

A narrowly advancing stock market can be compared to example *a*, where it looks initially as though the move through the line of defense (in stock market terms, *a resistance level*) is going to be successful, but because the move is accompanied by such little support, the overall price trend is soon reversed. In the military analogy, even if the two units had successfully assaulted the BB defense, it would not be long before army B would have overpowered them, for the farther they advanced without broad support, the more vulnerable they would have become to a counteroffensive by army B.

The same is true of the stock market, for the longer a price trend is maintained without a follow-up by the broad market, the more vulnerable is the advance.

At market bottoms, breadth is not such a useful concept for determining reversals because the majority of stocks usually coincide with or lag behind the major indexes. On the few occasions when breadth reverses its downtrend before the averages, it is actually a more reliable indicator than at tops. I'll begin this discussion with a rationale as to why the broad market normally leads the averages at market tops. The word "normally" is used because, in the vast majority of cases, the broad list of stocks does peak out ahead of a market average such as the Dow Jones Industrial Average (DJIA) or the S&P Composite. This rule is not invariable, however, and it should not be assumed that the technical structure is necessarily sound just because market breadth is strong. In most cases it will be, but if other indicators are pointing up weakness, this can override a positive breadth picture.

Advance/Decline Line

The most widely used indicator of market breadth is an *advance/decline (A/D) line*. It is constructed by taking a cumulative total of the difference (plurality) between the number of New York Stock Exchange (NYSE) issues that are advancing over those that are declining in a particular period (usually a day or a week). Similar indexes may be constructed for the American Exchange (AMEX) or NASDAQ issues. Because the number of issues listed on the NYSE has expanded since breadth records were first kept, an A/D line constructed from a simple plurality of advancing over declining issues gives a greater weighting to more recent years. For the purpose of long-term comparisons, it is better to take a ratio of advances versus declines, or a ratio of advances and declines divided by the number of unchanged issues, rather than limiting the calculation to a simple plurality.

The late Hamilton Bolton devised one of the most useful measurements of breadth. It is calculated from a cumulative running total of the following formula:

$$\sqrt{A/U - D/U}$$

where A = the number of stocks advancing
       D = the number declining
       U = the number unchanged.

Since it is not mathematically possible to calculate a square root of a negative answer (i.e., when the number of declining stocks is greater than the number of those advancing), the D and A are reversed in such cases, so that the formula becomes the square root of $D/U - A/U$. The resulting answer is then subtracted from the cumulative total, as opposed to the answer in the earlier formula, which is added. Table 27.1 illustrates this calculation using weekly data.

Inclusion of the number of unchanged issues is useful because the more dynamic the move in either direction, the greater the tendency for the number of unchanged stocks to diminish. Consequently, by giving some weight to the number of unchanged stocks in the formula, it is possible to assess a slowdown in momentum of the A/D line at an earlier date, since an expanding number of unchanged issues will have the tendency to restrain extreme movements.

The A/D line normally rises and falls in sympathy with the major market averages, but it usually peaks well ahead of them. There appear to be three basic reasons why this is so:

1. The market as a whole discounts the business cycle and normally reaches its bull market peak 6 to 9 months before the economy tops out. Since the peak in business activity is itself preceded by a deterioration of certain leading sectors such as financial, consumer

TABLE 27.1 Weekly A/D Line Calculation (Bolton Formula)

Date	Issues Traded (1)	Advances (2)	Declines (3)	Unchanged (4)	Advances + Unchanged (5)	Declines + Unchanged (6)	Col. 5 − Col. 6 (7)	√Col. 7 (8)	Cumulative A/D Line (9)
Jan. 7	2129	989	919	221	448	416	32	5.7	2475.6
14	2103	782	1073	248	315	433	−118	−10.9	2464.7
21	2120	966	901	253	382	356	26	5.1	2469.8
28	2103	835	1036	232	360	447	−87	−9.3	2460.5
Feb. 4	2089	910	905	274	332	330	2	1.4	2461.9
11	2090	702	1145	243	289	471	−18.2	−13.5	2448.4
18	2093	938	886	269	349	329	20	4.5	2452.9
25	2080	593	1227	260	228	472	244	−15.6	2437.3

spending, and construction, it is logical to expect that the stocks representing these sectors will also peak out ahead of the general market.

2. Many of the stocks listed on the NYSE, such as preferreds and utilities, are sensitive to changes in interest rates. Since interest rates usually begin to rise before the market peaks, it is natural for the interest-sensitive issues to move down in sympathy with rising rates.

3. Poorer-quality stocks offer the largest upside potential, but they are also representative of smaller, underfinanced, and badly managed companies that are more vulnerable to reduced earnings (and even bankruptcy) during a recession. Blue-chips normally have good credit ratings, reasonable yields, and sound underlying assets; thus, they are typically the last stocks to be sold by investors during a bull market.

The DJIA and other market averages are almost wholly composed of larger companies, which are normally in better financial shape. These popular averages, therefore, continue to advance well after the broad market has peaked out.

Interpretation

Here are some key points for interpreting A/D data:

1. Some A/D lines appear to have a permanent downward bias. It is, therefore, important as a first step to observe the relationship between an A/D line and an index over a very long period to see whether this bias exists. Examples include breadth data for the AMEX market, the U.S. over-the-counter (OTC) market, and the Japanese market.

2. Divergences between a market average and an A/D line at market tops are almost always cleared up by a decline in the average. However, it is mandatory to await some kind of trend-reversal signal in the average as confirmation before concluding that it will also decline.

3. It is normal for the A/D line to coincide or lag at market bottoms. Such action is of no forecasting value. When the A/D line refuses to confirm a new low in the index, the signal is unusual and very positive, but only when confirmed by a reversal in the average itself.

4. Breadth data may diverge negatively from the averages, but an important rally is often signaled when a down trendline violation is signaled along with a breakout in the market average itself.

5. In most cases, daily A/D lines have more of a downward bias than lines constructed from weekly data.

6. A/D lines may be used with moving-average (MA) crossovers, trendline breaks, and price pattern analysis. For longer periods, the 200-day MA appears to work reasonably well.

7. When the A/D line is in a positive trend, e.g., above its 200-day MA, it indicates that the environment for equities in general is a positive one, *regardless of what the major averages such as the DJIA or S&P Composite may be doing.* A positive A/D line is, therefore, a better bellwether for the market as a whole than a narrowly based blue-chip index. The opposite is true when the A/D line is in a declining trend.

Major Technical Principle   The longer and greater the negative divergence between the A/D line and the market average it is monitoring, the deeper and more substantial the implied decline is likely to be.

For this reason, divergences between the A/D line and the major market averages at primary peaks are more significant than those that occur at intermediate tops. For example, Chart 27.1 shows that the weekly A/D line peaked in March 1971, almost 2 years ahead of the DJIA, a very long period

CHART 27.1 The DJIA and the Weekly NYSE A/D Line, 1966–1977

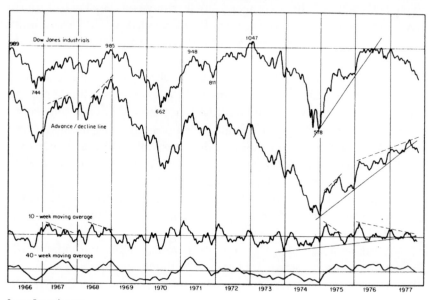

Source: From pring.com

by historical standards. The ensuing bear market was the most severe since the Depression. On the other hand, *the absence of a divergence does not necessarily mean that a steep bear market cannot take place,* as the experience of the December 1968 top indicates. This is also shown in Chart 27.1.

Positive divergences develop at market bottoms where the A/D line refuses to confirm a new low in the Dow. The most significant one occurred in the 1939–1942 period. The DJIA (shown in Chart 27.2) made a series of lower peaks and troughs between 1939 and 1941, while the A/D line refused to confirm. Finally in the middle of 1941, the A/D line made a post-1932 recovery high unaccompanied by the DJIA. The immediate result of this discrepancy was a sharp sell-off into the spring of 1942 by both indicators, but even then the A/D line held well above its 1938 bottom, unlike the DJIA. The final low in April 1942 was followed by the best (in terms of breadth) bull market on record. This positive action by the broad market is unusual. Typically at market bottoms the A/D line either coincides with or lags behind the low in the DJIA and has no forecasting significance until a reversal in its downtrend is signaled by a breakout from a price pattern, a trendline, or MA crossover.

A/D Lines Using Daily Data

Because daily A/D lines have a tendency toward a downward bias, some care should be used in comparing recent highs with those achieved 2 to 3 years ago. Daily A/D lines come into their own when they fail to confirm new highs in the market average that have occurred within an 18-month period. An example is shown in Chart 27.3a, where the A/D line peaks in April 1987 but the S&P Composite does not top out until late August. The S&P did not fall right away, but eventually followed the leadership of the A/D line. Quite often, a number of divergences will be set up. Initially, these might be well publicized, but since the widely expected decline fails to materialize, many technicians give up, stating that the divergence "won't work this time." Invariably it does work, though much later than most would anticipate. This was very much the case at the market peak in January 1973, which was followed by a 2-year divergence.

Because bottoms in the daily line usually coincide with or lag behind bottoms in the average, they are not very useful at this point for the purpose of identifying a trend reversal.

A more practical approach is to construct a trendline for both the A/D line and the market average. Violation of both lines usually signals that an important rally is under way. Some examples are shown in Chart 27.3b.

CHART 27.2 The DJIA and the Long-Term A/D Line, 1931–1983

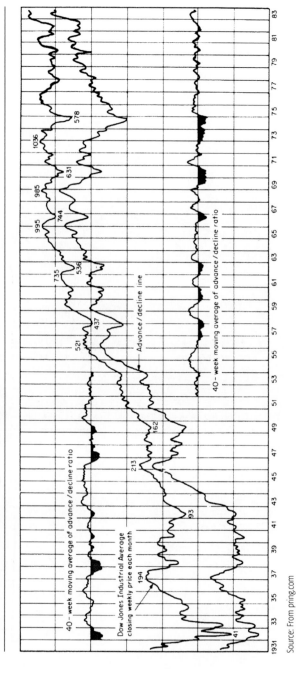

Source: From pring.com

CHART 27.3*a* The S&P Composite versus the Daily NYSE A/D Line, 1986–1988

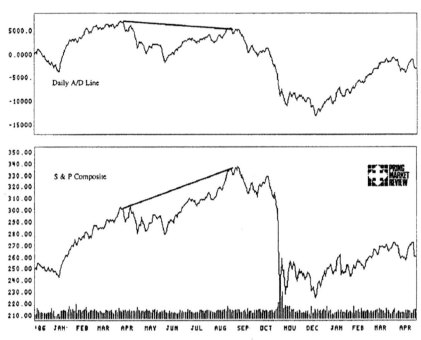

Source: From pring.com

CHART 27.3*b* The S&P Composite versus the Daily NYSE A/D Line, 1991–1995

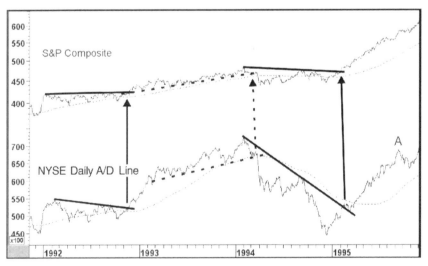

Source: From pring.com

Two resistance lines are violated at the end of 1992. Later on, the two dashed up trendlines are violated for a joint sell signal. Note that in this case the lines are penetrated at approximately the same time that both series cross below their respective 200-day MAs. This joint evidence adds to our weight-of-the-evidence approach and increases the odds of a valid breakout. Finally, both series violate down trendlines at the beginning of 1995.

When considering potential divergences or nonconfirmations, it is always important to give these relationships some room. For example, at point A it may have appeared at the time that the A/D line was going to experience a major negative divergence since it had yet to beat its early 1994 high. It would have been easy to jump to a bearish conclusion. However, this would not have been supported by the facts since the A/D line was well above its 200-day MA at this point. Moreover, there was no sign of a trend break in the S&P Composite that would confirm the negative divergence even had it existed. As it turned out, both series went on to make significant new highs, thereby pointing out the importance of giving the prevailing trend and this relationship the benefit of the doubt.

Charts 27.4 and 27.5 also compare the S&P Composite to the daily A/D line. The first shows a negative divergence that opened up at the 2007

CHART 27.4 The S&P Composite versus the Daily NYSE A/D Line, 2007–2009

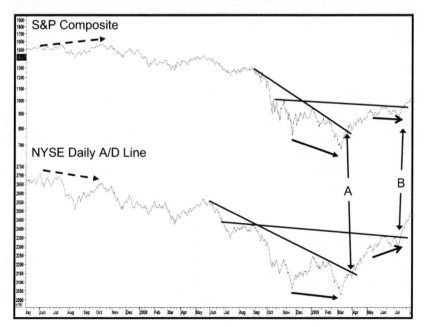

Source: From pring.com

CHART 27.5 The S&P Composite versus the Daily NYSE A/D Line, 2010–2012

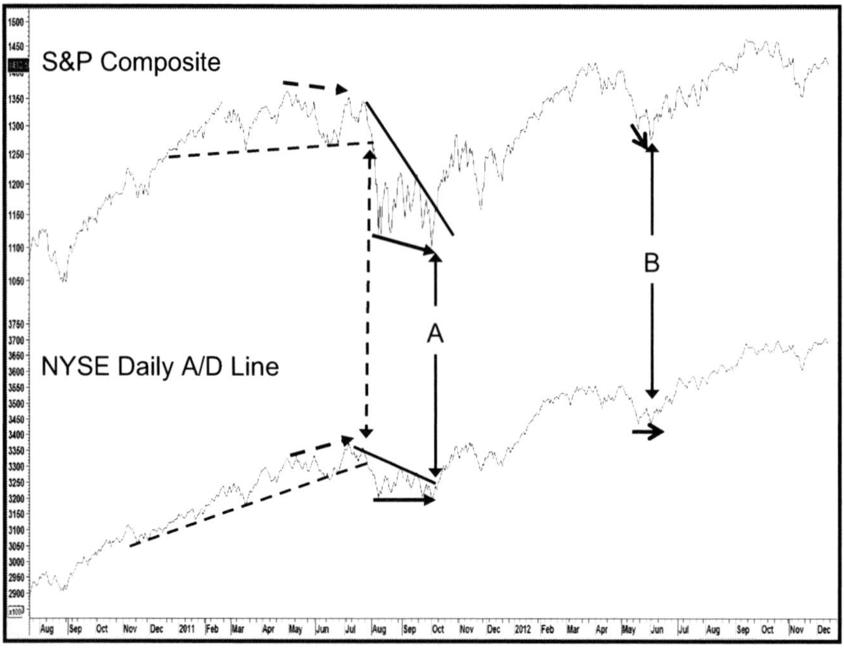

Source: From pring.com

bull market peak. I have highlighted the 2009 low, though this was not an actual divergence, as both simultaneously registered new lows, though that for the breadth indicator was clearly less intense. This slight discrepancy did represent a small warning that things might turn to the upside, but really required the kind of confirmation given at point B, where two down trendlines were penetrated on the upside. The action at A was a positive divergence as the A/D line experienced rising bottoms but not the price. This was again confirmed with two nice trendline violations, and a solid rally followed. Chart 27.5 shows a later period. First we see a confirmed negative discrepancy at the July 2011 intermediate top. This time, it's different because the S&P registered its high ahead of the line. It really does not matter which way this disagreement falls, though usually it comes from A/D line weakness. The key is that when both series confirm with a trendline break or reliable MA crossover, a discrepancy is a discrepancy and prices fall. Points A and B offer two examples of a rare situation whereby the A/D line bottoms ahead of the S&P. In the case of A, we see some actionable confirmation. However, in B's case, the drop was so steep that it was not possible to construct timely trendlines that could have served as actionable technical events.

Breadth Oscillators (Internal Strength)

For historical comparative purposes, the rate-of-change (ROC) method of determining momentum is useful in measuring price indexes because it reflects moves of similar proportion in an identical way. This method, however, is not suitable for gauging the vitality of the indicators con- structed from cumulative data that monitor internal market structure, such as those that measure volume or breadth. This is because the construction of such indexes is often started from a purely arbitrary number. Under certain circumstances, this might require an ROC to be calculated between a negative and a positive number, which would obviously give a completely false impression of the prevailing trend of momentum. The following sections provide a brief summary of some oscillators constructed from breadth data using a more suitable method of calculation.

Ten-Week A/D Oscillator

Chart 27.6 shows the DJIA and a 10-week oscillator calculated from a 10-week MA of the square root of the $A/U - D/U$ formula discussed earlier. A comparison of the A/D line to the DJIA illustrates the principle of divergence, as evidenced by declining peaks of momentum and rising peaks in the Dow at the 2007 peak. This was later confirmed by a break below the dashed up trendline. A positive divergence was also confirmed in the spring of 2009. Note that it was possible to establish different ranges for the oscillator depending on the primary trend environment. These are shown by the dashed parallel lines. Also, note the extremely high reading in the oscillator as it came off the 2009 low. This was a mega overbought and represented an early bird warning of a reversal to a bull market. You can also see an extreme but lower reading in the spring of 2003. That was also a mega overbought, but this time signaling the start of the 2003–2007 bull market.

CHART 27.6 The S&P Composite versus the 10-Week A/D Ratio, 2002–2013

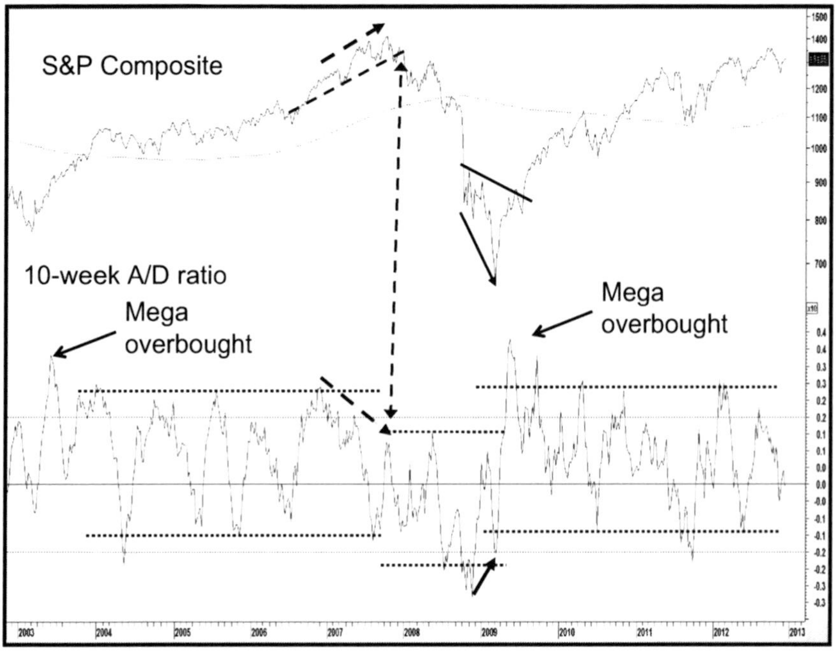

Source: From pring.com

Ten- and Thirty-Day A/D Oscillators

These indicators are calculated by taking a 10- or 30-day MA of the A/D or the $A - D$ ratio. An alternative calculation can be made by dividing the total of advancing issues by the total of declining issues over a specific time span. Their interpretation is exactly the same as with other momentum indicators, bearing in mind their relatively short time span. An example of a 10-day breadth momentum series is shown in Chart 27.7.

Note that this time we are comparing the oscillators to the A/D line itself rather than the S&P or DJIA. Both series experience a set of positive divergences between 1999 and March 2000. Then we see some negative divergences as the A/D line peaks out later that year. Note how the 10-day series is barely able to rally above the equilibrium point, indicating extreme weakness at the time of the actual rally high in September. Finally, both the 30-day oscillator and the line itself both violate up trendlines for a classic weight-of-the-evidence sell signal. One final negative divergence develops in January 2001.

CHART 27.7 The NYSE Daily A/D Line, 1999–2001, and Two Breadth Oscillators

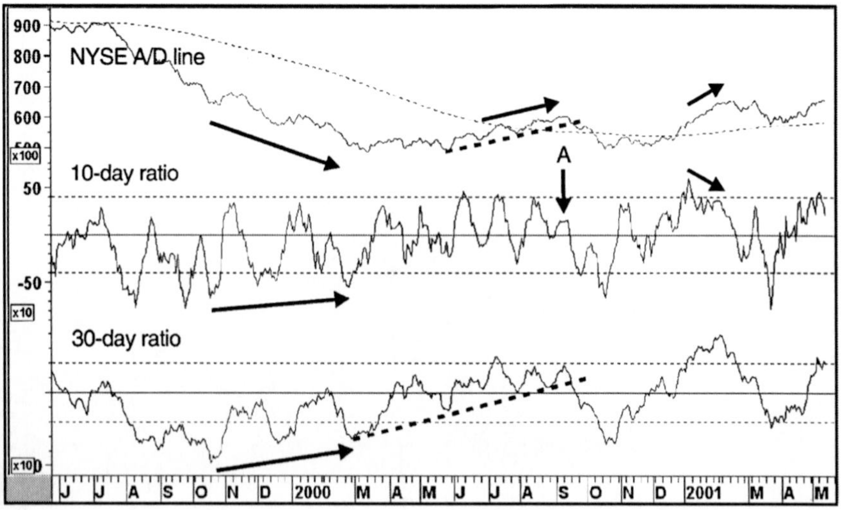

Source: From pring.com

The McClellan Oscillator

The McClellan Oscillator is a short-term breadth momentum indicator that measures the difference between a 19- and a 39-day exponential moving average (EMA) of advancing minus declining issues. In this respect, it is based on the same principle as the moving-average convergence divergence (MACD) indicator discussed in Chapter 14. The generally accepted rules are that buy signals are triggered when the McClellan Oscillator falls to the oversold area of –70 to –100 and sell signals are triggered when it rises to the +70 to +100 area. Since the calculation is based on a subtraction method and the number of NYSE issues has grown over the years, these bands are probably too narrow to be of practical use. My own experience suggests that its interpretation should be based on the same principles as those described in Chapter 13 using divergences, trendline analysis, and so forth. An example is shown in Chart 27.8 using breadth data from the NASDAQ exchange. Note the positive divergence that developed at the 2009 low. The dashed vertical arrows flag three important peaks—all were associated with a very low reading in the oscillator. At the 2000 peak, the indicator was actually in slightly *negative* territory, clearly an extreme reading for an extreme chart point.

Finally, the oscillator has been described here using two specific time frames for the EMAs for the calculation since these are the

CHART 27.8 NASDAQ 100 ETF, 2007–2010, and the McClellan Oscillator

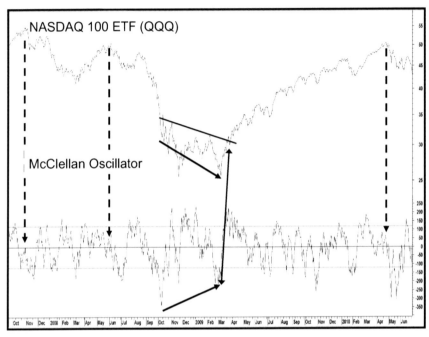

Source: From pring.com

generally accepted default values. However, there is nothing to stop the innovative technician from experimenting with different combinations of EMAs.

The McClellan Summation Index is a derivation of the McClellan Oscillator and is calculated as a cumulative total of the daily readings of the oscillator itself. The result is plotted as a slow-moving curve that changes direction whenever the raw oscillator (described earlier) crosses above or below its zero line. The slope of the summation curve is determined by the difference between the actual reading and the zero line. In other words, an overbought reading will cause the summation index to rise sharply, and vice versa. Many technicians use these changes in direction as buy and sell signals, but this can result in a lot of whipsaws. My own preference is to use an MA crossover. This is often less timely, but it filters out a significant number of false signals. A suggested time frame for this exercise is a 35-day simple moving average. An example is featured in Chart 27.9. Even here we see numerous whipsaw signals indicating that this approach is far from perfect.

CHART 27.9 S&P Composite, 1998–2001, and the McClellan Summation Index

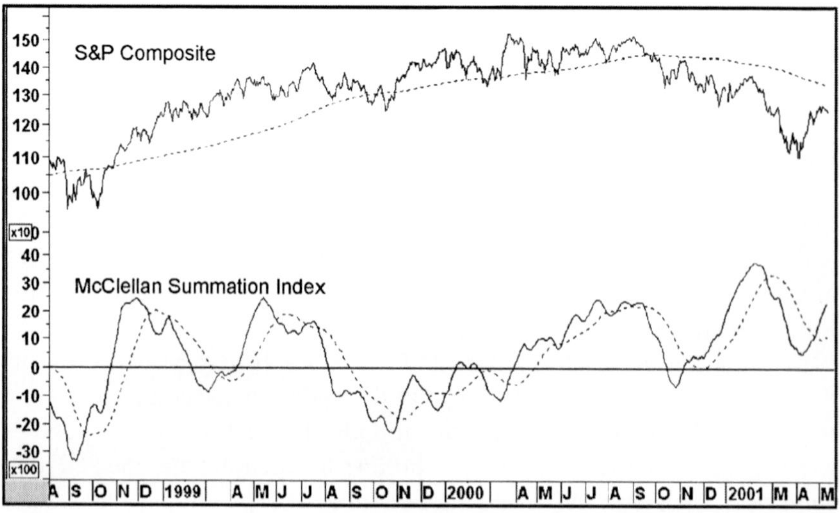

Source: From pring.com

High-Low Data

The popular press and many online data providers publish daily and weekly figures for stocks reaching new highs and lows. These statistics relate to the number of issues making new highs or lows over a 52-week period. There are various methods of measuring the high-low figures, but since the raw data are very jagged, displaying them in an MA format is usually better. Some technicians prefer to plot an MA of the two series individually, others an MA of the net difference between highs and lows.

> **Major Technical Principle**   A rising market, over a period of time, should be accompanied by a healthy, but not necessarily rising, number of net new highs.

When the major averages trace out a series of higher peaks following a long advance but the net number of new highs forms a series of declining peaks, this is a warning of potential trouble. This type of relationship indicates that the technical picture is gradually weakening because successive peaks in the market average are accompanied by fewer and fewer stocks making breakouts (new highs) from price patterns. The net number of new highs also takes into consideration stocks making new lows. In a bear market, a new low in the S&P Composite or other market average that is not accompanied by a declining number of net new highs is a positive sign.

In this case, a declining number of stocks reaching new lows implies fewer downside breakouts, i.e., a shrinkage in the number of stocks resisting the downtrend in the major averages. In Chart 27.10, for instance, the S&P falls to approximately the same level in December 1994 as it did earlier in the year, yet the number of new lows was far less. This indicated an improving technical position that was eventually confirmed when the index rallied above the solid trendline.

The bottom panel in Chart 27.11 shows a 10-day MA of the daily high/low differential. Note the negative divergence between this series and the average between 1989 and 1990, and also the fact that it was possible to construct a couple of (dashed) trendlines for the ratio and the S&P that were violated in early 1991. The implied trend of expanding net new highs was signaling that once the index itself responded with a breakout, prices were likely to move higher.

The Cumulative Net New High series in the second panel is constructed by cumulating the daily difference between the new highs and

CHART 27.10 The S&P Composite, 1993–1996, and 52-Week New NYSE Lows

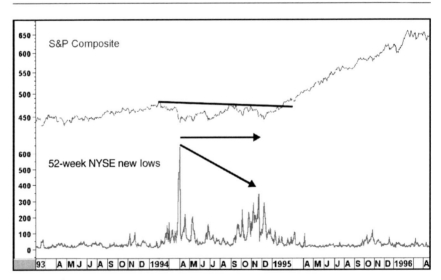

Source: From pring.com

CHART 27.11 S&P Composite, 1988–1993, and Two Net New High Indicators

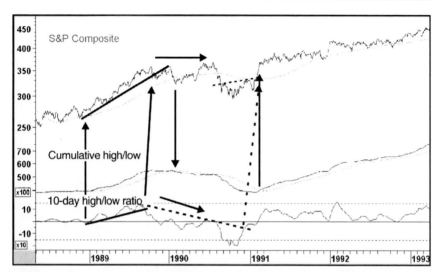

Source: From pring.com

lows in a similar fashion to the daily A/D line. For example, if there are 100 new highs and 20 new lows, the difference, i.e., 80, would be added into the total and vice versa.[1] I have found that using 100-day MA crossovers offers reasonably good signals of when the environment is positive or negative for the overall market. Signals of this nature generated between 1988 and 1993 are indicted by the solid perpendicular arrows in Chart 27.11.

Chart 27.12 shows more recent price action where the arrows point up the 100-day MA crossovers of the cumulative line.

Note that in early 2009 and late 2011 this developed more or less simultaneously with the 200-day MA crossovers of the S&P Composite. An alternative method of calculating high-low data is shown at the bottom of Chart 27.13, where an 8-day MA of net weekly new highs has been plotted against the S&P Composite. The light highlights indicate when this indicator falls below zero. Its main claim to fame is protection against a primary bear market, which it did very well in the 2007–2009 period. However, the drawback is that it often falls into negative territory at the end of a protracted short-term decline.

In this discussion we have limited ourselves to 52-week periods for the new high-low calculations. However, there is no reason why such

---

[1]Arms-Equivolume Corp., 1650 University Boulevard N.E., Albuquerque, NM 87102.

CHART 27.12 S&P Composite, 2006–2012, and Two New High Indicators

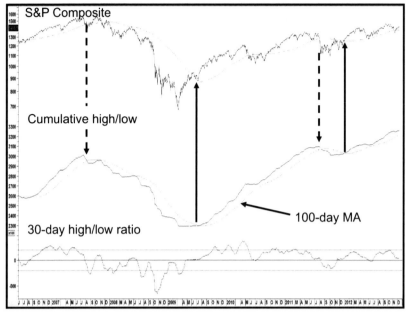

Source: From pring.com

CHART 27.13 S&P Composite, 2005–2012, and an 8 Day New High Indicator

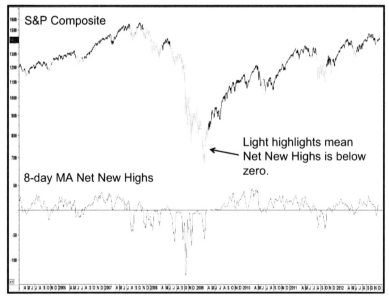

Source: From pring.com

CHART 27.14 Dow Jones UBS Commodity ETN, 2005–2012, and a Commodity New High Indicator

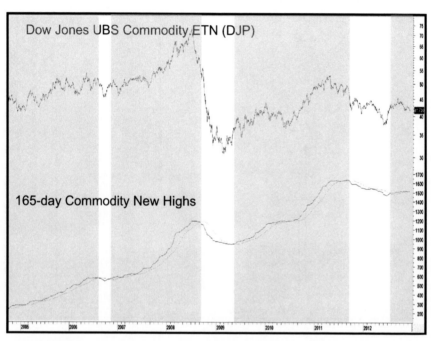

Source: From pring.com

calculations cannot be made for any time period or any basket of securities. For example, Chart 27.14 shows a cumulative line derived from the net new highs of a basket of commodities calculated over a 165-day time span.

The shaded areas represent when this series crosses above its (dashed) 100-day MA. It's by no means a perfect indicator, but does offer a view as to whether commodities are in a primary bull or bear market. Finally, Chart 27.15 shows a price oscillator calculated from a cumulative line of a basket of gold stocks. The legend explains the calculation. First, the line is calculated using a 65-day time span—in other words, the number of gold stocks registering net new highs over a 65-day period. The 15 and 65 indicate that the oscillator is calculated by dividing a 15-day MA of the cumulative line by a 65-day MA. As you can see, overbought/oversold reversals offer timely buy and sell alerts. We have used gold shares in this example, but there is no reason why this analysis cannot be extended to other sectors or markets.

CHART 27.15 Gold Miners ETF, 2007–2012, and a New High Oscillator

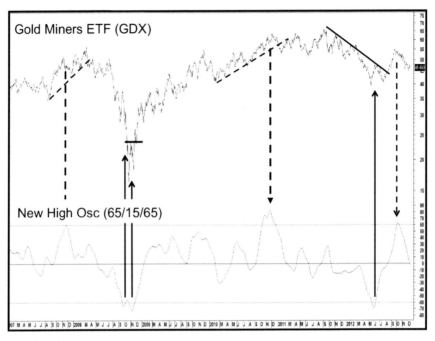

Source: From pring.com

Diffusion Indicators

A diffusion indicator is a form of oscillator constructed from a basket of items that measures the number or percentage of that universe that are in a positive trend. An example might be the percentage of the 30 stocks comprising the DJIA that are above their 30-day MAs. When all members are in a bullish mode, the picture is as positive as it can get. The implication is that the aggregate measure, the DJIA in our example, is vulnerable and, therefore, likely to peak out. The reverse set of conditions, in which none of the series is in a positive trend, produces the opposite effect; i.e., the aggregate index may be reaching its low point and could, therefore, be a "buy." This simple interpretation of diffusion indexes is a good starting point, but in practice, a diffusion measure is a form of momentum indicator, and is subject to the same benefits, drawbacks, and principles of interpretation outlined in Chapter 13.

What Is a Positive Trend?

In technical analysis, a market or stock that forms a series of rising peaks and troughs, or is above a trendline, may be classified as being in a positive trend. However, the only way trends can be monitored through this interpretation is on the basis of individual judgment, which would make the construction of a diffusion index covering many series over many years a very laborious process. For this reason, and because of the need for greater objectivity, a statistical measure that can easily be calculated on a computer is normally used.

The most common measurements calculate the percentage of a series that are above a specific MA or that have a rising MA. Another popular alternative is to take the percentage of a universe of series that have a positive ROC, i.e., a reading above 0 or 100. The choice of the time span for the MA or ROC is very important. The shorter the span, the more volatile the resulting oscillator.

In practice, it seems that the MAs and ROCs commonly used in other areas of technical analysis offer superior results. These are 30-day and 50-day for short-term trends; 13-, 30-, and 40-week for intermediate-term trends; and 9-, 12-, 18-, and 24-month for longer-term trends. The same exercise could also be accomplished with intraday data. One characteristic of using any raw series is that the resulting data usually needs to be smoothed. For example, the diffusion series shown in Chart 27.16 is calculated from the percentage of a basket of commodities and commodity indexes that are above a 24-month MA. This data, in turn, have been smoothed, and thus the solid line actually represents a 9-month MA of the percentage of groups above their respective 24-month MAs. The dashed line is a 9-month MA of the solid (24/9) series. The arrows show that timely primary-trend buy and sell signals are triggered as the diffusion indicator reverses direction and crosses its 9-month (dashed) MA.

How Many Items Should Be Included?

A natural tendency is to use as many items as possible to calculate a diffusion indicator, but this involves maintaining a very large database. My own experience shows that the same objective can be obtained from a relatively small universe of securities. The main thing to bear in mind is that the basket of items used in the calculation reflects the diverse nature of the index's components.

CHART 27.16 CRB Spot Raw Industrials, 1969–2012, and a Diffusion Indicator

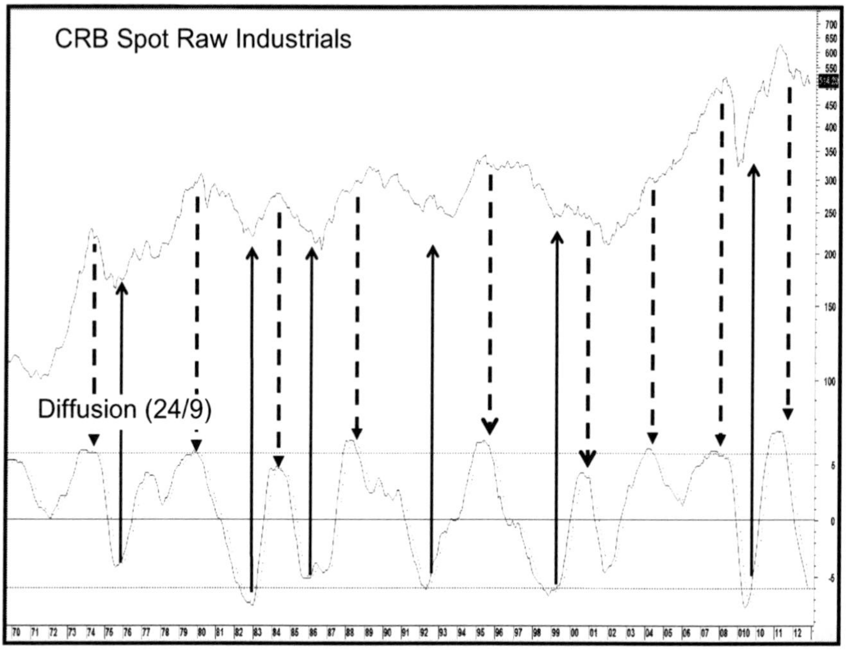

Source: From pring.com

Interpretation

When a diffusion indicator moves to an extreme, it reflects an overbought or oversold condition. However, such readings do not in themselves constitute actual buy or sell signals. The false sell signal for the diffusion series in Chart 27.16 in 2004 is an excellent reason to await a trend confirmation signal. Obviously, the odds favor a profitable investment made at the time of a zero reading, and vice versa. However, it is usually much safer to wait for a reversal in the trend of the diffusion index, or better still, for the confirmation of a trend break in the aggregate index being monitored.

> **Major Technical Principle** When a diffusion indicator reverses direction from an extreme reading, the index it is monitoring usually reverses as well. If it does not and the diffusion indicator continues to correct, it is a sign that many of the securities from which the diffusion indicator is constructed are themselves correcting.

CHART 27.17 DJIA, 2008–2012, and a Diffusion Indicator

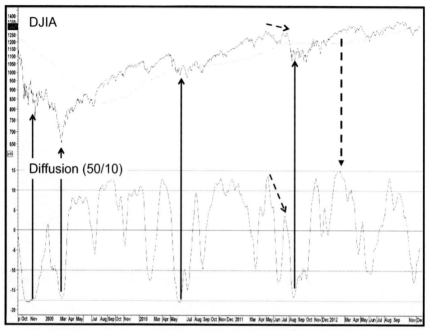

Source: From pring.com

   Chart 27.17 features a diffusion indicator constructed from a basket of Dow stocks. The basis of the calculation is the percentage that are above their 50-day MA. Since that would return a fairly jagged series, the data have been smoothed with a 10-day MA. There are two extreme levels, flagged by the dashed and solid horizontal overbought/oversold levels. The arrows show that reliable buy and sell signals are often triggered when the indicator reverses direction from a position beyond the extremes marked by the solid horizontal lines. The July 2007 high was instructive for although it was slightly below the April/May high, the oscillator was distinctly weaker. That sort of combination, whether the index reached a new high or not, is typically a strong sign of a very weak market.

Seasonal Breadth Momentum: The Seasons Defined

Every cycle effectively goes through four momentum stages before completion. This is shown conceptually in Figure 27.2. The first occurs after downside momentum has reached its maximum. At this point, the series

FIGURE 27.2 Seasonal Momentum Defined

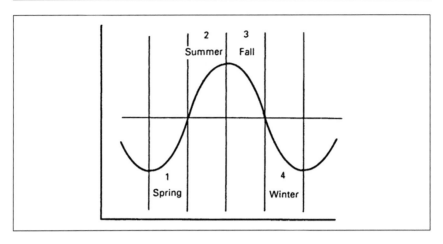

turns up but is still below its equilibrium level. The second is signaled when it crosses above its zero reference line. The third phase starts when it peaks out from above zero. Finally, phase 4 is triggered when the indicator crosses below the equilibrium point.

For simplicity's sake, the respective stages have been labeled as spring, summer, fall, and winter.[2] From both an agricultural and an investment point of view, the best results occur when planting (investing) is done in the spring and harvesting in late summer or fall.

In effect, spring represents accumulation, summer the markup phase, fall distribution, and winter the markdown phase. In situations in which a market can be subdivided into components, it is possible to take this approach one step further by calculating a diffusion index based on the position of the seasonal momentum of its various components, e.g., industry groups for a stock market average, commodity prices for a commodity index, etc. This seasonal momentum approach has two merits. First, it helps to identify the prevailing stage in the cycle, i.e., whether the stock market is in an accumulation, markup, distribution, or markdown phase. Second, it also helps identify major buying and selling opportunities.

---

[2]This approach was first brought to my attention by the late Ian S. Notley, Notley Group, Yelton Fiscal, Inc., Unit 211-Executive Pavilion, 90 Grove Street, Ridgefield, CT 06877.

Choice of Time Span

The choice of time span is critical for all momentum indicators, including those used in the seasonal momentum studies. For example, a series based on a smoothed 13-week ROC will have far less significance in terms of long-term investment strategy than a series based on a 48-month time span. This approach can be used for daily, weekly, and monthly data. I am sure you could expand this concept to include intraday data because the principle is the same. I have never done so, but encourage active traders to give it a try. As with most things technical, it seems that daily and weekly calculations, even when greatly smoothed, do not give as reliable a picture as calculations based on monthly data. That does not mean that shorter-term frames never work and that monthly ones always do. It's just that longer-term frames are less determined by random events and therefore have a *tendency* to operate more reliably. While our explanation of seasonal momentum is focused more on U.S. equities, this approach can also be expanded to commodities, bonds, and international markets. The indicators represented in the charts included in this chapter have been constructed by finding the number of a basket of 10 S&P Industry Groups in their respective winter, spring, summer, or fall positions and then smoothing that data with a 6-month MA.

Seasonal (Diffusion) Momentum for the Stock Market

Chart 27.18 shows all four seasonal momentum curves between 1980 and 2012. A high reading in the spring series, for example, indicates that the momentum of a significant proportion of the groups is in phase 1, i.e., below zero and rising, and therefore in a position to begin a major advance.

It is important to note that in most cycles there is a chronological sequence as the majority of groups move into spring from winter, subsequently landing in summer and finally fall. This is shown by the arrows. Bear market lows typically occur around the time winter momentum peaks. As with all momentum series, confirmation should come from the price, which in this case, is the S&P Composite.

The peaking out of spring momentum is sometimes associated with the first intermediate-term peak in the bull market, but it is *not* a primary-trend bearish sign. It simply means that the majority of groups are moving from the spring (accumulation) to the summer (markup) phase. It is when summer peaks that we get the first sign that the trend may be topping, but because it takes longer to build than to tear down, this sign of trouble is nowhere near as reliable as the winter peaking action at major lows.

CHART 27.18 S&P Composite, 1980–2012, and Seasonal Momentum

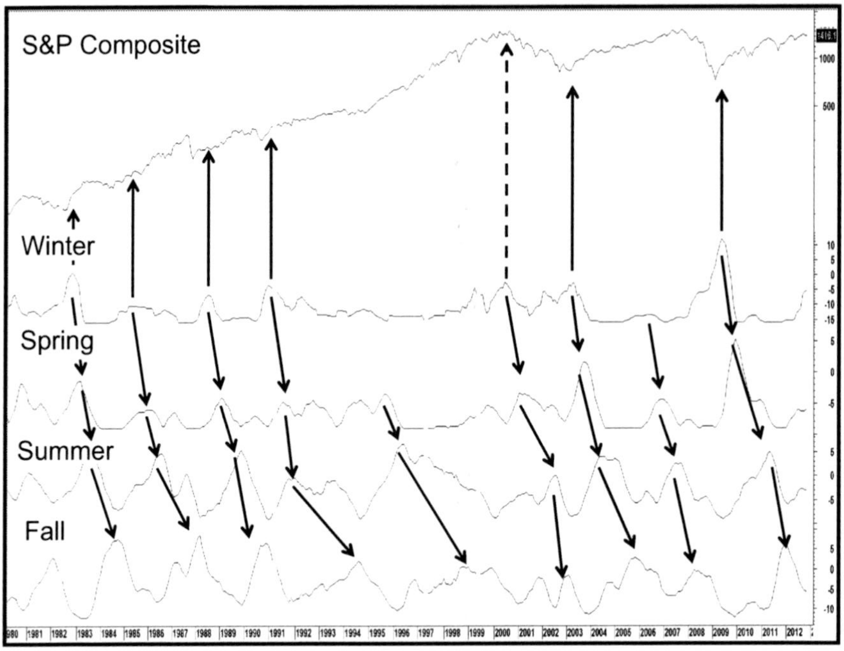

Source: From pring.com

When summer peaks, though, it does indicate that the environment has become much more selective as the smoothed momentum for more and more groups moves to the fall (distribution) phase.

Bear Market Bottoms

Major buying points occur when winter momentum reaches its peak and starts to turn down. Generally speaking, the higher the peak, the greater the potential for upside activity. This is because a movement out of winter momentum must flow into spring. A high and falling level in winter momentum, therefore, indicates that a significant number of groups have the potential to move into the spring position, i.e., to move to the point from which they have the greatest potential to rise. This is shown more clearly in Chart 27.18, but with a far greater history in Chart 27.19.

In this case, the universe from which the indicator is calculated is limited to 14 industry groups since that represents all of the available data. Nevertheless, reversals from above the horizontal line show

CHART 27.19 S&P Composite, 1923–2012, and Monthly Winter Momentum

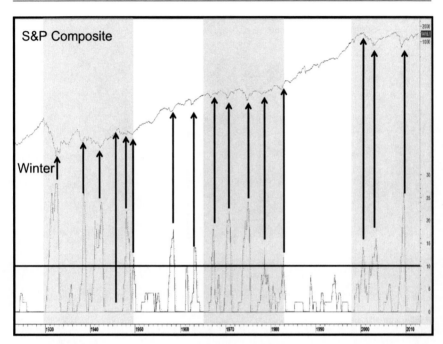

Source: From pring.com

consistent and reliable primary-trend buy signals. Note also that during secular bear markets, as flagged by the shaded areas, the number of groups moving into the winter position is usually far greater than in secular bull markets. Finally, you will notice that the winter position maxed out at around the same time the S&P was peaking. That was due to the fact since 1998 the market had been correcting internally as the index rallied due to the tech boom. By the time tech peaked, most groups were actually in a position to rally, which they did. The S&P sold off though, because its highly weighted tech component declined. This was a unique situation, but it does point out that while diffusion and indexes usually move in tandem, diffusion tells whether the advance or decline will be broadly based or not.

Chart 27.20 shows another "winter" exercise, but this time using the daily Know Sure Thing (KST) formula to identify short-term buying opportunities. There is no reason why it would not be possible to use the MACD or a smooth stochastic as a basis for constructing these indicators. In the case of the latter, the 50 level would correspond to the equilibrium zone for the KST.

CHART 27.20 S&P Composite, 2010–2012, and Daily Winter Momentum

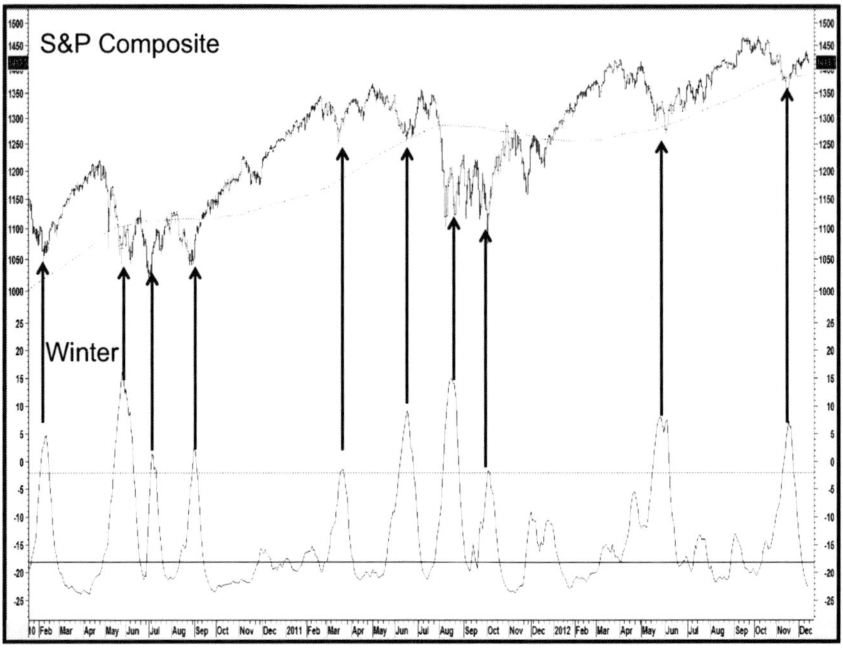

Source: From pring.com

A useful exercise is to take the total of groups in a positive trend (spring + summer) as shown in Chart 27.21.

Bull and bear markets are then signaled by reversals in this indicator. It's not perfect, of course, but when it peaks, it is warning us to be more selective in what we buy, even though the S&P may still work its way higher, as it did in the secular bull period of the late 1990s. Generally speaking, the lower the level of summer velocity when a reversal occurs, the greater the potential for a market rise.

Signs of a Market Peak

Market tops are far more elusive than bottoms, but often occur at some point between the peak in summer and fall momentum. Even a topping out in the fall momentum is not always sufficient to trigger a full-fledged bear market. It is only when a large and expanding number of groups fall below their zero reference lines, i.e., move into winter, that a bear market picks up downside momentum.

CHART 27.21 S&P Composite, 1980–2012, and Spring and Summer Monthly Momentum

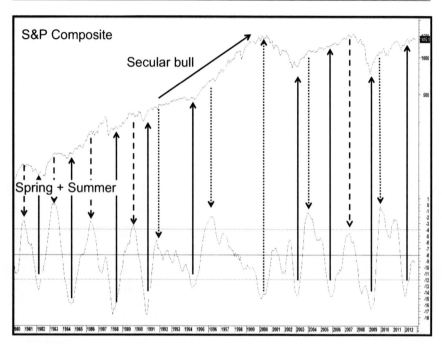

Source: From pring.com

Summary

1. Market breadth measures the degree to which a market index is supported by a wide range of its components.
2. It is useful from two aspects. First, it indicates whether the environment for most items in a universe (normally equities) is good or bad. Second, market breadth indicators signal major turning points through the establishment of both negative and positive divergences.
3. Indicators constructed from breadth data include A/D lines, breadth oscillators, diffusion indicators, and net new highs.
4. Breadth divergences are a fine concept, but should be confirmed by a trend reversal in the market averages themselves.
5. New highs and lows can be used to indicate the underlying strength or weakness of the prevailing trend. This data can also flag divergences or serve as a measurement of trends by cumulating the plurality of the highs and lows.
6. Seasonal momentum helps to point out major buying opportunities and explain the maturity of a primary bull and bear market.

Part III

OTHER ASPECTS OF MARKET ANALYSIS

28

INDICATORS AND RELATIONSHIPS THAT MEASURE CONFIDENCE

A negative divergence between an A/D line and a market average is a broad measure of a subtle loss of confidence by market participants. It is also possible, though, to gain an insight into confidence levels by observing relationships that compare what we might call speculative to defensive areas, as these, too, often serve in a more direct way as an indication of growing confidence or lack thereof. When these relationships are reflecting a trend of growing optimism, it is a positive sign and is an indication of higher prices. When they are deteriorating, an omen of weakness and lower prices is signaled.

> **Major Technical Principle** When a confidence ratio fails to confirm a new high in a market average, it is a sign of weakness that, when confirmed by price action in the average, leads to lower prices. Conversely, when a confidence ratio fails to confirm a new low in a market average, it is a sign of strength that, when confirmed by price action in the average, is usually followed by higher prices.

Figure 28.1 reflects the basic principles that can be applied to essentially all of the relationships described in this chapter in that the confidence ratios typically peak and trough ahead of prices. This does not happen in all instances of market turning points, nor is the lead/lag relationship constant. We should also add that not every divergence, whether negative

FIGURE 28.1 Confidence versus Price

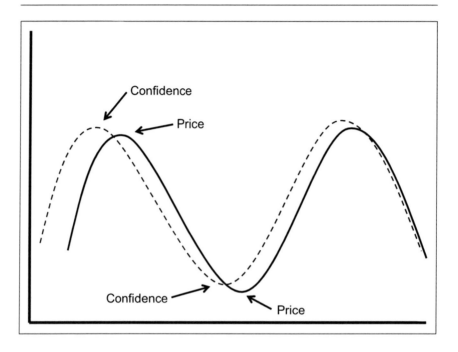

or positive, is necessarily followed by a change in trend of the price series being monitored.

The relationships in this chapter are focused on the U.S. market, but there is no reason why the curious reader cannot expand these principles to other equity markets, or indeed to the bond and commodity arenas.

The Consumer Staple/Food Models

The consumer staple sector embraces companies that produce, for want of a better term, necessities—things that consumers buy in bad times as well as good ones. Examples include manufacturers of food, household products, beverages, etc. In effect, they produce goods that people are unable or unwilling to cut out of their budgets, regardless of their financial situation. Consumer staple stocks are considered noncyclical, meaning that they are always in demand, no matter how poorly the economy is performing, because people tend to demand such products at a relatively constant level, regardless of price.

When investors are cautious, they tend to flock to these equities for four reasons:

1. Their lack of cyclicality makes for more accurate earnings forecasts than, say, highly cyclical and volatile mining stocks.
2. They tend to pay better dividends.
3. They generally have a consistent record of earnings and dividend growth.
4. Most of these companies have a solid balance sheet.

Because of these characteristics, consumer staples tend to do better during bear markets. Their relative action during bull markets has a tendency to be weaker as investors turn to more exciting sectors.

This knowledge can be put to profitable use with the aid of several indicators. For example, just monitoring the relative action of staples to the S&P offers some useful buy and sell signals. Chart 28.1 compares the S&P exchange-traded fund (ETF), the SPY, with the Spider Consumer Staple (symbol XLP) relative action.

CHART 28.1 S&P ETF, 1998–2012, and Consumer Staples RS Showing Divergences

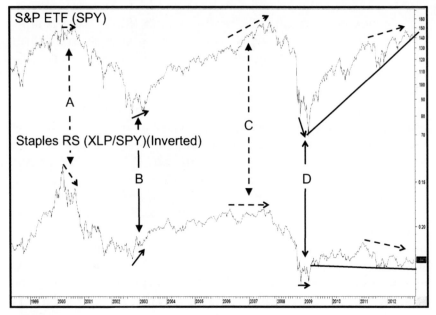

Source: From pring.com

CHART 28.2 S&P ETF, 1998–2012, and Consumer Staples RS Showing Trendline Violations

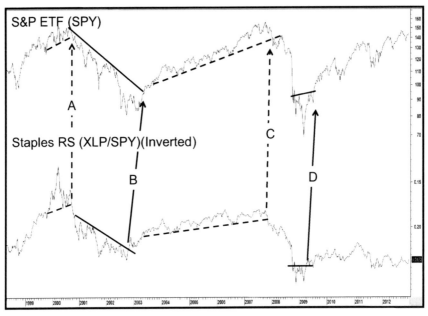

Source: From pring.com

In view of the fact that the relative strength (RS) line moves in the opposite direction to the S&P, it has been plotted inversely in the chart. This relationship often gives us advance warning of a change in trend as the inversely plotted RS line fails to confirm new highs and lows in the S&P. These divergences represent a subtle way in which confidence changes ahead of the overall market. Chart 28.2 codifies this in the sense that the divergences at A, B, C, and D were all confirmed with joint trendline breaks. Note that each instance was followed by a worthwhile move. The only exception was the potential divergence in the 2011–2012 period, but that had not been confirmed as the manuscript for this book was being submitted in mid-2013.

Another technique using the XLP/SPY relationship is to compare the momentum of the XLP relative action to that of the SPY. I use the daily Know Sure Thing (KST) formula presented in Chapter 15, but there is no reason why two moving-average convergence divergence (MACD) or stochastic indicators could not be overlaid to achieve similar results. An example using KSTs is shown in Chart 28.3, where the dotted line represents the XLP relative momentum and the solid one the KST for the SPY.

The light highlights indicate when the relative XLP momentum is above that for the SPY and when the SPY itself is responding by being

CHART 28.3 S&P ETF, 2006–2012, Comparing Two Momentum Indicators

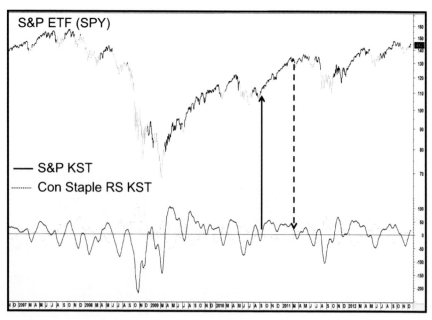

Source: From pring.com

below its 50-day MA advanced by 10 days. For a description on the technique of advancing moving averages, please refer to Chapter 11. During the bullish 2009–2012 period, this technique was not particularly helpful in that the declines were fairly truncated and therefore the sell signals developed fairly close to the final intermediate lows. On the other hand, for the most part, the bullish periods indicated by the dark highlights caught most of the upside action. Alternatively, the light shadings that occurred in the 2007–2009 bear market tell us that the model would have offered great protection against downside action, except for a relatively small decline at the start of 2009. The bottom line is that this approach works best when the signals are triggered in the direction of the prevailing primary trend.

An alternative method of presenting the same information is to subtract the S&P momentum from that of the relative XLP (Chart 28.4). In that way positive KST crossovers are represented on the chart by a move above the zero equilibrium line. Since this arrangement tells us when the relationship is overstretched, warnings of trend reversals, ahead of the actual zero crossovers, can be generated when the ratio reverses direction. Some examples have been flagged with the arrows.

CHART 28.4 S&P ETF Daily, 2008–2012, and a Differential of Two Momentum Indicators

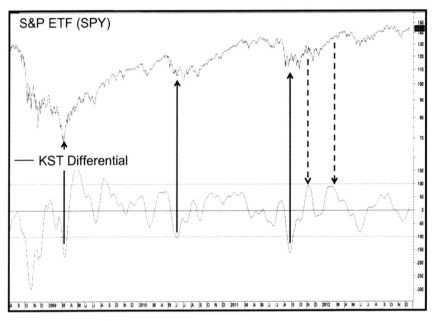

Source: From pring.com

However, you can also see that other extreme reading reversals fail completely in their trend signaling abilities. This will typically happen at the start of a new bull market, where momentum is particularly strong and countercyclical signals benign. The two "sell" signals in May and August 2009 are prime examples.

Finally, it's possible to extend the time frame to an intermediate one, as shown in Charts 28.5 and 28.6.

In these instances, the S&P Food Index, which is a member of the consumer staple sector, has been substituted for the consumer staples themselves because more history is available. The differential indicator in the lower panel is constructed by subtracting the intermediate KST of the S&P Composite from that constructed from the relative action of the food group. As you can see, reversals in the indicator from an extreme level, i.e., at or beyond +170 and –170, usually provide reliable signals of intermediate-trend reversals unless they develop at the start of a new primary trend. The light highlights reflect bearish trends when two conditions are in force. First, the relative food KST is above that for the S&P and the S&P itself is below its 40-week moving average (MA), which itself has been advanced by

CHART 28.5 S&P ETF Weekly, 1977–1994, and a Differential of Two Momentum Indicators

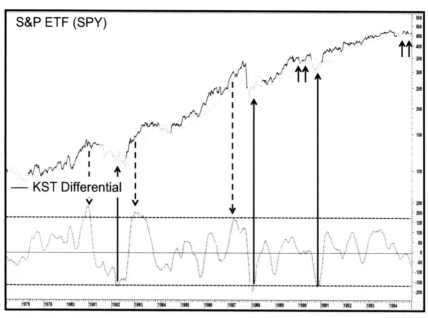

Source: From pring.com

CHART 28.6 S&P ETF Weekly, 1995–2012, and a Differential of Two Momentum Indicators

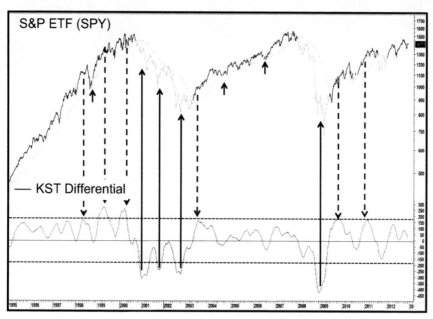

Source: From pring.com

seven periods. Again, the main criticism would come from bearish signals that are triggered in bull markets, where limited declines mean that the signals are triggered very near to the final low of the move, the 1987 decline being a principal example. Some additional instances have been flagged in the chart by the small solid arrows. The results using this system between 1976 and August 2012 returned annualized gains of 9.65 percent when this technique was in a positive mode and –0.60 percent when negative.

High-Yield versus Government Bonds

Another confidence relationship can be obtained by comparing the high-yield IBOXX Corporate High Yield Bond Fund (symbol HYG) to the Barclays 20-Year Trust, a government-bond ETF (symbol TLT). A rise in the ratio means that the prices of low-quality bonds are outperforming the relatively safe government sector. Such action indicates growing confidence by bond investors. Charts 28.7 and 28.8 compare the ratio to the ups and downs in the S&P Composite.

CHART 28.7 S&P ETF, 2007–2010, and a High Yield/Government Bond Ratio

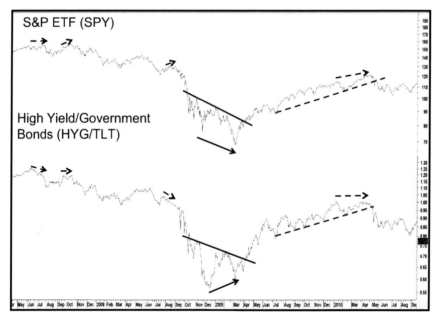

Source: From pring.com

CHART 28.8 S&P ETF, 2010–2012, and a High Yield/Government Bond Ratio

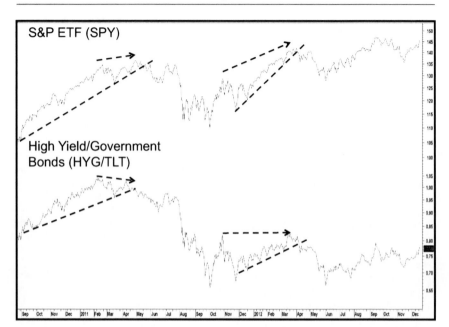

Source: From pring.com

Most of the time, both series are moving in the same direction. It is when they are not that a subtle warning of a change in trend is given. Usually, these prove to be negative indications, but the positive divergence in 2009 shows that it is not a one-way street. Once again, it is always useful to obtain some confirmation from the price as flagged by the various trendline combinations. Since the HYG has only been around since 2007, this relationship does not have a long-term track record. However, a similar relationship that has been around since the early twentieth century is the ratio between Moody's BAA corporate bonds and the constant 20-year maturity of U.S. government bond.

Chart 28.9 shows the actual ratio, with the arrows flagging extreme point reversals.

Solid arrows indicate bullish signals, dashed ones bearish indications, and dotted ones failed signals. The chart clearly indicates that there is a definite relationship between bond market sentiment and equity prices. The trick is knowing where the extreme points of the ratio are. But how do we know they won't become more extreme? A useful answer is to take the 12-month rate of change (ROC) of the ratio and set up some overbought

CHART 28.9 S&P Composite, 1923–2012, and a Government/Corporate BAA Ratio

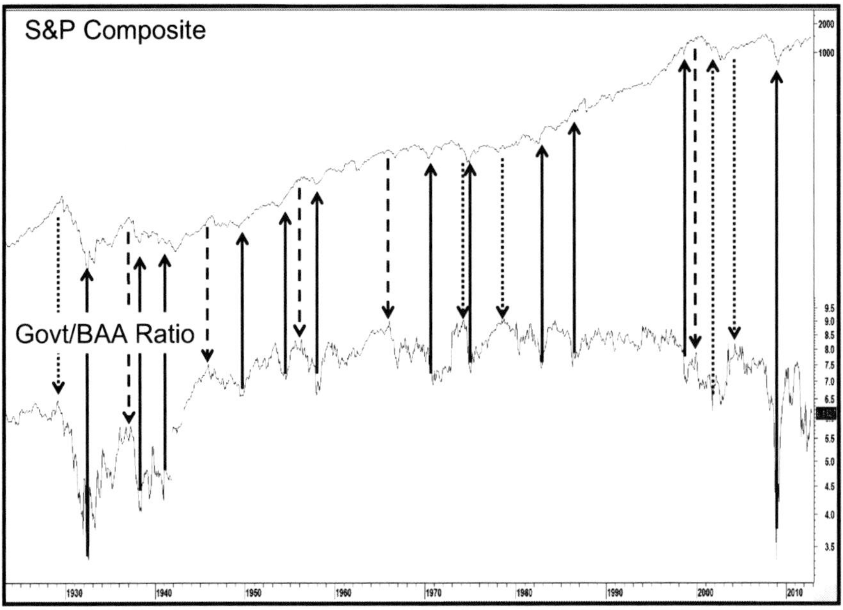

Source: From pring.com

and oversold zones at +15 and −15. Reversals that take place from a position beyond these levels then serve as our mechanism of primary-trend equity reversals. This is shown in Chart 28.10, where the extreme movements of the 1920s and the post-2007 period have been excluded so that the normal range can be appreciated. Once again, the two dotted lines indicate failed signals.

Chart 28.11 shows the post-2007 period that involved the 2008 financial crisis. These swings were enormous and certainly reflected the dramatic swings in investor confidence during these troubled times.

Finally, Chart 28.12 shows the ratio on a weekly basis, where divergences show up every few months or so. Also, changes in direction of the intermediate KST have provided useful signals of smaller trend reversals. I should add that prior to 2007, this relationship did not work as well as it has since, so it is possible that the 6 years of price behavior shown in this chart could turn out to be an aberration. Historical data for these and other bond series can be downloaded from the Federal Reserve website under "H.15 Selected Interest Rates Download."

CHART 28.10 S&P Composite, 1940–2007, and Government/Corporate BAA Momentum

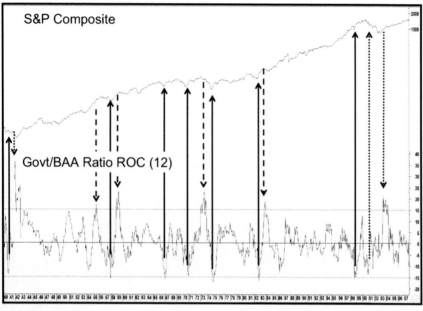

Source: From pring.com

CHART 28.11 S&P Composite, 1997–2007, and Government/Corporate BAA Momentum

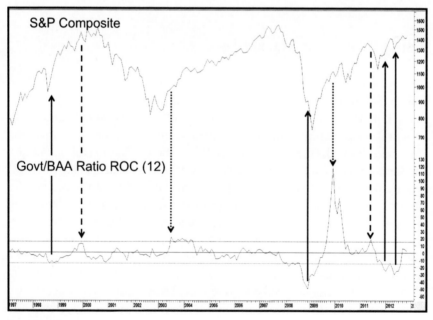

Source: From pring.com

CHART 28.12 S&P Composite, 2006–2012, and Two Indicators

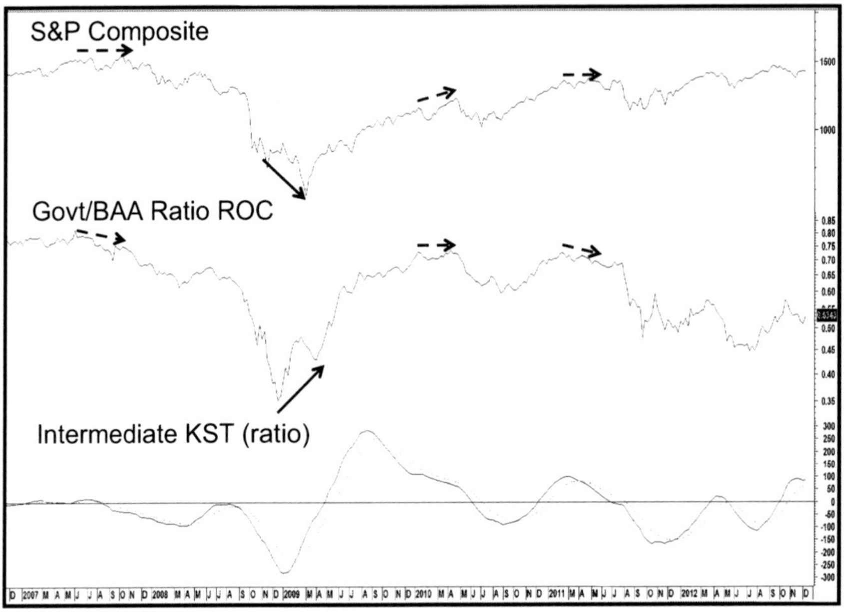

Source: From pring.com

Using Brokers as Market Leaders

The market as a whole discounts the economy, but brokerage stocks, which obtain their profits from market conditions, have a tendency to lead the market in both directions. For example, during bull markets, volume and therefore brokerage commissions tend to increase because traders and investors find it easier to take profits than losses. When these folks are making money, they also tend to make faster, more careless decisions. That also inflates trading. By the same token, more companies go public during the course of a bull market because they obtain a higher price for their stock. Underwriting fees can represent a large share of brokerage income. Finally, interest rates have a tendency to lead the stock market. That means that brokerage carrying costs decline at the start of an equity bull market and begin to rise prior to its ending. The bottom line is that a rising market means greater profits for brokerage companies and investment banks, and a falling market less so.

Each sector discounts or anticipates developments in its sector of the economy, so the leading role often played by the price of brokerages is no

CHART 28.13 S&P Composite, 1981–2012, and the Amex Brokers Index

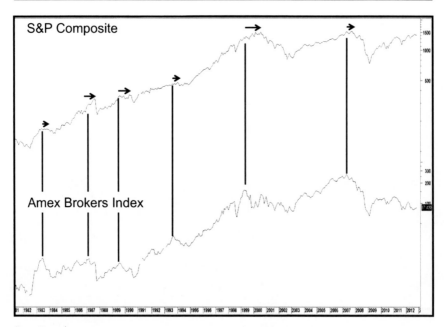

Source: From pring.com

exception to this rule. There are two principal ways in which it is possible to follow these stocks. The first is the Amex Brokerage Index (symbol XBD) and the second is the Dow Jones Broker Dealer, or more practically through the ETF that uses it as a tracking index, the IAI.

There are several ways in which the broker/market relationship can be analyzed. The first arises from positive and negative divergences. Chart 28.13 compares the S&P to the XBD.

The arrows show that brokers typically top out ahead of the overall market at primary-trend peaks. The leads are not constant, of course, but change from cycle to cycle. The width of the arrows roughly flag the lead times, and there does not appear to be a connection between the size of the divergence and that of the ensuing decline. For example, the divergence that took place in the 1989–1990 period was relatively large but the decline was fairly truncated. This compares to the devastating 2007–2009 decline that followed the very small 2007 negative divergence. Positive divergences, where the brokers fail to confirm new equity market lows, exist but are far more infrequent than negative ones. Chart 28.14 compares brokerage action to the market again, but this time, it reflects their *relative* action.

CHART 28.14 S&P Composite, 1978–2012, and the Amex Brokers Index Relative Action

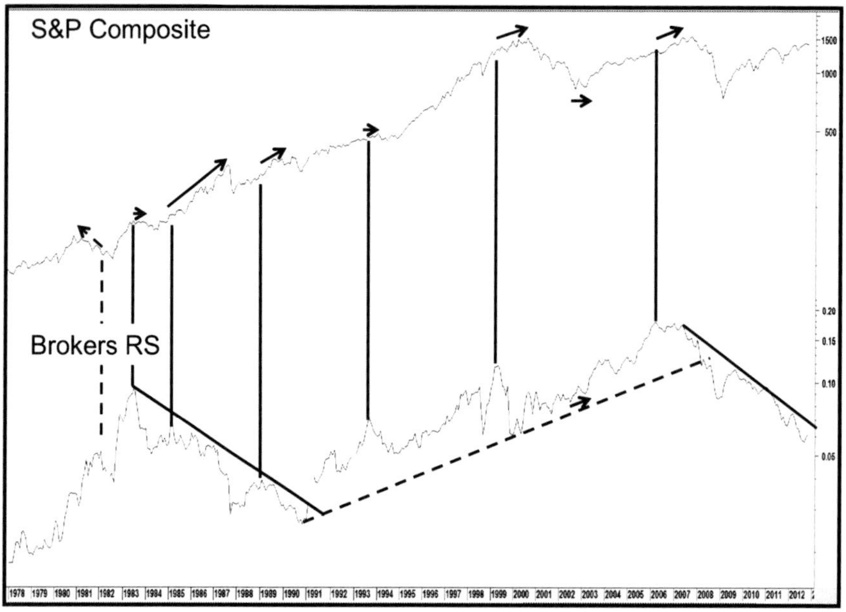

Source: From pring.com

The first thing to notice is the failure of brokers to identify the 1981 peak since the top in the RS line developed as the bear market was in its final stages. Other than that, the RS action, judging by the width of the arrows, provides a longer-term warning of tops than the absolute price data in the previous chart.

Chart 28.15 compares the Dow Jones Broker Dealer ETF, the IAI, to the S&P. Here you can see the negative 2007 divergence and the 2008–2009 positive one. Also featured in the chart is the July/August 2010 divergence, as flagged by the backward-pointing arrow on the IAI. This was an example of where the ETF lagged the market, thereby creating a disagreement. In such cases, price trumps everything, which means that when such disagreements develop, they are cancelled in the event that both series reverse their prevailing trend. In this case, it was a downtrend which was canceled by two upside trendline breaks.

The brokerage/market relationship is far from perfect, but it often gives a hint as to whether investors and traders are optimistic or pessimistic about the stock market's future performance.

CHART 28.15 S&P Composite, 2007–2011, and the Dow Jones Broker ETF

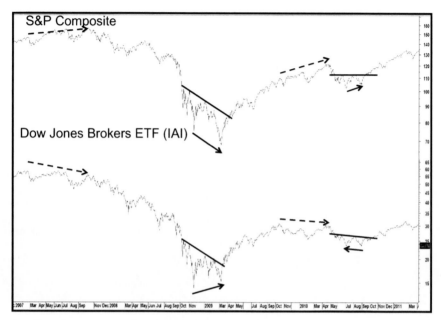

Source: From pring.com

Using Inflation-Protected versus Regular Bonds as a Commodity Barometer

Another useful relationship is to compare the prices of inflation-protected bonds (Barclays TIPS ETF) to the Barclays 20-Year Trust, or the TIP to the TLT. If the ratio is rising, it means that investors are favoring bonds protected by inflation over those that are not. If that is the case, it should mean that bond investors are anticipating inflation. Were they expecting deflation, the ratio would decline in view of the fact that the noninflation-protected instruments were outperforming their inflation-protected counterparts. In this respect, Chart 28.16 compares the ratio to the performance of the CRB Spot Raw Industrial commodity index. Prior to 2006, there was not much in the way of a relationship as commodities rallied and the ratio fell. However, at the start of that year both series violated trendlines and signaled higher commodity prices. Later in 2006 they started to move in similar directions, though the magnitude of each one was different as the more volatile commodity measure grabbed the majority of the price moves in both directions.

CHART 28.16 CRB Spot Raw Industrials, 2005–2012, and the TIP/TLT Ratio

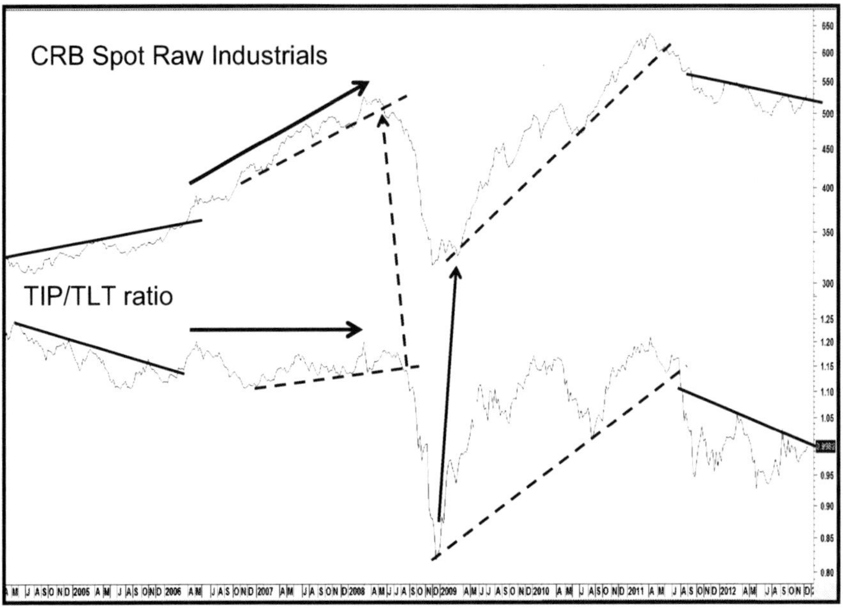

Source: From pring.com

The joint trendline breaks indicate signals for both trends reversing, and the two arrows indicate the confirmed negative divergence that developed in 2008. The more recent convergence of the price action can be better appreciated from Chart 28.17, which compares the intermediate KST for the two series.

It would be convenient to be able to conclude that one series is a consistent leader, but that is not the case, as the solid arrows show ratio leadership and the dashed ones when the commodity KST turned first. Turning points with no arrows indicate a coincidental relationship. Starting in 2001 there are many periods where it is not possible to distinguish between the two series because their trajectories are so similar. When you consider that the ratio contains such completely different data from the commodity index, the recent similarities between the two series serve as a sharp reminder that commodity and bond market participants are clearly on the same page.

Since the history of this relationship has only been available for a few years, it would be incorrect to place a great deal of weight on these conclusions. However, the fact that the connection between the ratio and commodity prices appears to be growing suggests that this form of analysis should be closely monitored as it appears to be quite promising.

CHART 28.17 Commodity Momentum versus the TIP/TLT Momentum, 2005–2012

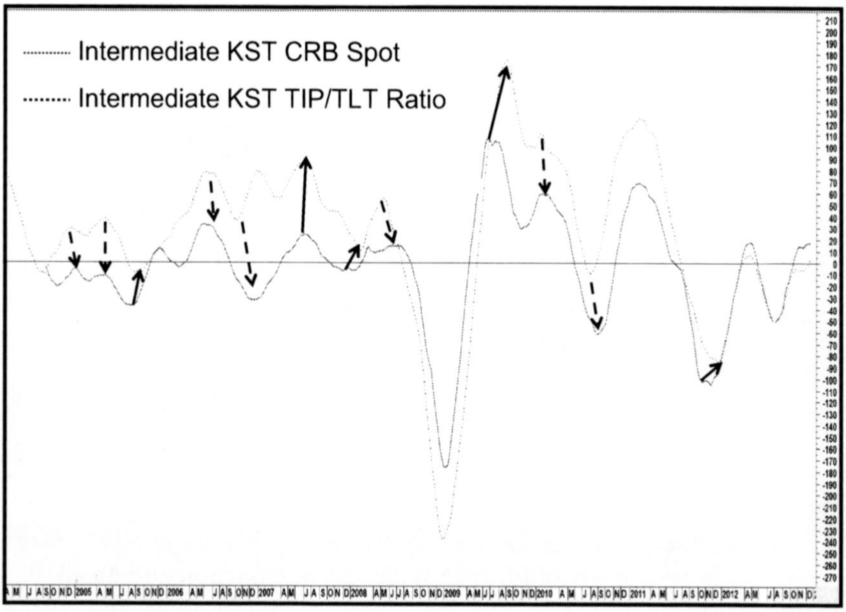

Source: From pring.com

Summary

1. Confidence ratios, such as the relative action of defensive stocks or quality bond market spreads, typically turn ahead of market averages such as the S&P Composite.
2. They can be used to trigger buy and sell signals through trendline analysis or momentum relationships.
3. Brokers have a tendency to lead the stock market at tops, less so at bottoms. Useful buy and sell signals can be derived from joint trendline violations.
4. In recent years there has been a strong relationship between the trend of commodity prices and the ratio between inflation-protected and regular bonds.

29

THE IMPORTANCE
OF SENTIMENT

I find more and more that it is well to be on the right side of the minority since it is always the more intelligent.

—Goethe

During primary bull and bear markets, the psychology of all investors moves from pessimism and fear to hope, overconfidence, and greed. For the majority, the feeling of confidence is built up over a period of rising prices so that optimism reaches its peak around the same point that the market is also reaching its high. Conversely, the majority is most pessimistic at market bottoms, which is precisely the point when it should be buying. These observations are as valid for intermediate-term peaks and troughs as they are for primary ones. The difference is normally of degree. At an intermediate-term low, for example, significant problems are perceived, but at a primary market low, they often seem insurmountable. In some respects, the worse the problems, the more significant the bottom.

The better-informed market participants, such as insiders and stock exchange members, tend to act in a manner contrary to that of the majority by selling at market tops and buying at market bottoms. Both groups go through a complete cycle of emotions, but in completely opposite phases. This is not to suggest that members of the public are always wrong at major market turns and that professionals are always correct; rather, the implication is that, in aggregate, the opinions of these groups are usually in direct conflict.

Historical data are available on many market participants, making it possible to derive parameters that indicate when a particular group has moved to an extreme historically associated with a major market turning point.

Unfortunately, there are several indexes that worked well prior to the 1980s but have been partially distorted because of the advent of listed options trading in 1973 and the introduction of stock index futures in 1982. The reason is that the purchase and sale of options and index futures substitute for short selling and other speculative activities that had been used as a basis for the construction of sentiment indicators.

Generally speaking, long-term data relating to market participants that have not been unduly affected by options trading before the early 1970s are limited. As with any data series of limited duration, a greater degree of caution should be exercised in its interpretation. Since a description of technical analysis would not be complete without some reference to investor sentiment, some of the more reliable indicators are considered here. Use of three or four indexes that measure sentiment is useful from the point of view of assessing the majority view, from which a contrary opinion can be taken.

Momentum as a Substitute for Sentiment

Individual stocks and many markets do not have published sentiment data from which indicators can be derived. In such instances, it is possible to substitute oscillators since there is a close correlation between overbought conditions and those of excessive bullishness and vice versa.

In this respect, the bottom panel of Chart 29.1 shows two momentum series.

Both are calculated by dividing the weekly close by a 13-week moving average (MA). The solid line is derived from the S&P Composite and the dashed one from the weekly percentage of bearish letter market advisors as published by Investors Intelligence.com. This latter series has been plotted inversely to correspond with the direction of equity market price movements. Thus, one is a momentum indicator derived directly from fluctuations in the S&P Composite and the other from sentiment data, which are, statistically speaking, completely independent. It is fairly evident that there is an extremely close correlation between them. The two trajectories are not identical, of course, but are close enough to prove the point that rising prices attract fewer bears and vice versa. We can also see a similar relationship in the bond market. Chart 29.2, for instance, compares a 10-week MA of a 14-week relative strength indicator (RSI) for bullish bond market traders as published by Market Vane against a 10-week MA for a 14-week RSI for the inversely plotted, government constant 20-year maturity bond yield. Again, the similarities between them are very close indeed.

The fact that sentiment and momentum indicators are closely related should come as no surprise because rising prices attract more bulls and falling

CHART 29.1 S&P Composite, 2009–2012, Comparing Momentum for Price and Sentiment

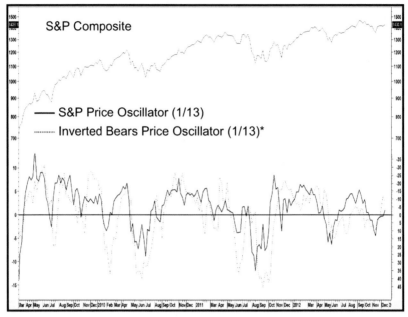

*Source Investorsintelligence.com

CHART 29.2 Government 20-Year Yield (Inverted), 2003–2012, Comparing Momentum for Price and Sentiment

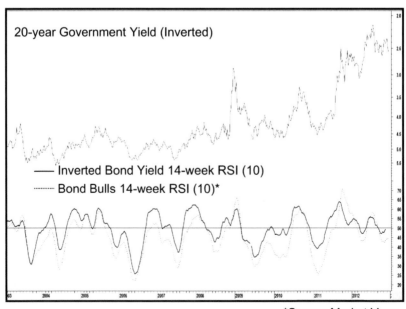

*Source Market Vane

ones more bears. I am not suggesting that every sentiment indicator and oscillator have this close relationship. However, it does point up the fact that if sentiment indicators are not available, momentum series can be useful substitutes.

Insider Trading

Stockholders who hold in excess of 5 percent of the total voting stock of a company and corporate officers or other employees who have access to important corporate information are required to file with the Securities and Exchange Commission (SEC) any purchases or sales within 10 days. As a group, these "insiders" are generally correct in their decisions, having a tendency to sell proportionately more stock as the market rises, and vice versa. An 8-week MA of the weekly insider sell/buy ratio is shown at the bottom of Chart 29.3. The chart shows that as prices work their way higher, insiders accelerate their sales as a percentage of purchases. Market peaks are signaled when the ratio rises for a period of a few months or more and then reverses trend. In this respect, a rise above the 70 percent level and a subsequent reversal in the direction of the index are sufficient under normal circumstances to induce a decline.

At market lows, the 60 percent level appears to offer the best warning of an impending advance. If the index either falls below the 60 percent level and then rises above it, or even just declines to briefly touch it, as in early 1978 or March 1980, a rally usually results.

Advisory Service Sentiment

Since 1963, Investors Intelligence (www.investorsintelligence.com) has been compiling data on the opinions of publishers of market letters. It might be expected that this group would be well informed and would offer advice of a contrary nature by recommending acquisition of equities at market bottoms and offering selling advice at market tops. The evidence suggests that the advisory services in aggregate act in a manner completely opposite to that of the majority and, therefore, represent a good proxy for an "anti-majority" opinion.

The most popular way to display this data is to compare the number of bulls or bears each week to the S&P Composite or some other average. That approach, though, does not take into consideration those looking for a correction. Chart 29.4 attempts to get around this problem by calculating the number of bulls minus the number of advisors who are bearish, i.e., the plurality of those with a firm opinion on the direction of the main trend.

CHART 29.3 DJIA 1978–2001 Specialists and NYSE Total Short Position.

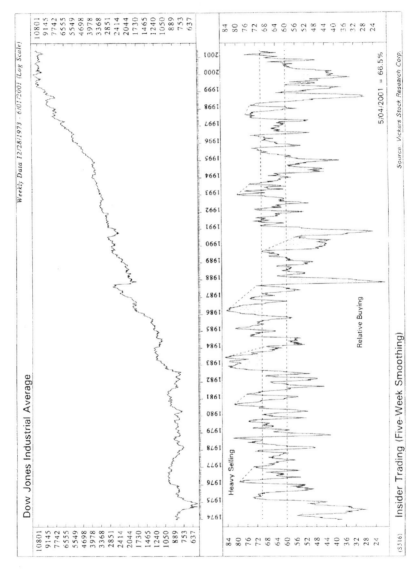

Source: From Ned Davis Research.

CHART 29.4 S&P Composite, 1995–2012, and Bulls Less Bears at Tops

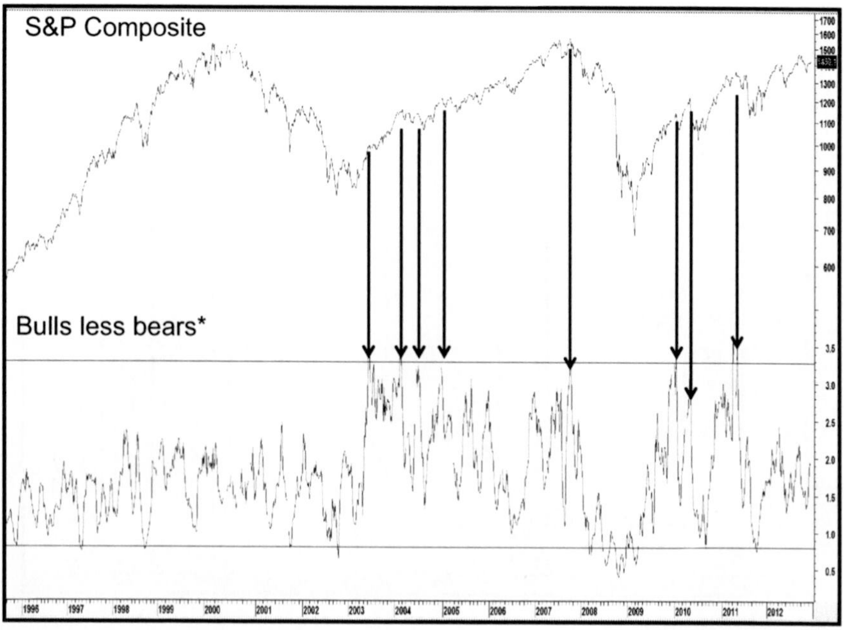

*Source: From Investorsintelligence.com

The arrows highlight points where the indicator reverses from a reading at or above 3.2. Such action indicates danger, but unfortunately, does not tell us how much. Thus, the late-2007 sell signal was followed by a severe bear market, whereas most of the others were fairly limited in their bearish warnings.

Chart 29.5 shows the same period, but this time from the aspect of the more reliable buy signals, triggered when the indicator reverses from the 0.8 level. There are two observations worth making. First, the indicator reaches this reading more often in a primary bear market and generates relatively weak signals. Second, when it does slip below 0.8 and starts to rise, this represents a high-probability rally signal.

Chart 29.6 takes a slightly different tack. First, it just represents the number of bearish advisory services that has been inversely plotted to correspond with stock market price movements. Second, the actual plotted series is a 9-week RSI that has been smoothed with an 8-week MA. Buy signals have been flagged with oversold upside reversals. The dashed lines, on the other hand, show that sell signals typically come after some form

CHART 29.5 S&P Composite, 1995–2012, and Bulls Less Bears at Bottoms

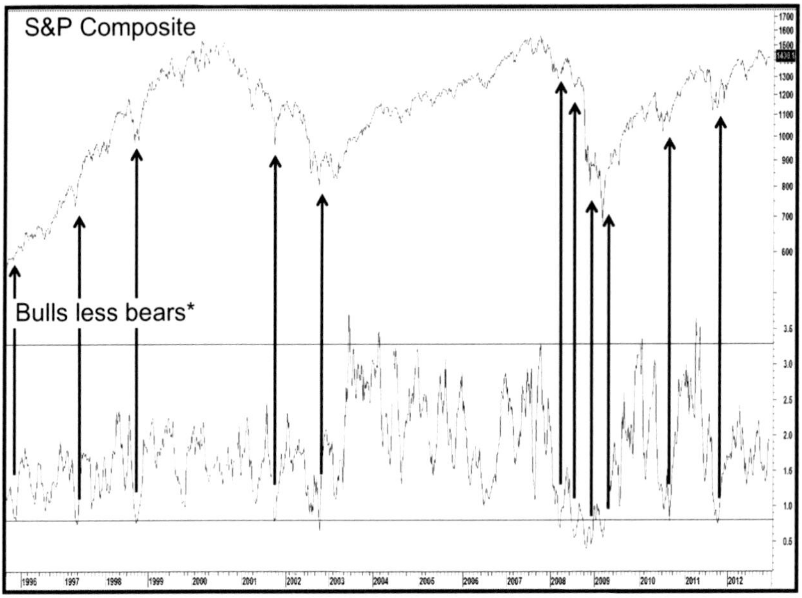

*Source: From Investorsintelligence.com

of negative divergence has materialized. If you look at the previous chart, you will also discover that bull market peaks are usually formed not at the point of maximum bullishness, but at some lower peak that develops afterward.

> **Major Technical Principle** An extremely high sentiment reading is not usually that bearish, as it is often a leading indicator. Bull market highs have a greater tendency to form when sentiment diverges in a negative way.

Finally Chart 29.7 shows that sentiment data, just like any other oscillator, occasionally lend itself to trendline analysis. The chart also reminds us that the principles of divergence can also be applied to the interpretation of this and similar data. For example, the market low of 1982 and high of 1987 were both preceded by a divergence.

CHART 29.6 DJIA, 1995–2012, and Inverted Bearish Momentum

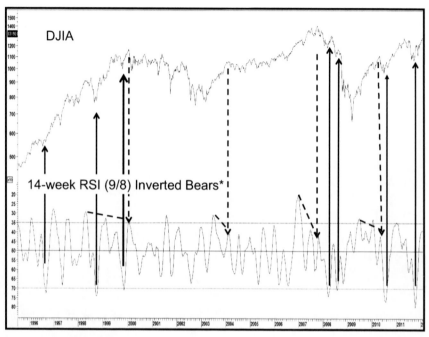

*Source: From Investorsintelligence.com

Quite often, the trend of sentiment can be as important as the level in identifying important market reversals. The chart shows many examples where it is possible to construct a trendline for the sentiment series. When the line is violated, a trend-reversal signal is given. The dashed vertical lines indicate sells, and the solid lines buy signals.

Market Vane and Bond Market Sentiment

Sentiment indicators are also published for the futures market. One of the most widely followed contains data issued by Market Vane. Each week, the firm polls a sample of market participants. The results are published as the percentage of participants that are bullish. The theory is that when a significant number of traders are bullish on a particular market, they are already positioned on the long side. That means that there is very little potential buying power left. The implication is that the price has only one way to go,

CHART 29.7 S&P Composite, 1976–2001, and Bears

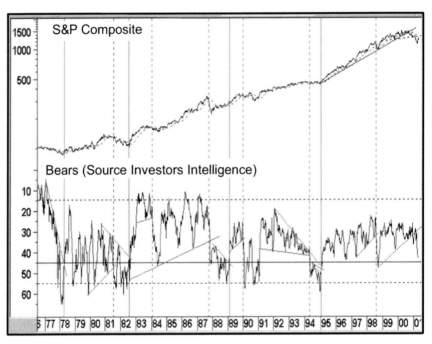

Source: From Investorsintelligence.com

and that is down. In a similar manner, if most participants are bearish, they have already sold or gone short. Since selling pressure has likely reached an extreme, prices can only move in one direction and that is north. An example in Chart 29.8 using reversals from the extreme levels of 85 percent and 15 percent indicates that such extended reversals offer good signals. Unfortunately, they are few and far between. An alternative method of interpretation is to construct trendlines for the sentiment series and observe when the price is reacting with a similar break of its own. Once again, we do not see a lot of signals, but when they are available, the result is quite effective.

One problem with these statistics is that they are based on the opinion of short-term traders, which makes them somewhat erratic, with implications limited to near-term price movements. A technique for surmounting this drawback is to calculate an MA of the raw data, say, with a 4-week span, which smoothes out week-to-week fluctuations.

An alternative is to plot a 10-week MA of a 14-week RSI as shown in Chart 29.9. In this instance, the overbought/oversold zones are constructed at 40 percent and 60 percent. The arrows show reversals from beyond those

CHART 29.8 20-Year Government Bond Yield, 1994–2012, and Market Vane Bond Bulls

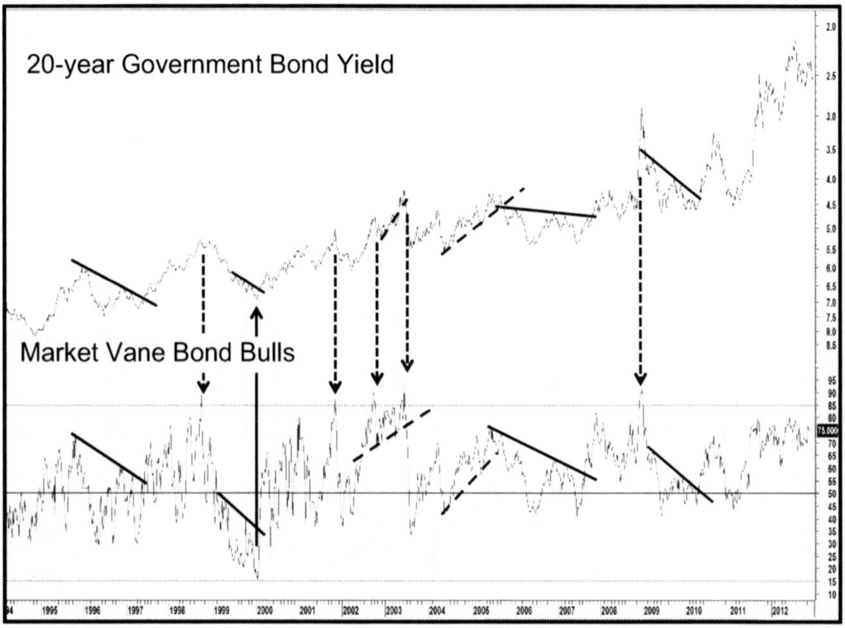

Source: From Market Vane.

levels that offer fairly consistent and reliable signals of changes in the trend of the 20-year yield series.

> **Major Technical Principle**   Quite often, the trend of sentiment can be as important as the level in identifying important market reversals. The same observation can be made for fundamental indicators, such as price earnings (P/E) ratios and so forth.

Combining Sentiment and Momentum

One useful approach for identifying early reversals in trend is to combine sentiment and momentum into one series, the combo. The bottom panel of Chart 29.10 shows an indicator that combines the Market Vane bulls with a 14-week RSI of the Barclays 20-year government exchange-traded

CHART 29.9 20-Year Government Bond Yield, 2000–2012, and Market Vane Bond Bull Momentum

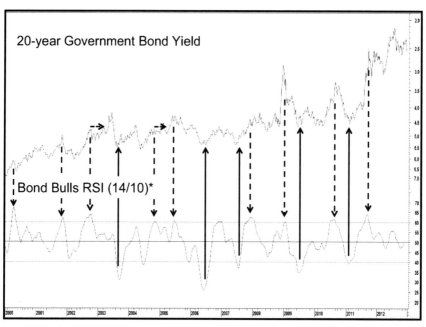

*Source: From Market Vane.

fund (ETF). Both series have been subtracted from 50 to allow for plus and minus numbers, with the total being divided by 2.

Buy and sell alerts occur when the 10-week MA of the combo, shown in the center window, crosses above and below its 6-week MA from below and above zero, respectively. In other words, a sell signal can only be generated from a reading above zero and a buy from below. Whipsaw signals have been indicated in the ellipses. When it is considered that the bulk of this period included choppy ranging action rather than persistent trends, it seems that this approach worked quite well.

Mutual Funds

Data on mutual funds are published monthly by the Investment Company Institute (ICI.org). The statistics are useful because they monitor the actions of both the public and the institutions. In recent years, money-market and tax-

CHART 29.10 Barclays 20-Year Trust, 2003–2012, and Two Momentum/Sentiment Indicators

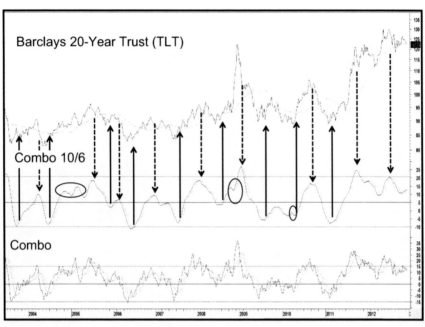

Source: From pring.com

exempt mutual funds have become widespread; therefore, the data used here have been modified to include only equity funds. Technical analysts usually calculate mutual fund cash as a percentage of assets. In a sense, this data should be treated as a flow-of-funds indicator, but it is discussed here as a measure of sentiment.

Mutual Fund Cash/Assets Ratio

Mutual funds consistently hold a certain amount of their portfolios in the form of liquid assets in order to accommodate investors wishing to cash in or redeem their investments. A useful indicator is derived when this cash position is expressed as a percentage of the total value of mutual funds' portfolios, a figure known as *total asset value* (see Chart 29.11).

The index moves in the direction opposite to the stock market because the proportion of cash held by mutual funds rises as prices fall, and vice versa. There are three reasons for this characteristic. First, as the value of

CHART 29.11 S&P Composite, 1970–2013, and Mutual Fund Cash/Asset Ratio

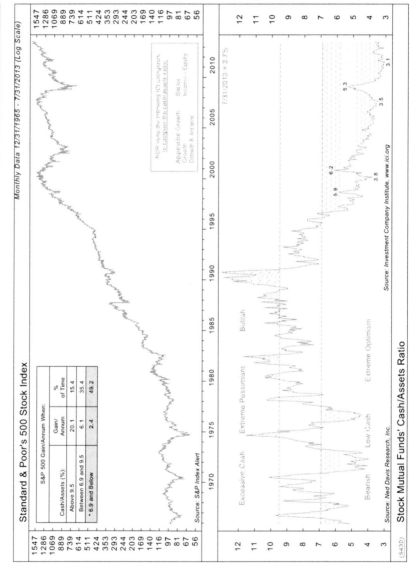

Standard & Poor's 500 Stock Index

Monthly Data 12/31/1965 - 7/31/2013 (Log Scale)

S&P 500 Gain/Annum When:		
Cash/Assets (%):	Gain/Annum	% of Time
Above 9.5	20.1	15.4
Between 6.9 and 9.5	6.1	35.4
* 6.9 and Below	2.4	49.2

Source: S&P Index Alert

NDR uses the following ICI categories to calculate the cash/assets ratio:

| Aggressive Growth | Sector |
| Growth | Income - Equity |
| Growth & Income |

Source: Investment Company Institute. www.ici.org

Excessive Cash
Extreme Pessimism
Bullish
Low Cash
Bearish
Extreme Optimism

7/31/2013 = 3.7%

Source: Ned Davis Research, Inc.

(S430) **Stock Mutual Funds' Cash/Assets Ratio**

Source: From Ned Davis Research.

a fund's portfolio falls in a declining market, the proportion of cash held will automatically rise even though no new cash is raised. Second, as prices decline, the funds become more cautious in their buying policy since they see fewer opportunities for capital gains. Third, the decision is made to hold more cash reserves as insurance against a rush of redemptions by the public. In a rising market, the opposite effect is felt as advancing prices automatically reduce the proportion of cash, sales increase, and fund managers are under tremendous pressure to capitalize on the bull market by being fully invested.

One of the drawbacks of this approach is that mutual fund cash data did, by and large, remain above the 9.5 percent level between 1978 and 1990 and lost a lot of validity as a timing device during this period. It is true that the market was in a rising trend, but one of the functions of an indicator of this nature is to warn of setbacks such as the 1980 and 1981–1982 bear markets, not to mention the 1987 crash.

One way around this problem, originally devised by Norman Fosback of Market Logic, is to subtract the prevailing level of short-term interest rates from the cash percentage levels themselves. In this way, the incentive for portfolio managers to hold cash due to high interest rates is neutralized. This adjustment to the cash/assets ratio is shown in Chart 29.12. It is a definite improvement on the raw data, but unfortunately, it, too, fails to explain the 1987 crash.

A final alternative, devised by Ned Davis Research, compares switch fund cash and mutual fund managers' cash to total mutual fund assets. This series is also adjusted for interest rates and appears to offer the best results of all. The labeled buy (B) and sell (S) signals in Chart 29.13 are generated when this series crosses below the lower dashed line; they remain in force until it crosses above the upper dashed (selling) line.

Margin Debt

Trends in margin debt are probably better classified as flow-of-funds indicators, but since the trend and level of margin debt are also good indications of investor confidence (or lack thereof), they are discussed in this section.

Margin debt is money borrowed from brokers and bankers using securities as collateral. The credit is normally used for the purchase of equities. At the beginning of a typical stock market cycle, margin debt is relatively low; it begins to rise very shortly after the final bottom in equity prices. As prices rise, margin traders as a group become more confident, taking on additional debt in order to leverage larger stock positions.

CHART 29.12 DJIA, 1965–2013, and Cash/Asset Ratios

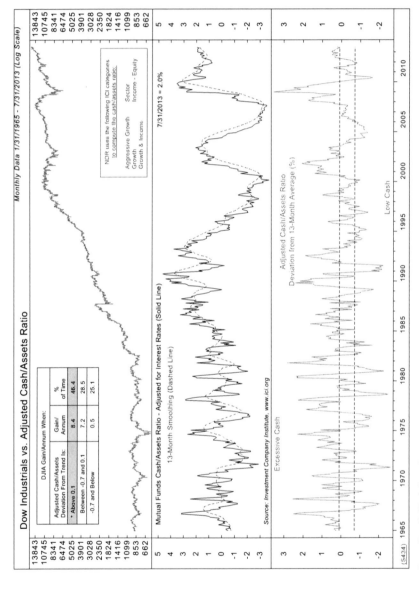

Source: From Ned Davis Research.

CHART 29.13 S&P Composite, 1965–2013, and a Switch Fund Cash/Asset Ratio

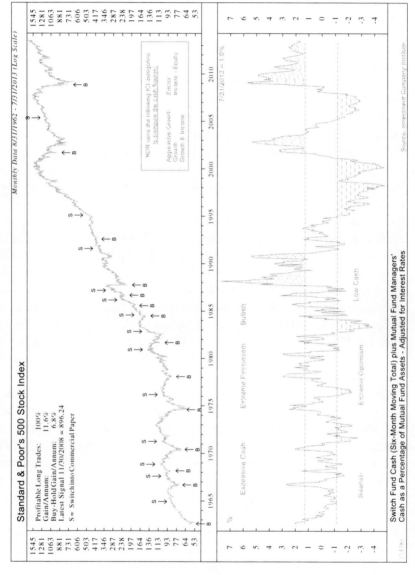

Monthly Data 8/31/1962 - 7/31/2013 (Log Scale)

Standard & Poor's 500 Stock Index

Profitable Long Trades: 100%
Gain/Annum: 11.6%
Buy-Hold Gain/Annum: 6.8%
Latest Signal 11/30/2008 = 896.24

S = Switch into Commercial Paper

NDR uses the following ICI categories to compute the cash figures:
Aggressive Growth   Sector
Growth   Income - Equity
Growth & Income

Excessive Cash

Extreme Pessimism)   Bullish

Bearish

Extreme Optimism

Low Cash

7/31/2013 = 1.9%

Source: Investment Company Institute

Switch Fund Cash (Six-Month Moving Total) plus Mutual Fund Managers'
Cash as a Percentage of Mutual Fund Assets - Adjusted for Interest Rates

Source: From Ned Davis Research.

625

During a primary uptrend, margin debt is a valuable source of new funds for the stock market. The importance of this factor can be appreciated when it is noted that margin debt increased almost tenfold between 1974 and 1987. The difference between stock purchased for cash and stock bought on margin is that margined stock must, at some point, be sold in order to pay off the debt. On the other hand, stock purchased outright can theoretically be held indefinitely. During stock market declines, margin debt reverses its positive role and becomes an important source of stock supply.

This occurs for four reasons. First, the sophistication of margin-oriented investors is relatively superior to that of other market participants. When this group realizes that the potential for capital gains has greatly diminished, a trend of margin liquidation begins. Margin debt has flattened or declined within 3 months of the vast majority of the 14 stock market peaks since 1932.

Second, primary stock market peaks are invariably preceded by rising interest rates, which in turn increase the carrying cost of margin debt, therefore making it less attractive to maintain.

Third, since 1934 the Federal Reserve Board (the "Fed") has been empowered to set and vary margin requirements, which specify the amount that can be lent by a broker or bank to customers for the purpose of holding securities. This measure was considered necessary in view of the substantial expansion of margin debt that occurred in the late 1920s. The liquidation of this debt pyramid contributed to the severity of the 1929–1932 bear market. When stock prices have been rising strongly for a period of time, speculation develops, often resulting in a sharp rise in margin debt. Sensing that things could get out of control at this stage, the Fed raises the margin requirement, which has the effect of reducing the buying power of the general public from what it might otherwise have been. Normally, it takes several margin-requirement changes to significantly reduce the buying power of these speculators. This is because the substantial advance in the price of stocks—which was responsible for the requirements being raised in the first place—normally creates additional collateral at a rate that is initially sufficient to offset the rise in reserve requirements.

Fourth, the collateral value of the securities used as a basis for the margin debt falls as stock prices decline. The margin speculator is faced with the option of putting up more money or selling stock in order to pay off the debt. At first, the margin call process is reasonably orderly, as most traders have a sufficient cushion of collateral to protect them from the initial drop in prices. Alternatively, those who are undermargined often choose to put up additional collateral or cash. Toward the end of a bear market, prices fall more rapidly, and this unnerving process, combined with the unwillingness or inability of margin customers to come up with additional collateral, triggers a rush of margin calls. This adds substantially to the supply of stock that must be sold, regardless of price. The self-feeding downward spiral of forced liquidation continues until margin debt has contracted to a more manageable level.

Most people think that the level of margin debt is the most important way to interpret this data. It is true that the higher the level, the greater the market's vulnerability when the numbers begin to contract. Perhaps a better way to express this statistic is to express the level of debt as a percentage of outstanding market capitalization. That way, the true vulnerability of the market would be represented in a more proportionate way. However, I believe that *it is the trend of margin debt that is all important* because trend reversals signal whether traders are confident, i.e., willing to take on more debt, or pessimistic, i.e., liquidating it. For this reason, margin debt is a useful indicator when expressed in relation to its 12-month MA, as shown in Chart 29.14.

Crossovers offer confirmation of major trend reversals. Most of the time, this relationship is reliable, but it does encounter whipsaws from time to time, as you can see from the ellipses.

CHART 29.14 S&P Composite, 1980–2012, and NYSE Margin Debt

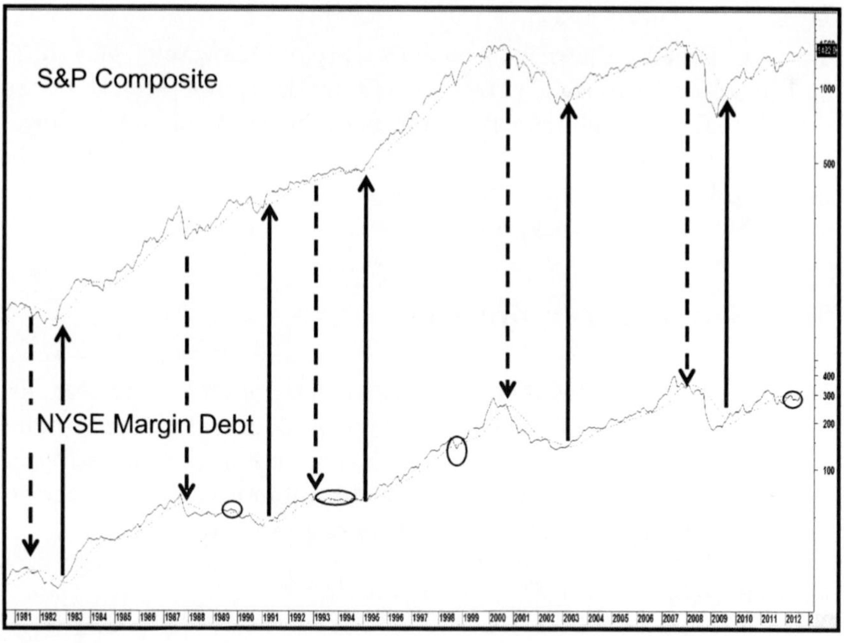

Source: From pring.com

CHART 29.15 S&P Composite, 1962–2012, and NYSE Margin Debt Momentum

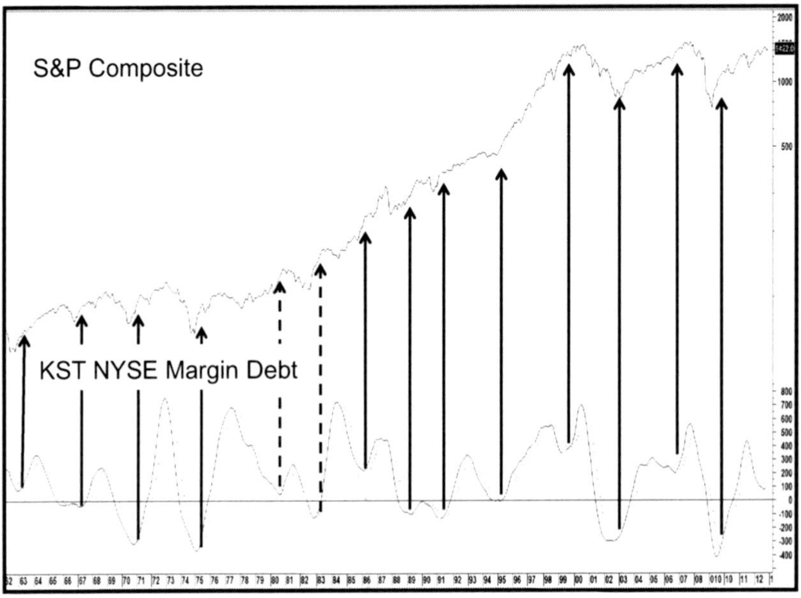

Source: From pring.com

An alternative, shown in Chart 29.15, is to plot a Know Sure Thing (KST) for margin debt (a moving-average convergence divergence [MACD] or stochastic could also be substituted) and use the positive 9-month MA crossovers as buy signals. As you can see, this technique has been pretty successful, but the two dashed arrows remind us that in technical analysis the probabilities are with us but never reach that perfect holy grail level of 100 percent.

Sentiment Using Option Data

Sentiment indicators based on short-selling data appear to have been distorted in recent years, in part because of the introduction of listed options and futures. The other side of the coin is that options can themselves be used as a basis for the construction of sentiment indicators. Their performance is far from perfect, but definitely worth consideration.

Put/Call Ratio

Perhaps the most widely followed option-derived indicator is the one that measures the ratio of the volume of puts to the volume of calls. A *put* gives an investor or trader the option to *sell* a specific stock index or commodity at a predetermined price over a specified period. In effect, the purchaser of a put is betting that the price of the underlying asset will go down. This is a form of short sale in which the trader's risk is limited to the cost of the put. (The risk on a short sale is theoretically unlimited.)

A *call*, on the other hand, is a bet that the underlying asset will rise in price. It gives a purchaser the option to *buy* a security at a predetermined price over a specified period.

It is normal for call volume to outstrip that of puts, and so the put/call ratio invariably trades below the 1.0 or (100) level. This indicator measures the swings in sentiment between the bulls and the bears. In theory, the lower the ratio, the more bullish the crowd and the more likely the market is to decline, and vice versa. A low ratio means that very few people are buying puts relative to calls, whereas a high one indicates that a larger number of traders than normal are betting that the market will go down.

For stock market data, a good source is the Chicago Board Options Exchange (CBOE) web site (www.CBOE.com), where it's possible to download historical data. My preference is for the Total Exchange Volume put/call data, as it is all encompassing. It is also possible to obtain other breakdowns such as indexes, equity volume, and so forth.

A 5-day MA of the ratio is shown in Chart 29.16.

Readings in excess of 125 seem to offer good indications of when pessimism has reached an extreme. Sell signals are not as prescient, and Chart 29.17 shows that they tend to end up with negative divergences rather than reversals from an extreme level.

Negative divergences appear at B, C, and D. A positive one can be observed at A. We also see a positive divergence at the 2009 bottom in Chart 29.18.

This one shows a different approach, with a 35-day smoothing of a 25-day MA of the raw data. The arrows flag reversals from overextended levels, which have had limited success. The two dotted arrows between 2004 and 2008 show how the bull market high was preceded by a series of weaker and weaker peaks in the ratio. Conversely, the two solid arrows a couple of years later flag a positive setup.

The VIX

The Market Volatility Indicator, or VIX, is a trademarked ticker symbol for the Chicago Board Options Exchange Market Volatility Index, a popular measure of the implied volatility of S&P 500 index options. It is often referred to as the fear index and represents one measure of the market's expectation of stock market volatility over the next 30-day period. The VIX is quoted

CHART 29.16 NYSE Composite, 2007–2010, and a CBOE Put/Call Ratio

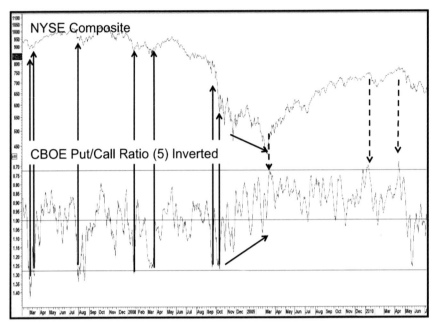

Source: From pring.com

CHART 29.17 NYSE Composite, 2007–2010, and a CBOE Put/Call Ratio Showing Divergences

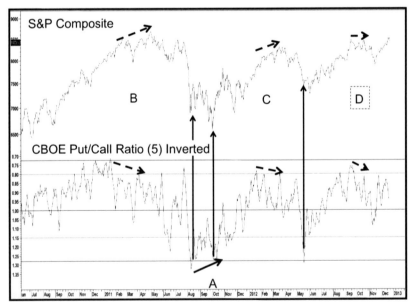

Source: From pring.com

CHART 29.18 NYSE Composite, 2004–2012, and a CBOE Put/Call Ratio Showing Divergences

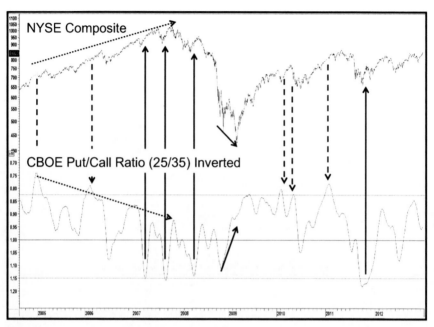

Source: From pring.com

as a percentage estimating the implied volatility of the market, which is the expected annualized movement of the S&P 500 over the next 30 days.

When prices are trending steadily upwards, there is generally a declining level of volatility as complacency sets in. Conversely, when a market is falling, a growing level of fear results in an expanding trend of volatility. As a contrarian indicator, the higher the VIX, the more bullish the market is and conversely, the lower the VIX, the more bearish the market is. Consequently, Charts 29.19 and 29.20 plot this indicator inversely so that its fluctuations generally match that of the market in terms of direction. Chart 29.19 indicates one use of the VIX with the aid of positive and negative divergences as the human emotions of greed and fear appear to lead prices.

Chart 29.20 uses the trendline technique with great effectiveness. This seems to be the best approach because the constant fluctuations of the indicator produce difficulties for moving-average and smoothed momentum techniques. Occasionally, the smoothing approach works very well. However, the results are so erratic that one needs to be very careful in utilizing it.

CHART 29.19 S&P Composite, 1990–2012, and the VIX

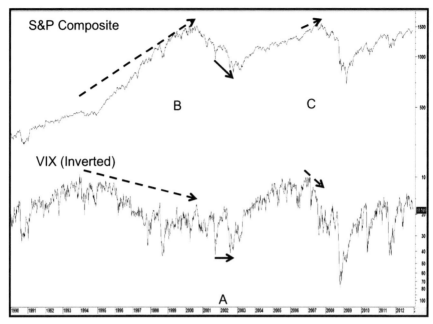

Source: From pring.com

CHART 29.20 S&P Composite, 2006–2012, and the VIX Showing Trendline Violations

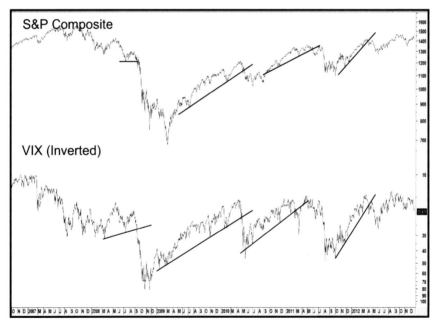

Source: From pring.com

Fundamental Indicators: One of the Best Indications of Sentiment

We saw in Chapter 23 (Chart 23.2) how the Shiller price/earnings ratio has fluctuated in gigantic swings in the last 100 years or so and that these movements were associated with changes in crowd psychology. At major market peaks, investors were willing to pay a huge price for equities, with a P/E generally in excess of 22.5, whereas this investment gauge typically bottomed in the 7 to 8 area. If investors were willing to pay high prices at peaks, it was because they were confident that the good times would continue to roll. On the other hand, fear at secular lows was so pervasive that they demanded bargains at fire sale prices.

We see the same thing with dividend yields, where low yields, less than 3 percent, are tolerated at peaks, but high yields of 6 percent to 7 percent become the order of the day at market bottoms because of the perceived risk and desire to be compensated for it.

Chart 29.21 compares the S&P to an inversely plotted 24-month rate of change (ROC) of the yield. The arrows show that peaks in this momen-

CHART 29.21 S&P Composite, 1950–2012, and Inverted Dividend Momentum

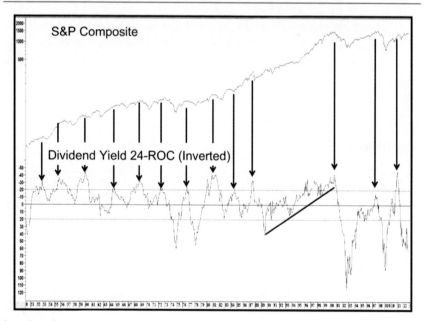

Source: From pring.com

tum indicator usually coincide with those of the market. The action in the mid- to late 1990s shows how optimism, as measured by this particular indicator, reached excessive levels and remained there for an extended period.

A Market's Reaction to News

Another extremely important, though imprecise, approach to appraisal of market sentiment is to observe the reaction of any market to news events, especially unexpected ones. This is a helpful exercise, since markets look ahead and factor all foreseeable events into the price structure. If a news event that would normally be expected to move the price does not do so, the likelihood is that all the news—good or bad—is already reflected in the price.

A classic example developed at the end of 1988 when the insider stock scandals began to appear, starting with the indictment of Denis Levine and Ivan Boesky. Under normal circumstances, the market would have been expected to sell off. But in this instance, it stalled for a while and then rallied sharply.

The discount rate was raised in the spring of 1978. This should have been a signal to sell, but the market rallied on record volume. In this instance, the fact that new highs quickly outpaced new lows just after a bear market low should have been the technical tip-off that the underlying structure was pretty sound.

Countless examples could be cited for many stocks and markets, but the principle remains that if a price does not respond to news in the expected way, it is probably in the process of turning. Evaluation of this factor is very much a judgment call, but it can act as a useful adjunct to an appraisal of the other technical indicators.

Summary

1. Sentiment indicators are useful supplements to the trend-determining techniques described in other chapters. They should be used for the purpose of assessing the consensus view from which a contrary position can be taken.
2. Since many sentiment indicators are subject to institutional changes, it is mandatory to consider them as a group rather than relying on one or two indicators alone.

    Because of the close tie between sentiment and momentum indicators, the latter can be substituted when sentiment data are not available.

30

INTEGRATING CONTRARY OPINION AND TECHNICAL ANALYSIS

"The law of an organized or psychological crowd is mental unity. The individuals composing the crowd lose their conscious personality under the influence of emotion and are ready to act as one, directed by the low crowd intelligence."

—Thomas Templeton Hoyle

"In any case, regardless of our political leanings, we should remember that the job of a contrarian is to challenge those beliefs that we hold most dear—the very beliefs that, because of our loyalty to them, we are least likely to subject to critical scrutiny."

—Mark Hulbert, July 25, 2012, MarketWatch

Contrary Opinion Defined

Humphrey Neil put together his own ideas and experience and joined them with the writings of Charles Mackay (*Extraordinary Popular Delusions and the Madness of Crowds*), Gustav Le Bon (*The Crowd*), and Gabriel Tarde to form the theory of contrary opinion. Today, it is widely understood that since the "crowd" is wrong at major market turning points, the only game in town is to be a contrarian! Unfortunately, whenever a concept or theory becomes popular, the basic idea is often distorted. This means that those who have taken the theory on its face value and not taken the trouble to study Neil and other writers are probably on shaky ground.

Neil pointed out that the crowd is actually correct for substantial amounts of time. *It is at turning points that the majority get things wrong.*

This last idea is really the center to Neil's thinking. Once an opinion is formed, it is imitated by the majority until virtually everyone agrees that it is valid. As Neil (1980) put it, "When everyone thinks alike, everyone is likely to be wrong. When masses of people succumb to an idea, they often run off at a tangent because of their emotions. When people stop to *think* things through, they are very similar in their decisions."

The word "think" has been deliberately emphasized because the practice of contrary opinion is very much an art and not a science. To be a true contrarian, you need to study, be patient, be creative, and bring to the table widespread experience. Remember, no two market situations are ever identical because history may repeat, but it rarely repeats exactly. In effect, it's not as easy as saying, "Everyone else is bearish; therefore, I am bullish."

Perhaps the best definition of contrary opinion comes from the late John Schultz, who, in a timely bearish article in *Barron's* just prior to the 1987 crash wrote, "The guiding light of investment contrarianism is not that the majority view—the conventional, or received wisdom—is always wrong. Rather, it's that the majority opinion tends to solidify into a *dogma* while its basic premises begin to lose their original *validity* and so become progressively more *mispriced* in the marketplace."

Three words have been emphasized because they encapsulate the three prerequisites of forming a contrary opinion. First, the original concept solidifies into a dogma. Second, it loses its validity and a new factor or series of factors comes into play. Finally, the crowd moves to an extreme, as reflected in a gross overvaluation. What he is saying is that at the start of a trend a few far-seeing individuals anticipate an alternative scenario or outcome to that being promoted by the majority. Later, as prices rise, others are persuaded that the scenario is valid. Then, as the trend extends, more and more people join the camp, perhaps being persuaded as much by the rising prices as the concept itself. Eventually, the concept or premise becomes a dogma so that everyone accepts it as gospel. By now, though, it has been so well discounted or factored into the price that the security or market in question is way overvalued. Even if the price is not overvalued, the concept begins to lose its original premise and a new scenario emerges. All those betting on the original one lose money as the market reverses to the downside.

These trends occur because investors tend to move as crowds and are subject to herd instincts. If left to their own devices, individuals isolated from their peers would tend to act in a far more rational way. Say, for example, you see stock prices starting to move up sharply after they had already moved up a lot. Even though you might know from your own experience that they cannot continue to go up forever, it would be difficult not to become caught up in the excitement, especially after they had rallied significantly from the level at which you first thought them irrationally high. Under such an environment it becomes very difficult to think independently from the accepted wisdom of the day.

> **Major Technical Principle** A good contrarian should not go contrary for the sake of going contrary, but should learn to think in reverse, to creatively come up with alternative scenarios to that of the crowd. In other words, try to figure out why the crowd may be wrong.

Why Are Crowds Irrational?

Neil wrote that there are several what he calls *social* laws that determine crowd psychology. These are as follows:

1. A crowd is subject to instincts that individuals acting independently would never succumb to.
2. People involuntarily follow the impulses of the crowd. (see the later section on why it is difficult to go contrary).
3. Contagion and imitation of the minority make individuals susceptible to suggestion, commands, customs, and emotional appeals.
4. When gathered as a group or crowd, people rarely reason or question, but follow blindly and emotionally what is suggested or asserted to them.

Why then is the crowd wrong at turning points? The reason is that when everyone holds the same bullish opinion, there is very little potential buying power left and very few people left who can perpetuate the trend. By the same token, if the market is *mispriced*, to quote John Schulz, other investment alternatives are becoming more and more attractive—little wonder that money soon flows from the overvalued, overbelieved situation to the more realistically priced one. The opposite would, of course, be true in a declining trend.

Take, for example, an economy deep in recession, business activity is declining rapidly, and layoffs and high unemployment are getting headlines in the nightly news. Stocks are extending their decline that began over a year ago, and the whole situation appears to be out of control in a self-feeding spiral. While everyone is looking down, it is the prerequisite of the contrarian to look up and ask the question, "What could go right?" This is where the alternative scenario comes in. Remember, people are rational. When they realize that hard times are coming, they adjust their plans accordingly. Businesses will cut excessive inventories, lay off workers, and pay off debts. Once this has been done, break-even points drop and businesses are in a great position to increase profits when the economy turns. All this economizing means that the demand for credit declines and so does its price—interest rates. Falling rates encourage consumers to go out and buy houses, and a new recovery gets underway. As Neil describes it, "In historic financial eras, it has been significant how, when conditions were slumping that, under the pall of discouragement, the underlying economics were righting themselves underneath to the ensuing revival and recovery."

The same is true in markets. No one is going to hold stocks if they think prices are in for a prolonged decline, so they sell. When all the selling is over, there is only one direction in which prices can go, and that's up! At that point, true contrarians have decided that enough is enough and that an alternative bullish outcome is likely and the underlying assumptions of the bear market are no longer valid.

Knowing when to go contrary is a key to the whole process because the crowd frequently moves to extremes well ahead of a market turning point. Many professionals knew the situation was getting out of hand in 1928 and in 1999 (for Internet stocks). In both cases, they had concluded that stocks were way overvalued and were discounting the hereafter. These opinions were correct, but their timing was early. Economic trends are often slow to reverse, and manias take prices well beyond reasonable valuations, often to ridiculous and irrational ones. In a sense, crowd psychology can be reflected graphically as a long-term oscillator, such as a rate of change (ROC) that moves to extraordinary levels not seen for decades. In normal times, a market turns when the indicator reaches its overbought level, but on rare occasions, the curve can run up to stratospheric levels. An example is shown in Chart 30.1 for the NASDAQ. The 18-month ROC in the lower panel moves up to a level dwarfing anything seen in the previous 20 years of trading history. Indeed, *it was twice as high as the best reading for the S&P Composite in 200 years of history.*

CHART 30.1 NASDAQ Composite, 1974–2001, and an 18-Month ROC

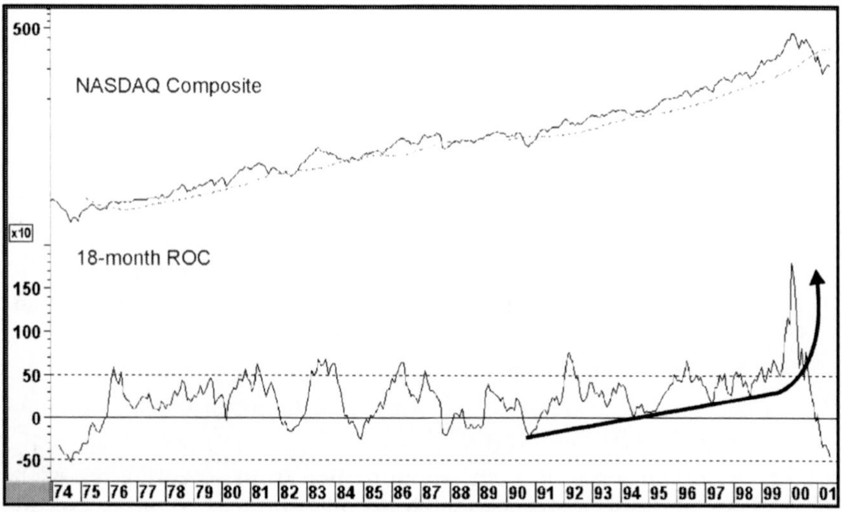

Source: From pring.com

If crowd sentiment is reflected in oscillators constructed from the price, then it follows that there are various levels or extremes to which crowds gravitate. The 1999 peak in the NASDAQ, the 1980 top in gold, and the 1929 peak are all examples of an extreme. However, since oscillators can be constructed from daily and weekly data, it follows that forming a contrary opinion is just as valid for shorter-term turning points. The difference is that the mood is not so all encompassing and intense as it is just prior to the bursting of a financial bubble.

Major Technical Principle Major turning points develop when the crowd moves to an overwhelming extreme. Short-term and intermediate-term turning points are associated with less intensive levels of crowd sentiment.

Bearing these comments in mind, it is now time to examine the kinds of signs that indicate when the crowd has moved to an extreme, either for small or large trends, and then see how technical analysis can be applied to such situations.

Why It Is Difficult to Go Contrary

Reading and learning about forming a contrary opinion is one thing, but actually applying it in the marketplace when your money is on the line is completely another. There are several reasons why it is not easy to take a position that is opposite to the majority:

1. It is very challenging for us to take an opposite view from those around us because of our need to conform.
2. If prices are rising sharply and we have already told friends of our reasons for being bearish, we are unlikely to continue in our contrarianism out of a fear of being ridiculed.
3. We often meet hostility when we go against the crowd.
4. There is always a tendency to extrapolate the past, from which we gain a sense of comfort.
5. A certain sense of security can be had from accepting the opinions of "experts" instead of having the confidence to think for ourselves. Chart 30.2 illustrates several quotations that three famous people probably wish they had never made. Never forget that most "experts" have a vested interest in the opinions they give publicly.

CHART 30.2 The S&P Composite, 1921–1935, and Market Comments

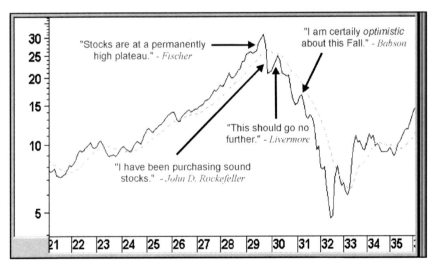

Source: From pring.com

6. We tend to believe that the establishment has all the answers. The United States' entry into Vietnam, the Soviets' into Afghanistan, and Neville Chamberlain's famous "peace in our time" speech just before the outbreak of World War II should make us think twice about this assumption.

Three Steps to Forming a Contrary Opinion

1. Figure Out What the Crowd Thinks

The first step is to try and get a fix on the consensus opinion of the market or individual security being monitored. If the crowd is not at an extreme, nothing can be done because we are only concerned with identifying potential trend reversals when crowd psychology has swung sharply in one direction or another. Bear in mind that the crowd is often right during a trend—it's at the turning point that the herd is almost always wrong. One method of gauging where the majority of market participants lie in their opinion is to refer to the sentiment indicators discussed in the previous chapter, or even an oscillator. Most of the time, these indicators are not telling us very much, but when they reach an extreme, a strong message is being given. Another possibility is to monitor valuations. If they are within the accepted norm, then there is little to be learned, but if they are approaching an extreme, then the crowd is giving us a valuable clue as to the way it is leaning.

Alternatively, a study of the media—particularly the financial media—can inform us of what people are thinking. If there is no clear-cut view, then there is not likely to be an extreme and there is little to be done.

However, as it becomes clear that a general consensus is forming and that consensus is approaching a dogma, it is then time to begin the creative process by thinking in reverse, and that involves the second step.

2. Form Alternative Scenarios

At this point, we know what the crowd thinks. It is up to us as true contrarians to come up with *plausible* reasons why it is likely to be wrong. In effect, we have to remove ourselves from the crowd and think in reverse. Such a process involves an understanding of the market we are watching. For example, Chart 30.3 shows the gold market at its secular peak in 1980.

CHART 30.3 Gold, 1970–1999

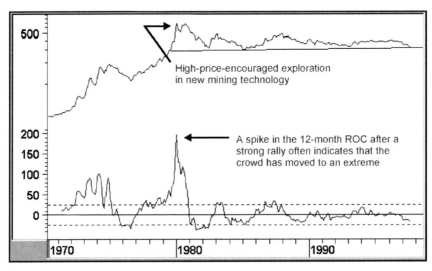

Source: From pring.com

At that time, the price had risen from obscurity when it first started to advance in 1968 to being quoted regularly on the nightly news. It seemed to the majority at the end of 1979 that inflation and gold prices would continue to rise forever. However, a realistic contrarian would have realized that the inflation would breed its own deflation as the rising trend of short-term interest rates, driven by rising commodity prices, would cause an economic recession. In addition, the high gold price would attract more mining activity and the adoption of more efficient technologies would enable the mining of higher-cost lodes. Once again, technical analysis can come to our rescue, as Chart 30.3 shows that the 12-month ROC for gold hit a generational extreme. Silver also had a huge run-up in this period from next to nothing to over $50. The talk was of a cornering of the market by Bunker Hunt and other operatives so that it appeared that the sky was the limit. In this instance, the contrarian may have come up with the scenario that a lot of silver had already been mined and was available in the form of silverware, which could easily be melted down and sold as silver bullion. As it turned out, the price was right and the silver market was flooded just at the time when high rates of interest caused margin liquidation in the silver pits.

Chart 30.4 shows bond yields and commodity prices. When yields are rising and it appears this trend will never end, an alternative scenario

CHART 30.4 Commodities and Bond Yields, 1970–1998

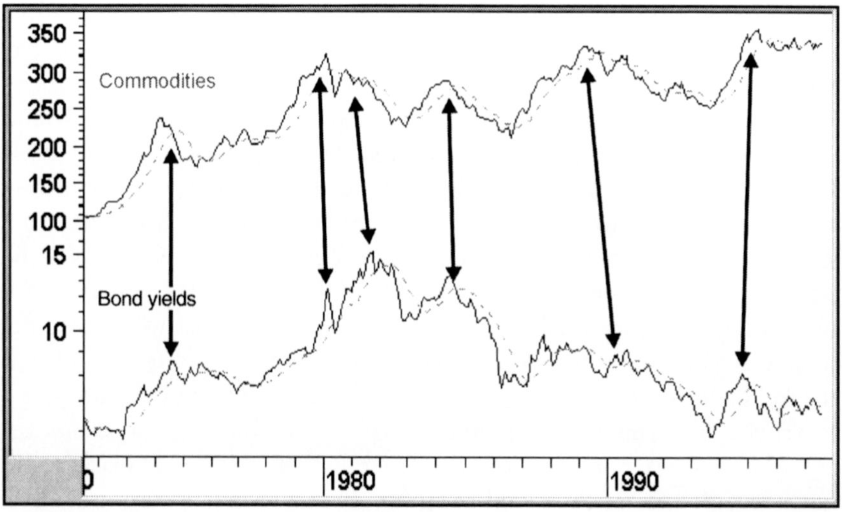

Source: From pring.com

is to use the knowledge that peaks in yields are often preceded by peaks in commodity prices, which in turn precedes a slow-down in economic activity. This is shown in the chart by the rightward sloping arrows. Thus, if it's possible to spot a top in industrial commodity prices, the alternative scenario of weaker business activity may well come to pass.

3. Figure Out When the Crowd Reaches an Extreme

When the crowd reaches an extreme the question is not usually whether, but when and by how much. In other words, when the crowd truly reaches an extreme, it is a forgone conclusion that the trend will continue. It is not even questioned by the crowd, only the *timing* and *amount* are in doubt. Such times are often associated with analysts making extreme forecasts that in the highly charged emotional atmosphere appear credible but that would previously have been greeted with mirth or great doubt.

Sentiment Indicators   Sentiment indicators, or long-term oscillators reaching an extreme, also represent one possibility for gauging that the crowd has reached an extreme.

The Media Sentiment indicators are not available for every market, so another useful exercise comes from a study of the popular and financial media. Most of the time, they are silent on financial markets or individual stocks, but when significant coverage appears, that is the time to pay attention. Major peaks and troughs are often signaled by cover stories in the popular and financial press. *Time, Newsweek, Businessweek,* and *The Economist* magazine are my particular favorites. Since many of these publications are going out of print due to technological developments, we will probably have to refer to their digital editions for such information. The more of them that give space to a particular market, the stronger the signal. It's not that the editors and writers of these magazines are idiots for publishing bear stories right at the low or bullish ones close to the absolute high. It lies more in the fact that they are journalists keeping the pulse of market conditions. As good journalists, it is their duty to give more space to articles when the emotions in and around the floors of the exchanges come close to reaching a crescendo. Generally speaking, cover stories are a fairly reliable indication of an impending turn, but they are not infallible, and often lead turning points by a week or so. As with any form of analysis, it's important to use a good dose of common sense. For example, there is the famous "Birth of the Bull" cover story in *Time* magazine several weeks from the 1982 market bottom (Chart 30.5). Just applying "contrary

CHART 30.5 S&P Composite, 1970–1999, and the Discount Rate

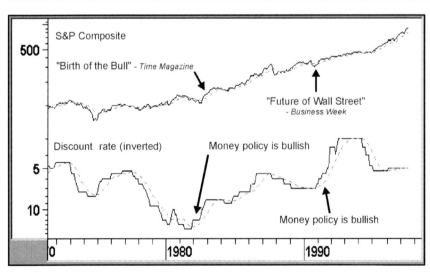

Source: From pring.com

opinion" blindly would have led to the conclusion that the bull market was over in the course of a few weeks. However, it is important to remember that it takes time for crowds to reach an extreme, as the long-term trend of rising prices adds more and more careless bulls to the fold. Also, bear markets are usually preceded by rising interest rates. In the fall of 1982 the Fed was following an easy money policy, not a tight one.

The exact opposite was true in 1990 (see Chart 30.5) when a *Businessweek* cover featured the troubled brokerage industry. In this instance, the prices of brokerage stocks had fallen sharply, but the Fed was engaged in an easy money policy, which is good for the equity market and certainly good for brokers, who get more underwriting fees and commissions in a bull market. In addition, the hard times they had just gone through would have resulted in substantially lowering their break-even points. Increased revenue from the bull market would then go straight to the bottom line.

One of the problems of cover stories is that the advent of electronic media is gradually sapping the life of their print brethren. *Newsweek,* which I referred to earlier, no longer has a print version. One substitute is to use Google Trends, where a graph similar to that shown in Chart 30.6*a* is displayed for a specific search. In this case, it was "gas prices." The various letters on the Google Search chart correspond to those on the price series

CHART 30.6*a* Google Search Gasoline Price(s)

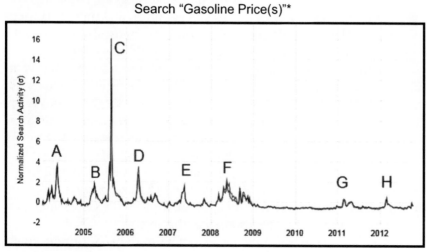

*Source: From Google Trends

CHART 30.6*b* U.S. Gasoline Prices, 2003–2012, and a Momentum Indicator

Source: From pring.com

in Chart 30.6*b*. Note that the intensity of the data does not necessarily correspond to the magnitude of the peak in gas prices and timing occasionally is early. That's why it's a good idea to also use an oscillator, such as the stochastic (24/15/10) featured in the lower panel of Chart 30.6*b*.

Charts 30.7*a* and *b* follow a similar path, but this time for a commodity price search. Here again, we note that extreme intensity does not translate into an extreme turning point. You can also see that points X and Y are the lowest during the search and Y certainly corresponds with a low (disinterest) in commodities. On the other hand, there seemed to be more interest in declining prices when the sharp 2008 decline was taking place. At the same time, interest was peaking momentum at B in Chart 30.7*b* and offered one of the lowest ROC readings in the whole 6-year period covered by the search. Combining sentiment in the form of the Google numbers with momentum paid off handsomely in this case.

Another way in which the media can point to major turning points is when it is possible to observe what I call a misfit story—when a heretofore "invisible" market is given the prominence it rarely, if ever, achieves.

CHART 30.7a Google Search Commodity Price(s)

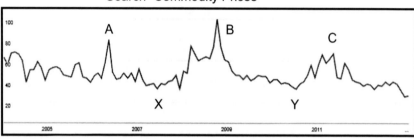

"Source: From Google Trends

CHART 30.7b CRB Spot Raw Industrials, 2005–2012, and a Momentum Indicator

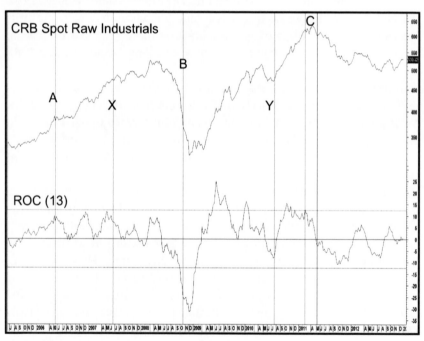

Source: From pring.com

For example, the financial media is always featuring stories on the stock or bond markets. That is normal and offering us no contrary bones. On the other hand, when we see a story in the popular press about an otherwise obscure market, then there is something to gnaw on. For example, in 1980, the sugar price peaked following a long and strong bull market. Close to the day of the high, the CBS Evening News led with a story on how traders were forecasting higher sugar prices. To my knowledge, sugar has never before or since been featured so prominently in the news. It was unusual and highly significant for the sugar market. Prominent stories in the U.S. press concerning specific "foreign" stock markets, currencies, etc., can also be valuable clues that these markets have reached an extreme. If you are long coffee, beware of media stories concerning food companies raising their price, as this unusual activity also tends to reflect major peaks.

Best-Selling Books   Another area to monitor is that of best-selling nonfiction books. If a financial book appears on the list, it is usually a sign that a particular market has attracted the attention of the majority and that the good or bad news has been fully discounted. Thus, Ravi Batra's book on the coming depression became a best-seller just after the 1987 crash, a classic sign of a bottom. The first edition of Adam Smith's *The Money Game* (Vintage, 1976) reached the same list just as the mutual fund boom was ending in late 1968. Perhaps the most unlikely of all was a book on money markets by William Donahue just as short-term interest rates were making a secular peak in 1981.

Politicians   A classic contrary indicator is the attitude of politicians, especially to bad news that is likely to adversely affect their election possibilities. Since politicians react to poll numbers and other trends in what we might term constituent psychology, they represent an excellent and reliable lagging indicator. They are the last to take action, and when they do, the next trend is usually underway. For instance, at the end of 1974, Gerald Ford introduced the famous W(in)I(nflation)N(ow) buttons, but consumer price inflation had, for all intents and purposes, peaked for that cycle. I remember watching the network news in the fall of 1981, right at the secular peak of interest rates. The news was full of stories of congressmen returning to Washington "determined to do something about high interest rates." They had earfuls of complaints from their constituents and were resolute to do something about it. The problem was that the economy was already weakening and rates had peaked. When politicians promote price controls, you can be fairly certain that the specific commodity is in the process of peaking. By the same token, when oil prices are spiking and politicians start to blame the "greedy speculators," it's time to liquidate and probably go short oil.

Unrealistic Valuations   A final pointer that the crowd has reached an extreme arises when a particular market reaches an historic level of over- or undervaluation (progressively more *mispriced* in John Schultz's definition). For example, it was reported that the real estate value of the emperor's palace in Tokyo was worth as much as all the land in California at the height of the Japanese real estate boom. In *Psychology and the Stock Market* (American Management Association, 1977), David Dreman noted that during the 1920s real estate boom in Florida, it was reported that there were 25,000 brokers in Miami, an equivalent of one in three of the population. This was not a valuation measure, but the statistic showed that things had clearly got out of hand. At one time in the 1990s tech boom, priceline.com, an online travel service, had a capitalization greater than the combined value of several of the airlines it represented. At its peak, the stock reached $160, but a year later it had fallen to just over $1.

Applying Technical Analysis

Since the crowd can and does move to an extreme well beyond normal experience, being early can be particularly harmful to one's financial health. This is where the integration of technical analysis and the theory of contrary opinion can be quite helpful. Let's consider a couple of examples. The Japanese bull market of the 1980s represents a classic mania where price earnings ratios and other valuation methods reached incredible extremes. The top had been called many times in the 1980s, but it never came. The crowd had clearly reached an extreme, but records continued to fall. In the end, the bubble was burst with the alternative scenario most likely to undo stock market bubbles—rising rates. Chart 30.8 shows that just after the 1990 top, both the Nikkei and Japanese short rates crossed their 12-month moving averages (MAs) for the first time in many years.

Both series also violated trendlines, thereby offering substantial technical evidence that the bubble had burst. Twenty-two years later, the Nikkei was still struggling at just over one-fourth of its 1990 high.

Charts 30.9 and 30.10 show two *Businessweek* cover stories in 1982 and 1984 concerning the bond market. The fact that the bond market should be featured so prominently after prices had fallen significantly was a sign that the crowd was at or close to an extreme. The next step was to appraise the technical position to see if there were any signs of a reversal. In the 1982 case, the 18-month ROC in Chart 30.10 had already completed and broken out of a massive 4-year base. Later on, the price broke out as well. This secondary breakout took place several months later, but it's

CHART 30.8 The Nikkei and Japanese Short-Term Interest Rates, 1982–1997

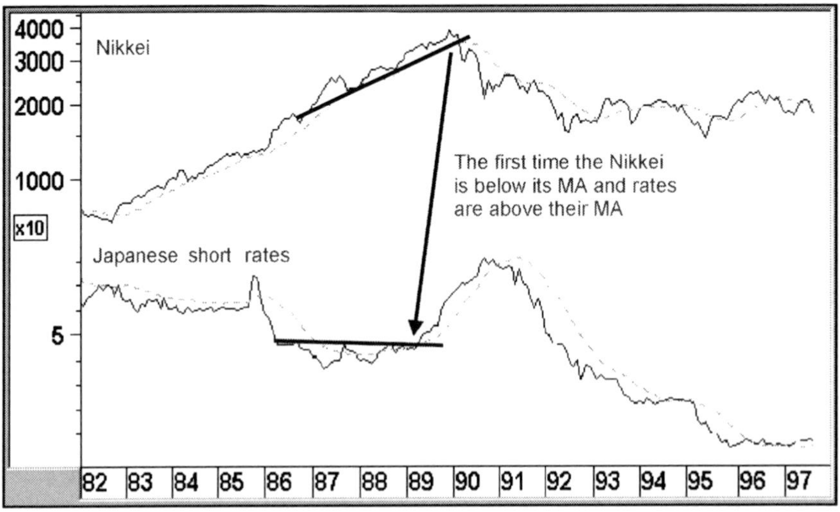

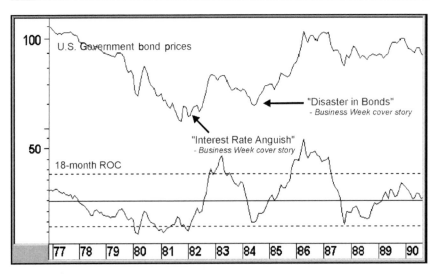

Source: From pring.com

important to remember that we are looking at the reversal of an extremely long trend and those sorts of things take time.

In 1984, the "Disaster in Bonds" cover story cumulated a 2-year decline. In this instance, the ROC was close to an extreme oversold condition

CHART 30.9 U.S. Government Bond Prices, 1977–1990, and an 18-Month ROC

Source: From pring.com

CHART 30.10 U.S. Government Bond Prices, 1977–1990, and an 18-Month ROC

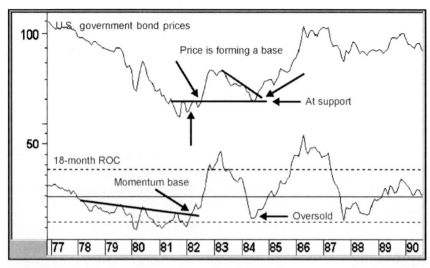

Source: From pring.com

and the price had reached support in the form of the extended trendline marking the previous breakout. The bear market trendline break was the triggering mechanism that indicated the crowd had now moved away from the bearish extreme and was now trending in the opposite direction. In both situations, the cover stories would have indicated that the bearish arguments were now well understood and discounted and that the trendline breaks were the signals that it was time to play the contrary "card."

Distinguishing Between a Short-Term or Long-Term Turning Point

Before we close our discussion on contrary opinion, it is important to understand that the crowd can move to a smaller, less intense level of extreme. This type of sentiment is associated with a price reversal of a short-term or intermediate-term nature. An example might be a 2- to 3-week run-up in the corn price, cumulating in a lead article in the commodities section in the *Wall Street Journal*. Such features are not uncommon—after all, some commodity is featured every day. The idea here is that when a commodity gains such attention, it usually comes after it has experienced a significant rally or reaction. The story develops because of excitement on the floor for that particular commodity and is reflective of the crowd reaching a short-term extreme. When confirmed by a technical indicator such as a 1- or 2-day price pattern, a trendline break, or a reliable moving-average crossover, this contrary position is usually well rewarded.

Another example might come from a recently released government employment report which indicates that the economy is stronger than most traders expected. Since bond prices react unfavorably to good economic news, they could sell off sharply. Speculators now reverse sentiment from positive to a state of discouragement. Not only are bond prices declining, but rumors of a pick-up in inflation causes prices to fall even further and sentiment to become even more bearish. The consensus mood among traders is now quite black. However, the chances are that this is only a small top. The alternative scenario in this case is to look through the gloom and examine the trend of employment and other economic numbers to see if the recent report was likely to be an aberration.

Summary

1. During the unfolding of a trend, the crowd is usually right. It is at the turning points that it is wrong.
2. Three prerequisites for justifying a contrary position are the original premise becomes a dogma, the premise loses its validity, and the market becomes progressively more mispriced.
3. Three steps to forming a contrary opinion are figuring out what the crowd is thinking, coming up with alternative scenarios, and determining when the crowd reaches an extreme.
4. It is difficult to go contrary in practice because of competing forces around us.
5. When the crowd reaches an extreme, the question is not whether, but when and by how much.
6. Signs that the crowd is at an extreme include cover stories, best-selling books, reaction by politicians, extremes in sentiment indicators, and gross over- or undervaluations.
7. Since mass psychology can move well beyond the norm, technical analysis should be used as a triggering device for signaling when the crowd is backing off from a bullish or bearish extreme.
8. Contrary analysis should be used as one more indicator in the weight-of-the-evidence approach.

31

WHY INTEREST RATES AFFECT THE STOCK MARKET

In this chapter we will examine why changes in the level of interest rates are an important influence on equity prices and apply technical analysis to credit market yields and prices.

Changes in interest rates affect the stock market for four basic reasons. First, fluctuations in the price charged for credit has a major influence on the level of economic activity and, therefore, indirectly on corporate profits.

Second, because interest charges affect the bottom line, changes in the level of rates have a direct influence on corporate profits and, therefore, the price investors are willing to pay for equities.

Third, movements in interest rates alter the relationships between competing financial assets, of which the bond/equity market relationship is the most important.

Fourth, a substantial number of stocks are purchased on borrowed money (known as *margin debt*). Changes in the cost of carrying that debt (i.e., the interest rate) influence the desire or ability of investors and speculators to maintain these margined positions. Because changes in interest rates usually lead stock prices, it is important to be able to identify primary trend reversals in the credit markets.

The Indirect Effect of Interest Rate Changes on Corporate Profits

Perhaps the most important effect of interest rate changes on equity prices comes from the fact that tight monetary policy associated with rising rates adversely affects business conditions, whereas falling rates stimulate the economy.

Given time, most businesses can adjust to higher rates, but when rates change quickly and unexpectedly, unless cash flows are extraordinary, businesses have to curtail expansion plans, cut inventories, etc., and this has a debilitating effect on the economy and, therefore, on corporate profits. Higher rates and smaller profits mean lower price earnings multiples and, therefore, lower stock prices.

When central banks become concerned about the economy, they lower short-term rates and a reverse effect takes hold.

The Direct Effect of Interest Rate Changes on Corporate Profits

Interest rates affect profits in two ways. First, almost all companies borrow money to finance capital equipment and inventory, so the cost of money, i.e., the interest rate they pay, is of great importance. Second, a substantial number of sales are, in turn, financed by borrowing. The level of interest rates, therefore, has a great deal of influence on the ability and willingness of customers to make additional purchases. One of the most outstanding examples is the automobile industry, in which both producers and consumers are very heavily financed. The capital-intensive utility and transportation industries are also large borrowers, as are all the highly leveraged construction and housing industries.

Interest Rates and Competing Financial Assets

Interest rate changes also have an impact upon the relative appeal of various asset classes. The most significant relationship is that of stocks to bonds. For example, at any point in time there is a balance between them, according to investors. However, if interest rates rise faster than dividend growth, bonds will become more attractive and, at the margin, money will flow out of stocks into bonds. Stocks will then fall in value until the relationship is perceived by investors to be more reflective of the higher level of interest rates.

> **Major Technical Principle** It is not the level of rates that is important, but their rate of change, because that has the greater influence on profits and equity prices.

The effect of interest rate changes on any particular stock group will depend upon the yield obtained combined with the prospects for profit growth. Most sensitive will be preferred shares, which are primarily held for their dividends and which do not generally permit benefit from profit growth. Utility stocks are also highly sensitive to interest rate movements since they are held as much for their current dividend yields as for potential growth. Changes in the level of interest rates, therefore, have a very direct effect on utility stocks. On the other hand, companies in a dynamic stage of growth are usually financed by corporate earnings and for this reason pay smaller dividends. These stocks are less affected by fluctuations in the cost of money, since they are purchased in anticipation of fast profit growth and future yield rather than an immediate dividend return.

Interest Rates and Margin Debt

Margin debt is money loaned by brokers for which securities are pledged as collateral. Normally, such borrowing is used for the acquisition of equities, but sometimes, margin debt is used for purchases of consumer items, such as automobiles. The effect of rising interest rates on both forms of margin debt is similar in that rising rates increase the cost of carrying the debt. There is, therefore, a reluctance on the part of investors to take on additional debt as its cost rises. When service charges become excessive, stocks are liquidated and the debt is paid off. Rising interest rates have the effect of increasing the supply of stock put up for sale with consequent downward pressure on prices.

Bond Yields versus Bond Prices

When a bond is brought to market by a borrower, it is issued at a fixed interest rate (coupon), which is paid over a predetermined period. At the end of this maturity period, the issuer agrees to repay the face amount. Since bonds are normally issued in denominations of $1,000 (known as *par*), this figure usually represents the amount to be repaid at the end of the (loan) period. Because bond prices are quoted in percentage terms, par ($1,000) is expressed as 100. Normally, bonds are issued and redeemed at par, but they are occasionally issued at a discount (i.e., at less than 100) or at a premium (i.e., at a price greater than 100).

While it is usual for a bond to be issued and redeemed at 100, over the life of the bond, its price can fluctuate quite widely because interest rate levels are continually changing. Assume that a 20-year bond is issued with a 4 percent interest rate (coupon) at par (i.e., 100); if interest rates rise to 5 percent, the bond paying 4 percent will be difficult to sell because investors have the opportunity to earn a return of 5 percent. The only way in which the 4 percent bondholder can find a buyer is to reduce the price to a level that would compensate a prospective purchaser for the 1 percent differential in interest rates. The new owner would then earn 4 percent in interest together with some capital appreciation. When spread over the remaining life of the bond, this capital appreciation would be equivalent to the 1 percent loss in interest. This combination of coupon rate and averaged capital appreciation is known as the *yield.* If interest rates decline, the process is reversed, and the 4 percent bond becomes more attractive in relation to prevailing rates, so that its price rises. The longer the maturity of the bond, the greater will be its price fluctuation for any given change in the general level of interest rates.

The Structure of the Debt Markets

The credit markets can be roughly divided into two main areas, known as the *short end* and the *long end.* The short end, more commonly known as the *money market,* relates to interest rates charged for loans up to 1 year in maturity. Normally, movements at the short end lead those at the longer end, since short rates are more sensitive to trends in business conditions and changes in Federal Reserve policy. Money-market instruments are issued by the federal, state, and local governments as well as corporations.

The long end of the market consists of bonds issued for a period of at least 10 years. Debt instruments are also issued for periods of between 1 and 10 years, and are known as *intermediate-term* bonds.

The bond market (i.e., the long end) has three main sectors, which are classified as to issuer. These are the U.S. government, tax-exempt (i.e., state and local governments), and corporate issuers.

The financial status of the tax-exempt and corporate sectors varies from issuer to issuer, and the practice of rating each one for quality of credit has, therefore, become widespread. The best possible credit rating is known as AAA; next in order are AA, A, BAA, BA, BB, etc. The higher the quality, the lower the risk undertaken by investors, and, therefore, the lower the interest rate required to compensate them. Since the credit of the federal government is higher than that of any other issuer, it can sell bonds at a relatively low interest rate. The tax-exempt sector (i.e., bonds issued by state and local governments) is able to issue bonds with lower rates than would normally be the case, in view of the favored tax treatment assigned to the holders of such issues.

Most of the time, price trends of the various sectors are similar, but at major cyclical turns some will lag behind others because of differing demand and supply conditions in each sector. Also, at the mature part of the cycle, when confidence is running high, we find that investors shrug off their fears of default in the search for higher yields obtained from lower-quality instruments.

Debt and Equity Markets

Bond and money-market prices typically top out ahead of the equity market at cyclical peaks. The lead characteristics and degree of deterioration in credit market prices required to adversely affect equities differ from cycle to cycle. There are no hard-and-fast rules that relate the size of an equity decline to the time period separating the peaks of bond and equity prices. For example, short-term and long-term prices peaked 18 and 17 months, respectively, ahead of the 1959 bull market high in the Dow. This compared with 11 months and 1 month for the 1973 bull market peak. While the deterioration in the bond and money markets was sharper and longer in the 1959 period, the Dow, on a monthly average basis, declined only 13 percent, as compared to 42 percent in the 1973–1974 bear market.

> **Major Technical Principle** Virtually every cyclical stock market peak in the last 100 years was preceded by, or has coincided with, a peak in both the long and the short ends of the credit markets.

A further characteristic of cyclical peaks is that high-quality bonds (such as Treasury or AAA corporate bonds) tend to decline in price ahead of poorer-quality issues (such as BAA-rated bonds). This has been true of most every cyclical turning point since 1919. This lead characteristic of high-quality bonds results from two factors. First, in the latter stages of an economic expansion, private-sector demand for financing accelerates. Commercial banks, the largest institutional holders of government securities, are the lenders of last resort to private borrowers. As the demand for financing accelerates against a less accommodative central bank posture, banks step up their sales of these and other high-grade investments and reinvest the money in more profitable bank loans. This sets off a ripple effect, down the yield curve itself and also to lower-quality issues. At the same time these pressures are pushing yields on high-quality bonds upward and are also reflecting buoyant business conditions, which encourage investors to become less cautious. Consequently, investors are willing to overlook the relatively conservative yields on high-quality bonds in favor of the more rewarding lower-rated debt instruments; thus, for a temporary period, these bonds are rising while high-quality bonds are falling.

At bear market bottoms, these relationships are similar in that good-quality bonds lead both debt instruments and poorer-quality equities. These lead characteristics are not quite as pronounced as at primary peaks and, occasionally, bond and stock prices trough out simultaneously. The trend of interest rates is, therefore, a useful benchmark for identifying stock market bottoms.

Charts 31.1a, b, and c show that primary stock market peaks and troughs between 1919 and 2013 were almost always preceded by a reversal in the trend of short-term interest rates. This is indicated by the solid lines for the peaks and dashed ones for the troughs, almost all of which slope to the right. Note that the interest rate series in the lower panels have been plotted inversely so that their movements are consistent with equity prices.

CHART 31.1a S&P Composite, 1914–1950, and Short-Term Interest Rates

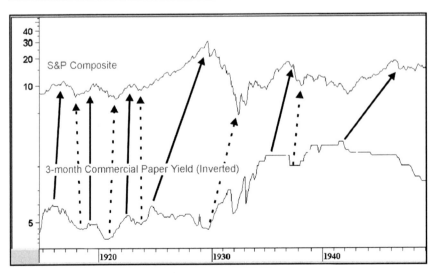

CHART 31.1*b* S&P Composite, 1956–1976, and Short-Term Interest Rates

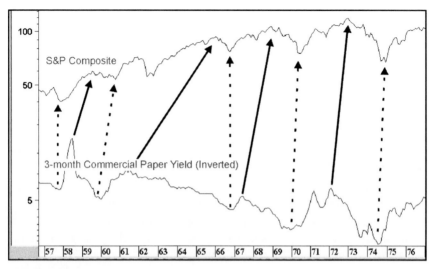

Source: From pring.com

CHART 31.1*c* S&P Composite, 1976–2012, and Short-Term Interest Rates

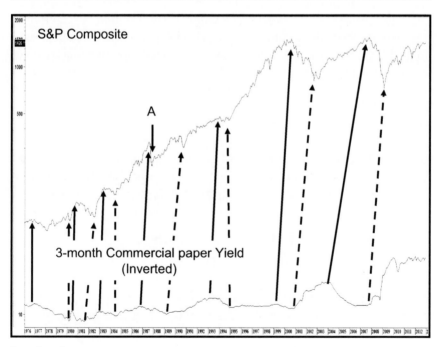

Source: From pring.com

A declining phase in interest rates is not in itself a sufficient condition to justify the purchase of equities. For example, in the 1919–1921 bear market, money-market prices reached their lowest point in June 1920, 14 months ahead of, or 27 percent above, the final stock market bottom in August 1921. An even more dramatic example occurred during the 1929–1932 debacle when money-market yields reached their highs in October 1929. Over the next 3 years, the discount rate was cut in half, but stock prices lost 85 percent of their October 1929 value. The reason for such excessively long lead times was that these periods were associated with a great deal of debt liquidation and many bankruptcies. Even the sharp reduction in interest rates was not sufficient to encourage consumers and businesses to spend, which is the normal cyclical experience. Although falling interest rates alone do not constitute a sufficient basis for an expectation that stock prices will reverse their cyclical decline, they are a necessary part of that basis. On the other hand, a continued trend of rising rates has in the past proved to be bearish.

There was one notable exception to the interest rate leading equity price rule and that developed in 1977 when the peak in equities preceded that of money-market prices. The 1987 low in equities at point A in Chart 31.1c was also out of sequence, most probably because the 1987 decline was not associated with business cycle weakness, as is normally the case.

The principles of trend determination apply as well to the credit markets as to the stock market. In fact, trends in yields and prices are often easier to identify, since the bulk of the transactions in credit instruments are made on the basis of money flows caused by a need to finance and an ability to purchase. Consequently, while emotions are still important from the point of view of determining the short-term trends of bond prices, money flow is generally responsible for a smoother cyclical trend than is normally the case with equities. That statement was true for most of the twentieth century, but with the advent of futures, bond and money-market participants have become more sophisticated in the discounting mechanism. Even so, cash or spot yields at the short end are still very much influenced by economic forces.

Relating Changes in Interest Rates to Equity Market Turning Points

I have already established that interest rates lead stock prices at virtually every cyclical turning. However, the leads, lags, and level of interest rates required to affect equity prices differ in each cycle. For example, 1962 experienced a sharp market setback with short-term interest rates at 3 percent.

On the other hand, stock prices were very strong in the latter part of 1980, yet rates never fell below 9 percent.

Earlier it was stated that it is not the level of interest rates that affects equity prices, but their rate of change (ROC). One method for determining when a change in rates is sufficient to influence equities is to overlay a smoothed ROC of short-term interest rates with a similar measure for equity prices. This is shown in Chart 31.2. Buy and sell signals are triggered when the interest rate momentum crosses above and below that of the Standard & Poor's (S&P) Composite. These signals are indicated by the arrows on the chart, dashed for sell and solid for buy.

We know that the stock market can rally even in the face of rising rates, but this relationship tells us when the rise in rates is greater than that of equities, and vice versa. At times, this approach gives some very timely signals, as happened at the 1973 market peak. At others, it is not so helpful. For example, it failed to signal the 1978–1980 rally. Even so, it is interesting to note that the total return on equities and cash during the 2-year period

CHART 31.2 S&P Composite, 1967–2012, and Equity Compared to Short-Term Interest Rate Momentum

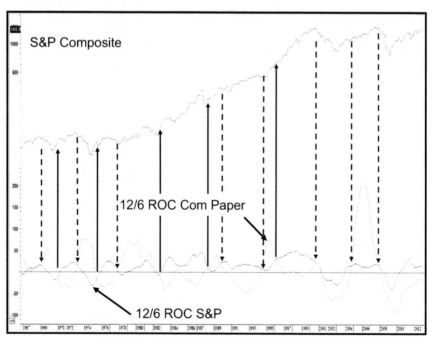

was approximately the same. This approach is far from perfect, as is clearly demonstrated by the confusing signals in the 1988–1990 period, not to mention its failure to trigger a buy signal in 2009 after having done a stalwart job of avoiding most of the 2007–2009 bear market. Generally speaking, it is better to be cautious when the interest rate momentum is above that of equities and to take on more risk when the reverse set of conditions holds true.

An alternative approach to the interest rate/equity relationship recognizes that rallies in equity prices are normally much stronger when supported by falling rates, and vice versa. It follows that if a measure of the equity market, such as the S&P Composite, is divided by the yield on a money-market instrument, such as 3-month commercial paper, the series will either lead or fall less rapidly at bear market bottoms and peak out ahead or rise at a slower pace at market tops, if interest rates are experiencing their usual leading characteristics.

An indicator constructed in this way, called the Money Flow Index, is plotted underneath the S&P Composite in Chart 31.3. The arrows point up the lead characteristics.

CHART 31.3 S&P Composite, 1967–2012, and the Money Flow Indicator

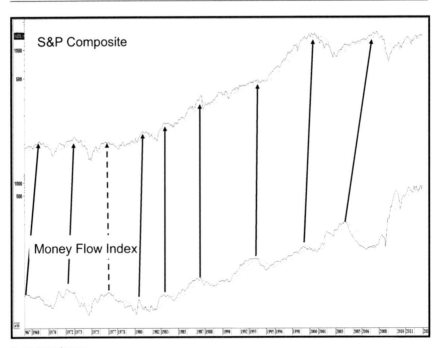

Source: From pring.com

Applying Technical Analysis to Short-Term Rates

Short-term rates are much more sensitive to business conditions than long-term rates. This is because decisions to change the level of inventories, for which a substantial amount of short-term credit is required, are made much more quickly than decisions to purchase manufacturing plants and equipment, which form the basis for long-term corporate credit demands. The Federal Reserve, in its management of monetary policy, is also better able to influence short-term rates than those at the longer end.

Short-term interest rates, when used with monthly data, generally lend themselves well to trend analysis. There are a number of series we could use, such as 13-week T-bills, certificates of deposit, 3-month euro-dollars, and the federal funds. I usually use the 3-month commercial paper yield because the series has a greater history. The following URL is a good source for many interest rate series, including the 3-month commercial paper yield (http://www.federalreserve.gov/releases/h15/update/default.htm), and is generally less volatile. In any event, most of these series, with the possible exception of T-bills, move closely together over the short run.

Chart 31.4 shows the commercial paper yield together with the growth indicator.

This series is constructed from four economic indicators: the Conference Board Leading Indicators and Employment Trends Index (www.conference-board.org), the CRB Spot Raw Industrial Material Index (www.crbtrader.com/crbindex/crbdata.asp), and the Commerce Department Capacity Utilization Index (www.federalreserve.gov/releases/g17/current). All four are expressed as a 9-month ROC and then combined and smoothed with a 6-month moving average (MA). It represents an example of how technical analysis can be applied to economic data. Positive zero crossovers indicate when the economy, as reflected by this composite indicator, is sufficiently strong to be consistent with rising short-term rates and vice versa. The dashed vertical lines indicate sell signals for rates (buy signals for prices) and vice versa. The growth indicator is not perfect and has occasionally experienced some whipsaws, but does offer a fairly independent variable from the price itself. Whenever it goes bullish for rates and they continue to edge lower, this means that the Fed is overriding economic forces (excessive and unnecessary easing). Such action generally results in higher interest rates and industrial commodity prices than would otherwise be the case.

The chart also features a 12-month MA of the yield, crossovers of which have generally offered reliable signals of primary trend reversals.

CHART 31.4 3-Month Commercial Paper Yield, 1955–2012, and the Growth Indicator

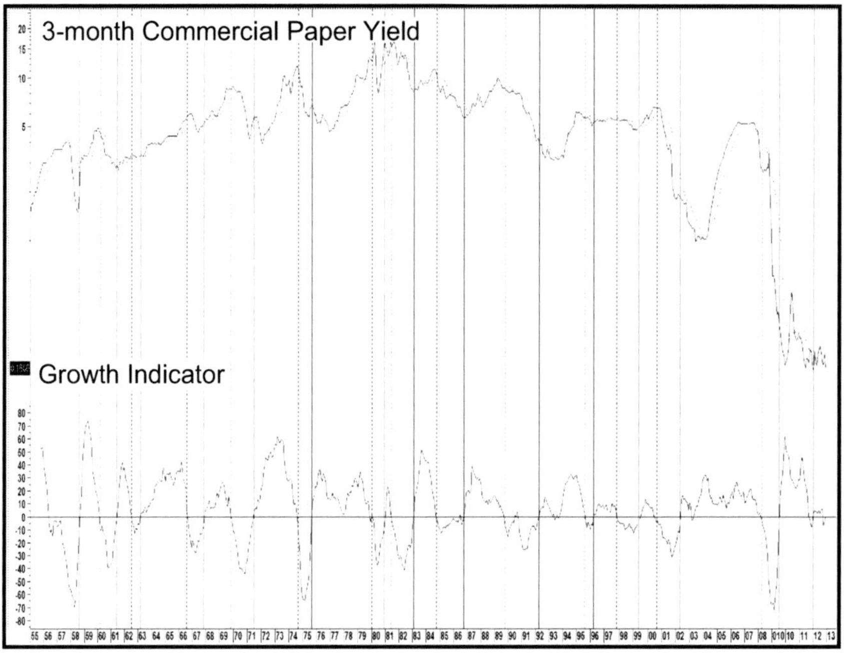

Source: From pring.com

Chart 31.5 shows the rate with an 18-month exponential moving average (EMA) and a long-term Know Sure Thing (KST). Once again, the bullish KST MA crossovers are flagged with the arrows. By and large, a KST MA crossover, when confirmed with an 18-month EMA crossover, has been reasonably reliable. When growth indicator signals are included, the results are even more impressive.

The Importance of Changes in the Discount Rate

Movements in the discount rate reflect changes in monetary policy and are, therefore, of key importance to the trend of both short-term interest rates and the equity market. Such action also has a strong psychological influence on both credit and equity markets. This is because the Fed does not reverse policy on a day-to-day or even a week-to-week basis, so a reversal in the trend of the discount rate implies that the trend in market interest rates is unlikely to be reversed for at least several months, and usually far longer. A corporation does not like to cut dividends once they have been raised. In a similar vein, the central bank wishes to create a feeling of continuity and

CHART 31.5 3-Month Commercial Paper Yield, 1958–2012, and a Long-Term KST

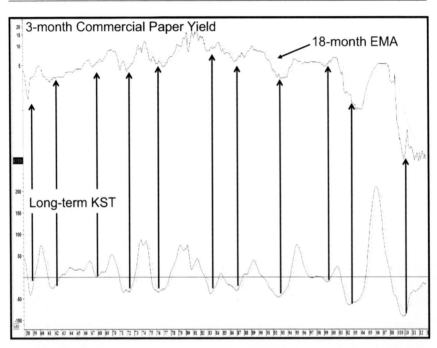

Source: From pring.com

consistency. A change in the discount rate is, therefore, helpful in confirming trends in other rates, which, when taken by themselves, can sometimes give misleading signals because of temporary technical or psychological factors.

> **Major Technical Principle**   Reversals in the direction of the discount rate offer reliable signals of primary trend reversals in short-term interest rates.

Effect on Short-Term Rates   Market rates usually lead the discount rate at cyclical turning points. In 2003, the Fed changed the basis on which the discount rate was offered. Consequently, the series plotted in Chart 31.6 represents the post-2003 data spliced to the originally reported series.

The objective of the chart is to show that a discount rate cut after a series of hikes acts as confirmation that a new trend of lower rates is under way. The same is true at cyclical or primary-trend bottoms. It is often a good idea to monitor the relationship between the discount rate and its

CHART 31.6 3-Month Commercial Paper Yield, 1970–2012, and the Adjusted Discount Rate

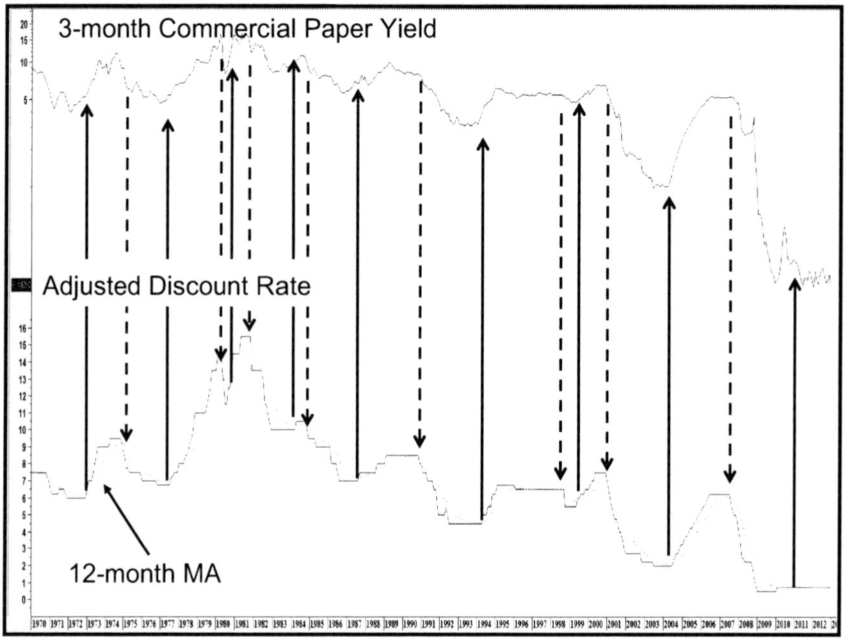

Source: From pring.com

12-month MA because crossovers almost always signal a reversal in the prevailing trend at a relatively early stage, as flagged by the arrows.

Effect on the Stock Market   Since the incorporation of the Federal Reserve System, every bull market peak in equities has been preceded by a rise in the discount rate, with the exception of the Depression, the war years of 1937 and 1939, and more recently, 1976. The leads have varied. In 1973, the discount rate was raised on January 12, 3 days before the bull market high, whereas the 1956 peak was preceded by no fewer than five consecutive hikes.

There is a well-known rule on Wall Street: *Three steps and stumble!* The rule implies that after three consecutive rate hikes, the equity market is likely to stumble and enter a bear market. The "three steps" rule is, therefore, a recognition that a significant rise in interest rates and tightening in monetary policy have already taken place. Table 31.1 shows the dates when the discount rate was raised for the third time, together with the duration and magnitude of the subsequent decline in equity prices following the third hike.

Cuts in the rate are equally as important. Generally speaking, as long as the trend of discount rate cuts continues, the primary bull market

TABLE 31.1 Discount Rate Highs and Subsequent Stock Market Lows, 1919–2012

Date of Discount Rate 3rd Hike		Months Between 3rd Hike and Market Low	Magnitude of Loss, %
November	1919	21	29.86
May	1928	49	77.45
August	1949	0	0
September	1955	27	9.04
March	1959	19	4.31
December	1965	10	15.92
April	1968	27	20.99
May	1973	16	36.47
January	1978	2	1.58
December	1980	19	18.06
February	1989	20	Gain of 4.7
November	1994	1	0
November	1999	34	28
September	2004	53	34

in stocks should be considered intact. Even after the last cut the market usually possesses enough momentum to extend its advance for a while. Quite often, the last intermediate reaction in the bull market will get underway at the time of or just before the first hike.

Most of the time, the cyclical course of discount rate cuts resembles a series of declining steps, but occasionally it is interrupted by a temporary hike before the downtrend continues. The *discount rate low* is defined one that occurs after a series of declining steps has taken place, and that either remains unchanged at this low level for at least 15 months or is followed by two or more hikes in 2 different months. In other words, if the series of cuts is interrupted by one hike, the trend is still classified as downward unless the rise occurs after a period of 15 months has elapsed. Only when two hikes in the rate have taken place in a period of less than 15 months is a low considered to have been established. Since the data are available for almost 100 years, they cover both inflationary and deflationary periods and are, therefore, reflective of a number of different economic environments.

Table 31.2 shows that there have been 17 discount rate lows since 1924. On each occasion the market moved significantly higher from the time the rate was cut.

TABLE 31.2 Discount Rate Lows and Subsequent Stock Market Highs, 1924–2012

Discount Rate Low	S&P Composite High	S&P Composite at Time of Cut	S&P Composite Price Peak	Time between Last Cut and Market High (Months)	Magnitude of % Gain	Average % Gain per Month
August 1924	September 1929	10.4	31.3	61	200.1	3.3
June 1932	July 1933	4.7	10.9	13	132.0	3.3
January 1934	February 1937	10.3	18.1	125	75.7	10.1
August 1937	June 1946	16.7	18.6	94	11.3	0.1
April 1954	April 1959	27.6	48.1	25	74.3	3.0
April 1958	December 1959	42.3	59.1	20	39.7	2.0
August 1960	February 1966	56.5	92.7	65	64.1	1.0
April 1967*	December 1968	91.0	106.5	20	17.0	0.9
December 1971	January 1973	99.2	118.4	13	19.4	1.5
November 1976	February 1980	101.2	115.3	27	13.9	0.5
July 1980	November 1980	119.8	135.7	4	13.3	3.3
February 1982	July 1983	146.8	167.0	5	13.8	2.8
August 1986	August 1987	252	329	12	3.5	2.5
July 1992	January 1994	424	481	18	13.4	.7
October 1998	August 2000	1098	1517	22	38.2	1.7
Average				35	48.6	2.5

*The April 1967 cut did not occur after a series of declines, but was associated with the 1966 business slowdown. The exclusion of this cut would improve the average results.
Source: www.pring.com.

A discount rate cut is only one indicator, and while it is invariably bullish, the overall technical position is also important. For example, the low in the discount rate usually occurs just after the market has started a bull phase. If the market is long-term overbought, the odds that the ensuing rally will obtain the magnitude and the duration of the average are slim. It should also be noted that while each discount rate low has ultimately been followed by a bull market high, this by no means excludes the risk of a major intermediate correction along the way. Such setbacks occurred in 1934, 1962, and during 1977–1978 and 1998. In the 1977–1978 period the market as measured by the NYSE A/D line did not correct, but moved irregularly higher. Chart 31.7 shows the relationship between the equity market and the discount rate for the decades spanning the turn of the century.

While cuts in the discount rate usually precede market bottoms, this relationship is far less precise than that observed at market tops. Note, for example, that the rate was lowered no fewer than seven times during the 1929–1932 debacle, whereas it was not changed at all during the 1946–1949 bear market.

CHART 31.7 S&P Composite, 1970–2012, and the Adjusted Discount Rate

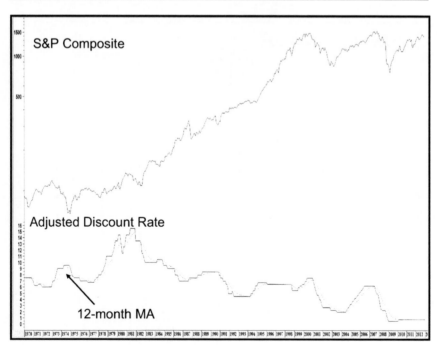

Source: From pring.com

Applying Technical Analysis at the Long End

Bond yield series tend to be very cyclical. We can take advantage of this situation by comparing a series such as Moody's AAA corporate bonds to an ROC. An example is shown in Chart 31.8, where the arrows show that overbought/oversold crossovers of the 12-month ROC have consistently flashed excellent buy and sell signals. This approach cannot be used as an actual system because offsetting signals may not be given. For example, during the 1940–1981 secular or very long-term uptrend, no buy signals were given between the 1950s and 1981. This contrasts to the post-1981 secular downtrend where several buys were triggered. It is a classic example of how oscillators tend to move and stay at overbought levels during a bull market and reverse the process during bear markets. In this case, the bull market was the secular trend and the overbought readings represented primary trend peaks.

CHART 31.8 Moody's AAA Corporate Yield, 1955–2012, and a 12-Month ROC

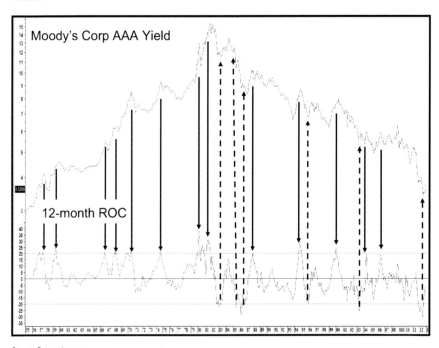

Source: From pring.com

CHART 31.9 The 30-Year Government Bond Yield, 1997–2001, and a Smoothed RSI

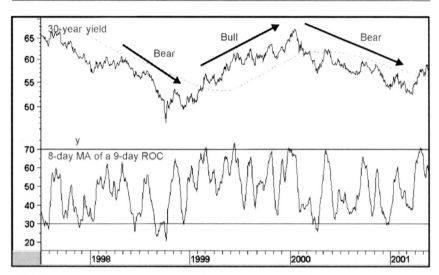

Source: From pring.com

Chart 31.9 expresses a similar idea, except that this time the oscillator is a short-term one, an 8-day MA of a 9-day relative strength indicator (RSI). The arrows above the yield show the primary trend environment. You can see quite clearly that overbought conditions are far more common in the bull phase and oversold during the bear trends. Note also that the 200-day MA can serve as an additional arbitrator of the direction of the primary trend. At the tail end of the chart the oscillator reaches an overbought condition and the yield crosses above its MA, suggesting the probability that a new bull market is under way.

Finally, Chart 31.10 compares a perpetual contract of the U.S. Treasury bond futures against two ROC indicators. Between the opening of the year 2000 and the end of the chart, the primary trend was bullish. The four arrows attached to the 10-day ROC indicate oversold or close to oversold conditions. Each was followed by a worthwhile rally. The ellipse in the furthest right part of the chart indicates a failure to respond to an oversold condition and offers the first hint that a new bear market has begun. Several joint trendline breaks in the price and momentum are also indicated on the chart. The adoption of this combination is quite useful because the 10- and 45-day spans are separated by a considerable distance. In this way characteristics not shown by the 10-day series may show up in the 45-day one and vice versa. Of course, it's even better when all three are indicating a trend reversal, as was the case in April 2000.

CHART 31.10 The 30-Year Government Bond Yield, 1999–2001, Two ROC's

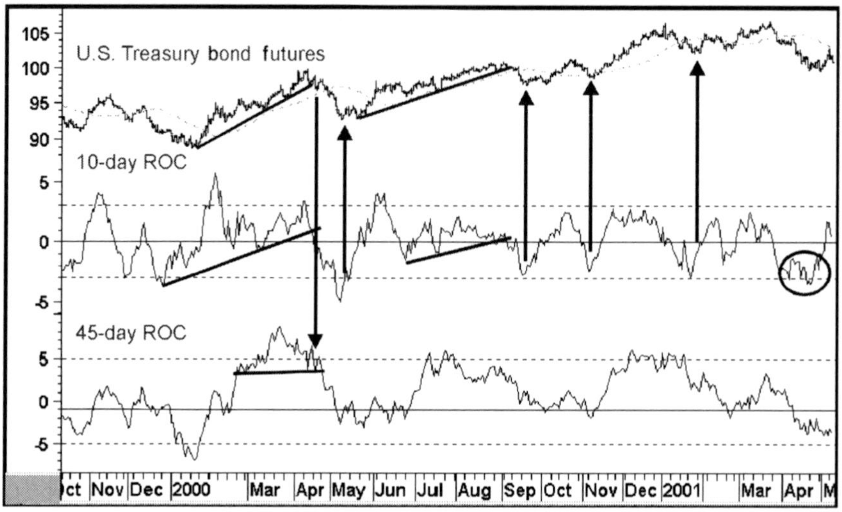

Source: From pring.com

Summary

1. Interest rates influence stock prices because they affect corporate profitability, alter valuation relationships, and influence margin transactions.
2. Interest rates have led stock prices at major turning points in virtually every recorded business cycle.
3. It is the ROC of interest rates, rather than their actual level, that affects equity prices.
4. Short-term interest rates generally have a greater influence on stock prices than long-term ones.
5. Changes in the trend of the discount rate offer strong confirmation that a primary trend change in money-market prices has taken place.
6. Reversals in the trend of the discount rate offer early bird warnings of a change in the primary trend of stock prices.

32

USING TECHNICAL
ANALYSIS TO SELECT
INDIVIDUAL STOCKS

A useful systematic approach for stock selection is what is known as *the top-down approach*. In this case, the "top" represents an analysis of whether equities in general are experiencing a primary bull or bear market. Since most equities rise during a bull trend and decline during a bear trend, the first step establishes whether the overall environment is likely to be positive or negative.

The next involves an appraisal of the various sectors and below them, industry groups, since equities in the same industry generally move together, as do industry groups in their sector. Once an attractive industry group has been isolated, the final stage involves the selection of individual stocks. This approach is discussed later, but first, some general observations.

All investors and traders would like their selections to appreciate rapidly in price, but stocks that may satisfy this wish tend to be accompanied by a substantially greater amount of risk than most of us are willing to accept. Stocks that move up sharply in price usually have a high beta (i.e., they are very sensitive to market movements), a very small float (i.e., are illiquid and very price sensitive to a small increase in volume), or a very strong earnings momentum, resulting in constant upward revisions in the price/earnings multiple. Others may be experiencing a turnaround situation in which the price has fallen to unrealistically low levels so that the slightest good news has an explosive effect on the price.

These are all fundamental factors and really fall outside the scope of this book. However, it is important to understand that investors can be very fashion conscious when it comes to stock ownership. After prices have been bid up to unrealistically high levels and the media are covering positive developments in cover stories, major articles, etc., the chances are that the bullish arguments are understood by virtually all market participants. At this point, effectively everyone who wants to buy has already done so and the stock is said to be *overowned*. This happened to the pollution control group (waste management) in the late 1960s, the so-called glamour growth stocks in 1973, the oils in 1980, and technology in the spring of 2000. When the news is so bad that it appears that profits will never recover, or that the company might file for bankruptcy, the opposite condition sets in and the stock is said to be *underowned*. Real estate investment trusts in 1974, tire stocks in 1980, and financials in 2009 are examples of underownership. Not all companies move to such extremes, but it is important to recognize that this psychological pendulum nevertheless exists.

A position of overownership usually develops over several major advances after a *secular rise*. Similarly, a position of underownership, in which a stock becomes totally out of fashion, usually takes many years to evolve.

Stock Selection from a Secular Point of View

General

It makes sense to start off with a very long-term or secular point of view, gradually working down to the short-term aspects. Ideally, the selection process should begin by determining whether the stock in question is in a secular advance or decline in order to gain some idea of where it might be in its ownership cycle. Chart 32.1 shows Cominco, a Canadian mining company, that went through many cycles between the 1970s and the turn of the century. Stocks in resource and basic industries such as Cominco are called *cyclical* stocks since they offer great profit opportunities over one or two business cycles but are rarely profitable using the buy-hold approach.

Because of the long-term growth characteristics of the global economy, most stocks exhibit characteristics of a long-term secular advance interrupted by mild cyclical corrections or multiyear trading ranges.

An example is shown in Chart 32.2, featuring Coca-Cola. A couple of secular trends are evident. The termination of the first was signaled by a

CHART 32.1 Cominco, 1970–2001

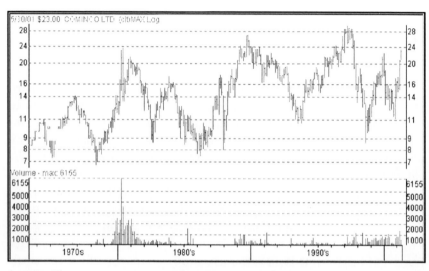

Source: From Telescan

CHART 32.2 Coca-Cola, 1980–2012, and Relative Strength

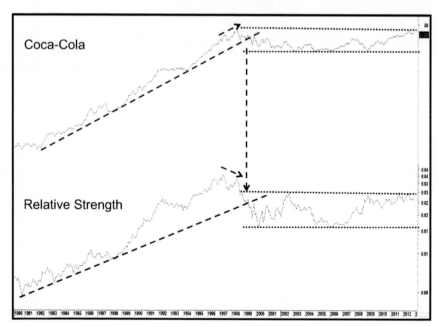

Source: From pring.com

joint trendline break in the price and the relative strength (RS) line in 1999. Note this was preceded with a negative divergence where the price touched a new high but the RS line did not. The second was a sideways trading range for the ensuing 13 years. The direction of the ultimate breakout may well be signaled by the RS line.

All the RS lines in this chapter are relative to the S&P Composite unless otherwise stated. I have incorporated them into most of the charts in this chapter for two reasons. First, RS trends and divergences can be very helpful in understanding the strength or weakness in the underlying technical structure. Second, when a stock is purchased, it is far better for it to be in a trend that is outperforming than underperforming the market. Chart 32.3 offers a classic example of this.

During the 20-year period covered by the chart, Reliant Energy was in a secular uptrend. This looked good on the surface, but a quick glance at the RS line indicates that it was in a secular downtrend in terms of relative performance. Note that it was possible to construct two trendlines for the price. The dashed one is an extremely good example of why it is a smart idea to extend a trendline once it has been violated. Note how the extended line became formidable resistance several times in the mid-to-late 1990s. Even when the price broke above the line at the turn of the century, the retracement move found support there.

CHART 32.3 Reliant Energy, 1980–2001, and Relative Strength

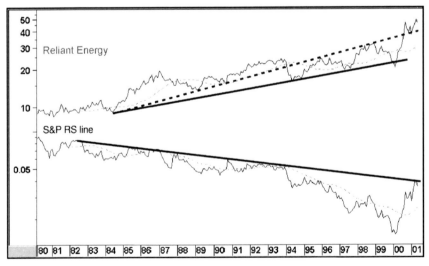

Source: From pring.com

CHART 32.4 ADM, 1980–2001, and Relative Strength

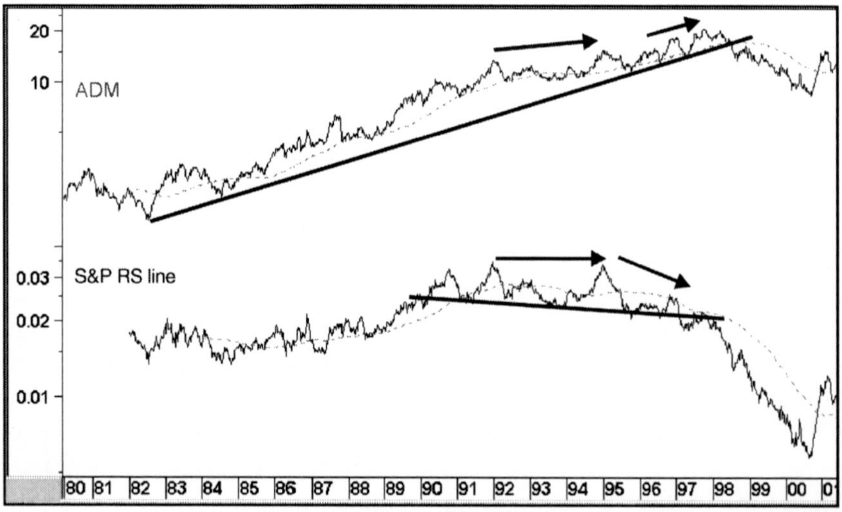

Source: From pring.com

Finally ADM experienced a secular break to the downside in 1998 (Chart 32.4). Its RS line also completed a downward head-and-shoulders top. Note that in ADM's case, advance warning of potential weakness was given first by the failure of the RS line to confirm the new high in the price in 1995 (at the tip of the horizontal arrow) and then to diverge negatively with the late-1997 high.

These examples point up the differing life cycles and characteristics of individual stocks. Investors who are able to identify secular trend reversals in price and relative action are in a position to profit from extremes in the ownership cycle. Consequently, a very long-term chart can provide a useful starting point for stock selection.

Major Price Patterns (Long Bases)

In Chapter 8, the relationship between the size of the formation and the ensuing price move in both terms of magnitude and duration was established. The bigger the base, the further they can race! Or the greater the top, the more they'll drop!

By definition, there are few points in a stock's lifetime where this condition is prevalent, but when it can be spotted, it is well worth while taking action based on this information. Sometimes, as in the 1940s and the 1982–1983 period, for example, there are an unusually large number of such issues breaking out of large bases. The more this is so, the stronger the foundation for the next bull market. The 1940s were followed by the very strong 1950s and early 1960s, and the 1982 low was followed by the 18-year secular bull, with its final top in early 2000.

Chart 32.5 shows an example for Andrew Corp. breaking out from a 6-year base in 1991. A good rally, more than meeting the objective of the pattern, followed. Later on, the joint penetration of 6-year up trendlines indicated that the strong advance was unlikely to continue. In the case of the price, this was followed by a consolidation, and for the RS line, an actual trend reversal.

Applied Materials experienced a breakout from a 10-year base (Chart 32.6) in late 1992. The uptrend in the price continued until at least the spring of 2001, but the RS up trendline was temporarily violated in 1998 and 2000.

Large tops are, of course, the opposite of large bases, and we see one such animal in Chart 32.7 featuring Coeur D'Alene Mines. Interestingly,

CHART 32.5 Andrew Corp, 1980–2001, and Relative Strength

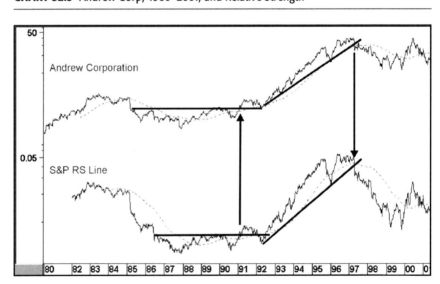

Source: From pring.com

CHART 32.6 Applied Materials, 1980–2001, and Relative Strength

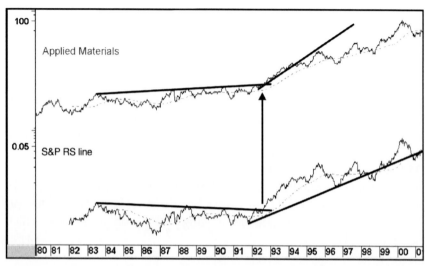

Source: From pring.com

CHART 32.7 Coeur D'Alene, 1980–2012, and Relative Strength

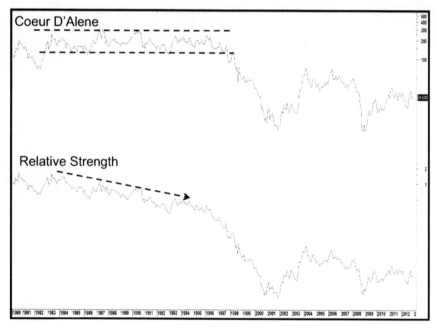

Source: From pring.com

a clue of impending weakness was given by the persistent decline in the RS line. That's not always the case, because it has been known for RS trends to reverse to the upside during the formation of a trading range. However, in this case, there was no indication whatsoever that the fortunes of the RS line was about to change for the better until well after the downside price break.

Compare that example to Chemed in Chart 32.8. Once again we see a multiyear trading range in the form of a consolidation reverse head-and-shoulders pattern. Throughout the formation of the range, the RS line was in a clear-cut downtrend, leaving the impression that the pattern would break to the downside. Then, as the right shoulder was forming, the RS line violated a 4-year (dotted) down trendline and started to rally at a more accelerated rate than the price. At the time of the breakout, the RS line was well below its late-1982 high, but had already violated a 20-year (solid) down trendline, thereby supporting the breakout by the price which developed in late 2003.

CHART 32.8 Chemed Ordinary, 1980–2012, and Relative Strength

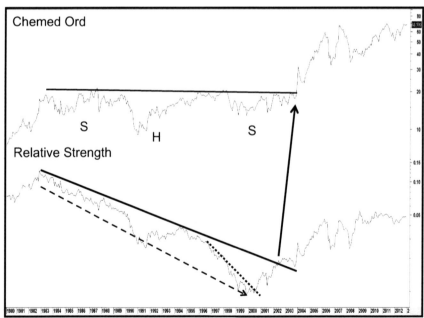

Source: From pring.com

Some Basic Principles of Stock Selection During a Primary Bull Market

General

A bull market has been defined as an environment when most stocks are moving up most of the time for an extended period. In this case, the extended period should be expected to last between 9 months and possibly as long as 2 to 3 years. A bear market is exactly the opposite, except the average bear market typically unfolds over a shorter period. When exposure to equities is being contemplated, it is clearly better for both investors and short-term traders with a 2- to 3-week horizon to be buying when the primary trend is positive. It is true that some stocks experience primary bull trends when the overall market is in a primary bear trend, but the law of probability indicates that it is much more difficult to make money when swimming against an overall negative environment. We must also bear in mind, of course, that because of the group rotation process, different stock groups are experiencing different phases of their bull and bear cycles simultaneously. Thus, while the S&P, for instance, may have just embarked on the first downleg of a new bear market, lagging groups, such as mines, may still be experiencing the final leg of their bull market. The selection process at this stage of the cycle is much more difficult, but there are still some opportunities offering substantial upside magnitude at this juncture. A lot will depend on whether commodities are in a secular bull or bear market. If it's a bull trend, the inflationary part of that specific business cycle associated with the trend will generally experience greater magnitude and duration.

The performance of specific issues can differ widely, not only over the course of the total market bull move, but during its various stages as well. This concept was described in Chapter 22, which described the sector rotation process.

The first step is to decide whether the market is in a primary bull or bear trend using the principles outlined earlier. If it is fairly evident that a bull market began some time ago and there are few signs of a top or evidence of a bear market, intermediate lows are a good place to begin the analysis. I'll have more to say on that one later, but for now, let's assume that there is ample evidence that a new bull market is just beginning. Signs would include the observation that A/D line had been falling for a year or more. We would also probably see a confirmed new trend of declining interest rates and an oversold condition in the long-term momentum indicators, lots of media coverage on weakness in the stock market and the economy, layoffs at major brokerage firms, and so on.

If all of these conditions were present, it would be an odds-on probability that the market was either at or very close to a bear market low based on the principles outlined earlier in this chapter.

Selecting Stocks Close to a Bear Market Low

The next step would be an examination of the technical position of the various industry groups, especially the early-cycle leaders, to make sure that they are technically sound on both an absolute and relative basis. Finally, an examination of the stocks within the groups found to be the most sound should be undertaken.

In this respect, the obvious starting point would be an analysis of the relative positions of the various industry groups in terms of the sector rotation process described in Chapter 22. Some sectors do not fit conveniently into the chronological sequence that makes up a complete cycle, and not all that do respond in the way expected in every cycle. However, an analysis of the energy and financial sectors or the banks/aluminum ratio would be a good point to determine whether the environment was an inflationary or deflationary one. The next step would be to analyze the groups that were akin to the sector that looked more promising. We will do that later, but for now, let us assume that we have been lucky enough to identify a bear market low.

The 1990 bottom met these requirements. The S&P Composite actually fell for a relatively short period of time, yet the New York Stock Exchange (NYSE) daily A/D line had been falling for over a year by the time the market bottomed in late 1990. One of the good-looking groups falling into the early leader category at the end of 1990 was the brokerage industry. What made them especially appealing as a contrary play was the *Businessweek* cover story cited in Chapter 30 questioning the future of the industry.

Technically, Chart 32.9 shows that the index completed a base in early 1991.

The RS line was ahead of the game because it experienced an 8-year down trendline break a couple of months earlier right at the turn of the year. The index itself had simultaneously violated a smaller down trendline and crossed above its 24-month moving average (MA) as the RS line was breaking out. The RS line also crossed above its 24-month MA. Both long-term monthly Know Sure Things (KSTs) triggered bullish signals as well. Note how the RS line made a slightly lower low in 1990 than in

CHART 32.9 S&P Brokerage Index, 1982–1993, and Three Indicators

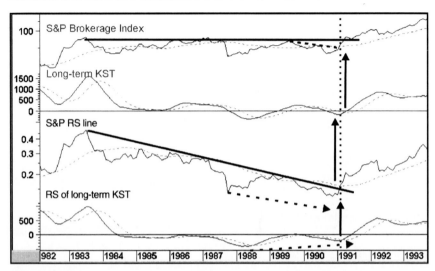

Source: From pring.com

1987 but the RS KST did not. This positive divergence added icing to the bullish case, indicating the probability of an emerging bull market to be pretty high. The dotted vertical line on this chart indicates the approximate point where the initial trend breaks took place. They are replicated on Charts 32.10 through 32.15, which feature individual stocks.

Merrill Lynch (symbol MER), formerly the largest broker and now no longer with us as a separate trading entity, is featured in Charts 32.10 and 32.11.

It violated a 2-year down trendline for the absolute price and an 8-year down trendline for the RS line against the S&P. Since both KSTs were turning bullish and the absolute one was actually completing a reverse head-and-shoulders pattern, MER would have qualified as a buy. Later on, the 8-year down trendline for the absolute price was penetrated on the upside, and that completed the bullish picture. Chart 32.11 shows the price together with an RS line against the Brokerage Index itself. A rising line means that the stock is outperforming the index and vice versa. It is fairly evident at the opening of 1991 that this stock has broken its downtrend and was, therefore, likely to outperform both the S&P and the Brokerage Index.

Legg Mason, featured in Chart 32.12, was also in a bullish position since both the absolute and relative prices had broken out from bases and their respective KSTs had gone bullish. Indeed, the relative KST was actually diverging positively from the RS line.

CHART 32.10 Merrill Lynch, 1983–1993, and Three Indicators

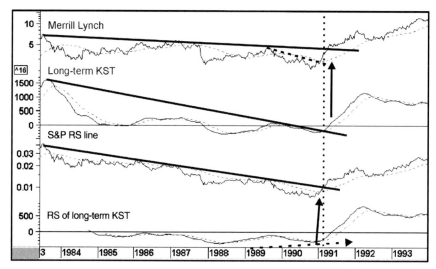

Source: From pring.com

CHART 32.11 Merrill Lynch, 1986–1991, Relative to the Brokerage Index

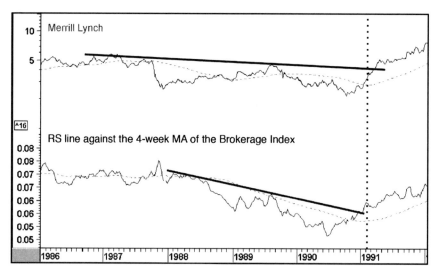

Source: From pring.com

CHART 32.12 Legg Mason, 1986–1993, and Three Indicators

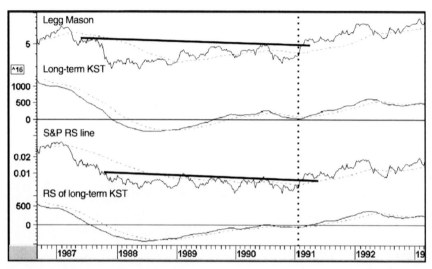

Source: From pring.com

CHART 32.13 Legg Mason, 1986–1991, Relative to the Brokerage Index

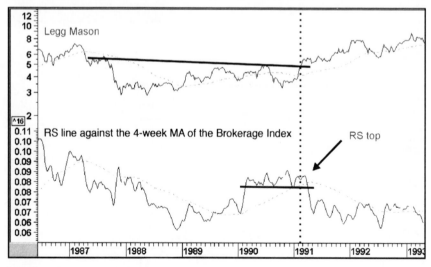

Source: From pring.com

CHART 32.14 Raymond James, 1985–1993, and Three Indicators

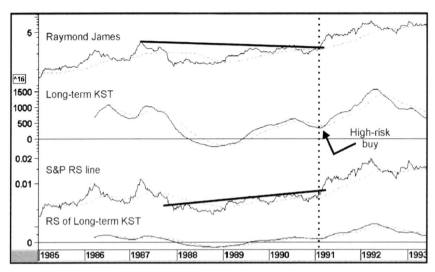

Source: From pring.com

CHART 32.15 Raymond James, 1986–1993, Relative to the Brokerage Index

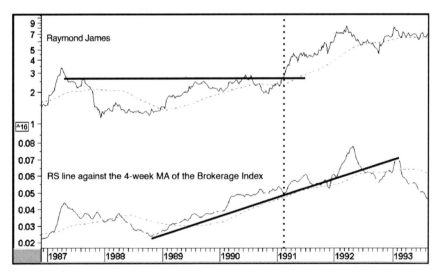

Source: From pring.com

This sideways action was actually potentially more bullish than that of MER, which was reversing from a downtrend. However, Chart 32.13 shows us that RS line against the Brokerage Index was actually tracing out a top. Unfortunately, that was not known at the time of the breakout (i.e., at the dotted vertical line).There was little doubt by the early spring of 1991 that a switch to another broker would have made sense since the RS line completed the top and dropped below its 65-week estimated moving average (EMA).

Finally, Raymond James, featured in Chart 32.14, came away from the 1989–1990 bear market virtually unscathed. At the time of the broker breakout, both the absolute and relative lines were completing large bases.

Unfortunately, this was not a low-risk situation like Merrill because the long-term KST for the absolute price was reversing from a moderately over-bought condition, which, on the one hand, made it less attractive. On the other hand, it often pays to go with the leader because strong stocks have a habit of getting stronger. This is because there are usually some good fundamentals that enabled them to be strong stocks in the first place. The arbiter in this case would have been the RS line against the Brokerage Index in Chart 32.15. Just after the breakout, it started to accelerate away from its 65-week EMA and up trendline and outperformed the Brokerage Index for the next year.

Using a Change in the Cycle to Select Stocks

Throughout the stock cycle, groups are continually changing leadership. One way of detecting this is to create a ratio of a leading and lagging group. Chart 32.16 shows such a series—aluminums against property casualty insurers.

When the line is rising, it is bullish for aluminum producers relative to insurance stocks, and vice versa. We are looking for changes in the direction of the ratio, which offer a proxy for a change in leadership from early-cycle, liquidity-driven issues to late-cycle, earnings-driven sectors. It is fairly evident from looking at the chart that this is a pretty jagged relationship subject to numerous whipsaws. One way around this is to construct a smoothed long-term momentum indicator, such as a KST—the moving-average convergence divergence (MACD) or stochastic (24/15/10) can also be substituted. Note that the indicator in the bottom panel is similar in its trajectory since it is the long-term monthly KST for the inflation/deflation ratio discussed in Chapter 22. It's a preferred measure and acts as a check, but for a "down and dirty" substitute, the more narrowly based aluminum/insurance ratio works fine. KST MA crossovers of the ratio are then used as a proxy for when a change in leadership might be taking place.

CHART 32.16 S&P Aluminum/Property Casualty Ratio, 1984–2012, and Two Indicators

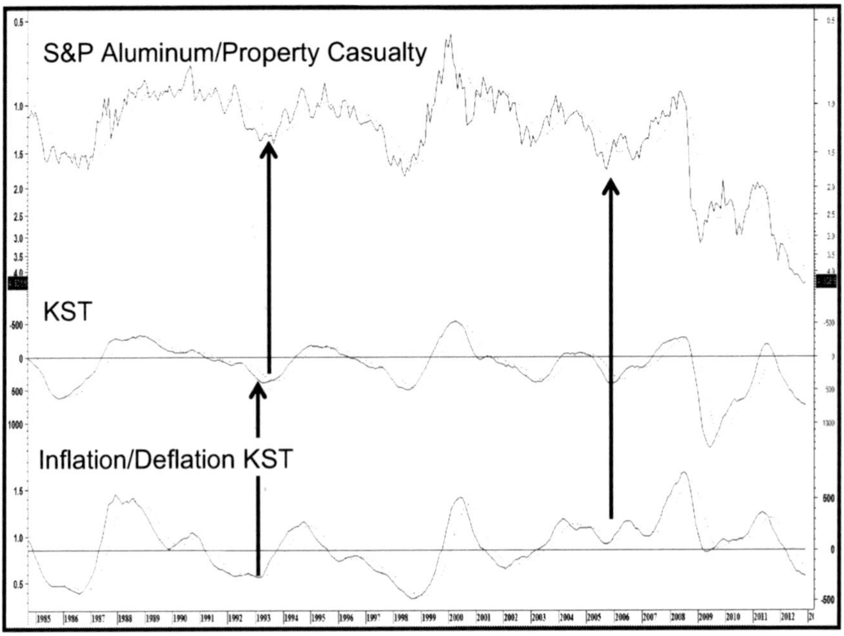

Source: From pring.com

In most situations, the ratio bottoms out during the course of the cycle rather than at a bear market low. An exception developed during early 2009 because of the relative collapse of financials in the 2008–2009 crisis. For this exercise, we are interested in the point in the cycle when the ratios bottom, since that gives us a clue that the inflationary part of the cycle is underway. The arrows on the chart flag two such reversals in 1993 and the very end of 2005. The upside reversals indicated a switch to lagging or earnings-driven stocks. In these instances, both rallies lasted a couple of years. At the time it was not possible to note breakouts in resource-based stocks in 1993, as this was the early stage of the tech boom, but in Chart 32.17 the lagging technology sector appears to offer some potential.

In both cases a certain amount of stalking was necessary as the absolute and relative down trendlines were not violated for several months after the aluminum/insurance ratio signal was given. Eventually, the lines were violated and in the case of the 1993 signal, a worthwhile rally followed. There are lots of computer hardware stocks, but one well-known seasoned issue is IBM, featured in Chart 32.18. See how both KSTs bottomed and the absolute and relative trendlines violated on the upside in 1993 and 2005.

CHART 32.17 S&P Computer Hardware, 1986–2012, and Three Indicators

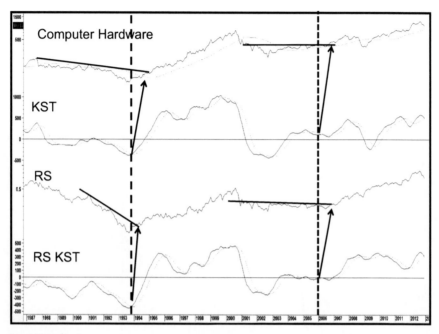

Source: From pring.com

CHART 32.18 IBM, 1987–2010, and Three Indicators

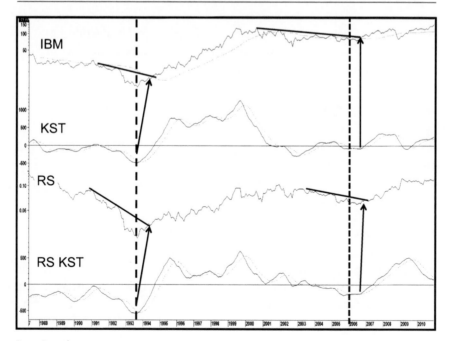

Source: From pring.com

CHART 32.19 Apple, 1987–2012, and Three Indicators

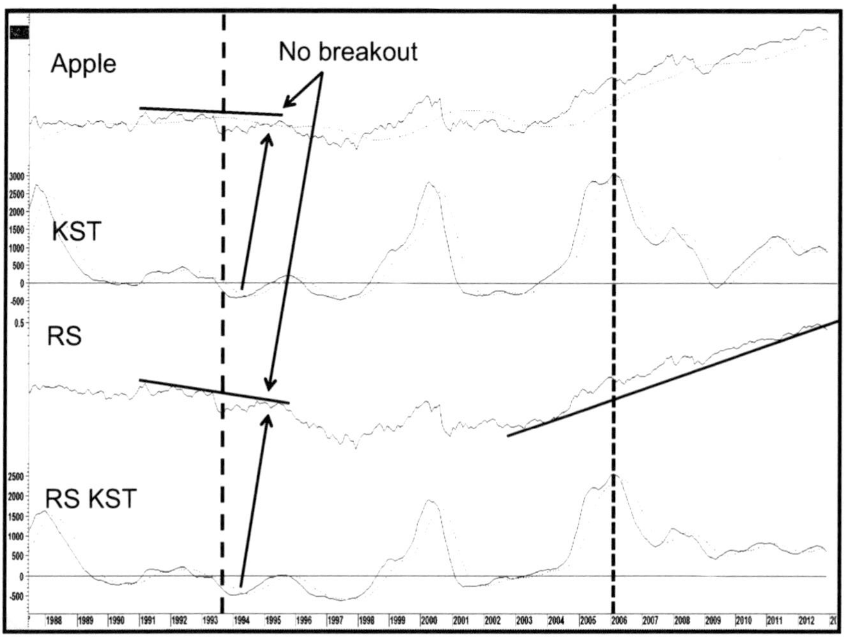

Source: From pring.com

Apple (Chart 32.19) is another industry giant, but while its KSTs bottomed in a sympathetic way to computer hardware action, neither the price itself nor its RS experienced an upside breakout.

Short-Term Analysis

Short-term traders will need to adopt one more stage to the analysis, and that is to make sure that prior to a purchase, the stock in question is in a technically strong short-term position as well as being in a constructive mode from a long-term point of view.

Chart 32.20 shows McKesson with a short-term and long-term KST, both based on daily data.

In this case, the long-term KST uses the same time frames as the monthly formula, but multiplied by 21 to correspond to the approximate average trading day in a month. The vertical thick black line indicates the low point separating the bear market on the left from the primary bull trend on the right. The letters mark the short-term KST buy signals that

CHART 32.20 McKesson, 1999–2001, and Two Indicators

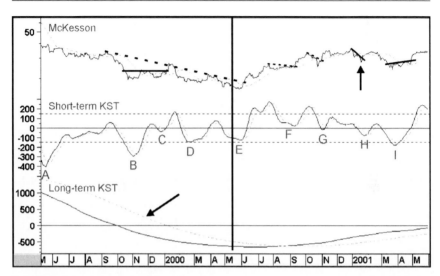

Source: From pring.com

developed close to or below zero. Other smoothed short-term oscillators, such as a stochastic, smoothed relative strength indicator (RSI); MACD; etc., could, of course, be substituted for the KST. Note that none of the signals labeled A to D had any form of upside magnitude, with the exception of C. Even here, the nice trendline break in the price was followed by a whipsaw breakout, simply because this was a bear market environment. This again emphasizes the point that the best signals go with the trend. This is not the same thing as saying that all short-term bear market buy signals result in whipsaws and all pro-trend moves will be successful. For example, the buy signal at H took place during the bull move but was essentially a false signal. Again, we could filter this one out because it was not possible to construct a meaningful trendline as it was at F, H, and I.

E, of course, was the most successful, but at the time, the long-term KST had not crossed above its MA. However, one of the principles of interpretation allows us to anticipate a reversal if the KST has flattened and if a trendline break in the price or short-term KSTs is sufficient to anticipate a reversal. In this case, an 8-month down trendline in the price had been violated, and the short-term KST had gone bullish and diverged positively with the price twice. Consequently, there would have been enough evidence to draw the conclusion that the odds favored a long-term KST buy signal being triggered.

CHART 32.21 IBM, 1993–1994, and Two Indicators

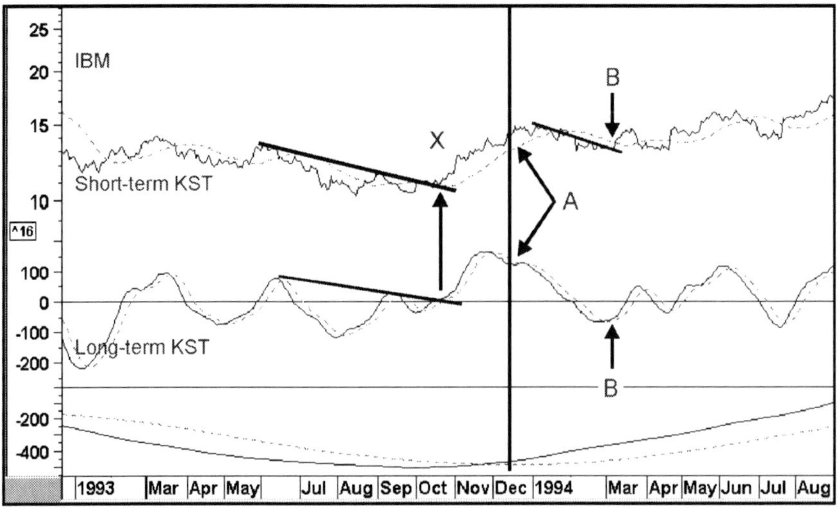

Source: From pring.com

Sometimes, when a computer scanning exercise returns a long-term smoothed momentum buy signal, the short-term situation is overbought. Chart 32.21 offers an example for IBM at arrow A. In such situations, it doesn't matter too much for a long-term investor, but for a short-term trader, entering when the price is overbought can prove disastrous. Chart 32.21 shows that the first opportunity to buy once the long-term KST had crossed its MA came under the cloud of a short-term overbought situation.

The next one came at B when the price broke above a small trendline and the short-term KST triggered a buy signal. Even this was not the greatest of signals, but at least the entry price was lower than that when the long-term series went bullish. The best signal of all developed at X when the price violated a down trendline and the short-term KST went bullish. Note also that the KST was barely below zero at the time, which was a tip-off for the sharp rally that followed. Since the long-term KST had reversed to the upside at this point, it would have been reasonable to use all this positive evidence to conclude that the probabilities strongly favored a long-term MA crossover.

I am not going to say that anticipating a long-term buy signal will work every time, but it is certainly true that on many occasions the first rally coming off a bear market low often turns out to be very worthwhile.

Summary

1. Most stocks go through ownership cycles, which normally take a long period to complete. It is important to identify whether a stock is in a secular uptrend or downtrend in order to better understand its position within its ownership cycle.
2. Substantial profit potential is available to the long-term investor who can identify stocks that are breaking out from extended bases when they are accompanied by expanding volume and an improving long-term trend in RS.
3. A bull market generally carries most stocks with it, but the performance of individual issues can vary enormously, both over the course of the primary upmove and within it.
4. Once a favorable market environment has been established, the process of selecting stocks should begin with the selection of industry groups with a positive long-term technical position.
5. Following the isolation of attractive sectors and subsequently groups, it is important to look for stocks that are also showing positive technicals.

33

TECHNICAL ANALYSIS
OF INTERNATIONAL
STOCK MARKETS

Equities are bought and sold throughout the world for essentially the same reasons, so the principles of technical analysis can be applied to any stock market. Unfortunately, the degree of sophistication in statistical reporting of many countries does not permit the kind of detailed analysis that is available in the United States, although things are improving rapidly. Even so, it is possible to obtain data on price, breadth, and volume for most countries. Information on industry groups and interest rates is also widely available.

In this chapter we will concentrate on longer-term trends for the purpose of gaining perspective, but the analysis can just as easily be used to identify intermediate-term and short-term trends.

Identifying Primary Global Trends

Chart 33.1a shows the Morgan Stanley Capital International (MSCI) World Stock Index, which is constructed from a selection of blue-chip stocks from many different countries weighted by capitalization.

This series has been adjusted to U.S. dollars and is widely published in the financial press. Other world indexes published by Dow Jones and the *Financial Times* can be adopted into the analysis, but the MSCI has been chosen because of its extensive history going back to the 1960s. In addition, MSCI indexes are available for direct investment in individual country and regional exchange-traded funds (ETFs), as is the World Index (symbol

CHART 33.1*a* MSCI World Stock Index, 1964–1992, Showing 4-Year Cycle Lows

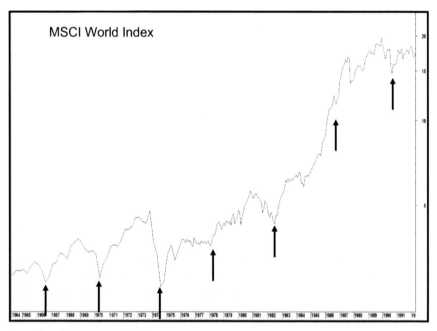

Source: From pring.com

ACWI) itself. The World Index is a good starting point from which to analyze the cyclical trends of the various stock markets, just as the S&P Composite might be used as a starting point for the U.S. market. This is because the stock markets around the globe *tend* to move in the same direction, just as the majority of U.S. stocks reflect the primary trend of the S&P most of the time. Generally speaking, improvements in technology and communications have broken down geographical and trading patterns, and countries have become more interdependent, with the result that their stock markets and business cycles are now more closely related than they used to be. A giant leap in this direction appeared to take place after the 1987 crash, in which all markets participated on a synchronized basis. This was later reinforced almost 10 years later when the so-called "Asian meltdown" reverberated around the world. The introduction of international and specific country closed- and open-ended mutual funds in the 1980s and 1990s and their U.S.-based expansion in the opening decade of the current century is a striking example of this growing sense of international awareness. There are exceptions, though, because it is possible for different economies to be in a different state of expansion than others. An example might be the performance of neighbors Greece (ETF symbol GREC) and Turkey (TUR) in the 2011–2012 period in that the Greek economy was retrenching and the Turkish economy expanding. As a result of the variations in the long-term economic, financial, and political situations between countries, a good world bull market in equities may be brief or almost nonexistent for a country undergoing financial distortions, such as Hong Kong between 1986 and 1990. Country performance can also differ because of the makeup of specific markets. For example, the Swedish and Finish indexes performed superbly in the latter part of the 1990s because they were dominated by technology companies. Countries with substantial natural resources such as Canada (EWC) and Australia (EWA) tend to outperform when commodity prices are rising and so forth. An additional factor emanates from demographics. Regions and countries with a population pyramid skewed toward older people (Europe and Japan, for example) have a built-in disadvantage compared to countries such as Indonesia, India, Turkey, etc., whose population is skewed toward younger people, where growth characteristics such as family formation, consumer spending, and so forth are far more dominant.

Charts 33.1a and b show the existence of the international 4-year cycle, as indicated by the arrows. The troughs in 1962, 1966, 1970, 1974,

CHART 33.1b MSCI World Stock Index, 1992–2012, Showing 4-year Cycle Lows

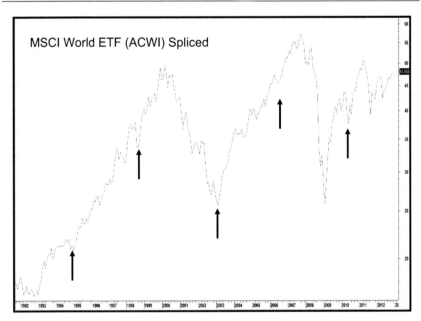

Source: From pring.com

1978, 1982, 1986, 1990, 1994, 1998, and 2002 are all separated by approximately 4 years. I say approximately since the actual bottoms do not fall in the same month. The 1986 "bottom" was more or less nonexistent and was essentially a 6-month trading range. This demonstrates the fact that in a secular bull market, such as the 1980s, the cycle low is not so much a bottom as a buying point prior to further gains. The same sort of thing happened in 1994, where the sideways correction was more obvious, the 2006 and 2010 4-year cycle "lows" also provided good buying opportunities.

The reason why this cycle works is because global equity prices revolve around the 4-year business cycle. Partial proof of that is provided in Chart 33.2, which compares the ACWI to a derivative of the amplitude-adjusted Organization for Economic Cooperation and Development (OECD) composite leading indicators. That derivative is a simple 1/15 price oscillator. The dashed line is a 1-period moving average (MA) of that derivative advanced forward by 3 months. The solid arrows indicate when the derivative crosses above its advanced moving average from a sub-zero position. The dashed ones indicate the same thing, but point up that equities did not respond positively to expanding economic conditions in the normal way. One of the reasons for using the price oscillator derivative calculation is that the data are reported with a 2-month time lag, so this

CHART 33.2 MSCI World ETF (ACWI) Spliced, 1984–2012, and a Global Economic Indicator

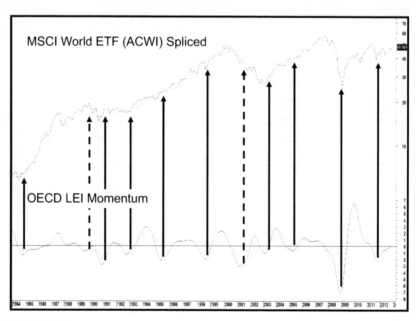

Source: From pring.com

CHART 33.3 MSCI World ETF (ACWI) Spliced, 1966–2012, and a Long-Term KST

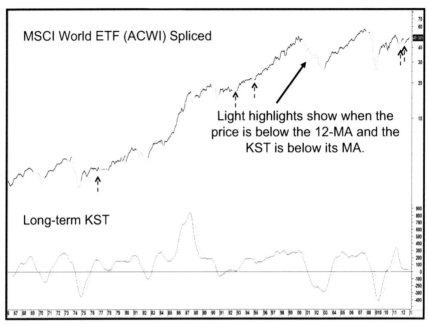

Source: From pring.com

technique allows the indicator to reverse sooner than would otherwise be the case.

Chart 33.3 shows the MSCI World ETF, spliced to the actual index prior to its listing. Also included in the chart is the long-term Know Sure Thing (KST). The light plot indicates those periods when the KST is below its 9-month MA and the ETF price is also below its 12-month MA. As you can see, this system would have sidestepped all the major bear trends. It also triggered several false negatives, as indicated by the small dashed arrows. The 12-month MA was used in the model because crossover signals are one of the most reliable over the history of the index. The model, therefore, offers an overall objective indication as to whether global equity prices are in a primary bull or bear market.

New Highs/Lows and Diffusion Indexes

The World Index can also be used with net new high data. Chart 33.4 was constructed using the popular MetaStock program.

CHART 33.4 MSCI World ETF (ACWI) Spliced, 1996–2012, and a Net New High Oscillator

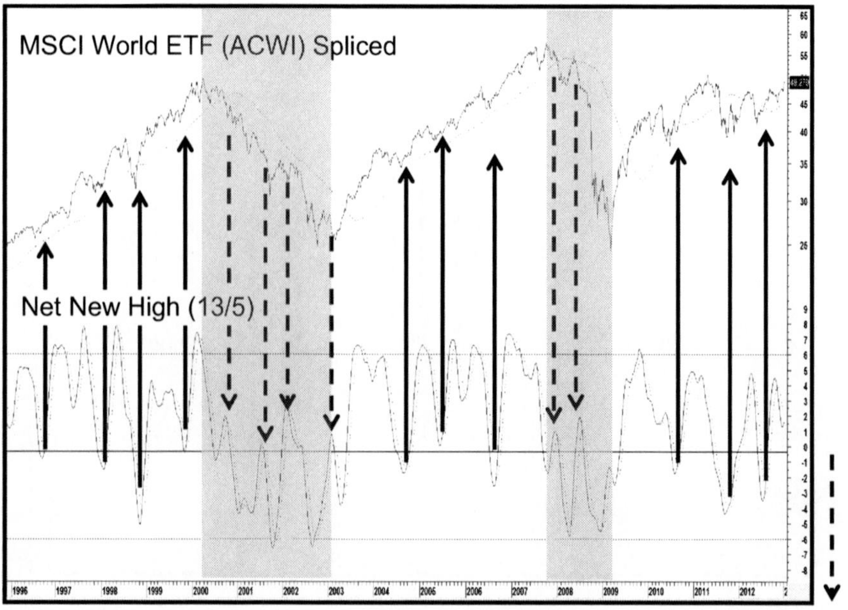

Source: From pring.com

In this instance, new highs and lows are calculated for a basket of individual stock markets. Instead of the normal time span of 52 weeks, I chose a 13-week period and smoothed the data with a 5-week simple moving average. Thirteen weeks is, of course, a quarter of a year and appears to work quite well. The arrows indicate pro-trend signals, the direction of the primary trend being determined with the benefit of hindsight. So, for example, reversals to the upside are only generated when the indicator drops below zero or, in the case of 2005, very close to zero during primary bull markets. In a similar way, sell signals in bear markets are flagged with the dashed arrows and can only develop when those reversals develop from a position above zero. The shaded areas flag the two bear markets that developed during the 1997–2012 period represented on the chart. Chart 33.5, on the other hand, draws our attention to the fact that contratrend signals have a much lower chance of succeeding.

New lows on their own are featured in Chart 33.6. The plotted data is, in fact, a 4-week MA of a basket of individual country indexes touching a new low over a 13-week time span. The horizontal lines show two levels of tolerance. During a bull market, a reversal from the lower line triggers a buy signal. During a bear market, the requirement is a reversal from the

CHART 33.5 MSCI World ETF (ACWI) Spliced, 1996–2012, and a Net New High Oscillator

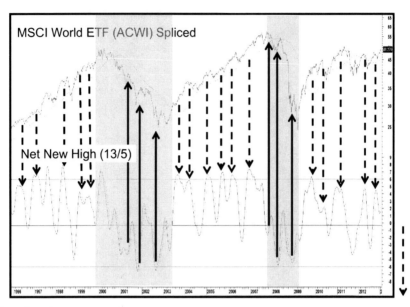

Source: From pring.com

CHART 33.6 MSCI World ETF (ACWI) Spliced, 1996–2012, and a Net New Low Indicator

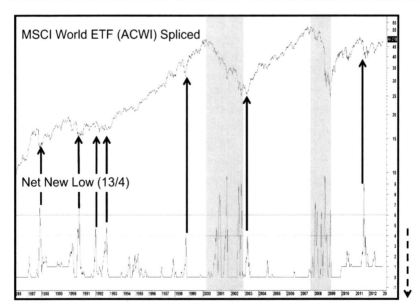

Source: From pring.com

CHART 33.7 MSCI World ETF (ACWI) Spliced, 1969–2012, and a Diffusion Indicator Showing Buy Signals

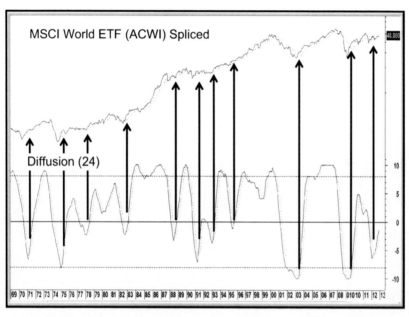

Source: From pring.com

upper horizontal line and above. Even then, the rallies are somewhat puny when compared to those signaled during bull markets.

Chart 33.7 shows a different representation.

In this case, it is a diffusion indicator that measures a basket of individual country indexes in local currencies that are above their 24-month MAs. The 24-month time span is used as an attempt to reflect half of the 4-year (24-month) business cycle. Buy indications develop when the indicator reverses from a below-zero reading and crosses above its 9-month MA. The 11 signals in the approximate 40-year period covered by the chart certainly reflect that 4-year business cycle idea, though, of course, they are not evenly spaced. Chart 33.8 shows the exact same diffusion series, but this time from the sell side. That is, when the indicator moves above the overbought zone and crosses through its MA on its way back to the equilibrium area. During extended bull markets, some of these signals result in false negatives, which have been flagged by the dashed arrows. Note that in neither case did the price slip decisively below its 12-month MA. On the other hand, this approach more than made up for this deficiency by calling major tops that developed in 1969, 1973, 1990, 2000, and 2007.

CHART 33.8 MSCI World ETF (ACWI) Spliced, 1969–2012, and a Diffusion Indicator Showing Sell Signals

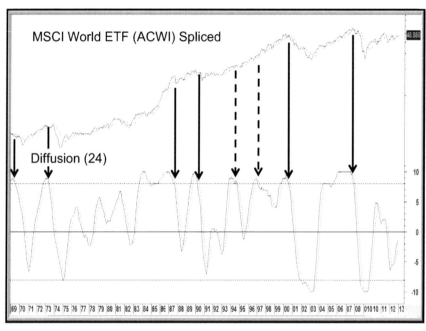

Source: From pring.com

Chart 33.9 features a way of identifying trend reversals in the MSCI Emerging Market ETF (symbol EEM). It's a diffusion indicator constructed from a basket of emerging-market ETFs.

The number 40 in the legend refers to the fact that we are looking at the number of individual emerging-market ETFs above their 40-day MA, and the 8 tells us that the final plot is an 8-day smoothing. The arrows flag when the indicator rallies through its oversold zone. The solid arrows reflect successful signals and the dashed ones false positives. The same exercise is undertaken in Chart 33.10, but this time from the sell side. Of course, it would be possible to construct similar measures using weekly or monthly time spans for the purpose of monitoring longer-term trends.

Global A/D Line

The global A/D line in Chart 33.11 is a daily A/D line plotted on a weekly basis. It is constructed from 20 country and regional ETFs. The history only

CHART 33.9 MSCI Emerging Markets ETF (EEM), 2010–2012, and a Daily Diffusion Indicator Showing Buy Signals

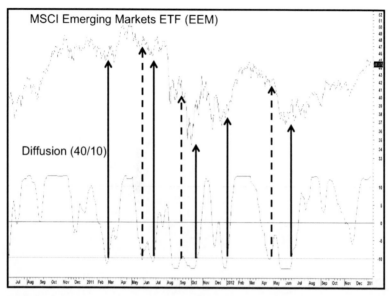

Source: From pring.com

CHART 33.10 MSCI Emerging Markets ETF (EEM), 2010–2012, and a Daily Diffusion Indicator Showing Sell Signals

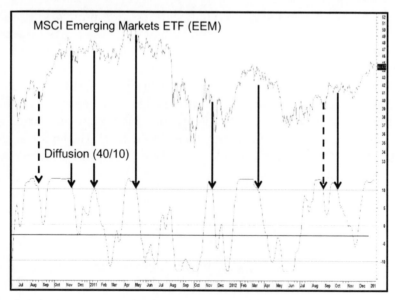

Source: From pring.com

CHART 33.11 MSCI World ETF, 2007–2012, and Two Breadth Indicators

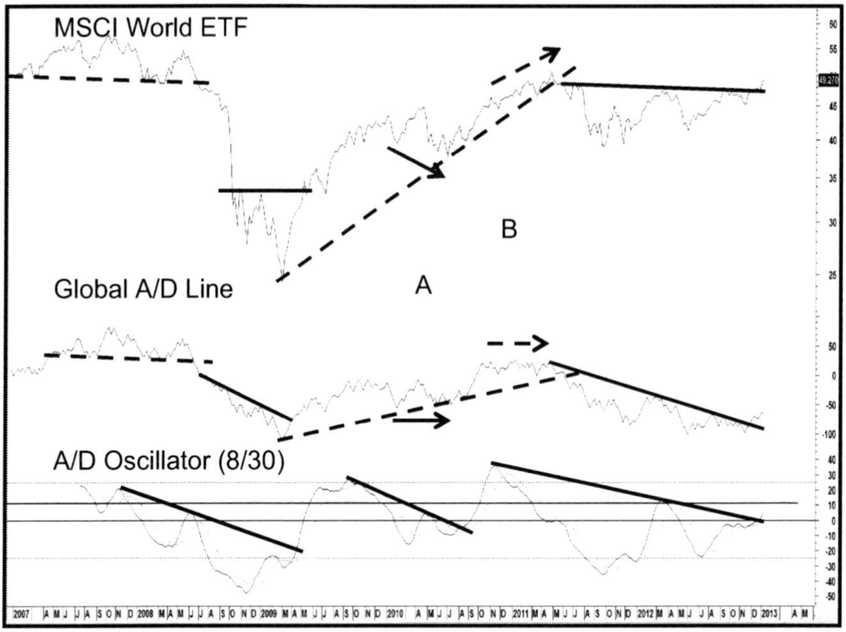

Source: From pring.com

covers 5 years of data, but it is certainly showing some promise as a useful analytical tool. Occasionally, as at points A and B, it throws up positive and negative divergences. However, its main use comes from the fact that its jagged action allows the construction of trendlines, which when confirmed by the price itself, offer timely buy and sell indications. The indicator in the bottom panel is a price oscillator constructed by dividing an 8-week MA of the A/D line by a 30-week MA. It's also possible to construct trendlines on this series, and we see three useful ones in the chart. The indicator also lends itself to overbought/oversold reversals more in identifying reversals in the A/D line than for the price itself.

Relative Strength and Momentum

Today there are a variety of ways in which investments or trades can be executed in specific markets. Individual stocks can be purchased through brokers with an international presence, through American depositary receipts (ADRs), etc. In recent years the exchanges of most countries have established futures markets on key indexes. Exposure can also be achieved through closed and open-ended mutual funds that specialize in individual countries or regions.

The most popular instrument, the exchange-traded fund, is now available for virtually every country in the world. Some ETF families also include sector funds for individual countries. China and Brazil are just two examples.

The key to selecting better-performing stock markets is the adoption of relative strength analysis using the principles outlined in Chapter 19. Chart 33.12 shows the relative strength (RS) line for the S&P Composite against the MSCI World Index with a long-term KST of the same series. The KST reversals were, for the most part, timely signals, though in several instances it would have been more advisable to wait for some trendline confirmation, as we can see, for instance, in the confusing

CHART 33.12 S&P Composite RS versus the World ETF, 1975–2012, and a Long-Term Monthly KST

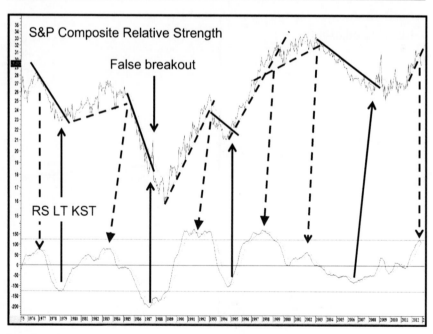

1990–1992 period. Generally speaking, the KST reversal trendline confirmation approach works very well. However, in 1987 and 2009 this approach resulted in a couple of nasty whipsaws. Both situations were involved with sharp global sell-offs, so the relative rally reflected a temporary rush to (relative) safety.

Chart 33.13 shows the same arrangement for the Nikkei. In order to make the comparison relevant, the Nikkei has been adjusted into U.S. dollars. The most striking part of the chart lies in the two distinctive periods on either side of 1990: a secular bull prior to that date and a secular bear after. The differing characteristics for the relative KST in the bottom panel are also evident, with the secular bull rarely falling below zero and never to an oversold condition, while the opposite was true for the post-1990 period. The chart also demonstrates the power of long trendlines when they are violated, because both dashed trendline penetrations ushered in an extensive period of deterioration. As we leave the chart, the dollar-adjusted series was tantalizingly close to a 20-year upside breakout. Not only was that 1990–20?? down trendline a long one, but it had been

CHART 33.13 Nikkei Dollar Adjusted, 1966–2012, and Two RS Indicators

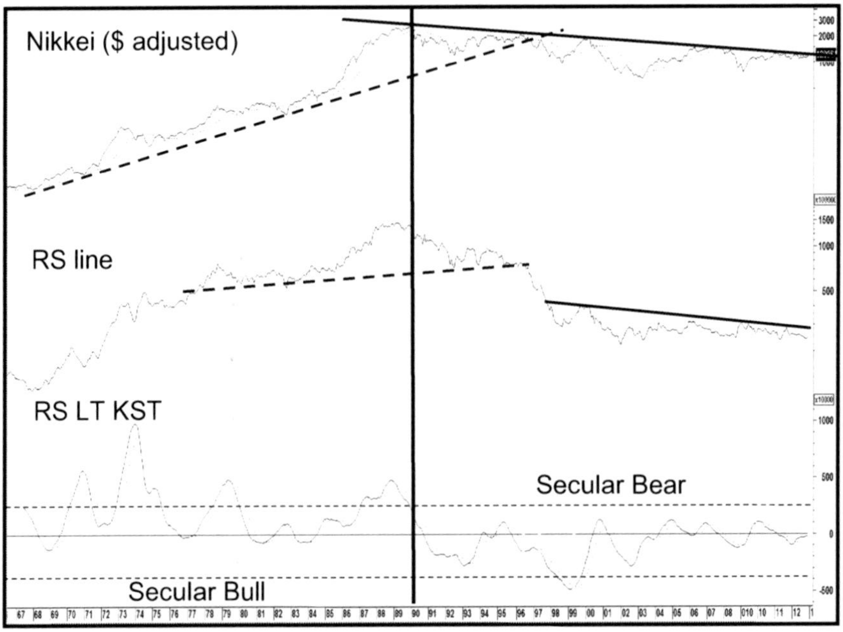

Source: From pring.com

touched or approached on numerous occasions. That means that when it is eventually violated, the Japanese stock market should, at least in nominal terms, experience a very big move. Let's say that happened but was not accompanied by the relative strength line. In that event, it would mean that money was to be made in Japanese equities but capital could be applied more efficiently elsewhere.

Chart 33.14 shows the German DAX Index together with its 18-month rate of change (ROC). Overbought re-crossovers have a 60-year history of offering primary-trend sell signals. They are certainly not perfect, as the two dashed arrows point out, but generally speaking, downside penetrations of the +50 percent level offer reasonably consistent signals. Note also the 1960 move above the 200 percent level, cited in Chapter 23 as a sign of a secular peak. Indeed, it was because the DAX did not take out its 1960 high for 24 years. In this instance the secular bear experienced an initial sharp drop, and this was followed by a multidecade trading range, not unlike the post-1980 secular bear for the gold price.

CHART 33.14 German DAX, 1950–2012, and an 18-month ROC

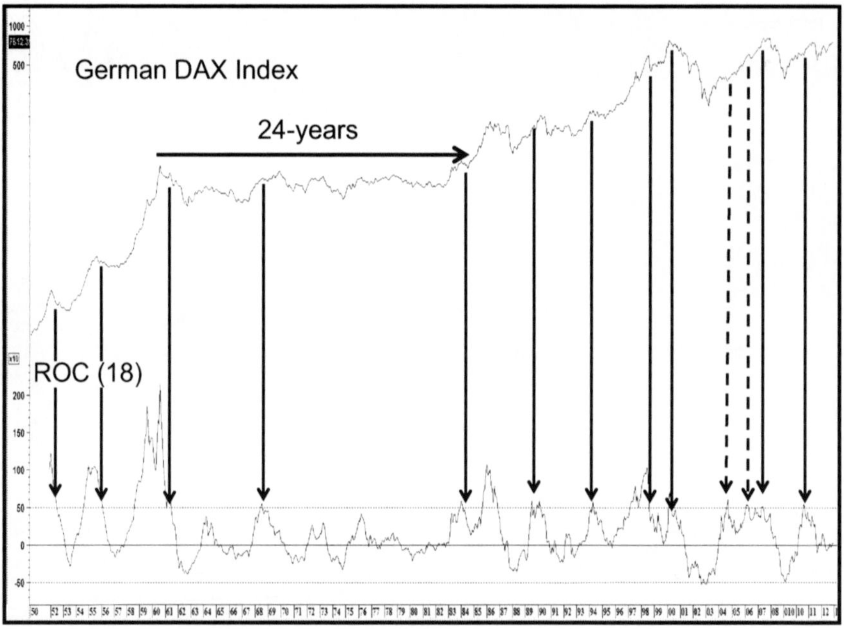

Individual Country Breadth Analysis

Breadth data are now published for many countries, but in many instances A/D lines appear to have a downward bias, probably because many stocks included in the breadth numbers are highly illiquid. For this reason, I prefer to produce my own data selected from a basket of stocks reflecting broad industry participation in each country. Unfortunately, space is limited in this book, so we are only able to scratch the surface. I certainly advise readers in emerging countries to experiment with some of the ideas expressed here and in Chapter 27.

Chart 33.15 features a Brazilian A/D line constructed from 30 leading Brazilian stocks.

You can see how it was possible to construct trendlines for both this indicator and the Brazilian index, the Bovespa, and observe divergences. At point A1 two things are happening. First, the A/D line makes a new high but the Bovespa does not. This is usually a bullish phenomenon, and

CHART 33.15 Bovespa, 1999–2009, and a Brazilian A/D Line

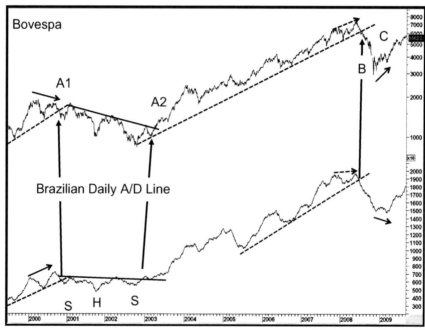

Source: From pring.com

we would normally expect the Bovespa to follow through on the upside. However, in technical analysis, a discrepancy is a discrepancy, so when both dashed up trendlines are violated, we need to respect that, and as you can see, both series declined. As time moved on, the A/D strength extended as the line formed a reverse head-and-shoulders pattern but the price trended down. Note the two trendline breaks at A2. Finally, at the top in 2008, it is the A/D line's turn to be weaker, as you can see from the two small arrows. Then at B both series violate major up trendlines and a bear market was signaled at B. Note how the line lagged the Bovespa at the bear market low. This did not tell us much, as it is normal for breadth indicators to lag the market average.

Chart 33.16 shows a 45-day A/D ratio.

This relatively long-term parameter means that the indicator reflects intermediate trends and is quite deliberate in its trajectory. It is, therefore, more prone to allowing trendline construction. Point A is especially interesting because the oscillator was clearly in a constructive mode as it was experiencing many positive divergences with the price during August and most

CHART 33.16 Bovespa, 2008–2009, and a Brazilian Breadth Oscillator

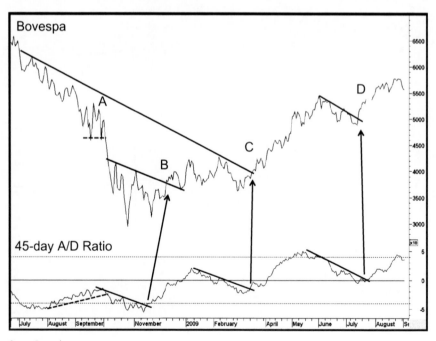

Source: From pring.com

of September. Then the ratio broke below its up trendline and the Bovespa broke to a new low. This is what I call a destructive breakdown, as the potentially very bullish action by the momentum indicator is ruptured. Such situations are typically followed by a sharp decline, which often turns out to be the final one for the move. At points B, C, and D we see joint trendline breaks, which are then followed by a rally of some kind. That at B was a weak one because the basing action was not really complete at that point.

Chart 33.17 features an A/D line I developed for the Indian market because the National Stock Exchange's published figures resulted in a downward bias and, therefore, not helpful for analytical purposes. Chart 33.17 also shows a 65-day oscillator. When all three indicators break trend, there is a greater probability that the signals will be valid. That was certainly true for those triggered at A, C, and D. The signal at B was a bit more problematic because it developed under the context of the strong 2003–2008 primary bull market. As a result, the decline was quite scary but relatively brief.

Diffusion indicators, of course, are another possibility. In this respect, Chart 33.18 features an indicator that monitors a basket of Saudi stocks

CHART 33.17 The Nifty, 2005–2006, and Two Breadth Indicators

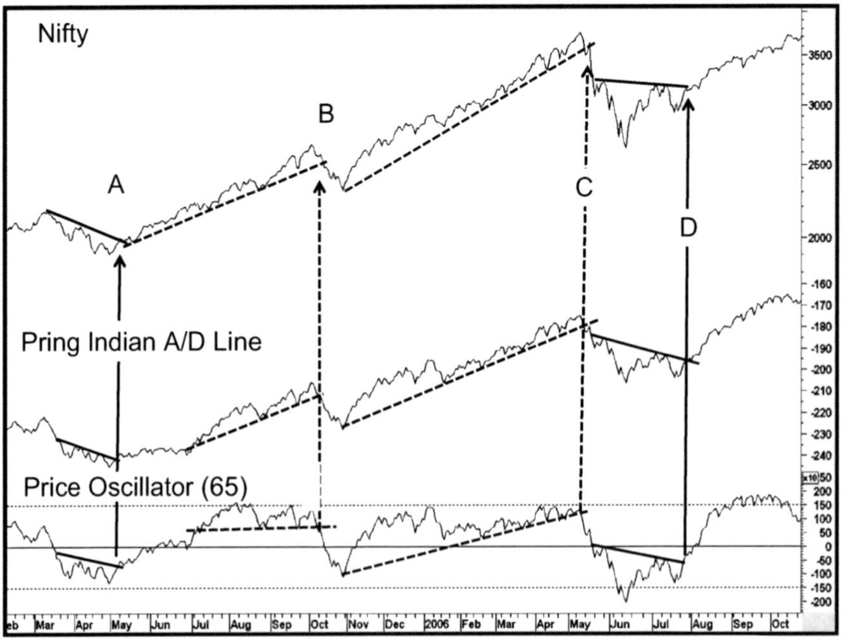

Source: From pring.com

CHART 33.18 The Saudi General, 2006–2008, and a Saudi Diffusion Indicator

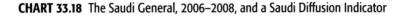

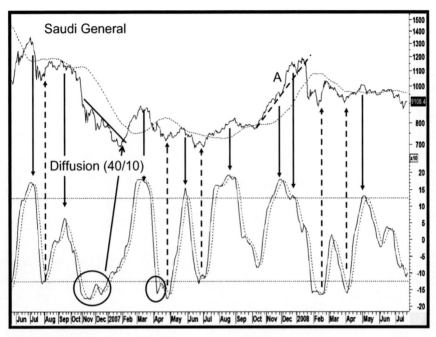

Source: From pring.com

that are above their 40-day MAs. The arrows flag the overbought and over-sold crossovers, the signals for which are expected to have an effect for 4 to 6 weeks. In most of the instances, this is the case. Sometimes these buy signals prove to be premature, as we can see from the two ellipses. However, in most cases, there is the possibility of constructing a trendline and waiting for its violation as a confirmation.

Finally, a useful technique for any market is to calculate the number of stocks in a selected basket whose intermediate KST is below zero (winter and spring positions). When that series reverses from a high reading, it indicates that many stocks are moving to the mark-up phase, i.e., starting a new intermediate uptrend. Such activity, therefore, offers an indication of a strong technical position. Of course, it's also possible to undertake the same operation using the moving-average convergence divergence (MACD) or a stochastic.

Chart 33.19 shows such an exercise based on a basket of Indian stocks compared to the principal Indian market average, the Nifty. In this case, the number 8 in the legend tells us that the raw data have been smoothed with an 8-week MA.

CHART 33.19 The Nifty, 2004–2009, and a Momentum Indicator

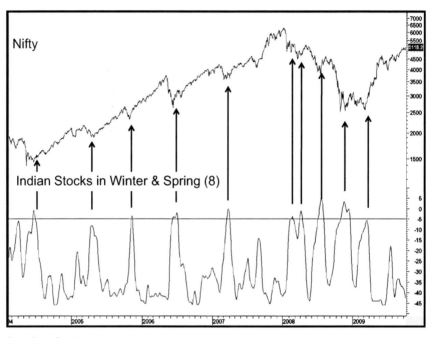

Source: From pring.com

Summary

1. There is a definite 4-year global equity cycle.
2. Recent technological innovation and other factors have led to a much closer relationship between equity markets around the world.
3. Diffusion indexes, net new highs, and other breadth-based indicators incorporating individual country indexes can be used for identifying trend reversals in the World Index.
4. Relative strength is the best tool for identifying markets that are likely to outperform or underperform the world stock indexes.

34

AUTOMATED TRADING SYSTEMS

In recent decades, there has been a substantial increase in the use of personal computers for the purposes of technical analysis. Not surprisingly, this has encouraged many traders and investors to use their own mechanical, or automated, trading systems. These systems can be very helpful as long as they are not adopted as a substitute for judgment and thinking. Throughout this book I have emphasized that technical analysis is an art, the art of interpreting a number of different and reliable scientifically derived indicators. I believe that mechanical trading systems should be used in one of two ways. The preferred method is to incorporate a well thought-out mechanical trading system to alert the trader or investor that a trend reversal has probably taken place. In this method, the mechanical trading system is an important filter, but represents just one more indicator in the overall decision-making process. The other way in which a mechanical trading system can be used is to take action on *every* signal. If the system is well thought out, it should generate profits over the long term. However, if you pick and choose which signal to follow without other independently based technical criteria, you run the risk of making emotional decisions, thereby losing the principal benefit of the mechanical approach.

Unfortunately, most mechanical trading systems are based on historical data and are constructed from a more or less perfect fit with past, in the expectation that history will be repeated in the future. This expectation will not necessarily be fulfilled because market conditions change. A well thought-out and well-designed mechanical system, however, should do the job reasonably well.

> **Major Technical Principle**   It is better to design a system that gives a less-than-perfect fit but more accurately reflects normal market conditions.

Remember that you are interested in future profits, not perfect historical simulations. If special rules have to be invented to improve results, the chances are that the system will not operate successfully when extrapolated to future market conditions.

Advantages of Mechanical Systems

One of the great difficulties of putting theory into practice is that a new factor, emotion, enters the scene as soon as money is committed to the market. The following advantages therefore assume that the investor or trader will follow the buy and sell signals consistently:

- A major advantage of a mechanical system is that it automatically decides when to take action; this has the effect of removing emotion and prejudice. The news may be atrocious, but when the system moves into a positive mode, a purchase is automatically made. In a similar vein, when it appears that nothing can stop the market from going through the roof the system will override all possible emotions and biases and quietly take you out.
- Most traders and investors lose in the marketplace because they lack discipline. Mechanical trading requires only one aspect of discipline: the commitment to follow the system.
- A well-defined mechanical system will give greater consistency of profits than a system in which buying and selling decisions are left to the individual.
- A mechanical system will let profits run in the event that there is a strong uptrend, but will automatically limit losses if a whipsaw signal occurs.
- A well-designed model will enable the trader or investor to participate in the direction of every important trend.

Disadvantages of Mechanical Systems

The disadvantages of using mechanical systems are as follows:

- No system will work all the time, and there may well be long periods when it will fail to work.
- Using past data to predict the future isn't necessarily a valid approach because the character of the market often changes.
- Most people try to get the best or optimum fit when devising a system, but experience and research tell us that a historical best fit doesn't usually translate into the future.
- Random events can easily jeopardize a badly conceived system. A classic example occurred in Hong Kong during the 1987 crash, when the market was closed for 7 days. There would have been no opportunity to get out, even if a sell signal had been triggered. True, this was an unusual event, but it's surprising how often special situations upset the best rules.
- Most successful mechanical systems are trend-following by nature. However, there are often extended periods during which markets are in a nontrending mode, which renders the system unprofitable.
- "Back-testing" won't necessarily simulate what actually would have happened. It is not always possible to get an execution at the price indicated by the system because of illiquidity, failure of your broker to execute orders on time, and so forth.

Design of a Successful System

A well-designed system should try to capitalize on the advantages of the mechanical approach, but should also be designed to overcome some of the pitfalls and disadvantages already discussed. In this respect, there are eight important rules that should be followed:

- Back-test over a sufficiently long period with several markets or stocks. The more data that can be tested, the more reliable the future results are likely to be.

- Evaluate performance by extrapolating the results over an earlier period. In this case, the first step would involve the design of a system based on data for a specific time span, such as 1977 to 1985 for the bond market. The next step would be to test the results from 1985 to 1990 to see whether or not your approach would have worked in the subsequent period. In this way, rather than "flying blindly" into the future, the system is given a simulated but thorough testing using actual market data.

- Define the system precisely. This is important for two reasons. First, if the rules occasionally leave you in doubt about their correct interpretation, some degree of subjectivity will permeate the approach. Second, for every buy signal there should be a sell signal, and vice versa. If a system has been devised using an overbought crossover as a sell and an oversold crossover as a buy, it might work quite well for a time. An example is shown in Figure 34.1a. On the other hand, there could be long periods during which a countervailing signal is not generated, simply because the indicator does not move to these extremes. Failure to define the system precisely can, therefore, result in significant losses, as shown in Figure 34.1b.

- Make sure that you have enough capital to survive the worst losing streak. When devising a system, it is always a good idea to assume the worst possible scenario and to make sure that you start off with enough capital to survive such a period. In this respect, it is worth noting that the most profitable moves usually occur after a prolonged period of whipsawing.

- Follow every signal without question. If you have confidence in your system, do not second-guess it. Otherwise, unnecessary emotion and undisciplined action will creep back into the decision-making process.

- Use a diversified portfolio. Risks are limited if you place your bets over a number of different markets. If a specific market performs far worse than it ever has in the past, the overall results will not be catastrophic.

- Trade only markets that show good trending characteristics. Chart 34.1 shows the lumber market between 1985 and 1989.

FIGURE 34.1 Overbought/Oversold Crossovers

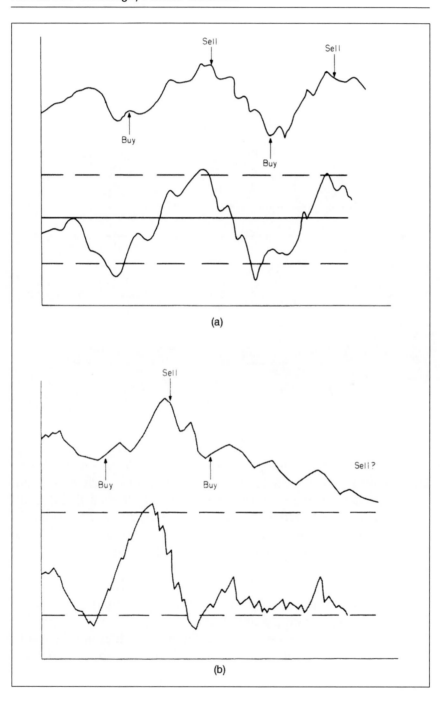

CHART 34.1 Lumber, 1985–1989

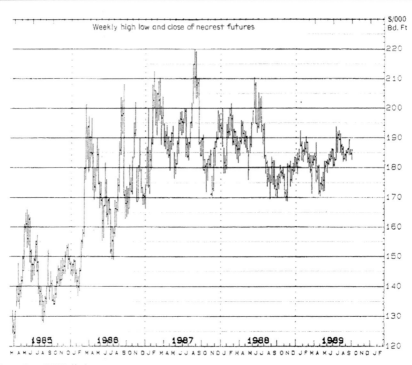

Source: From CRB Weekly charts.

During this period the price fluctuated in a volatile, almost haphazard, fashion and clearly would not have lent itself to a mechanical trend-following system. On the other hand, the Commodity Research Board (CRB) Spot Raw Industrial Materials Index (Chart 34.2) shows an example of both a downtrending and uptrending price trend. Although it is subject to the odd confusing trading range, it has, by and large, moved in consistent trends.

- Keep it simple. It is always possible to invent special rules to make back-testing more profitable. Overcome this temptation. Keep the rules simple, few in number, and logical. The results are more likely to be profitable in the future, when profitability counts.

CHART 34.2 CRB Spot Raw Industrials, 2007–2011

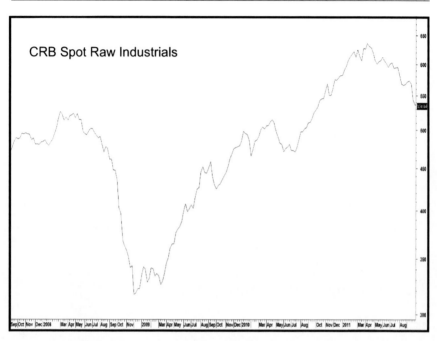

Source: From pring.com

FIGURE 34.2 Trade-off Between Timeliness and Sensitivity

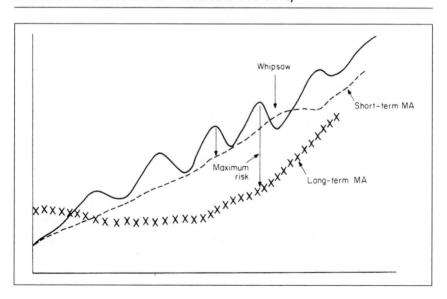

FIGURE 34.3 MA Crossovers in Trendless Markets

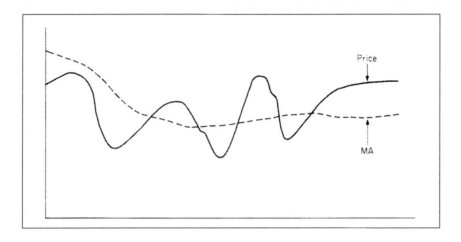

Trading Range and Trending Markets

There are basically two types of market conditions: trending and trading range. A trending market, as shown in Figure 34.2, is clearly suitable for moving-average (MA) crossovers and other types of trend-following systems.

In this kind of situation, it is very important to define the risk since an MA is a trade-off between volatility and sensitivity. In Figure 34.2, the maximum distance between the short-term MA, shown as the dashed line, and the series, shown as the solid line, is the maximum risk. Unfortunately, the short-term MA whips around and gives several false signals. Although the risk of the individual trade defined by the crossover of this MA is small, the chances of unprofitable signals are much greater. On the other hand, a longer-term MA, shown by the X's, offers larger maximum risk but fewer whipsaws.

MAs, as shown in Figure 34.3, are virtually useless in a trading range market since they move right through the middle of the price fluctuations and almost always result in unprofitable signals. Oscillators, on the other hand, come into their own in a trading range market. They are continually moving from overbought to oversold extremes, which trigger timely buy and sell signals. During a persistent uptrend or downtrend, the oscillator is of relatively little use because it gives premature buy and sell signals, often taking the trader out at the beginning of a major move. The ideal

FIGURE 34.4 Relationship Between Profits and Risk Per Trade Based on Opportunities

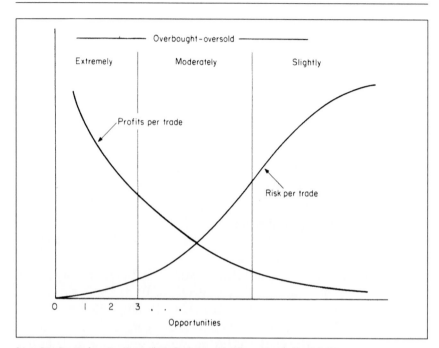

Source: From Perry Kaufman. New Commodity Trading Systems, John Wiley and Sons Inc New York 1987.

automated system, therefore, should include a combination of an oscillator and a trend-following indicator.

The risk and reward for oscillator-type signals generated from overbought and oversold extremes are shown in diagrammatic form in Figure 34.4.

The number of potential trading opportunities is represented on the horizontal axis and the risk on the vertical axis. There are very few times when an oscillator is extremely overbought or extremely oversold, but these are the occasions when the profit per trade is at its greatest and the risk the smallest. Moderately overbought conditions are much more plentiful, but the profits are lower and the risk higher. Taken to the final extreme, slightly overbought or oversold conditions are extremely plentiful, but the risk per trade is much higher and profits are significantly lower. Ideally, a mechanical trading system should be designed to take advantage of a situation in which profits per trade are high and risk is low. Execution of a good system, therefore, requires some degree of patience because these types of opportunities are limited.

Turning points in price trends are often preceded by a divergence in the oscillator, so it is a good idea to combine signals from extreme oscillator readings with some kind of MA crossover. This won't result in a perfect indicator, but it might help to filter out some of the whipsaws.

Guidelines for Appraising Results

When the simulated results of a mechanical system are being reviewed, there is a natural tendency to look at the bottom line to see which system would have generated the most profits. However, top results do not always indicate the best system. The reasons for this are as follows:

- It is possible that most, or all, of the profit was generated by one signal. If so, this would place lower odds on the system's generating good profits in the future since it would lack consistency. An example of an inconsistent system is shown in Table 34.1, which represents signals generated by a 10-day MA crossover of an oscillator that was constructed by dividing a 30-day MA by a 40-day MA (a form of moving-average convergence divergence, or MACD). The market being monitored was Hong Kong during the 1987–1988 period. The system would have gained nearly 1,200 points, compared to a buy-hold approach, which would have lost 800 points. However, this excellent gain would have actually resulted in a loss had it not been for the fact that a prescient short-sell signal occurred just before the 1987 crash.
- Another consideration involves the identification of the worst string of losses (the largest drawdown). After all, it is no good having a system that generates a large profit over the long term if you don't have sufficient capital to ride out the worst period. There are two things to look for in this respect: the string of losing signals and the maximum amount lost during these adverse periods.
- A system that generates huge profits but requires a significant number of trades is less likely to be successful in the real world than is a system based on a moderate number of trades. This is true because the more trades that are executed, the greater the potential for slippage through illiquidity and so on. More transactions also require more time and involve greater commission costs.

TABLE 34.1 Hang Seng 3-Month Perpetual 30/40 Oscillator Performance, 1987–1988

| Date | Trade | Price | Current Trade | | Profit or Loss | Cumulative | |
			Points	Percent	Points	Percent	Dollars
08/19/87	Sell	3559.900	0.000	0.000	0.000	0.000	0.000
09/30/87	Buy	3843.900	-284.000	-7.978	-284.000	-7.978	-79.78
09/09/87	Sell	3696.900	-147.000	-3.824	-431.000	-11.802	-114.97
09/25/87	Buy	3918.900	-222.000	-6.005	-653.000	-17.807	-168.12
10/14/87	Sell	3999.000	80.100	2.044	-572.900	-15.763	-151.11
12/15/87	Buy	2099.900	1899.100	47.489	1326.200	31.726	252.02
02/04/88	Sell	2269.900	170.000	8.096	1496.200	39.822	353.38
02/22/88	Buy	2374.900	-105.000	-4.626	1391.200	35.196	290.77
03/28/88	Sell	2459.900	85.000	3.579	1476.200	38.775	336.97
04/08/88	Buy	2639.900	-180.000	-7.317	1296.200	31.458	239.14
04/19/88	Sell	2584.900	-55.000	-2.083	1241.200	29.374	213.32
06/06/88	Buy	2612.900	-28.000	-1.083	1213.200	28.291	200.18
07/05/88	Sell	2702.900	90.000	3.444	1303.200	31.736	241.52
07/06/88	Buy	2774.900	-72.000	-2.664	1231.200	29.072	208.45
07/18/88	Sell	2722.900	-52.000	-1.874	1179.200	27.198	185.80

Total long trades	7		Total short trades	7
Profitable longs	4 (57.1%)		Profitable shorts	1 (14.3%)
Total buy stops	0		Total sell stops	0
Biggest gain	1899.100		Biggest loss	-284.000
Successive gains	3		Successive losses	3
Total gain or loss	$1179.200		Average gain or loss	84.229
			Total gain or loss	18.58%

Source: *Pring Market Review*/MetaStock.

The Best Signals Go with the Trend

In virtually every situation, the best signals invariably occur in the direction of the main trend. It is easy to pick out the direction of the primary trend in hindsight, of course, but in the real world we have to use some kind of objective approach to determine the direction of the main trend.

One idea might be to calculate a 12-month MA and to use the position of the price relative to the average as a basis for determining the primary trend. The trading system would be based on daily and weekly data and would be acted upon on the long side only when the index was above the average; short signals would be instigated when it was below.

There are two drawbacks to this approach. First, the market itself may be in a long-term trading range in which MA crossovers do not correctly identify the main trend. Second, the first bear market rally quite often occurs while the price is above its 12-month MA. In effect, the buy signal associated with that rally would be operating against the main trend. By and large, though, most markets trend, and this approach will filter out a lot of the countercyclical moves.

An alternative is to use a long-term momentum series, such as the monthly Know Sure Thing (KST), calculated along the lines discussed in Chapter 15. When the KST is rising and the price is above its 12-month MA, a bull market environment is indicated, and all trades would be made from the long side. When the KST is falling and the price is above its 12-month MA, the chances are that the primary trend is in the process of peaking; no positions would be instigated. If you already had some exposure, the topping-out action of the KST would indicate that some profits should be taken, but total liquidation of the position would probably be better achieved at the time of a negative MA crossover. A trade would be activated only when the KST and the price, vis-à-vis its MA, were in a consistent mode. For example, when the KST peaks out and the market itself falls below its 12-month MA, a bear market environment is indicated and only trades on the short side should be initiated. If you do not have access to the KST, the MACD, using an 18/20/9 combination on monthly data, is a close substitute.

A Simple Technique Combining an Oscillator with an MA

A technique that enables investors to take advantage of both trending and trading range markets is to combine an MA and an oscillator in such a way that buy signals are triggered when the oscillator has fallen to a predetermined oversold level and the price itself subsequently crosses above an MA.

The position is liquidated if the price crosses below the MA. On the other hand, if the oscillator crosses to an overbought level prior to an MA crossover, part of the position will be sold in recognition of the possibility that the market might be experiencing a trading range. The other part of the position will continue to ride until an MA sell signal is triggered.

This approach will make it possible to capitalize on the potential of a trending market, but some profits will be taken in case subsequent market action turns out to be part of a volatile trading range.

Recognizing that oscillators often diverge at important market turning points, an alternative might be to wait for it to move to an extreme for a second time before buying on an MA crossover. The same rules as previously described would be used for selling.

Marketplace Example

Now it is time to take an actual example of a system by combining these two techniques. The security I chose is a continuous contract for U.S. T-bonds, an MA, and a price oscillator, as shown in Chart 34.3. A price oscillator was calculated by dividing a short-term MA by a longer-term one. In this case, I used a one-period MA, that is, the close as the shorter average and the 10-day simple MA as the longer-term one. The 10-day average is plotted in the upper panel with the oscillator underneath.

CHART 34.3 Treasury Bonds and a 1/10 Price Oscillator

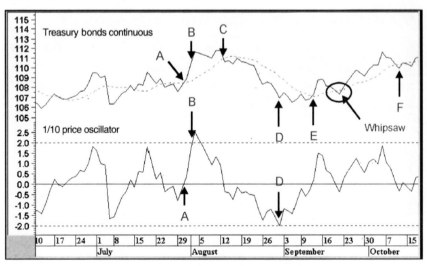

Source: From Martin Pring, *Trading Systems Explained*, Marketplace Books, Columbia Maryland, 2008.

Chart 34.3 shows the way the system works. It is really very simple: Buy when the price crosses above the 10-day MA (as it does in late July at point A). Then sell when it crosses below the average or when the price oscillator reaches a specific predetermined level. The oscillator reaches the designated overbought level a few days later (B). In this case, I selected the +2 and –2 percent. This means the overbought and oversold lines are the equivalent of the price being 2 percent above and below the 10-day MA. Then, in early August, the price crosses below the average and this initiates a short signal (C). The position covered at the end of the month is fairly close to the actual low as the oscillator touches its oversold zone (D). The next buy signal comes on an MA crossover in early September (E). The oscillator never has a chance to move to the +2 percent level because the MA crossover comes first. The next short signal is a whipsaw, followed by the final buy that resulted in a small profit (F).

I optimized (optimization is the systematic search for the best indicator formula) this system by using one variable for the MA and the oscillator, and another for each of the overbought and oversold conditions. The best overall returns were given by the 26/2/–4 combination, as you can see in Table 34.2. This was not the one I finally chose, however, because I like to see identical levels for the overbought and oversold triggering points. The rationale for this arises from the fact that oscillator sensitivity to overbought and oversold conditions depends on the direction of the primary trend. In a bull market, oscillators move to higher overbought levels and rallies are generated from moderate oversold levels. If you know you are in a bull market, you could skew the

TABLE 34.2 Treasury Bonds Price Oscillator Optimization Results, 1981–1998

Profit	Percent	Total	Win	Lost	Average	OP1	OP2	OP3
6039	160.39	387	126	261	2.6001	26	2	–4
5680	156.80	388	137	251	2.2558	26	2	–2
5573	155.73	365	131	234	2.2056	28	2	–2
5362	153.62	425	133	292	2.7005	24	2	–4
4968	149.68	426	145	281	2.3202	24	2	–2
4452	144.52	365	119	246	2.6470	28	5	–2
4389	143.89	365	119	246	2.6598	28	6	–2
3052	130.52	387	127	260	2.4372	26	2	–3
2980	129.80	353	110	243	2.7424	30	5	–2
2833	128.33	365	118	246	2.4860	28	2	–3

TABLE 34.3 Treasury Bonds Using the 28/2/–2 Combination, 1981–1998

Buy/Hold profit	1.12	Days in test	6291
Buy/Hold pct gain/loss	111.83	Annual B/H pct gain/loss	6.49
Total closed trades	365	Commission paid	0.20
Avg profit per trade	0.00	Avg Win/Avg Loss ratio	2.21
Total long trades	183	Total short trades	182
Winning long trades	70	Winning short trades	61
Total winning trades	131	Total losing trades	234
Amount of winning trades	4.15	Amount of losing trades	–3.36
Average win	0.03	Average loss	–0.01
Largest win	0.10	Largest loss	–0.06
Average length of win	8.05	Average length of loss	4.52
Longest winning trade	21	Longest losing trade	18

triggering points to the upside, and vice versa. Unfortunately, we never learn that the primary trend has reversed until sometime later. Also, if we go with numbers skewed to a bull market environment, the system is definitely going to be under pressure when a bear market begins. It makes sense to evenly balance the overboughts and oversolds. That is why I chose the 28/2/–2 combination. I could have chosen the 26/2/–2 combo, but the profit was only slightly better. The 28-day MA generated fewer signals, and fewer signals mean fewer chances for mistakes.

On the face of it, the number of losing signals of 234 to 131 winners looks pretty grim. However, when you look at the more detailed report of Table 34.3, the average win was 2.2 times greater than the average loss, which shows this system did a reasonable job of cutting losses short.

The top panel of Chart 34.4 shows the equity line. The starting amount of $1 was increased to $2.55. Even though the system trailed the buy-hold approach, there were no major drawdowns in terms of peak-to-trough equity. The one in 1994 of 10 percent was the worst. Not bad, considering the 150 percent gain was achieved at a 9.4 percent annualized rate.

Other tests on many closed-end mutual funds covering the 1980s and 1990s have shown that the 28/5/–5 combination of a 28-day MA and a close divided by a 28-day MA using +5 and –5 as the overbought/oversold triggering points worked consistently well.

CHART 34.4 Treasury Bonds, 1981–1998, Featuring the 28/2/–2 Price Oscillator System

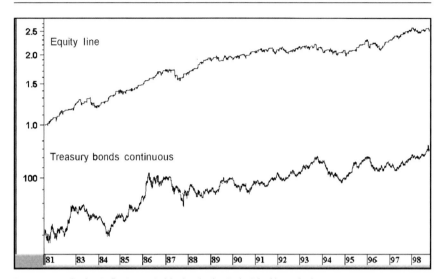

Source: From Martin Pring, *Trading Systems Explained*, Marketplace Books, Columbia, Maryland, 2008.

The Triple Indicator System

One important principle that should be followed when designing a system incorporating several triggering mechanisms is to make sure it incorporates different indicators based on different time frames. The contrasted time frames are important because prices at any one time are determined by the interaction of many different time cycles. We cannot make provisions for all of them, of course. If we can ensure there is a good time difference that separates the indicators used in the construction, we will at least have made an attempt to monitor more than one cycle.

A system I devised in the late 1970s combines an MA crossover with a signal from two rate-of-change (ROC) indicators. These are a 10-week simple MA, a 6-week ROC, and a 13-week ROC. Thus, we have two different types of indicators: a trend-following MA and two oscillator types. The system also consists of three different time frames. The buy and sell rules are very simple. Buy when the price is above the 10-week MA and both ROCs are above zero. Sell when all three go negative, that is, when the ROCs cross below zero and the price crosses its MA. Signals cannot be generated unless all three agree. This is because we want to make sure the various cycles reflected in the three different time frames are all in gear.

CHART 34.5 British Pound System and a 10-Week MA

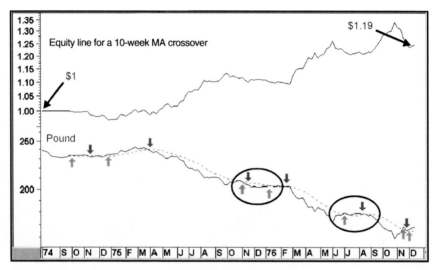

Source: From Martin Pring, *Trading Systems Explained*, Marketplace Books, Columbia, Maryland, 2008.

Originally, when I introduced this system, it was applied to the pound/dollar relationship because it was one that trended very consistently.

Let's take a close look at Chart 34.5 to see how it works by starting off with a simple 10-week MA crossover between mid-1974 and 1976. Buy signals are once again indicated by the upward-pointing arrows and short positions by the downward-pointing ones. There were 13 signals for a total profit of $0.19 on an initial $1 investment, from both the long and the short side. This compares to the buy-hold approach, with a loss of almost $0.70. Taken on its own, this was a fairly commendable performance, but let's remember that for a significant portion of the time, that is, most of 1975 and 1976, the British pound was in a sustained downtrend. It is true there were a number of whipsaws in late 1975 and early 1976. These are shown in the two ellipses, but they were of minor consequence as it turned out.

The next step is to introduce a 13-week ROC. Buy and sell signals are triggered when the 13-week ROC crosses above and below its zero reference line. This approach, shown in Chart 34.6, nets a gain of $0.23 with six signals. This was better than the results with the MA crossover, especially since fewer signals dramatically reduced the potential for whipsaws. Even so, there were a couple of nasty whipsaws in 1976.

CHART 34.6 British Pound System and a 13-Week ROC

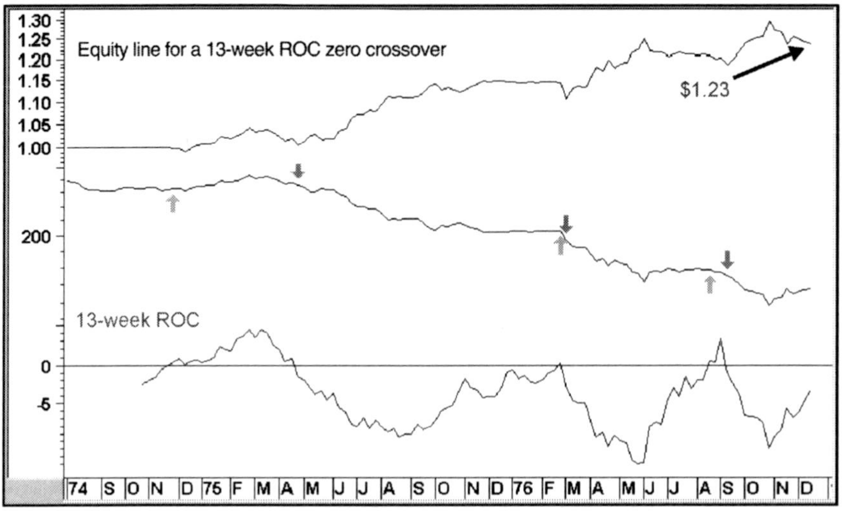

Source: From Martin Pring, *Trading Systems Explained*, Marketplace Books, Columbia, Maryland, 2008.

The next step is to introduce a second ROC indicator to filter out some of the whipsaws. A 6-week ROC was chosen mainly because it spans approximately half the time span of the 13-week series. The result was an improved $0.24, but the number of signals increased to 12. The 6-week ROC is shown in the middle panel of Chart 34.7.

Putting the Indicators Together

I put all three indicators together in Chart 34.7 so you can see how their integration improves things. The actual result was a slight increase in profit over the previous 6-week ROC test. However, the important thing was that the signals were reduced to only three. A closer look at Chart 34.7 shows that the first sell comes in October 1974, as the 6-week ROC follows the others into negative territory. Then, in December, the 13-week ROC crosses above zero, and this is closely followed by an MA crossover. Finally, the 6-week series moves above zero for a buy signal. All three then move into negative territory in April 1975. The MA and 6-week ROC go bearish simultaneously, and this is then followed by the 13-week series. The system stays bearish all the way through late 1976. It almost goes bullish when the price crosses its average and the 6-week ROC goes positive in February 1976.

CHART 34.7 British Pound System and Three Indicators

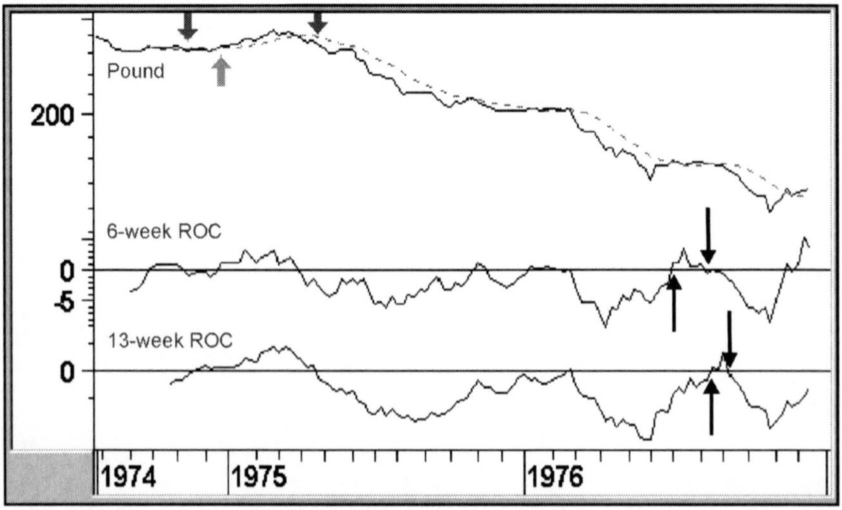

Source: From Martin Pring, *Trading Systems Explained*, Marketplace Books, Columbia, Maryland, 2008.

However, the 13-week series, which had been bearish, now goes bullish, but by this time, the currency had slipped below its MA and the 6-week series fell below zero. As a result, all three indicators were never in agreement. The same is true in the July–August period of 1976 when the two ROC indicators take turns in being bullish and bearish. This was a type of a negative complex divergence described in Chapter 13. The combination of all three indicators works extremely well in this environment.

This is about as good as it gets.

Appraising the System

I originally introduced this approach in my book *International Investing Made Easy* (McGraw-Hill, 1981) with some hesitancy because there was obviously no guarantee it would continue to operate profitably. It was subsequently reintroduced in the third edition of this book in 1992 with the same proviso. What I said was, "It is important to understand this approach will not necessarily offer such large rewards in the future. The example of the British pound must be treated as the exception rather than the rule, but it is introduced to give you an incentive to experiment along these lines."

CHART 34.8 British Pound System Results, 1983–1998

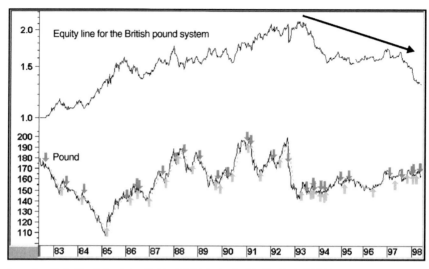

Source: From Martin Pring, *Trading Systems Explained*, Marketplace Books, Columbia, Maryland, 2008.

The system continued to work extremely well, as you can see by looking back at the equity line in the upper panel in Chart 34.8. However, I am glad I used the cautionary statement, because once we move past 1993, the system fell apart. Just look at the declining equity line between 1993 and 2002 in Chart 34.8. Indeed, though it made money for the next 10 years, the peak 1993 equity has never been surpassed. The initial drop was due to the many whipsaws arising from the trading range that followed the drop from $2.00 in 1993. This goes to show that even if a system works well for 20 years, as this one had, market conditions can and do change, so you must be prepared for such instances. Obviously, we do not know until sometime after the fact that the market environment was different. Is there anything we can do to avoid such situations? One possibility is to run a very long-term MA or trendline through the equity line.

In Chart 34.9, I have plotted a 300-week simple MA against the equity line of the three-indicator pound system when applied to the Hang Seng Index. I used 300 weeks because I felt it necessary for the system to undergo a fairly long period before it can be considered out of touch. The idea is when the equity line crosses below the MA something is seriously wrong with the system, and it should be at least temporarily abandoned. At this point, it would make sense to reappraise it and see if it could be improved, and I do not mean by introducing special rules to block out a bad period.

CHART 34.9 British Pound System Applied to the Hang Seng Index, 1981–2012

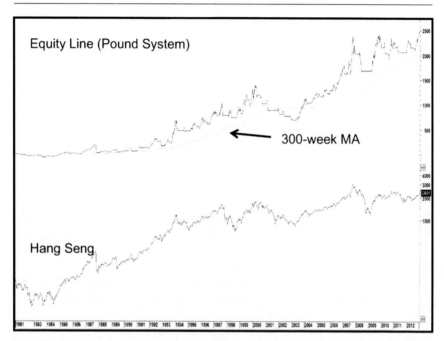

Source: From pring.com

You could also wait until the equity line crosses back above the MA again, but in the case of the "busted" pound system, as far as the pound was concerned, even that approach was problematic. Unfortunately, such eventualities are unavoidable, which is why it's a good idea to diversify among securities and systems in order to reduce risk.

Introducing an Intermarket System

The Relationship

So far, we have just considered particular securities or markets in isolation, using statistically derived data from that security alone. An alternative approach is to adopt a tried and tested intermarket relationship as a cross-reference.

Better results are often obtained in this way. An intermarket relationship develops when one market consistently influences another. The first step is to rationalize why such a relationship exists in the first place.

Perhaps the most basic one is between equities and short-term interest rates. This was described in Chapter 31, where it was established that changes in the trend of short-term interest rates lead equity prices.

What we do not know is the lead time or the magnitude of the ensuing stock rally. The answer is to classify the trend of money-market prices, which is what the inverted short rate actually is, with an MA crossover. When a rising trend of money-market prices has been established, it is then time to look at the trend of equities to see when they respond. The rationale is that a rising trend of money-market prices sets the scene for an equity bull market. However, this is not confirmed until the S&P Composite crosses above its MA. Just think of this as something akin to an unconscious swimmer receiving mouth-to-mouth resuscitation. You know the treatment is good for the patient, just as falling rates are good for equity prices. However, we do not know how much treatment is required and whether the patient will recover until he or she is able to breathe by him- or herself. In our analogy, the stock market is shown to respond to the interest-rate treatment when it crosses its MA.

Here is how it works. Look at Chart 34.10. In October 1981, the inverted commercial paper yield crosses above its 12-month MA (shown in the ellipse), indicating the environment is now bullish for equities. However, the equity market does not respond by bottoming out until

CHART 34.10 S&P Composite, 1980–1988, versus 3-month Commercial Paper Yield

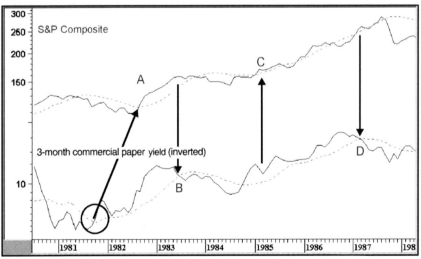

August 1982. When the S&P rallies above its 12-month MA (A), it indicates that the market is responding to the positive interest rate environment. In this case, the crossover comes in August 1982. At that time, both trends are bullish and so is the system. It remains positive until either series moves back below its average, which, in this case, developed in June 1983 (B). It then goes bullish again in January 1985 (C).

Finally, the inverted yield falls below its average in early 1987 (D). The market continues to rally, but the system is no longer bullish. In most instances, it would be better to generate the sell signals after the S&P crosses below its average. In this instance, though, the 1987 crash was over before the average was penetrated. Since the risk increases as the money-market series crosses below its average, it is probably best to act on the signal in two parts. This would involve taking off half the position as the money-market series goes negative and then liquidating the rest when the S&P crosses its average.

Figure 34.5 compares the risk and reward for the system between 1900 and 2009 to that for the S&P Composite. The vertical axis measures

FIGURE 34.5 The 120% Rule Risk versus Return

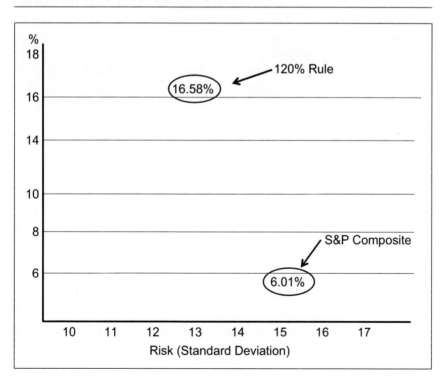

the monthly reward on an annualized basis, and the risk is measured on the horizontal axis. In this sense, risk is measured as volatility. The best place for any system to be is in the top-left corner, often referred to as the northwest quadrant. This is where the reward is high and the risk, or volatility, is low. In the case of this system, you can see that the risk was slightly lower than that for the S&P, but the reward was substantially higher. At Pring Turner Capital, we call this the 120 percent rule because it has had such an excellent and consistent track record for over 100 years.

The system says nothing about periods when the market is above its average and rates are not, since those are obviously bullish periods as well. However, once rates move above their 12-month MA, there is a real danger that the next correction could be the first downleg in a bear market. It is true that sooner or later the S&P Composite will cross below its MA, thereby stopping us out, but why run the risk when good returns and little volatility can be had under more favorable conditions? During those periods when both were in a negative mode, the annualized loss was 9.58 percent.

If you are a short-term trader, you probably feel this approach is worse than useless. However, it can be put to very good use if you realize that when the system is bullish, short sell signals are more likely to result in losses. They are not just going against the main trend, but are occurring in one of the most positive equity environments you can get. By the same token, this knowledge can be used to take positions yourself on the long side when a short-term buy signal is triggered. I am not going to say that sharp corrections will never happen when this system is positive, because there have been periods such as 1971 when a fairly large retracement move did materialize. It is merely that when the system is positive, the odds favor strong short-term rallies and whipsaw reactions.

Using Margin

All the systems described here were tested on a cash basis with no margin. You might think that it makes sense to go out and apply a system using lots of margin. That way the gains would multiply. In actual fact, this is not necessarily the case. Chart 34.11 shows a simple 10-day MA crossover system using no margin, and Chart 34.12 shows it using a 10 percent margin requirement. Since the initial trades were losers, the account was wiped out in just over a year. Remember: Leverage works both ways.

CHART 34.11 American Century Gold Fund, 1989–1998

CHART 34.12 American Century Gold Fund, 1989–1998

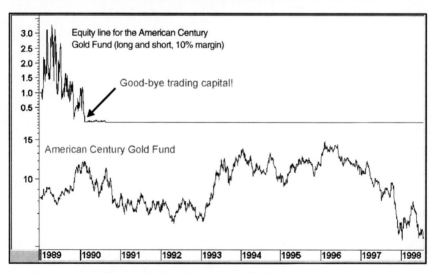

Summary

1. There are two ways in which systems can be used: act on each signal without question, or use the signals as a filter so the current system becomes one more indicator in the weight-of-the-evidence approach.
2. The principal advantage of a mechanical system is that it removes subjectivity and encourages the adoption of discipline.
3. No system will ever work all of the time. It is important to understand the pitfalls of automated systems so that they can be programmed out.
4. Systems should be designed to take account of the fact that there are two different types of market environment: trading range and trending.
5. Because no system works perfectly, it should be exhaustively tested before being applied to the marketplace.
6. The use of any system should involve diversification to spread the risk for any period where it does not operate successfully for a specific security.
7. Incorporating a tried and tested intermarket relationship into the system acts as a cross reference and usually enhances results.
8. The use of margin exaggerates the results, both on the upside and the downside. The actual performance will depend on the chronological sequence of the good and bad signals.

35

CHECKPOINTS FOR IDENTIFYING PRIMARY STOCK MARKET PEAKS AND TROUGHS

Primary bull market tops and bottoms are elusive affairs, largely because the points at which we expect them to develop are the ones that appear to be the most unlikely at the time. When most people are lucky enough to identify a bull market peak, they assume that prices will immediately decline. This is not normally the case because of the numerous and confusing cross-currents necessary for the development of true distribution. This topping-out process usually requires a trading range environment, which reflects the tremendous battle between bulls and bears. First one comes out on top and then the other. By the time the distribution has been completed, both sides are exhausted. Even though the bears eventually win, most lose their original conviction because of the numerous false rallies that they did not anticipate. These advances develop under an environment of extreme optimism, which also make them all the more convincing to those caught short or who have already sold out.

We know that the news is favorable at market peaks, but when a typical top is staring us in the face, the widespread contagion of optimism deludes us into expecting conditions to get even better. The opposite is true of bottoms: The news is bad, but we expect it to get worse before prices hit their low. Alternatively, we expect the other shoe to drop, just like traumatized earthquake victims anticipate a killer aftershock. If it seems inconceivable, given the prevailing conditions and likely outlook, that prices will rise, they probably will.

As an initial step, and this would apply to any security, it's a good idea to make an attempt to figure out the current position of the cycle using monthly data calculated from your favorite long-term smoothed momentum curve, e.g., the Know Sure Thing (KST), stochastic (20/14/10), moving-average convergence divergence (MACD), etc.

Though by no means infallible, these series have a strong tendency to reverse direction around the time of a primary peak or trough. If you spot a reversal of or some observe stalling action, it's then a good idea to revert to evidence provided by other indicators.

The Mechanics of a Peak

A classic market peak should involve a battle between early- and late-cycle leaders. As the top begins, liquidity-driven issues peak out and begin their bear market (see Figure 35.1).

On the other hand, late-cycle leaders are still in the terminal stages of a bull trend and are helping to push the averages higher. If strength in the earnings-driven sectors outweighs weakness elsewhere, the averages move to new bull market highs. This is the principal reason why breadth divergences are so prevalent at market peaks. In 1973, the commodity boom had the effect of prolonging the bull market, as far as the averages were

FIGURE 35.1 Sector Rotation in the Cycle

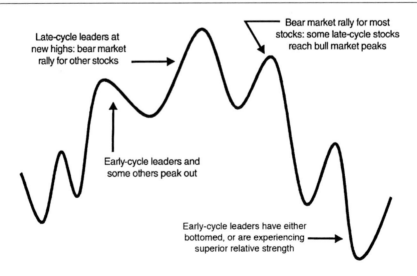

concerned, but the NYSE A/D line had peaked 9 months earlier. In 2000, it was the unprecedented strength in technology stocks, another lagging sector, that propelled the averages higher, but under the surface, the average stock peaked 2 years earlier in 1998.

What Is a Peak?

The objective of this chapter is to offer a checklist of characteristics present at a typical market top or bottom. In reality, there are no "typical" turning points because no two situations are exactly the same. However, there are enough characteristics to enable us to identify the intricate tapestry of a market top or bottom.

It's possible to categorize three types of market peaks. The most important are those that develop after a prolonged bull market, extending over several business cycles. These are the secular turning points described in Chapter 23. Around the time of the peak, it is possible to point to some kind of speculative bubble, often concentrated in a few sectors. At such times old rules are thrown out and virtually everyone becomes an overnight investment genius. Such peaks are very hard to pinpoint at the time because they have defied virtually every traditional rule. Eventually, new rules or rationalizations are developed to justify the final ascent to the equity summit. In this way traditional valuations are surpassed by several degrees. Normal extreme technical benchmarks are also exceeded, and divergences are so plentiful that they are ignored because *they no longer work*. Finally, contrarian positions based on observation of normal crowd behavior prove futile, as the majority march on to new extremes of irrationality. Old rules are thrust aside and ridiculed as new-era thinking predominates. The rallying cry of the bulls is almost always inculcated in the mantra that "this time it is different." In all cases, the leveling factor that brought investors back to reality was a good dose of rising short-term interest rates. Three such peaks possessing at least some of these characteristics developed in 1929, 1966, and 2000. The 1990 secular peak in Japanese equities also qualifies. In 1929, stocks lost close to 90 percent of their value in 3 years. The bear market that followed the 1966 peak lasted a lot longer and consisted of several mini-bull and mini-bear markets. When stocks are adjusted for inflation, the bottom, as measured by the major averages, did not take place until 16 years later in 1982. The top established in 2000 is likely to be of similar importance to the 1929 and 1966 experiences, since many of the valuation, sentiment, and technical characteristics cited in Chapter 23 were present.

There are really two factors that cause the ensuing bear market to be so devastating or lengthy. The first is a direct result of the long and persistent bull trend and falls under the title "careless investment decisions." It is the function of the bear to cleanse the system of these poorly thought-out and precariously financed positions. Such is true of every market peak. It is just far more prevalent at these super-cycle turning points. Second, it appears that the pendulum of human emotions, the ultimate arbitrator of prices, moves to an extreme of extremes. If such a level is reached on one side, an extreme of an extreme is likely to develop on the other. It almost appears as if a prerequisite for a huge bear market is an exceptionally large speculative bull market.

The second peak is what we might term a *recession-associated top* (RAT). It is the most common and best fits the primary trend description described in Chapter 1. In such situations, the unwinding of distortions in the economy brought about by the recovery is sufficient to trigger an actual recession where profits are under attack. In each cycle, the sector responsible for the distortion will be different. In the early 1970s, it tended to be real estate; in 1974, bloated inventories from the commodity boom were the primary culprit. In 1990 and 2007, the financial sector was under pressure, and so forth. Since these RAT-type bear markets are associated with economic contraction and recovery, which take time to accomplish, they usually last 1 to 2 years, are broadly based, and can be quite severe. The most severe of these bear markets develops under the context of a secular bear market.

The third kind of peak precedes so-called growth recessions or double-cycle peaks as described in Chapter 2. They are usually followed by shallower and shorter bear trends. Growth recessions involve the slowing down of the economy but not an actual contraction. In this process, several industrial sectors will experience recessionary conditions, but strength elsewhere will offset this weak activity so that the overall economy escapes the indignity of the "R" word. These weak sectors, therefore, experience a true 1- to 2-year bear market, whereas others merely experience a major trading range. Growth recessions are more likely to develop during a secular bull market.

Examples of double-cycle bears are 1984 and 1994. Other bear trends are associated with a slowing in some of the economic indicators and are preceded by an unhealthy level of speculation. They take the form of severe technical corrections, but are so dramatic that the change in psychology is sufficient to correct much of the speculative juice. The 1962, 1987, and 1998 declines come to mind as good examples.

All of the characteristics listed in the following section do not appear at every market peak, and neither is their intensity of the same magnitude. They are presented solely as a guide for things to watch out for at major highs.

Characteristics of Primary Market Peaks

1. In order for a bull market top to form, it must be preceded by a bull market. Thus, it must be possible to look back and identify a rally of at least 9 months duration.

Monetary and Sector Rotation Factors

2. Almost all market peaks are preceded by a trend in rising short-term interest rates. The lead times vary from a couple of months to years. If interest rates have not begun their ascent, the odds of a top are greatly reduced. For examples, refer to Charts 31.1a and b in Chapter 31.
3. Watch out for hikes in the discount rate. Has the "three step and stumble" rule, discussed in Chapter 31, been triggered? If so, the distribution process may well be under way, and the reward of owning stocks is usually outweighed by the risk.
4. In many instances, market tops are preceded by a peak in the Dow Jones Utility Average. This is because this is a very interest-rate-sensitive market sector.
5. Observation of the long-term relative momentum for a selection of early- and late-cycle leaders often points up a bull market peak. This will be true if the long-term smoothed relative momentum for financials, utilities, and consumer nondurables (staples) peaked out some time ago. By the same token, a characteristic of a market peak is either continued strength in late-cycle leaders, such as basic industry and resource stocks, or an actual peaking of their smoothed momentum.

Technical Factors

6. When interest rates start to rise, this adversely affects financials and preferred shares. Consequently, it is normal for the NYSE A/D line to peak out ahead of the Dow Jones Industrial Average (DJIA) and S&P Composite. The length of the divergence often has a related effect on the size of the ensuing bear market.

7. If the NYSE daily A/D line and or the Value Line Arithmetic Index are below their 200-day moving averages (MAs), this indicates that the broad market is probably in a primary downtrend. Even if the DJIA and S&P Composite are at new highs, this weak breadth position is telling us that the market has become very selective. Under such an environment, it is more difficult to find stocks that are advancing. Cutting back on equity exposure, therefore, makes excellent sense because your odds of success are less. The opposite would be true in a declining market, where the A/D line is advancing.

8. An alternative way of looking at the technical position of market breadth is net new high data. Has the number of net new highs diverged negatively with the major averages? If it has not, this may not be a top. If it has, then fewer stocks are driving the market higher, and this is a sign of weakness. If the number of new highs has shrunk considerably, it is very difficult to make money because the selection process is becoming progressively more difficult.

9. Momentum typically leads price, especially at market tops. Occasionally, it is possible to identify multiyear tops or trendline violations in several long-term rate-of-change (ROC) indicators. For example, if you can spot trendline breaks in the 12-, 18-, and 24-month ROCs, this indicates that the cycles they reflect are all starting to turn. The more trend breaks from different time spans, the stronger the signal. Sometimes, an individual ROC moves between specific benchmarks, and these have traditionally offered good timing points for major tops or bottoms. Charts 21.5 and 21.6 offer some useful benchmarks for a 9-month ROC of the S&P Composite. Always make sure that any momentum signals are confirmed by some kind of trend-reversal signal by the price itself.

10. Another way in which momentum can signal a maturing bull trend is with the use of a long-term smoothed oscillator such as the KST or by an identifiable peak in the Special K. In the case of the KST, market tops are typically signaled by a reversal to the downside from an overbought condition. This is represented in Chart 35.1 by the vertical lines, where the KST crosses below its 9-month MA.

The chart shows that this approach works well when a normal cyclical bull market is experienced. However, during a secular bull market, such as the one that developed in the 1990s, this indicator gives premature sell signals. These are flagged with the dashed vertical lines—all the more reason to make sure that such signals are confirmed by a trend break in the price.

CHART 35.1 S&P Composite, 1952–2012, and a Long-Term KST

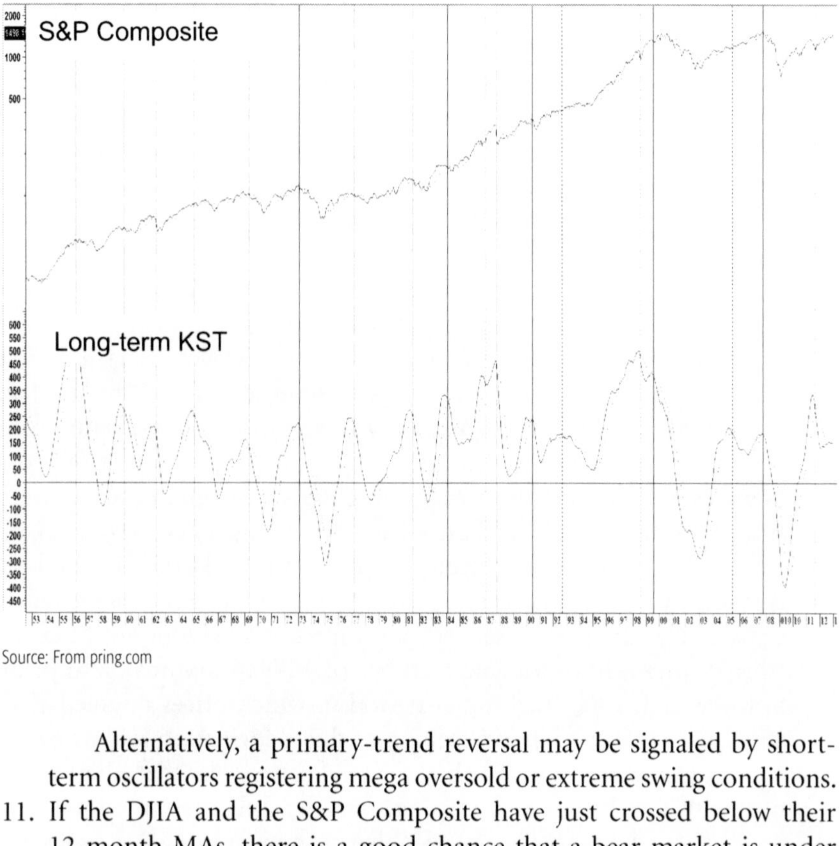

Source: From pring.com

    Alternatively, a primary-trend reversal may be signaled by short-term oscillators registering mega oversold or extreme swing conditions.

11. If the DJIA and the S&P Composite have just crossed below their 12-month MAs, there is a good chance that a bear market is under way, provided, of course, that other indicators are in agreement. Quite often, a negative 7-month MA crossover will work as well as a 12-month time span. Also, in the trend-reversal department, monitor the current position of the Industrials and Transports as called for in Dow theory.

Psychological Factors

12. If key companies report excellent earnings and the prices of their stocks decline, this adverse response to good news indicates extreme technical vulnerability. Whenever a stock or market index fails to respond to good news, this is a sign of technical weakness. Remember, if good news cannot send a security higher, what will?

13. On the sentiment side, a reading in the *Investors Intelligence* percentage of bears would be in the 10 to 20 percent range. Another sign might be the market's failure to respond favorably to a prominent earnings report that was well ahead of expectations. Such signs often develop during the course of a primary trend, say at an intermediate turning point, so it's their collective rather than their individual warnings that should be heeded. Finally, in the sentiment area, if the level of margin debt has recently crossed below its 12-month exponential moving average (EMA), this tells us two things. First, traders are losing confidence. Second, the market is no longer being supported by an expansion in margin debt, and worse, the implied contraction in margin exposure will put downward pressure on stock prices. Consequently, a 12-month downward EMA cross is usually an excellent long-term sell signal. The problem is that the data are published with a 2-month lag.

14. If the media are full of optimistic news and stories of huge returns are being publicized, this is indicative of a topping environment. Supplementary evidence in this direction might evolve from magazine cover stories on the market itself, especially ones citing a new paradigm, or concerning companies or groups that have been leaders in the bull market. In very strong trends, such as the 1990s tech bubble, such signs can be early. For example, an unprecedented amount of cover stories developed in the late summer of 1999, 6 months or so prior to the March 2000 final top, a period in which prices doubled. The good news is that a correct reading of this information told us that a major peak was at hand. The bad news, of course, was that what would normally have been a really strong signal worked after an unduly difficult delay. It is a stark reminder that some major market peaks are associated with a substantially less intensive peak in bullish sentiment than previous lower peaks. Consequently, it is not possible to conclude that just because a new high is not accompanied by a higher level of optimism that everything is okay. The whole situation regarding negative divergences and the action of other indicators must be considered.

15. When the market is rallying, there is always a substantial amount of doubt. However, as equities approach a peak, the question of whether the security in question is a good investment is not even debated. Instead, for the stock market, for example, the debate revolves around which sectors will do well, how high prices will go, or what the next levels of resistance are. In such an environment, forecasts that would previously have been ridiculed for their excessive optimism are given widespread publicity and credibility.

16. Since brokerage companies thrive on bull markets, they become very prosperous during these times. If you see reports of any of these companies moving into larger and more expensive office accommodations, this is often a sign that the uptrend is in a very mature stage. Alternatively, this could show up in the exchange or the back office of brokers being overwhelmed with backlogged orders.

Chronological and Cycle Factors

17. A quick review of the three markets in relation to their 12-month MAs will offer a quick reference for the current stage of the cycle. A market top should see the 3-month commercial paper yield above its 12-month MA. The "three steps and stumble" rule (see Chapter 31) will probably have been triggered as well. Bond yields in the corporate and governmental sectors should be in a similar position. The S&P Composite should be above its average, and the CRB Spot Raw Industrials should be above its average as well. In cases where stocks have fallen quite some way from their peak, it is possible that the S&P would already be below its 12-month MA. If the CRB Spot RM Index has also recently crossed below its average, then little support from commodity-based equities is likely, and at the tail end of the cycle, this usually means a bear market.

18. The 4-year stock cycle has been extremely reliable in offering a buying opportunity once every 4 years. It follows that if the current year is 2 or 3 years from the previous 4-year low, the odds favor a bull market peak. If some of the other signs discussed here are present, this will obviously increase the probability of a top.

19. Is it possible to observe three identifiable intermediate advances that have already taken place? If this is the top of the third, it may be a primary peak. This is by no means infallible, because some bull markets consist of two advances and some more than three. However, when combined with others, these signs can be quite a useful benchmark.

Primary Market Bottoms

Bear market bottoms develop under exactly the opposite conditions as tops. The news is bad, sentiment is extremely bearish, and the long-term momentum indicators are usually extremely oversold. Perhaps the key difference between a major low and a major high is that in almost all cases, bear markets are shorter than bull markets. We have to say "in almost all cases" because the 1929–1932 bear market lasted for 3 long years, whereas the average primary decline has mercifully been much shorter. Characteristics of a major low are as follows.

Monetary and Sector Rotation Factors

1. Bear market lows are invariably preceded by a peak in short-term interest rates. I say "short-term rates," but in almost all cases, a peak in long-term rates also precedes an equity bottom. It is just that changes in the level of short-term rates have a much larger influence on equities than yields at the long end because they reflect liquidity conditions deriving from short-term business decisions. Borrowing costs at the short-end change on a week-by-week basis. Because long-term bonds lock in rates for a considerable period, their effect on the economy is more gradual. The interest rate lead time varies from cycle to cycle, but generally speaking, the longer the lead, the stronger the ensuing bull market. In 1966, for instance, interest rates and equity prices reversed almost simultaneously, whereas the lead was almost a year in 1920 and 1982. The 1967–1968 bull market was tame in comparison to the bull markets of the 1920s and 1980s. This is not the same thing as saying that every time the lead is a year or more, the market will experience a mega rally—merely that there is a rough tendency for that to be the case. The reason for this phenomenon lies in the fact that the longer the lead, the weaker the economy. That weak economy has its pluses since it encourages firms to lower their break-even levels, so when the economy rebounds, new revenues fall to the bottom line.

2. The industry group structure at market bottoms should reveal an improving trend of relative strength and relative smoothed long-term momentum favoring early-cycle leaders, such as utilities, most financials, and most consumer staples (nondurables). To that list you could add homebuilders, telecom, and brokerage stocks. There should also be a pattern of deteriorating relative strength and relative smooth momentum in some of the lagging groups, such as resources, basic industry, and technology. Quite often, when the long-term smoothed *relative* momentum of the S&P Financial Index bottoms, this is quite close to a market bottom. The weakness in earnings-driven stocks is used more as a confirmation.

Technical Factors

3. Positive divergences between the A/D line and the major averages are much rarer than negative ones at market tops. Indeed, the line often lags at most bear market lows. However, when divergences do develop, they are usually followed by an above-average bull market. That was true of the divergence between the (Bolton) weekly A/D lines at the 1942 and 1982 lows (see Chart 27.2). Such a divergence was also present at the 2009 low.
4. Net new highs can also diverge with the averages, but seem to work better when smoothed with a moving average Chart 27.12 also shows a positive divergence in the 30-day high/low ratio at the 2009 bear market low.
5. Other confirming signs would be record volume coming off the low, as in 1978, 1982, and 1984. Also, most bottoms involve a rally and subsequent test of the low. When the second rally surpasses the first, a series of rising peaks and troughs is signaled. This approach was one of the few in the 1929–1932 bear market that had not previously experienced a whipsaw. It is generally a reliable signal, especially when combined with Dow theory buy signals. Another confirming but extremely important signal is the ability of the S&P Composite to rally above its 12-month MA.
6. In extended bear markets, the final low is usually confirmed by a bottoming in smoothed long-term momentum. In this instance, the Coppock Index, described in Chapter 13 and featured in Chart 13.8, is probably the most reliable, as it appears to work with amazing consistency on a number of different markets. During shallow bear markets not associated with recessions, smoothed long-term momentum can often prove to be agonizingly slow. Long-term ROCs will occasionally prove to be better substitutes when it is possible to observe momentum price pattern breakouts or upside penetrations of down trendlines. If you are able to identify a bullish secular environment, the analytical test for a bear market low does not have to meet such a stringent level, as would be the case in a secular bear trend.
7. If short-term oscillators are signaling mega overbought or extreme swing conditions, as described in Chapter 13, this is also a sign that psychology has changed for the better.

Economic Factors

8. Normally, it is a prerequisite of a bottom for the economic news to be at or close to its worst. Chart 35.2 shows the 9-month trend deviation indicator for the Conference Board Coincident Indicators. The same concept is shown in Chart 35.3, which compares the S&P to a composite economic indicator. Note that the Master Economic Indicator bottoms pretty closely to major stock market lows associated with recessions.

CHART 35.2 The S&P Composite, 1956–1980, and the Coincident Indicator (deviation from trend)

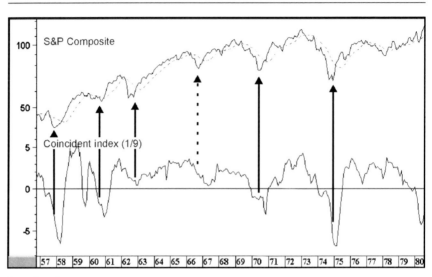

Source: From pring.com

CHART 35.3 The S&P Composite, 1978–2000, and the Coincident Indicator (deviation from trend)

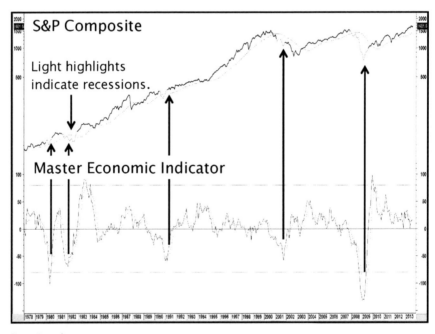

Source: From pring.com

Chronological and Cyclical Factors

9. In terms of the financial market chronological sequence, it is normal for a stock market bottom to be preceded by the 3-month commercial paper yield crossing below its 12-month MA. At the actual bottom, the S&P will be below its 12-month MA, but so, too, will the CRB Spot Raw Material Index. If the yield and commodity index are below their average and the S&P is above its, then the S&P crossover confirms that a bottom is in place, and the markets are in the correct sequence for a Stage II, as described in Chapter 2.

10. Is it possible to observe three discernible intermediate declines during recession-associated bear markets? This is by no means infallible, but often a good sign.

11. Does the market meet most of the characteristics cited previously in a year in which the 4-year stock market cycle is due to bottom? If so, the odds of a major bottom are greatly increased. If the year ends in the number 4, this is also a positive sign since years ending in a 5 are the most bullish of the decade. Hence, 1954, 1974, 1984, and 1994 were major bottoms (the first bottom developed at the end of 1953), all of which were followed by 5 strong years. With the exception of 1984, all were also 4-year cycle lows.

Psychological Factors

12. Sentiment is typically very bearish at a major bottom. This can show up in extreme readings in advisory sentiment, public short ratios, or the put/call ratio reversing from its overbought level.

13. Sentiment is also reflected in the media, and here cover stories are a great place to build a contrary case. Occasionally, brokers use the buying opportunity derived from the bear market as the basis for an ad campaign. Such ads do not necessarily indicate the wisdom of brokerage houses, although they are certainly courageous for taking a bullish stance. Rather, it is recognition of the fact that the decline in equity prices has caught the attention of the public. Remember, when everyone thinks alike, it is time to expect a market turn.

14. How does the market respond to bad news? During the decline, it would be normal for it to sell off on bad news, such as an unexpectedly poor earnings report, huge layoffs, a major bankruptcy, and so on. However, if it starts to shrug off such news and actually rises, the psychology has probably changed.

Summary

If it were necessary to summarize these characteristics for peaks and troughs into a few vital points, they would probably be as follows:

1. Crowd psychology has moved to a measurable extreme.
2. Interest rates have already reversed their trend.
3. Long-term momentum is at an extreme or has already reversed from one.
4. The technical position of leading versus lagging groups is consistent with the direction of the turning point in question.
5. These conditions have been confirmed with the completion of a price pattern and the penetration of a long-term MA, for example, 12-month, 200-day, and so on.

EPILOGUE

The suggestion was made at the outset that the keys to success in financial markets are knowledge and action. The knowledge part of the equation has been discussed as comprehensively as possible, but the final word has been reserved for investor action, since the way in which knowledge is used is just as important as understanding the process itself.

Indicated in the following are some common errors that all of us commit more often than we would like to admit. The most obvious of these can be avoided by applying the accompanying principles.

1. *Perspective.* The interpretation of any indicator should not be based on short-term trading patterns; the longer-term implications should always be considered.

2. *Objectivity.* A conclusion should not be drawn on the basis of one or two reliable or favorite indicators. The possibility that these indicators could give misleading signals demonstrates the need to form a balanced view derived from *all* available information. Objectivity also implies removing as much emotion from the trading and investing process as possible. If incorrect decisions are being made, they will almost always come from a position of mental imbalance. Every effort should therefore be made to reduce the emotional content of any decision on both the buy and sell sides.

3. *Humility.* One of the hardest lessons in life is learning to admit a mistake. The knowledge of all market participants in the aggregate is, and always will be, greater than that of any one individual or group of individuals. This knowledge is expressed in the action of the market itself, as reflected by the various indicators. Anyone who fights the tape or the verdict of the market will swiftly

suffer the consequences. Under such circumstances, it is as well to become humble and let the market give its own verdict. A review of the indicators will frequently suggest the future direction of prices. Occasionally, the analysis proves to be wrong, and the market fails to act as anticipated. If this unexpected action changes the basis on which the original conclusion was drawn, it is wise to admit the mistake and alter the conclusion.

4. *Tenacity.* If the circumstances outlined previously develop, but it is considered that the technical position has *not* changed, the original opinion should not be changed either.

5. *Independent thought.* If a review of the indicators suggests a position that is not attuned to the majority view, that conclusion is probably well founded. On the other hand, a conclusion should never be drawn simply because it is opposed to the majority view. In other words contrariness for its own sake is not valid. Since the majority conclusion is usually based on false assumptions, it is prudent to examine such assumptions to determine their accuracy.

6. *Simplicity.* Most things done well are also done simply. Because the market operates on common sense, the best approaches to it are basically very simple. If an analyst must resort to complex computer programming and model building, the chances are that he or she has not mastered the basic techniques and therefore requires an analytical crutch.

7. *Discretion.* There is a persistent temptation to call every possible market turn, along with the duration of every move a security is likely to make. This deluded belief in one's power to pull off the impossible inevitably results in failure, a loss of confidence, and damage to one's reputation. For this reason, analysis should concentrate on identifying major turning points rather than predicting the duration of a move—there is no known formula on which consistent and accurate forecasts of this type can be based.

APPENDIX
The Elliott Wave

Introduction

The Elliott wave principle was established by R. N. Elliott and was first published in a series of articles in *Financial World* in 1939. The basis of the Elliott wave theory developed from the observation that rhythmic regularity has been the law of creation since the beginning of time. Elliott noted that all cycles in nature, whether of the tide, the heavenly bodies, the planets, day and night, or even life and death, had the capability for repeating themselves indefinitely. Those cyclical movements were characterized by two forces: one building up and the other tearing down.

The principal part of the theory is concerned with form or wave patterns, but other aspects include ratio and time. In this case, pattern does not refer to the types of formation covered in earlier chapters, but to a waveform. Ratio refers to the concept of price retracements and time to the period separating important peaks and troughs.

Chapter 15 described several techniques based on the Fibonacci number sequence. This same sequence forms the basis for retracement and time development in Elliott theory.

The Fibonacci Sequence

This concept of natural law also embraces an extraordinary numerical series discovered by a thirteenth-century mathematician named Fibonacci. The series that carries his name is derived by taking the number 2 and adding to it the previous number in the series. Thus, 2 + 1 = 3, then 3 + 2 = 5, 5 + 3 = 8, 8 + 5 = 13, 13 + 8 = 21, 21 + 13 = 34, and so on. The series becomes 1, 2, 3, 5, 8, 13, 21, 34, 55, 89, 144, 233, and so on. It has a number of fascinating properties, among which are the following:

1. The sum of any two consecutive numbers forms the number following them. Thus, 3 + 5 = 8 and 5 + 8 = 13, and so on.
2. The ratio of any number to its next higher is 61.8 to 100, and the ratio of any number to its next lower is 161.8 to 100.
3. The ratio 1.68 multiplied by the ratio 0.618 equals 1.

The connection between Elliott's observation of repeating cycles of nature and the Fibonacci summation series is that the Fibonacci numbers and proportions are found in many manifestations of nature. For example, a sunflower has 89 curves, of which 55 wind in one direction and 34 in the opposite direction. In music, an octave comprises 13 keys on a piano, with 5 black notes and 8 white. Trees always branch from the base in Fibonacci series, and so on.

The Wave Principle

Combining his observation of natural cycles with his knowledge of the Fibonacci series, Elliott noted that the market moves forward in a series of five waves and then declines in a series of three waves. He concluded that a single cycle comprised eight waves, as shown in Figure A.1 (3, 5, and 8 are, of course, Fibonacci numbers).

The upper part of the cycle consists of five waves. Waves 1, 3, and 5 are protrend moves and are called impulse waves. Waves 2 and 4, on the other hand, are called corrective waves because they correct waves 1 and 3. The declining part of the cycle consists of three waves, known as a, b, and c.

FIGURE A.1 Typical Cycle

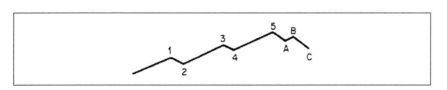

FIGURE A.2 Complete Cycle with Subwaves

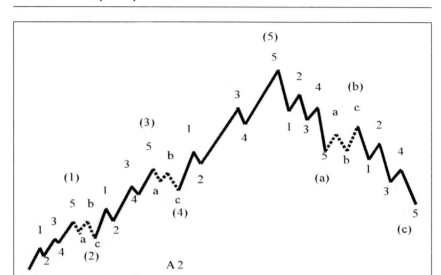

The longest cycle in the Elliott concept is called the grand supercycle. In turn, each grand supercycle can be subdivided into eight supercycle waves, each of which is then divided into eight cycle waves. The process continues to embrace primary, intermediate, minute, minuette, and subminuette waves. The various details are highly intricate, but the general picture is represented in Figures A.1 and A.2.

Figure A.2 shows a complete cycle with its subwaves. The determinant of whether a wave divides into five or three is the direction of the next largest wave. Corrections are always three-wave affairs.

Figures A.3 and A.4 show Elliott in historical perspective. Figure A.3 illustrates the first five waves of the grand supercycle, which Elliott deemed to have begun in 1800. Some Elliott wave theoreticians believe that the grand supercycle peaked at the end of the twentieth century.

FIGURE A.3 The Grand Supercycle

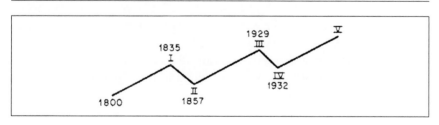

FIGURE A.4 Supercycle

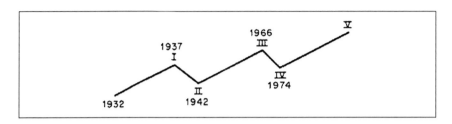

As the wave principle is one of form, there is no way to determine when the three corrective waves are likely to appear. However, the frequent recurrences of Fibonacci numbers representing time spans between peaks and troughs are probably beyond coincidence. These time spans are shown in Table A.1.

More recently, 8 years occurred between the 1966 and 1974 bottoms, the 1968 and 1976 tops, and the 1990 and 1998 bottoms. Also, there were 5 years between the 1968 and 1973 tops, for example. By the same token, there are many peaks and troughs that are not separated by numbers in this sequence.

It can readily be seen that the real problem with Elliott is interpretation. Indeed, every wave theorist (including Elliott himself) has at some time or another become entangled with the question of where one wave finished and another started. As far as the Fibonacci time spans are concerned, although these periods recur frequently, it is extremely difficult to use this principle as a basis for forecasting; there are no indications whether time spans based on these numbers will produce tops to tops or bottoms to tops, or something else, and the permutations are infinite.

We have hardly scratched the surface, and in some respects the old maxim "A little knowledge is a dangerous thing" applies probably more to Elliott than to any other market theorist. Its subjectivity in itself can be dangerous because the market is very subject to emotional influences. Consequently, the weight given to Elliott interpretations should probably be downplayed. Those wishing to pursue this theory in greater detail are referred to the classic text on the subject, by Frost and Prechter, called *Elliott Wave Principle* (Gainsville, GA, New Classics Library, 1978), since the theory has been described in this Appendix only in its barest outline.

TABLE A.1 Time Spans Between Stock Market Peaks and Troughs

Year Started	Position	Year Ended	Position	Length of Cycle (years)
1916	Top	1921	Bottom	5
1919	Top	1924	Bottom	5
1924	Bottom	1929	Top	5
1932	Bottom	1937	Top	5
1937	Top	1942	Btoom	5
1956	Top	1961	Top	5
1961	Top	1966	Top	5
1916	Top	1924	Bottom	8
1921	Bottom	1929	Top	8
1924	Bottom	1932	Bottom	8
1929	Top	1937	Top	8
1938	Bottom	1946	Top	8
1949	Bottom	1957	Bottom	8
1960	Bottom	1968	Top	8
1962	Bottom	1970	Bottom	8
1916	Top	1929	Top	13
1919	Top	1932	Bottom	13
1924	Bottom	1937	Top	13
1929	Top	1942	Bottom	13
1949	Bottom	1962	Bottom	13
1953	Bottom	1966	Bottom	13
1957	Bottom	1970	Bottom	13
1916	Top	1937	Top	21
1921	Bottom	1942	Bottom	21
1932	Bottom	1953	Bottom	21
1949	Bottom	1970	bottom	21
1953	Bottom	1974	Bottom	21
1919	Top	1953	Bottom	34
1932	Bottom	1966	Top	34
1942	Bottom	1976	Top	34
1919	Top	1974	Bottom	55
1921	Bottom	1976	Top	55

GLOSSARY

Advance/Decline (A/D) line   An A/D line is constructed from a cumulative plurality of a set of data over a specified period (usually daily or weekly). The result is plotted as a continuous line. The A/D line and market averages usually move in the same direction. Failure of the A/D line to confirm a new high in the market average is a sign of weakness, whereas failure of the A/D line to confirm a new low by the market averages is a sign of technical strength.

Advisory services   Privately circulated publications that comment upon the future course of financial markets, and for which a subscription is usually required.

Bear trap   A signal that suggests that the rising trend of a security has reversed, but which soon proves to be false.

Breadth (in the market)   The term *breadth* relates to the number of issues participating in a move. A rally is considered suspect if the number of advancing issues is diminishing as the rally develops. Conversely, a decline that is associated with fewer stocks falling is considered to be a bullish sign.

Bull trap   A signal that suggests that the declining trend of a security has reversed, but which soon proves to be false.

Customer free balances   The total amount of unused money on deposit in brokerage accounts. These are "free" funds representing cash that may be employed in the purchase of securities.

Cyclical investing   The process of buying and selling stocks based on a longer-term or primary market move. The cycle approximates to the 4-year business cycle, to which such primary movements in stock prices are normally related.

Divergence   A nonconfirmation that is not cleared up. Negative divergences occur at market peaks, while positive divergences develop at market bottoms. The significance of a divergence is a direct function of its size—that is, over time and the number of divergences in a given situation.

Insider   Any person who directly or indirectly owns more than 10 percent of any class of stock listed on a national exchange or who is an officer or director of the company in question.

Margin   Occurs when an investor pays part of the purchase price of a security and borrows the balance, usually from a broker; the margin is the difference between the market value of the stock and the loan that is made against it. In the futures markets, margin is a good-faith deposit for a contract for future delivery.

Margin call   The demand upon a customer to put up money or securities with a broker. The call is made if a customer's equity in a margin account declines below a minimum standard set by the exchange or brokerage firm. This happens when there is a drop in price of the securities being held as collateral.

Members   Members of a stock exchange who are empowered to buy and sell securities on the floor of the exchange either for a client or for their own account.

Momentum   The underlying power or thrust behind an upward or downward price movement. Momentum is represented on a graph as a line that is continually fluctuating above and below a horizontal equilibrium level, which represents the halfway point between extreme readings. Momentum is a generic term embracing many different indicators, such as rate of change (ROC), relative strength indicators (RSIs), and stochastics.

Moving average (MA)   A simple MA is constructed by taking a mean average of a time series over a given period. When the price crosses above or below the MA, a buy or sell signal is given. MAs often serve as support or resistance points.

Moving-average convergence divergence (MACD)   An oscillator that measures the distance between two simple or exponentially smoothed MAs.

Nonconfirmation   A market is said to be "in gear" when most averages and indicators that form a part of it confirm successive highs or lows. For example, when the Dow Jones Industrial Average (DJIA) makes new highs, but the A/D line does not, a nonconfirmation is said to occur. If other indicators or averages also fail to confirm, conditions are regarded as bearish until the nonconfirmations are cleared up, and vice versa.

Odd lots Units of stock of less than 100 shares; these do not customarily appear on the tape.

Odd-lot shorts Odd lots that are sold short. Since odd lots are usually the vehicle of uninformed traders, a high level of odd-lot shorts in relation to total odd-lot sales often characterizes a major market bottom. A low level of odd-lot shorts compared with total odd-lot sales is a sign of a market top.

Option The right to buy or sell specific securities at a specified price within a specified time. *A put* gives the holder the right to sell the stock, and a *call* gives the right to buy the stock.

Overbought An opinion about the level of prices. It may refer to a specific indicator or to the market as a whole after a period of vigorous buying, after which it may be argued that prices are overextended for the time being and are in need of a period of downward or horizontal adjustment.

Oversold An opinion about the level of prices. It is the opposite of overbought—that is, a price move that has overextended itself on the downside.

Price/earnings ratio The ratio of the price of a stock to the earnings per share—that is, the total annual profit of a company divided by the number of shares outstanding.

Price patterns When a trend reverses direction, the price action typically traces out a formation known as a *price pattern*. The larger and deeper the pattern, the greater is its significance. Patterns that are formed at market tops are called *distribution formations*; that is, the stock or market is assumed to be undergoing distribution from strong, informed hands to weak, uninformed buyers. Price patterns at market bottoms are known as *accumulation formations*. Price formations may also represent temporary interruptions of the prevailing trend, in which case they are called *continuation patterns*.

Rally A brisk rise following a decline or consolidation of the general price level of a security price.

Reaction A temporary contratrend price weakness or consolidation following an upswing.

Relative strength (RS) comparative An RS line is calculated by dividing one security's price by another. Usually, the divisor is a measure of the market, such as the DJIA or the Commodity Research Bureau (CRB) Commodity Index. A rising line indicates that the index or stock is performing better than the market, and vice versa. Trends in RS can be monitored by MA crossovers, trendline breaks, and so on, in the same way as any other price trend.

Relative strength indicator (RSI)   An oscillator measuring the internal momentum of a price series. The RSI is designed to oscillate between 0 and 100. It can be calculated for any time span, but 14 days is the most commonly used period. It should not be confused with comparative RS, which measures relative performance between two different spans.

Secondary distribution or offering   The redistribution of a block of stock some time after it has been sold by the issuing company. The transaction is handled off the exchanges by a securities firm or group of firms. The shares are usually offered at a fixed price, which is related to the current market price of the stock.

Security   A generic term applied to any freely traded entity, such as a stock, bond, currency, commodity, or market index.

Short covering   The process of buying back stock that has been sold short.

Short-interest ratio   The ratio of the short position to the average daily trading volume of the month in question. A high short-interest ratio above 1.8 used to be considered bullish, but recent distortions due to the active trading of stock index futures and options have made this a less useful indicator than it once was.

Short position (interest)   The total amount of short sales outstanding on a specific exchange at a particular time. The short position is published monthly.

Short selling   Short selling is normally a speculative operation undertaken in the belief that the price of the shares will fall. The security is simply sold before it is bought. This process is accomplished in the stock market by borrowing stock from a broker in order to sell shares one does own. Most stock exchanges prohibit the short sale of a security below the price at which the last board lot was traded. This is not the case in the futures markets.

Specialist   A member of a stock exchange who acts as a specialist in a listed issue and who is registered with the exchange for that purpose. The member agrees to efficiently execute all orders and, insofar as reasonably practical, to maintain a fair and orderly market in the issue or issues for which he or she is a specialist.

Trendlines   Trendlines are constructed by joining a series of descending peaks or ascending troughs. Greater significance is attached to the trendline violation the more times it has been touched, the longer the line remains viable, and the less steep its angle. A trendline break does not necessarily signal a trend reversal, but can also result in a consolidation.

Yield curve   The structure of the level of interest rates through various maturities. Usually, the shorter the maturity, the lower the interest rate. Thus, 3-month T-bills usually yield less than 20-year government bonds. The slope of the yield curve relates to the speed, which rises as the maturity increases. In periods of tight money, short-term rates usually yield more than longer-term rates, and the curve is then called an *inverse yield curve*.

BIBLIOGRAPHY

Achelis, Steven B. *Technical Analysis A to Z*, Probus, Homewood, Ill. 1995.

Appel, G. *Winning Stock Market Systems*, Signalert Corp., Great Neck, N.Y., 1974.

Arms, Richard W. *The Arms Index* (TRIN), Dow Jones-Irwin, Homewood, Ill., 1989.

_____. *Volume Cycles in the Stock Market: Market Timing Through Equivolume-Charting*, Dow Jones-Irwin, Homewood, Ill., 1983.

Ayres, L. P. *Turning Points in Business Cycles*, August M. Kelly, New York, 1967.

Benner, S. *Benner's Prophecies of Future Ups and Downs in Prices*, Chase and Hall, Cincinnati, 1875; reprinted in *Journal of Cycle Research,* vol. 8, no. 1, January 1959.

Bernstein, J. *The Handbook of Commodity Cycles: A Window on Time*, John Wiley and Sons, Inc., New York, 1982.

Bollinger, John A. *Bollinger on Bollinger Bands*, McGraw-Hill, New York, 2001.

Bressert, Walter *The Power of Oscillator Cycle Combinations*, Bressert and Associates, Tucson, Ariz. 1991.

Bretz, W. G. *Juncture Recognition in the Stock Market*, Vantage Press, New York, 1972.

Bulkowski, Thomas N. *Encyclopedia of Chart Patterns*, John Wiley and Sons, Inc., New York, 2000.

Colby, Robert W., and Thomas A. Meyers. *The Encyclopedia of Technical Market Indicators*, Dow Jones-Irwin, Homewood, Ill., 1988.

Coppock, E. S. C. *Practical Relative Strength Charting*, Trendex Corp., San Antonio, Tex. 1960.

De Villiers, Victor. *The Point and Figure Method of Anticipating Stock Price Movements*, 1933 (available from Traderslibrary.com).

Dewey, E. R. *Cycles: The Mysterious Forces That Trigger Events*, Hawthorne Books, New York, 1971.

Dewey, E.R., and E. F. Dakin. *Cycles: The Science of Prediction*, Henry Holt, New York, 1947.

Dorsey, Thomas J. *Point and Figure Charting*, John Wiley and Sons, Inc., New York, 1995.

Drew, G. *New Methods for Profit in the Stock Market*, Metcalfe Press, Boston, 1968.

Edwards, Robert D., and John Magee. *Technical Analysis of Stock Trends*, John Magee, Springfield, Mass., 1957.

Eiteman, W. J., C. A. Dice, and D. K. Eiteman. *The Stock Market*, McGraw-Hill, Inc., New York, 1966.

Elder, Alexander. *Trading for a Living*, John Wiley and Sons, Inc., New York, 1994.

Fosback, N. G. *Stock Market Logic: A Sophisticated Approach to Profits on Wall Street*, The Institute for Econometric Research, Fort Lauderdale, Fla., 1976.

Frost, A. J., and Robert R. Prechter. *The Elliott Wave Principle: Key to Stock Market Profits*, New Classics Library, Chappaqua, N.Y., 1978.

Gann, W. D. *Truth of the Stock Tape*, Financial Guardian, New York, 1932.

Gartley, H. M. *Profits in the Stock Market*, Lambert Gann Publishing, Pomeroy, Wash., 1981.

Gordon, William. *The Stock Market Indicators*, Investors Press, Palisades Park, N.J., 1968.

Granville, J. *Strategy of Daily Stock Market Timing*, Prentice Hall, Englewood Cliffs, N.J., 1960.

Greiner, P., and H. C. Whitcomb. *Dow Theory, Investors' Intelligence*, New York, 1969.

Hamilton, W. D. *The Stock Market Barometer*, Harper & Bros., New York, 1922.

Hayes, Timothy. *The Research Driven Investor*, McGraw-Hill, New York, 2001.

Hurst, J. M. *The Profit Magic of Stock Transaction Timing*, Prentice Hall, Englewood Cliffs, N.J., 1970.

Jiler, W. *How Charts Can Help You in the Stock Market*, Commodity Research Publishing Corp., New York, 1961.

Kaufmann, Perry. *New Commodity Trading Systems*, John Wiley and Sons, Inc., New York, 1987.

_____. *Trading Systems and Methods*, Wiley Trading, New York, 2013.

_____. *Smarter Trading*, McGraw-Hill, New York, 1995.

Krow, H. *Stock Market Behavior*, Random House, New York, 1969.

Kirkpatrick, Charles II and Dahlquist, Julie. *Technical Analysis: The Complete Resource for Financial Market Technicians*, FT Press, Upper Saddle River, N. J. 2010.

McMillan, Lawrence G. *McMillan on Options*, John Wiley and Sons, Inc., New York, 1996.

Merrill, A. A. *Filtered Waves: Basic Theory*, Analysis Press, Chappaqua, N.Y., 1977.

Morris, Greg. *The Complete Guide to Market Breadth Indicators: How to Analyze and Evaluate Market Direction and Strength*, McGraw-Hill, New York, 2005.

_____. Candlestick Charting Explained: Timeless Techniques for Trading Stocks and Futures, McGraw-Hill, New York, 2006.

Murphy John J. *Intermarket Technical Analysis*, John Wiley and Sons, Inc., New York, 1991.

_____. *Trading with Intermarket Analysis, Enhanced Edition: A Visual Approach to Beating the Financial Markets Using Exchange-Traded Funds*, Wiley Trading, New York, 2012.

_____. *Technical Analysis of the Financials Markets*, New York Institute of Finance, New York, 1999.

Nelson, S. *ABC of Stock Market Speculation*, Taylor, New York, 1934.

Nison, Steve. *Japanese Candlestick Charting Techniques*, New York Institute of Finance, New York, 1991.

Pring, Martin J. *The All Season Investor*, John Wiley and Sons, Inc., New York, 1991.

_____. *Martin Pring on Price Patterns*, McGraw-Hill, New York, 2004.

_____. *The Definitive Guide to Market Momentum*, Traders Press, Cedar Falls, IA, 2009.

_____. *The Investor's Guide to Active Asset Allocation: Using Technical Analysis and ETFs to Trade the Markets*, McGraw-Hill, 2006.

_____. *Breaking the Black Box* (book and CD-ROM tutorial combination), McGraw-Hill, New York, 2002.

_____. *How to Forecast Interest Rates*, McGraw-Hill, New York, 1981.

_____. *How to Select Stocks* (book and CD-ROM tutorial combination), McGraw-Hill, New York, 2002.

_____. *International Investing Made Easy*, McGraw-Hill, New York, 1981.

_____. *Introduction to Candlestick Charting* (book and CD-ROM tutorial combination), McGraw-Hill, New York, 2002.

_____. *Introduction to Technical Analysis* (book and CD-ROM tutorial combination), McGraw-Hill, New York, 1998.

_____. *Investment Psychology Explained.* John Wiley and Sons, Inc., New York, 1991.

_____. *Learning the KST: An Introductory CD-ROM Tutorial*, www.pring.com, 1997.

_____. *Martin Pring on Market Momentum*, McGraw-Hill, New York, 1995.

_____. *Technician's Guide to Daytrading* (book and CD-ROM tutorial combination), McGraw-Hill, New York, 2002.

_____. *Momentum Explained, vol. I* (book and CD-ROM tutorial combination), McGraw-Hill, New York, 2002.

_____. *Momentum Explained, vol. II* (book and CD-ROM tutorial combination), McGraw-Hill, New York, 2002.

Rhea, Robert. *Dow Theory*, Barrons, New York, 1932.

Pring, Martin, Turner, Joe, and Kopas, Tom. *Investing in the Second Lost Decade*, McGraw-Hill, New York, 2012.

Pruden, Hank. *The Three Skills of Top Trading: Behavioral Systems Building, Pattern Recognition, and Mental State Management*, Wiley Trading, New York, 2007.

Shuman, J. B., and D. Rosenau. *The Kondratieff Wave*, World Publishing, New York, 1972.

Smith, E. L. *Common Stocks and Business Cycles*, William Frederick Press, New York, 1959.

_____. *Common Stocks as a Long-Term Investment*, Macmillan, New York, 1939 (now available in reprint from Fraser, Burlington, Vt., 1989).

_____. *Tides and the Affairs of Men*, Macmillan, New York, 1932.

Technical Analysis Societies

International Federation of Technical Analysts (IFTA) [www.IFTA.org]
(From here links are available to major technical societies around the world.)

Useful Web Sites

Bigcharts.com For commentary, charts, and industry group information.

Wealth-lab.com For charting, discussion, and rankings of automated systems plus unique system testing software.

Quote.Yahoo.com For charting for U.S. stocks international indexes, etc.

Investorlinks.com For multiple links to financial sites

Stockcharts.com   Free charting, with special emphasis on sectors. Multitude of indicators and analytical screens chart formats and indicators.

Freestockcharts.com   Charting of stocks and a substantial number of indicators. Remembers your favorite chart arrangements, etc.

MarketWatch.com   Latest financial news, timely articles, and quotes.

Sentimentrader.com   Subscription-based service providing, among other things, a unique collection of sentiment and commitment of traders charts.

Online Interactive Technical Analysis Course

Martin Pring's Interactive Technical Analysis Course (Pring.com)   A 15-hour complete course on technical analysis, including an interactive quiz with each training module.

INDEX

Note: **SG** indicates pages in Study Guide.

G

H

N

T

ABOUT THE AUTHOR

Martin J. Pring is the chairman of Pring Turner Capital group as well as the strategist for the Pring Turner Business Cycle ETF (symbol DBIZ). He is the founder of Pring.com, which provides research for financial institutions and individual investors around the world. The site also features a 15+ hour interactive online video training course on technical analysis. Since 1984, he has published the *InterMarket Review*, a monthly newsletter offering a long-term synopsis of the world's major financial markets, and in 2013, he joined Golden Gate University as an adjunct professor teaching a virtual graduate level course on technical analysis.

More from the investor *Barron's* refers to as the "technician's technician"!

The **definitive guide** to technical analysis—tuned up to give you the edge in today's global economy

Apply Pring's **winning methods** with this hands-on study guide

Earn steady profits—despite the next ten years of secular bear markets

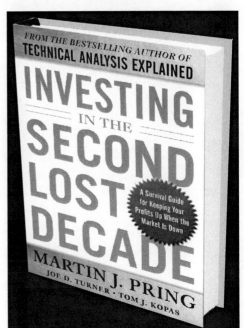

CPSIA information can be obtained at www.ICGtesting.com
Printed in the USA
BVOW02*1249091016

463685BV00004B/1/P